Between Sex and Power

The institution of the family changed hugely during the course of the twentieth century. In this major new work Göran Therborn provides a global history and sociology of the family as an institution, and of politics within the family, focusing on three dimensions of family relations: on the rights and powers of fathers and husbands; on marriage, cohabitation and extra-marital sexuality; and on fertility and birth control. Therborn's empirical analysis uses a multi-disciplinary approach to show how the major family systems of the world have been formed and developed. His truly global scope covers the family in:

* Europe and the New World
* West Asia and North Africa
* South and East Asia
* Sub-Saharan Africa
* Creole America and Southeast Asia.

Therborn concludes by assessing what changes the family might see during the next century.

This book will be essential reading for anybody with an interest in either the sociology or the history of the family.

Göran Therborn is Director of the Swedish Collegium for Advanced Study in the Social Sciences and University Professor of Sociology at Uppsala University.

International Library of Sociology
Founded by Karl Mannheim
Editor: John Urry
Lancaster University

Between Sex and Power

Family in the world, 1900–2000

Göran Therborn

Routledge
Taylor & Francis Group

LONDON AND NEW YORK

First published 2004
by Routledge
11 New Fetter Lane, London EC4P 4EE

Simultaneously published in the USA and Canada
by Routledge
29 West 35th Street, New York, NY 10001

Routledge is an imprint of the Taylor & Francis Group

© 2004 Göran Therborn

Typeset in Baskerville by Exe Valley Dataset Ltd, Exeter, Devon
Printed and bound in Great Britain by The Cromwell Press, Trowbridge, Wiltshire

British Library Cataloguing in Publication Data
A catalogue record for this book is available from the British Library

Library of Congress Cataloging in Publication Data
Therborn, Göran, 1941–
    Between sex and power: family in the world, 1900–2000 / Göran Therborn.
      p. cm. – (International library of sociology)
    Includes bibliographical references.
    1. Family–History–20th century.   2. Family– Cross-cultural studies.
    3. Patriarchy–History–20th century.   4. Marriage–History–20th century.
    5. Sex–Social aspects.   6. Fertility, Human–Social aspects.
    I. Title.   II. Series.

HQ518.T47 2004
306.85´09´04–de22   2003017723

ISBN 0–415–30077–0 (hbk)
ISBN 0–415–30078–9 (pbk)

Contents

List of illustrations   ix
Preface   xi

Introduction: sex, power and families of the world   1

PART I
Patriarchy: its exits and closures   **13**

1 Modernities and family systems: patriarchy around 1900   **17**

Collisions and continuities in Europe 20
At the frontier: gender governance of European settlement 29
The duality of Creole society: colonial and Indo- and
    Afro-American families after the upheavals 34
Colonial thrusts 37
Imperial threats 56
The world of patriarchy around 1900 70

2 A long night's journey into dawn   **73**

Prologue: when the earth moved: three moments of change 73
Act 1: reform, revolution or neither 79
Act 2: the constitutional moment 92
Act 3: '1968' and feminist globalization 99

3 The patriarchal burden of the twenty-first century   **107**

South Asian marriage arrangements 108
Backlash in West Asia and North Africa 112
African traditions and their ruination 116
East Asian changes and recidivism 119

Southeast Asian hesitations 123
Euro-American post-patriarchy: inequality 126
Patriarchy into the twenty-first century 129

PART II
Marriage and mutations of the socio-sexual order   **131**

Meanings of marriage 131

4   Sex and marriage in 1900   **137**

Fin-de-siècle scenes 137
The rule of universal marriage 139
The peculiarities of Western (European) marriage 144
The Creole Americas and their non-marriage 156
The global significance of marriage in 1900 160

5   Marital trends of the twentieth century   **162**

The rise of the Western honeymoon 162
Asian ageing 172
African specificity through colonialism and national crises 177
The world of marriage in 2000 181
The great disruption – and the smaller ones 187

6   The return of cohabitation and the sexual revolution   **192**

Boundaries blurred: marriage and non-marriage 192
The sexual revolution 207
From outlaw to married citizen: a note on rights to homosexuality 223

PART III
Couples, babies and states   **227**

7   Fertility decline and political natalism   **229**

The world's demographic transition, 1750–2050 229
Family systems and their fertility 239
Damming a tide: governmental birth promotion 251

8   The politics and sociology of birth control   **260**

Family systems and the second wave of fertility control 260
Assessing the waves: Europe and the Third World 265
The political demography of family planning 271
Moving against oneself? 284
Summing up: the routes to fertility decline – convergent or divergent? 289

Conclusions: the century gone, the century coming   **295**

The global dynamics of family institutional change 295
Times coming 306

Appendix: a note on primary sources   316
Notes   318
Bibliography   323
Index   365

Illustrations

Figure

7.1   A framework for understanding fertility control   243

Tables

3.1   Types of sexual unions in Nigeria, 1998   117
3.2   Who decides a wife's visit to relatives, 2000?   118
3.3   Women's average income relative to men's in post-patriarchal
        societies, 2000   128
4.1   Eastern and Western European marriage systems *c.* 1900   145
4.2   Female age at first marriage and percentage of women never
        married in North America, Oceania and Britain around 1900   147
4.3   The percentage of children born out of wedlock among live
        births in Europe, and in ex-British settlements, 1896–1900   149
5.1   Peaks of Western European female celibacy   162
5.2   Years of peak numbers marrying in Western Europe since 1815   164
5.3   Percentage married among American women aged 20–24,
        1900–2000   166
5.4   East–West European marriages in 1985   168
5.5   Sexual unions in Mexico in 1930 and 1970   169
5.6   Sexual unions in Jamaica, 1975–76   171
5.7   Extra-marital births in Uruguay, 1900–2000   172
5.8   Married girls in Iran aged 15–19, 1976–96   176
5.9   African polygyny around 2000   178
5.10   The household structure of the black population of South
        Africa, 1996   179
5.11   Children aged 10–14 in African households with both parents,
        and with no parent present, 1995–2000   180
5.12   The urban population of sub-Saharan Africa, 1900–2000   181
5.13   Western European women never married by the age of 45–49,
        c. 1900 and 2000   182
5.14   Female mean age at first marriage in Europe in 2000, east and
        west of the Trieste–St Petersburg line   183
5.15   Marriage propensities in Africa and Asia, 1990–2000   184

5.16   Marital status of women aged 35–39 in Creole America and
       some other countries for comparison   186
5.17   Children living with both parents until the age of 16:
       Swedish birth cohorts, 1900–83   187
5.18   Crude divorce rates around the world, 1950–99   190
5.19   Total divorce rates in Europe, 1995–2000   191
6.1   Trajectories of extra-marital births in Europe, North America
       and Oceania, 1960–2000   199
6.2   Mother's partnership situation at first birth in Europe and the
       Western New World in the 1990s   201
6.3   Family status of women in the EU, 1996   203
6.4   Forms of sexual union in Brazil, 1960–2000   204
6.5   Cohabitation in Hispanic America, *c*. 1980 and 2000   205
6.6   Periods of female pre-marital sex: Europe, the USA and New
       Zealand in the mid-1990s   209
6.7   Teenage African women in the 1990s and their sexual experience   213
6.8   Current African sexual orders   214
6.9   Girls married by age 18 and 20 and female median age at
       marriage in South Asia and in some other countries of young
       marriage and strict sexual control   216
6.10   Teenage Latin American women in the 1990s and their sexual
       experience   219
7.1   Total and marital fertility rates in the Western European family
       system around 1900   230
7.2   Total and marital fertility rates outside the Western European
       family around 1900 and early twentieth century   231
7.3   The demographic shift: fertility decline in Third World
       countries, 1965–80   237
7.4   The timing of the two-to-three child norm worldwide   238
7.5   Fertility in Communist and in Capitalist Europe, 1951–85   258
8.1   Desired number of children in family regions of the world,
       mid- to late 1970s   264
8.2   Timing of extra-European post-World War II fertility decline
       by geocultural family system   266
8.3   Total fertility rates in the developed world, 1965–2000   285
8.4   Completed fertility in Europe by female birth cohorts   288
8.5   Expected number of children by young European and
       American women   289
8.6   Ethnic fertility in women in the USA, 1999   289
8.7   Fertility in major countries or regions of the world,
       1896/1900–1995/2000   293
9.1   Regional population prospects of the world, 2000–50   309

Box

8.1   World routes of fertility decline   290–91

Preface

When you read this, at least eight years will have passed since my friend and distinguished colleague Frank Castles, then at the Australian National University, asked me to write a book on the institution of the family in the world from 1901 to 2001. It was meant to be part of a huge Australian research programme, celebrating the Centenary of Australian statehood. The offer was made, not to a family sociologist, but to a comparativist social scientist, whose only pertinent merit was a study of the rise of children's rights in the OECD countries (Therborn 1993).

I missed the Centenary date of 2001, without, I think, in any way hampering its solemn celebrations. The task was daunting. However, I was soon enraptured by the topic, and whatever you may think of the ultimate outcome, I myself have learnt a lot. I am very grateful to Frank Castles for the challenge. The empirical spadework with my own hands has left me with a feeling of some familiarity with the vast field.

My eminent predecessor in the area, William J. Goode, Si to his friends, sadly and suddenly passed away in May 2003. He had started reading, and cheerfully commenting on, my manuscript, but I never knew his final judgment: I missed my most important deadline. Our theoretical perspectives are fundamentally different, but I admired him as a very great scholar, and I liked him, and miss him, as a most amiable person.

The Swedish Collegium for Advanced Study in the Social Sciences is a great place to work at, and I would like to thank our Chairman of the Board, Professor Sverker Gustavsson, for his unwavering support. The project was launched from the Australian National University, and its hospitality during two research visits, and the friendly collegiality of its Research School, with its arc of brilliance from political philosophy to demography via political science and sociology, and its excellent library resources, have been crucial to this work.

I also have an intellectual debt to my students at Pompeu Fabra University in Barcelona, and to my distinguished friend Vicenç Navarro, who invited me to give a course there in the summer of 2000. The course gave me reason to re-think the synopsis of the book.

My wife Sonia has been a most important collaborator on this project, in all stages of it, from conception, drawing on her psychological experience, to data collection, data storage and references. Rather than a conventional academic project, this has been a small family enterprise.

As always, all mistakes are the responsibility of the author. But let me hope that you, the reader, will share some of the pleasure that the author has enjoyed in writing this book.

Göran Therborn
Uppsala, July 2003

Introduction

Sex, power and families of the world

Sex is a basic driving force of human biology; power is a key feature of human sociology. They are entangled, not worlds apart. Power can be observed in the animal kingdom, while the forms of human sexuality are socially constructed and variable. Both are convertible currencies, and merge into one another. Sex may lead to power, through the conduit of seduction. Power is also a basis for obtaining sex, whether by force or lubricated with money and what it can buy. The family is an enclosure in the open battlefields of sex and power, delimiting the free-for-all by staking out boundaries, between members and non-members, substituting rights and obligations for free trade and perpetual combat. As such, the family is a social institution, the most ancient, the most widespread of institutions.

Two American sociologists have argued in an important book that the family, or at least the American family, is in transition from being an institution to becoming a 'companionship'. That was in 1945, so if they were right there should not be much left of the institution. But they were using the word 'institution' in a narrower sense than in most contemporary social science. To Burgess and Locke (1945: 27), an 'institutional family' would typically be one 'in which its unity would be determined entirely by the social pressure impinging on family members', whereas the unity of 'the family as companionship' would develop out of 'mutual affection and intimate association'. An institution in this book is a set of norms, defining rights and obligations of members and boundaries between members and non-members. The kinds of affection and intimacy which refer to a family are still governed by such a norm complex, and a breach of norms – which certainly occurs – does not mean that the norms have disappeared.

The family is suspended between sex and power, as biological and social forces. But it is, of course, not a safe haven or an escape from power and sex. A family is always an outcome of sexual relations past or current: no sex, no family. But it is a regulator of sexual relations, determining who may, who must, and who must not, have sexual relations with whom. Power relations are inscribed in the rights and obligations of family members. Indeed, it makes good analytical sense to view an institution in terms of an equilibrium, between the pattern of rights and obligations, on one hand, and the distribution of power resources among the members, on the other. This balance or equilibrium is what explains the resilience of an institutional form, in this case a certain kind of family, once established. Those privileged by it can maintain their status because their resources of control and of sanction match their rights, while those who have few power resources have more duties than rights.

Institutional change is then induced by events or processes which upset a given balance between, on one hand, rights and duties, and, on the other, powers and dependencies. Fathers may lose their property, children may get a chance to go to school, women may get opportunities on the labour market, religious traditions may weaken, states or international organizations may intrude into families, curtailing the rights of fathers and husbands, providing rebelling daughters with routes of escape. Or, the forces pushing existing equilibria out of joint may work in the opposite direction: family property – and the control and transmission of it – may become more important, as in China in recent decades; women may be pressured away from the labour market – as has at least been attempted from the Elbe to the Yellow Sea; religious support of the rights of fathers and husbands may become stronger; within living memory French fathers had the right to hand over disobedient children to state penitence.

The privacy of family life has always been linked to societal authority, through institutionalized rights and duties prescribed and proscribed by organized religious bodies, buttressed or licensed by political authorities or directly by state legislation. But the links may be distant and/or tenuous, largely lost in the labyrinths of individual family power structures, or modified by provincial or local customs. A global view of the family will have to catch something of the diversity in which these powerful canons of authority exist.

Each present has its past. The family is an ancient institution, its origins going beyond history. But this is a study of the family from experiences and preoccupations of the turn of the twentieth and twenty-first centuries. While written in a scholarly rather than an opinionated mode and with the perspective of an individual author, this work is, of course, coming out of a period which has seen what Juliet Mitchell (1966) on the barricades, referring to women, called 'the Longest Revolution', and Francis Fukuyama (1999), from the opposite side of the frontline, termed 'The Great Disruption'. It is appearing at a time, when 'heterosexual marriage' is envisaged as 'largely undermined by the rise of the pure relationship and plastic sexuality' (Giddens 1992: 154), and when it apparently makes sense, to talk about 'The End of Marriage' (Lewis 2001) or of 'What comes after the family' (Beck-Gernsheim 1998). If all this were true, one might, perhaps, at least understand, if not necessarily agree with, the great US economist who compares 'the disaster' of 'the failure of the family system in America' to the Irish Potato Famine (Akerlof 1998: 308). We have to face the fact, that the 'Western family' is widely seen by writers with loud voices and strong opinions to be in 'great disorder' (Roudinesco 2002).

Ancestors

The *problématique* of this book is, then, naturally different from that of preceding classics, on whose shoulders I am sitting, looking out at the past, at the present, and into the future. Nearest in time, closest in affinity, even with a certain personal proximity is William J. Goode's (1963) magnum opus *World Revolution and Family Patterns,* which sought to 'describe and interpret the main changes in family patterns that have occurred over the past half-century in Japan, China, India, the West, sub-Saharan Africa, and the Arab countries, and to relate them to various alterations in other institutional areas' (Goode 1963: v) – a daring enterprise that Goode carried out with enormous empirical acumen, helped by a vast network of distinguished informants, and concluded with unfailing wisdom. His book is a landmark of comparative social science.

However, in the world of scholarship and of intellectual engagement with ideas, recognition, respect and admiration do not add up to adulation, and may very well leave room for critique. With the hindsight of four decades, I can see three major sets of problems with Goode's work. First, his focus of change – in other words his dependent variable – is a tendency 'towards some type of conjugal family pattern – that is, toward fewer kinship ties with distant relatives and a greater emphasis on the "nuclear" family unit of couple and children' (Goode 1963: 1). Fortunately, it does not prevent his actual analysis from going beyond this perspective, into marriage patterns, husband–wife and parent–child relations, divorce. But it does blur the perception of other issues, and its formulation gives Goode's key variable of investigation an elusive character. 'The most important characteristic of the ideal typical construction of the conjugal family is the *relative* exclusion of a *wide* range of affinal and blood relatives from its everyday affairs. There is *no great* extension of the kin network.' 'The locality of the couple's household will no longer be *greatly* determined by their kin . . . The choice of mate is *freer* than in other systems . . .' (Goode 1963: 8, italics added). Even the ideal type is formulated in terms of more or less.

The perspective does not systematically address the question of to what extent this means anything more than an argument that the rest of the world is approaching a pre-modern Western European conjugality. As it is formulated as a direction of change, its assessments become heavily dependent on the particular vantage point from which the pace of change is observed. Forty years later, it is easy to see that many of the most dramatic family changes – as seen today – actually occurred after the early 1960s, when Goode was finishing his book. This ageing of perspective is reinforced by Goode's abstention from alternative ideal types and from attempts at gauging the amount of change from one to the other.

Second, Goode's explanatory master variable, 'the social forces of industrialization and urbanization', is left with its meaning and mode of family influence unclear. 'With reference to the modern world, it does not seem possible or useful to distinguish clearly between the *separate* effects of urbanization and industrialization' (original italics); ' . . . the core element of industrialization is a social factor, the freedom to use one's talents and skills in improving one's job' (Goode 1963: 169, italics omitted). 'The prime social characteristic of modern industrial enterprise is that the individual is ideally given a job on the basis of his ability to fulfil its demands, and that this achievement is evaluated universalistically' (Goode 1963: 11, italics omitted). The major explanation seems to be an economic culture of achievement and universalism, difficult to handle in comparative historical research under any circumstances, and not operationalized in indicator terms. Its ideal typical idyll, moreover, does not seem to capture the processes of proletarianization and of capital accumulation with which actual historical industrialization was associated. Here again, Goode is far better than his theory, though, in injecting something of a class perspective into the Parsonian 'pattern variables'. As it is the 'upper-strata' who control the new jobs of industry, they can continue to control their young, he notes, for example (Goode 1963: 17).

Third, Goode's basic explanatory argument is a straightforward functional one, of 'The "Fit" Between the Conjugal Family and the Modern Industrial System' (Goode 1963: 10ff). The more limited conjugal family opens mobility channels, which the industrial system requires. Its 'emphasis on emotionality' compensates for the 'unremitting discipline' and the emotional insecurity of industrial work. In these and related ways, 'the needs of the industrial system are . . . served by the conjugal family pattern' (Goode 1963: 15). Goode is explicitly aware of the severe limitations of this functionalism, mainly set out in terms of 'theoretical harmony' or 'fit' (Goode 1963: 10–11), he acknowledges the possibility of family systems affecting industrialization, and he concedes a significant role to 'ideology': the ideology of the conjugal family, of individualism and of egalitarianism (Goode 1963: 18ff).

For all the daring and brilliance of its author, *World Revolution and Family Patterns* is entrapped in the prevailing theoretical paradigm of its time and place, Parsonian structural functionalism, and with its vista in part dazzled by remaining glimmers of evolutionary kinship anthropology. The functionalist cloud hanging over Goode's investigations prevents any systematic attention to paths of effect, to secularization, to schooling, to political conflict and changes of political power, for instance. Moreover, its story ends before the dramatic changes of family patterns in the last third of the twentieth century.

The most fascinating feature of Goode's work on the family, which also includes, *inter alia,* a major treatise on divorce, to which we shall have reason to return (Goode 1993), is his worldwide curiosity and knowledge. Indeed, in a future history of comparative social science, sociologists of the family deserve central attention. The opaque currents of theoretical fashion and institutional power have tended to push family studies to the periphery of general social science, empirical as well as theoretical. However, in the field of large-scale, historically conscious, perceptive as well as wide-ranging empirical research, family sociology has an impressive pedigree.

Goode has remained a beacon of comparative family sociology, but family studies more generally by no means peaked with his achievements. Much epochal work appeared later, mainly, but not exclusively, in other disciplines:

history, anthropology, demography and economics. Anyone engaged in family studies today is indebted to a large number of great scholars and their large-scale collective projects, such as Ansley Coale and the Princeton European Fertility Project, and the late Peter Laslett and his Cambridge Group on the History of Population and Social Structure; to collective histories, such as the global study edited by André Burguière *et al.*, and that by Gordon Anderson, the networked, ongoing Eurasia project spanning East Asia to Western Europe (of George Alter *et al.*), and the European work by David Kertzer and Marzio Barbagli; to individual historians, like John Gillis, Karl Kaser, Michael Mitterauer, Joan Scott and Louise Tilly; to the global historical anthropologist Jack Goody; to social and historical demographers like P.N. Mari Bhat, John Caldwell, Jean-Claude Chesnais, Gavin Jones, Dirk van de Kaa, James Lee, Ron Lestaeghe, Peter McDonald and Wang Feng; to feminist development economists such as Esther Boserup and Bina Agarwal; to lawyers and legal historians like David Bradley, John Eekelaar and Mary Ann Glendon. Family studies have also attracted a great deal of policy-oriented research, among which the large-scale comparative projects by Franz-Xavier Kaufmann *et al.*, and by Sheila Kamerman and Alfred Kahn stand out.

One, quite often praised, family theorist will be absent from the discussion: Nobel Laureate Gary Becker (1991). This is not to pick a disciplinary quarrel: Becker's assumption-driven modelling, typical of neoclassical economics, appears fatally parochial in any comparative perspective, historical or spatial. For example, according to Becker (1991: 118) 'Divorce is more likely when the wife's wage rate is high relative to that of her husband'. While that may make common sense, it has nothing to offer if we want to explain the actual history of divorce rates in the world, the spectacularly high rates among Muslim Malays until about 1970, where most women were non-waged, the traditionally high divorce rate among Arab populations where virtually no married woman ever had a wage, or why Scandinavia has lower divorce rates and higher female wage rates than the USA. What use do we have for explaining different marriage rates and sexual bonding by a proposition that 'A person enters the marriage market if he expects his marital income to exceed his single income' (Becker 1991: 119)? Comparative research is focused on the variability of common sense, of institutional parameters, and from that perspective Becker, for all his intellectual powers, seems stuck in mid-Western America.

All the pages allotted me would hardly suffice to give a fair assessment of the work of these, and other relevant, eminent predecessors and contemporary colleagues. Instead, let us briefly look back on the family tree.

Before William J. Goode, two figures of family sociology stood out from the rest, Frédéric Le Play and Edward Westermarck, both extremely influential and successful in their time, but now largely forgotten outside their native countries (France and Finland, respectively), except by a small body of specialists. Both were excluded from the canon of disciplinary classics long ago. Le Play never made it into the rival French pantheons of Emile Durkheim and René Worms. With the arrival of Bronislaw Malinowski into the centre of disciplined anthropology as well as onto the anthropology chair at the London

School of Economics, where Westermarck was teaching, Westermarck became a pre-classic. While doubts about the value of their eventual resurrection for the advancement of the social sciences appear quite legitimate, in this context of a sociological history of the family, a bow to these ancestors seems proper.

Frédéric Le Play (1806–82) has left an enduring legacy to historians and anthropologists of the family, less visible in the US-dominated family sociology, and less relevant to contemporary North Atlantic family concerns: that is a typology of family structures, enveloped in the crisis concerns of Le Play's time and milieu, the Counter-Enlightenment of mid-nineteenth-century French social Catholicism. The ideological wrap has been discarded, but Le Play's structural analysis has been elaborated and put to use. A late twentieth-century French *maître-penseur*, Emmanuel Todd (1990), has even made it the basis for far-reaching explanations of ideological and political developments in Europe.

Le Play distinguished three family types from their parent–married child relations: the 'patriarchal family', now usually referred to as a (patrilineal) 'joint family'; the *famille souche*, translated into English as 'stem family'; and the 'unstable family', in twentieth-century language called the conjugal or the nuclear family. In the patriarchal family, which Le Play found 'among Eastern nomads, Russian peasants, and the Slavs of Central Europe', the married sons remained with or near their father, who still exercised authority over them and their children. Le Play's own preference was for the stem family, a sedentary agrarian structure found in Western Europe, in England in particular, after it was undermined by the inheritance laws of the French Revolution – stipulating equal inheritance rights among the children – and by proletarianization. In the stem family the father retains control over property transmission, but only one married child stays with the parents, inherits and carries on the paternal home, while the others receive a dowry and set out on their own.

Because of their inheritance rules, freedom of testation, and unified marriage property under the command of the husband/father, Le Play (1855: 18) was very positive towards the British: 'The Anglo-Saxon race has . . . appreciated the necessity of firmly maintaining the organization of the family under the tutelary aegis of paternal authority'. 'It is in England . . . that paternal authority and the family . . . appear to offer their most commendable traits' (1866: 297). Among the European industrial working class Le Play saw an 'unstable' family prevailing, meaning a family formed by marriage, growing with children, shrinking with adult children leaving the home, and dissolving upon the death of the parents: that is, a neolocal conjugal family, establishing its own household upon marriage.

This scheme, with its focus on inheritance rules and their effect on family organization and interaction patterns, has turned out to be a fruitful comparative structural approach to family systems (cf. Skinner 1997). Its distinction of the Eastern European patrilineal joint family from the family patterns of Western Europe has been corroborated by later specialist historians (Kaser 2000).

Le Play was a mining engineer, with annual research leave from the French Ministry of Public Works, which he used to study not only European mining and metallurgy, but also European social conditions. His major work, *Les Ouvriers Européens* (The European Workers) appeared in its first edition in 1855. It dealt with a wide gamut of living conditions in workers' and farmers' families, with a focus on the family budget, and was based on direct observation. His family typology is only sketched there (Le Play 1855: 18–19), and was formulated more clearly later (Le Play 1866, 1871). During the Second Empire Le Play was a distinguished public figure. A handy introduction in English to his bulky oeuvre is the short biography and text selection edited by Catherine Bodard Silver (Le Play 1982).

Edward Westermarck (1862–1939) was part of the Liberal Finnish–Swedish elite in the then Russian Grand Duchy of Finland. His first important work, *The History of Human Marriage* (1891), an expanded English edition of his 1889 dissertation, was prefaced and proof-read by Alfred Wallace, the great evolutionary naturalist, and the British Vice-Consul at Helsingfors had helped him with the English language. It was a great success, going into five editions and several translations. It brought its author a professorship (of practical philosophy) in Helsingfors (today's Finnish-speaking Helsinki), and a part-time sociology professorship at the London School of Economics (1907–30).

Westermarck later undertook extensive fieldwork in Morocco, but the first edition of his book on marriage was based on library research, and on a questionnaire to missionaries and similar informants about extra-European cultures and customs. Its time-frame is almost infinite, starting with mating and parenting among animals, birds in particular, and aiming at capturing human history from the 'savages' to late nineteenth-century 'civilized' legislation. Its spatial stretch is global. Its argumentation has a certain anecdotal style to it, the immense area covered making brevity a necessity; customs from different epochs, of small tribes and large empires are immediately juxtaposed to each other, and systematic statistical data are lacking. It was a style attacked and abandoned by the new discipline of anthropology, for intensive observation of bounded small-scale societies. Nevertheless, the author's range of knowledge is enormously impressive, and the book is a powerful analysis based on extensive empirical evidence. It deals with several topics of direct relevance to this book, such as the liberty of choosing a marriage partner, husband–wife and parent–child relations, possibilities and practices of divorce.

In its own time, its impact seems to have been, above all, in dispelling prevailing myths of primitive promiscuity (the main theme of Westermarck's (1889) dissertation, its interest in sexual selection, its instinct explanation of the incest taboo: 'an innate aversion to marriage between persons living very closely together from early youth' (Westermarck 1903: 544). But Westermarck also had something to say on a key theme of this book.

In 1891 he concluded: 'Marriage has thus been subject to evolution in various ways, though the course of evolution has not always been the same. The dominant tendency of this process at its later stages has been the extension of the wife's rights. . . . The history of human marriage is the history of a relation in which women have been gradually triumphing over the passions, the prejudices, and the selfish interests of men' (Westermarck

1891/1903: 549–50). A grandson of Westermarck might have written that in 1991, and still have been in the middle of the process of change. As for the prospects for 2091, we shall see below.

Themes

This book has three main themes, which reflect how the author is trying to make scholarly sense of his time and context. Patriarchy, and the relative rights and duties of parents and children, of men and women, is the first. The 'rule of the father' is here seen more broadly than by Le Play, referring to male family powers, whether of fathers, maternal uncles in matrilineal societies, husbands, or other family members qua males. Its main focus will be on parent–adult child (on other parent–child relations see Therborn 1993) and husband–wife relations. Parental power will largely concentrate on the control – degree or absence – of children's marriages and household formation, as a most important aspect of control over the life-course of the next generation, but it will also pay attention to specific intra-family discrimination of daughters, from infanticide or malnutrition and neglect to disinheritance. In this perspective, parental power and control will be taken as manifestations of patriarchy, without singling out or excluding maternal matchmakers and commanding mothers-in-law, as long as they are delegated by or linked to paternal power. Male sexual power without paternal significance will be referred to as phallocracy, which may be taken as a younger brother of patriarchy.

Paternal power is the core meaning of patriarchy, historically and etymologically, and we shall have to take stock of its operation, many times, in many places. It tells us something noteworthy of recent changes in the UK that an influential British feminist theorist in 1990, and throughout eight reprints in the 1990s, could dismiss paternal power as irrelevant at best: 'This inclusion of generation in the definition [of patriarchy] is confusing. It is a contingent element and best omitted' (Walby 1990: 20). With that reservation, the approach to patriarchy in this book owes much to contemporary feminism, and to its critique of twentieth-century masculinist silence on the subject.

Powerful fathers are also husbands, so it seems both logical and practical to extend the notion of patriarchy to the power of husbands. We shall look at their various prerogatives, legal and/or actual: in family decision-making as 'head of the family', in control of their wives' activities and mobility, in polygyny and sexual double standards. We shall also pay attention to the discrimination against daughters and to special sacrifices demanded from women for male sexual reasons, such as the crushing of girls' feet in imperial China, euphemistically called 'foot-binding', or genital mutilation. But patriarchy in this book will not be cut loose from the family and made synonymous with the subordination, discrimination, or social disadvantages of women in general. Gender discrimination and gender inequality should be seen as a broader concept than patriarchy, with the latter's family tradition and historical connotations. A significant erosion, and even disappearance of the latter does not necessarily entail the end of the former, and has not actually done so, as we shall see.

A second main topic of this endeavour concerns the role of marriage, and non-marriage, in regulating sexual behaviour, and sexual bonding in particular. Single living and informal sexual bonding, in cohabitation or otherwise, are not recent inventions. They were widespread in northwestern Europe and in Latin America and the Caribbean at the time of Le Play and Westermarck. The latter also noted, more than a century ago, that 'the proportion of unmarried people has been gradually increasing in Europe' (Westermarck 1903: 541). Historically, marriage rates have actually gone both up and down, and the current North Atlantic rates of non-marriage, extra-marital births, and unmarried cohabitation are by no means unique in modern history, as global analysis will show.

Current customs and debates in Europe, the Americas and Oceania under-line that contemporary family sociology cannot neglect the sexual revolution of the 1960s and 1970s. Marriage should be seen, not (only) as an institution *sui generis*, but as a major part of a mutating socio-sexual order. We shall pay special attention to the sexual position of adolescents worldwide, as adolescence is the normal entry into that order, in one variant or another.

The third part of the book deals with the past, present and future prospects of fertility and birth control, with their implications for ageing and for geo-political shifts. It thus relates also to the beginning of population decline in Europe, the rapid ageing of Japan, and the emerging scarcity of children in some parts of the world, following an enormously successful global effort at birth control.

In particular, we shall try to understand the link between, on the one hand, the sexual intimacy of individual couples, and, on the other, the national, continental and inter-continental waves of fertility change. This will take us to issues of politics, social movements, states and supranational organizations; again, we shall have to be very aware of the multi-sided, multi-level politics of patriarchy and of marriage and sexuality as well.

These three themes we shall pursue through a century, from about 1900 to 2000 and beyond. However, tradition did not end in 1900, nor did modernity begin in 1901. Substantial changes of patriarchy had already occurred by 1900, although not as much as Westermarck hoped or Le Play feared, and the origins of collective patterns of birth control can be traced back to the seventeenth century. While generally starting the investigative clock around 1900, the pre-story is not to be interpreted as pre-history, as some kind of 'primordiality'.

The themes of this book cross academic disciplines, and the author has tried to follow the tracks of the former, rather than the boundaries of the latter. The search area is indicated by sociology, law and demography, but tools and experiences of anthropology, history and political science have also been called for, because the task is not just the normative structures of the family institution, but their actual operation and their limits, across the globe and during a century or more.

Going for the world

History has its ironies, even in the small world of scholarship. The Parsonian functionalist – usually a creed of complacent American mainstream moderate conservatism/liberalism – William Goode talked about 'world revolution' in the early 1960s. True, the 'world revolution' Goode referred to did not fly the red flag. It was made up of industrialization and urbanization, as social forces 'affecting every known society'. In contrast to the assumed universality of that 'revolution', we shall here be on the look-out for something sounding much more anodyne, for 'globality'.

Globality, in the sense used here, refers to connectivity, variability and inter-communication of social phenomena, as opposed to the commonality, singularity and one-way direction of universal forces. That is, to the connections between different forces and events in different parts of the globe, to the worldwide variability of causal processes as well as of institutional forms and outcomes, to the significance of communication between actors on different continents.

In this sense, this is a global history and a global sociology of the family. It is global also in a literal meaning of planetary circumference. Goode left out Latin America and the Caribbean, non-Arabic West Asia, and Southeast Asia. By a good American, Europe was subsumed with the New World as the 'Western Cultural Complex', given an original extension to the Urals, without the legacy of the October Revolution being allowed to weigh significantly upon it. The Cold War set its limits to what open American minds might write. Historically, this subsumption of Europe under the 'Western' rubric veiled the important historical family differences between Eastern and Western Europe, as well as the special features of the overseas settlements.

The collective work of Burguière *et al.* (1986), for all its resources of regional expertise, falls short of a planetary picture, with a partial view of Latin America, and a total neglect of non-Arab West Asia and of Southeast Asia.

How may one then reach for empirical globality, as a lone researcher, with no specialist colleagues to call in? By an analytical framework and some hard work. Any serious, globally comparative family analysis would have to start with families of families, with family systems. Otherwise, the myriads of different individual families would be unmanageable. But what families of families, what typology of families? There seem to be three major alternatives. One would be a structural one, distinguishing features of the institutional structure, possibly linking up with Le Play's typology. Another would be to focus on the normative underpinnings of different family systems in history. Most of this normative basis would be religious – Christian, Muslim, Hindu, Confucian, Buddhist, etc. – or secular rationalist.

While both would be feasible, this study has opted for a third kind of guide, a geocultural road map. A purely structural compass does not seem to be the most adequate for grasping and explaining structural changes over a long time, and in three thematic dimensions. Religious and other wide and deep value systems differ not only in their conceptions of the family, but also in their normative interest in it, and in their normative significance to it. Most important is that religious practices of social institutions may differ strongly from place to place. A Christian marriage in Africa, for instance, is often very different from one in Europe, and a Muslim family in the Punjab is far from identical to one in Java. Processes of secularization have furthermore changed the relevance of religion to family systems.

'Geoculture' is a term coined by Immanuel Wallerstein (1991) in analogy with geopolitics, for the 'underside', the 'cultural framework' of the world system. But once in the public domain, the notion may be used for other purposes than world-system analysis. In our context it is attractive as indicating a geographic cultural anchorage of norms and institutions. To view family systems as geocultures means to treat them as institutions or structures taking their colouring from the customs and traditions, from the history of a particular area, a cultural wrapping which may remain after structural, institutional change, leaving imprints on the new institution. Geocultures in this sense may be small or large, and their boundaries are not self-evident, although they should be related to the patterns of political power, because of the importance of power in sustaining and in changing social institutions. On the other hand, we are here looking for a tool, a heuristic device helping us to manage the complexity of family forms on the planet. The task is to study patriarchy, the socio-sexual order, and fertility over a century, not to provide the typology of modern family systems.

From these considerations, I have found it useful to distinguish five major and two important interstitial family systems in the modern world. The major ones derive from a specific value system, of religious/philosophical origin, and shaped by the history of the area. The interstitial ones have gained their character from encounters with different value systems. These family systems may be, and will be, sub-divided in various ways, but their number has to be small, and their area large, to be practical. The major family systems are those of:

Africa (sub-Saharan)
European (including the New World settlements)
East Asia
South Asia
West Asia/North Africa.

Interstitial family systems of global weight are those of:

Southeast Asia, from Sri Lanka to the Philippines and with Indonesia at its centre, where the rigid patriarchies of Confucianism, Islam, and Catholicism were mellowed by Buddhist insouciance in family matters, and by Malay customs.
Creole America, coming out of the American socio-economic history of Christian Europeans running plantations, mines and landed estates with African slaves and servile Indian labour. Alongside the strict patriarchal

white high culture, that history developed a particular black, mulatto, mestizo and uprooted Indian family pattern. While most distinctive in the Caribbean, the pattern may be seen throughout the Americas, from the Afro-American ghettos of the USA to the Andean peripheries of South America.

Behind the divisions are certain findings which will be demonstrated later, for example that territorial geocultures have a tendency to prevail, in their bearing upon the family features under study, over religious divisions, such as between Muslims, Christians and Animists in Africa, or between Hindus and Muslims in South Asia. Across the areas there are major divides, which sometimes have to be drawn differently for different periods or different purposes. In Africa it is often meaningful to follow a northwest to southeast diagonal, although the continent's ethnic mosaic makes any neat patterning almost impossible. In Europe there is a historical east–west family division, along a line from Trieste to St Petersburg, going back to the early Middle Ages, but one may also occasionally find a rationale for a northwest versus the rest, or for a Western Europe versus New World distinction. Whereas in East Asia the first subdivision is clearly between China and Japan, in South Asia the non-political, non-religious geocultural north–south divide is decisive, bringing the extremely patriarchal north of the Indian Hindu centre together with Muslim Bangladesh and Pakistan, versus a south of both Hindus and Muslims with milder patriarchal manners, by comparison. But within all areas many national pictures will be shown, because of national productions of power as well as because many sources are nationally generated.

Though no addict of crime fiction, I subscribe to one of its rules, in contrast to many of my colleagues, particularly those in the USA: do not reveal your findings in advance.

Part I

Patriarchy: its exits and closures

Our Father, who art in Heaven . . .
> (Matthew 6: 7–15)

. . . paternal authority is the most necessary, the most legitimate of all social powers.
> (Le Play 1866: 189)

Patriarchy has two basic intrinsic dimensions. The rule of the father and the rule of the husband, in that order. In other words, patriarchy refers to generational and to conjugal family relations or, more clearly, to generational and to gender relations. Although patriarchy shaped father–son relationships in asymmetric ways, as well as those of mother-in-law versus daughter-in-law, the core of patriarchal power was, above all, that of father to daughter and of husband to wife. The power of the father over his son was usually a mitigated version of his power over his daughter, and the power of the mother-in-law was delegated, by the father-in-law and/or by the husband.

The analysis here will be deployed in a narrative, a story about the world situation in 1900 and its change, and non-change, over the course of a century. But underlying it is a conception of patriarchy as a cluster of variables. The Family Father of Roman law had three basic powers: *potestas*, including the 'right of life and death', over his children as long as he lived; *manus* over his wife; and *dominium* over his property. When *manus* was becoming obsolete by the beginning of the imperial, or what is today called the Christian, era, the wife remained under the *potestas* of her father (Evans Grubbs 2002: 20ff).

The cluster used here, inspired by modern feminism and by comparative history and anthropology, covers patriarchy in a more specific manner. With regard to paternal/parent–child relations we shall take notice of formalized rules of child obedience and deference, and we shall look at genealogical and basic inheritance rules, i.e. whether there is a paternal bloodline only (patriliny); whether adult children are allowed to make their own marriages; and whether upon marriage they are expected to remain in the paternal household. The power of (prospective) mothers-in-law will here largely be subsumed under parental patriarchy.

Regarding husband–wife relations, the main aspects are: the presence or absence of institutionalized sexual asymmetry, such as polygyny and different adultery rules; of marital power hierarchy, in norms of husband headship and family representation; and of heteronomy, i.e. of the wife's duty to obey, and the husband's control over his wife's mobility, decisions and labour. West African evidence, in particular, has shown that hierarchy and heteronomy may vary independently of each other. Historically we shall have to rely mainly on evidence of institutionalization, on legal and social norms, and on observed patterns of behaviour. Recent survey research has made possible more specific insights into patriarchal marriage forms, collecting from large samples answers to questions about beating; visits to friends, neighbours and relatives; decisions on large daily purchases, on food to cook, on contraception, etc.; and on household divisions of labour. The main push of this analysis comes from Third World research (cf. Oheneba-Sakyi 1999; Blanc 2001; Jejeebhoy 2001).

Further attention will be paid to the possibility of discrimination against daughters by infanticide, maltreatment, neglect and inheritance systems, and to special physical sacrifice demanded of girls and women, such as infibulation or cliterodectomy, foot-crushing or foot-binding, and *sati* (widow immolation).

Patriarchy in this general sense of asymmetric male power of kinship has several variants of organization – of descent, of matrimonial patterns, of kinship nomenclature; these are central foci of classical mid-twentieth-century anthropology, a terrain which will here largely be left unexplored. Let it be mentioned only that in matrilineal kinship systems – where ancestry and inheritance run from mothers to children – patriarchal-equivalent power is usually invested in the maternal uncle. Patriarchy in the sense used here is de facto frequently accompanied by another principle of hierarchy – seniority – then institutionalized in the superiority of the older brother over the younger, and, generally, of the older over the younger incumbent of the same position in the generation-cum-gender system. The classical Chinese rites of mourning and the imperial Chinese penal codes provided highly elaborate illustrations of the institutional complex of patriarchy-cum-seniority.

Patriarchy has also an important extrinsic aspect: its relationship to other powers of this world. In some societies, African in particular but in principle also in imperial China, patriarchal power was supreme on earth, and religious practices are geared to veneration of and contacts with one's ancestors and their spirits. Orthodox Confucian rules and, even more telling, the penal codes of imperial China put filial piety above loyalty to the state and its laws, explicitly endorsing or permitting, respectively, a cover-up of crimes by fathers or other higher-ranking family members. The imperial penal codes had two exceptions to this rule: treason and rebellion (Bodde and Morris 1967: 41).

In other societies, patriarchy is explicitly subordinated to the authority of the Church or to institutionalized religious rituals before God and, in addition or alternatively, to the monarch or the state. The Russian Tsar kept some patriarchal features till the end of Tsardom, but in Western Europe revolutions pushed explicit patriarchal models of monarchy out of fashion from the time of John Locke and the English 'Glorious Revolution'. With

Hobbes, Locke and Rousseau a new political theory of the family developed in Western Europe (Abbott 1981). Louis XVI was still referred to as the 'father of the people', but Danton expressed the family self-portrait of the Revolution: 'It is the people who has produced us; we are not its fathers, we are its children!' (Delumeau and Roche 1990: 256, 335). The Victorian British cult of the family had patriarchal implications, like most family cults. But its political metaphor was one of representation, rather than a model of rule. 'England', Prime Minister Disraeli said in 1872, 'is a domestic country. . . . The nation is represented by a family – the Royal Family' (St John-Stevas 1957: 259).

1 Modernities and family systems
Patriarchy around 1900

In the beginning of our story all significant societies were clearly patriarchal. There was no single exception. Overwhelming opinion among the powers that be was well expressed by an enlightened, aristocratic Dutch Liberal, then Minister of Justice, P.W.A. Cort van der Linden, who said in parliament in 1900: 'The character of marriage is nevertheless, in my view, incompatible with a principled equality between man and woman' (Sevenhuisen 1987: 235).

The world was not equally patriarchal, though. The powers of fathers, brothers, husbands, and of adult sons, although virtually everywhere overwhelming, did differ across classes and cultures. Furthermore, our story does not begin 'Once upon a time there was traditional patriarchy'. Such a notion is generally vacuous, ignoring the great variety of 'traditions' and their historical mutations, and it is particularly inadequate to capture the situation in 1900, when a worldwide wave of recent family change had just rolled onto the stone tablets of historical archives. Indeed, the Paris World Exhibition of 1900 was also the occasion for a (third) international congress on the conditions and the rights of women (Dhavernas 1978: 75).

Major, or at least significant, legal changes to the family institution took place in the last quarter of the nineteenth century in a number of countries. Japan and Germany issued new civil codes in 1898 (*Meiji Minpo*) and in 1900 (*Bürgerliches Gesetzbuch*, passed in 1896). Married Women's Property Acts had given economic legal capacity, or at least protection (cf. the critical view of Sachs and Wilson 1978: 7ff), to women in the common law world, beginning in Mississippi in 1839, scoring an important victory in New York in 1848, spreading into the settlements of Australia and New Zealand, and climaxing in the English Act of 1882. Similar acts were passed in the Nordic countries between 1874 (Sweden) and 1889 (Finland) (Blom and Tranberg 1985). More indicative of times changing was perhaps new legislation protecting the earnings of married women, such as the first English Married Women's Property Act of 1870 (Gravesen 1957), incorporated also in the subsequent Nordic laws.

Changes of penal law could also be highly pertinent. One example is the Swedish Penal Code of 1864, which abolished the previous stipulations against violence to and insults to parents, offences that formerly could be punished by death. Breaches of the Fourth Commandment disappeared from the state's statute book, although it was made explicit that assault of parents should be regarded as 'aggravating' in cases of assault (Odén 1991: 94ff). More implicit was that with the same Code, the husband's ancient right to spank his wife ended. True, serious conjugal beatings were sanctioned with double fines, following medieval law (Hafström 1970: 52). Instead, legislation protecting children began to appear. A key European event in this respect was the British Prevention of Cruelty to, and Better Protection of Children Act of 1889; this was inspired by a notorious case of child maltreatment in New York in the early 1870s, in which the child could be legally rescued only with the help of a law against cruelty to animals (Therborn 1993: 251). Class polarization under-cut patriarchal solidarity even in France, which also in 1889 passed a law making it possible for paternal power to be forfeited by maltreatment of children, having brutal and alcholic proletarian fathers in mind (Delumeau and Roche 1990: 376–77).

Colonial family legislation had started, although more by providing options and by attempts at stigmatization than by effective interference, in spite of pressure from zealous Christian missionaries. British India had by 1900 seen a series of such largely symbolic acts, prohibiting *sati* (the immolation of widows) in 1829, and infanticide (in 1870), allowing widows to remarry (1856), allowing inter-caste marriages (1872), and trying to raise the marriage age (1891) (Lardinois 1986b: 354ff). In British Africa English marriages were offered, without much success, since the Gold Coast Marriage Ordinance of 1884 (H.F. Morris 1968: 35ff) However, nineteenth-century challenges to established patriarchy outside Europe and European settle-ments arose also in pre-colonial societies. Siamese (today we would say Thai) women were given increased freedom to marry in the 1860s (Hahang 1992: 58). In 1884 Choson Korea decreed a limitation of early marriage and gave permission for women to re-marry (Kwon 1999: 45). In late Qing China – during the Hundred Days of Reform under Emperor Guangxu in 1898, after the disaster of the Sino-Japanese war of 1895 and before the return of the conservative Empress Dowager Cixi and the disastrous Boxer Rebellion – the leading reformist intellectual of a dying empire, Kang You-wei, presented the emperor with a 'Memorial with a request for a ban on the binding of women's feet', with the conjunctural argument that foot-binding 'weakened the race hereditarily' and stood in the way of an 'increase of military strength' (Dikötter 1995: 18).

Most legal and social changes went in a de-patriarchalizing direction, but not all. The *Meiji Minpo* was rather a generalization of samurai patriarchy to all commoners, and the Egyptian 1875 codification of Hanafi (one of the four major schools of jurisprudence in Sunni Islam, predominant in the Ottoman Empire) family norms – an enterprise which introduced the modern Arab concept of family law, 'Personal Statute' (*al-ahwal al shakhsiyya*) – seems to have meant a rigidification of Muslim patriarchy (Botiveau 1993: 17, 194). The Napoleonic Civil Codes adopted in Hispanic South America (and in Spain in 1884), hardly contained any emancipation from patriarchy, and the assertion of civil (over ecclesiastical) marriage in Argentina, Chile and Uruguay in the 1880s had no feminist implications. In 1891, the Argentine Supreme Court stated: 'As long as marriage lasts, women in general lack civil capacity and are under the tutelage and the power of their husbands' (Lavrín 1995: 195–96).

Social stabilization in late Victorian Britain, after the convulsions of the industrial revolution, meant a strengthening of the patriarchal institution of marriage – if not of patriarchal power within marriage – and family. 'By the turn of the century', historian John Gillis writes in a major work, 'the clergy could congratulate themselves on the return of the people to their altars. . . . People were not only marrying more conventionally, but earlier and more often.' Female labour market participation had started to fall after 1870. 'Young people were once again subject to adult authority both in and outside the family . . . teenagers stayed at home longer, leaving it only to be married' (Gillis 1985: 232, 245, 261, respectively).

Feminist movements, often supported by male socialists and radicals, had arisen in the Americas, in Oceania and in Europe, pioneered there by Britain and growing most strongly in Scandinavia. An International Council of Women had been launched in Washington DC in 1888, which by 1900 had spawned eleven national councils, from Norway to New Zealand and from Canada to Argentina. More powerful were the new inter-continental female moral crusades: the World's Women's Christian Temperance Union, of US origin (1884) and a formidable force in North American and, even more, in Australasian politics and social life; and the orginally British Federation for the Abolition of State Regulation of Vice (from 1875), directed against regulated/tolerated prostitution (R. Evans 1979: 249ff). Women's issues were high on the agenda of Indian modernists, and in 1893 Annie Besant moved to India: a British convict with ideas about contraception, a future leader of theosophy from a base in Madras, and a future annual President of the Indian Congress Party. Political rights had been won by women in New Zealand, in outback Australia, and in patches of the USA west of the Missisippi, i.e. in peripheries of the Anglo-Saxon overseas settlements.

The Western European pattern of post-pubertal marriage had long provided a social basis for local youth cultures, of entertainment and courtship, and also, as in the charivari, an occasional force of moral sanction and ridicule. This youthful social space was widespread all over Northern and Western Europe, more peer-controlled in Scandinavia and in Germany, less so in France (Gillis 1975; Shorter 1977: chs 4 and 6; Mitterauer 1986). In the 1830s youth emerged as a socio-political category in Europe, with Giuseppe Mazzini's national-republican Young Italy movement, soon spawning a networked Young Europe. Around 1900 youth movements in Europe and in the European settlements overseas were generally overshadowed by class movements and actions and their political economy, but there was a very significant social presence of youth in the labour movement, and 'youth' and 'young' were about to spread as a rallying-cry outside Europe and its offshoots, to Young Ottomans, Young Turks, Young Tunisians, Young India, that is, to male youth.

Sociologically, the family institution had to adapt to the long-distance mass migration, from Europe to the Americas and to Oceania, from China across the South China Sea, but also traversing the Pacific. Indian families had moved across the Indian Ocean to East and South Africa, to the Caribbean, and to Fiji. Country-to-city migration had acquired major proportions in Europe. Massive proletarianization, whether from population increase, technical changes or from the force of superior property ownership, and the emergence of a sizeable salaried 'service class' had by 1900 radically changed the premises of family relations in major parts of Europe, the USA and other European settlements. The same processes were at least beginning to affect Japan, some industrial centres of India, and new mining centres, such as Southern Africa and Chile. In the Americas, the USA, Cuba and Brazil in particular, the final end of slavery set the recently emancipated black population out on a new course of, severely socio-economically constrained, family options.

In the following we shall make a brief tour of the world around 1900, looking at the main public issues of generational and gender relations, and making an assessment of the relative strength of patriarchy in different parts of the world. We shall make our stops according to our previously identified world pattern of family systems, but let us also take notice of the different roads to modernity, the layout and the effects of which are already clearly visible by 1900.

Collisions and continuities in Europe

The European family system, to different degrees in its major western, eastern and other variants, had by 1900 been put under very heavy strain by a socio-demographic revolution that began in the eighteenth century. Demographically it is recorded in a move to a sustained, long-term, higher population growth. The threatening pauperization of this new proletariat was delimited by another world-historical innovation, the Industrial Revolution, and by mass extra-continental migration. By 1900 in northwestern Europe these social convulsions had not only undermined the agrarian property context of the European family, but had also started to re-settle the latter in an urban–industrial mode.

Second, the European family was the context and the target of the worldwide powerful discourses on the family at the close of the nineteenth century, the most influential anti-patriarchal ones being John Stuart Mill's *The Subjection of Women* (1869), Henrik Ibsen's *A Doll's House*, August Bebel's *Socialism and Woman* (both of 1879), and the most powerful patriarchal tract, *Rerum novarum*, the 1891 Encyclica of the infallible Pope Leo XIII. 'Like the polity, . . . the family is truly an association [veri nominis societas est], which is governed by its proper power [potestate propria], which in this case is that of the father [paterna]', the Pope proclaimed (Rodríguez 1964: 269).

Profound, dramatic social changes and sharp, highly articulate ideological conflict affected the European family. Relatively speaking, this was, before its nineteenth-century challenges, a very moderately patriarchal system. Supreme value was invested in a transcendental God, and not in patrilineal ancestors. While parents had an important say in marriage matters in the upper classes and in the southern and, above all, eastern parts of the continent, free choice of spouse was a central religious norm of the Catholic Church since the Counter-Reformation Council of Trent. The two major Enlightenment codifications, the Prussian Code of 1794 and the French Code Napoléon of 1804 – two major countries outside the Tridentine norms, Prussia as Protestant and France as the explicit warden of Gallic patriarchy in defiance of the Church – assumed the key roles being played by the parties themselves, while providing parents with certain powers of veto. Both required parental consent to the marriage even of legally mature sons (Glendon 1977: 29, 31). The European practice of adult marriage and of a separate household gave the protagonists a social basis of autonomy. Monogamy was the norm, and women could move in public, heterosocial places, although normally not into positions of public authority.

The sexual libertinage of the eighteenth-century upper classes of Europe was not exclusively a male privilege. Lady Montagu (1994/1716–18: 22) tells us about Vienna court society ''tis the established custom for every lady to have two husbands, one that bears the name and another that performs the duties'. Marriage was a sacred act, a sacrament, but no sacred obligation. Indeed, in Catholicism it was clearly morally secondary to the celibacy of priests, monks and nuns. Kinship was generally weak, open and delimited, outside a small minority of upper-class lineages, usually without organization, with bilateral ties and inheritance rights (maternal as well as paternal), and usually not extending beyond two steps from ego, beyond grandparents/ grandchildren, nephews/nieces, uncles and aunts, or first cousins.

In the Scottish Enlightenment, first in Hume (1742) and then underlined in Millar (1771), there emerged the idea that the position of women was an indicator of social progress. An evolutionist, 'modern' twist was given to the old feudal European notion of chivalry, which did not assume any equality among the sexes. Hume (1742/n.a.: 77) put it thus:

> . . . nature has given man the superiority above woman, by endowing him with greater strength both of mind and body . . . Barbarous nations display this superiority by reducing their females to the most abject slavery. . . . But the male sex among a polite people discover their authority in a more generous, though not a less evident manner, by civility, by respect, by complaisance, and, in a word, by gallantry.

Patria potestas and *manus mariti*, fatherly and husbandly power, were firmly institutionalized, buttressed by Church law and religious teaching, by secular law, and by village mores, under the sanction of public ridicule (Shorter 1977: 220). The Anti-Enlightenment counter-revolution was aggressively patriarchal: 'Paternal authority is the foundation of morality and of society', the important mouthpiece of French conservatism, *Journal des Débats*, asserted in 1800 (MacMahon 2001: 134).

From the perspective of an interest in patriarchy, the picture of the European family and its relations to the tremendous social changes of the continent in the eighteenth and nineteenth centuries becomes almost the inverse of the family portrait by mid-twentieth-century functionalist sociologists, of industrial and urban revolutions leading to (conjugal) family revolutions. As we shall see, however, in the experiences of Japan and of East Asia generally, this conclusion does not warrant adoption of the same correlation of socio-economic and family change with the causal arrows turned around, with the northwestern nuclear family providing the preconditions for the industrial revolution. Over the long term, a picture of adaptive continuity emerges, in spite of enormous changes in patterns of property, labour and residence, but not of a 'modern equilibrium'. The relative stability of European patriachy from 1600 to 1920/50 contrasts with the major changes in the last 50–80 years of the twentieth century.

In other words, we have here two research questions. How is the basic continuity of moderate European patriarchy by 1900 to be explained in view of the profound social and economic changes? Second, how should we account for, and evaluate, the forces of institutional conflict and change?

By 1900, the European family had been subjected to at least three tremendous social and economic changes, the onslaught of which went roughly from the northwest to the southeast. The first one was proletarianization, the growth of non-propertied classes, dependent on the sale of their labour. Proletarianiz-ation is pertinent to patriarchy because the proletarian father has no property to transmit to his children, and because his fatherly power is subject to the superior powers of owners of land or capital. In Saxony, by the nineteenth century a leading area of German industrialization, proletarians increased from 24 per cent of the total population in 1550 to 58 per cent in 1750, and 71 per cent in 1843. Most of this increase was rural. The rural proletariat increased its share of the total population from 22 to 55 per cent between 1550 and 1843 (Tilly 1984: 33).

Urbanization, secondly, challenged traditional authorities of all kinds including patriarchy, by its display of heterogeneity, its offers of options, and its escapes from social control. High cultures of the world had for millennia had a range of urbanization between an eighth and a sixth of its population, 'urban' referring to concentrated settlements with 2,000 inhabitants or more. Between 1800 and 1900 pan-European urbanization in this sense jumped from 16 to 41 per cent of the population (Bairoch 1997: II, 193, 195).

Industrialization, finally, challenges patriarchy, and any family arrange-ments in existence, primarily by its large-scale severing of work-place from residence, thereby undercutting paternal control. While general employ-ment statistics have generally been unable to distinguish domestic, proto-industrial manufacturing from factory production, there is no doubt that Europe saw an epochal industrial revolution in the course of the nineteenth century. Agriculture, which in developed, stratified pre-industrial societies usually occupied 75–85 per cent of the population (Bairoch 1997: I, 597), had in all Europe, including Russia, come down to employing only 56 per cent of the population by 1900 (Bairoch 1997: II, 189). Industrial employment in the broad sense (manufacturing, mining, construction, utilities and transport) around 1900 constituted a good quarter of the Italian labour force, a third of the French, almost two-fifths of the German, and half of the British labour force (Flora *et al.* 1987: national tables).

We should add a fourth, socio-political challenge, which was crystallizing in the last quarter of the nineteenth century, also, by and large, along the northwest–southeast axis, though with a strong Central European qualification. That was the nation-state, above all in the shape of obligatory public schooling (cf. Therborn 1993: 248ff). This took children away, for some time, from the rule of the father, something which caused bitter conflicts with the militant religious patriarchies of the supra-state Catholic Church and sub-state Dutch Calvinist Fundamentalism.

The reproduction of European patriarchy in the face of the challenges of proletarianization, urbanization and industrialization rested on four key components. One was the development of the 'family wage economy' (Tilly and Scott 1987/1978). The early proletarian, industrial as well as proto-industrial artisan, family developed a survival strategy based on the pooling of the contributions, waged or not, of all family members, of children as well as of wife/mother. The *pater familias* was no longer a landowner allocating labour and transmitting property, but he was still head of a striving family enterprise. While having no longer any significant property to promise and to distribute, he usually controlled important access to employment. He also had another powerful sanction: he could throw out disobedient, low-waged youngsters onto a city of usually acute housing shortage. This patriarchal family-wage economy survived the coming of obligatory public schooling: it was postponed until the end of schooling (Tilly and Scott 1987/1978: 207ff).

Second, European-type patriarchy provided low-status niches for many proletarians who could not fit into the family wage economy. Celibacy was no sin, and children born out of wedlock, while clearly low class, were neither a disaster nor a threat to the established order. Parts of Europe, like many Alpine communities and northern outlying Portugal, could develop these patterns of deviance without in any significant way being either challenged by or challenging pious regional Catholicism.

Third, the normative pattern, and the character of its centre of power was extremely important. Eighteenth-century aristocratic court society had let go of many family norms in favour of general sexual libertinism. However, this kind of society was crucially dependent on royal largesse, which made courtly favour much more important than the management of the family estate. The French Revolution, with its definite cutting of aristocratic *plumage,* and the rise of bourgeois capital re-asserted European family norms, powerfully and profoundly. Eighteenth-century *libertinage* was perceived as an aberration, leading to cataclysmic social disaster. The rising new mode of production, industrial capitalism, was not just a system of market rationality. It had a heavy social anchor in the patriarchal family, as Thomas Mann portrayed so well in *Buddenbrooks* (1903).

The estate-managing, providing family man became the norm of the European nineteenth century. He was bourgeois, true, but he was not *ancien régime*, nor of a strange religion or foreign ethnicity. He was the persona of modern success and of universalistic respectability, well sustained by religion, law and public opinion. While the secularization of schools created religious conflicts in Catholic and Calvinist countries, which had to be dealt with in some form of *modus vivendi* or other, public mass schooling was generally committed to inculcating patriarchal values in pupils, such as obedience, discipline, deference, to supporting existing patriarchal norms, not subverting them. Nor did it pose any conflict between the demands of the nation-state and the old ways of the father and mother.

To 'respectable' workers and even to the mainstream of European trade unionism and socialism, the family man was the normative hero. In this way, patriarchal normativity was carried, across a cultural bridge above a social cataclysm, from the peasant village to the urban working-class block.

Fourth, and finally, what made the large-scale reproduction of patriarchal norms possible was industrialization. Uniquely successful and extensive, European industrialization created a broad industrial working class out of the proletarians. And the industrial working class was, towards the end of the nineteenth century, with the declining relative importance of the textile and garment industry, becoming increasingly male. Married women had generally tended to avoid factory labour, with its totalitarian demands (Tilly and Scott 1987: 148ff; Beuys 1980: 391). This working class, even if not highly skilled, soon acquired resources sufficient to, more or less, follow the family norm of the ruling class. Proletarianization did not, in the end, mean pauperization, marginalization and family dissolution, tendencies which were very much present in large European cities of the nineteenth century, in informal unions, births out of wedlock, and in abandoned infants. The latter were a major phenomenon of Catholic Europe, and of Moscow and St Petersburg, whose institutions at their nineteenth-century peak received 26,000 infants a year (Tilly *et al.* 1992: 18). In Lombardy in the first seven decades of the nineteenth century, about 400,000 children were abandoned, a good half of them in Milan (Hunecke 1994: 125).

By 1900 the male breadwinner working-class family had emerged *de facto*, and had established itself as the normative aspiration of the European working classes. This new working-class family was most striking in the country with the most convulsive and dramatic, but also economically most extensive and successful industrialization – Britain (Johnson 1976; Mitterauer and Seider 1982: 132ff; Barbagli 1984: ch. III; Gillis 1985: pt III; Gillis 1997: pt II)

Now, the bourgeois family, however powerful, was not a self-evident norm. Europe, after all, was a continent of revolutions and of normative and civil wars. For reasons which still remain obscure, the great French Revolution and its heritage did not pose a challenge. On the contrary, the Napoleonic tradition had bequeathed a militant patriarchy, with the notorious paragraph 213 of the 1804 Civil Code stipulating wifely 'obedience' to her husband, a clause inserted upon the personal insistence of the emperor (Glendon 1977: 182n) and a wide-ranging *puissance paternel* (fatherly power). Republican Revolutionary tradition saw itself in an exclusively patrilineal descent, threatened by a clerical sway over women, subscribing for long that 'the tradition of the French family is the respect for the head [le chef] of the family' (Dhavernas 1978: 91, quoting a Senator of 1936). Fathers' legal 'right to correction' included the possibility of sending disobedient children into state prisons or penitentiaries, herein continuing, after the Jacobin interlude, a pre-Revolutionary institution (*lettres de cachet*). About a thousand children a year, mainly Parisian, were punished in that way in the second half of the nineteenth century (Delumeau and Roche 1990: 337). French feminism was very weak, and confined to a small circle of the *haute bourgeoisie protestante* and of dissident Freemasons (Evans 1979: 126ff), i.e. marginal Republican milieux.

The ideological challenges to European patriarchy came from two sources, from Protestant Radicalism and from (atheistic) Socialism. John Stuart Mill's (1869) treatise on *The Subjection of Women* is the first major manifestation of the former, and was instantly a 'feminist bible', published in the same year all over the (former) British Empire and translated into French, German, Swedish and Danish (R. Evans 1979: 18–19). Mill's main point is that gender subordination has become 'one of the chief hindrances to human improvement'. Gender equality would mean not only 'the unspeakable gain in private happiness to the liberated half of the species', but would also entail 'an increase of the general fund of thinking and acting power, and an improvement in the general conditions of the association of men with women' (Mill 1869/1970: 95).

The Norwegian playwright Henrik Ibsen came out of a similiar milieu, although without John Stuart's formidable father, and was very much concerned with individual moral issues. Ibsen's play *A Doll's House* placed the question of love and convention at a summit of dramatic choice. Nora, who finally leaves a conventional marriage for an uncertain future, soon became a global heroine of Radicals.

Already the so-called Utopian socialists of the 1830s and 1840s, the French Saint-Simonistes and the Fourieristes, had a feminist orientation. But the first important connection between the Socialist labour movement and the cause of women was estalished by August Bebel, soon to become the leader of the most developed labour movement of the world, German Social Democracy. Bebel's treatise *Die Frau und der Sozialismus* (Woman and Socialism) appeared in 1879 and rapidly became the most read Socialist tract, after the *Communist Manifesto*. It is actually a work of social history, with a futuristic socialist coda, more than the reasoned plea of Mill. Its critical edge and its politics are directed against the double dependency of women: upon the world of men, and upon the relations of property. The former provides the common interests with the bourgeois women's movement, the latter with the male labour movement.

Bebel, Ibsen and Mill were all minoritarians of their time. Prevailing opinion was better expressed by the formidable Protestant Prussian conservative historian Heinrich von Treitschke, one of Bebel's explicit targets: 'The real vocation of woman will always be the house and marriage. She should bear and educate children' (Beuys 1980: 389).

However, the most powerful counterblast to left-wing liberal or socialist individualism came from the sacred guardian of European patriarchy, the

Pope. The 1891 Encyclica of Leo XIII was meant to confront the modern times head on, as indicated by its opening and title *Rerum novarum*, 'On New Things'. It contained a social message to capitalist industrialization, inspiring social Catholicism ever since. In retrospect its equally strong patriarchal emphasis, part of its polemics against socialists, tends to be forgotten. The sacred basis of paternal power was something that the Encyclica wanted to hammer home among the faithful (Rodriguez 1964: 268–70).

The legal and political issues of European patriarchy focused on the legal capacity and rights of married and unmarried women. Common law married women were considered merged with their husbands; in continental civil law as fully subject to the power of their husbands. Maidens were traditionally under the law of their father whatever their age, in Scandinavian law until 1857 in Denmark and 1858 in Sweden. The institution of a matrimonial guardian was abolished in Sweden in 1872. In northwestern Europe married women had by 1900 recently gained the right to manage their own property and income – in England in 1870 and 1882. True, the Swedish law of 1874 was originally petty and custodian in this respect, in contrast to the Norwegian law of 1888, which provided married women with full legal economic maturity, like the Danish law of 1899 (Blom and Tranberg 1985: 43, 54, 190). France and the Latin countries of the Napoleonic Code were still exceptions, as well as Russia and Eastern Europe. Only in 1907 did French married women gain a legal right to dispose of their own wages (Dhavernas 1978: 8ff), and only then were legally mature children and men freed of the obligation to have their parents' consent to marriage, although a man under 30 and a woman under 25 still had to formally and respectfully solicit the advice of the parents (Coester-Waltjens and Coester 1997: 16). However, French law maintained until 1965 a stipulation, referred to by the highest private law court of the land (*Cour de Cassation*) as late as 1962, that a married woman had to have her husband's permission to work outside the home (Dhavernas 1978: 103–4).

At the centre of European family normativity around 1900 was the new Civil Code for the German Reich. The main purpose of the Code was to unify German law, corresponding to the proclamation of the Reich in 1871. The preparation was mainly in the hands of judges and jurists from the ministerial bureaucracy, drawn from the circle of the liberal German *Bürgertum*. After the publication of a first draft in 1888 it was revised by a second commission, and then finally by a special commission of the Reichstag. The central political govenment does not seem to have taken any active part in the process (Staudinger 1995: I Buch, Einleitung, Teil IV). In the final parliamentary debate, the leader of the Social Democrats, August Bebel, was very much engaged, not without some occasional success (Berathung 1896). The Code was adopted in 1896, and in effect from 1 January 1900. It was preceded by significant partial reforms, such as lifting the requirement for parental consent to marriage for daughters over 25 and sons over 24 (in 1875), and introducing legal majority for women (in 1884).

In family law, the Code substituted 'parental' (*elterliche*) for 'fatherly' power (*väterliche Gewalt*), which according to authoritative interpretation (Staudinger

1908: vol. IV, 824) was in principle invested in both parents. But without further ado the Code goes on to regulate how this parental authority should be exercised by the father (Bürgerliches Gesetzbuch 1907: §§1626ff). The mother is later included in a subsidiary role, with power being transferred to her by the death of the father, but in case of a parental disagreement, §1634 made clear that the view of the father should prevail.

'To the husband belongs the decision in all affairs of the married life in common', said §1354, but added in the same paragraph, 'The wife does not have the obligation to carry out the decision of her husband when the decision constitutes an abuse of his right'. And regardless of the preceding paragraph, §1355 continued, the wife has the right and the duty to 'direct the common home'.[1] Against the first-mentioned paragraph the Social Democrats put the alternative 'In all common matters of married life the spouses are equal'. The left Liberals (*Freisinnigen*) would have been satisfied if the paragraph was deleted. Neither proposal had any chance, and in the third and final reading in the Reichstag, the paragraph of husbandly power was passed without further debate (Berathung 1896: 191ff, 366).

By 1896 the subjection of women had nevertheless ceased to be self-evident in Europe, even in the German Reichstag. The speaker for the Law Commission, the main author of the draft code, Professor Planck, a high Prussian civil servant, accepted the position of women as a measure of 'the whole cultural level' of a people. In his opinion the draft code ameliorated the situation of women considerably. He then pointed to, inter alia, the equal economic capacity (*Geschäftsfähigkeit*) of women, and the new concept of parental power (Berathung 1896: 197ff).

The wife's work outside the home was not made dependent upon husbandly approval, as it was not only in the French law of Napoleonic vintage but also in the Swiss Civil Code of 1907 (Lalive and Keppler 1968: 1072). Conservative to many in the 1890s already, though, was the marriage property rule, which retained the Prussian–Saxon regime of 'administrative community' (*Verwaltungsgemeinschaft*), meaning that all wealth of the couple was to be administered by the husband (Staudinger 1995: IV Buch, Einleitung, 6–8).

A draft proposal that children between 21, the age of legal majority, and 25 should have their parents' consent to marry was subject to a heated parliamentary debate, which was more about parental consent to marriage in general than about a specific year of matrimonial majoration. Lutheran Conservatives and National Liberals pleaded in favour of parental consent, against spirited interventions by Bebel, supported by the Catholic Centre, and were in the end successful (Berathung 1896: 356ff).

In terms of the times, German patriarchy was relatively moderate and judicially regulated. It fits this moderate character, that a First Draft paragraph about children owing 'obedience' to their parents – a general rule in seventeenth- and eighteenth-century continental European law and carried into the modern world, also outside Europe, by the Code Napoléon – was dropped in the further commission work (Staudinger 1908: 799), and did not reappear in the two final parliamentary readings (Berathung 1896). But it was still flanked by strict rules of male exclusion, e.g. by a Prussian law of 1851 prohibiting women from participating in political meetings and from joining political associations, and by the continuing exclusion of women from higher education. A handful of women had been granted special access to university education, and in 1900 Baden, in the Liberal southwest, was the first state of the Reich to allow women to matriculate as ordinary students. In dominant Prussia this happened only in 1908, eleven years after women's entrance to the University of Vienna (Albisetti 1996: 51, 53), and the same year as the ban on political activity by women was lifted (R. Evans 1979: 105, 109). Nowhere in Europe in 1900 had women the right to vote.

By 1900, little had happened to patriarchy in Eastern Europe, for long more patriarchal than the West, with patrilineal kinship, patrilocal house-holds, and inheritance basically among sons or other male relatives only. The area was still overwhelmingly rural although industrial developments started in the last third of the nineteenth century. The Orthodox Church condoned arranged marriages, which were still very frequent, even among the ordinary peasantry. (The Tsarist family law left marriage matters to the religious authori-ties.) In Russia the practice was rooted among the serfs, and their emancipation in 1861 does not seem to have made much change to family matters. The Emancipation Decree explicitly stated that local customs and traditions of household norms should be followed (Moseley 1959/1976; Czap 1976; Johnson 1976; Kaser 2000: 124ff). The Great Reform of 1861 maintained the peasant commune, now as an institution of male family heads, for collective ownership of land, responsible for redemption payments to the landlords, and invested with powers of re-partitioning among households according to family needs. Outside the peasantry, the Russian Civil Code of 1864 gave daughters a right to inherit a fourteenth of the immovable property of their fathers, and an eighth of movable property. A widow could claim a seventh of the immovable property of her deceased husband, and a fourth of his movable property (Kaser 2000: 127).

In the revolutionary movement towards the end of the century, some women and feminists distinguished themselves; they were often university-educated in Switzerland like Vera Figner and Alexandra Kollontai (cf. Alpern Engel 1976). Switzerland, i.e. the cantons of Zürich, Bern and Geneva, was the pioneering provider of university education for women, more often foreign than Swiss, and the Russian medical student Nadezhda Suslova was, in 1867–68, the first European woman to receive a regular academic degree (Albisetti 1996: 46, 48, 48n).

In the Balkans, an extended patrilineal family was significant among southern Slavs, Serbs, Montenegrins, Croats, Bulgarians and Albanians; this was the *zadruga*, in which even an adult married husband could be under the rule of his father or his older brother (Byrnes 1976; Kaser 1995).

Legally, Eastern European family matters were basically under religious jurisdiction, including that of the religious minorities of the Russian Empire, although the latter also got a general marriage law in 1894. In Greece the legal tradition continued Roman–Byzantian traditions. Added to the basics of religious law in Eastern Europe was a set of territorial variations, reflecting the different political historical trajectories of the areas in 1900 under one monarch.

There were also some variations on the common theme of patriarchy. Serbia had stiffened the Roman law, with its conception of husbandly power, '*manus mariti*', taking as its model the Austrian Civil Code of 1811, and adding both old Serbian concepts, like '*stareschina*' (elder of the house) to the status of the husband, and Napoleonic ones, like '*autorisation marital*'. Bulgaria, on the other hand, for all its Orthodox patriarchy, included a marriage regime of separated property and the unimpeded business capacity of the wife, as well as a symmetric regulation of divorce (Bergmann 1926; Crusen *et al.* 1937: vol. IV).

At the frontier: gender governance of European settlement

The Europeans who went out to settle in the Americas, Australasia, or northern and southern Africa – although the latter two regions will be largely left out of treatment here – brought with them their, mainly Western, family norms, legal, religious and customary. But the settlers were rarely representative of their country of origin. They tended to include larger proportions of adventurers, misfits and dissenters, in short, of institutional innovators. The conditions of overseas settlement also differed. The familiar ancient village or small community was left behind, and an unknown expanse of land opened up. Neighbours were few and far between. We are in this section talking only about European settlements based on genocide and ethnic cleansing. The different family pattern in societies where the natives maintained a major presence will be dealt with later. For a long time there were, as a rule, many more men than women, complicating family demography. Royal and ecclesiastical authority did not disappear, but it was very distant, in the last instance overseas.

However, this susceptibility to institutional change should not be collapsed into twentieth-century modernity, as one of the world's great family historians allowed himself, saying 'The [US] American family was probably "born modern" because the colonial settlers seemed to have seized privacy and intimacy for themselves as soon as they stepped off the boat' (Shorter 1977: 238). For one thing, some of the settlers were what now would be called Christian Fundamentalists, such as the New England Puritans and the Dutch Calvinist Afrikaners, i.e. they were militantly patriarchal. Pressures of change in New England, for instance, were first met with fulminating sermons and draconian statutes, including the death penalty for sins against the Fourth Commandment (Mintz and Kellogg 1988: 17). In the Spanish conquest of America, priests and monks of the Catholic Church accompanied the *conquistadores* at the landings and the first battlefields.

As time wore on and socio-economic conditions diverged with the distance of oceans and generations, countervailing tendencies of institutional orthodoxy also emerged. Alongside the adventurers, the dissenters, the escapees, who continued to pour in, there were now settled communities, cities, and bi- or even multi-generational local elites with aspirations of respectability.

In Hispanic America patriarchy was reinforced in 1776 by the royal so-called Pragmatic Sanction, making paternal consent a requirement for a valid (white) marriage. This move by Enlightened Bourbon Absolutism had its social edge against informal and inter-ethnic unions, and its ideological thrust against the Spanish Church, which in contrast to the Portuguese and the French, had been very loyal to the Council of Trent and its strict rule of free choice of marriage partner (Socolow 1989: 211ff; Navarro 1999: 47). Independence did not loosen the norms of patriarchy in either northern or southern America, once the immediate revolutionary upheavals had calmed down. US state codifications of family norms tended rather to rigidify those in existence (Sachs and Wilson 1978: 76). Mid-nineteenth-century officious legal commentary in the USA emphasized marriage as an institution or a status, rather than as a contract (Grossberg 1985: 21ff). The early new Civil Codes of Latin America, such as the Chilean one of 1858 – drawn up by one of the sub-continent's great intellectuals, Andrés Bello – followed the Code Napoléon in proclaiming the wife's duty of obedience to her husband. Among the late nineteenth-century waves of mass immigration, the patriarchal family and kin and ethno-religious communities were crucial supports in crowded cities of raw capitalist industrialization, or for that matter on the homesteads. Under the new free labour regime in Brazil, family migration was especially promoted for coffee share-cropping in São Paolo and for more intensive, diversified agriculture in the south.

Nevertheless, with these qualifications and contradictions, it is true that in the second half of the nineteenth century patriarchy was being attacked and eroded more powerfully and extensively in the New Worlds than in the Old. The political discontinuity of American independence, and also the legislative autonomy of the British colonies, made the door to new legal arguments, irrespective of precedent and ancient custom, more easy to open. Religious churches had been disestablished in the USA, and the bonds between the Church and the states of independent Latin America, although everywhere re-established, were riven by controversy from the beginning. The Church was, after all, colonial and not nationalist. At the end of the nineteenth century, all institutional authority in the New Worlds was being swamped by the enormous influx of immigrants, young free men and women of different nationalities, languages, religions and customs. While there was hardly any frontal challenge, existing institutions could hardly corral this rapid human flood.

Into this welter of change stepped a newly emerging social force, organized women. Settler women had always had important economic functions, and an extra scarcity value. Social control of them had almost always been more difficult than in the villages of Old Europe. With the widening differentiation of the overseas settlements, between established settlers and rough, new male immigrants, women were often regarded as important, nay crucial, norm-carriers, as carriers of 'civilization' and manners, and in their effect on new single males as well as in themselves. For these and, possibly, other reasons women's access to education tended to be much easier in the New World. Beginning in the west, in Iowa in 1855, US women got access to university studies in the third quarter of the nineteenth century. By 1880 women made up a third of US college and university students (Stevenson 1991: 121–22). The newest of the New Worlds was at the head though. In 1893 over half of New Zealand university students were female (R. Evans 1979: 61).

It was the size of the New World intake, more than the dates, that was impressive. The comparative figures I have are from about 1920 or the years after, but they should tell us something about the situation around 1900 as well. In the 1920s, women constituted 36 per cent of the university student population in the USA, 23–25 per cent in Chile and Cuba, and 15 per cent in Argentina (Miller 1991: 54). The only European country on a par with Chile was the UK, possibly even slightly ahead, but clearly behind the USA. Most European countries had 10–15 per cent women students; with Germany and Sweden at the lower end, and the Netherlands and Italy at the higher; Spain underlined the distance between the two Hispanic worlds, with 4 per cent female students in 1920. Germany reached the Chilean 1920s level only after World War II, in East Germany by 1950, and West Germany by 1970 (Fischer *et al.* 1985: 6, 82).

Disestablished Anglo-Saxon Protestantism was significant for its support of women's education in the New World. This can be seen from its role in overwhelmingly Catholic Latin America. The Argentine mid-nineteenth-century educationalist and President Sarmiento took US education as a model, and also brought US teachers to Argentina. A key figure of feminism in the La Plata region (of Argentina and Uruguay), Maria Abella de Ramirez, was graduated from such a 'normal school' (teachers' college) in 1894 (Cassina de Nogara 1989: 31). In Chile the leading secondary girls' school, the Colegio de Santiago, had been founded by Methodist missionaries in 1881. The new, egalitarian Cuban education system of 1901, under US occupation, was given a boost by Harvard University offering a summer school to a thousand Cuban teachers (Miller 1991: 50, 52).

In Argentina, Chile, Uruguay and Cuba these pioneering women, though often daughters of Freemasons and usually educated outside the Catholic circuit, were not isolated grouplets, as in France, or, for varying reasons, in the heartlands of the Iberian rule of the Americas. This was not the case in Brazil, with its underdeveloped, elitist school system, in the beleaguered Hispanicism of Peru, nor even in Mexico, which was changing in other respects but where little immigration and bitter conflicts with the USA also meant that the traditions of New Spain remained more powerful than in the end-of-world periphery of the Southern Cone.

Disestablished Protestantism provided New World women with a public moral force, which no New World Catholicism allowed; nor, for that matter, did any Old World state Protestantism, although Norway, on the northwestern periphery of Europe, harboured some considerable similarities. Catholicism always emphasized the male clergy above the congregation, and its outlets for female activity were either very narrowly circumscribed as a public activity, in the form of charity, which was a major feature of late nineteenth-century Catholic America, or confined within the walls of nunneries, whereto a great deal of female dissent and cause commitment was directed. Sin was more serious to Protestants than to Catholics, as the former lacked the handy solutions of the confessional.

While certainly bruising male sentiments and interests, New World feminist moral crusaders could base themselves not only on Protestant theology, but also on 'polite society' of established settlement. Often there was an important ethno-religious component. The women activists were British Protestants, and their male targets were very likely to be non-British Catholics, Irish, Slavs and Italians.

The world's first powerful women's movement was the Woman's Christian Temperance Union, founded in 1874, springing from the American Midwest. By 1900 it had 200,000 members in the USA. Its main role in history is not the shortlived and disastrous legal prohibition of alcohol, but its pushing of a feminist agenda. Its main successes occurred in New Zealand and Australia, to where the movement spread in 1885. This was the movement which succeeded in giving women the right to vote, in New Zealand in 1893 and in the new Commonwealth of Australia in 1901 (Evans 1979: 58ff). Except for a few American states west of Mississippi, Australia and New Zealand were the only parts of the world where women had political citizenship at the beginning of the twentieth century. The merit belongs, above all, to a force of female Protestant anti-alcohol campaigners. When and where the traditonal backbone of Christian patriarchy had been bent, these self-righteous women alone had the capacity to appeal across the gender barrier to the male upholders of inherited institutions. In the Catholic countries, the male secular Republicans had good reasons to fear the hold of the clergy over a large part of a feminine electorate, but until 1929 in Ecuador no male Catholic political elite could overcome its patriarchal instincts to allow women the right to vote.

With respect to family law also, the New World led the Old. At issue was, above all, in the common law world the legal 'death' of married women, absorbed by their husbands, and in the Napoleonic civil law countries the *patria potestas,* the supreme power of the husband and father. It was also the question of to what extent marriage was a contract and to what extent a social institution. Catholicism held it to be a sacrament, a sacred institution. Protestantism saw marriage as 'a worldly thing' (Luther), but as an institution of social importance, superior to, overriding individual interests. In the 1840s the women's movement gathered momentum in the United States. Married women's economic rights were at the centre of women's demands. But there were also other issues. A very important one in the decades leading up to the Civil War was the abolition of slavery. Abolitionism was very much carried by morally concerned northern middle-class Protestants, female as well as male.

What became the feminist historical landmark of the Seneca Falls meeting and Declaration in 1848 was planned as part of the campaign for marriage property reform in the state of New York. The Declaration took its language from the Declaration of Independence, holding 'these truths to be self-evident', 'that all men and women are created equal', as a baseline for a list of egalitarian demands, including the right to vote (Evans 1979: 46–47).

While the rise of a mass women's movement, reinforced by mass female entry into higher education, was a major event in the history of patriarchy, there were no further breakthroughs of women's rights in the USA before the turn of the century. In the aftermath of the Civil War the alliance of abolitionism and feminism fell apart. Women were kept out of electoral politics, save in a few remote areas like Wyoming, and states still maintained bars against women entering professions, such as law (Sachs and Wilson 1978: 97ff). In the racist backlash after the Civil War and the end of Reconstruction, the status, as opposed to contract, character of marriage was often given a new emphasis, as a legal rationale for a wave of racist marriage laws, against inter-racial marriage (Grossberg 1985: 136ff). Although common law, in contrast to European civil law, is generally reluctant to regulate and to intervene in internal family relations, American states passed laws explicitly proclaiming wifely subordination, laws which in some cases remained on the statute books into the 1970s (Sachs and Wilson 1978: 149).

When in the early 1870s the colourful New York feminist Victoria Woodhull publicly took republican contractualism to its logical conclusion there was an outrage: 'I have an inalienable, constitutional, and natural right to love whom I may, to love as long or as short a period as I can; to change that love every day if I please, and with that right neither you nor any law you can frame have any right to intervene' (Stevenson 1991: 154, emphases omitted). It would take more than a century before such a statement could enter mainstream opinion in New York.

In one other area US patriarchy was clearly curtailed by the end of the nineteenth century. Judges had come to recognize the interests of children, that children could be abused by parents, and that children's interests were relevant to custody cases, the number of which was mounting with wider possi-bilities of judicial divorce. In practice this was evolving into maternal preference in custody disputes (Grossberg 1985).

Statute-based, legislature-made law is usually more difficult to change than judge-made law. While the Argentine Civil Code of 1869 refrained from admonishing the wife to obey her husband, in contrast to the Uruguayan Code of the year before and the Chilean of 1858 (Bergmann and Ferid 1955), it still put her squarely under *patria potestad* (the Spanish legal term for male family power), like her sisters in all Latin America who had living fathers/ husbands. Widowed and separated women could obtain 'fatherly power' over their children in the late nineteenth-century post-colonial codes from Argentina to Mexico (Arrom 1985; Lavrin 1995: ch. 6). The Mexican Code of 1884 gave daughters legal majority and the right to marry at 21, although not, if unmarried, to choose their own residence before the age of 30. Its Positivist liberalism gave the couple the right to choose their own property regime, but it also took away each child's legal right to an equal share of four-fifths of the estate, and an earlier change had freed parents from providing their daugthers with a dowry (Arrom 1985).

In the Southern Cone of the Americas, particularly in Chile and Argentina, debates about the subordination of women in family law and demands for change gathered some momentum in the last 10–15 years of the nineteenth century, only to become completely lost in the male legislative labyrinths. Change would take a long time to come.

The duality of Creole society: colonial and Indo- and Afro-American families after the upheavals

What I am here calling Creole society was the product of unequal encounters and deep interpenetration between, on one hand, a socially significant ruling class of European colonizers, and, on the other, a socially significant class of ruled non-Europeans. 'Socially significant' here means that we are not referring to people on the margin of the social system in question, such as temporarily posted colonial administrators or soldiers, or occasional colonial subjects, visiting, trading or being chased, or alternatively, as expellees in reservations or other outlying peripheries. 'Deep interpenetration' is referring to the profound effects of these two, or more, classes upon each other, especially upon their most intimate social relations, their family and gender systems. Creole societies in this sense created dual, sometimes triangular family systems – white, non-white and mixed – each very different, but each crucially shaped by the other(s).

In modern history there are two main types of Creole societies, societies to be found chiefly, albeit not exclusively in the Americas. The first one, with the most blurred boundaries, we may call, from its main locale, Indo-American, coming out of long, extensive, asymmetrical encounters of Europeans and American Indians, i.e. between colonizers and natives. The other, stemming from traumatic meetings of imported unfree labour and settler-owners, is mostly Afro-American, produced by slave-trade or slave-hunting in Africa and plantation slavery in the Americas. The former had historically involved forced labour, and both relations were typically exploitative and domineering, in one way or the other. The Caribbean Hindu family, also a product of imported indentured plantation labour, and significant in Trinidad and Guayana above all, seems to have been less uprooted.

Though there were tendencies in that direction in French Canada, spawning *les Métis*, the Indo-Creole family system is mainly an outcome of the Spanish conquest and colonization. As the Swedish historian of the region, Magnus Mörner, once put it: 'the Spanish conquest of America was a conquest of women'. Ideal typically Indo-Creole society comprised the 'white' colonial settlers and rulers, a clearly minoritarian but not marginal segment, a gradually very important, historically growing mestizo population, and a huge set of local Indian communities, whose family folkways had to a considerable, though varying extent been affected by the conquest, its demographic as well as economic-political disaster, and by their relations both to the whites and to the mixed-bloods (cf. Heydt-Coca 1999).

For the global family historian, who is constrained not only by limits of his competence but also by necessary priorities among too large a set of populations or territories, the most important Indo-Creole societies are those which produced large mestizo populations. This rested on two conditions, the presence of high-culture, sedate Indians, and secondly, on a certain limitation of European settlement. The former condition highlights the valleys, high plateaux, and surroundings of the Andes and their northern continuation, from current Paraguay to central Mexico. While we should expect to see its influence operating on white high society in the centres of Mexico City and Lima, its full bloom in the mestizo sense we should find in the colonial peripheries of this vast area, in Central America (save Costa Rica), in Colombia, Ecuador and in old Alto Peru, i.e. Bolivia and Paraguay of today.

Slavery, in the sense of unfree labour, is ancient and has taken many forms, including ones very important to the operation of large-scale social systems (Patterson 1982). Its operation in, say, the Muslim world in the sixteenth to eighteenth centuries, would have demanded the attention of a world student of families in that period. However, here we are concerned with a specific and socially particularly devastating kind of slavery, plantation slavery. Its large-scale deployment originated in the Americas and has, on the whole, remained specific to that area (Blackburn 1997).

The Afro-Creole society I am referring to was created by plantation slavery. Three major regions of the Americas have been shaped by the latter and characterized by an Afro-Creole society. From north to south, the first is the south of the United States, where cotton and tobacco were the major products of slave labour. Second, the Caribbean, or the West Indies as the more popular English naming goes, including parts of Venezuela and Colombia, less so Central America, centred on its highlands and turned more to the Pacific than to the Atlantic. British Jamaica and Spanish Cuba were the centres of Caribbean sugar plantation slavery. Finally, Brazil, from Bahía down to Rio de Janeiro but with its classical centre in Bahía in the northeast with its sugar plantations (Freyre 1933/1970).

Common to Creole family formation, Indo- as well as Afro-Creole, were the following characteristics. Among ruling Europeans, Creole society meant a strengthening, a rigidification of patriarchy. White women were secluded from any kind of productive work as long as there was a male provider and his slaves or servants around. The white Creole concern with 'purity of blood' called for strict chaperoning and parental control. The result was a European family pattern of an unusual segregation and hierarchy of the sexes.

The scarcity and the inaccessibility of white women was, on the dark side of Creole society, compensated for by the prevailing norm and practice, by violence if need be, of the sexual accessibility of black, Indian, mestiza and mulatta women. For slaves, marriage was often prohibited, and in any case informal mating strongly encouraged. Male sexual predation became almost institutionalized among the white rulers. Within their racial boundaries, this provided role-models for the classes and races of the ruled males. And besides models from above, what prize of masculine prowess other than sexual exploits was there for male slaves, who not only had no property but had no community and no family of their own? For non-white women, sexual relationships with white or at least lighter-skinned males did not necessarily involve violence and male exploitation. In terms of both social and economic life-chances, the common colonial Cuban saying, 'rather mistress of a white man than wife of a negro' (Martínez-Alier 1974: 129) had its rationale. Slave resistance led to high mortality and low birth rates, which in the Caribbean and in Brazil, above all on the sugar plantations, led to a continuous natural decline of the slave population, sustainable only by continuous import (Higman 1991). Among mulattos, free blacks and mestizos, the Creole family had distinctive featuress in its instability and informality, in active, little-controlled sexuality, informal, unstable unions, male absenteeism, and matrifocality. The patrilineal, patriarchal, ritually formal white family had its opposite in the loose, matrilineal informality of coloured Creoles.

Catastrophic colonial conquest with ensuing imposition of Christianity broke the back of the major Indian cultures, usually patriarchal and patrilineal and not seldom polygamous. On the other hand, they did reproduce themselves as mutated and subdued communities. They were not shattered socially, like the slaves from Africa, or new interstitial social systems, like the mestizo and the mulatto worlds outside the British American dichotomous divide of whites and non-whites. Nor were the Indians integrated into Latin America, remaining far from the priest, and even further from secular authority, even though subjected to them. Indian families have tended to have at least an official and superficial informality, with widespread unofficial cohabitation, alterations of its traditional lineages, sometimes polygamy of one form or another.

The Creole family system conceptualized here builds upon a number of works with different, separate approaches and concerns, developed in and about different parts of the Americas. Key areas and topics have been the master–slave societies of northeastern Brazil (Freyre 1933/1970; Kuznesof 1991; Borges 1992), of the southern USA, about which there is an immense literature (e.g. Dollard 1937/1957; Groves 1944; Gutman 1976; Wyatt-Brown 1986; Morris 1995; Patterson 1998), and of the West Indies (Patterson 1967; Martinez-Alier 1974; Charbit 1987; Stolcke 1992, with a comparison to Brazil; Barrow 1996; Ortmayr 1997); and the Hispanic *conquistador* society in general (Das and Jesser 1980; Lavrín 1989; McCaa 1994), and more specifically *mestizaje* and the triangle of white European–mestizo–Indian family relations from Paraguay (and northern Argentina), along the Andes to Guatemala and Mexico (Tumin 1952; Fals-Borda 1962; Price 1965; Gutierrez de Pineda 1976; Angulo-Novoa 1980; Mayer and Bolton 1980; Hawkins 1984; Deere 1990; Potthast-Jutkeit 1997; Heydt-Coca 1999; Barrig 2001).

By 1900, this Creole bifurcation of races and families had been put under serious challenge. The French Revolution, through a series of convulsive local revolutions, led to the end of slavery in Haiti. British abolitionism totally changed the parameters of Jamaica, which because of its low fertility and propensity to population decline was extraordinarily dependent on the slave trade. In 1865 the outcome of the American Civil War put an end to US slavery, and in 1888 the Golden Act of Brazil finally ended the world's last plantation slavery. The Indo-Creole family lived a lesser drama, but nevertheless also one calling for fundamental reflection and redefinition. The convulsions of the Wars of Independence were finally leading up to some new national stability. New immigration was on the political agenda, and streams of immigrants were coming in, although without comparison with the areas of genocidal settlement.

By and large, the white elite of Creole society maintained its gender-family system intact for the rest of the nineteenth century. As a specific social system it was never under threat, whatever the fantasies of the Ku Klux Klan. Slow, genteel decline, economically and politically, befell the plantocracy of the US south, the Caribbean, and the Brazilian northeast, and also the lily-white elites of old New Spain and other centres of Hispanic colonialism. Occasionally, exit was the best or the only option, from Haiti, from Peru, or from Cuba. But nobody wanted, or at least nobody ever tried, to draw the white patriarchy into the informality of the coloured worlds. In the southern United States, the carefully engineered racial and gendered transformation of the plantation south meant a calibrated reproduction of the race, class, gender system in place, incorporating anomalous poor whites within the strictly segregated compound of white family and society (e.g. Janiewski 1996). In Brazil, which was never obsessed with any colour line, an elitist free labour Republic basically reproduced the elites of the slave-owning Empire.

The coloured side of the Creole gender-family system did pose a challenge to patriarchy, as a blatant violation of it. However, this side was the side of poverty and of illegitimacy, in the social and not only technical sense. The end of slavery and of other forms of colonial exploitation did not reinforce the populations of colour and their specific family relations, except perhaps politically in Haiti and the Caribbean, but that whole region was becoming a backwater and the first out-migration area of the Americas. Though they did in part indicate the future of the European family, in 1900 nobody thought of Haiti or Jamaica as social models for the future.

Colonial thrusts

In ways parallel to the upheavals of industrial capitalism and its unhinging of the old estates order in Europe, to the encounters of mass migration with disestablished feminine moralism in the New Worlds of settlement, and to the challenges to dual Creole societies by slavery abolition and the growing consolidation of non-Indian nation-states, late nineteenth-century Afro-Asian societies and their family systems were confronted with a new and seemingly unstoppable surge of European and US colonialism and imperialism. No analysis of the family in the world of 1900 would be valid unless it takes the impact of the latter into account.

The actual operation and impact of colonialism were complex and con-tradictory. Nationalist notions of conquest, occupation, oppression, exploitation and racist humiliation are all true, but also partial, as clichés, stereotypes, caricatures. Imperialist motivations of civilization, law, peace, progress all turned out to be ridiculously hollow and hypocritical in the second half of the twentieth century, but they were not completely absent either. After all, no less a nationalist than Gandhi (1948: 212) for a long time saw the British Raj in India as a 'beneficial to the ruled'. Now, in the early twenty-first century, that explicit, violent imperialism is having a renaissance in the United States, and in its chorus of satellites, a sharp double-edged blade of critical capacity is required in order to understand what is going on, and to act adequately upon it.

Psychoanalytically inspired analysts of colonialism have related patriarchy and colonialism through conceptions of sexual domination. The classic here is Frantz Fanon's (1952) *Peau Noire, Masques Blancs* (Black Skin, White Masks), written by a 27-year-old black physician from Martinique. A succinct summary formulation may be taken from the Bengali writer Ashis Nandy (1983: 4): 'The homology between sexual and political dominance which Western colonialism invariably used . . . beautifully legitimized Europe's post-medieval models of dominance, exploitation and cruelty as natural and valid. Colonialism . . . produced a cultural consensus in which political and socio-economic dominance symbolized the dominance of men and masculinity over women and femininity.'

This perspective captures one important, psychological aspect of colonialism, its sexual rapaciousness in relation to colonized women, its sexual fears of the colonized male, its contempt for the 'effeminate' Bengali middle class, its respect for 'martial races', like the Punjabi Sikhs or the Gurkhas, its arrogant paternalism in its perception of 'child-like races'. However, this pan-sexist conceptualization of modern colonialism falls short for at least two reasons of pertinence to our story.

First, empirically very important but theoretically secondary, is its failure to distinguish between what we have here called Creole societies, based on decisive, extensive interaction between colonizers and colonized, and, on the other, what we may name colonial societies proper or simple, in which colonial rule is mainly superimposed upon a conquered society. For family analysis this distinction is crucial. In simple colonial societies, the family system of the colonized is not smashed as in plantation slavery, and the zone of extra-familiar sexuality and of informal sexual unions is marginal and relatively insignificant in terms of numbers, while large and central in the Caribbean and similar parts of the Americas. The tendencies in that direction in the early Dutch colonies of the South African Cape, Ceylon and the East Indies were reversed in the course of the nineteenth century, among the frigidly racist Boers, and were also swamped by the colonial extension of Dutch Indonesia. However, colonial concubinage remained important enough to be a note-worthy policy issue in the early twentieth century (cf. Stoler 1997).

Second, the sexual psychology of colonialism shortcuts institutions and institutional effects, and in particular the institution of the family and the social status of women. The fatal flaw of this perspective is that it completely fails to account for some notable normative effects of colonialism. On the whole, modern colonial rule, and the modern threat of colonial subjugation, in so far as they induced any normative change at all, tended to strengthen the position of women, children and of young people, at the expense of elderly and adult men. In order to understand why this was the case, we have to see colonialism as the asymmetric encounter of two social systems of family and gender relations.

With respect to patriarchy, colonial power and penetration mediated an encounter of the patriarchal, male-dominated European family system with, by and large – minor and marginal exceptions apart, such as matrilineal societies in West Africa, in today's Kerala, and in highland Sumatra – *more* patriarchal and misogynous kinds of family. To the colonial rulers, all male, of course, this surplus male power in the colonies was no problem, nor a concern in itself, although there were some 'abhorrent' practices: *sati*, widow immolation on the funeral pyre of her husband, was the one catching most attention. Furthermore, colonial power in the eighteenth and nineteenth centuries was more often than not established by siding with one local potentate, or aspiring potentate, against others. The British were soon to develop the doctrine of 'indirect rule', developing it into a fine art, which the instinctively more 'direct' and 'assimilationist' French had de facto come to adhere to, in great part, by the turn of the century (Suret-Canale 1971: ch. III; Thobie 1991: 299ff; Conklin 1997).

However, colonial rulers were also men with a sense of mission, having a mandate of social change. Since the Enlightenment, educated Europeans harboured the idea that a significant aspect of European civilization was the 'gallant' treatment of women, in contrast to the manners of less civilized peoples. As James Mill (1817: vol. 1, 279) put it in the first volume of his *History of British India*: 'Among rude peoples women are normally degraded; by polished ones they are exalted' (cf. Osterhammel 1998: ch. XII). Moreover, the European colonizers had an increasingly influential home front. Militant Christianity made up most of the colonizers, troops in the nineteenth century, spearheaded by a vanguard of missionaries, fearless, well informed, and normatively aggressive. Their zeal was directed not only against the false gods of the heathens but also against their abominable sins against Christian monogamous patriarchy. In the colonies the missionaries were not mainly ranting preachers of a strange religion, but to a very considerable extent educators, nurses, doctors and social workers.

The colonized families never made up a nation. Colonial power entered through the fissures of internecine elite conflicts, of multicultural polities, and of warring inter-ethnic social systems. The historic battle of Plassey in 1757, which in retrospect decided the British rule of India, was actually a messy, small-scale affair, the outcome of which was determined by the secret alliance with the British of one Bengali aspirant to power and wealth. The overall context was an unbalanced triangle of powers, the Mughal Nawab of Bengal, formally a governor on behalf of the Mughal sultan in Delhi, and his extensive kin, in frequent conflict among themselves; the Bengali bankers and money-lenders, on whom the Nawab had become increasingly dependent; and, thirdly, the British East India Company, granted extensive commercial privileges by the Delhi sultan.

Among the colonized there was always a significant part of the local elite, who saw or learnt to see colonial rule as a road to social change, very much including family change. The epitome is the case of Rammohan Ray

(1772–1833), a Bengali Brahmin with a multi-generational record of high service to the Muslim Mughal Empire. Ray, or Roy in some transliterations, was given the title of Raja by the Mughal emperor. He became an important administrator to the new rulers, the British East India Company, first entering it by lending money to junior British clerks (Robertson 1995: 18–19), adding English to his education in Sanskrit, Arabic and Persian, as well as Bengali. Ray was many things, a Vedantic scholar, a deistic religious reformer, and the founder of the first modern Indian organization for social change, Brahmo Samaj, in 1828. In this context, however, Rammohan Ray has a place primarily because of his propagation of large-scale family reform (Das and Mahapatra 1996: 96ff), to which we shall come back soon.

Colonial criticism of local practices generated an anti-colonial defence of the latter. Nineteenth-century India is full of examples of this, which could also be seen, for instance, in the re-assertion of the veil in Algeria after the ultra-colonialist coup of 13 May 1958, and in Iran after the Shah (cf. Fanon 1962: chs 1 and 3). However, nationalism, as we shall see, on the whole brought forward women demanding rights.

But colonial rule was not just political and normative rule. It also involved socio-economic changes and policies, and their effects, unintended as well as intended. These policies included redefinitions of property, the introduction of cash crops, often through coercive cultivation (much developed by the Dutch in their East Indies), forced labour (widespread in Africa), mining, some industrialization, and a new infrastructure of ports and railroads. Moreover colonialism entailed limited but significant educational opportunities, and a new clerical labour market. In many ways the situation and the options of the colonial generation of children and of men and women differed from the pre-colonial ones. This must have been corroding the power of fathers, but the effects on the relative position of wives to husbands and of daughters to brothers were more complex. In so far as women had an economic autonomy as subsistence farmers – very often the case in Africa – or had some specific rights in matrilineal societies, their prospects tended to narrow by the colonial promotion of male cash crop cultivation and by European notions of father/husband rights (Boserup 1970: ch. 3).

Colonialism also had important effects on general population development. The social dislocations in the wake of colonial conquest, the dreadful punitive raids following resistance and rebellion, and the deadly effects of the first wave of forced labour caused a decline of the population in German Cameroon, and in French and Belgian Congo in the last decades of the nineteenth century, and a slowdown, or maybe a halt, of population growth in the whole of sub-Saharan Africa (Caldwell 1985: 483). Later on, colonial power came to contribute positively to population growth, through policies of vaccination, sanitation and hygiene, and through economic development.

Nineteenth-century colonialism thrust into three major family systems of the world: the Indian, or in current terms the South Asian; the African; and the civilizationally interstitial Southeast Asian. We shall look at them in turn.

South Asia: the elites and the others

Most of today's South Asia was colonial British India by the end of the nine-teenth century, although there were still some substantial, quasi-independent polities left on the sub-continent, like Hyderabad, Mysore and Rajputana. The vast social complex, which this study, with the liberality of a global sociologist, has called the South Asian family system, was divided by religion (Hindu, Muslim, Sikh, Jain, Parsee, and even Christian and Jewish), by caste, by a north–south linguistic divide and cultural gradient, and by regional and local customs. On the whole, however, this complex configuration of family forma-tion and operation, was strongly patriarchal and misogynous. Marriages were generally arranged, and girls had to be married off before puberty, which meant child, often small child, marriages. Polygamy was legitimate, but occurred among a small minority, certain categories of Brahmins, for instance. Residence upon marriage was with the groom's family, and inheritance was patrilineal – with a few exceptions, such as the famous upper caste of Nayars in current Kerala, and some peoples in Assam. Girls and women were gener-ally held strongly inferior to males and had no space of autonomy, except as prostitutes and professional entertainers. On the contrary, female seclusion, *purdah*, was the norm among the higher castes.

Upon this common theme there were religious, caste, regional and local variations. The sub-continent also housed several deviant ethnicities of marginal importance to the area. The general rule was that Hindus tended to be more patriarchal and sexist than adherents of the other religions, the higher castes much more so than the lower ones, and 'Aryan' northerners more than 'Dravidian' southerners.

Hindu patriarchy was enshrined in a 2,500-year-old tradition of law, having its paramount authority in the Code of Manu of the centuries around the birth of the Christian era (Mayne 1953: chs I–II). Male–female relations are given a particular shape and colouring by men's and women's different relationship to the Gods. Marriage is a sacred act, the way to pay one's debts to one's ancestors. For males there is an alternative of ascetic renunciation, functionally equivalent to Christian monkhood, but not for women. A woman who does not marry breaks a holy rule, and is punished accordingly.

Upon birth a human being has three debts, to the Gods, to the sages, and to the ancestors. Marriage and procreation pay off the latter, but the other two require special sacrifices and rituals, and the acquisition of learning, respec-tively. However, these duties can only be performed by men; a woman's only form of a virtuous life is devotion to her husband. Manu said: 'The husband must constantly be worshipped as a god by a faithful wife, even if he be destitute of charater or seeking pleasure elsewhere or devoid of good qualities. . . . A woman attains paradise not by virtue of any austere penance but as a result of her obedience and devotion to her husband' (Kapadia 1966: 253). In brief, a pious woman's only path to heaven is to worship her husband. Marriage is woman's fakirhood.

It is this high-intensity normative conjugal hierarchy which is the basis for the indissolubility of a Hindu marriage, and for the death of widows, physical or social. Islam, by contrast, does not exclude women from direct access to God, and regards marriage as a worldly contract, although the major part of Arab patriarchy in the times of the Prophet also enters into the divine law of Muslims. During the centuries of being ruled by Muslim lords many Indians converted to Islam, but with the possible exception of the spread of female seclusion, the family norms of the rulers do not seem to have affected the non-converted very much. Rather, the caste rules tended to follow the converted and their descendants into Islam and Christianity.

Between the northern and the southern parts of the Indian sub-continent there ran a divide of marriage customs, which has turned out to be of enduring significance in twentieth-century India. In the northern core of Mughal India there was a strong Hindu norm of kin and village, exogamy, whereas Muslim custom on the contrary favours cross-cousin marriage. The implications of this are graphically brought out by Irawati Karvé (1953: 130), who wrote the classical, trail-blazing study on the regional variations of kinship and family in India:

> Early marriage out of the native village to a complete stranger is a terrible crisis in a girl's life. . . . Hundreds of folk-songs bear witness to the agony of a girl parting for ever from her parents' home. The husband is a shadowy figure, the real people are the parents-in-law . . . who are ready to find fault with her at the slightest gesture. . . . Only when a girl becomes the mother of a boy does she feel completely at home in her husband's house.

In southern India, on the other hand, marital alliances are usually between kindred families, with certain specific exchange rules, and often between cross-cousins. Dravidian languages, according to Karvé, have no terms to designate in-laws as different from parents and siblings. Her north–south contrast may include some black-and-white stereotyping, but is a good piece of *Verstehen*. This is how she sums up the south Indian couple: 'The southern man may be more natural in his attitude to women. He is the cross-cousin and the playmate of his future wife, not her lord and master.' But this is still India, Karvé (1953: 220) continues: 'There is also compulsion in this type of marriage as there is a complete absence of unrestricted choice of mate'.

'North' in Karvé's work refers to the Hindu population of what is now Pakistan and Bangladesh, and the current Indian states of Punjab, Haryana, Uttar Pradesh, Bihar and West Bengal. 'South' comprises Kerala, Karnataka, Tamil Nadu and Andhra Pradesh. In between, Karvé placed a heterogenous central zone, running from Rajasthan in the northwest via Gujarat and Maharashtra (the colonial Bombay Presidency) to Orissa, while indicating the closeness of Rajasthan and Gujarat to the northern pattern, of Maharashtra to the southern, and the ethnic fragmentation in Orissa. While the poles, with their hard core in Punjab and on the Malabar coast of Kerala, respectively, are clear, the areas in between are sometimes mapped differently. On the north–south family divide in India see further Dyson and Moore (1983), Kolendra (1987) and Goody (1990: ch. 8).

Kerala, mainly the former princely states of Travancore and Cochin, has a strongly deviant family structure. Both the 'core' (Karvé) upper caste of Nayars – traditionally warriors, with colonial peace increasingly civil servants and professionals – and the largest caste, the 'untouchable' Ezhavas or Thiyas,[2] are matrilineal and matrilocal. The head of the family is the oldest female, although there is also a powerful role for the eldest male. At least among the Nayars women have considerable sexual autonomy, as their husbands do not live with them, but in the joint family of their respective mothers, and do not have rights in their children. Part of this was too much for the patriarchal British to accept, and in the first quarter of the twentieth century colonial power intervened in favour of husbands and fathers, but here we are still in 1900 (Karvé 1953: 258ff; Jeffrey1992: ch. 2).

The nineteenth-century colonial impact on this world was confined mainly to a small, urban, upper-caste, middle- and upper-class elite, i.e. to a part of the upper castes who were the strictest practitioners of sanctified patriarchy. India upon conquest was a complex, highly stratified, sophisticated civilization, with well-developed urban and proto-industrial traditions, imposed upon a huge peasantry, with and without land rights, working an often rich and fertile land. Colonial rule had at most a marginal effect on the great majority of the enormous population. In the first two-thirds of the nineteenth century there seems to have been an urban decline in India, the Mughal cities of Agra, Delhi, Ahmedabad, Lucknow, and others declining, while the growth of the three centres of British India, Calcutta, Madras and Bombay, did not fully compensate. By 1900 it seems that India was as urban as it was in 1800, i.e. having about 11 per cent of its population in cities (Ramachandran 1989: 60ff).

India had been an industrial centre of the pre-industrial (pre-1800) world, exporting a characteristic cotton cloth to Britain, but after the Napoleonic wars in Europe it rapidly lost out to its colonial master, with its mechanized spinning, fed by US raw cotton. The expansion of colonialism in India economically meant de-industrialization (Bairoch 1997: vol. II, 850ff). In the latter part of the nineteenth century India was slowly recovering from that blow. British-owned jute mills in Calcutta and Indian-owned cotton mills in Bombay became the new industrial centres, and by 1900 the Indian was one of the major cotton textile industries of the world, although with a labour productivity much lower than Japan's (Litten 1984: 255n, 257n). In contrast to the cases of Europe, North America and Japan, the labour force of the Indian textile industry was overwhelmingly male, which restrained the family impact of this very delimited industrialization, with its kinship networks of labour recruitment, even further (Litten 1984: 49–51, 60–62).

The British Raj did affect the Indian countryside by its property assessments, its collection of tax revenue, its pushing of cash crops, etc., but the ancient, well-entrenched family norms seem to have been affected little or not at all by these socio-economic changes. The population grew after the consolidation of colonial rule, from about 1830 to 1890, whereupon higher mortality slowed down population growth and lowered life expectancy (Dyson 1989: 9; Bhat 1989).

At the intellectual elite and Bengali urban clerical level, however, British–Indian interaction and cultural change were intense and major, respectively. The colonial rulers met in India an ancient high culture, which gave rise to a British Sanskritic scholarship, in the work of William Jones (1746–94), the Asiatic Society in Calcutta of 1785, and the Sanskrit College in Calcutta of 1821. At the intellectual elite level, what happened was a mutual attraction, of Britons for (ancient) Indian civilization, and of Bengalis for British (modern) civilization. By the second half of the 1830s this mutual attraction of civilizations had succumbed to the asymmetry of power. In 1835 Thomas Macaulay, who knew no non-European language, could write in an official memoir on Indian education: 'a single shelf of a good European library was worth the whole native literature of India and Arabia' (Zastoupil and Moir 1999: ix). In the same year English replaced Persian as the official language of Bengali administration and courts.

Rammohan Roy (or Ray) was the first outstanding Bengali intellectual attracted by British and Christian civilization. He was typical of his early nineteenth-century milieu in a stereotypical rather than a statistical sense. A Bengali Brahmin of the *Kulin* category he was married three times before the age of nine (Robertson 1995: 15), educated in Arabic, Sanskrit and Persian, before learning English. In 1811 his sister-in-law was forcibly burnt alive upon his brother's funeral, which made him a sworn foe of *sati*. Himself an ambitious Sanskritic scholar of the *Vedas*, Roy in 1823 made a contribution to the inter-civilizational debate in favour of English, rather than Sanskrit education (Roy 1823/1999).

Out of the interaction of the Indian, above all Bengali, and the ruling British elites, both of them bifurcated (the Indians between the modernists and the traditionalists, the British between the pragmatic rulers and the civilizers, increasingly Christian missionaries), there ensued in the course of the nineteenth century a string of Indian family legislation. Its writ rarely ran beyond a part of the anglicized middle and upper classes in Calcutta and other significant colonial cities.

The first target of this kind of change was *sati*, the upper-caste Hindu custom of a widow throwing herself onto the funeral pyre of her husband. This was a ritual following from the asymmetrically sacramental character of Hindu marriage, indissoluble and unrepeatable by a woman, leaving the surviving widow only the option of being a social outcast. The Portuguese prohibited it in Goa in 1510, and several Indian states tried to curb it. Nor was it condoned by the Muslim Mughals, but the practice survived, particularly in Bengal, the core of British India (Lardinois 1986b: 353ff). The East India Company in 1813 made it illegal if forced and if involving a widow under the age of 16 (Mani 1993: 273, 281). After Rammohan Roy's agitation the British Governor Bentinck prohibited the ritual in 1829, hardly successfully but nor without effect. The annual average of 580 *satis* in the Bengal Presidency in 1815–28 did come down (Kapadia 1966: 172).

The status and possible role of widows were at the centre of the next campaign by Indian reformers, in this case egged on by a successor of Roy, Isvarachandra Vidyasagar. Because of the rule of pre-pubertal marriage of girls and the frequently much higher age of their grooms, social death as a widow befell a large number of women while still in their youth, by today's standards, or even still in their childhood. The reform campaign led to a law of 1856 allowing Hindu widows to remarry, but the social price remained high. A few daring men who married a widow were excommunicated from their kin and caste (Kapadia 1966: 175). In 1872 a similar elite piece of legislation, the Special Marriage Act, tried to legitimate inter-caste marriages by allowing civil marriage among Hindus, Buddhists, Sikhs and Jains, but de facto this had any bearing only upon interstitial ethno-religious outsiders to the mainstream of colonial society. Among upper-caste Hindus it had no legitimacy, and the legal permission of inter-caste marriage remained a moving target of Indian legislative reformers for the first half of the twentieth century (Mayne 1953: 74–75; Kapadia 1966: 118–19). On the other hand, widow remarriage was tolerated among lower castes, irrespective of Vedic law as well as of colonial intervention (Kolendra 1987: 323ff).

Female infanticide was another misogynous old custom, practised above all in the northwest, among the Rajputs and others. In 1870 it became the object of a delegitimating legislation, again largely ineffectual. The ratio of males to females in today's northern states of Punjab, Haryana and Rajasthan in 1901 was 120, 116 and 110, respectively. The average for the southern Indian states of Maharashta, Andhra Pradesh, Tamil Nadu, Karantaka and Kerala was then 101 (Dyson and Moore 1983: 38).

The final, and most controversial reform act of the nineteenth century – although all the pieces of legislation mentioned had both its Indian proponents and opponents – was the 1891 Age of Consent Act, which stipulated a minimum female age of marriage at 12. By that time modern nationalism had emerged in India, and its leaders, B.G. Tilak, Lajpat Rai and others, first of all, vigorously opposed the bill. Questions of women's status should wait until after independence, if they were to be considered at all, something which even the cosmopolitan religious reformer Swami Vivekananda, lionized at the World Parliament of Religions in Chicago in 1893, was now denying (Chakravarti 1990: 73–78; Bose and Jalal 1997: 109ff; Chowdhury 1998: chs 3, 5). The nationalists opposed the 'Westernization' of Indian women, the 'coarseness and degeneration in the female character' following from men and women 'meet[ing] together, convers[ing] together at all times, eat[ing] and drink[ing] together', thereby losing their Indian spiritual character (Chatterjee 1990: 242–43, quoting Bhudev Mukhopadhyay from 1882). On the other hand, in spite of nationalism's strident neo-patriarchy, the first major manifestation of Indian nationalism – directed against Lord Curzon's proposal in 1905 to partition Bengal in order to drive a wedge between Hindus and Muslims – was also the occasion for the first (small-scale) mass appearance of Indian women in a public protest (Ray 1995).

In India, as elsewhere, the colonial ruler was often torn between, on one hand, his realpolitik of aligning himself with whatever local power was prepared to collaborate, and his own religious and other social conceptions, on the other, conceptions pushed with great vigour by the Christian missions and their principals. Thus, while the Age of Consent bill bowed to the latter, in the notorious Rukmubai case the colonial courts bowed to the former, ordering a girl who was married against her will to join her husband (Chakravarti 1990: 73).

By way of conclusion, in 1900 the South Asian family system was affected by colonialism only at its urban elite fringe. Here the debates of the century had been very lively, but with a new nationalist discourse arising, explicitly defending all ancient indigenous customs, it is difficult to say whether the reformers had scored any lasting points in the public debate. But for those who had both the resources and the will, there was now on the statute books at least a contested legitimation of the pre-modern Indian patriarchy. Education of girls and women had also advanced, usually pioneered, even in intellectual Calcutta, by Christian missionaries (R. Ray 1995). In 1883 two Bengali women obtained BA degrees at the University of Calcutta, which compares well with the German Reich, where no woman was allowed to take the secondary school final exam, the *Abitur*, qualifying for university entrance, until 1895 (Albisetti 1996: 45).

Africa: the morning of colonial shock

The sub-Saharan African family constitutes the major alternative, not only to the European but, as Jack Goody (1976) has taught us, to the Eurasian family systems. The American Indian 'question' had largely been solved by genocide. It is the 'major' alternative, in the sense of both incidence and structural differentiation, as large-scale, not just elite, polygamy, with bridewealth paid to the bride's family rather than female dowry and female inheritance, as a set of family systems, where land was abundant and labour more scarce, where land was largely worked by women with hoes, rather than by men with ploughs, where fertility was more important than legitimacy (cf. Boserup 1970).

Within these distinctive but very general parameters, the African family is not easily subsumable under one rubric, not only because of the continent's extremely rich and variegated ethnic mosaic, but also, and first of all, because it includes some major variants of male family power in a social context wherein family and kinship were all-important in 1900. Trying to sum up in a couple of broad strokes the main lines of differentiation, we may distinguish two different cleavages.

One is *descent*, which clearly divides into patrilineal and matrilineal family systems, and, indeed, societies. Well before modernity, but after Roman Antiquity, European kin has been mainly bilateral, with relatives symmetrical on both father's and mother's side, traits which seem to stem from Germanic tribes and from the Christian Church (Goody 2000: 15). In modern times only aristocratic lineages and dynasties, and the large extended *zadruga* of Russia and the Balkans, have had a patrilineal orientation in Europe. Those traditions are now virtually gone, although both Russia in the northeast and Iceland in the northwest still use the patronymikon – for example son or daughter of Peter – as a rule for naming children. But outside Christian Europe, bilaterality has been rather rare, difficult as it is to organize a strong and extensive kinship on its basis. Patrilineality has then been the rule, matrilineality the exception in recorded history.

In pre-colonial Africa, kinship was extraordinarily important, in the absence of corporately organized religion – save in Christian Abyssinia – and of enduring, institutionalized states. Matrilineality means that genealogy and inheritance run through mothers and grandmothers. Although kin power is usually held by a male, over the conjugal family by the wife's oldest brother, matrilineality makes the role of the husband ambiguous and difficult, and de facto the system often allows important roles to women. The Ashanti, a major people of Ghana, for instance, have a system of female co-chiefs, *Ohema*, translated by their first British recorder as 'Queen Mother' (Rattray 1923: 81ff). Some important African peoples are matrilineal: the Akan group of peoples prevailing in Ghana and present also on the Ivory Coast, and many peoples in a vast area of Central Africa, including the Bakongo of Congo and the Bemba of Zambia (Radcliffe-Brown and Forde 1950). Most peoples of West, South and East Africa are patrilineal, in which descent and inheritance are concentrated on the father's side. (The European pattern of bilateral kinship exists mainly as a tendency in certain peoples in certain periods.) Patrilineality simplifies matters for patriarchy and male power.

The other division is *conjugal*, which takes on a unique range of variability in Africa. Around 1900 the normative space of married women was narrowly circumscribed virtually everywhere outside Africa, with mainly a few marginal, if colourful, exceptions here and there, like the Nayar women on the Malabar coast of India or some niches among the very rich or the very aristocratic of Europe and North America. Africa, by contrast, ran a gamut from strong explicit subordination and strict surveillance, if not seclusion, to widespread economic entrepreneurship and parental custody. The African pattern of mass polygamy, in contrast to the elite polygamy of the Arab world, or of Asia, tends generally to include some conjugal autonomy, as the wives are not locked up under eunuch guard, but have their own individual residence and a crucial economic role.

With regard to conjugal relations there is major continental cleavage, a diagonal division. By and large, this sets the coastal areas of West Africa, including the big patrilineal Yoruba and Ibo peoples, against the rest of Africa, and in particular Eastern and Southern Africa. Northern, super-Saharan Africa will be dealt with as part of the Islamic Arab and West Asian world, and equatorial Central Africa tends to form a heteroclite area in between, like the central zone of regional Indian kinship differentiation above.

Along the West African coast there was a pre-colonial tradition of female autonomy, under male sovereignty, manifested in autonomous trading and other economic activities, although the important trade, in slaves, gold, ivory and kola nuts, was mostly in male hands (Coquery-Vidrovitch 1997: 95). In contrast, there are peoples among whom women are subject to very tight male superordination and control, such as the Luo in Kenya, the Shona and the

Ndebele in Zimbabwe, and the Zulu in South Africa. The matrilineal peoples usually allow for some female autonomy, but many of the matrilineal societies of the Congo region seem to keep women in very subordinate positions, as the main subsistence providers and barred from all important decision-making (Jacobson 1967, 1977; McGaffey 1983), although historically, the power of distinguished women in the Congo seems to have fluctuated (Hilton 1983). Public power in matrilineal societies is usually in male hands (see Epilogue in Appiah 1992: an illuminating account of his father's funeral in 1990, in the royal court society of the matrilineal Asante in Ghana).

The Kikuyu (or Gikuyu) people of Kenya have a remarkable patriarchal myth of creation, which seems to indicate a tension underlying Kikuyu patriarchy. In the beginning, Gikuyu, the founder of the people, was given a beautiful wife with whom he had nine daughters. The Divider of the Universe then provided him with nine young men who married his daughters. The daughters were ruling the men, treating them unjustly, whereupon the husbands rebelled, by first making the women pregnant and then attacking their rule. The strong but now handicapped women had to surrender, and since then the man is the head of the Kikuyu family (Kenyatta 1938/1961: 3ff).

How the African family systems were affected by the slave raids (Hilton 1983) need not concern us here, as the trade, which had been the economic base of many African polities in Dahomey and in the Niger Delta, was slowly fading out in the course of the nineteenth century. That century seems nevertheless to have seen the export of about three million slaves across the Atlantic (Iliffe 1995: 131). The colonial conquest was extremely rapid, fuelled by inter-imperialist rivalries. In 1879 nine-tenths of Africa was ruled by Africans; two decades later the overwhelming part was under European rule (Oliver and Atmore 1994: 100). Only Ethiopia could resist successfully, defeating the Italian army in 1896.

By 1900 colonial power had had little time to impact the African family, but there were already visible marks. The armed invasions, the forced labour regimes which were soon set up, and the general social dislocations that followed in their wake brought mid-century population growth more or less to a halt; it only resumed in the 1910s (Caldwell 1985), and in East Africa probably only by 1925–30 (Cordell and Gregory 1987). Exact figures for whole populations are impossible to obtain, but indicators of the death toll of early colonial rule exist for specific groups of indentured labourers, on railway construction in the Congo and Cameroon and on plantations in the latter. They show annual death rates of between 10 and 20 per cent of the workers (Caldwell 1985: 474–75). In a few cases the colonial conquest assumed genocidal proportions. In King Leopold's Congo, the population has been estimated to have been halved between 1880 and 1920, a loss of perhaps about ten million people (Hochschild 2000: 233). The Hereros of today's Namibia lost four-fifths of their people to the Germans (Boahen 1989: 95). The German suppression of the Maji Maji rebellion in Tanganyika (today's Tanzania) in 1905–6 seems to have caused hundreds of thousands of deaths (Caldwell 1985: 472).

Large-scale mining and male labour migration had begun in Southern Africa: for diamonds in Kimberley in 1868, for gold at the Witwatersrand in 1886. Cash crops had begun to replace the slave trade in West Africa, first of all by cultivating oil palms, and soon also cocoa, grounduts, coffee and cotton. The tapping of wild rubber was a major, and viciously coercive, operation in King Leopold's Congo. Mining, cash cropping and new agricultural techniques like the introduction of the plough had the general effect of offering opportunities to men but not to women, who were locked into the traditional subsistence economy (Boserup 1970: ch. 3). On the cocoa farms of the Gold Coast, wives became labourers on lands controlled by their husbands exclusively (Tashjian and Allman 2002). Even domestic urban labour (for white settlers) in South Africa was overwhelmigly male (Coquery-Vidrovitch 1997). Rural African male control of women, white bans of unmarried women into Southern African colonial cities, and female African family choice combined in producing male domestic labour for the colonials (Barnes 2002; Jackson 2002).

The new options for young men were met by the patriarchs by raising the brideprice and/or, as among the Mossi of what is now Burkina Faso, successfully resisting its monetization (Iliffe 1995: 236). Whatever the longer-term relative price effect on brides of the commodification of the African economy – and it has been argued (Kitching 1983: 229) that they have been to shorten the period of saving and waiting for the bridegrooms – the short-term effect of colonial wage-labour and hut taxation was to raise the price significantly. In Buganda around 1900, the brideprice had quintupled in a few years after the introduction of a British hut tax (Haydon 1960: 92). A similar development took place in Leopold's Congo (McGaffey 1983: 179).

The two great proselytizing Eurasian religions, Christianity and Islam, were both spreading rapidly across Africa in the nineteenth century. Islam made its largest gains in the first half of the century, primarily on the West African savannah, among the Hausa, the Bambara and others, but also later in Sudan and into the Great Lakes region. Growing European power and involvement favoured Christian missions, which became very active and successful from mid-century, although the French in Senegal and elsewhere and the British in northern Nigeria accommodated well with Islam, in the latter region even to the point of barring the entry of Christian missionaries (Lugard 1922/1965: 592ff). In contrast to its basically anti-modernist role in Europe, Christianity became a major force of modernization in Africa, above all because of its great contribution to education. As in Europe, the Protestant churches, of all denominations, were most active, particularly in offering education to girls (Coquery-Vidrovitch 1997: 144ff, 155–56).

Later on we shall return to the effects of Christianity and of Islam on the African family. At this point an important difference between the early colonized elites in Africa and their Bengali colleagues referred to above, the two generations of Rammohan Roy and of Isvaracandra Vidyasagar, may be noticed. While the cosmopolitan elite of Bengal were very outspoken critics of Bengali patriarchy and misogyny, petitioning the colonial authorities for legislation of change, the new Christianized African elite were bending in the opposite direction.

If there was any group in British Africa resembling the Calcutta *babus*, it was the Freetown 'Creoles', the descendants of the freed slave colony of 1787 and later black African settlers there. Around the turn of the century some of them came to play an important part in southern Nigeria. It was from this, very anglicized, pre-nationalist elite group that the first defence, with some authority, of the African family came. In 1888 Bishop Sawyer of the 'Diocese of the Native Pastorate' argued that the Bible contained no attacks on polygamy, and in fact condoned it in the Old Testament. At the Pan-Anglican Congress in 1908, another Creole, Reverend James Johnson, later an assistant bishop, argued that while infanticide, cannibalism and witchcraft were repulsive practices which of course had to be suppressed, native marriage forms should not be attacked, and polygamists should not be excluded from the Church (Spitzer 1972: 134–35n).

The genital mutilation of girls might conceivably have been regarded as 'repugnant to natural justice, equity and good conscience' – as the widespread so-called repugnancy test was formulated in the colony of Sierra Leone (Philips and Morris 1971: 73n) – but it was not as visible as widow-burning or foot-binding and did not become a public issue until the late 1920s–early 1930s in Kenya, where it spawned a vigorous anti-colonial reaction among the Kikuyu (Natsoulas 1998), and then late into the twentieth century. In varying forms of severity it was a widespread practice in Africa in a broad belt from Senegal (though not among its main ethnic group, the Wolof) via northern Nigeria, the contemporary Central African Republic to the Horn, and with an eastern north–south extension from Tanzania to Egypt, including the Copts (Coquery-Vidrovitch 1997: 206–7). Infibulation – the worst form, involving excision of the entire clitoris, the labia minora and majora, and the sewing up of the remnants of the labia majora – is concentrated among pastoralist or agro-pastoralist peoples in a narrower and shorter belt from Chad to Somalia and Eritrea (Hicks 1996).

Missionaries sometimes provided shelter to runaway maltreated women, and preached monogamy to non-receptive ears. But colonial power itself tended to buttress patriarchy through its policy of maintaining and, in the case of the British, particularly in northern Nigeria, symbolically reinforcing the traditional chiefs. As Lords Milner and Lugard put it 'the British policy is to rule the subject races through their own chiefs' (Lugard 1922/1965: 194). Colonial officials could therefore clash with the missionaries. In 1908, for instance, a Colonel Lambskin accused the Christianity successfully carried to the Baganda people in Uganda of leaving 'women at liberty to roam about to do as they liked, with the result of promiscuous sexual intercourse and immorality', thereby being a main cause of the prevalence of syphilis in the region (Musisi 2002: 104). The French paid less respect to the pre-colonial royal traditions, but also made use of local chiefs (Suret-Canale 1971: 75ff), and by 1900 Republican 'assimilation' was on the retreat in favour of more utilization of local customs and powers, of 'autonomy' (Thobie and Meynier 1991: vol. 2, 299ff).

Family matters were regulated by customary law and practice also under colonial occupation, de facto and under the British method of Indirect Rule as a matter of principle, subject to the 'repugnancy' test. It was the British, however, who also began, just before 1900, to issue a set of colonial Marriage Ordinances, the exact content of which varied from the jurisdiction of one colonial governor to another. The main purpose was to offer an English or part-English alternative to a customary marriage, in principle monogamous, difficult to dissolve, and with English inheritance. In practice, in so far as Ordinance marriage was resorted to at all – and it became a status symbol in Buganda and some other areas – it was usually combined with a customary law marriage, the rights and obligations of which were usually preponderant (Morris and Reid 1972: 216ff). In some cases, such as the Rhodesian Ordinance of 1901, the main thrust was a support of women's rights within the customary system. There was silence on polygamy, but there was a stipulation that no woman should be married against her will and even a procedure of judicial redress that she could resort to (Jeater 1993: 74ff).

In 1900, Africa had just been conquered. Its family system was poles apart from that of the conquerors. The brutal but multi-faceted colonial modernity had just dawned on Africa. Many things had fallen apart, but how they were to be put together again was still unclear.

The interstices of Southeast Asia

In family as well as in modern political terms Southeast Asia is an interstitial area between the major patterns: in between and affected by South Asian civilizations, Buddhist, Hindu and Muslim, and by East Asian Chinese, and also by ancient European colonization, Portuguese, Spanish and Dutch, while maintaining a vigorous and diverse regional tradition, from Javanese and other Malay to Thai, Burmese and Sinhalese. Around 1900, the Dutch ruled their 'East Indies'; the Spanish had just lost the Philippines, not to the Filipinos but to the Americans; Vietnam, Laos and Cambodia were under French rule; Burma, Ceylon and Malacca with Singapore under British; while Siam was manoeuvering to avoid being swallowed by the imperial crocodiles.

By and large, this was an area of tolerance, where patriarchy was less hard than in the core Asian civilizations of East, South and West Asia. Buddhism, the main religion of Ceylon, Burma, Thailand, Laos and Cambodia, embedded family rules in a mellow glow of informality and this-worldly insouciance. Pre-missionary and pre-colonial Malay culture, from the Malacca Peninsula to today's Philippines, accorded women rights to property – the bridewealth was usually paid to the bride herself – and a new couple more often than not resided in the wife's village. Malay kinship is generally bilateral (Jones 1994: 220), like European. Sexuality was relatively loosely regulated, and divorce was very frequent, easy to get on the wife's initiative as well as on that of the husband (Reid 1988–93: vol. 1, ch. 4). The rigid edges of Islam, which swept the Malay archipelago in the fifteenth and sixteenth centuries, were rounded by Malay *adat* (custom). Christianity, which arrived in the Moluccas with the

Portuguese, captured the Philippines with the Spanish conquest from 1571, and later on, especially in the nineteenth century, was pushed by Dutch missionaries, also had to adapt to Malay mores.

Even in quite patriarchal Vietnam – which largely belongs to the East Asian, Sinic civilization – orthodox North China Confucianism was mellowed by local custom, in part coming from the Buddhist southwest and an earlier normative commonality with Burma and Siam (Gledhill 1968: 206; Pham van Bich 1999: 38ff). It was the peasant wives who did the small cash trading, and kept control of the proceeds. In describing a marital relationship, the Vietnamese linguistic order is to begin wth the wife. In the *Baba* and *Peranakan* culture of Chinese merchants in the Straits settlements, the central place of the matron is manifest in the family photographs of the early twentieth century (Pernakan Museum in Singapore).

This relativization of patriarchy should not be interpreted as some sort of gender equality, though. The high cultures of the region were all very hierarchical, often with exquisitely elaborated rituals of super- and subordination. The 'Indic kingdoms' of Java and Bali were famous for their permeation by cultivated inequality. In this obsession with rank, that women generally were inferior to men was self-evident. But there are specific practices and institutions which by the modest world standards of 1900 may justify a designation which a Thai lawyer has used for his own late twentieth-century society, 'a feminist patriarchal system' (Hahang 1992: 27).

In both Buddhism and Malay custom, marriage, though a norm – particularly for Malays – is both secular and informal, with low and porous walls to the outside. Therefore, in contrast to the Euro-Christian and other Asian religious family systems, Buddhist and Malay marriage added little to the general inferiority of women. Neither in Malay *adat* nor in, for example, Sinhalese law were married women merged with their husbands, but had an adult capacity to engage in trade and to manage property (Goonsekere 1979: 135ff; Reid 1988: ch. 4). Divorce was easy, also for women. In the nineteenth and first half of the twentieth centuries the (non-Christian) Malay world had by far the highest divorce rates in the world. In Java, in the last third of the nineteenth century, for instance, around a half of all marriages ended in divorce (Jones 1994: 187). But divorce as a rule ended in a new marriage, and widow remarriage was the norm (Boomgaard 1981: 141).

Bilateral kinship also gave the wife's father a right to intervene, recognized by Kandyan law in Ceylon and in the Code of Rama I in Siam (Goonesekere 1979: 116; Kasensup 1956: 279). A perceptive seventeenth-century Spanish Jesuit, Alcina, noticed the wife's possibility of taking recourse with her family of origin in pre-Christian Filipinas (Cannell 1999: 66). The general weakness of wider kinship in much of Southeast Asia lessened the burden of patriarchy. The arrangement of marriages in Java, for instance, usually involved only two nuclear families (Geertz 1961: 55), and in Burma there was a positive avoidance of joint families, i.e. of the norm in East, South and West Asia (Spiro 1977: 122).

While Southeast Asian women were thus in some respects better off than their European sisters, in others their position was weaker. Parents of the former had the major say in the choice of marriage partner. The largest leeway in partner selection was in Burma and in (large parts of) Siam, where the young usually had a veto, and could sometimes even impose their will on their parents (Spiro 1977: 154; Hahang 1992: 46–47). Java, on the whole, had the same norm as in India: girls had to be married off before or on reaching puberty, i.e. child marriages. Ceylon, Burma, Siam and the Philippines, on the other hand, had a custom of more adult marriage. In 1901 mean age at first mariage was 18 years in Ceylon, and 21 (in 1903) in the Philippines (Xenos and Gultiano 1992: 28–29).

Polygamy was generally legitimate in the region, although practised mainly among the elite, and the explicit treatment of women as sex objects, to be given as gifts, occurred in Java for example. Women could also be sold as slaves, as in Burma among other places (Cady 1958: 61). The law of Siam distinguished three categories of wives: the major wife, the minor wife and the slave wife (Wichiencharoen and Netisastra 1968).

Siam was feeling the approaching and encroaching colonial heat: it had just lost its suzerainty over Cambodia and Laos to France, over the southern part of the Malacca peninsula to Britain, and was itself about to become the only independent state in the region. The rulers of the country were aware of the necessity to modernize in order to keep the predators at bay. Like many other countries in a similar situation at the time, reformist intellectuals raised the issue of the position of women, as either holding down the country or as a lever for lifting it. In 1907 a Thai writer, Thianwan, published a series of articles under the slogan 'For the Advancement of Women', calling for education and for an end to prostitution slavery and polygamy (Barmé 1999). In contrast to his Egyptian contemporary and fraternal spirit Qasim Amin, Thianwan did not preach mainly to the deaf and hostile, but had some resonance in the royal palace of King Chulalongkorn and one of his wives, Saowapha.

One issue of modernization came to centre around polygamy. In 1912 the new King Vajiravudh commissioned the draft of a new Marriage Law, and a debate ensued about whether polygamy should be banned, or at least put discreetly beyond the law, like the French mistress pattern. Prince Svasti, later Chief Judge, was for one or the other of those two options, arguing that polygamy was 'bringing disgrace on our country'. The King himself presented a memorandum in favour of keeping polygamy regulated: not by defending it as an ancient custom or as a good institution – on the contrary, the King explicitly pitied the 'minor wife', the wife sold by her parents, and condemned her treatment as chattel. His arguments in favour of maintaining polygamy as a legitimate institution of marriage was pragmatic: it was a deep-rooted practice which the law should respect, and law should not be used to 'deceive the world'. Polygamy also meant that all children were legitimate and cared for, in contrast to the European production of 'illegitimate' children. Thirdly, it opened up the possibility for the legal protection of 'minor wives'. The debate did not end with the King's memorandum of 1913, but Siamese polygamy was not legally proscribed until 1935 (Wichienharoen and Netisastra 1968).

The colonial context around 1900 was as diverse as the cultural traditions of the region. Indo-China had recently come under French domination, and Burma under British. The latter had also recently taken control over all the sultanates of Malacca. Ceylon harboured important colonial trading-posts since the Portuguese entered the Indian Ocean, with the Dutch supplanting the Portuguese in the mid-seventeenth century. Since the wars of the French Revolution the island was ruled by the British. In the course of the nineteenth century the Dutch had tightened and extended their grip of the 'East Indies', first gaining full control over Java, then expanding into Borneo (Kalimantan), Celebes (Sulawesi), Western New Guinea (Irian Jaya) and Sumatra, and finally, in the first decade of the new century, winning a tough war against Aceh on northern Sumatra. Bali was fully conquered in 1906. On the other hand, in the Philippines the first modern anti-colonial revolt had risen and was gaining ground, when the uprising against the Spanish was hijacked by the American army, and the Philippines annexed to the United States. In the world's first anti-colonial novel, José Rizal's *Noli me tangere* (Don't touch me, of 1887), the predatory sexuality of Spanish friars and priests plays an important part.[3] In the meantime, the Portuguese were still keeping a toehold in East Timor.

The family impact of colonialism in Southeast Asia did not run very deep by 1900. But there were two exceptions. The clearest one was the Catholic conquest of most of the Philippines, and Christian inroads into some smaller Indonesian islands. Hereby the Malay pattern of extensive divorce was eclipsed (Javillonar 1979). But even in the Philippines, with its firmly implanted colonial church, Christian marriage was grafted onto pre-colonial norms, e.g. of brideprice, and rituals (Cannell 1999: 63ff), as in the Andean 'Indies'.

The other exception was ethnic mixing, although part of it followed more from trading relations than from colonial power, such as the spread of Chinese migrants, historically *huashang* (traders) (Wang 1991: 4ff) throughout the region, giving rise to extensive ethnic inter-marriage particularly in the Philippines and in Siam. The strong Chinese component gave the social category of mestizo a different connotation in the Filipinas than in Ibero-America. In Ceylon, Eurasian intimate relations had given rise to a special pre-British social category of *Burghers*. On the whole, until well into the twentieth century, the colonial powers in Asia were positively tolerating informal Eurasian unions by severely restricting the possibilities of lower rank personnel to marry, whether in the army, the administration or in private enterprise. In the Dutch East Indies of the 1880s about half of the European male population was unmarried and living with Asian 'housekeepers' (Stoler 1996: 218).

However, in contrast to Creole America, this inter-racial informal sexuality was a minor phenomenon in Asia, far from having a significant effect on regional family relations. In the 1890s there were 62,000 civilian 'Europeans' in the Dutch East Indies, most of them Eurasians, making up less than half of one per cent of the population of Java and Madura. The Chinese were much more important numerically, amounting to 1.2 million in 1930. Since 1848, when marriages between Christians and non-Christians were allowed, the Dutch colonial government permitted a formalization of Eurasian unions, and from the turn of the century it was actively encouraging it (Ricklefs 1981: 119, 147; Stoler 1996, 1997: 199, 218–19).

The force of colonialism was mounting. From a woman's point of view its direction was rather positive, to the limited extent that it had any family concerns at all. In Southeast Asia, like elsewhere, the colonial powers refrained from any general attempt at transforming the family norms of the colonized, although the British tried in Burma, under the mistaken assumption that there was no Burmese law (Hla Aung 1968; Huxley 1988). Christian missionaries were, of course, more ambitious, and with extended Dutch colonial control they were fanning out into the Outer Islands of the Indies. But their religious and family effect was quite limited outside the Philippines and Vietnam, where a tenth of the population had become Catholic by the 1920s (Marr 1981: 83).

The new colonial economy of cash crops, plantations, mining and oil extraction must have had important effects on family patterns, but their complexity defies a short non-specialist treatment. The plantations had significant ethnic implications, drawing large numbers of Chinese to the Dutch Indies and to British Malacca, and Tamils to Ceylon and also to Malacca. The very profitable system of forced cash crop cultivation, *cultuurstelsel*, which the Dutch forced upon Java from the 1830s, and which at its height provided the Dutch state with a third of its revenue (Ricklefs 1981: 117), was de facto a cruel, occasionally famine-producing system of exploitation. But as it was imposed on existing villages and on their local power structure and distribution of labour, the family changes from it can hardly have been major.

Colonial public policy was taking new turns in the region around 1900. In the Philippines, the Americans were replacing the Spanish. Among other things, this meant a push for education, increasingly in English, and a legalization of divorce.

In the Netherlands there had been a reaction against colonial exploitation. First ignited by what may be regarded as the first modern Dutch novel, *Max Havelaar*, by a pseudonymous former colonial civil servant, Multatuli ('I have carried much'; in fact, Eduard Douwes Dekker). Published in 1860 it draws a lurid picture of colonial greed, corruption and injustice. By 1899 a prominent Dutch political adviser, C.Th. van Deventer, published a famous article in the most important journal in the Netherlands at the time. Under the title 'A Debt of Honour' van Deventer argued that the Dutch were in debt to the Indians (today's Indonesians) for all the wealth they had extracted from the Indies. In 1901, the new Dutch government under the fundamentalist Calvinist Abraham Kuyper, proclaimed the 'Ethical Policy' for the Indies. Concern for the welfare of the colonized was now said to be a cornerstone of Dutch policy.

The framework was, of course, unchanged: colonial power and colonial enterprise, now in rapid expansion, and the colonial war against the Sumatran Muslim realm of Aceh was pushed with vigorous brutality. But colonial ethics was not just rhetoric: there was a new effort at, *inter alia*, health and education investment. The latter, in particular, bore significantly upon family relations. The interest in the well-being of the population resulted in a series of social studies, one focus of which was the risk of pauperization among the Eurasian part of the 'European' population. Early marriage was another focus which led to an ineffectual clause of criminal law against sexual intercourse with minors (Blackburn and Bessell 1997).

Like almost everywhere, European colonialism and European colonial Christian missionaries in Southeast Asia meant a lift for formal education, and for the education of (elite) women in particular. The first palpable effect seems to have come from the co-educational Dutch parish schools of the eighteenth century in Ceylon, giving rise to, among other things, a school of female poetry. British and American missionaries continued the effort in the following century, and by 1900 there were in Ceylon several female physicians (Jayawardena 1986: 117ff), a species then absent in central European countries. In 1911 about one-tenth of Ceylonese women were literate (Marecek 2000: 144), an Asian record second only to Japan.

Local male elites outside Ceylon were usually less open to female education. This was clearly the case in the Dutch Indies, where the issues of education, child marriage, polygamy, and the absolute marriage norm in general were brought into the public by a remarkable young Javanese woman of princely status, Raden Adjeng Kartini (1879–1904), whose letters to the wife of the Dutch colonial education officer and other Dutch ladies were published posthumously by a high Dutch colonial official.

In 1913 Dutch patrons set up the Kartini Fund to promote female education in Java, and in 1964 Kartini was proclaimed *pahlawan nasional* (national hero) of Indonesia. Kartini criticized the seclusion of young upper-class girls, the hierarchy, by sex and by age, of siblings, the coercion of marriage, Muslim polygyny, and expressed a longing for education. In the end, Kartini was pressured to decline a scholarship to study in the Netherlands and obeyed her beloved father in marrying a much older, but circumspect man. She died soon after her first child was born (Jayawardena 1986: 140ff; Tiwon 1996: 49ff).

Imperial threats

The main non-European states coeval with the first surge of European modernity were never properly colonized – China, Japan and the Ottoman centre of the Islamic world. A few others – Siam, Persia – survived by diplomatic skill and luck in inter-imperialist rivalry; still a few others by military capacity – Abyssinia which defeated an Italian invasion in 1896 most clearly – or by more general inaccessibility and lack of promise of profit, like Afghanistan. But in the last two-thirds of the nineteenth century, all these states were overtaken by North Atlantic modernity and came under acute imperialist threat.

To the European Enlightenment – Voltaire first of all, and the great philospher G.W. Leibniz – China was an object of inspiration, as an advanced civilization characterized by wisdom and tolerance. In the Swedish debates on freedom of the press in the 1760s, China was invoked as a model to follow.[4] Adam Smith was more critical of isolationist China, and by the end of the eighteenth century an agrarian stagnation had set in, with an ensuing

Malthusian overpopulation. The international political effects appeared after some time lag. In 1793 and in 1816 British missions to the imperial court were, respectively, condescendingly and brusquely dismissed. It was the Opium War of 1840–42, whereby the British broke China open to the unhampered British sale of opium from India, which showed that the wheels of history had turned. A set of other imperial powers descended upon China, forcing trade opportunities and a number of other concessions. In 1853 an American fleet appeared in the bay of Edo. Japan was drawn into the maelstrom. In the West, the Ottomans, who had never isolated themselves, had been on the defensive throughout the eighteenth century. Napoleon's brief conquest of Egypt in 1798 shook the main Muslim empire, and with Greek independence in 1830 – ensured only by concerted efforts of the major European powers – a secular European rollback began.

This seemingly endless series of intrusions and defeats demonstrated the superiority of European civilization, and led to extensive searches for the reason behind it. Embassies and study missions were dispatched to Europe and North America, foreign experts were invited. A great amount of Western literature was translated. Profound autocritical reflections were elaborated. Most of the interest was naturally focused on looking for the bases of Western military and economic power. However, the conviction soon developed that this power rested on broad and complex social foundations, which were very, very different from Chinese, Japanese or Ottoman society. When looking at these social foundations, the different pattern of family and gender relations was apparent. The family, and the position of women, therefore came to occupy a quite significant place in the Asian preoccupations of how to deal with the challenges and the threats of Euro-American power.

The much more respected position of women in Europe, their public appearance, and the freedom of the young to marry according to their own choice were noticed by early Asian visitors or compilers of knowledge about Europe. That men and women dined together in public, and that women appeared in theatres and other public places amazed and amused Mehmet Efendi, the Ottoman envoy to France in 1720–21 (Osterhammel 1998: 349). 'Their custom is to esteem women and think lightly of men. Marriages are left to mutual arrangement', stated a Chinese memorial of the 1750s to the Emperor on European customs (Teng and Fairbank 1954: 20). From Paris in the 1820s, the young and very open-minded imam to an Egyptian student group, Rifa 'a al Tahtawi (1834/1989: 78) reported: ' . . . men are the slaves of women, regardless of whether the latter are beautiful or not, and are fully devoted to the latter.'

The first Japanese ambassador to the United States, in 1860, was stunned by the presence of family ladies at a reception at the US Secretary of State, and by male courtesy to women. 'The way women are treated here is like the way parents are respected in our country', one of the Japanese visitors wrote in his report (Miyoshi 1979: 76). The Chinese diplomat to various capitals in Europe from 1877, Li Shuchang, wrote down in his notebook: 'In the West young people also ask for their parents' consent to marry, but they choose themselves their future spouses' (Li Shuchang 1988/1901: 20–21).

Two major geocultural family systems of the world were facing this imperialist but not-yet-colonial challenge: the East Asian one, with its important Chinese and Japanese sub-variants (Korea was conquered by the Japanese and Vietnam by the French); and the West Asian/North African Islamic one, also sub-divided, between Sunni and Shia, first of all.

East Asia: the family in reactive modernities

In the second half of the nineteenth century the political and intellectual elites of China, Japan and Korea became aware of their weakness in front of foreign powers closing in, determined not to let them alone. Prevailing imperialist *Zeitgeist* in Europe and the United States with regard to the ancient Asian polities was nicely expressed by the *Edinburgh Review* in 1852: 'The Japanese undoubtedly have an exclusive right to the possession of their territory', the British journal graciously conceded, 'but they must not abuse that right to the extent of debarring all other nations from a participation in its riches and its virtues' (Beasley 1990: 28).

The question was how to get wealth and strength, now that old methods had turned out deficient. In East Asia, lacking any strong transcendental religion to fall back upon, this self-questioning led to an extraordinarily radical rejection of previous culture by an important part of the intellectual elite. This rejection first ran its course in Japan in the 1870s and 1880s, peaking in a vice-ministerial proposal of basing education in Japan upon the English language, and followed a couple of decades later in China. In Korea the current was weaker, and in Vietnam it became convoluted in the new colonial power, although it meant a wide opening to Christian missions and an abandonment of the demotic Vietnamese script as well as the Chinese script of high culture, for Roman letters. Everywhere the acculturation was soon reined in by a new conservative nationalism, as well as by the weight of ancient traditions, but the cultural clashes were tremendous.

The Japanese path

The Japanese were the first, the most vigorous, and the most successful to embark on a route of reactive modernization. A new regime was emerging from the complex and ironic intra-elite political convulsion known as *Meiji Ishin*, the Meiji Restoration – restoring the Emperor as the only pivot of the polity, and restoring the prestige of the country. The Charter Oath issued in the name of Emperor Meiji proclaimed in 1868: 'Evil customs of the past shall be abandoned and everything shall be based on the just laws of Nature. Knowledge shall be sought throughout the world so as to strengthen the foundations of Imperial rule' (Hirakawa 1998: 94).

From the very beginning, the new regime saw itself in a threatening international context, and confronted with the urgent task of 'enriching the country and strengthening the army'. The accent of this task could be put either on the former part, training for participation in an industrial, Spencerian race for progress, or on the latter, arming for war. With the former there would be a drive for 'enlightenment and civilization', in the latter an instrumental conception of knowledge would be combined with an emphasis on fostering national loyalty and devotion. In the first decade of the Meiji period, the first orientation prevailed, but by the third decade the political accent was clearly on the second part of the task.

Without being explicitly the hottest bones of contention, family and gender relations were a central part of the 'restoration', or reformation, programme, and strategically located in both periods. 'Women are people too', it was recognized (Sievers 1983: 15).

One component of the vast, comprehensive set of policy decisions for national enlightenment and national mobilization was the law of 1872 on compulsory elementary education, which also included girls, in order to form 'good wives and wise mothers', a phrase originally coined by Nakamura Masanao, a Christian-influenced Meiji progressive (Sievers 1983: 22).[5] It took some time for it to be effectively implemented, but in 1890, 30 per cent of eligible girls were at school. By 1910 schooling had become virtually universal (Noulte and Hastings 1991: 157–58). The same year the buying and selling of daughters for prostitution was prohibited in the wake of a public and international scandal.

To the leading intellectuals of the Meiji Enlightenment the position of women was an important issue, to which they devoted great attention. They were among the first travellers abroad, and among the first enthusiastic learners of English and other European languages. First among equals was Fukuzawa Yukichi (1835–1901), a scholar of 'Dutch learning' who had been on the first official mission abroad, in 1860. Fukuzawa was a prolific and very influential writer on a number of social and political topics (Miyoshi 1979: 167ff). With respect to the family he was primarily engaged in fighting for monogamy. In his 1866 report on conditions in the West, he stressed: 'It is in accordance with the Way of Heaven that there should be one husband and one wife in the house. This constitutes what is called the family' (Hane 1984: 97). While concubinage was the main critical target of the group – which included the translator of J.S. Mill's *The Subjection of Women*, and Mori Arinori, assassinated as a progressive Minister of Education in 1889 – Fukuzawa also came out against parents marrying off daughters against their will, and for wifely autonomy and right to property, and also for the remarrying of widows (Sievers 1983: ch. 2; Hane 1984).

In the early 1880s there were also female voices to be heard in public, attacking patriarchy and its stunting of women's growth: 'daughters raised in boxes'. Foremost among these was Kishida Toshiko, who gained a platform by means of a short-lived Liberal party (Sievers 1983; Mackie 1998: 129). By the mid-1880s the political skies over Japan were darkening.

The 'Meiji Six', as Fukuzawa's group called themselves, were also basically nationalists. Although in the beginning they thought 'there is nothing in which we can take pride vis-à-vis the West' (Fukuzawa, cited in Pyle 1998: 101), there was always an instrumental streak to their feminism, and a correlation of their positions with the winds of high politics, which was moving away from industrial 'enlightened peace' (the meaning of the imperial name Meiji) in the direction of strengthening and testing the army.

The first major domestic victory of the neo-conservative forces was the Imperial Rescript on Education of 1890, which most directly meant that neo-Confucian ethics was now given a leading role in the school curriculum. It is important in our context for its founding of the Japanese imperial 'family state' (*kazoku-kokka*). The Emperor, the state and the family were now brought together in a system, which was to be energetically and pervasively propagated in the ensuing decades. In the language of this particularly solemn declaration from the throne: 'Our Imperial Ancestors have founded the Empire on a basis broad and everlasting. Our Subjects ever united in loyalty and filial piety have from generation to generation illustrated the beauty hereof. . . . Ye, Our Subjects, be filial to your parents, affectionate to your brothers and sisters; as husbands and wives be harmonious, as friends true . . .' (Pyle 1998: 109).

The Meiji family was summed up normatively in a Civil Code, the drafting of which began in the 1870s, in the period of Enlightenment, under the actual direction of an imported French legal adviser, Gustave Boissonade, and Kumano Binzo, a Japanese former student of law in France. A new, codified legal system was a precondition for a revision of Japan's unequal treaties with foreign powers, so the law-drafters were told to to hurry up, and their work led up to the promulgation of a Code in 1890.

This Code, soon known as the Old Code, met with a barrage of neo-conservative criticism, however. The attack was headed by Hozumi Yatsuka, the Dean of the Law School of the Tokyo Imperial Unversity, a major proponent of the imperial family–state concept. 'Loyalty [to the Emperor] and filial piety will perish with the enactment of the civil code', Hozumi wrote, ' . . . the spirit in which this civil code is drafted will bring repudiation of the national religion and destruction of our house system. The words *house* and *household head* appear briefly, but the draft obscures the true principles of law, and thus, is worse than a dead letter. Alas, these men are trying to enact a civil code centered on extreme individualism . . .' (cited in Hirakawa 1998: 74–75).

The 'Old Code' was submitted to almost immediate revision, under the chairmanship of the Prime Minister, Ito Hirobumi, and the committee also included the new Minister of Education. Neither belonged to the neo-Confucian camp, but the tide was definitely with the latter in the mid-1890s, after the victorious war against China.

In the final version of the Code (§57), the samurai concept of *ie*, 'house', was both the portal to the family stipulations, but also their foundation and raison d'être. The house is defined as a 'family group united under the headship of one person'. Normally it would consist of a patriarchal head, his wife, their first-born married son and his wife, sometimes other married sons, unmarried children, and the children of the second, or third, generation. A headship is inherited by male primogeniture, but in case there are no sons, a daughter may become the head (§970), although the usual pattern then would be for her husband to be married into the house and its headship (§736).

As in almost all countries, the general rules here hide significant regional differences. Late nineteenth-century Japan contained also areas with male ultimogeniture, with succession by the eldest daughter's husband even if she had a younger brother, and with the old head moving out of the house upon the eldest son's marriage. The extended family – more often of the 'stem' variant, with only one married son, than of the 'joint' one – were more frequent in the northeast, where it constituted a majority of households, than in the southwest and central Japan, where the extended family made up a large minority, perhaps a third, of households (Hayami and Ochiai 1996).

As a rule, women entered the house of their husbands upon marriage. In fact, however, they were often entered into the socio-legally important family register only after having borne a son (Sievers 1983: 116). Although individual acquisition of property is possible, the property of the house belongs to the head, who has a duty to support its members. The head has a veto over the residence of house members. His consent is also necessary for marriage (§750). In the officious comments on the law, it is laid out that non-consent does not invalidate a marriage, but it would mean a removal from the public family register, a kind of social excommunication (Kono 1970: 81).

Parental consent to marriage was also necessary, unless the 'man has completed his thirtieth year or the woman her twenty-fifth year' (§772). This form of the rule was taken from a draft of the German Civil Code, which later was rescinded there as too patriarchal. The minimum age of marriage was 18 for the groom and 16 for the bride (§765). The average marriage age was much higher than the minimum: women in their early twenties, men in their late twenties in 1886 (Hayami and Ochiai 1996: figs 5A–B). The samurai tradition of marriage arranged with the help of go-betweens spread among the commoners in the Meiji era (Hendry 1981: 23).

A marriage could only be monogamous (§766), but concubinage is indirectly recognized and regulated by references to its offspring, who could enter the house only with the consent of the head (§735). A recognized child of a concubine, a *shoshi*, seems to have the same or similar rights of inheritance as a legitimate one, while other out-of-wedlock children are behind daughters of the former categories, even if male (§970).

French and German influence had led to the introduction of a number of contractual elements into the family institution. Parental power, invested in the father (§877), could be lost by a court decision because of abuse (§896). The husband was the manager of his wife's property, but had to have her consent for contracting a loan or for alienating her property (§801–2), and the law explicitly allowed other property arrangements by mutual contract at the time of marriage (§793). Indeed, the Japanese law-makers did not find it necessary, or desirable, to enter any French insistence on wifely obedience into the effects of marriage (§§788–92). Divorce by mutual consent was granted without ado in secularized Japan, but persons under 25 had to have parental permission (§§808–9). Ill-treatment or gross insult by either party, and by, or of, ascendants of either party, bigamy, and adultery by the wife were valid grounds for judicial divorce (§813).[6]

It is the final Code's emphasis on the patrilinear, patrilocal extended family, and its clauses requiring the consent of the head of the house as well as of parents, which most clearly express Meiji Japanese patriarchy. Conjugal relations, perhaps because less important, are less hierarchical than the Napoleonic law of Latin Europe and Latin America – not to mention Serbian subordination – and provide more individual autonomy than the English common law tradition before its late nineteenth-century reforms.[7]

The adapted samurai patriarchy coalesced with the modernizing state, bent on national expansion, and with emergent capitalist industrialization into a unique comprehensive system of hierarchy, devotion, and male domination. The patriarchy of the family fed into, and was itself nourished by, the state through the vigorously pushed cult of the emperor, whose ancestors were the ultimate ancestors of the Japanese (Pyle 1998; Thomas 1998: 125).[8] The new textile industry was largely worked by indentured young female labourers, contracted out by their parents for one- to five-year contracts, housed and surveilled in factory dormitories (Sievers 1983: ch. 4).

The blocked exits out of China's past

Traditional China conceived itself as the centre of the world, the 'Middle Kingdom', and it was undoubtedly the source and the centre of an ancient civilization. Japan by contrast was a side-branch of the Sinic civilization, and once a cultural borrower from the latter, a historical precedent of which the Meiji borrowers from the West were well aware. But the polity of this proud self-sufficient civilization was more fragile. Instead of an image of one imperial lineage – reproduced as long as it actually was through concubinage legitimacy – going back to the Sun Goddess, Chinese historiography dealt with the cyclical rise and fall of dynasties. The dynasty ruling in the nineteenth century was not even (Han) Chinese, but Manchu, a not quite assimilated ethnicity with a language and customs of its own.

On the other hand, China bore the first brunt of the Western onslaught, promising much larger and more lucrative markets than the Japanese. But it took the country a long time, at least a century, to find a new equilibrium. How long Communism will last in China is still in the stars, but no regime before it managed to cope with the modern challenges to China. The extraordinary radicalism, nay iconoclasm, and creativity of its early twentieth-century modernist intellectuals never acquired a sufficient social base and an adequate political expression. Nor did China produce a cohesive and far-sighted neo-conservatism of the Meiji sort. Beneath the violent vicissitudes which ensued, the Chinese family plodded along, more or less like before.

Patriarchy was, as we have seen above, at the very core of Chinese civilization. The father–son relationship was the pivotal social bond, and filial piety, *hsiao*, the essence of moral obligation. In contrast to the legal Roman concept of *patria potestas*, fatherly power, *hsiao* is an ethical concept, denoting a son's duty of unconditional obedience (Hamilton 1990). Elaborate hierarchies of generation, gender and age permeated Chinese society, and the Sinic culture of East Asia.

Kinship norms are summed up in rules of mourning, of which there were five basic degrees, but where the second was subdivided into four, prescribing different length, garb and consequences: the death of a father is the first degree, that of a wife 2a, a son 2b, a first cousin 3. The Criminal Code also applied this hierarchy, adding an age distinction to the mourning hierarchy of generation and gender. A younger brother beating an older brother is punished – by two and a half years of penal servitude plus 90 blows of bamboo – whereas an older beating a younger is not punished at all (Bodde and Morris 1967: 38).

The ideal Chinese family was a patrilineal 'joint family', with a patriarch, married sons, and immature children or grandchildren. Under conditions of high mortality and widespread poverty this was, of course, far from universal practice. How far the latter differed from the norm has been the subject of controversy among specialists, but it seems clear that a family larger than the nuclear was a major phenomenon in early twentieth-century China, and at least in some regions the predominant pattern (Fei 1939: ch. III; Wolf 1985; Zang 1993: 41).

Patrilineality meant that daughters did not really belong to the family. Raising them was a burden, as they were to leave with a dowry into the family of their future husbands. Female infanticide was frequent (Fei 1939: 52), girls could be sold by poor parents to prostitution, or they could be given away as future minor wives to be reared by their future parents-in-law (Wolf and Huang 1980).

Marriages were arranged between families, and child betrothals were frequent, but the actual marriage age was later than in India, in the later teens for women (Fei 1939: 53; Wolf and Huang 1980: 135; Zang 1993: 38).

Strictly speaking, Chinese patriarchy was not polygamous. Bigamy already was punishable by 90 strokes of bamboo by Qing law (V. Chiu 1965: 32). Nor was it monogamous. Concubinage was legitimate and common among the upper classes. It differed in two respects from the European, particularly Latin, mistress system. First, the concubine lived in the household of the patriarch, and jealousy of the wife was an offence. Second, the children of the concubine were as legitimate as those of the wife. On the other hand, institutionally, the concubine had a lower, weaker social position than the wife.

Marriage in China was a secular arrangement, and divorce was easy, by mutual agreement or on the part of the husband, but not very frequent (Tai Yen-hui 1978: 90; Wolf and Huang 1980: 185). As the Chinese concept of divorce literally meant 'oust wife', there was no provision for wife-initiated divorce. The seven grounds for morally justified husbandly divorce ranged from failure to serve his parents to loquacity and jealousy (Chiu 1965: 61ff). Although these reasons are broad enough to give every husband a chance to get rid of his wife, the Chinese is a minutely regulated patriarchy, and not a blank cheque of male power, as the Muslim institution of *talaq*, of a husband's repudiation. Under certain conditions a wife cannot be ousted, the most important being if she has no family to return to. Furthermore, a *nouveau riche* was not allowed to divorce the wife he married when he was poor (Chiu 1965:

70–71). China furthermore had the unique institution of obligatory divorce for beating or cursing parents-in-law, incestuous adultery, the selling of a wife for prostitution, etc. (Tai Yen-hui 1978).

Widows were not morally expected not to remarry, but the Qing Code only said that she could not be forced to remarry (Bernhardt 1996: 52).

At least in terms of normativity, patriarchy seems to have become more stringent in the last dynasties, the Ming (1368–1662) and the Qing (1644–1911) (Hamilton 1990; Bernhardt 1996). However, there seem to have developed some pro-feminine tendencies in the eighteenth and early nineteenth centuries, critical of polygamy, stressing the value of women's domestic role, opening up literate culture to some elite women (Spence 1990: 146; Dikötter 1995: 14ff).

Around the turn of the twentieth century, traditional China was clearly in agony. The war with Japan, over influence upon Korea, had ended in disaster for China in 1895. The Japanese acquired territorial port 'concessions' in China, like the Western powers. Taiwan had to be ceded to Japan, and Korea became a Japanese satellite. These final decades of the Qing dynasty were times intellectually effervescent, even though, at the end of the day, ineffectual.

The most impressive intellectual of these difficult years was Kang You-wei (1858–1928). While his supreme concern was the survival and preservation of China, family and gender relations had a very important place in his thought and action, like the case of his Japanese counterparts. On the immediate, practical level Kang was in this respect mostly concerned with the tortuous binding of women's feet. In 1883 he organized the first anti-footbinding society in China, in his home town near Guangzhou (Canton) (Wang 1998: 35).

Anti-footbinding societies spread among progressive circles in eastern China in the late nineteenth and early twentieth centuries, not only for purposes of propaganda but more practically for providing marriage outlets for women without bound feet. Even in these circles the presumption of parental arrangement could be upheld. As the Anti-Footbinding Society of Hunan put it in the first paragraph of its statutes: 'The purpose of organizing this society is to make opportunities for members to arrange marriages for their children so that girls who do not bind their feet will not become social outcasts' (Buckley 1993: document 74).

Footbinding in China acquired the same notoriety as *sati* in India, and, much later, genital mutilation in Africa, but also conflicting interpretations and evaluations (see further Ebrey 2003: ch. 9). As Kang put it: 'There is nothing which makes us objects of ridicule so much as footbinding. . .' He also believed that it fatally weakened the nation: 'I look at Europeans and Americans, so strong and vigorous because their mothers do not bind their feet and therefore have strong offspring' (Croll 1990: 51). The Protestant missionaries lined up against it in the second half of the nineteenth century, and the cause eventually found its crusader in Mrs Archibald Little, a British feminist writer married to a British China merchant. In 1895 she founded in Shanghai the Natural Foot Society, a European ladies' committee aiming at the Chinese upper classes. Only in 1902, after the humiliating defeat of the Boxer Uprising, did natural feet finally gain imperial support, although the Manchus themselves had never adopted this custom. The Japanese, who had never adopted the custom either, banned it in their new colony of Taiwan.

In his high-profile erudition, circumspection, cosmopolitan horizon, and commitment to loyal change, Kang You-wei was unique among his coevals. In his posthumously published *The Book of One World*, an evolutionist utopia of the route from the current Age of Disorder to one of Complete Peace and Equality, he included a vision of male–female equality, governed by temporary 'contracts of intimacy', and with children cared for by society at large, in a world where national boundaries had disappeared (Ono 1989: 42–43; Wang 1998: 34ff). But he did not have much impact on his torn society.

One of Kang's most radical disciples, Tan Su-tung, placed gender relations within a general agenda of social change by calling for the creation of four *tung* (good connections): between upper and lower classes, between China and foreign countries, between male and female, and between oneself and others (Teng and Fairbank 1954: 157).

After the Sino-Japanese war, Chinese students were going to Japan in increasing numbers to learn of modernity. For all the Chinese national humiliation, Japan came to constitute the major conduit for modernist ideas of social and cultural change into China. An early female exponent of this was Qiu Jin, who upon her return to China in 1906 became a prominent spokeswoman for women's rights, in general, in the family and in society, but with a particular edge against footbinding and a drive for girls' education. In 1907 she was executed as a revolutionary (Buckley 1993: document 74b).

Little positive came out of all this within the range of contemporary experience, although the Chinese Empire dissolved in 1911. The reform-minded Emperor Guangxu was effectively ousted from power in 1898, and subdued by the formidable ex-concubine Empress Dowager Cixi, who in 1900 gambled on the Boxers, in the end smashed by a combined European imperialist force. Belated Manchu attempts at reform never reached very far.

Cracks began to appear in traditional custom in the cities, with industry and foreign trade (Dikötter 1995: 18–19), but these fissures were small in comparison with the life of villages, ravaged but normatively unperturbed by the political vicissitudes. Symbolic is a draft of a new Family Code, launched in 1907 and delivered in 1911, just before the Republican Revolution, and never decided upon. Re-drafting continued up to the Guomindang Code of 1930, the writ of which barely reached beyond the Chinese parts of the treaty ports. China – like Korea, in its way – in 1900 was still basically Confucian, under scattered modernist attack.

Islam under pressure

The Islamic world, in contrast to the Indian and the Sinic, developed in a conflictual symbiosis with Europe, not only with the other 'peoples of the book', i.e. Jews and Christians, but also with the culture of Ancient Greece, which in the European Middle Ages was re-exported to Europe. While in this sense of actual contact there was more of an affinity with Europe, in another respect there was a sharp divide. Islam was a direct rival of Christianity, in a sense that the polytheistic Hinduism or secular Confucianism never were. Islam and Christianity are both monotheistic, monopolistic and endowed with ultimate, sacred truths.

Islam is a legal system as well as a religion, and family law, or the law of personal status, is the heart of the legal system. In 1900 this law had been frozen for about a thousand years, since the foundation of the major schools of Islamic law in the eighth and ninth cenuries (Makdisi 1981: 2). Nor was the stern patriarchy of medieval Islam mitigated by custom, although the Central Asian incursions, of the Seljuks in Iran and of the Mamluks in Egypt, had brought some less misogynous practices into the Arab world (Keddie 1991).

Changes of this widely ramified, archaic and sacred normative complex were bound to be slow and difficult, particularly among the population at large. For the elite of these highly stratified societies there were more degrees of freedom, as usual.

The family of Muslim West Asia and North Africa was patrilineal and patrilocal, with a strong endogamic tendency. Marriages with paternal first cousins were often strived for, and quite frequent, albeit rarely a statistical norm. The patriarchal joint family, including more than one married son, was an ideal, reached or approximated to varying extent during a family life cycle. Marriages were arranged, and child marriages, or child betrothal, were common. Girls were usually married off by puberty, and Ottoman law had a minimum age of nine.

The Hanafi law school, which prevailed in the Ottoman Empire, alone among the schools of Islamic law, Shia as well as Sunni, gave a girl upon maturity the right to call for nullification of her child marriage, provided that it had not been sexually consummated. Muslim law generally held that girls should not be married against their will, but their acquiescence was always the presumption. Polygamy was religiously sanctioned but, as in the rest of Asia and in contrast to sub-Saharan Africa, was mainly an elite phenomenon, comprising a few per cent of males only: 4 per cent in Algeria in 1903, for example (Goode 1963: 104). Divorce was easy for husbands – just a one-sided repudiation, the only legal restriction being that if it had been uttered or occurred three times, it was irreversible (Baron 1991: 285) – and very difficult or virtually impossible for women against the will of their husbands. The Maliki school of law, predominant in the Mahgreb, is the only one acknowledging the possibility of judicial divorce because of serious ill-treatment by the husband (Pearl 1979: 108–9). Divorcees, as well as widows, could re-marry.

However, Islamic law did not allow unconstrained male domination. Its property regime gave women not insignificant powers, indeed in some respects greater ones than early nineteenth-century Western European law. Daughters had a right to inherit half of the son's share; in Shi'i law they inherited all if they had no brother. With regard to land and camels this right was often evaded, however. According to the norm the *mahr*, the dower the bridegroom had to pay upon signing the marriage contract, and the deferred portion agreed upon then, should be paid to the bride, not to her father. In practice this stipulation was often violated, but it was also followed (Keddie 1991; Barakat 1993: 110). In marriage, wife and husband had separate property, and their economic transactions, at least among the urban propertied classes, were regulated by formal contracts. This property regime gave many women a chance to make a divorce deal with their husbands. Married women had a legal capacity of their own, which has made old Ottoman court records fascinating sources of family history (e.g. Marcus 1989: ch. 5).

Gender segregation and female seclusion were general rules of the Islamic household, and veiling was the norm among urban middle- and upper-class women. This was an ancient West Asian custom, which has been traced back to Assyria in the thirteenth century BC (Keddie 1991: 3). If the generally curious and well-informed Lady Montagu, wife of an eighteenth-century British ambassador to Istanbul, is to be believed, cloaking could and was used as a cover for widespread erotic intrigues. As Lady Montagu (1994/1717: 71) put it: 'This perpetual masquerade gives them [Ottoman ladies] entire liberty of following their inclinations without danger of discovery'.

This once culturally flourishing and militarily vigorous world was clearly decaying in the nineteenth century. In military terms the Ottoman Empire had been on the defensive since the aftermath of their unsuccessful siege of Vienna in 1683. Culturally, the area had been a stale backwater since about the times of Ibn Khaldoun, i.e. the fourteenth century. Politically it was made up of the vast, and loosely linked Ottoman Empire, the lands of which included current Iraq in the east, Saudi Arabia in the south, Algeria in the west, and Serbia and Bosnia in the north, and everything between. The Ottomans were flanked by two other Muslim polities, Qajar Persia to the east, and Makhzen, today's Morocco, to the west, both also in bad shape.

European imperialism and European nationalism came to shake this world to its foundations. It began in earnest in 1830, when European-fuelled and militarily supported nationalism gave Greece independence from the Sultan, and when a new colonial expansion began with the French conquest of Algeria. And so it continued until the end of World War I, during which time British-supported Arab nationalism reached the southeastern parts of the crumbling empire, to be wrapped up in British and French colonial 'mandates'. After the war, a secular Turkish nation-state rose from the Ottoman ruins.

Egypt became the frontier of modernity in the Islamic world. According to protocol it was part of the Ottoman Empire, to whose Sultan it paid an annual tribute, but for practical purposes it was independent in the nineteenth century, until its occupation by the British in 1882. Egypt was invaded by Napoleon in 1798, as part of the Anglo-French conflict. The French army devoted much effort to demonstrating its friendliness to Islam – though soiled by a profanation of the al Azhar mosque immediately after storming the city – and its relations to the population of Cairo seem to have been amiable. A great Egyptian chronicler, Abd-al-Rahman al-Jabarti, recorded the French occupation. One of the things he noted was the bad behaviour of the women accompanying the French army, moving around with their faces unveiled, without chaperone, even on horseback. Worse, this behaviour spread to some Muslim women around the French. When the French had to withdraw, in 1801, several women connected with the French were killed on the spot (al-Jabartî 1979/1798–1801: 320–21, 366).

While leaving no lasting manifestations of modernity, the French invasion had shattered the *ancien régime* of Egypt, and soon after their departure power was taken by an Ottoman commander of Albanian descent, Muhammad Ali, who set the country on a path of change, which included the dispatch of a group of students to Paris in 1826. Muhammad Ali was an energetic but autocratic innovator, who managed to get the Ottoman Sultan to grant him hereditary rule over Egypt, but none of his successors had his ruthless ability.

Among the urban elite, however, French and other European manners began to gain influence, even in matters of family and intimacy, fed by a continuous, if thin, stream of French education. Romantic love marriage, and the existing obstacles to it, became a major theme of the new Cairo theatre. Although the opera and the theatre practised gender segregation, meeting places for the young began to appear. The great Muslim religious reformer Mohammed Abduh, the *mufti* (highest judge) of the country, held pre-marital mixing to be permitted by Islamic law. The Coptic Church accepted it, and the patriarch in 1895 instructed his priests to ensure that they were not marrying anybody against his or her will. The age of girls' marriage seems to have edged upwards in the course of the nineteenth century (Baron 1991: 281–82), although the census of 1907 can hardly be taken as very reliable. The trade in Circassian slave girls, favourite concubines of upper-class males, was forbidden in 1877. In Istanbul, the first prohibitions of this trafficking were proclaimed in 1847 and again in 1856 (Eyrumlu 2001: 345).

By 1900 there had been no modern reform of ancient Sharia law in any Muslim country. The Ottoman Empire undertook a large project of codification of Islamic civil law in 1869–76, which got an Egyptian adaptation in 1875, but it included no change of family law. It is still the basis of civil law in Palestine and Jordan (Botiveau 1993: ch. 4). The first modern reforms of famly law were promulgated in 1917, at the end of the Ottoman Empire. They raised the female minimum marriage age to 17, and allowed for a clause in the marriage contract giving the wife a right to sue for divorce if her husband should take another wife (Botiveau 1993: 145, 195n).

On the issue of consent, Islamic law did not crack easily. In 1904 there was a famous legal case. A legally adult woman of high social origin married a successful nationalist journalist against her father's will. The latter challenged the marriage on the ground that the two were not of equal status, which they should be according to Islamic law. The father won the case (Baron 1991).

In the 1890s a small feminist movement could be discerned among the Egyptian elite, a current in which Arab Muslim women were little visible, though. The first women's journal in Arabic was founded in Alexandria in 1892 by a Syrian Christian woman, the sharp feminist poet and essayist Aisha Ismat al-Taimuriya, a Turco-Circassian who wrote articles about the barriers to female education (Taimuriya 1990: 125ff). The key figure of Cairene elite feminists in the 1890s was a French woman, Eugénie Le Brun Rushdi, married to an Egyptian and a convert to Islam (Badran and Cooke 1990: xxx–xxxi).

The most remarkable feminist tracts of the whole empire were written by a male Egyptian judge of Kurdish background and French education, Qasim Amin. The intellectual context was similar to that of contemporary East Asia, i.e. an international more or less social Darwinist literature about what accounted for the weakness or the strength of nations. Arousing great interest at both ends of Asia was Samuel Smiles' *Self-Help*, which was translated into Arabic in Beirut in 1880, nine years after the Japanese translation (Mitchell 1988: 108; Beasley 1990: 89). 'The worth and strength of a state', Smiles had written, 'depend far less on the form of its institutions than on the character of its men'.[9] The competitive world of Herbert Spencer, immensely popular in Japan, also entered into Qasim Amin's work. Among Francophone intellectuals there was a French work entitled *What Accounts for the Superiority of the Anglo-Saxons?*, published in Paris in 1897 and in Cairo in Arabic two years later. The answer was character and education (Mitchell 1988: 110, 198n).

If a country's weakness, in a ruthless struggle for survival, depended on the character of its men, the critical eye would go directly to the prime agency of character formation, the family. By the late nineteenth century this had become a well-known theme in progressive elite circles, in Istanbul, among Namik Kemal and his influential literary circle (Enqinün 2000), as well as in Cairo.

What made Amin (romanized as Emin by his German translator) outstanding in the Ottoman world were two things. One was an articulate programme, prudent and circumspect, as could be expected from a sophisticated judge, for the *Liberation of Woman*, the title of his first book (Emin 1899/1928) on the topic. It focused on the promotion of female education, but also included unveiling and conjugal marriage, and was critical of polygamy and unilateral divorce. Second, Amin was the most articulate Muslim secularist of the empire. While keeping a respectful stance towards Islam, and always relating to the Koran and Sharia, Amin held that a new social order had to be based on science and use utility, rather than tradition, as its yardstick: 'Scientific progress leads to moral progress', as he put it in his subsequent book, *The New Woman*, in 1901 (Sharabi 1970: 92ff; Hourani 1983: 164ff; Baron 2000: 148ff).

Qasim Amin was widely attacked and had no direct impact. He died in 1908. But he became an icon of Egyptian feminism, annually commemorated (Badran and Cooke 1990: 352).

The Ottoman reform attempt, *Tanzimat* (a word meaning reform, restructuring), of the mid-nineteenth century centred on state–citizen relations, like religious equality before the law, and on economic development. It made no attempt at changing family relations, although ideals of companionate marriage did emerge among the urban elite, as we noted above. Muslims generally, and Muslim girls in particular, were very little present in the plethora of foreign schools which proliferated in the last decades of the empire, which were usually staffed by missionaries but often religiously cautious or nonconfessional. A Muslim religious suspicion is detectable, but neither the state nor the Muslim clerics offered any educational alternative (Davison 1990: ch. 9).

Persia had early, sporadic contact with Europe – Montesquieu's famous *Lettres Persanes* had some slight link to reality – and in the early nineteenth century these contacts were intensified, primarily with Britain – against a mounting Russian threat – including via British Bengal. However, this early curiosity and attempt at modernization did not come to much, and Persia was to follow the Ottomans at a distance (Fazlhashemi 1999; Eyrumlu 2001). The city of Teheran remained a public space basically closed to women at least until the 1930s, whereas the large numbers of Christian and Jewish women, under less rigid surveillance than their Muslim sisters, made a certain opening up of Istanbul and Cairo to women easier, as they had featured in urban life since the late nineteenth century (Eyrumlu 2001: 339ff).

In the western part of the Islamic world, the sultanate of Morocco remained highly traditional until its twentieth-century colonial conquest, and the reform of Tunisia was impeded by the indebtedness of the ruling Bey and his ensuing subordination to the French. Financial profligacy and irresponsibility, leading to dependence on foreign creditors, backed up by imperialist military power, haunted the Islamic polities of the nineteenth century, as well as late imperial China. At that time the consequences were even more sinister than becoming dependent on International Monetary Fund credits today.

Summing up the situation in the heartlands of Islam around 1900: in its cosmopolitan, multicultural metropolises, Istanbul and Cairo, a debate of a new family had started among the elite. Romantic marriage had emerged as a cultural topic – if hardly as a practice – and at least among progressive intellectuals female education had become a programme. In Cairo the first generation of women feminists was just emerging, and in Istanbul the future leading feminist, Halide Edip Adivar, graduated in 1901 as the first Turkish Muslim from the American School for Girls.

However, there had been no institutional change, apart from a possible rise in the marriage age of girls. The veil was still *de rigeur* among respectable urban women, and gender segregation governed respectable entertainment, the opera, the theatre and restaurants. Medieval Muslim patriarchy was submitted to criticism, and religious reformers, like Mohammed Abduh, *mufti* of Egypt, were trying to relate Islam to modern science. While raising the issue of gender segregation, Abduh was little concerned with family issues. Courts and clerics remained adamantly patriarchal. With respect to family and gender relations, in 1900 the Muslim world of West Asia and North Africa was still on the eve of modernity.

The world of patriarchy around 1900

The world around 1900 was a patriarchal world. The laws of fathers ruled the world of children, including grown-up children, at least if unmarried. In matrilineal societies, the oldest maternal uncle was usually the functional equivalent of male generational authority. Wives were institutionally subordinate to husbands virtually everywhere, although West Coast African wives frequently had economic autonomy. Marriages were normally parentally arranged everywhere, except in the North Atlantic area of northwestern Europe and North America (and the European offshoot in Oceania). Among the major Amer-Indian populations, among the Creole elites of the Americas, in Mediterranean Europe, the Balkans, Russia and all over Asia and Africa, marriage was first of all a parental affair, above all for the bride. Among the Creole populace, where non-marital sexual unions were common, male power was more phallocratic than patriarchal.

Polygyny was normatively permitted all over Africa and Asia, except Japan, which had just outlawed it. In many bourgeois and aristocratic milieux of Latin Europe and America mistress-keeping was almost institutionalized. Divorce was a unilateral male privilege in China and in Muslim countries, and difficult elsewhere. Female seclusion was a Muslim and northern Indian norm, and 'respectable' female movement in public spaces was restricted almost everywhere, save perhaps the West Coast of Africa. The restrictions varied enormously, though. In northwestern Europe and North America, sexually ambiguous spaces were usually off-limits to non-escorted women; these included restaurants, theatres and other places of entertainment, and the streets after dark. In a vast swathe of land from the Gangetic plains of the defunct Mughal Empire to the Atlantic coast of *Makhzen* or Morocco, women of the conservative upper classes were normatively expected to leave their house (and its female quarters) only on the rarest of occasions, such as their marriage, their father's death, and at their own burial. There were likely to be some further occasions, but each time, upon leaving the house, they had to be wrapped up and veiled.

Most societies took special tolls of women. As daughters they had fewer, or no, inheritance rights. As sexed beings, they were subjected to genital mutilation in many parts of Africa. In major parts of China their feet were broken and bound up, as a tribute to the male sense of female beauty. Wife-beating was legitimate in most parts of the world. Widows were socially dead in India, and were often prevented from re-marrying in China.

Even if generally patriarchal or male-dominated, the world of 1900 was highly differentiated. The poles were the northwestern European family system – prevailing also in North America and in European Oceania – on one hand, and China, on the other. Norms of free choice of marriage, which of course did not exclude parental pressure, of new household formation upon marriage, and a less bounded kinship system taking in the maternal as well as the paternal side made the northwestern European family stand out as significantly less patriarchal, relatively speaking. In Sweden, married women were still legally under the 'guardianship' (*målsmanskap*) of their husbands, and the new German Civil Code, which entered into force with the new century, stipulated as the general rule, that 'to the husband belongs the decisions in all affairs of the married life in common'. The common law tradition of married women having no individual legal existence had been broken in England only in 1882, with the Married Women's Property Act. The further south and east one ventured from northwest Europe, including within Europe itself, the more rigid were the patriarchal rules one would find.

China and the other East Asian heirs of Sinic Confucian civilization – Korea, Vietnam, Japan (albeit already in forceful motion) – had the most elaborate ideology and ritual of patriarchy, with 'filial piety' or respect for the father as the paramount family norm. But patrilineal, father to son kinship, and patrilocal residence were the rule all over Eurasia, from the Balkans to Korea, and into Japan, as well as in most parts of Africa and among the larger Indian populations of America. Southeast Asia, by contrast, like most of Western Europe, had bilateral kinship, and new couples were not always expected to reside with the father of the husband. The popular Creole family was inscribed in a circle of male socio-economic power, male-dominated sexual asymmetry and frequent male violence, but often had a maternal focus, of mothers and their children.

This whole world was going to change in the twentieth century, but not in any evolutionary or even manner.

2 A long night's journey into dawn

Patriarchy, the law of the father, was the big loser of the twentieth century. Probably no other social institution has been forced to retreat as much. Institutionalized religion has also lost much ground: secularization was already well under way by 1900, among Latin European liberals and among the industrial working class all over Europe. However, the late twentieth century saw a worldwide, though minoritarian, re-assertion of religion, in Christian, Muslim and Jewish fundamentalism, in Hindu and Buddhist nationalism, and in post-Communist re-affirmations of religion, from Polish Catholicism to Chinese Falun Gong.

Popular rule – the principle, but not necessarily the practice – has largely succeeded the upper-class 'constitutional monarchies' of West and Central Europe, and the less constitutional monarchies of Russia, the Ottoman Empire, Iran, Siam, Qing China, Yi Korea and Meiji Japan, and is a big winner. However, again in principle if not in practice, popular rule was the self-conception of the Americas of the nineteenth century. At the beginning of the twenty-first century, popular rule and self-determination, while the talk of the town, are still delimited by geopolitical power politics, with different accounts for Kuwait and Palestine, among others.

Secularization and democratization were advanced in the course of the twentieth century, but clearly behind a process which has not even got a proper designation. We might name it *de-patriarchalization*. But the twentieth century was more than a century of change in the long reign of patriarchy. The second half of the twentieth century, and its last quarter in particular, was the period of the most rapid and radical global change in the history of human gender and generational relations. This chapter will give an overview of the processes of change, before, in the next chapter, taking stock of what has been achieved, and what not.

Prologue: when the earth moved: three moments of change

Initiations of change were concentrated in three short periods of social and political international concatenation: around World War I, in the aftermath of World War II, and in the aftermath of '1968'. The 1910s and 1920s saw the first real break of patriarchal rule in the modern world. Scandinavia could claim institutional priority, with Sweden in the lead of implementing, in a new Marriage Law of 1915, a Scandinavian programme of family law reform, drafted before the war. The Russian October Revolution and the new Soviet Union provided a more powerful, revolutionary attack on patriarchy, outlawing it in 1918, while the Civil War in Russia and the World War outside were still going on. In spite of their geographical proximity in the European north, the Scandinavian and the Russian/Soviet breakthroughs were completely independent of each other. The patriarchal traditions they attacked were also part of two clearly different variants of the European family system, with the revolutionaries facing a much harder nut of patriarchal power, than the reformists of the northwest.

Significant legal changes occurred in the 1920s in the Anglo-Saxon world too, in Britain, the British Dominions and the USA, but they did not amount to a rupture with the rule of husbands and fathers. Nor did other revolutions in the world of this time, although openings began to appear in the fortress of patriarchy.

The second period, right after World War II, had its actual centre in East Asia, where the elaborated patriarchal traditions of Confucianism and of the feudal *samurai* norms were attacked head on, by US occupation-emboldened Japanese reformers and by Comintern-taught Chinese Communists. Through the efforts of the radical legal staff of General McArthur, the post-militaristic Japanese Constitution of 1947 included a ringing affirmation of gender equality. This was not just a constitutional decoration, but was translated into a new, egalitarian Civil Code a year later. The Chinese Communists followed their Russian comrades in giving a high and early priority to revolutionizing the family. A new Marriage Law, proclaimed in May 1950, was the first major institutional transformation by the Communist revolution, after its victory half a year earlier. Eradicating millennial patriarchy was, of course, a protracted and difficult operation, which has not been fully completed in the past half-century, but in China and in Japan an epochal process of change was set in motion around 1950.

The Communist take-over in Eastern Europe also involved immediate and radical anti-patriarchal family legislation, emphasizing gender equality, free marriage choice, secularization of marriage, and women's right to work outside the home. At the level of institutional family norms, this meant a turn of the tables of European patriarchy. Before World War II, East–Central Europe had a much more patriarchal family system than the western part, but now the ancient European family divide running from Trieste to St Petersburg/Leningrad got a new meaning.

Elsewhere in the world, changes were at most embryonic. The Asian wave of de-colonization took place under the auspices of a two-gendered conception of human rights, reflected in the constitutions of independence. But family change was not high on the agenda in New Delhi, Colombo or Jakarta, not to mention Karachi, Baghdad and Damascus.

The Allied occupation of Germany was not concerned with German patriarchy, held irrelevant to Nazi belligerence, although it monitored and vetted

German legislation and constitution-drafting. Latin women, in America and in Europe, belatedly got the right to vote in the aftermath of World War II, but they did not get equal rights in marriage.

Nevertheless, a global preparation was made, apart from the delimited regions of change in East Asia and Eastern Europe. The United Nations Declaration of Human Rights, of 1948, did include very advanced formulations on family and gender. At a time when arranged marriages dominated all Asia and Africa and were still important in Eastern Europe, and when a large number of US states prohibited inter-racial marriages, and when only the Scandinavian and the Soviet family codes had instituted egalitarian marriages, the UN Declaration stated (in article 16):

(1) Men and women of full age, without any limitations due to race nationality or religion, have the right to marry and to found a family. They are entitled to equal rights as to marriage, during marriage, and its dissolution.
(2) Marriage shall be entered into only with the free and full consent of the intending spouses.

The third moment began in the late 1960s, picking up speed in the first half of the 1970s, to an international climax in 1975, whereafter a global process of change continued for a couple of decades. The year 1975 had been declared an International Women's Year by the UN General Assembly, which inspired a spate of scrutinizing reports in a number of countries, two major international conferences, the most important one arranged by the UN in Mexico, the other in East Berlin, the setting up on all continents of public national agencies concerned with gender relations, and new legislative initiatives. The legislative impact was most immediate – and prepared – in the civil law countries of Western Europe, where in 1975, Austria, France and Italy passed their first post-patriarchal marriage laws, followed within a year by West Germany, and within a decade by the rest of the region, of which Greece, the Netherlands and Switzerland constituted the *arrière-garde*. While British gradualism did not require any sharp de-patriarchalizing breaks in the 1960s and 1970s, there was important reform legislation in Australia and Canada, and a series of crucial Supreme Court decisions in the USA.

The decision to hold an International UN Conference had established a global agenda, and the General Assembly afterwards declared a Decade for Women (1975–85). Major normative changes ensued in Latin America. The Decade ended in Nairobi, which boosted African efforts at reining in the flourishing forms of patriarchy in Africa, efforts finally breaking through in Southern Africa, with its belated liberation from colonialism and racism, situated in a much more gender-conscious context than the independence wave of the early 1960s. The UN commitment stimulated governmental concern with gender inequality as well as local feminist movements in South Asia and West Asia/North Africa, although the actual effects on the family seems to have been quite limited.

Forces of change and of resistance

Many different forces were involved in these three moments, on the international as well as on the national level. The eruption of the three moments
does not derive from the same social volcano, but they are linked.

Probably to the surprise of many today, international Communism played a
crucial, if not overwhelming, role in all three. The Bolshevik Revolution set a
model of Communist gender and family modernism, which was repeated by
later comrades in East Asia and Eastern Europe – adding enormous political
weight in the second moment of de-patriarchalization – and later still in Cuba,
connecting with the third moment. Less well known is that there was a
Communist initiative behind the idea of an International Women's Year. The
idea seems to have come from the Communist women's front organization, the
Women's International Democratic Federation, presided over by a leading
Finnish Communist, Hertta Kuusinen. In 1972, this organization – from its
official observer status, together with other non-goverment observers – put a
proposal to the UN Commission on the Status of Women via the Romanian
Commission delegation. The Commission adopted the proposal, and submitted
it to the UN General Assembly, which endorsed it: 1975 was to be the International Women's Year, dedicated to Equality, Development and Peace (Pietilä
and Vickers 1996: 76).

The enormously important UN Year and Decade for Women were, of course,
also outgrowths of the work on human rights, including women's rights, which
began right after World War II and became a permanent, if for some time low-
profile, part of the UN apparatus (Winslow 1995). The UN Commission on
the Status of Women was set up in 1947.

For the century as a whole we might identify four broad ideological currents
behind determined thrusts into the fortresses of patriarchy. Most obviously,
there is the feminist women's movement, which was the main force of the
Decade for Women, which pushed the Anglo-Saxon advances that, after all,
did take place in the first years of the twentieth century, and which constituted
a very significant, if hardly decisive, part of Scandinavian pioneering.

Second, the Socialist labour movement, above all in its Marxist and
Anarchist streams, in power spearheaded by Communism, has provided a
heavyweight proponent of an egalitarian family. This commitment, which has
had its ups and downs on the agenda, should probably be seen as part of a
general cultural modernism, as well as of egalitarianism. After the *Communist
Manifesto*, the most widely read book of the classical Marxist working-class
movement was interestingly enough *Woman and Socialism* by August Bebel, the
leader of German Social Democracy. In classical Marxist parlance, what today
is better understood as 'modernity' was referred to as the 'bourgeois-
democratic revolution'. At the fourth anniversary of the October Revolution,
Lenin put the issue of women's rights into this context.

The bourgeois–democratic element of the revolution means that the social
relations . . . of the country are purged of mediaevalism, serfdom,

feudalism. . . . Take religion, or the denial of rights to women, or the oppression and inequality of the non-Russian nationalities. These are all problems of the bourgeois-democratic revolution. . . . There is not a single country in the world . . . where these questions have been completely settled on bourgeois-democratic lines. In our country they have been . . . by the legislation of the October Revolution. . . . In our country we no longer have the base, mean, and infamous denial of rights of women or inequality of the sexes, that disgusting survival of feudalism and mediaevalism which is being renovated by the avaricious bourgeoisie and the dull-witted and frightened petty bourgeoisie in every other country of the world without exception.

(Lenin 1922/1947: 748–49)

Third, we may discern an important current of secularized Liberalism, mainly of Protestant Christian or Jewish – seldom Catholic[1] – provenance, which was crucial to the Scandinavian pioneers, provided core male support for Anglo-Saxon feminism, and operated in the US civilian occupation staff in Japan as well as in the UN Commission of Human Rights. Intellectually, this is the very important tradition of John Stuart Mill and Henrik Ibsen, whose tract *The Subjection of Women* (1869) and whose play *A Doll's House* (1879), respectively, had an immediate impact on the educated world.

Finally, there is stream of nationalist developmentalists, who provided the first writers against patriarchy and male oppression outside Europe and the Americas. We met the generation, from around the previous turn of the century, in Chapter 1: Fukuzawa Yukichi in Japan, Qasim Amin in Egypt, Thianwan in Siam, and Kang You-wei in China. In power, developmentalist nationalism gave rise to the reforms of Kemal Atatürk in Turkey of the 1920s and to the equal rights constitutionalism of post-World War II independence in Asia and Africa, and, in the third historical moment, played an active part in global birth control and gender relations reform policies.

Patriarchy is about power. There are, then, good reasons to expect politics to have been enormously important to family changes in the twentieth century. But the erosion of patriarchy, like political changes, have also to be seen as outcomes of wider socio-economic and cultural processes.

We shall return to the broader context of societal transformation below. But here a word of warning should be given against any ambitious social evolutionism. The pioneering breakthrough of the walls of patriarchy in Scandinavia, carried by a large socio-cultural consensus, took place in an area which in social and economic structure was hardly in the global vanguard. True, there had been very rapid and successful economic developments in the latter part of the nineteenth century and in the years leading up to World War I. The region belonged to the richer part of Europe at the time, but only Denmark was among the most prosperous continental countries, all of them well behind Britain. On the eve of its new Marriage Act, Sweden was about 75 per cent rural and almost half of its economically active population were engaged in agriculture (Norway and Denmark had almost 40 per cent, and Finland 70 per cent), much more than most of Western Europe (SCB 1969: table 4; Jörberg and Krantz 1976: table 4).

Industrialization and urbanization are not of much help in explaining why Scandinavian family norms changed radically about 50–60 years before those of the rest of Western Europe. Nor do they help us to explain why China in 1950 embarked on a policy of radical family change – with 80 per cent of its population in agriculture and 88 per cent in the countryside, both figures similar to or higher than the Afro-Asian Third World average (Bairoch 1997: III, 738–60) – while South Asia, West Asia, North Africa and most of sub-Saharan Africa did not. The crucial things here are the parameters of family and political systems. Other things being equal, industrial labour and urban residence do tend to undermine the law of the father, but few things are equal in this world.

Of course, political and family changes can rarely be taken as endogenous, as unrelated to social and economic processes. It is not by chance, for instance, that major family reform in Scandinavia occurred in the early twentieth century rather than in, say, the early nineteenth century, that a Communist revolution succeeded in China in the mid-twentieth century and not in the mid-nineteenth century, that a feminist revolution swept North America in the 1960s and 1970s, rather than in the 1760s and 1770s. Only a certain threshold of socio-economic change makes political and ideological breakthroughs possible and viable. My two points here are: First, that family systems have a different sensitivity to, or resilience against, socio-economic changes, or, for that matter, juridico-political changes; and second, above all, the contingency of politics means that the amount of social and economic change leading to normative, institutional change by political intervention, through reform or through revolution, will differ widely.

Secularization and internal church liberalization seem to hold more explanatory promise, because of their more direct link to family norms. The Protestant state churches of Scandinavia, which in accordance with Lutheran theology in principle always had recognized the legitimacy of secular family legislation, but which had always taken a keen interest in family matters, and which at least up to the mid-nineteenth century had vast powers of social control, put up little or no resistance to the proposals of reform.

In Britain, family law reform is usually viewed as beginning with the English Matrimonial Causes Act of 1857. Its main, modest, achievement was to move marriage disputes from ecclesiastical to secular courts, and to allow for fault divorce, e.g. for adultery. Six thousand clergy mobilized against it, rounding up ninety thousand signatures from their flocks, but Parliament stood firm (Gravesen 1957: 11). This by no means signified the end of Anglican clerical influence on English family law, but it set a modern stage of secular–clerical confrontations and compromises.

With a multi-religious cultural mix, even at the individual and family level, East Asia, a region of profound change, is first of all a secular civilization, without any important religious authority. As the dismantling of patriarchy has never originated in religious sources, but in more or less secular ones, meeting either religious resistance or resigned acquiescence, secularization has been a major force of change.

Schooling and education, of girls in particular, has had a great impact, putting off child marriages, providing some kind of personal autonomy. We shall come back to this in Chapter 7 as well. In 1950, two-thirds of all Chinese and 77–85 per cent of the rest of Third World Afro-Asia were illiterate (Bairoch 1997: III, 748), with the crucial female rates still higher. The most patriarchal parts of the world did not make much progress in this respect until 1970–74. At that time in Ethiopia almost all (99.6 per cent) young women (aged 15–34) were illiterate, while Pakistan kept four-fifths in full scriptural ignorance, Bangladesh and Morocco three-fourths, Algeria, Ghana, Haiti, India and Syria about two-thirds, Turkey and Zambia two-fifths, and Brazil one-fourth (UN 1991: table 4). But from 1980 to 2000 many balls started rolling. Illiteracy rates of females aged 15 and over, which in spite of rapid population growth means a ballast of the past, declined from 74 to 48 per cent in Northern Africa, from 73 to 51 per cent in Africa between the Limpopo River and the Sahara, from 65 to 50 per cent in South Asia, and from 48 to 25 per cent in western Asia (UN 2000a: chart 4.5). In Ethiopia by the mid-1990s, female gross school enrolment was a fifth of the girls' age group, and in India almost two-thirds (UN 2000a: table 4A).

Act 1: reform, revolution or neither

The consensual vanguard

The vanguard of the dismantling of explicitly patriarchal marriage only happened to coincide in time with World War I. It was in fact driven by an entirely peacetime regional dynamic, but this took place only among some small populations in one of the outpost of the world. On its own, without the war context, it would have had little significance.

The pioneers, largely anonymous even in their own countries, were a set of law professors of a Scandinavian Law Commission, entrusted by the national governments of Scandinavia with the task of reforming family law. The little band of male academics, in the second half of their work period reinforced by a woman from each Scandinavian country, coming from stodgy conservative law faculties, although including a few bright liberal minds, was not completely on its own. The leading Danish jurist in the decades around 1900, Carl Goos, was inspired by Mill on women's rights and was in the early part of his career connected with the culture radicals around the Brandes brothers, but in the 1890s he became a minister of a Conservative government.

The jurists were not acting in a social vacuum, although the overall context was not politicized, which made passage easier, given the strength of conservatism. There were also, particularly in Denmark and Norway, less strongly in Sweden, significant and articulate women's movements raising demands for reform. Would-be reformers were also lucky in that the Lutheran state churches of Scandinavia all recognized the sovereignty of the state in matters of marriage – marriage being a 'worldly thing' (Luther) – and that the church hierarchy was undergoing a modernizing, liberalizing change, most clearly visible in Sweden.

The outcome of the deliberations of the Commission, set up in 1909, were proposals for an individualist and an explicitly egalitarian conception of marriage. The former was manifested most directly in divorce by mutual consent and because of no-fault irretrievable damage. That principle was installed in a Norwegian law of 1909, and the more general notion that marriage was for the well-being of the individuals who contracted it was elaborated in laws on the contraction and dissolution of marriage, in Sweden in 1915, in Norway in 1918, in Denmark in 1922, and finally in Finland, which as a Grand Duchy of the Russian Empire had not taken part in the Law Commission, in 1929.

An egalitarian conception of marriage had wide legal ramifications, into property rights and inheritance, and complications because of the factual economic domination of husbands. Apart from the basic principle itself, legislation on this matter involved a number of possible points of controversy. The Danish legislation, which actually started first, in 1919, did not reach fruition as the Law on the Legal Effects of Marriage till 1925, two years earlier than the corresponding Norwegian law. The Finns waited till 1929, but were then the most consistent.

Sweden had taken the initiative in a Scandinavian coordination of family law reform, and it was the first implementer of the Commission proposals. The shifting political constellations of the reform process underline the broad, if not universal, consensus behind it. The Nordic initiative had been taken by the country's first Liberal government, akin to the then government parties of Denmark and Norway. But the government bill on the Contraction of Marriage was presented in 1915 by a right-wing government, emerging from a bitter political fight over armaments, the position of the King, and international orientation. Among Liberals and Social Democrats the Swedish government of 1915 was called 'the Royal Courtyard Government' (*borggårdsregeringen*), after a Royalist pro-armaments demonstration, which led to the fall of the Liberals. Nevertheless, the new government had no qualms about continuing family liberalism, in the form of instituting no-fault divorce, subject to certain delaying rules of separation and mediation, and with careful attention to provision of alimony after separation and divorce. The social guardianship (*vårdnad*) of children would be decided by the court, implicitly in the interests of the children. Going against the official Legal Advisory Council, the Conservative Minister of Justice proposed that in cases where the social guardianship went to the mother, the legal-economic one (*förmynderskap*) would too.

The die-hard Right was against the bill, but waged no serious resistance. It was passed even in the First Chamber, elected with a high property census, by 83 votes to 51.

The Marriage Code revision dealt primarily with the legal effects of marriage during its duration, but also elaborated the consequences of death and divorce. The government bill was put out in December 1919 by a Liberal–Social Democratic coalition. The main government spokesmen (Liberal Justice

Minister Löfgren and Social Democratic Minister-without-Portfolio Undén) stressed that 'The main aim is to create full equality between husband and wife in marriage'. In most respects the revision did so. The husband's legal guardianship (*målsmanskap*) over his wife was abolished, and all restrictions of the latter's legal and economic capacity were abolished. The social guardianship over children in marriage was invested in both parents, and due to an individual Social Democratic intervention in the parliamentary debate, no judicial redress was made available in case of parental conflict. In one significant respect equality was not attempted. The father was still alone the legal economic guardian of children in wedlock, till a new Parental Code was adopted in 1949 (Finnish legislation had achieved this in 1929).

This time there was more resistance than in 1915, but again the Second Chamber Conservative leadership concurred with the Liberals. Though several reactionaries fulminated against the new ideas of 'a few jurists and feminist women', the real fight was not about male headship, but about a new conception of marital property, and the bulk of the opposition came from propertied farmers. In order to deal with the contradiction between legal equality and economic inequality, the Swedish Law Commission and the government proposed a new legal institute, of deferred community of property in marriage (*giftorätt*), replacing the previous separate property regime. The new proposal meant that the spouses had a latent right to half of the total of married property – unless there was a specific contract of separate property – which was activated upon divorce and death, a right which was safeguarded by certain clauses about economic management during the marriage. This meant a considerable amount of economic security for the economically weaker spouse, usually the wife. Conservative farmers were afraid that this rule would endanger the inheritance of family farms, although a special clause made it a right for a child to bail out other heirs to keep the property undivided. In the end the new Code was passed by a two-thirds majority even in the First Chamber. Children under the age of legal maturity (21) were given certain rights too, to keep their own earnings after the age of 15, and to decide their own employment after the age of 18.[2]

But then as later, such as in its 1981 establishment of an Ombudsman for Children (Flekköy 1993), it was Norway that was the avant-garde of children's rights. A 1896 Child Protection Act put neglected or truant children in the care of the state. The 1909 Divorce Law introduced the welfare of the child as the criterion for solving conflicts over custody, a principle then adopted by the new Nordic marriage laws. In 1915, the concept of illegitimate children was abolished, and children of extra-marital birth were given a right to paternity, and his/her father's name and inheritance. Norway was soon followed by Iceland in this, a country of many extra-marital births, whereas the Swedish 1917 legislation recognized only the right to paternity (Therborn 1993).

A crucial element in the large post-patriarchal consensus in Sweden and in the Nordic countries was the legal context: a liberal, individualistic conception of law, which had established itself as a mainstream of professional legal opinion, including leading Conservative politicians. Pertinent also were some aspects of the, by Western European standards, late modernization of Scandinavian law. There was, for instance, in the Swedish 1919–20 debates a conspicuous absence of the obsession with family headship and final family authority, which characterized Napoleonic and German family law, and which was still important to British lawmakers in the 1920s. In the Nordic countries, the authority of the husband, derived from seventeenth- and eighteenth-century laws, was now widely regarded as obsolete.

Legal individualism in Scandinavia had no strong clerical counterpart, in contrast to the case in other Christian countries. Lutheran Protestantism recognized in principle state family legislation as fully legitimate. The state churches had lost their traditional social control with proletarianization, industrialization and urbanization, and were now trying to adapt to a secularized world. They were often unhappy with the reform proposals, but they raised no serious resistance.[3] The large denominations of Protestant dissent were allied to the political Liberals, and did not do battle for patriarchal marriage as a legal institution.

Because of the absence of clericalism, proto-democratic Scandinavian politics was, in the first decades of the twentieth century, more or less dominated by Liberal parties, with a strong Social Democratic, later also Communist or Left Socialist, current to their left, and an often weaker right-wing stream to their right. The peaceful context, and the simple non-federal structure made the politics of domestic reform easier than in many other countries. Pre-war social polarization and the civil war with its aftermath delayed reform in Finland.

A significant women's movement, with something of a mass membership, had emerged in the Scandinavian countries, and they were also recognized by the governments as bodies to be consulted. Finnish women won the right to vote in 1906 (in the wake of the Russian upheavals of 1905), Norwegian in 1907, Danish in 1915, and Swedish in 1921, it having been first decided in 1919. Norwegian and Danish women had most political influence, well connected with male left liberalism, especially in Norway. But the Swedish women's organizations also made themselves heard in the preparation of the new marriage law, and four female experts were officially consulted. In 1914 the Danes took the initiative to a Scandinavian feminist meeting with a view to pressing for family law reform, and in 1915 a female member was added to each of the national commissions on family law.

Finally, the lawyer-politicians who presented the reform bills often invoked a sense of social evolution, which family law had to adapt itself to. They referred to women's higher education, increasing gainful employment, and to their interest in a new law. Legislation was conceived as an adaptation to ongoing social change, not as an instrument of enlightenment against outrageous and obsolete practices. The contrast to the legal dismantling of patriarchy in Eastern Europe and East Asia is striking in this respect. On the other hand, the reference for change was purely national. From a cross-national, Western European and American perspective there was, as we noticed above in the survey of patriarchy round 1900, nothing special about women's education and employment in Scandinavia at the time.

Feminism and the Communist revolution

The Russian Revolution is a beacon in the world history of patriarchy, and it was often perceived and portrayed as such by its contemporary enemies, viewing it as a destroyer of the holy institutions of marriage and family. While its actual achievements were much more modest than those boasted by its protagonists and decried by its antagonists, it did send a beam of red light across the world, setting an example for Communist revolutions, most importantly in China, as well as severely shaking the deep roots of Russian patriarchy.

Emancipation of women and children was hardly a popular demand among male Russian workers and peasants. In fact, no such demands figure in the local workers' and peasants' assembly resolution of March and April 1917 analysed by the great French historian Marc Ferro (1967: vol. 1, 174, 187). Women of the popular classes did not, at this time, have any articulate political expression of significance. True, the revolutionary intelligentsia did include some forceful women, some of whom, like the Bolshevik Alexandra Kollontai, were also feminists. But the revolutionary parties, then as well as later, were overwhelmingly male, and exclusively male-led. In brief, 'feminism', in a latter-day, loose, anachronistic sense, was neither popular, nor carried by revolutionary women. Nevertheless, feminism was a principle of Marxism. As such it was first elaborated, as *Woman and Socialism*, in Prussian prison, by August Bebel (1879/1979), the leader of German Social Democracy, with great popular success. Marx's closest comrade Friedrich Engels (1884) in his tract on the *Origins of the Family, of Private Property and of the State*, took Lewis Henry Morgan's *Ancient Society* (of 1877) as his starting-point for a historical–materialist treatment of the family.

Lenin, the leader of the Russian Revolution in October 1917, was both a ruthless revolutionary strategist of power, and a principled Marxist, committed to radical social transformation. To the former, feminist issues were irrelevant, but to the latter they were important. They were not just an ideological boast of a successful revolutionary in power. In April 1917, when Lenin first made his call for transforming the February Republic into a state of proletarian revolution, while not including a destruction of patriarchy in the shortlist of revolutionary slogans, he did write and publish the following, in an elaboration of 'The tasks of the proletariat in our revolution', in a section about the establishment of a people's militia, demanding that it should 'extend to all citizens of both sexes':

> Unless women are brought to take an independent part in political life generally, but also in daily and universal public service, it is idle to speak of a complete and stable democracy, let alone Socialism. And such 'police' functions as care of the sick and homeless children, food inspection, etc. will never be satisfactorily discharged unless women are on equal footing with men, not nominally but in reality.
>
> (Lenin 1917/1947: II, 36)

Six weeks after the Russian Revolution, in full Civil War, the Soviet of People's Commissars issued a decree allowing for no-fault divorce. At about the same time (on 20 December 1917), the institution, and public offices for, civil marriage was established (Schlesinger 1949: 33n). In October 1918 there followed a full family law, with a consistent emphasis on husband–wife equality, including in the choice of a family name and in joint parental authority. Equal gender pay was also installed, and the Land Code of 1922 gave men and women equal access. A socio-political language of gender neutrality was pushed (E. Wood 1997: 50ff). Abortion was legalized in November 1920. A major point of the Russian Family Code of 1926 was the legal recognition of de facto marriages, with attached provisions for alimony and child support in case of a break-up, a clause which in the last instance was deleted from the Ukraine Family Law of the same year (Schlesinger 1949: 356).

Whatever else it was, the feminist dimension of the Bolshevik Revolution was neither opportunistic nor an ideological decoration. It was an assertion of principle, very difficult to realize against strong resistance as well as tenacious resilience, from which later Soviet leaders retreated, but which they never could quite abandon.

Attacks on patriarchy soon entered onto the agenda of the new Communist International, the Comintern. The launching of the International and its first two congresses made no reference to the family or to women, but the third congress, in June 1921, passed several resolutions on the issue, couched in the form of tasks of the member parties. The main one referred to 'family enserfment' (*l'asservissement familial*), 'not only in the bourgeois capitalist countries, but also in the countries where there exists already a soviet regime' (*Quatre premiers congrès* 1934/1969: 145). The fifth congress in 1924 adopted a programme of 'Total equality between men and women, before the law and in social life; a radical reform of marriage and family legislation' (Scott 1978: 78). The German veteran socialist feminist Clara Zetkin played a key role in the feminist concerns of the Comintern.

The Soviet power itself took feminism and anti-patriarchy into Central Asia and the Caucasus with a revolutionary *khudzum* or storm in the late 1920s (Schlesinger 1949: doc. 10; Massell 1978). The ruthless land collectivization drive from 1929 also used feminist arguments in its propaganda – on posters kept in the Uppsala University Library, for instance – presenting the *kolkhoz* as an exit from patriarchy. Parental authority was under ideological attack in the 1920s, and physical punishment of children was forbidden, a measure strongly resented by many peasant fathers (Geiger 1968: 53f, 99). Communist children got their official martyr in 1932, in the figure of Pavlik Morozov, who denounced his *kulak* father and who was subsequently killed by local peasants (Geiger 1968: 54).

A large part of the Soviet population naturally experienced the anti-patriarchal onslaught in ways similar to how Francis Fukuyama (1999) viewed the less dramatic upheavals in the USA half a century later, as a 'great disruption'. The all-male Communist leadership under Stalin, which was causing and governing many disruptions, began to lower the feminist flag in the 1930s, extolling family stability and motherhood, and in 1936 making divorce complicated and expensive. In 1944 a new Family Law made a strong demarcation between marriage and non-marriage, between marital and non-marital children, and divorce dependent on judicial approval. In a peculiar twist of wartime Stalinist traditionalism, co-education, once a central revolutionary tenet of education, was abolished, for a time, in August 1943, referring to 'the different requirements of their [i.e. boys' and girls'] vocational training, practical activities, preparation for leadership and military service' (Schlesinger 1949: doc. 16).

East Slavic patriarchy, and even more so Caucasian and Central Asian, was strongly entrenched, and the ideology of 'totalitarianism' is of no use in assessing the actual power of Communist feminism. The patriarchal and patrilocal family of the USSR survived Lenin, Stalin and de-Stalinization, at least partly. Among couples interviewed in 1962 in the Leningrad Wedding Palace four-fifths had asked for their parents' consent to their marriage, and two-fifths were going to live with parents(-in-law) upon their marriage. Three-quarters of brides interviewed in the same place in the late 1960s had been introduced to their spouses by their parents. While marital choice, subject to parental approval, had by then become the norm, the Soviet press of the 1970s carried articles denouncing paternal interference in marriage matters (Fisher 1980: 41ff).

In the late 1970s, one in eight young rural Soviet Estonians held that parental approval was obligatory before getting married, as did a good quarter of young Russians, more than half of Georgians, and nine out of ten young Uzbeks (Jones and Grupp 1987: 242). In 1970, a quarter of rural married couples of the Soviet Union were living with their parents (Bridger 1987: 96).

The legal family revolution of the Bolsheviks was very much ahead of Russian societal time, and Soviet family practices did not immediately dance to political music, however loud and powerful. But normative politics was also sustained by a forceful push of extra-family female economic participation, as *kolkhozniks* as well as waged workers. After the implosion of Eastern European Communism as a system of political economy, its contribution to the dismantling of patriarchy might be seen as Communism's lasting legacy.

Variants of limitations

In other areas of the European family system, normative changes were minor, in spite of the fall of dynastic regimes in Germany and Austro-Hungary, and the rise or enlargement of an East-Central European band of states from Romania to Finland. The latter was part of the Nordic compact, since the Red revolution and the White alignment with Wilhelmine Germany had both failed, but for the rest pre-national legal pluralism or German 1896 family law governed the family institution until the next war (cf. Therborn 1995: 106–7). Only in Europe north of Belgium, Switzerland, Italy and Hungary did women get the right to vote (UN 1991: table 3).

In Italy, the quasi-revolutionary situation after the war led, in the field of family and gender relations, to no more than the belated adoption of a pre-war bill abolishing the legal incapacity of married women with respect to their own property or earnings. The rest of Napoleonic patriarchy was maintained (Ungari 1970), and a female vote was stopped by the Senate.

The English Royal Commission on Matrimonial Causes was coeval with the Scandinavian Law Commission and submitted its report in 1912. While it did recommend an enlargement of grounds for divorce, including desertion, cruelty, insanity and refusal to sex, it was still, in contrast to the report of the Scandinavian lawyers, couched in a supra-human, religious conception of marriage. Its reception was steeped even more in these terms, and only in 1937 did the British Parliament act (Davies 1957: 320ff). The 1925 Guardian-ship of Infants Act has been remembered as a milestone proclaiming the best interests of the child as the crucial judicial criterion in parental disputes of guardianship. As such, that is a major blow to patriarchy. But, as Stephen Cretney (1998) has recently made clear, the final Act removed an original draft of equal maternal and paternal authority. Patriarchy still ruled Britannia.

In the USA, where family law is first of all a state matter, it seems that significant advances towards equal guardianship of children were made. By World War II the states that had introduced such laws included New York and the northeast, Illinois and the midwest, and California (*Corpus Juris Secundum* 1944: vol. 39, §6n). Changes were also made with regard to the husband's headship of the family, inherited from common law or asserted by statute, but here the picture is more diverse, and husband normative headship remained widespread (*Corpus Juris Secundum* 1944: vol. 41, §§4–9n).

Among the WASP middle and upper middle classes, the chaperon of un-married young women disappeared in the interwar period, and the specific American 'dating' culture began to develop as a respectable road to marriage without close parental surveillance. In the 1923 edition of Emily Post's *Etiquette* book, there was a chapter on 'Chaperons and Other Conventions'. Four years later the chapter had changed into 'The Vanishing Chaperon and Other Lost Conventions', and by the 1930s this monitor of morals was definitely relegated to the past tense, as 'The Vanished Chaperon. . .' (D'Emilio and Freedman 1988: 258). Unmonitored dating in a car had by the 1920s become an estab-lished pattern of American youth, reaching well into 'Middletown' or Muncie, Indiana (Lynd and Lynd 1929/1956: 137–38).

China: an aborted revolution

In China, the ancient empire imploded in 1911, succeeded by a fragile and fraught republic. To world history, this was similar to the end of Rome. A new order did not take quite as long a time as it did 14–15 centuries earlier, but nor did it spring out of the forehead of the republic.

Late Imperial China had instituted a legal Codification Commission, two members of which took the opportunity for drafting a new Japanese-inspired Family Code, finished just before the Revolution but made public only in

1916. Through a number of further drafts, a new Family Law was finally enacted in 1931, by the embattled Guomindang government. That was the year when the modern classic of Chinese denunciation of the emotionless Chinese extended family and its romantically cruel and tragic arranged marriages appeared, in Ba Jin's (also romanized as Pa Chin) *The Family.*

The government had inserted a paragraph in the Code (§972), that marriage should be concluded by the parties themselves. On the other hand, leaning on German and Swiss jurisprudence, the new Chinese law accorded the husband/father a decisive family vote (§1089) (Valk 1939). In practice, the writ of the Guomindang government in the 1930s ran no further than some administrative centres and port cities. The perceptive Russian–American observer of Goumindang China in the late 1930s, Olga Lang (1946: 122), noticed the stir: 'a revolution in human relations', but 'in love as in every other sphere the old pattern has persisted'. In Yenan the Communists were already proclaiming radical family reform (Meijer 1971: appendix I). Neither had much impact before 1950, although the American modernizationist Marion Levy (1949), noting the discrepancy between legal stipulations and actual practice, found enough change to call Chinese kinship and family 'transitional'.

An urban bridgehead in revolutionary Turkey

In the Ottoman Empire, as in the other countries of 'reactive modernization', an intellectual critique of and debate about the position of women developed in the last decades of the nineteenth century, with the reformers presenting it as an indicator of modernity or civilization. After the Young Turk revolution of 1909 this discourse was stepped up. The main ideologue of the new regime, the pan-Turkic nationalist Ziya Gökalp, an admirer of Emile Durkheim, was even proclaiming that feminism was a 'creation of the Turks' (Göle 1995: 61). The foremost female intellectual of the country, Halide Edip Advar, published an important feminist novel, *The New Turan,* in 1912. In the new century urban women began to access education – Istanbul high schools in 1911 and the university in 1916 – and found jobs as primary school teachers, a development much furthered by the demand for female labour during the war. Nevertheless, the circles of emancipation were very limited, largely confined to the multi-cultural and multi-ethnic capital, and the then similar cities of Salonica and Izmir (cf. Duben and Behar 1991).

The disaster of the war, the Greek occupation of Izmir/Smyrna, and the Allied occupation of Istanbul finally broke the long-decaying Ottoman Empire, and brought forth much more radical nationalists and social reformers than the Young Turks. In May 1919, Halide Edip was the first woman to speak in public, enthralling an immense crowd in the ancient Istanbul Hippodrome in protest against the Greek occupation of Izmir (Yerasimos 1992: 158ff).

In this bleak hour, the incipient Turkish nation was 'saved' by the ablest of the Ottoman generals, Mustafa Kemal Pasha, who defeated the Greeks, re-negotiated the peace treaty with the victors of World War I, expelled the last Sultan, and set up the Republic of Turkey. Mustafa Kemal embarked upon a frantic effort at national modernization: 'The civilized world is far ahead of us. We have no choice but to catch up' (Mango 2002: 438). The whole legacy of Arabo-Islamic culture, except for Islam as a private religious matter, was discarded by decree: the Islamic state, the Arabic alphabet, the Muslim calendar, the Ottoman dress – although in contrast to the fez for men, the veil for women was not prohibited by law – and the name system. When, in 1934, he proclaimed that everybody had to acquire a European-type surname, Mustafa Kemal himself chose the name of Atatürk, 'Father Turk'. (Atatürk was a divorcee with no children of his own, but he had three adopted daughters, taught by a Swiss *gouvernante* and protected by a black eunuch.)

Family law reform had been on the agenda of the Young Turks, and was much pushed by Ziya Gökalp, but only modest and ineffectual changes came out of it, including a law in 1917 which has nevertheless lived on among Muslims in Lebanon and Israeli Palestinians (Coulson and Hinchcliffe 1978: 49). After 'the War of Independence', there was an upper-middle-class women's movement in Istanbul for a change of the patriarchal Islamic family law. Soon after, Mustafa Kemal ordered a new law commission to import the Swiss Civil Code into Turkey, which took effect in 1926. The Minister of Justice, who had studied law in the homeland of the new Code, said that with it Turkey will 'close the doors to an old civilization, and will have entered a contemporary' (Duben and Behar 1991: 213).

Swiss family law dated from the early twentieth century, and was moderately patriarchal by contemporary standards. Transposed to Turkey, it meant a ban on polygamy and on unlimited, unilateral male divorce, while allowing for divorce by mutual consent, and equal male–female inheritance rights. On the other hand, the husband was 'the head of the family', who alone represented his wife against third parties, who could deny his wife the right to work outside the home, and who had the decisive right with regard to the children. Against these male rights, however, the wife had the right of legal appeal against abuse by her husband (Bergmann 1938: 769ff)

Atatürk was personally committed to women's rights, in particular their right to move and work in public, and Turkish women won the right to vote and to run for public office (in 1934) well ahead of French and other Latin European women. The new republic gave rise to an educated class of women, and to a professional female elite, of judges for example. But the Kemalist revolution did not penetrate the entrenched family and gender traditions of the rural popular classes. While already by 1929–30, 75 per cent of Istanbul girls aged 7 to 11 attended primary school – almost the same proportion as Istanbul boys (Duben and Behar 1991: 216) – only a third of all Turkish children attended primary school in 1950, and little more than two-fifths in 1960 (UNESCO 1964: table 9).

In the countryside, where the majority of the population lived until the mid-1980s, the patriarchal, patrilocal extended family remained the norm, comprising about a third of all households, virtually unchanged from the 1840s to the 1970s (Duben 1982: 77ff). Marriages continued to be arranged, for half of all men and two-thirds of all women according to the Turkish Fertility Survey of the late 1960s (Timur 1978a: 236–37). In the small towns, a study from the 1970s reported that two-thirds of the brides saw their husbands for the first time on their wedding-day, which happened only to a fifth of village brides (Cosar 1978: 133). Indeed a study in the 1970s found that 46 per cent of female university graduates had arranged marriages (Kandiyoti 1982: 114). The ban on polygamy was circumvented by rural religious weddings, the children of which, illegitimate according to the state authorities, were on occasions legitimized post-hoc by the state (Cosar 1978: 127). Nevertheless, even in provincial towns, the Kemalist revolution left a more visible public female presence than in neighbouring Iran, which also had a moment of modernization of gender relations in the second half of the 1930s (Eyrumlu 2001).

Even many highly educated Turkish women stayed at home (Kandiyoti 1982), and in the last years of the twentieth century only about 10 per cent of Turkish women were economically active outside the family, somewhat less than in Egypt and Syria, but about the same or perhaps somewhat higher than in Iran[4] (UN 2000a: table 5d). Since the 1980s, Turkish female opinion has been polarized between, on one hand, a modern Islamic current, family-oriented, with a strict dress code of its own, but also educated and outspoken, and, on the other, a more articulate feminism and an organized secularist professional defence (Göle 1995: ch. III).

In 1994 a judicial decision cleared the way for Turkish women to seek a job against the will of their husbands, and in 2001 the husband-as-head-of-the-family clause was finally dropped from Turkish law, but only for marriages after 1 January 2002. Married couples were given different options until 2003. The new law was not uncontroversial, in spite of a constitutional provision for gender equality, and the Minister of Justice had to threaten to resign to get it through the coalition (which was wiped out in the 2002 election). The Islamic party voted against it (*Süddeutsche Zeitung*, 26 November 2001: 6). In terms of gender development, according to the United Nations Development Programme, Turkey ranks 71, just behind Sri Lanka and Lebanon, and just ahead of Peru, Paraguay and Oman, but far behind Bulgaria and Romania. In terms of 'gender empowerment' Turkey is currently far down, well below all Latin America, but clearly ahead of Egypt and Bangladesh (UNDP 2002: tables 22 and 23).

The Kemalist revolution was an important and iconoclastic moment of 'reactive modernization', and a model for the ancient rival of the Ottoman Empire, Iran, under Reza Pahlevi, but less so for the ex-subjects of the Ottomans, the Arabs. Its basic limitations were its abstention from any agrarian reform, and the slow pace of Turkey's industrialization and economic development. The social and demographic distance between Istanbul – even Muslim Istanbul – and Anatolia was enormous. It may be illustrated by the fertility gap. In 1885, the fertility rate of Muslim women in Istanbul was 3.5, a level reached by all Turkish women only in the last years of the 1980s (Behar 1995: 37ff).

The Mexican Revolution and Latin America

Latin America family law had been basically modelled after the French Code Napoléon, with its emphasis on male headship and wifely duty and obedience (Bergmann 1928). The Brazilian Civil Code of 1890 required parental consent to marry (Borges 1992: 358–59n), whereas the Liberal *Reforma* in Mexico emancipated all children at the age of 21 (Arrom 1985). The law in Latin America pertained mainly to the Creole upper middle and upper classes, whereas informal unions prevailed among the popular classes, and more or less traditional community customs among the Indian populations (see also Chapter 4).

The protracted, bloody convulsions of the Mexican Revolution (1910–17) left a significant impact on official family norms, and a less clear effect on family practices. The revolution included a feminist current – partly inspired by Mediterranean Anarchism (Fowler-Salamini 2002: 42) – which organized two feminist congresses in 1916, and a pan-American one in 1923. Socialist governors of the state of Yucatán made it sympathetic territory to feminism. Family law became a state affair according to the 1917 Constitution, and Yucatán and the Federal Capital pioneered a dismantling of blatantly patriarchal legislation, and permitted divorce. But a Federal Law of Family Relations of 1917 gave married women a legal capacity, to make contracts and to act as guardians, for instance.

In 1928, a new family code took effect for the Federal District (Mexico City), which for its time was the most progressive in the world, after the Soviet and the Scandinavian. It stated explicitly that 'men and women have the same legal capacity', which included the right for women to practise law, and the right to leave the parental home upon the age of 21, the same age as for men (Macías 1982: 119ff). But the really advanced clause was article 167, decreeing that 'Husband and wife have the same authority and voice in the house'. In contrast to the Swedish law it did provide a judicial solution in cases of conflict. Article 169 gave the wife the right to have a job, to practise a profession or to do business, but like the West German law thirty years later, it made this right dependent upon fulfilment of her domestic duties, in the defence of which the husband was provided with the right to judicial appeal (Bergmann 1940: 509ff).

Land reform was a central issue of the Mexican Revolution, inscribed in the Constitution of 1917 and concretized in the *Ejido* Law of 1920, providing for collective communal land tenure, held by *ejido* communes, but cultivated in the form of individual plots. Large amounts of land were transferred in this way, particularly in the second half of the 1930s under President Cárdenas, from landowners to peasants. However, in contrast to the Bolshevik Land Code of 1922, the Mexican land reform was set in motion within the pre-revolutionary family structure. Among the *ejidatorios,* land should be divided equally between the *jefes de familia*, i.e. among men. In a 1927 specification of the law, the exclusively male membership of the commune was made explicit, supplemented with a provision for 'single women or widows who are supporting a family'. Only in 1971 did women get equal rights as rural commune members (Stephen 1997: ch. 4).

Mexican feminism lost most of its revolutionary power through internal dissension and tenacious male resistance – spearheaded by the post-revolutionary Confederation of Catholic Associations – to which was added an anti-clerical fear of religious women. In 1938–39 women's suffrage seemed en route to pass, with presidential support and a Constitutional amendment ratified by the states of the federal polity, but in the bitter conflict within of the ruling party about the presidential succession, the issue of women's political rights disappeared from the Congress agenda. Mexican women only won the right to vote in 1953 (Morton 1962; Sánchez Korrol 1999).

Mexican family relations have been characterized by a social norm of patrilineal joint families, with a strong *macho* (masculinist) component of gender relations, including polygyny in non-urban areas, and in urban shanty towns as well as among the wealthy upper class (Nutini 1965; Lomnitz and Perez-Lisaur 1991). Female single-living was still illegitimate in Mexico City in the 1970s (Macías 1982: 120). However, the daughters of poor agricultural labourers or small farmers did get an exit option. Since the 1930s, internal Mexican migration was predominantly female (Oliveira 1991).

The profound Mexican Revolution did have an important feminist component, but the meandering path of the victorious revolution leaves the actual impact of the revolution upon the practices of patriarchy and of *machismo* a very difficult one to disentangle. In terms of the current gender development index, Mexico, ranking 49, is well behind Argentina (33), Uruguay (37), Chile (39), and Costa Rica (41), but well ahead of Brazil (64), and the Andean countries (UNDP 2002: table 22).

The Turkish and the Mexican revolutions were very different: the former a nationalist project from above, the latter a social revolution from below. What they had in common was an anti-clerical modernism, which included new family norms. In different ways, both largely preserved pre-revolutionary rural patriarchy, much more strongly in Turkey than in Mexico, but the more unified Turkish political leadership opened political access to women earlier, and professional space more widely. While Kemalism set an example to Iran, the Mexican Revolution seems to have offered surprisingly little inspiration to the rest of its region.

Southern Cone feminism, the most vigorous south of Mexico, did not achieve a breakthrough in this early history of assaults on patriarchy. After all, the World War was an ocean away, and even in Europe it did not open up any significant inroads into patriarchy and male domination. Some advances were made though, like the Brazilian Civil Code of 1916, which at least emancipated grown-up children, while explicitly maintaining male headship of the family (articles 233 and 380) (Bergmann 1928: 67ff). There was also an interesting initiative on child welfare, from the first American Child Congress in Buenos Aires in 1916 to the still-existing American Child Institute in Montevideo (cf. Guy 1998). But on the whole, official Latin American norms remained strongly patriarchal, like Latin Europe. In North American Québec, the French Code of wifely obedience still went on ruling (Bergmann 1928: 107).

It should be remembered that Paris, France was the centre of the world to the Latin American elites. In comparison with their masters, some Latin American males were less misogynous. While no Latin European country had accorded women the right to vote by World War II, four Latin American ones had: Ecuador (1929), where the conservatives for once overcame their prejudices and betted more rationally on women's Catholic conservatism at that time, Brazil (1932), Uruguay (1932) and Cuba (1934).

Act 2: the constitutional moment

In the aftermath of World War II, the principle of equality between the sexes had reached the attention of constitution-makers in Japan, in post-Fascist Western Europe, in the arc of new Communist countries from Germany to Korea, and decolonized India and Indonesia. It was enshrined in the United Nations Declaration of Human Rights, adopted in 1948, transcending the gulf of the erupting Cold War.[5] For some time, and especially at the global level of the UN, it was mainly an elite symbolic expression. But in Japan, and in China and the other new Communist countries, the constitutional clauses entailed a serious commitment to institutional change. In West Germany, a *pétard* was inadvertently put under national patriarchy, in the form of a general clause of gender equality, later detonated by a Constitutional Court taking it seriously. The UN, for its part, put up an ideological-cum-administrative machinery, in the form of a Commission of the Status of Women, which would prepare an agenda of worldwide change, and, most concretely, the third act of the twentieth-century drama of dismantling patriarchy.

Let us begin in East Asia, where the most important scenes of Act 2 took place.

Asia: the East and the rest

US occupation liberalism and the Soviet-inspired Communist revolution together made East Asia the key area of the post-World War II constitutional assault on patriarchy.

The Japanese 'embrace of defeat' (Dower 1999), and their rapid repudiation of pre-war and wartime values included a rejection of the *ie*, the house system of a patriarchal extended family, enshrined in the 1898 Civil Code, and a new Civil Code was passed in 1947, carefully based on conjugal symmetry (extending to the surname, article 750), while not proclaiming a norm of equality (Supreme Court of Japan 1959). According to the American occupation official supervising the rewriting, the German-born and educated jurist Alfred Oppler (1976), the Japanese reformers were more radical than the Americans had envisaged. Before that, the new Japanese Constitution of 1946 included, in its article 24, a statement of the 'essential equality of the sexes', a radical statement for its time. It had a fascinating background.

The new Japanese Constitution was de facto secretly drafted by a group of Americans on the staff of General McArthur and then pressured upon a reluctant Japanese government, which managed to make some subtle changes in the official Japanese-language version. Gender equality was pushed by an extraordinary member of the group, Beate Sirota, a young woman born in Vienna, raised in Tokyo before the war (where her pianist father was teaching), and educated in the USA during the war. In the final process of negotiating the draft and its translation, with the Japanese government, her occasional siding with the Japanese counter-proposals was used by the American team for an appeal to Japanese reciprocation. The sex equality clause was accepted (Dower 1999: 365, 380). Indeed, the final version of article 24 of the Japanese Constitution is a ringing tribute to marital autonomy and equality:

> Marriage shall be based only on the mutual consent of both sexes and it shall be maintained through mutual cooperation with the equal rights of husband and wife as a basis. With regard to choice of spouse, property rights, inheritance, choice of domicile, divorce and other matters pertaining to marriage and the family, laws shall be enacted from the standpoint of individual dignity and the essential equality of the sexes.

Japanese women won the right the vote and to run for office in the autumn of 1945, upon the insistence of US occupation authorities, and radical women found a public arena, from radio broadcasting to the 1946 Diet, for advocating family law reform, and legalization of birth control. In spite of the opposition of the new Prime Minister Yoshida, and other conservatives, the samurai 'house' system – socially undermined among the urban popular classes but for the rest still in operation – was abolished by a new Civil Code in the full spirit of the new Constitution, developed in the course of 1947 and taking effect from 1 January 1948. Even after adoption the Code remained controversial, and right-wing attempts were made to revise it, but it stayed, sustained by post-war social and economic processes (see further Dore 1958; Kono 1970: 91ff; Oppler 1976: ch. 9; Hopper 1996: ch. 10).

The victory of the Chinese Communists in 1949 meant that a full-scale assault on the most ancient and elaborate patriarchy of the world was mounted. The Communist Party at the time of revolution was a movement of young rebels, and among embattled, peripheral 'Soviets' of the early 1930s, the freedom and equality of marriage had already been proclaimed (Müller-Freienfels 1978: 351). Fomenting the class struggle during the protracted civil war had also entailed efforts at breaking up the authority and power of the patriarchal clans, encouraging denunciations by the poor and the downtrodden, women and men, at village 'struggle meetings' against local landowners and bullies. At least in some areas in 1947–48 this was called the 'Divide the Family Campaign' (Crook 1959: 145ff).

In national power, the first major institutional change, outside those of government itself, that the Chinese Communists embarked upon was a new Marriage Law, proclaimed in May 1950. It was meant to herald a revolution:

Article 1.
The feudal marriage system, which is based on arbitrary and compulsory arrangements and the superiority of man over woman and ignores the children's interests, shall be abolished.

The New Democratic marriage system, which is based on the free choice of partners, on monogamy, on equal rights for both sexes, and on the protection of the lawful interests of women and children, shall be put into effect.

Article 2.
Bigamy, concubinage, child betrothal, interference with the re-marriages of widows, and the exaction of money or gifts in connection with marriages, shall be prohibited.

Article 3.
Marriage shall be based on the complete willingness of the two parties. Neither party shall use compulsion, and no third party shall be allowed to interfere. . . .

Article 7.
Husband and wife are companions living together and shall enjoy equal status in the home. . . .

Article 9.
Both husband and wife shall have the right to free choice of occupation and free participation in work or in social activities.

(Meijer 1978: appendix)

Other equality clauses concerned property and inheritance, use of surname, equal rights of children, including a stipulation (article 16) against discrimination of stepchildren. Disputed no-fault divorce was subjected to judicial mediation and decision.

Impotent people were not allowed to marry (article 5b), and one important concession to traditional clan exogamy was made: article 5a stated that 'marriage between collateral relatives by blood (up to the fifth degree of relationship) is to be determined by custom'.

The Communist leadership meant the Marriage Law very seriously, and was therefore also worried about resistance to it, which was tenacious and sometimes ferocious. In February 1953 the government issued a directive, signed by Prime Minister Chou En-lai, about enforced efforts, including a mass movement campaign. 'At this time', the directive said, 'when the women are struggling for freedom of marriage against the surviving thoughts and ugly customs of the feudal marriage system . . . everywhere the Party and the Government organ . . . shall be responsible for providing these women with the protection they need, to help them and to give them shelter for a time' (Meijer 1971: appendix IX).

Three and a half million cadres were deployed in the campaign, holding local meetings and studies of the law, and distributing pamphlets. In November of the same year, the Central Committee had to admit, though, that the campaign had had an 'uneven' success, and that the reform would take a long time. Only in 15 per cent of the territory was the new law followed. In a quarter of it, 'Distrust and misconceptions of the Law are still abundant. Suicide by and murder of women still occur to a considerable extent.' (The Central Committee report is included as appendix X in Meijer 1971.) On the eve of the revolution, Marion Levy Jr (1949) had published his functionalist study of Chinese family change as *The Family Revolution in Modern China*. That was somewhat premature.

In spite of the land reform, which officially gave women equal land rights (Yang 1965/1959: 142), and massive extra-domestic female employment, estimated at 80–90 per cent by the end of the 1950s, including part-time and seasonal employment (Croll 1995: 79), Chinese patriarchy has taken decades to melt down, and has not fully disappeared yet, as we shall see in the next chapter. Parental direction of marriages remained important for a long time, particularly in the countryside, sustained by customary rules of clan and village exogamy, which made youthful courtship difficult (Parish and Whyte 1978: 69ff). The 'People's Communes' experiment included a push for communal eating and communal childcare, and was intended, among other things, to undermine the family. In this, as well as in its economic respects, it all failed though (cf. Meijer 1971: ch. 15), and after the last Maoist experiment, 'The Cultural Revolution', the family household came to the fore again, as a major vehicle of market-driven economic development. In another sense, the 'Cultural Revolution' had brought family relations into focus in a brutal and nasty way, punishing children for the sin, the 'crime', of their parents having once been middle or upper class, and its overcoming opened individual prospects again (cf. Xinran 2002).

But it may also be said, that even if traces are still visible, China in a few decades has dismantled the central institution of a two- to three-thousand-year-old social order.

Communist Vietnam got a special family touch after 1945, when Ho Chi Minh emerged as a national leader, as 'Uncle Ho', but the French colonial war delayed family legislation until 1959. South Korea reappeared under American protection as the most loyal heir to the Confucian tradition, in spite of its large Christian minority, and during the Cold War the oppression of women was no longer a US policy concern. The 1958 Family Code stipulated that parental consent was required for marriage, and remained in force until 1979. Only in the revision of 1989, valid since 1991, was the principle of husband–wife equality accepted. A wide range of traditional exogamy rules still apply (Bergmann and Ferid 1993; Nahm 1993: 334ff; Park and Cho 1995).

The radical Indian nationalism of Mahatma Gandhi included an outspoken anti-patriarchal component: 'I am uncompromising in the matter of women's rights', Gandhi wrote in *Young India* in 1929, 'in my opinion she should labour under no legal disability not suffered by man' (Sarkar 1977: 97). But it did not hold a transformation of the Indian family a key to societal transformation.

The Constitution of independent India included non-discrimination on grounds of sex (articles 15 and 16), but that did not mean a commitment to equal family rights. The secular nationalist idea of a uniform civil code was given up in view of the violent communal tension around Partition (into Pakistan and India), and family reform efforts concentrated on changing Hindu law, under consideration since a first Law Committee Report in 1941. The issue stalled in the Constituent Assembly, under pressure from strong religious mobilization, but important government figures were also adamantly against reforming the family, including Home Minister Patel and President Prasad who threatened to veto the Hindu Code Bill if passed (Agarwal 1994: 208ff). The times turned in 1952, with the electoral victory of the Congress Party, and Nehru's secular leadership managed to push through a Hindu Marriage Act (1955), a Hindu Succession Act (1956) plus two other laws, on guardianship and on adoption. Polygamy was prohibited, inter-caste marriage and divorce were allowed, a principle of equal inheritance rights was laid down. But freedom of marriage remained a non-issue – apart from allowing marriages between castes and within lineages (*gotras*) – and the actual changes by the other stipulations were minor and slow, including inheritance rights (Agarwal 1994). Muslims, Parsees, Christians and Scheduled Tribes maintain their own family laws (little reformed in the Muslim case).

Indonesia also based its Constitution on general principles of equality, while continuing a religious and customary legal pluralism in family matters. But from a basis in the colonial civil code, the Supreme Court began to intervene in favour of bilateral, as opposed to patrilineal, kinship, and for daughters' rights of inheritance (Sarkar 1977; Soewondo 1977; Lev 1978).

Germany and Eastern Europe

In Western Europe, outside Scandinavia and, to a lesser extent, Britain, a moderate patriarchy, centred on the husband–father, rather than on the head father, was firmly institutionalized until long after World War II, until the 1970s in fact. Legally mature children, under 25 or under 30, respectively, were still required by Belgian and Dutch law to ask for parental consent to marriage.[6] The vote for women of democratic Latin Europe, from then francophone Belgium to Italy, did not entail any immediate changes of family rights. Nor did the new Western European constitutions, which did include cautious clauses of gender equality, imply a social revolution, unlike in Japan.

Most impact was felt in Germany. Germany was under Allied occupation, and the Allied Control Council vetted German laws, judiciary and education, *inter alia*. However, the German family system was not regarded as a prop of German belligerence, and was left out of occupational efforts. The Nazi divorce law of 1938 was regarded as too little familistic – allowing no-fault divorce – and the British, French and Soviet Controllers were inclined to repeal it, but in the end they were persuaded by the Americans to let it stay, shed of some racist elements (Glendon 1977: 214ff). While the whole tradition of Japanese conservatism was discredited and considered defeated in the war –

because of the absence in Japan of any clearcut division between tradition-alism and the militaristic imperialism which launched the Pacific War – German traditionalism could re-affirm itself as non-Nazi. The patriarchal family – counterposed to the modern, totalitarian state – was at the very core of this assertive traditionalism. The family constituted a 'holy space' according to the Cologne Principles (1945) of the new Christian Democracy (Hintze 1995).

German constitution-drafting was undertaken by a German commission – watched and checked by the Control Council – in which Social Democratic and Liberal forces were strong, together with the Christian Democrats and other conservatives. The outcome was a compromise, from which the progressive forces benefited more than the conservatives, thanks to the controversial interventions of the new Constitutional Court.

To the later bitter surprise of German conservatives, the new West German Constitution of 1949 had put a bomb under German patriarchy in the form of an innocuous-sounding clause stating that men and women 'are equal before the law'. The conservative political majority of West Germany had no intention of revising the old Civil Code because of that statement in the Constitution, and instead drew comfort from other stipulations they had managed to insert.

But a vague and general equality clause turned out to be a lever of change, thanks to the egalitarian vigilance of the constitutional judges. Paragraph 3, II, 1 of the West German Constitution declared that men and women 'are equal before the law' (*sind gleichberechtigt*), and that nobody should be discriminated against because of his or her sex. Conservatives took heart from paragraph 6, I, which put 'marriage and family under the special protection of the state', and from 6, II, stating that the 'care and education of children are the natural rights of parents', as well as their duty. The Catholic Church was extremely active – 'exercised massive pressure' (Eschenburg 1983: 503) – trying to influence the constituting process, followed more cautiously by the Lutheran. The main Catholic conservative demand of the Constitution was a strong affirma-tion of 'parental rights' (*Elternrecht*), in general but above all as a means to ensuring proper religious education and confessional schooling, in accordance with the Papal Encyclica of 1929, *Divini Illius Magistri,* making confessional education a duty of Catholic parents. The final wording did not measure up to their demands, but Adenauer, the leader of Christian Democracy and also a *Realpolitiker,* did not want to push the issue (Schwarz 1986: 593–94).

The Constitution gave the legislators four years to change family legislation in accordance with the equality clause. But the conservative coalition did nothing to implement it, whereupon the Constitutional Court declared that article 3, II was a 'genuine legal norm', and as such binding the legislator. The result was the half-hearted Equal Rights Act of 1957, which did introduce more normative equality between husband and wife, in their internal relations, but which gave the father the decisive voice of parental authority. It also re-affirmed the 'rule' of the housewife marriage, and only allowed the wife to work outside 'to the extent that it is compatible with her duties in marriage and family'. In 1959 the Constitutional Court struck down these stipulations as unconstitutional. The legislature was given until 1965 to mend its patriarchal ways. It did not. Only in 1976, with a Social Democratic–Liberal majority, was a marriage law of gender equality passed (Helwig 1982; Vogel 1989a,b; Schwab 2001).

The new Italian Constitution included a principle of gender equality, but also, like the German one, a restrictive clause (in this case §29) making equality subordinate to the preservation of the unity of the family. That 'unity' was, of course, invested in the husband head, reaffirmed in the traditionalist Fascist Code of 1942. The Italian Constitutional Court did not use the equality principle on family matters till the beginning of Act 3 in the modern history of patriarchal erosion (Librando 1978).

In the Communist advances in Eastern Europe after World War II, gender equality and the secularization of marriage were very early demands and policy measures. In Bulgaria, a first edict to that effect was issued in October 1944, and in Poland in September 1945, in both cases followed up by a full law some months later, in 1945 and in January 1946, respectively. The four-party National Front of Czechoslovakia, in which the Communists had a strong influence, included economic gender equality in its action programme of 27 March 1945. In the Soviet zone of occupied Germany, family reform began in 1946, and the Soviet military administration in Germany (SMAD) dispatched monitoring teams to check implementation of the new, egalitarian gender regulations. Gender equality, in the family and elsewhere, was stipulated in all the new Eastern European constitutions after 1945, preceded or very soon followed by egalitarian family legislation: in Bulgaria in 1945, in Albania in 1948, in Czechoslovakia, GDR and Poland in 1950, and in Hungary in force from 1 January 1953; the latest was the Romanian one of February 1954 (Loewenfeld and Lauterbach 1963–72; Scott 1978: ch. 4; Ganghofer 1992).

These normative changes suddenly put Eastern Europe at the forefront of dismantling patriarchy, still well entrenched in the Western part, except Scandinavia. In the USSR itself, however, the emphasis of the moment was fertility and family stability, a national conservatism not unnatural after the tremendous war casualties. In 1944 the Soviet government released an edict on 'strengthening the family', including introducing the Napoleonic interdiction of extramarital paternity suits, making divorce expensive and difficult, and banning (most) abortions. Unlike in the West these national concerns did not include any transcendental family moralism. Unwed mothers were provided with a child allowance, and the option of leaving their child to a public institution (Juvilier 1978).

The United Nations

The new inter-state organization, the United Nations, included freedom of marriage and equality of marriage in its Declaration of Human Rights of 1948, well ahead of most of its member states:

> Article 16. (1) Men and women of full age, without any limitations due to race nationality or religion, have the right to marry and to found a family.

They are entitled to equal rights as to marriage, during marriage, and its dissolution.

(2) Marriage shall be entered into only with the free and full consent of the intending spouses.

The Declaration as a whole was passed by forty-eight votes to nil, with eight abstentions. The marriage article, in the separate article-by-article vote, was opposed by six countries, headed by Saudi Arabia. Most of the others probably went along with it, understanding 'equal' rights as not meaning 'identical', as a Pakistani delegate put it to Eleanor Roosevelt, who apparently shared that interpretation herself (Glendon 2001: 154, 161).

The UN Declaration of Human Rights was a product of a group of people largely formed by the Depression and the war, above all a Canadian law professor at the UN Secretariat, John Humphrey, who wrote the first draft, a very prominent French jurist, René Cassin, who formulated most of the final text, and Eleanor Roosevelt, who first chaired the Commission with great political prestige and diplomatic skill, adroitly succeeded by a younger Lebanese philosopher–diplomat, Charles Malik (see further the wonderful monograph by Mary Ann Glendon 2001).

Many of these clauses of equality got no further than the paper they were written on, and others took a long time to be implemented, often meeting tenacious, though devious rather than head-on, resistance. However limited and uneven the impact of post-war egalitarian constitutionalism, it should not be dismissed as irrelevant. Communist cadres and West German judges, among others, took it quite seriously, and explicit patriarchy was being de-legitimized and put on the defensive in a large number of countries. The stage was set for a new offensive against the ancient rule of fathers and husbands.

In Latin America, general gender rights were little affected by the World War, which in the southern hemisphere mainly took the form of a dutiful declaration of war against the enemies of the United States – and in the Brazilian case the dispatch of an air squadron to the European theatre of war. But political rights were extended, as in Latin Europe. Women finally got the right to vote, in Argentina and Venezuela in 1947, in Chile in 1949, in Mexico in 1953, in Peru in 1955, in Colombia in 1957, and, finally, in Paraguay, where elections did not matter very much under the dictatorship of general Stroessner, in 1961.

Act 3: '1968' and feminist globalization

The third thrust was an international, increasingly global socio-cultural movement, spearheaded by the youth rebellion of the 1960s, and, in particular by the first female cohorts of mass high education in North America and Western Europe. Largely through the UN machinery – the International Women's Year of 1975 and its global roll-call in Mexico – this movement spread to a global wave of feminism.

The West awakens

'1968' had its epicentre in Paris, and to the original student rebels, the March 22 Movement, the sexual restrictions of student life were a significant reason for rebellion. By the 1960s, French patriarchy was one of the most explicit and strongly institutionalized of the rich world. Imperial Napoleonic male domination had been incorporated into mainstream Republican tradition. The French had inherited, from the Code Napoléon, a much stronger patriarchal power than the German Code of 1896/1900, or even the Prussian Code of 1794. French family law had its progressive aspects, allowing for divorce and safeguarding daughters' inheritance, but it was originally virulently patriarchal, to the point of allowing fathers to send their children to state imprisonment. Over time the Code Napoléon had mellowed by gradual revisions. In 1935 the paternal '*droit de correction*' providing fathers various means to 'correct' disobedient children was abolished, and in 1938 the Popular Front had abolished the infamous paragraph of wives owing 'obedience' to their husbands. But what it put in its place was a norm that the husband was the '*chef de famille*', and as such he could still prohibit his wife from various activities.

The French High Court, the *Cour de Cassation*, was keeping the banner of patriarchy flying throughout the 1960s. In 1962 it upheld the husband's right to prohibit his wife from taking a job. In 1969 it refused a woman, who had first been denied a divorce, to set up an abode of her own, as her husband was publicly maintaining a mistress. The Court based itself on §108: 'The married woman has no other domicile than that of husband' (Dhavernas 1978: 103, 113–14).

The conservative French legislator did give married women an unconditional right to work in 1965, but the *chef de famille* doctrine was reaffirmed. Then in 1970, the post-Gaullist government hit upon the brilliant idea of cautious reform by introducing the German idea of 1896 of a decisive vote by the husband/father in case of family disagreement. The West German Constitutional Court had eleven years earlier declared the clause incompatible with the German 1949 Constitution, which had not prevented the Belgians from taking it up in 1965 (Lohlé-Tart 1975: 152). But now it was too late: the French parliament rejected the proposal, and, after last minute debate, acceded to the principle of conjugal and parental equality (Dhavernas 1978: 107ff). 'Paternal power' (*puissance paternelle*) was replaced by 'parental authority' (*autorité parentale*). But it took another fifteen years for equality to work itself out in all nooks of French family law (Rieg 1992: 429).

By the early 1970s, explicit husband/father superiority, or at least ultimate family authority (as in Belgium, the Netherlands and Switzerland), was still the rule in Western European civil law south of Scandinavia, although Germany and France had just started to move (cf. Kirk *et al*. 1975; Chloros 1978). In the Netherlands a stipulation that persons under 31 should seek parental advice before marrying had just been taken off the books (in January 1970), but Belgian adults under 25 were still held to do so (until 1983, Coester-Waltjen and Coester 1997: 16n).

Then a spate of egalitarian legislation appeared: in 1975 in Austria and Italy, and in 1976 in Belgium. New West German legislation substituted in 1979 'parental care' (*elterliche Sorge*) for 'parental power' (*elterliche Gewalt*) (Schwab 2001: 202). With democratization, normative family equality reached Spain in 1975, Portugal in 1977, and finally Greece, after the electoral victory of the Socialists, in 1983. In 1978, the Council of Europe passed a resolution on the equality of spouses (Boulanger 1990: 39ff, 259). The last countries of the region to strike down patriarchal norms were the Netherlands, which in 1984 discreetly discarded the remnants of the ultimate authority clause (inserted in 1947), and Switzerland, where a major francophone (Protestant) contribution tipped a referendum balance in favour of husband–wife equality (Grtossen 1986: 256ff). It had taken that principle 64 years to travel from Scandinavia to West-Central Europe.

In England, the 1973 Guardianship Act, introduced by a Tory government, gave mothers the same parental rights as fathers (Cretney 1998: 181). The Anglo-Saxon legal tradition lacks the legal formulation of normative principles characteristic of the Civil Law tradition, which makes it easy for the historian to pin down the stand of normative officialdom, which, of course, can never be taken for actual practice. But this seems to be a final legal exit from patriarchy, although it is not listed as a landmark decision by, for example, Sachs and Wilson (1978: 228). Before 1973, a series of laws had been enacted with a view to ensuing some basic spousal equality in spite of economic inequality. The 1964 the Married Women's Property Act guaranteed a right to keep household savings, the Matrimonial Homes Act of 1967 gave a non-owning spouse certain residence rights, the Matrimonial Proceedings and Property Act of 1970 gave legal economic value to unpaid domestic labour (Cretney and Masson 1990: ch. 12).

Australian legal developments, albeit complicated by the country's federal structure, have tended to run parallel to English ones. The 1975 the federal Family Law Act finally introduced matrimonial equality into Australian law (Finlay 1979). Similar changes occurred at about the same time in Canada, including a new Civil Code of Québec in 1980. Opinion studies from the 1980s onwards have shown de-patriarchalization in Québec to have leapt ahead of Anglo-Canada (Wu and Baer 1996).

The United States was another centre of the late 1960s movement. Its courageous Civil Rights movement finally brought democracy to the southern part of the country, till then a racist apartheid regime. American feminism, as in the nineteenth century, was in many ways a global vanguard.

With its state-fragmented family legislation and its powerful judicial system, American de-patriarchalization is difficult to follow and to summarize. It was driven more by Supreme Court decisions than by legislation. The changing times are indicated by the fact that most crucial decisions were taken by the Burger Court, the Supreme Court presided over by the Conservative Nixon appointee Warren Burger, succeeding the Liberal Earl Warren as President of the Court in 1969.

As in Western Europe, US legislation in the 1960s was full of patriarchal clauses. For instance, 32 states held in 1969 that the wife's domicile followed her husband's (Kanowitz 1973: 197). A number of them had male headship clauses, including Texas (abolishing it in 1967), Washington (leaving the patriarchal barricades in 1972) and California (also leaving in the 1970s). In 1981 the US Supreme Court struck down the last bastion of legal patriarchy, Napoleonic Louisiana, in *Kirchberg* v. *Feenstra* (Glendon 1989: 147, 183n; Baer 1996: 36, 133). Before that, in *Roe* v. *Wade* (1973), and *Planned Parenthood of Central Missouri* v. *Danforth* (1976), the Court made clear that a husband had no right to veto an abortion (Clark and Glowinsky 1995: ch. 3). Other male preference laws were nullified in the 1970s, in *Reed* v. *Reed* in 1971, *Stanton* v. *Stanton* in 1975, and *Orr* v. *Orr* in 1979 (Baer 1996).

However, the USA remains a country of contradictions. It was the first and so far the only country to see a successful anti-feminist backlash in the area of the European family system: the proposal of a gender-equality Equal Rights Amendment to the sacred US Constitution, first introduced into the US Congress in 1923, passed by the Senate in 1950 and in 1953, and finally passed by Congress in 1972. But in spite of a prolonged state ratification process, from 1979 to 1982, it failed to pass, lacking the ratification of three states. Fifteen states failed to support male–female equal rights: the hard South from Alabama to Virginia, but not Texas, Mormon Utah, Missouri and Illinois, burdened by a stringent two-thirds majority clause (Baer 1996: 61).

The global reach

The United Nations gave Act 3 of de-patriarchalization a strong global dimension. Like the later UN Convention on the Rights of the Child, the idea of which originated in the Polish Politburo of the 1970s (Therborn 1996), although in a more indirect manner, the tremendously important UN Women and Development Decade originated in the Communist left and in Cold War diplomacy. The starting-point was the idea of an International Women's Year, which came out of a Geneva meeting of the UN Commission on the Status of Women in 1972, and first of all from feminist non-government organizations (NGOs) surrounding the meeting. The initiative seems to have come from the Communist Women's International Democratic Federation and its Finnish President, Hertta Kuusinen. The initiators then got a Romanian official dele-gate to table the motion. Romania was at that time the favourite Communist country in the West, distancing itself from the USSR. The Commission adopted the proposal, and submitted it to the UN General Assembly, which endorsed it. The year 1975 was to be International Women's Year, dedicated to Equality, Development and Peace. The Finnish government chief delegate to the UN Commission, Helvi Sipilä, was appointed Secretary-General of the Year and it was decided to make a conference in Mexico City the focal point of the Year.

It was a tremendous success. A total of 133 states participated with about 1,200 delegates, at levels varying from prime ministers (like Sirimavo Bandaranaike of Sri Lanka and Olof Palme of Sweden) to diplomats, and including some controversial celebrities of the time, like Ashraf Pahlavi, sister of the Shah of Iran, and Imelda Marcos, 'First Lady of Plunder' of the Philippines. The Conference elected another Romanian delegate Rapporteur-Général, Maria Groza. Some 4,000–6,000 activists took part in the off-stage Tribune. The Third World Group of 77 dominated the politics, Zionism came to constitute a divisive issue, with Western Europe and the former British Empire lining up as a minoritarian guard around Israel.

But above all, the Tribune witnessed a confrontation between North American feminism, well represented by Betty Friedan, and Third World feminine Leftism, eloquently voiced by Domitila Barrios, from the Housewives Committee of the Bolivian Siglo XX tin mine. The Tribune as well as the Conference stayed on the feminist track, but the social and economic issues of poverty, exploitation and imperialism raised by Domitila Barrios found a resonance among Latin American feminists (Miller 1991: 198ff).

The main outcome of the Conference was a feminist 'World Plan of Action', a formidable document in 219 paragraphs, prepared at great speed by Sipilä and the UN Secretariat and discussed at pre-Conference seminars, which finally had to be adopted en bloc, as there was no time to deal properly with the 894 amendments tabled. The main emphasis of the plan was on education and social development, but it also tackled issues of family rights, with a special pointer against child marriages, and denials or restrictions of the inheritance of widows (§129). Women's rights 'in all the various forms of the family, the nuclear family, the extended family, consensual union, and the single-parent family' was also stressed (§127). It was also significant that the plan called for new governmental agencies dealing with gender equality and with women's rights and opportunities, for research, and for recurrent reviews of changes in the world (UN 1975: annex).

The plan proposed that the Year should be followed up by a Decade for Women, which was accepted by the General Assembly in December 1975. So the Mexico conference came to inaugurate an international Decade for Women of 1975–85, including two further global conferences, in Copenhagen in 1980 and in Nairobi in 1985. It was normatively underpinned by the UN Convention of the Elimination of All Forms of Discrimination Against Women, of 1979. After the Decade itself, momentum was kept up by the Population Conference in Cairo in 1994 and the Women's Conference in Beijing in 1995. With the Women and Development Decade, and its global entanglements of international organization and movements with national states and NGOs, women's rights and life-chances became hot political issues all over the world (Miller 1991; Eekelaar and Nhlapo 1998; Berkowitz 1999; Edwards and Roces 2000; V. Guzmán 2001).

The UN Decade for Women turned out to be extremely important in spawning feminist action in the Third World. At the mid-Decade conference in Copenhagen about 7,000 participants assembled for the NGO Forum, while in Nairobi at the end of the Decade there were 14,000. Extensive reviews of what had changed, and what had not, since Mexico were made, and new forward strategies were drawn up (UN 1975, 1976, 1980; Pietilä and Vickers 1996).

The Decade established a global agenda of reforming gender and family relations, and the Beijing Conference in 1995 was a celebration, a consolidation, and a platform for further forays into the labyrinths of male power, not least in China.

From the Mexico conference and from the UN Decade followed national reports, offices, ministries, investigations, and international comparisons, benchmarks, indices, and international models and money for social movements. Work on a Convention on the Elimination of All Forms of Discrimination Against Women was speeded up, to be adopted in 1979. Most UN members ratified it in the early 1980s, but there was also a second wave of ratifications in the mid-1990s, including many African countries, from Algeria to South Africa, as well as India. In 1999, the UN General Assembly adopted an Optional Protocol to the Convention according to which states could allow citizens to petition the UN Committee to inquire into violations of the Convention by state governments. By the spring of 2000 most Western European countries (the UK excepted), several Latin American countries, including Mexico, Argentina and Cuba, Ghana and Senegal in Africa, Indonesia and the Philippines in Asia had adopted the Protocol, providing a global edge against all forms of discrimination against women (UN 2000a: chart 6.2).

In Cuba a new, strongly egalitarian Family Code was adopted in 1975, before the Mexico conference, emphasizing equal parental responsibility and the household obligations of both spouses, even if one of them was not working outside the domestic sphere. Cohabitation was put on an equal legal footing with marriage (Bergmann and Ferid 1928: 541ff; 1989). Cuba retains the notion of 'family head' (*Jefe de familia*) as a socio-statistical category, but self-defined by family members. In 1995, 36 per cent of all Cuban households declared a female head, with 51.5 per cent in Havanna. Most interesting here is perhaps, that two-thirds of these female family heads were married or cohabitees. About 30 per cent of all current married or cohabiting family heads in Cuba are women (calculated from Benítez 1999: 68, 77).

After the Mexico conference many governments gave financial support and encouragement to various women's organizations and initiatives. Under UN auspices three regional official conferences followed, in Venezuela, Havana and Mexico (UN ECLAC 1988), and from 1981 there began a series of biannual Latin American and Caribbean feminist meetings (Miller 1991: 214ff; Stephen 1997: 15ff).

In South America the new dictatorships of the 1970s held up the process of change, even though feminist discourse gradually spread there too, and only after the fall of the military juntas were patriarchal laws abolished or overturned. In 1987 Argentina changed to equal rights of spouses and parents, and to allowing divorce (Torrado 1993: 276ff). The new Brazilian Constitution of 1988 overturned the male headship clauses of the family code, which then was rewritten in 2001. In the juridical discussions of the 1980 Pinochet Constituition in Chile, the old principle of male family headship was reasserted, and an advanced proposal of equal gender rights was stopped in the final stage of the process. With the return to democracy, the patriarchal clauses of the family code were finally rescinded in 1994. Divorce is still taboo, but a marriage can be 'nullified' (Fries and Matus 1999).

Other Latin American countries moved also in the 1980s towards legal family equality: Venezuela in 1982, Peru in 1984, and Ecuador in 1989, for instance (cf. Binstock 1998). In Mexico family legislation belongs to the states, and the equality ruling in the Federal District spread only gradually and unevenly to the rest of the United States of Mexico (Bergmann and Ferid 1993). In 1994 the Zapatista movement in Chiapas issued its 'Revolutionary Law of Women', with a catalogue of rights, including that of not having to 'marry by force', which still needed to be asserted apparently (Stephen 1997: 14).

African family law had its constitutional moment of equality in the early 1960s, written in the sand, as the Ivory Coast stipulations against polygamy or of conjugal equality (Levasseur 1976). The UN Decade, with its culmination in Nairobi in 1985, and the 1979 UN Convention of the Elimination of All Forms of Discrimination Against Women (CEDAW) gave a new impetus. The 1982 Zimbabwe law on Legal Majority, common to women and to men, was a major blow to Southern African patriarchy, followed a decade later by the South African Constitution. Towards the end of the UN Decade African reform began to leave the paper world and, at least, to enter that of judicial proceedings, still available to a minority only (cf. Eekelaar and Nhlapo 1998).

In Asia, India, with its thin progressive leadership and heavy conservative society, established a Committee on the Status of Women in 1971, which in 1975, for the UN Conference, issued a quite critical report (Robinson 1999: 148–49). The bloody military dictatorship of Indonesia, the establishment of which in 1965 had a violent anti-feminist slant directed against the devilish Communist women (Tiwon 1996: 64ff), issued in 1974 an ambiguous Marriage Law, proclaiming both equal rights (§31:1) and husband headship (§31:2). While claiming monogamy as the basis of marriage (§3:1), it also allows religiously permitted polygyny (§§4–5), which, of course, is the case for the overwhelmingly Muslim population (Supriadi 1995; Parawansa 2002).

Sri Lanka was, in 1981, one of the first Asian countries to ratify CEDAW, without qualifications, and its 1978 Constitution enshrined gender equality (Goonesekere 1995). The South Asian states have also ratified CEDAW, to what effect it may have: Bangladesh in 1984, India in 1993, and Pakistan in 1996; so have also most of the Arab states: Egypt in 1981, Yemen, Iraq, Tunisia and Libya in the 1980s, Algeria, Jordan, Kuwait and Morocco in the 1990s. Syria had, by 2000, not ratified the Convention, but it had submitted a Plan of Action to the UN. Out of the Convention on the eve of the new century were Afghanistan, Iran, Saudi Arabia, Somalia and the United States (UN 2000a: chart 6.1).

In 1989 the UN adopted an elaborate and soon well-monitored Convention on the Rights of the Child (UN 1989), after an original 1978 proposal by the Polish government (see further Therborn 1996). Its widespread ratification – outside the USA – and the substantial non-governmental as well as official reporting to its monitoring committee provides another indicator of the delegitimation of patriarchy (Franklin 1995; Therborn 1996; Bartley 1998). How far the Convention's writ on children's right to provision, protection and, in this context most important, participation has reached outside the little world of welfare states, universal schooling, and of general citizen access to a law-bound judiciary and to effective, rule-bound administration is another question. At least it has provided a focused perspective to socially concerned elites across the planet, and it has played a significant part in the increasingly serious attention paid to genital mutilation of girls in Africa and to the 'missing girls' of northern India.

Act 3 of de-patriarchalization was enacted across the whole planet, with variable gusto and meaning. It meant a global official discrediting of patriarchy, above all in husband–wife and in parent–daughter relations. The Child Convention did not enter directly into the relations of parents to adult children, and the latter's right to marriage, for instance. The most immediate substantial impact of Act 3 was in the 'West', from Western Europe to Australia, where the process was carried by forceful social movements. Its coupling with democratization in South America and Southern Africa in the 1980s and early 1990s provided de-patriarchalization with a strong socio-political impetus there. In the rest of the world, the direct effect was much more limited, even if almost everywhere visible, at least in elite politics, administration and adjudication.

3 The patriarchal burden of the twenty-first century

The secular changes of the twentieth century, for all their character of an epochal turn, do not mean that patriarchy has disappeared from the earth. In large areas of the world it is still strongly entrenched. And neo-patriarchal movements, usually with religious argumentation, have appeared.

In a global perspective one of the most powerful expressions of patriarchy, as understood in this book, is paternal and/or parental power over children's marriage. A marriage is one of life's most important decisions, and therefore one where the difference between autonomy and heteronomy weighs most heavily. All available evidence indicates that the autonomy of marriage has increased during the twentieth century. Nevertheless, parents still have a major say regarding their children's marriage, in at least half, probably more, of the populations of Asia, in many parts of Africa, in pockets of Europe – not only among recent immigrants – and also among Indian peoples of the Americas. Parents also play a significant part in the marital life of many adult children through post-marital household patterns. The extended family is a major phenomenon in most regions of the world outside Europe, North America and Oceania.

Within the couple, the principle of male headship has been widely challenged. But the norm has not disappeared everywhere, and in many parts of the world, husbands still control not only all major family decisions but also whether the wife may leave her house or not. Nor have special gender sacrifice and institutionalized violence against girls and women disappeared. While violence against women has become an issue in Africa and Asia, wife-beating is still legitimate in many social milieux. Sexual double standards are still in force.

Let us make a worldwide overview of major patriarchal burdens carried on into the twenty-first century before finally making a summary overall assessment of the past century of change. There are three large areas of the world where patriarchy is well entrenched on the threshold of the twenty-first century: first, South Asia, its northern parts, Hindu and Muslim, in particular; second, West Asia/North Africa, with Turkey a significant but far from complete exception, and including, with some reservations, Central Asia; third, most of sub-Saharan Africa, with partial exceptions on the West Coast and in the south.

East Asia, which when our story began was the most elaborate patriarchy of the world, has undergone radical change, and the power of fathers and husbands has been seriously eroded, without evaporating. Southeast Asia, never a rigid embodiment of patriarchy, still contains important elements of it. In the rest of the world, explicitly patriarchal norms have, on the whole, been effectively abolished, recently or earlier. But male advantages remain in a number of fields, with a tendential increase in post-Communist Europe.

South Asian marriage arrangements

South Asia appears to be the largest bastion of arranged marriages at the start of the twenty-first century. Marriage without parental sanction, although legally possible and, of course, occurring, is a legal and administrative hassle, even in the capital city of New Delhi. A love marriage, if not approved by parents, is a shameful affair of legal trickery, in the hands of seedy touts – though often helped by the temples of the reformist Hindu Arya Samaj organizaton, which provide officiants. In the process the prospective couple runs the risk of parental intervention, with the help of the police (Mody 2002).

South Asian marriage is normally a family business, although the relative activity and power in the process varies among father, mother, older siblings, other relatives and, not necessarily least, the prospective bride or bridegroom. It is largely governed by caste rules, prescribing endogamy in the caste or, usually, sub-caste and exogamy of *gotra* or clan, although there is a trend towards widening of caste endogamy, but mainly within overall caste boundaries, i.e. from sub-sub-caste to sub-caste or caste endogamy (Shah 1998: ch. 8; Dube 2001: ch. 4).

In India the marriage market is no metaphor. It can be seen in action and full bloom in the multipage 'Matrimonials' Sunday section of the *Hindustan Times*, or other major newspapers. The columns are usually titled by caste, or by the occupation/education of the grooms or brides on offer. This important Delhi newspaper in 1999 offered 43 pre-set categories for their marriage ads, 18 by profession, from 'Banks/Financial Institution/Insurance' to 'Working Girls', and 25 by 'Religion/Community/Caste'. Here are a few examples selected at random from the *Hindustan Times* on 18 April 1999:

Grooms wanted for
AGARWAL [a caste]. **Suitable match for Aggerwal, Singhal** [sub-castes]. M.A. (Economics), PG Diploma in Computer Application, fair complexion girl, 23/154, of highly educated family, decent marriage. . . .

BUSINESSWOMEN. **Groom for beautiful, slim, Khatri** [a caste] **BA,** Fashion Computer Diplomas girl, 22/162. Father leading businessman, owning substantial residentialization, property.

S[CHEDULED]C[ASTE/S[CHEDULED]T[RIBE] **Suitable match for fair, slim,** Central Govt. Employed SC girl 28/152/8500, Post-graduate. Father Gaz. Officer in the Railway. . . .

Brides wanted for

ARORA [a caste]. **Wanted slim beautiful charming** educated bride for Software Developer with Microsoft MCA qualified, slim, fair, handsome, 178/25 yrs, 67 kgs. Contact . . . . Father owns Pvt. Ltd. Co. Boy also Director in father's co. Bride should be from Punjabi Arora or Khatri family. . . .

ENGINEERS. **Wanted good looking well educated** status family girl, preferably Delhiite, for Vaish Engineer boy, 34/165, well settled, having own business, income high five figures, small family, own house. Father retired Senior Govt. Officer, caste no bar, expected shortly. . . .

N[ON-]R[ESIDENT]I[NDIAN]S. Suitable match for Educated Rajput (Swarankar) boy, 27 yrs/5.9. Family well settled and having own business in America. Girl should be fair, slim, and educated. Parents visiting Delhi. 5/68, W.E.A. Padam Singh Road. . . .

OTHER CATEGORIES. **Alliance invited for handsome Graduate** boy, 28/176 cms., earning five figures, employed as Asst. Business Manager with newspaper Co. (parents inter-caste married, Bisa Agarwal, well educated, cultured beautiful match preferred) Contact. . . .

Among the roughly 1,600 'Matrimonials' in the *Hindustan Times* of 18 April 1999 I found two written in the first person, and two more written in the third person but without any reference to an alliance or a match, and without any reference to family, occupation or income. More than 99 per cent of the ads vaunted socio-economic offers and desires. Indian marriage is a professional sport.

This blatant instrumentalism is, of course, the baseline of materialist strategies, from which the crimes of dowry blackmail, dowry violence and dowry murder spring. The reproduced tradition of hypergamy, of women given on to higher status patrilineal households, further strengthens Indian patriarchy.

The power of South Asian parents is not easy to assess in straightforward terms. To what extent are parents the 'agents' of young people, in the same sense as any money-seeking athlete, musician or writer has an agent? On the macroscopic level at which this global study has to operate, that question cannot be given a fully satisfactory answer. However, given the original asymmetry of power between children and parents, the burden of proof should be on those who would advocate that parental intervention in their children's marriage is only instrumental to the instrumentalism of the children. Otherwise, an assumption of patriarchal heteronomy seems warranted. However, such an assumption does *not* entail assumptions of necessary conflicts, of parental neglect of what they see as the 'best interests' of their children, or of children's lack of bargaining capacity and possible veto powers. Contemporary South Asian marriage strategies include a great deal of complexity, subtlety and variation (cf. the situation in Lahore in Fischer and Lyon 2000).

Autonomous marriage decisions by adult children are clearly regarded as objectionable in South Asia, unless they concur with parental wishes. The degrading hassles of the Delhi court dealing with rebellious children who only want to marry of their own choosing is a good indicator. That in a working-class neighbourhood of metropolitan Calcutta in the 1990s 'Love marriages are considered shameful' (Tenhunen 1998: 80), or held as deviant among 'untouchable' *Dalits* in the metropolitan slum of Madras (Chennai) (Wit 1996: 166), may be taken as a parental generation shaming (part of) a children's generation. Arranged marriages have legitimacy on their side. In 1974, the Committee on the Status of Women in India (1974: 414), reporting to the UN conference in Mexico, had found in a national survey, that 74 per cent of Indians believed that marriages should be arranged by parents.

But challenges are, of course, being made. Couples are turning to the seedy judicial go-betweens and consultants at the family court of New Delhi in order to marry of their own choice. And in March 1997, a Lahore (Pakistan) court dismissed a demand by the parents of a young woman that her non-sanctioned marriage should be voided. Her behaviour – to marry against her parents' wishes – could not be approved, the judges said, but there was no law according to which the marriage could be voided (*Die Zeit*, 14 March 1997, p. 10).

The problem remains South Asian, rather than Hindu or Muslim, Indian, Pakistani or Bangladeshi. On the whole, there are valid reasons for treating the secular Hindu state of India together with the Muslim countries of Bangladesh and Pakistan, the former officially secular, the latter explicitly Muslim. If one should make a divide, the line would run between the south of India, on one hand, and the north together with Bangladesh and Pakistan, on the other. Male domination is much stronger in the north, particularly in the northwest of northwestern India and Pakistan, than in the south, with the northeast of West Bengal and Bangladesh in between (cf. Agarwal 1994: ch. 8; Jejeebhoy and Sathar 2001).

Purdah, female seclusion, is an upper-caste practice common to Hindus and Muslims, still frequent in conservative rural milieux. In the early 1970s purdah was a dominant phenomenon in northwestern India, practised by two-thirds of women in the states of Haryana and Rajasthan, by around 40 per cent in the other northern states, but only by 4–5 per cent in the southern states of Tamil Nadu, Kerala and Karnataka (Committee on the Status of Women in India 1974).

The northern part of South Asia demands extra sacrifices of girls and women, with excess female child mortality (by neglect more than by infanticide), much more seclusion, more patriarchal joint households, stricter norms of patrilocality, and more discrimination of widows (Dyson and Moore 1983; Kolendra 1987; Malhotra *et al.* 1995; Basu 1999; Das Gupta *et al.* 2000: table 1; Das Gupta 2001). In Bangladesh, Nepal, and Pakistan female life expectancy at birth is slightly lower than that of males; in India as a whole the female advantage is only one year. But in the big Indian states of the north, Uttar Pradesh, Bihar and Orissa, female life expectancy is also shorter than male. This is an abnormal pattern indicating mistreatment of females. Among the rich countries women tend to live 5–7 years longer than men, in China and Indonesia the female advantage is 4 years, in Egypt 3 years, in Saudi

Arabia 2.5 years and in Iran 2 years. The only social area in the world resembling South Asia in sapping the superior biological strength of the female sex is sub-Saharan Africa, particularly in the AIDS-ravaged southern part, but also including Nigeria and other West African countries (Vijayanunni 1998: table 54; UNDP 2002: table 22).

From practices of infanticide, neglect and maltreatment follows a male population surplus, which in India has tended to grow in the course of the twentieth century, with rather dramatic turns for the worse in some northern states in the second half of the century, and spreading in the last decades to the southern state of Tamil Nadu. By the census of 1991 there were 108 Indian men to 100 Indian women (Vijayanunni 1998: table 60).

In the early 1990s a fairly large (almost 3,000 interviewees) survey of women aged 20–39 was made to compare religious, national and regional contexts of patriarchy. The areas of investigation were Muslim Pakistani Punjab, Muslims and Hindus in northern Indian Uttar Pradesh (UP) and in southern Indian Tamil Nadu. In no area did a majority of the women have a say in deciding their marriage, but the range of those who had ran from 42 per cent among Tamil Nadu Hindus to 10 per cent among UP Hindus. After marriage two-thirds to nine-tenths lived with in-laws, but by the time of the interview this kind of residence constituted a majority only in Punjab and among Hindus in Uttar Pradesh. Most Tamil Nadu women could go unescorted to the market or the village community centre, but only a third in Punjab and UP. Less than one in five of UP women had a say concerning food for the family, whereas in Punjab and in Tamil Nadu a great majority had. A good third of the women had been beaten by their husbands, among UP Hindu women almost half had (Jejeebhoy and Sathar 2001: tables 3–4). The overall pattern is clear: a strong, persistent patriarchy, with a regional rather than a national or religious gradient. On every score Tamil women of southern India, both Muslim and Hindu, do better than their sisters in northern India or in Pakistan.

A pervasive norm of female subordination runs through the whole South Asian sub-continent, although like any norm it may be breached or evaded. Two vignettes from opposite corners may illustrate the burden of misogynous traditions. Both are from young women in the countryside, where three-quarters of the Indian population lived in the early 1990s: one from the high caste Rajputs in the conservative northern state of Uttar Pradesh in the mid-1970s; the other about 'untouchable' Paraiyars in the patriarchally more relaxed southern state of Tamil Nadu in the 1980s.

A young Rajput woman: 'I can talk to my husband even in the presence of others, but my mother could not talk to her husband when we were very young children. . . . Although, so far, I have never eaten in the presence of my husband, I can talk to my husband anytime I want. . . . My mother could not serve meals to her own husband [because of pollution norms]. . . . Now I can serve my husband myself' (Minturn 1993: 84).

Among the Paraiyars and other Tamil castes, the general rule of female quietness and respectfulness is supplemented by a taboo for a woman to speak her husband's name. He is like a god, whose name must not be pronounced.

In the 1980s, Robert Deliège (1997: 231) did find some young women daring to mention their husband's name, but he doubted whether they ventured to address him by his name.

The entanglement of patriarchy and misogyny with caste and religion through rituals and rules of pollution and purity provides male domination with a deep social anchor, largely out of reach for a secular bureaucracy and its discourse of equal rights.

Backlash in West Asia and North Africa

This is the region of the world where the confrontations between modernist thrusts to de-patriarchalization and religiously grounded patriarchal counter-blasts have been most violent. In the last quarter of the twentieth century, the battles were most often won by the latter. The devastating Israeli attack in 1967 was a humiliating defeat for Arab secular nationalism. The partial redress through the Egyptian Ramadan war (of 1973) seemed to vindicate the Islamicist currents, also deliberately pandered to by Arab rulers from Egypt to Morocco as a dagger against the secular left, still strong among students and intellectuals (see further Ajami 1981). In the 1970s the veil, or the head cover, re-emerged among women of the region. Communist modernization in Afghanistan was defeated by a major international mobilization of Islamic reaction, bankrolled by the Saudis and armed by the United States. The de-patriarchalizing reforms of the Shah of Iran were drowned by an Islamic revolution. Attempts at major changes of official family norms in North Africa, from Egypt to Morocco, have been forced to backtrack by vigilant and forceful religious conservatism.

It does not mean, though, that the war of attrition has been won by the *muhajedeen* of patriarchy: it goes on, with various outcomes. A recent, belated expansion of girls' schooling has taken place throughout the region west of Afghanistan, which has pushed up the age of female marriage quite con-siderably (see Chapter 4), something which sooner or latter will mean more female autonomy. The global discourse of women's rights and gender equality has entered the region, and one of its most interesting effects has been the rise of an explicitly 'Islamic feminism' (cf. Tohidi 2002: 868ff, on Iran). Since 1994 Turkish women have had the right to seek a job without their husband's permission, thanks to a judicial decision. In 2001 Turkey finally removed the legal doctrine of male family headship, against strong resistance from the secular nationalist right and from Islamic conservatives, a legal change in force from 1 January 2002. The legal formulation had been imported from Switzerland with the Civil Code of 1926, but the Swiss themselves – no feminist avant-garde – did away with it in 1974.

However, outside Turkey, patriarchal norms permeate the legal system of the area, as well as family practice. Patriarchal practice also rules the bulk of the Turkish population, where the 1993 Demographic and Health Survey found that only a third of marriages had been arranged by the spouses them-selves – including through abduction/elopement (Remez 1998). Even in the European diaspora, for instance in Sweden, heavy parental involvement in children's marriages is the rule, although the eventual spouses usually have their say too (Berg 1994).

An Egyptian-American writer, Hisham Sharabi (1988), has characterized contemporary Arab society as one of 'neopatriarchy', referring both to its failed modernity more generally and to its contemporary family. A woman's marriage in this Islamic world, except legally mature women in Egypt belonging to the Hanafi School of Islamic jurisprudence, is conducted by a male guardian, which nowadays is often a formality, but which means crucial veto powers. Forced marriages are proscribed, but consent may be implied, and under special circumstances of temptation a Moroccan judge is allowed to order a marriage (Nasir 1990: ch. 3C; cf. Welchman 2001).

If we look at the most important Arab country, Egypt, we certainly find an old patriarchy vigorously alive under new conditions. By the early 1990s only a third of married women under 30 had arranged their marriage themselves, ranging from 16 per cent among the illiterate to 46 per cent among those with ten or more years of education (Nawar *et al.* 1995: 154). There is a class stratification of arranged marriages, but individual choice is not a general middle-class norm (cf. Rugh 1984: 135ff; Mensch *et al.* 2000). Almost half of rural and a third of urban women marry a relative, primarily a cousin (Zanaty *et al.* 1996: table 8.3). Egyptian youths usually live with their parents, or some other relative, until they marry.

Inside marriage, the husband decides the important issues, although almost half of Egyptian women in 2000 said they decided daily purchases. Only one in eight said they could decide whether to visit a relative, whereas a quarter had the experience that their husband had to decide that. A majority held that the wife's visit to a relative was something she and her husband decided jointly (DHS 2000, Egypt). Husbands have a legal right to prevent their wives from leaving the house, unless stated otherwise in the marriage contract (Hoodfar 1997: 74). However, a Nasserite decree of February 1967 rescinded the possibility to call upon the police against a wife who had left the house without her husband's permission (Nowaihi 1979: 101).

Patriarchal norms are still being successfully inculcated, according to a large survey of adolescents, aged 16–19, in 1997. Nine-tenths held that a wife needs to ask her husband's permission for everything. That may have included interpretations of fact, as well as a norm. But 75 per cent of the boys and 56 per cent of the girls held that in cases of spousal differences of opinion, the wife must comply (Mensch *et al.* 2000: table 8). In the Demographic and Health Survey of 1995, nine-tenths of all women aged 15 to 19 agreed to at least one of a range of reasons for a husband to beat his wife: 76 per cent found wife-beating justified when 'wife answers back', 70 per cent when she refuses sex, and 64 per cent when she talks to other men (Zanaty 1996: table 14.18). Wife-beating is no theoretical issue in Egypt. A third of married women have been beaten in their marriage, and half of these had been beaten in the past year (Zanaty *et al.* 1996: tables 14.19 and 14.20).

Female genital mutilation was almost universal among Egyptian women in the 1995 Demographic and Health Survey.

Changes are occurring, but slowly and non-linearly. Education is giving women more resources and some escape from all-embracing family control. Male migration to the Gulf makes young childless wives more dependent on their in-laws, but tends to strengthen the independence of other married women (Hoodfar 1997).

The amended Sadat Constitution of 1971 proclaimed Islam as the 'state religion' of Egypt, in spite of its ancient and significant Coptic Christian minority, and 'Islamic shari'a a principal source of legislation'. The state dependence of the religious establishment made the latter clause indeterminate. That was used to push through a divorce law in 1979, making polygyny *per se* a valid reason for divorce. But the constitutional clause opened up an arena for religious challenge, which the normally fully pliant National Assembly took advantage of in 1982, examining current laws in the sacred light of medieval stipulations. The divorce law, called the Jihane Act, after the wife of the now-murdered President Sadat, was abrogated in 1985 and replaced with a more restrictive one (Botiveau 1993: chs 6–8). But in 2000 a new divorce law gave a woman the right to file for divorce against the will of her husband and without having to claim a grave fault on his part. Such a *khul* divorce requires a renunciation of all financial claims on the husband. Conservatives complained against it, for violating rules of Islam. But in December 2002 this complaint was dismissed by the Constitutional Court (*Middle East Times*, 20 December 2002).

Attempts at family law reform in Algeria have been stalled by religious reaction. Independence brought education and large-scale professional entry to Algerian women, who in the mid-1990s made up half of the country's physicians and a third of its lawyers and judges (Turshen 2002: 891). But as in Kemalist Turkey this was largely an upper middle-class advance, which left the bulk of the population in traditional family patriarchy. More than half of Algerian women in a survey of the 1970s had had no say at all in their marriage (Coester-Waltjen and Coester 1997: 22). The authoritarian rulers of the country had no commitment to gender equality, and in the fratricidal post-Independence struggles for power, victorious contenders were keen on not offending conservative tradition (Minces 1978). In Algeria as in the rest of the Arab world, Islamic reaction was getting stronger after the 1967 Israeli war and the deepening crisis of secular nationalism.

The still-valid 1984 Family Code reflects this male accommodation between authoritarian secularism and religious conservatism. As in all Arab countries, a woman needs a guardian in order to marry, usually her father. This does not necessarily mean an arranged marriage, and the bride's consent is legally required – although according to Muslim law it may be taken as implied – but it assures a paternal say in a daughter's marriage. Normal minimum marriage age was raised to 18 for women (21 for men). The Code (§39) requires the wife to obey her husband. Polygyny is permitted, although it is a valid ground for a wife's divorce. Husbands have a right to divorce by repudiation (*talaq*), whereas divorce is difficult for wives. Independent Algeria has always had a feminist women's movement, which originally could draw strength from female participation in the war of national liberation, and which later was inspired by French and international feminism. It has staged a series of protests against Algerian patriarchy, before as well as after the Code, but so far to little avail. In the late 1980s the movement was also overwhelmed by pro-patriarchal manifestations by women from the then-allowed Islamist movement (Kopola 2001: part II). In 1997 the government began investigating a reform of the Family Code, but so far the latter remains valid, guilty of explicit patriarchy.

That the ancient monarchical polity of Morocco has been very cautious in modernizing its *mudawana* or Law of Personal Status is perhaps less surprising than the Algerian stalemate (Lahrichi 1985). As in Algeria there was a governmental attempt to move in the late 1990s, raising the female minimum marriage age from 15 to 18, making polygyny at least more difficult, perhaps doing away with the ancient stipulation that a bride needs a male matrimonial guardian to make her marriage contract. However, a vigorous clerical protest in 1999 put the reforms on hold until 2003, when the new King restarted the process.

Tunisia, under a united, secularist, top-down authoritarian leadership, has moved furthest from traditional Arab patriarchy. Its Code of Personal Status, issued in 1956, a year after Independence, prohibited polygyny outright – still the only Arab country to do so, although the Syrian Code of 1953 and the Iraqi one of 1959 required a judge's permission (Barakat 1993: 113) – as well as unilateral husbandly repudiation. The minimum age of marriage was raised to 15 for girls and 18 for boys, and the freedom of marital choice was provided with legal support. As was to be expected, the Code met considerable religious resistance, which foundered on the rock of united secular, modernist power. But here too the legitimacy of women's rights declined after the disaster of 1967 (Tessler *et al.* 1978).

The highest profile religious backlash to secular modernization in West Asia was the 1979 Islamic Revolution in Iran. In fact, however, its impact has been limited. A religious reaction had been taking place for a decade in the region, and the Shia minority orientation of Iranian Islam limited its international appeal. In terms of patriarchy Iranian Islamism has been a complex compound of orthodox, misogynous strictures, of surveillance of women, of gender segregation, and references to ancient sacred tradition, on one hand, and a continuing modernist dynamics, on the other. The marriage age of girls was lowered to 13, and could go lower than that as girls were proclaimed mature at the age of 9, but since 1986 the actual age of marriage has shot upwards. The principle of a husband's right to unilateral repudiation has been endorsed, but subject to court registration and a judicial norm of attempting reconciliation. Polygamy has been endorsed, but remains a marginal phenomenon. More difficult, and sensitive, to evaluate, is the regime's encouragement, particularly after the war with Iraq, of 'temporary marriages', a peculiar Shia institution, which has lately spread to Sudan (Bergmann and Ferid 1991: Iran; Sanasarian 1992; Mir-Hosseini 1993).

The crucial problem of patriarchy in West Asia and North Africa is not Islam. It is the weakness and the venality of the secular forces, largely hammered home by their powerful Israeli and American enemies – most recently with the destruction of the Palestine Authority; enemies because of the nationalist anti-imperialism of the former. Islam does not possess the internationally unified, doctrinally single-minded mobilization for patriarchy, which Papal Catholicism waged from the mid-nineteenth century to the late twentieth century. By comparison, Islam has always been fragmented, theologically as well as organizationally.

African traditions and their ruination

Africa contains traditions of the most autonomous women of the world, such as marketing women of the West Coast, quite established by the time of the colonial arrival of Europeans. But it also, and mainly, includes strongly patriarchal areas. And, as we noticed above, spousal autonomy did not mean equality, but a free space under an overarching male superiority.

Family and kinship was by far the most important institution in the African tradition, which largely lacked distinctive, differentiated religious and political ones. Urbanization and the uprooted poverty of the decades-long economic crisis have worn and torn upon the extensive African family, but its norms are still in place, structuring social life.

The normative tone is well given by the 1981 African Charter on Human and Peoples' Rights, a quite original blend of international human rights doctrine and an assertion of African culture. In line with the former, a number of individual rights – mainly politico-judicial and in practice more honoured by their breach than by their defence – are recognized, but no individual family right, to marry for instance. True to international convention, the Charter does stipulate (article 18: 3) that 'the State shall ensure the elimination of every discrimination against women', a clause which has been used in recent efforts at dismantling discrimination. But the Charter also includes a catalogue of duties, and here the family idea finds its expression:

> Article 27: Every individual shall have duties towards his family and society, the State and other legally recognized communities and the international community.
>
> Article 28: Every individual shall have the duty to respect and consider his fellow beings . . . .
>
> Article 29: The individual shall also have the duty:
> 1. To preserve the harmonious development of the family and to work for the cohesion and respect of the family, to respect his parents at all times, to maintain them in case of need;
> 2. To serve his national community . . . .
>
> (Steiner and Alston 1996: 1215ff)

The family is the first duty, before state and nation. It is a collective, whose cohesion is a major concern. The key members of the family, the only ones mentioned explicitly, are the parents.

In the second half of the twentieth century there has been a more or less continental drift away from parental arrangement of marriages towards a more complex pattern of both individual choice and parental involvement. The tradition of a brideprice paid to the father of the bride has eroded in many parts of Africa, but in some sense or other it is still operating or taken into account, even in South African 'townships' (Mathabane 1995), and by current South African law reform (Nhlapo 1998: 633). It is a potent indicator that marriage is still a family affair.

Post-colonial legal pluralism means that one can marry according to modern statutory law, to religious, for instance Islamic, law, or to customary law (see Table 3.1). Upon recent legislation an 'Act wife' (as she is referred to in Nigeria) is usually basically equal to her husband, in marital rights and obligations, in divorce, and in inheritance. But customary marriage still dominates, and in African customary law a wife is almost always clearly subordinate. As the colonial collection and codification of customary law in the 1930s were based on information from male elders, many of whom were already worried by what they saw as tendencies to female escape, these modern customs may perhaps be more patriarchal than some pre-colonial customs (cf. Mamdani 1996; Koker 1998: 333ff). The repertoire of sexual unions in contemporary Nigeria provides a sense of patriarchal proportions.

Together, Islamic and customary marriages make up the great majority, and they are ruled by patriarchal norms. Only in the Igbo urban southeast is statutory marriage clearly dominant. In the north almost all marriages are Islamic, and in the Yoruba west, customary marriage dominates the urban picture, whereas cohabitation reigns in rural Yorubaland. My Nigerian psychologist colleague Bola Udegbe suggests that the latter may follow from the high regional brideprice.

In the countries influenced by the French civil law tradition, the Napoleonic stipulation of the husband as the *chef de famille* tends to be kept, even after its belated deletion in France in 1970: for instance, in the family code of Senegal (§152), although §154, giving the husband the right to prevent his wife from working outside the house, was rescinded in 1989; in the 1987 family code of Congo/Kinshasa (then Zaïre); and in that of Mali. The Mali code (§85) is also noteworthy for stating that: 'The parents have the right to agree to its [the child's] marriage, to give permission to its marriage contract' (Bergmann and Ferid 1998).

General constitutional clauses of gender equality are often taken back by other clauses upholding customary family law, such as in Zimbabwe, Zambia,

Table 3.1 Types of sexual unions in Nigeria, 1998 (as a percentage of all unions)

Statutory marriage	Customary marriage	Islamic marriage	Cohabitation
17	24	46	13

Source: Udegbe (2001). The data are derived from a survey of 1,475 individuals by the Male Responsibility Study of University College Hospital in Ibadan. It sampled the three major regions of Nigeria, and urban as well as rural populations, but it is not a representative national sample in the statistical sense.

Kenya, Ghana and Botswana (Ncube 1998: 516n). The post-apartheid South African constitution also protects customary law, but democratic South Africa has moreover put in place an elaborate legal and judicial instrumentarium of a Bill of Rights and of specific legislation which provide a basis for extensive de-patriarchalization, although many South African daughters, wives and widows may still be barred from making use of it (Nhlapo 1998; Sinclair 1998; Sloth-Nielsen and van Heerden 1998). In Zimbabwe a crucial step forward was the 1982 Legal Majority Act, which provided all citizens, female as well as male, full legal capacity from the age of 18 (Ncube 1998).

African custom is for male control of women, although outside parts of northern Nigeria it rarely resembles the seclusion of Arab or northern Indian mores. As a recent Demographic and Health Survey shows (Table 3.2), it is still around.

The three African countries in Table 3.2 are from the (historically more patriarchal) east and the south, and any claims to being representative of Africa would have a flimsy base. Nevertheless, the truncated data of the table do indicate that wifely subordination is still a major phenomenon of African social life. Wife-beating is also frequent in Southern and Eastern Africa (cf. Green 1999). It has an amazing legitimacy. Among women born in 1975–80, 38 per cent in Malawi, 53 per cent in Zimbabwe and 79 per cent in Uganda agreed to at least one of five reasons given for a husband to beat his wife: neglecting the children and going out without telling him were the most popular reasons; adultery was not on the list (DHS 1999–2001).

As will be dealt with in some detail in the next chapter, polygamy, formal polygyny as well as informal philandering, are major features of the current sexual order in Africa. Much of it might better be termed phallocracy, and in the urban slums it is what remains of a patriarchal system in ruins, but it is part of the male domination complex, which in this book is summed up as patriarchy.

In the countryside, customary authority – the chiefs – is the major pillar of patriarchy. Nationalist politics weakened it, but the post-Independence crises have often left the chiefs the only authority around. In Ghana, for instance, the position of Chief is currently being re-evaluated and its prestige enhanced

Table 3.2 Who decides a wife's visit to relatives, 2000?

Country	Women saying husband (%)
Malawi	36
Uganda	42
Zimbabwe	21
Egypt	26
Turkmenistan	10
Nepal	34
Colombia	11
Haiti	7
Peru	13

Source: DHS 1999–2001.

by highly educated heirs taking it up, which of course also may entail internal reform. One of the basic Constitutional Principles (no. XI) of democratic South Africa stated that 'The institution, status, and role of traditional leadership, according to indigenous law, shall be recognized and protected by the Constitution'.

East Asian changes and recidivism

The Confucian ethic, with its supreme norm of 'filial piety', is the most patriarchal of all the major normative systems of the world. Around the turn of the twentieth century, Confucian East Asia also had the most elaborate patriarchal family system among all the main family systems of the world, although the Japanese Family Code of 1898, as we noticed above, did include some contractual elements into its attempt at generalization of the old samurai family onto the whole population. But changes were dramatic and radical in twentieth-century East Asia.

East Asia is, of course, first of all China, the centre of its ancient civilization, the source of Confucianism, and the dominant country in terms of population, almost ten times more populous than Japan, and over twenty-five times more than South Korea. The marital freedom and equality installed by the Communist revolution have taken time to materialize, and new political restrictions have entered family life: of state-planned work assignments until recent post-Maoist times, work-place political controls, and heavy-handed family planning. But ancient patriarchy has been largely dismantled, although traces of it are still being planted.

One of the most systematic overviews of Chinese marriage change is an early 1980s survey of 5,436 married women in the five big cities of Beijing, Chengdu, Nanjing, Shanghai and Tianjing (Zang 1993). For rural China, i.e. most of China, diverse regional data have to be pieced together. According to the metropolitan interviewees, parental arrangements went down from over half before 1938 to a third of marriages during the 1937–40 Sino-Japanese war, and virtually disappeared in the 'Great Leap' from 1958. The major entry into marriage has become introductions by non-relatives, whereas own initiatives were sufficient for somewhat less than a third of the women who married in the early 1980s. Even in the largest cities of China a dating culture has been slow in emerging (cf. Evans 1997: 86–87). The high labour force participation of both sexes has meant that work-place friends have become the most important go-betweens (Dai Kejing 1990: 184). Parents are still involved, albeit no longer decisive in urban milieux, and so are friends and colleagues. Chinese marriages are collective concerns (Lee and Wang 1999: 81).

Patrilocal residence upon marriage was still the norm among city newly-weds of the 1980s; it actually increased again after 1965, although historically there has been a growing tendency towards residing with the bride's parents (Zang 1993: table 5). The census of 1990 found that between a fifth and a quarter of the Chinese population aged 30 to 49 lived in three-generation households (Guo 2000: 107). Seventy per cent of Shanghai couples married in 1989–90 resided with in-laws a month after their wedding, four-fifths of them with the groom's parents (Davis 1993: table 3.3).

The sense of filial obligation remains strong. A 1994 survey in the provincial city of Baoding (Whyte 1996: table 1) found that more grown-up children disagreed (49 per cent) than agreed (38 per cent) with the statement 'Young people should pay more attention to their own careers than to caring for their parents'. There was also, among grown-up children, a 2:1 opinion that people should be more concerned about caring for their parents or parents-in-law than for their own children.

In the countryside, which in 2000 still holds two-thirds of the Chinese population, pre-revolutionary family changes had not been significant, and the new Marriage Law of 1950 met with strong resistance. It caused considerable social disruption, with mass applications for divorce from arranged marriages, and tenacious attempts, sometimes violent, by parents and husbands to keep their previous rights. The new concept of free choice ran against ingrained norms and strategies of family formation, and against the deeply rooted value of filial piety. In a rural survey in China in 1990, half of all men and 40 per cent of all women reported that their marriage was self-decided (Rahman 1995: 95). On a national level, it has been estimated that by 1990, 80 per cent of the women born after the revolution have had the opportunity to choose their marriage partner (Li 1994).

Oppressive patriarchal practices continued, known to us through recurrent denunciations in the Chinese press, but new family patterns gradually spread across the vast countryside. Child marriages tended to disappear, albeit not completely, and while parental arrangements seem to have kept the upper hand in the 1950s and 1960s, perhaps even up to the 1980s (Domenach and Hua 1987; Aijmer and Ho 2000: 132), they now normally have to enlist the clear consent of the intended spouses (Parish and Whyte 1978: 174; Croll 1981: ch. 2).

One way of parental control that has recently increased, with greater prosperity and with social commodification, is based on economic family transfers upon marriage, of bridewealth – to the bride's family, 'salt and vinegar money', compensating her family for the cost of her upbringing – as well as of conspicuous dowries (Domenach and Hua 1987: 86ff; Siu 1993; Kipnis 1997: chs 3, 5). At the same time the rise of bridewealth demands indicates a growing value of daughters, as labour in the new family market economy, as care-givers and, increasingly, also as scarcity value.

This increased value of daughters, however, though derives from the son preferences at birth, which with the new birth control policy, selective abortion and, to a minor extent, the old practice of female infanticide, have created very skewed sex ratios. Whereas in a normal human population, the ratio of boys to girls (at birth) is around 105–7:100, in China in 1995 the ratio was 117:100 reaching 127 and 133 in the central provinces of Henan and Hubei. For the population as a whole the sex ratio was 106:100 in 1990, slightly lower than the Indian ratio of 108:100 (Li and Peng 2000: 68–71). By 2000, the overall Chinese sex ratio had increased to 107:100 (China, National Bureau of

Statistics 2001). By contrast, in Japan the male: female ratio for the whole population was 96:100 and among infants 105:100 (figures from the 1995 census: Japan Statistics Bureau 2001: table 9).

Equal inheritance rights of sons and daughters, and inheritance rights of widows are granted by law, and were legislatively re-asserted in 1985. But equal rights are still widely negated in practice, even in less misogynous southern China (Aijmer and Ho 2000: 139, 142n).

The new market economy has also involved a market in women and children, purchased in or abducted from poor rural areas, for domestic service, prostitution or forced marriages (Evans 1997: 169ff). The 1997 revision of the Criminal Code treats this as a very serious crime, under certain circumstances even meriting the death penalty (Palmer 2000: 96ff). The long battle between Communist state legislation of individual freedom and equality in family matters, on one hand, and the recurrent patriarchal urges of Chinese 'civil society', on the other, is far from over and fully won by the former.

Also on the increase with market industrialization are stem or extended families, contrary to the old Western idea of 'modernization', a process to be found in north China (Selden 1993) as well as in the southern parts (Harrell 1993; Johnson 1993), simultaneous with growth of a separate but adjacent residence for newly-weds. This is partly conspicuous consumption in conformity with old cultural patterns, revived with the retreat of Communism, and partly due to the labour demands of family enterprise. Patrilocal or virilocal residence remains the norm, i.e. residing (for some time) with the husband's parents, or near them, in their village. Ritual veneration of ancestors, once a major prop of Chinese patriarchy, is returning (Kipnis 1997: chs 4–5; Aijmer and Ho 2000: chs 8–9).

A contemporary wedding custom of north China underlines this situation in an often quite nasty way. Towards the end of the wedding banquet, in the parental home of the groom, the bride's relatives and friends leave, and a rowdy party of teenaged boys from the groom's village appear, teasing and twisting the bride, demanding candy, cookies and cigarettes. Sooner or later the bride breaks into tears. The groom is present, but never intervenes to protect his bride, although he tries to please the rowdies by handing out goodies (Kipnis 1997: 94ff) reporting from a village in Shandong province).

In summary, the Communist revolution and its dramatic trajectory has had a strong impact on Chinese patriarchy, through its land reform, abolishing lineage and landlord ownership, through its massive promotion of female labour force participation outside the family confine, through its marriage and inheritance laws, and commitment to gender equality. Marriage has become a free choice for the great majority of Chinese – in the cities overwhelmingly so. The gender division of labour has become much less unequal, partly through a high labour force participation rate, which in 1990 ensured that women provided almost half (45 per cent) of all non-domestic labour (Tan and Peng 2000: table 12.9). Household labour is no longer an exclusively female task, but now has a significant male input. Urban comparisons between the USA and China show less gender bias in domestic cooking and laundry in China than in the USA (Xu 1998: 191; cf. Parish and Farrer 2000: 249). On the labour market, the gender gap of remuneration, after controls for education and other background factors, is also relatively small at 11 per cent, which is smaller than among OECD countries (2002: ch. 2) and much smaller than in Taiwan (33 per cent) (Tang and Parish 2000: 286). An active Women's Federation, backed up by new 1990s legislation on the 'Protection of the Rights and Interests of Women' is resisting the male bias of managers (Wang 2000).

My knowledge is insufficient for a comparison between (mainland) China and Taiwan, which with its soaring economic development has also changed considerably. While now a centre of production of East Asian youth culture, Taiwan has preserved a good deal of traditional Chinese patriarchy, with 40 per cent of households in 1985 being extended to the parental generation of the adult couple, residing mostly with the husband's parents (Lee and Sun 1995: table 1). At least in its first surge, economic development widened the gap of education, income and prospects of sons to daughters (Greenhalgh 1985), although by international standards Taiwan is not a particularly unequal society, and educational differences have declined in the 1990s (Chiang 2000: table 11.1). Two indicators point to more patriarchy in Taiwan than in urban mainland China: parental co-residence is less frequent in the latter, and household labour is more evenly divided between wife and husband (Tang and Parish 2000: ch. 11).

However, old East Asian patriarchy has not been quite done away with, and in the new social context of a market economy, social commodification, and Communist ideological implosion, some ancient forms of patriarchal culture are reappearing, including ancestor worship, economic inter-familial marriage transactions and extended families.

In Japan, the feudal 'house' concept of family, and its official registration rules, were not rooted in the commoner population, and a certain process of informalization and nuclearization took place before the Pacific war (Kono 1970: 90). Normally, though, marriages were arranged, often by special go-betweens, and parental consent was crucial. Only after the war did major changes begin in this respect. Contemporary Japanese language makes a distinction between *miai* and *ren'ai*, usually translated as arranged marriage and love marriage, respectively. The predominance of the former was broken only by the age cohorts born after the war, starting to marry in the late 1960s (cf. Natsukari 1994: fig. 8.4). A survey of the mid-1950s showed that about three-quarters of marriages in large cities were arranged (Pharr 1977: 231). In the late 1960s *miai* fell below half, and among couples married around 1990, 85 per cent characterized them as 'love marriages' (Japan Foreign Press Center 1994: 21–22).

In the post-war period, arranged marriages in Japan increasingly changed meaning, referring more to the use of go-betweens and the matching of social and family criteria, than to parental decision (Hendry 1981; Applbaum 1995). Material considerations also play an important role in 'love marriages'. In a 1988 survey, 76 per cent of women in their twenties mentioned a husband's occupation and 87 per cent his income as an 'important' or 'very important' criterion for spouse selection (Natsukuri 1994: 147).

A considerable amount of patriarchal and/or parental weight has remained in the Japanese family, as a 'modified stem family' (Kumagai 1995). A fifth of all married couples are living with parents, and almost a third of 40–44-year-olds did so in 1995 (Japan Statistics Bureau 2000: tables 7 and 9; 2002: table 2.19). Typically, a contemporary Japanese wedding includes two ritual moments expressing the respect of bride and bridegroom to their parents (Edwards 1989).[1] But within the family the post-war 'salaryman' father has declined in status, absent as he often is, and the professional mother and housewife has gained status, although she is now also often working outside the family unless her children are small (Kumagai 1995). Nevertheless, according to the 1995 census, half of all married Japanese women under the age of 34 are full-time housewives.

In traditionally strongly Confucian Korea, major inroads into patriarchy occurred only with and after dramatic economic transformation of South Korea from the 1960s onwards. In the 1990s, most South Korean marriages were basically decided by the couple themselves, although go-betweens are common and parental approval has to be asked for. In 1991 a law of equal inheritance between sons and daughters was finally passed. (I.H. Park and L.J. Cho 1995; Hampson 2000). Family rituals are regulated by law, and promoted by governmental neo-Confucianism (Kendall 1996: 68ff). The oldest son still remains under his father's headship until the latter's death, even if he, as is now common, takes up a separate residence (Lett 1998: 83).

Son preferences are strong, and with birth control expressed in high male: female ratios, as in China, mainly by means of selective abortion (C.B. Park and N.H. Cho 1993; Das Gupta *et al.* 2000: table 1). However, in Korea, in contrast to China, this tendency seems to have been reined in. For the southern nation as a whole the sex ratio at birth remained at its 1990 level of 110:100 throughout the 1990s to 2000, and in the most misogynous province, Daegu, the ratio declined from 130 to 113:100 (Korea National Statistics Office 2001: table 19). In spite of Korea's stronger patriarchal traditions a smaller proportion of Korean than of Japanese couples are living with parents, little more than 10 per cent (Korea National Statistical Office 2001: table 16). The household division of labour also seems somewhat less unequal in South Korea than in Japan (Tsuya and Bumpass 1998).

Southeast Asian hesitations

The different cultures of Southeast Asia, from the Philippines to Sri Lanka, had in common that their patriarchy was looser, more mediated and mitigated, than the hard core of Asian patriarchal civilizations of Confucian East Asia, Indic South Asia and Muslim pastoralist West Asia. Southeast Asia included bilateral inheritance, bifocal household location upon marriage, more leeway for young couples, whether through later marriage, as in Sri Lanka, through Buddhist informality in Burma/Myanmar and Siam/Thailand, or through the legitimacy of massive-scale divorce among Muslim Malays.

Social change has been less dramatic and profound than in East Asia, while at least economically more rapid than in South Asia. On the whole, the impression one gets of Southeast Asia is that parents still have an important role in the marriage decisions of the young. But the emphasis is clearly more on parental consent, and possible veto, than on parental arrangement. The soaring sex trade has also given a new twist to the ancient tradition of polygamy and conspicuous male sexual consumption, a topic we shall return to in a later chapter on sex and marriage.

Like the rest of the Third World these days, Southeast Asia is also caught up in the entanglements of global and national feminism, confronting tenacious national fortresses of male power. Since 1999, newly democratic Indonesia, the heavyweight country of the region, has had a Ministry for Women's Empowerment. Among the unresolved tasks of that ministry is the 1974 Marriage Law, which, while in several ways formally egalitarian, stipulates (in article 31:3) that the husband is the 'head of the family', condones, under certain conditions, male polygamy, and allows for female marriage at the age of 16, requiring parental consent for people under 21 (Bergmann and Ferid 1976: Indonesia; Soewondo 1977; Robinson 2000; Parawansa 2002: 72). Half of all Indonesian women married before the age of 21 in 1995 (Jones 2002: 228).

The Asian Marriage Survey in Indonesia in 1979–80 highlighted a strong gender difference in parental arrangement, a common differential but not always as strong. Among wives born in 1953 and later about 60 per cent said their marriage had been arranged by their parents, while only a third of husbands said so. Part of this difference may be due to gendered interpretations, as couples diverged significantly in their assessment of parental involvement (Malhotra 1991).

The Suharto dictatorship resurrected/reinvented a pompous Javanese wedding ritual, including feudo-patriarchal rites of deference to senior authority, family and non-family, and introduced a special, formalized marriage culture among the military and the civil service (Pemberton 1994: ch. 5). This involved requiring permission from superiors to divorce and to take a second wife. It refrained from interfering with the custom of supplying men of power with ample sexual services, though – an ancient, pre-colonial custom in the archipelago (Suryakusuma 1996). Indeed, the sex industry expanded vigorously under the 'New Order', accounting for 1–2 per cent of the gross domestic product (GDP) before the crisis of the late 1990s, officially employing 75,000 prostitutes – a number the scholarly experts of the field think should be doubled or trebled. The Dutch colonial port and transport hub of eastern Java, Surabaya, is apparently still the capital of prostitution (Hull *et al.* 1999).

The Malay marriage custom was for long similar to that of South Asia, in the sense of very young, pubertal or pre-pubertal marriages for girls, parentally arranged. However, the mass practice of divorce (Jones 1994), without parallel in the world, with frequent re-marrying, indicated an underlying independence of the young generation, absent in South Asia. In the last third of the twentieth century the marriage age rose, and the divorce rate went down. The change was most dramatic among the Malays of Malaysia (and of Singapore). At the time of Malaysian independence in 1957, 54 per cent of Malay girls aged 15 to 19 were married; in 1991 5 per cent were. The mean age at first marriage had risen from 18 to 25 (Leete 1996: table 7.4). While this maturing of brides points to mounting independence, some state laws and courts of the legally pluralistic Malaysian federation still allow for the old Muslim practice of marriage of a virgin by her male guardian (Ahmad 1998: 15).

Substantial parental control of marriages, but usually short of unilateral arrangement and with normally most initiative coming from the youngsters themselves, seems to be the major pattern of the region. In Burma/Myanmar, which because of its society being cordoned off from the rest of the world is not likely to have changed much recently, this pattern of marital selection is traditional (Spiro 1977). In the Thai Marriage Survey of 1979–80 two-thirds of the women reported that their choice had been decisive in their marriage (Montgomery *et al.* 1988: 377), but parental consent remained a norm (Hahang 1992). The importance of the parental generation is underlined by the practice – at least in the northern countryside – of bridewealth being paid by the groom (and his family) to the bride's family, as the 'price for the mother's milk' (Whittaker 1999: 56–57). The family cycle normally includes a period of living with the parents of either spouse (Limanonda 1995: 71ff).

To north Vietnam, a significant input in the selection of a mate by the intending spouses seems to have arrived in Hanoi only by the late 1980s, and a rural study of 1990 found an overwhelming parental control over children's marriages (Pham Van Bich 1999: 127). What emerged very strongly from Vietnam was an intrusive involvement of the work-place organization, permitting or prohibiting couples from courting and marrying, a feature found also in China, although there also denounced by higher party organs (Bélanger and Khuat Thu Hong 2001). Officially, the Vietnamese Marriage Law of 1959 emphasized freedom of choice, but for the political authorities, and for family strategists, the class and political family background of a potential bride or groom was crucial. The 'New Cultured Family Campaign' launched in 1975, with the end of the American war and with the UN Women's Year, emphasized family equality and mutual support. The 1980s reforms of the regime have put an end to this political control of people's marriages. On the other hand, *doi moi* reforms have also meant commercialization of social relations, which under conditions of patriarchy and poverty has included a significant trafficking in women, largely to China but also to Thailand, and for local consumption (Le Thi Quy 2000).

While freedom of marriage has certainly increased and Confucian patriarchy been seriously eroded in Vietnam, there is still a strong and asymmetric inter-generational bond. Husband and wife may actually have come closer to each other, but the lineage is still often stronger than the couple. With the implosion of Communist and nationalist ideology, ancestor worship has returned. The old tradition of widespread long spousal separation, of labour migration, has been maintained and was reinforced by Communist state work assignments and urban migration control (Pham Van Bich 1999: 174f, 223ff).

The predominantly Catholic Philippines are the Southeast Asian antidote to Vietnam, in terms of mate selection. But the Philippines are also part of Asia, and arranged marriages, while becoming rare, have not quite disappeared (Cannell 1999). While unilateral parental decisions have been rare for a long time – and are of course incompatible with Catholic teaching – a third of Philippine daughters in the 1970s had sought parental approval for their marriage (Domingo and King 1992: table 7.1). Marital legislation was changed to equality in 1987, though, while Sri Lanka still maintains the principle of male headship (Bergmann and Ferid 1992: Sri Lanka).

The resurgent stridency of Islam, which in Southeast Asia has been relatively modest and politically kept under control, seems to have had contradictory effects on family and gender relations. On one hand, there is, in Indonesia and Malaysia, a spread of a specific female dress code, with an emphasis on headscarves and body-wrapping dresses, and a re-assertion of male rights to control how women behave. On the other hand, the new Islamic movement is a modern movement, spearheaded by educated young males, openly questioning their parents' heterodox customs (Jones 1994: 41ff).

Southeast Asia keeps a considerable patriarchal ballast, particularly in its largest countries. But although its changes, from a relatively favourable starting-point, have been hesitant it clearly belongs to the less patriarchal part of Asia. In a five-country study of married women aged 15–39 in the mid-1990s, the difference between South and Southeast Asia came out very clearly. On a six-point scale of domestic economic power – referring to purchases and to employment – ranging from a maximum female power (6) to complete patriarchy (0), Pakistan scored 1.3, India 1.65, Malaysia 3.05, the Philippines 4.01, and Thailand 4.33 (Mason 1998: table 6.4). Region, and regional family systems, rather than religion provides the dividing line. For instamce, in the Philippines, Muslim women of the southern Zamboanga had more intra-family economic power than the Catholics of Metro Manila (Mason 1998: 119).

Euro-American post-patriarchy: inequality

In Europe, the Americas and Oceania, a bulk of patriarchal norms were still in force in the 1960s, and where they had been dethroned they were in important areas still reproduced *sotto voce*, like parental marriage involvement in the Soviet Union and surviving patriarchal customs in the Balkans. However, the 'Western' 1968 Movement and its global extension swept away the stipulations of female subordination, as we saw above. There are still pockets of old patriarchal practices of father-inherited, father-housed and father-led families – among the Albanians in northern Albania and in Kosovo and Macedonia, in part also in Montenegro, Bosnia and Serbia (Kaser 1995: 450ff), on the Russian periphery, and in the Amerindian Andes, although the recent indigenous protest movement from Chiapas to Bolivia has brought forth an important female Indian leadership. But the nations of the different variants of the European family system have entered a new historical stage, of post-patriarchy.

The fall of Eastern European Communism meant an enormous impoverishment of the bulk of the population. In 2001 GDP in Russia and in most of the ex-USSR was down at its 1970s level (14 per cent below 1980), and much more unevenly distributed (UN Economic Commission for Europe 2002: table 8.1). Much of this impoverishment and mounting inequality have fallen on women and children (UNDP 1999a; UNICEF 1999), but are we here facing a patriarchal backlash? There have been attempts at such – by secular housewife ideologues and by revitalized religious forces, cheered on by some loud-mouthed anti-feminists – which could tap a substantial reservoir of tacit housewife preferences (as shown by Hungarian and Polish surveys in 1988–90; Einhorn 1993: 65 and ch. 6). But I have seen little hard evidence of a re-patriarchalization. Victorious Polish Catholicism made judicial divorce more difficult and costly, and restricted the right to abortion, but does not seem to have strengthened the powers of fathers and husbands (Kurczewski 1994; Szlezak 1994). Nor does the new Russian Family Code (Khazova 1998; Bergmann and Ferid 2001). The European Communist dismantling of patriarchy still looks irreversible, in contrast to significant cases of Chinese recidivism.

While the power of fathers and husbands does not seem to have increased, that of pimps certainly has. Trafficking in women has become a significant Eastern European trade, in this respect similar to China. In the mid-1990s, about 2 per cent of Latvia's employed women were selling sex (Ellman 2000: 136).

Post-patriarchy means adult autonomy from parents and equal male–female family rights – not just as proclaimed rights but as justiciable claim rights. This is a major historical change, virtually unknown and unpractised anywhere before, and as we have just seen, it is a recent change. However, it does not in itself mean gender equality. Men and women, as family members as well as in their individual capacity, are embedded in social and economic relations of inequality, often of recently increasing inequality. This study is limited to an analysis of the family, and it does not deal with the wider issue of socio-economic inequality, a topic I am pursuing in other contexts (Therborn 2003, 2004). But an indicator of the magnitude of the problem as it impinges upon post-patriarchal family and gender relations seems to be called for. Perhaps the best available single indicator is a measure of female to male mean income (Table 3.3). A post-patriarchal society gives men and women equal rights to act, but their relative income taps their ability to act.

The measure is crude, even adjusted for part-time employment, so little significance should be attached to small numerical differentials. Nevertheless, I think Table 3.3 is illuminating. Even in post-patriarchal societies, women have at most only barely three-quarters of men's economic resources of action, and this is likely to be an overstatement, as entrepreneurial and capital income is not included. Weighting by population numbers, it is fair to say that post-patriarchal women have little more than half (55–60 per cent) of the economic resources of men.

Table 3.3 Women's average income relative to men's in post-patriarchal
 societies, 2000 (%)

Panel A. Age groups 25–54, income adjusted for part-time employment[a]

Country	%	Country	%	Country	%
Austria	54	Greece	48	Sweden	72
Belgium	55	Ireland	38	Switzerland	45
Denmark	74	Italy	43	UK	47
Finland	71	Netherlands, the	47	Australia	48
France	71	Portugal	73	Canada	51
Germany	51	Spain	44	USA	62

Panel B. Unadjusted for part-time employment, all economically active[b]

Country	%	Country	%	Country	%
Western Europe		*Eastern Europe*		*Anglo New World*	
France	62	Czech Rep.	58	Australia	69
Germany	50	Hungary	58	Canada	62
Italy	44	Poland	61	USA	62
Spain	43	Romania	58		
Sweden	68	Russia	64	*Latin America*	
UK	61			Argentina	36
		East Asia		Brazil	42
		Japan	44	Chile	37
		China	66	Mexico	38
				Uruguay	51

Sources: Panel A calculated from OECD (2002: tables 2.4, 2.5, 2.15); Panel B calculated from
UNDP (2002: table 22).

Notes:
a Income is employment income, the female/male ratio of the hourly earnings of all wage and
   salary earners, and the gendered employment rates are recalculated assuming part-time is
   half-time employment.
b The income is an estimate based on the ratio of the female to male non-agricultural wage
   and the male/female shares of the economically active population. National dates may differ
   from 1991 to 2000.

Eastern Europe would be little affected by adjustments for part-time employment, if they had been comparatively possible, as it is a small phenomenon
there. But Japan, where as many women (25–54 per cent) work part-time as in
the UK (38 per cent), and also Mexico, would do worse than it does in the
table. But East Asia is hardly post-patriarchal, and the region is inserted
mainly as a memorandum item. Australia, Canada and the UK look very
different depending on whether or not large-scale part-time employment
among women is taken into consideration. The same would apply to European
countries like the Netherlands and Switzerland.

The optimists may find hope in the fact that in the OECD area young
women (aged 25–34) are more educated than men. In Hungary and Poland
women make up two-thirds of those having a tertiary education in the age
group. In France, Italy, Spain, Sweden and the Anglo New Worlds it is well
above half, in Japan slightly more than half. Switzerland, a century ago a

pioneer of higher female education, is now the redoubt of male educational exclusivity, Swiss women constituting only a third of the younger population with a tertiary education. Germany, UK and Korea maintain a smaller male advantage (OECD 2002: table 2.3). In Russia, Argentina and Chile women are also more educated (UNDP 2002: table 22). In China, on the other hand, women make up three-quarters of the country's illiterates (16–17 per cent of the population in 1995) and one-third of the students in higher education (Tan and Peng 2000: 155). Pessimists may object that the current information society is not a learned society. Above a certain level, and along several paths, a long education may not lead to a long radius of possible action.

Patriarchy into the twenty-first century

Compared to the world of 1900 patriarchy has had to retreat everywhere. The legal rights of women and children have been extended in all countries, and the expansion of education and paid work has extended autonomy. Dramatic socio-economic, political and cultural changes have undercut the authority of fathers and elders. However, the most important feature of the twentieth-century change of patriarchy is not its universal tendency. It is the variation in outcome as well as in timing.

The distance travelled has been greatest in East Asia, where the once-elaborate Confucian patriarchy and the 1898 modernization of the Japanese samurai family have been reduced to cultural residues. Enormous forces of violence and of new social construction were involved here: the fall of the Chinese Empire and the Communist Revolution, the bombing and destruction of all major Japanese cities and the US occupation; the wars, revolutions and economic take-offs of Korea and Vietnam. Eastern Europe was also shattered by war and revolution, which by mid-century put this, historically the most patriarchal part of Europe, in the forefront of European emancipation from patriarchy.

By contrast, changes have been modest by world standards in South Asia, West Asia and Africa, which are now the most patriarchal areas of the world. The socio-political convulsions of the century have been much more limited, in spite of liberation from colonialism, and, except for the oil wealth of some small populations, socio-economic developments have been less dramatic. Sub-Saharan Africa and South Asia are still predominantly agrarian in employment, and Central Asia relatively so, whereas West Asia and North Africa are less agrarian than Southeast Asia and Latin America (UN 2000a: chart 5.5). South Asia and Eastern Africa are also among the least urbanized parts of the world: in 2000 India was 28 per cent urban, Pakistan 33 per cent, Eastern Africa 25 per cent, but Western Africa 40 per cent, Northern Africa 49 per cent and Iran 65 per cent; the world average is 48 per cent (UNFPA 2002: 72ff). West Asian/North African patriarchy has its strong politico-religious props, whereas South Asian and sub-Saharan African patriarchy are being sustained by rural–agrarian structures and processes, for want of a strong political push in the opposite direction.

Southeast Asian patriarchy has not declined dramatically either, despite rapid economic growth lately. But it was not very stern to begin with.

Europe and America have finally developed into post-patriarchal societies – an epochal change. But the variation of timing is remarkable. The dismantling of patriarchy had its first Western European breakthrough in Scandinavia in the 1910s, but a decisive victory in the region had to wait another 60–75 years. In the Americas, there is the same time-span between the onslaught of the Mexican Revolution and the landmark institutional changes of the last quarter of the century.

Patriarchy, in the sense of a strong parental influence over children's marriages, a clear hierarchy of husband over wife, and institutionalized disadvantages of daughters, is still a major force in the world. While there are always individual and local exceptions, patriarchy governs at least a third, probably around 40 per cent, of the human population in South Asia, West Asia with Turkish qualifications, large parts of Central Asia, North Africa and most of sub-Saharan Africa except southern Africa and the West Coast. Substantial patriarchal minorities are also to be found in other parts of the world, in rural hinterland China above all, in rural Vietnam and other interiors of Southeast Asia, among Balkan Albanians and Serbs, among recent Afro-Asian immigrants to Europe and the New Worlds, in the Andean regions of Latin America, and among US Mormons. But their numbers are either rather small on a world scale, or, in China, impossible to estimate.

The post-patriarchal societies, where patriarchal practices have become normatively deviant, relegated to ethnic, religious or local enclaves, may be very generously defined to include all Europe, save some parts of the Balkans and of outback Russia, North America, Latin America except parts of the Andes, Japan and Korea with some extra generosity, and Oceania: in other words, currently the most economically developed parts of the world, with their close Eastern European and Southern American neighbours. Together they make up about 30 per cent of the world population, less than the clearly patriarchal part.

In between the patriarchal and the post-patriarchal regions and cultures of the world is a final third of humanity, mainly most of China and of Southeast Asia, but also recent transitional areas like Southern Africa and Turkey, and West Coast Africa and Andean America. Here, parents, and not seldom other relatives, have a significant say in marriage matters, the asymmetry of sexual rights is pronounced, and husbands tend to be dominant. At the same time, young people and married women have a recognized autonomy, and sexual pairing is a decision above all by the couple themselves.

In brief, despite tremendous, epochal changes, the burden of paternal and husband domination brought into the twenty-first century is a heavy one. Humanity's long patriarchal night is dawning, but the sun is still visible only to a minority.

Part II

Marriage and mutations of the socio-sexual order

'Marriage', said the Prophet 'is my way'.
> (Muhammed, quoted in Haddad 1998: 15)

The purpose of marriage is to unite two families with a view to harmonizing the friendship of two clans.
> (*The Book of Rites*, cited in Chiu 1966: 4)

Restraints upon marriage, especially among the lower class, are evidently detrimental to the public, by hindering the increase of the people; and to religion and morality, by encouraging licentiousness and debauchery among the single of both sexes.
> (W. Blackstone, cited in Gillis 1985: 142)

Sex is one of the things Middletown has long been taught to fear.
> (Lynd and Lynd 1929/1956: 169)

Meanings of marriage

Marriage has come in many shapes. Among the Akan people of contemporary Ghana, for example, a connoisseur has distinguished 24 typified heterosexual liaisons, according to varying kin involvement and knowledge, inter-family exchanges, rituals performed, and the social status of the partners (Vellenga 1983: 145). Ancient Hindu law distinguished eight forms of acquiring a wife, and listed them in a ranking of virtue, enamoration or falling in love being among the least virtuous, as number six (Mayne 1953: 121).[1] While not very concerned with classifications, a significant focus in this study is certainly on variations, in space and in time.

Human marriage is a socio-sexual institution, a part of the wider institutional complex of the family. As such it pertains to a specific sexual order, as well as to the more general social order. We may discern five major functions of marriage, of historically and culturally varying importance. No rank order of intrinsic significance will be made here. However, our main focus will be on marriage as a sexual order, a choice deriving from early twenty-first-century experiences, as well as from its relative neglect by previous family sociology and family economics.

Imagine a set of sexed bodies, moving around, encountering each other, attracting each other at random. Marriage imposes a certain order on this movement, sociologically speaking, a set of monopolies and trading restrictions into the sexual economy, if we use the perspective of an economist.[2] A sexual approach to marriage is, furthermore, an ancient tradition. An old Chinese account of the origins of marriage ran like this: 'In the beginning, men differed in nothing from other animals in their way of life. As they wandered up and down in the woods, and women were in common, it happened that children never knew their fathers but only their mothers.' Indiscriminate sexual intercourse was then abolished and marriage was instituted by the Emperor Fou-hi (Westermarck 1891: 8).

In order to understand the operation of marriage as a sexual order, we need to get an overview of the whole sexual terrain, locating marriage within a larger space of pre-marital and extra-marital sex, including homosexuality. In other words, we need to get a handle on the *sex–marriage complex*. This can, of course, only be done approximately, and only a few broad lines of historical development are within the scope of this book.

Whether marriage exists or not in a particular case may be a matter of dispute, serious enough to have to be settled in court (for some recent cases in East Africa, see Kabeheri-Macharia and Nyamu 1998 and Rwezaura 1998). But whatever more is required, sexual intercourse is a seal of marriage, and impotence is a valid ground for divorce even in strongly patriarchal and misogynous societies. According to the classical Hanafi school of Islamic jurisprudence, the husband's impotence was a wife's only possible reason for getting a divorce.[3] The Puritan tradition of Protestant Christian dissent rejected an ecclesiastical conception of marriage for a minimalist informality having two elements: a promise (of monogamy and fidelity) and a sexual consummation (Laslett 1965/1971: 152f). New England colonial laws and courts upheld the principle of no sex, no marriage, annulling non-consummated unions (Morgan 1966: 34).

However, marriage as a regulation of sexuality, its first function, and of romantic love, should be analysed comparatively in view of what it does not regulate, as well as in terms of its forms of regulation. It is the interface of sexuality and normativity, of drives, norms and actions, which we shall focus on as the sex–marriage complex. While extra-marital heterosexual practices and liaisons are clearly on the increase in many parts of the world, there is also a noteworthy drive for marital regulation and legitimation of homosexuality.

Second, marriage is also an arrangement of procreation, a way of caring for the offspring of sexuality, defining their legitimate descent, and the main or ultimate responsibility for their upbringing. In this vein, marriage may be seen as a natural order, characteristic of most birds and some mammals, including most, but not all, humans. The first great sociological historian of marriage, Edward Westermarck (1891: 19–20), held that 'marriage is nothing else than a more or less durable connection between male and female, lasting beyond the mere act of propagation till after the birth of the offspring'.

Third, marriage has historically been a major vehicle of social integration/ social division. The incest taboo and other variable rules of exogamy, of marrying out, have led to networks and alliances by inter-marriage, the focus of

Claude Lévi-Strauss's (1949/1969) classical analysis of systems of exchange of women among different male descent groups, while rules of marrying in – whether within a village, religion or 'race' – have created deep rifts in the social web of humankind. Part of these alliance transactions are often transfers of wealth, nowadays more important among the poor of this world, than among the rich. The dissolution of marriage, divorce, is still referred to as a major indicator of social disintegration or 'disruption' (cf. Fukuyama 1999).

Marriage bears upon two other aspects of a society: social status and house-holding. Marriage is a major mechanism for settling the social status of adults. This holds for males above all, whereas many societies until quite recently never treated a woman as an adult, or not before she became a grandmother, or at least the mother of a son. Most cultures have therefore treated weddings as a major rite of passage, sub-Saharan Africa and Buddhist Southeast Asia housing the main exceptions.

There is a historical political economy of sex–marriage family systems. Let us here formulate some hypotheses about this imbrication of sex–marriage order and political economy. Below we shall use them as tools of guidance.

Marriage rules and the control of sexuality, of female sexuality in particular, should be stronger among the propertied than among the property-less classes. Among the propertied, rules of inheritance should affect both age and frequency of marriage. Under the general norm of male supremacy, hier-archies of race/ethnicity and class will tend to evolve hierarchical male–female sexual relations, while excluding or minimizing marriage. The respect of formal rituals of marriage should vary with the internalization of the official value system, and with the proximity/distance to the agents of social control. Household production means stricter marriage norms than in economies where the household is only a consumption unit. Under conditions of house-hold production, the gendered division of labour should affect marriage patterns through its demand for male or female labour. Migration affects marriage and sex patterns, through the sex ratio of a given local population, and through its structuring of encounters and exits.

The major religions and value systems of the world have invested marriage with different meanings (on religious law in these matters, see Bergmann 1926: vol. I).

Among Christians the meaning of marriage has been the object of millen-nial disputes. In the Orthodox and Catholic interpretations, it is a holy act, a sacrament, a gift of divine grace. But the criteria for a properly constituted marriage was for long unclear and controversial within the Catholic tradition itself, because the Church also recognized that mutual consent of bride and groom to marry was per se a valid criterion, unless voided by the Church. This complex situation, with the established possibility of clandestine marriages, kept medieval ecclesiastical courts busy (Smith 1986: 52ff). The Counter-Reformation Council of Trent set out the Church doctrine: marriage was a sacrament and as such to be governed only by Church law. It should normally be contracted before the parish priest. There was no reference to parental consent, only to that of the direct parties themselves. Marriage was indissoluble, once sexually consummated. The Orthodox Church had always held that marriage could only be concluded by priestly blessing. Adultery, impotence, and a few other reasons were accepted as grounds for Orthodox divorce, while widow remarriage was clearly frowned upon.

Protestantism saw marriage as a worldly contract, though to be concluded by a clergyman according to church rules. Extensive sexual surveillance and jurisdiction were established in the Protestant world, from Calvin's time in Geneva and onwards, reaching their full deployment in the seventeenth century. In Sweden they were enshrined in the Church Law of 1686. Divorce was possible, for instance under conditions of adultery and abandonment. In the Anglican Protestant tradition the recognition of formless marriages by consent remained in some force until the 1753 Hardwicke Act in Parliament, setting down the criteria for a valid Anglican marriage, in England and Wales, excluding the overseas colonies, and Scotland and Ireland, which had their own rules. The practice of English marriage law from the fourteenth to the nineteenth centuries was summed up by its great historian Lawrence Stone (1995: 33) as a 'mess'.

While the Lutheran and Calvinist Protestants had developed their own ecclesiastical norms of proper marriage, they did in principle recognize marital jurisdiction by secular authorities. But in the Catholic countries, a bitter conflict between secular national authorities and a strong supranational Church developed from the French Revolution onwards. The Code Napoléon, the legal model of Latin Europe and Latin America, required a civil procedure for a valid marriage, and in the late nineteenth century the Papal contestation of it was a major issue in most Catholic countries (an excellent overview of Christian disputes on marriage was given by the British Jesuit G.H. Joyce (1948)).

In Hinduism, marriage is a religious obligation and a holy institution, a sacrament, and as such in principle indissoluble, even by death.

> In India marriage is a sacrament and no normal man or woman must die without receiving this sacrament. It is a custom among many communities that if a woman dies a spinster, a marriage ceremony is performed with the corpse and the woman is then burnt with the honours due to a married woman. There is greater freedom for man, but if a man who has gone through the initiation ceremony dies without marrying, he is supposed to become a ghost.
>
> (Karve 1953: 130)

A widow in Hindu tradition is socially dead, tolerated only as a perpetual mourner – to become Buddha, Gautama had abandoned his wife and son. Buddhism, as a classical canon, in contrast to all other religions or major ethical teachings, has rather little to say about marriage, which is something wholly of this world. Theravada (or Hinayana) Buddhism (currently dominant in Sri Lanka, Thailand and Myanmar) does not even provide a religious marriage ceremony (Limanonda 1995; Morgan 1996).

Islam and Confucianism both view marriage as a dissolvable worldly contract, but as such governed by strict rules of procedure and boundary. As Islam makes no distinction between religious and secular law, and as Islam, like Judaism – to whose original marriage conceptions Islam is very similar[4] – is a very legalistic religion, marriage resides squarely within the domains of Islamic law. Marriage is a focal concern of the latter. 'Almost every legal concept revolves around the . . . status of the marriage', says one recent textbook author (Pearl 1979: 42). Islam sees marriage primarily as an institution for regulating human sexuality, which in itself is not seen as something negative or second to celibacy. The Prophet himself was married, unlike Jesus. 'Marriage', said the Prophet, 'is my way [sunna].' 'The messenger said, Young man, those of you who can support a wife should marry, for it keeps you from looking at strange women and preserves you from immorality' (Haddad 1998: 15, 26n). Extra-marital sex is a major offence, by men as well as by women. The Koran (Sura 24: 2) is very strong on this point: 'The man and the woman guilty of adultery and fornication, flog each of them with a hundred stripes; let not compassion move you in their case' (Haddad 1998).

In the Confucian tradition, in this respect summarized by Master Meng (Meng-tzu, or Mencius, 551–479 BC), the relation between father and son is the primary of the 'Five Relationships' in human life, and filial piety the cardinal virtue. Mencius listed them and gave them their main ethical meaning in the following way: love between father and son, just dealing between ruler and subject, distinction between husband and wife, precedence of the old over the young, and good faith between friends (Mencius 1963: 118; Tu 1998: 125). 'Distinction', or 'separation' as it is sometimes also translated, between spouses seems to relate mainly to the household division of labour (Tu 1998: 127). Marriage is located within this setting, as the institution for the continuation of the line of the ancestors. Mencius said: 'there are three contraventions of the rule of filial piety, and of these the greatest is to have no progeny' (Mencius 1963: 140). But marriage has also another important function. According to the major normative code of the Confucian tradition in Imperial China, *The Book of Rites*: 'marriage ritual is the proper mergence of two family names in order to offer sacrifices to ancestors and carry on family lines' (Dai 1990: 183); 'The purpose of marriage is to unite two families with a view to harmonizing the friendship of two clans' (Chiu 1996: 4).

Ontological and normative conceptions of the chain of being which links the living, the dead or departed members of the community, the spirits, and God or Gods, constitute a central part of African religions. This gives the inter-generational family relation a strong religious charge. Marriage as institutionalized procreation, then, is a religious, moral duty (Mbiti 1989: 130). The person who leaves no descendants then breaks the link of life. The memory of one's descendants also assures one of a life after death. Marriage conveys a right to the outcome of female fertility, and this is crucial, more than sexual monopoly or biologically based legitimacy. In African marriage in 1900, there was also more of an economic aspect than in the other major cultures of the world, as the major part of predominant subsistence agriculture was carried out by women (Boserup 1970). Marriage was a crucial form of labour supply.

4 Sex and marriage in 1900

Fin-de-siècle scenes

Many different reportages could be made about sex and marriage around 1900. The period was in Britain seen as a time of 'sexual anarchy', of never-married old women, emancipated 'new women' – against whom a prominent author (Walter Besant) wrote an anonymous book of male revenge – and of homosexual men (Showalter 1960/1992). In Europe, prudish and hypocritical Victorian Britain glued its eyes to the homosexual trial of Oscar Wilde, while not quite recovered from the Bradlaugh/Besant[1] contraceptives trial in 1877; in fin-de-siècle Vienna, there were the erotic society portraits of Gustav Klimt and the novel sexual theory of Sigmund Freud; and in the embattled Third French Republic, with its *galanteries* and its *demi-mondes*, ordinary whores supplemented the virtues of the French family and enhanced the pleasures of its *chefs*. The Second Congress of Feminine Organizations and Institutions met in Paris in 1900, and debated, *inter alia*, §340 of the Code Napoléon, prohibiting any search for paternity outside marriage. The outcome of the congress debate was, that under certain circumstances a single mother should have a right to claim child support (Fuchs 1992: 90ff).

Henrik Ibsen had begun a questioning of the institution of marriage, and August Strindberg had brought to light a self-destructive psychological dynamic of married couples in Swedish short stories (*Giftas*, Marrying) and on the international stage. A third Scandinavian writer, whose words spread in the new century to Beijing and Tokyo in the east and to New York and Buenos Aires in the west, was Ellen Key (1911), who attacked conventional marriage from an original maternalistic Darwinism, in favour of free sexuality and a dedication to parenthood.

From the USA the rich heiresses of the robber barons were emerging onto the Atlantic marriage market, while at home Thorstein Veblen (1899/1953: ch. 13) was bringing up the malaise at leisure of the upper-middle- and upper-class housewife. The sexual radicalism of the New York avant-garde of the 1870s had been subdued, and the Societies for the Suppression of Vice and the Department for the Suppression of Impure Literature – associated with leading feminist organization, and the Women's Christian Temperance Union – were on the rampage: Tolstoy's *Kreutzer Sonata* was one of their most famous catches (D'Emilio and Freedman 1988: 159ff).

In Asia, the interface with the West started swinging, as in the variegated upper-class nightlife of the *Rokumeikan* entertainment complex of Tokyo, which with its dedication to Western dancing gave its name to a time of frivolity, 'the Rokumeikan era' (the 1880s above all; Seidensticker 1983: 68ff, 97ff), or in more blunt fashion the new centres of inter-continental prostitution, such as Tokyo's Yoshiwara district, Singapore's Malay Street, Shanghai and Surabaya (Henriques 1968: ch. 8). Local prostitutes had a much more significant place in the sexual order than today. In many cultures, for instance in Europe and in urban middle- and upper-class Latin America, prostitutes often provided the first sexual experience to young males. A visit to a brothel was a respectable rite of passage, to which a father could invite (and pay for) his son, as Marcel Proust's father did, and as Jorge Luis Borges' father offered to do. In Mexico City in 1905, registered and apprehended unregistered prostitutes made up 12 per cent of the female population aged 15 to 30 (Macías 1982: 44). But the Spencerian Minister of Education, Justo Sierra, dedicated himself to the education of middle-class girls, either for 'school life' (as teachers), or for the 'life of the household' (*vida del hogar*) (Barcelo 1997: 89). At the other end of the Latin New World, the Anarchist paper *La Protesta* was introducing discussions of free sex and free love into Buenos Aires and the Rio de la Plata region (Lavrín 1995: 129f).

The new Japanese Civil Code of 1898 stipulated monogamous marriages, thereby also giving rise to the notion of illegitimate children, while still providing some recognition of the old custom of concubinage. The great, if failed, intellectual reformer of the dying Chinese Empire, Kang Youwei, pleaded in his 1902 utopia of a universal commonwealth for a substitution of pure relationships, or 'contracts of intimate relations' for the ancient institutions of family and marriage (Teng and Fairbank 1954: ch. XVI; Ono 1989). In India an elite debate raged about the age of marriage, or more specifically the age of sexual consummation of marriage. Hindu law had no minimum age of marriage, but the Indian Penal Code of 1860 prohibited marital sex with wives under ten. The conservative view of the matter was that sexual initiation, and with it the celebration of the *garbhâdhâna* sacrament, was mandatory after the first menstruation, while the modernists argued that the Scriptures left the matter open (Kapadia 1966: 145ff; Robinson 1999: 42ff).

In 1902–3 all the colonies of South Africa, led by the Cape, outlawed sexual relations between white women and non-white men (Simons 1968: 106–7). Further northeast, in Uganda, the *lukiko*, the royal council of Bugandai, was trying to stabilize the brideprice, which was going up because of the inflationary effect of the colonial hut tax (Haydon 1960: 92).

The marital scandals of the time, in Egypt as well as in India, pitted strong women against the marriage norms of contemporary patriarchy. In India there was the case of Rukmabai, the friend of an Indian feminist named Ramabai, a young woman who had been married off as a child. Upon her father's death she refused to go to her husband, who then went to court demanding the restitution of his conjugal rights. In the first instance he lost, in the second he won, and public opinion was mobilized in his favour (Chakravarti 1990: 73ff).

In Egypt Safiyya Abd al-Khaliq al-Sadat also lost her court case, in 1904, against her father. Safiyya was legally of age, but her father–guardian had the right to challenge her marriage against his will, on the ground that it was a socially unequal match. Safiyya's husband Ali Yusuf was a journalist, for a nationalist newspaper, and her father was a notable (Baron 1991: 275).

In Europe by that time, on the other hand, the adulterous woman had become a literary heroine – Emma Bovary, Anna Karenina, Ana Ozores, Effi Briest – from France to Russia, from Spain to Prussia (see further Ruiz-Doménec 2003).

There is a certain titillating piece of truth in calling the then new century 'the century of sexuality' (Person 1999), even though a *scientia sexualis* began to emerge in the nineteenth century (Foucault 1976). After all, Havelock Ellis's monumental, multi-volume *Studies in the Psychology of Sexuality* started to appear in 1900,[2] and in 1905 Freud published his *Drei Abhandlingen zur Sexualtheorie*.[3] But there are no indications of a revolution in sexual practices.

All over Europe extra-marital births, related to the number of unmarried women in the very fertile age range of 20 to 30, were going down. How much of this was due to contraceptive practices, and how much to sexual precaution is unknown, but formal marriage was being strengthened, at the expense of informal cohabitation, among the popular classes of urban industrial Europe. More stability and formality were following upon the convulsions of nine-teenth-century migration and industrialization. In rural Germanic Europe, and on its Latin and Slavic fringes, the ancient custom, particularly in the less economically differentiated areas, of collectively termed 'night bundling' (*Kiltgang*), of pre-marital erotic, but usually not sexual, pairing of unmarried youth, was dying (Wikman 1937). But it had not yet been succeeded by the dance-hall youth culture, or individual 'dating', developing in the USA from the 1920s onwards.

The rule of universal marriage

There was a rule of universal marriage, but the rule was not a universal one. It held in most parts of the world, but not all – not in Western Europe, hardly in European settlements overseas, and definitiely not in Iberian America and the Caribbean. It held wide sway nevertheless, from St Petersburg to Tokyo, from the Kola Peninsula to the African Cape, for girls and women, above all.

There are no systematic global statistics from that time, but a combination of quantitative evidence and historical-cum-anthropological findings make some generalization possible. In China, there were by 1929–31 hardly any never-married women at all above the age of 34 (0.0–0.1 per cent), but around 6 per cent of males had not been married by the age of 40. This was hardly a post-imperial novelty, although statistics for 1900 are lacking. In the first two decades of the nineteenth century, 96 per cent of all noble women in the imperial capital of Beijing were married by the age of 30 (Lee and Wang 1999: tables 5.2 and 5.3). In Taiwan in 1915 and in Korea in 1925, respectively, 0.5 and 1 per cent of women had never married by the age of 45–49; in Japan in

1925 the figure was 2 per cent (the same for men); and in Russian Central Asia in 1897, 0.4 per cent (Mosk 1983: tables 1.2 and 3.8).

Chinese girls tended to marry in their late teens, at 17–19, and boys mostly at 20 (Lee and Wang 1999: tables 5.1 and 5.4). In some parts, in Taiwan in particular, there was a practice of child marriage among poor people. A girl child was adopted and reared as a daughter-in-law by her future husband's family. Polygyny or marriage-cum-concubinage was common mainly among the Qing nobility, but only among a third. One or two married males in a hundred among the total population were polygynous (Lee and Wang 1999: 76–77). On the other hand, in the upper or upper middle strata, it was not rare. Among lineages with genealogical records, it could range from 8 to 26 per cent of the men (Lee and Wang 1999: 184n), and among the fathers of college and high schoool students questioned in the 1930s, 16 per cent had a polygynous father (Lang 1946: 221).

The Japanese married later. According to the first national recording, in 1886, women married at 19, with a hefty increase in the next statistic 22 years later, to 23 (Kumagai 1995: 143). The regional differences were substantial, being about six years (Hayami and Ochiai 1996: figs 5A–B). Japan seems to have harboured some patterns of non-marriage and of informal or semi-official unions, however, as its marriage rate officially registered for 1900–4 is relatively low: 8.2 marriages per thousand population, staying below 9 until the 1940s, except for 1920–24 (Taeuber 1958: table 84). A marriage rate of 8–9 per thousand population is similar to the current American one, and was in the 1900s well below the Western European pattern of 12 per cent in Sweden, 16 in England and France, and 17 in Germany. There may be some statistical discrepancies here, and later Japanese census data show virtually universal marriage. But there was probably something more, perhaps due to belated adaptations to the new house registration system, *koseki*, enshrined in the new family code.

Japan, uniquely in the Afro-Asian area, had a not insignificant number of 'illegitimate' births around 1900. The Japanese learnt of illegitimacy from Europe and coined a new word for it to be included in the new household registration system set up in the Meiji era. But the phenomenon of children born to an unmarried mother – other than to a recognized concubine whose children were seen as legitimate – was not unknown in Tokugawa Japan. With the opening of society and with industrialization and urbanization the rates increased strongly in certain areas – in new cities of outlying Hokkaido, in the Tokugawa economic capital of Osaka and surroundings, and in the capital Tokyo. The average rural illegitimacy rate was 4 per cent, but the new Hokkaido city of Haokdate had a rate of 43 per cent in 1897, Osaka 23 per cent, and Tokyo 13 per cent. Hokkaido and the region from Osaka to Kyoto also had the highest marriage age (Hayami 1980).

In India in 1901, 96 per cent of women in the age group of 20–24 were already married. The singulate mean age at marriage (SMAM) was 13 for girls and 20 for boys. India then included today's Bangladesh and Pakistan. In the big northern states of India, in Bihar, Orissa and West Bengal, girls were betrothed by the age of 11, to husbands who were 10 years older on average. Given the negative view of the British colonial officials to child marriage, this may very well have been an overestimate (Xenos and Gultiano 1992: appendix tables 1–2). Hindu as well as Muslim law allowed for polygyny, but it was always a minor elite phenomenon (Kapadia 1966: ch. 3).

A debate about child marriage, and about the dismal fate of child or young widows, who were socially dead and prohibited from remarrying, had started in nineteenth-century India. It had brought some colonial legislation: the 1856 Widow Remarriage Act, explicitly allowing widows to remarry, and the stipulation of of the 1860 Penal Code that sexual intercourse with a wife below the age of 10 was punishable rape. But in practice hardly anything had changed by 1900, and a distinction between marriage and sexual consummation was already a Hindu social norm, with an unknown rate of violation. Among the lower castes children were apparently not seldom married off even before their birth (Kapadia1966: 146ff).

Child marriages were also common in the Dutch East Indies, today's Indonesia, particularly in Java, in part a legacy of the Indic civilization on the archipelago. From the stability of later data and from contemporary colonial reports, it seems likely that about half of West Javanese girls were married before the age of 16 (Jones 1994: 84ff; Blackburn and Bessell 1997). For want of an exact statistic, we may also listen to the bitter correspondence of a Javanese woman who later was adopted as an Indonesian national saint: 'I want to be free . . . so that I may never . . . never be forced to marry . . . But marry we must, must, must.' Raden Adjeng Kartini, who had won a scholarship to Holland, was married off and died in childbirth ten months after her marriage, in 1904, at the late age for Java of 24 (see Tiwon 1996: 55).

Southeast Asia encompassed a variety of marriage customs, including relatively late marriages in the Philippines (a SMAM of 21 in 1903), and a mean marriage age of 18 in Ceylon. The Indian age hierarchy was observed in Ceylon, with males a good 7 years older, but in the Philippines the bride–groom age difference was 4 years (Xenos and Gultiano 1992: appendix tables 1–2). The region also seems to have shown some variation on the major Asian theme of marital universalism apart from the Buddhist informality and the absence of a civil register in Burma and Siam. Later into the century, but long before marriage by everybody began to be at least marginally questioned, Ceylon in 1921 had 8 per cent of its women registered as non-married by the end of their fertile age, and (mainly) Catholic Philippines had 5 per cent spinsters in 1939 (Chesnais 1992: table 13.4).

In the Muslim heartlands of West Asia and North Africa, marriage was universal, although the modal age could vary. Statistics of the time are fragmentary, though. The Egyptian census of 1907 found that in the female age group of 20–29, 94 per cent had married, and 57 per cent already before their twentieth birthday. Forty-six per cent of urban Algerian Muslim women had married in their teens in 1903 (Goode 1963: 110). Polygyny, while legitimate, was a small minority practice: in Egypt, at most 6 per cent of married men had more than one wife (Baron 1991: 283), and in Istanbul about 2 per cent of married Muslim men (Quataert 1991: 162). It could occasionally be more widespread, as indicated in the inheritance records of Palestine Nablus from the mid-eighteenth to the mid-nineteenth century (Tucker 1991: 239), but its high cost kept it socially restricted (cf. Marcus (1989: 199ff) on eighteenth century Aleppo).

The rich Ottoman elite had for many years satisfied a large part of their sexual appetite by buying Circassian slave girls, whose children usually obtained their freedom without any stigma of illegitimacy. But under external pressure this outlet was drying up towards the end of the nineteenth century; an Anglo-Egyptian Convention of 1877, for instance, outlawed the slave trade (Baron 1991: 283).

Shia Islam in Iran had institutionalized a temporary marriage, *sighele*, the length of which could run from a few hours to many years (legally to 99 years). The scope of it seems to be unknown. Part of it might be seen as similar to prostitution, part of it to the East Asian or the Creole concubine relations. The offspring of a temporary marriage was legitimate, and part of its purpose was to produce an heir in a barren marriage (Roudolph-Touha 1979: 213ff), in this respect similar to secondary unions for the same purpose in Africa (e.g. Schapera (1950: 182ff) on the Tswana of today's Botswana).

Eastern Europe also belonged to the world of universal marriage. Eurasia stopped at the eastern shores of the Gulf of Finland. Women who had not married by the age of 50 amounted to 4 per cent in Russia and and 2 per cent in the Ukraine in 1897. The mean marriage age was 20 in Russia and close to 21 in the Ukraine. The gender age difference was minimal – negligible in the Ukraine, little more than a year in Russia (Coale *et al.* 1979: table 4.2). The marital age had climbed upwards in the nineteenth century, aided by the emancipation of the serfs. Landlords had previously pressured it down, with rules and fines (Czap 1976).

Eastern Europe also comprised Hungary and the Balkans. Never-married women amounted to 4.8 per cent in Hungary in 1900, 4.0 per cent in Greece (in 1907), 2.8 per cent in Romania, 1.6 per cent in Bosnia (in 1910), and less than 1 per cent in Bulgaria and Serbia. Mean age at marriage was around 20, somewhat lower in Serbia, and higher in Greece and Hungary at 22–23 (Sklar 1974; Botev 1990; Tomka 1999). The average annual marriage rate for 1900–4 was 17 per thousand population in Russia and 21 in Serbia (B.R. Mitchell 1998a: table 6, Europe).

In sub-Saharan Africa, kinship provided the core of all social relations, political and religious as well as economic. Separate political structures were absent, weak or, in their colonial form, alien and superficially imposed. African religions were practised in kin and family contexts, although local religious specialists were included. Islam has no church, although West Africa had important Muslim orders or brotherhoods. In this setting, marriage should be expected to be virtually universal, for women at least. The earliest censuses of African populations date from the second half of the 1950s, but there seems to be no anthropological or historical evidence countering an expert historical demographer of the 1960s concluding that 'almost everyone gets married in tropical Africa' (Walle 1968: 197).

Age at marriage varied considerably in sub-Saharan Africa. Girls were married in their early teens in the savannah and sahel regions of West Africa, and also in central Congo and northern Mozambique. Along the Atlantic coast, in the south and most of the east, marriage was usually later, in the mid- to late teens. Men married much later, having to accumulate means to pay bridewealth, very often only in their late twenties, and occasionally later. There were at least some peoples, where, like in China, there were some males who were squeezed out of the marriage market altogether (Walle 1968: tables 5.4 and 5.5, referring to the 1950s; Lestaeghe 1989).

Marriage was a very serious business in 1900. It involved substantial economic transactions between the families of origin involved. In Africa, the groom's family paid bridewealth to the bride's family. This transfer was, and often still is, the key criterion of a proper African marriage, as it is not marked by any important religious ceremony in African indigenous religions. In northern India, and among its higher castes in particular, the exchange goes in the opposite direction, in the form of a dowry brought by the bride. While it typically includes personal items, such as jewellery, fine clothes and household utensils, the dowry is also expected to bring wealth to the groom's family, into which the new couple is entering. In China too the bride's dowry was usually the major transaction, but among the lower castes and in the southern parts of India, brideprice or bridewealth was often paid as well, a practice most deeply rooted in southern China (Lang 1946: 126). The Japanese betrothal payment, *yuinô*, goes from the groom's family to the bride's (Edwards 1989).

Muslim customs usually involved two-sided transactions, but the most important is usually the dower, *mahr*, paid or legally pledged by the groom and his family to the bride (not to her family). It is a key stipulation of Muslim marriage law, as it is meant to provide a certain elementary security for the bride, in case of divorce or death. Weddings tended to be big and expensive, though of course varying with class (Esposito 1982; Nasir 1990). Sub-Saharan Africa is an exception, usually holding much more grand burials (see further Goody 1976, 1990).

There was little youth in this world around 1900, and what there was can hardly have been very attractive. Girls of India – married off before their menarche – had mostly no youth at all, going directly from childhood to a patriarchal marriage. Many girls of Java and of West Asia were in the same situation, as were the child-betrothed 'minor wives' of China. Seclusion separated the sexes in South and West Asia, and sex segregation was the rule of social life everywhere else – outside Euro-American areas. Adult sexual control was strict and, seemingly, effective, save in some African populations. African age groups could constitute some sort of youth culture to young women as well as to young men. Girls were going to school in Japan, and as in the Philippines married late by Asian standards. The textile industry, from Japan to the Ottoman Empire, and silk-making, from the Pearl River Delta in southern China (Stockard 1989) to Bursa in Anatolia (Quataert 1991), recruited young female, unmarried labour. Japan actually pioneered industrialization by female labour: in 1900, 60 per cent of the Japanese factory labour force was female (Stearns 2000: 108). But it all occurred under conditions of chaperoning and with hardly any leisure.

Young men had more freedom, both because they married later than women – 7 years on average in South Asia and 10 years in Ottoman Istanbul (Duben and Behar 1991: 224) – and because they were males. In the Buddhist countries they had a specific youth culture of temporary monkhood. Wage-labour entailed opportunities of class comradeship, but under harsh conditions. Coffee and tea houses were open to them, as were brothels. But being unmarried they were dependent on their families of origin, and clearly subordinates in strongly hierarchical societies.

Youthful, pre-marital sex must have been rare under these systems of surveillance, apart from variable numbers of males taking recourse to prostitutes. Some African populations did allow for pre-marital sex, though. The Tallensi of what is now Ghana and the Nkundo of Congo, for example, had rules distinguishing women who a man may have sex with but could not marry, due to kinship rules (Radcliffe-Brown 1950: 61).

The peculiarities of Western (European) marriage

In European social history there is a dividing line running from Trieste to St Petersburg, setting apart a Western marriage pattern from the rest of Eurasia, from Africa, and from the pattern of major parts of the Americas. A British–Hungarian statistician-cum-demographer, John Hajnal (1965), was the first to see it, although an East–West family division was noticed by the family sociologist Frédéric Le Play (1855/1982). Later research has qualified and supplemented the finding, but not erased it. Its extent has been demarcated more clearly by June Sklar (1974) and by the Austrian historians Michael Mitterauer and, above all, Karl Kaser (2000), who has provided plausible reasons for it, going back to the early Middle Ages. Research since Hajnal has found a great variety of marriage patterns within modern Western Europe, in particular in Spain (Reher 1997: 155–56), Portugal (Livi-Bacci 1971: 41ff), and Italy (Barbagli 1984: appendix I) (cf. Laslett 1983: table 17.5; Ehmer 2002; Kertzer 2002).

By and large, the 'Hajnal Line' corresponds to current national borders more than to the political boundaries of 1900. If one conceives of Europe as beginning in the Mediterranean, we may say that the line runs through the Ionian Sea and the Adriatic,[4] along the border between Slovenia and Croatia, and the old boundary between Austria and Hungary, which currently divides the Austrian provinces of Styria and Burgenland. It then continues between Slovakia and the Czech lands, historically the border between Hungary and Bohemia, after which it bends eastwards through contemporary Poland, demarcating Cracow and the southeast in order to locate the rest of Poland and the Baltic Republics in Western Europe, as well as Finland, northwest of St Petersburg.

The Western European marriage system, which in modified, weakened form was transplanted to the overseas settlements of the Americas and Oceania, has three characteristics as a sex–marriage complex: late marriages, a high proportion never marrying, and (outside the Mediterranean) a combination of a significant, non-hierarchical sexual informality – expressed in pre-nuptial conceptions, non-marital births, and informal cohabitation – with a strongly normative sexual order (Table 4.1).

The divide is very clear, and it also holds for the Western European countries not listed in Table 4.1 (Belgium, the other Nordic countries, Scotland). West of the line, the average age of first marriage is 24 or higher, east of it is 22.5 or lower. West of the line between a tenth and a fifth of women never marry, east of it at most 4–5 per cent never marry. The Eastern European marriage pattern, in terms of age and frequency, is closer to that of Central and East Asia than of northwestern Europe. Hungary was in this respect closer to Kazakhstan than to the other half of the Double Monarchy. Demographically, if not culturally, Asia did begin with the road east from Vienna, as Austrians sometimes said at the time.

The key pillar of the Western European pattern of late marriages and high celibacy was the principle of 'neo-locality', i.e. that a marriage should

Table 4.1 Eastern and Western European marriage systems *c.* 1900 (female mean age at first marriage, and percentage never married by age 45–49)

Western Europe	Age at marriage	Never married (%)	Eastern Europe	Age at marriage	Never married (%)
Austria	27	11	Bosnia	20.5	2[d]
Baltic lands	26	9[a]	Bulgaria	21	1
Czech lands	25	9[b]	Croatia	20	2
England	26	15	Greece	–	4
Finland	25	15	Hungary	22.5	5
France	25	12	Romania	20	3
Germany	26	10	Russia	20	4
Italy	24	11	Serbia	20	1
Netherlands, the	27	14	Slovakia	21	–
Polish lands	24	8[c]	Ukraine	21	2
Portugal	25	20	Caucasus	18	1[e]
Spain	24	10	Central Asia	17	<1[f]
Sweden	27	19	Kazakhstan	18	<1
Switzerland	26	17			

Sources: the main source is Coale *et al.* (1979: table 4.2), supplemented by Sklar (1974: tables 1–2), on Czech and Polish lands, and on Bosnia and Slovakia, by calculations from Kaser (1995: table 22), using Hajnal's (1953a: 170) method for calculating the age at first marriage (SMAM), and by Botev (1990: tables 1–2) on Greece.

Notes:
a Arithmetic mean of then Russian provinces Estonia, Latvia and Lithuania.
b Arithmetic mean of then Austrian Bohemia and Moravia, and referring to the age group of 40–49.
c Mean of then Russian Vilna and Vistula, German Posen and West Prussia, and Austrian Galicia.
d 1910.
e The average of Armenia, Azerbaidjan and Georgia.
f Current Kyrgyzstan, Tajikistan, Turkmenistan and Uzbekistan.

normally be the initiation of a new household, a principle distinguishing it not only from African and Asian, but also from Eastern European family formation. Medieval and early modern Western Europe were basically settled lands, which meant that neo-locality had to be tied in with a system of inheritance, of the transfer of property, i.e. land above all, from one generation to the next. The inheritance pattern most clearly sustaining the West European marriage was one in which the land was transferred to one heir only, usually but not always the oldest son. The other siblings could be, and were normally, entitled to inheritance too – daughters being endowed with a dowry upon marriage, for instance – but this had to be catered for without dividing up the land, including the tenancy. The new household did not have to wait for the death of the previous owner or tenant. There developed contracts of retirement, whereupon a father left his land to his heir, while securing a cottage, or other accommodation, and provisions from his successor.

This basic system had several variants, in historical time as well as in local space, but it set Western Europe apart from the rest of the Eurasian continent. In the latter, equal male inheritance prevailed, with land either partible, after the death of the father, or held collectively, under a household head. The divide in Europe has been traced back to the early Middle Ages, and its modern trajectory seems to coincide with the medieval German move eastwards, the *Ostkolonisation* (Kaser 2000: ch. 2). In the west, the Atlantic was no boundary. The Western European family very clearly comprised the Nordic islands and the British Isles, and extended south towards the Straits of Gibraltar.

Setting up a new household upon marriage required a certain amount of resources of the new couple, differing from one class to another. In a landed society, it meant, first of all, access to land, which in a mostly settled society meant access rights, mainly by inheritance or (tenant) succession. Access was possible not only by parental death, but also through retirement agreements with the parental generation, a common phenomenon of agrarian Europe (Gaunt 1983). When only one son (or daughter if no son) could inherit the land, which was very often the case, the other siblings were forced to try to accumulate resources for marriage some other way, and many of course failed.

Women and men of the labouring classes were expected to have saved enough, from meagre wages, to be able to acquire and to deck out their own housing and not seldom to have learnt a trade, in order to marry. The severe normative restrictions on marriage – constraints which, of course, could be 'worked' in various ways – were mitigated somewhat by an old and widespread practice in Western Europe, of children and young people, and the offspring of farmers, circulating as waged servants among non-parental households.

The principle of neo-local marriage has a strong socio-economic flexibility, which sustains its institutional equilibrium. It can be applied to the vastly different social stations of very unequal class societies. It can adapt itself – or, rather, be adapted by social actors – to changes in farm prices, wages or mortality rates, by tightening or loosening the requirements of marriage (cf. Wrigley 1987: part III). The mechanism was discovered by the first demographers-statisticians of Europe. 'From the days of Süssmilch [i.e. 1740] till the middle of the last [nineteenth] century', Westermarck (1921: 390) wrote in the fifth edition of his *History of Human Marriage*, 'it was regarded almost as a statistical axiom that the number of marriages varies inversely with the price of corn'. What changed with industrialization was not the marital adaptation mechanism, but the indicators of good and bad times.

The Western European settlers overseas modified their marriage pattern substantially, under the impact of less restricted access to land, better economic opportunities generally, and, particularly in the plantation and estate economies from the southern United States southwards, hierarchical race relations and racially unbalanced sex ratios. The latter kind of society, as noted above, gave rise to a new family system, the Creole, which will be dealt with separately. The settlers of the White British Empire and its successors tended to marry more and earlier than in Britain, and thereby also to produce more children (Table 4.2). But they stayed within their original Western European parameters of marriage.

The sexual order outside marriage

The peculiar Western European marriage system was sustained sexually by four additional features of the sexual order. At one end was outright repression. In several areas landless labourers were by law, and by landed support of the law, forbidden from marrying. At the other was toleration of informal cohabitation. In between were a legitimacy of celibacy and prostitution. Emigration was also from the mid-nineteenth century an important outlet from the areas of highly restrictive marriages, such as Ireland, Galicia, northern Portugal, and large parts of Scandinavia.

Repression of marriage was the case, for instance, in Alpine parts of Bavaria and Austria (Mitterauer and Sieder 1982: 123) and in Iceland (Pinson 1992). Even if not forbidden, labour and housing markets, and church control could make deviant coupling difficult or unattractive.

Table 4.2 Female age at first marriage and percentage of women never married in North America, Oceania and Britain around 1900

	Marriage age	*Never married by age 50*
Australia	24	9
Canada	25	11
New Zealand	25.5[a]	8
USA (whites)	24	8
Great Britain	26	15

Sources: Marriage age. Australia: McDonald (1975: table 43); Canada: Festy (1979a: table I.8) referring to women born in 1846–50; among the cohort born in 1886–90 the age had gone down to 24; New Zealand: Festy (1979b: table B); US and Britain: Haines (1996: table 3). Non-marriage, referring to the generation born 1851–55 for the non-European countries: Festy (1979b: table A), for the USA a concurring figure is found in Haines (1996: table 2); for Great Britain, Hajnal (1965: table 2).

Note:
a Refers to women born between 1886 and 1890.

The religious orders and the clergy provided a cultural alternative to marriage in Catholic countries. Around 6 per cent of the adult population of eighteenth-century Spain were living in religious celibacy (Quale 1988: 236). That way out was not available to Protestants, whose clergy was usually positively expected to be married. However, all Christian Europe was alike in not attaching any religious stigma to celibacy, in not seeing an intrinsic value in fertility, nor in practising any kind of ostracism of solitary persons, which may often be found in other parts of the world.

Finally, large-scale prostitution furnished alternative sexual outlets, from the enormous sex industry of big cities, like Rome (which in the Renaissance became 'the capital of prostitution', Goody 2001: 115), Venice, Paris (*'cette grande courtesane'*, Balzac) and London, to the well-spread supply of village whores. The little and late urbanized Lutheran countries of the north had never had any large-scale sex trade. But in the late nineteenth century Sweden introduced an experiment with regulated prostitution. In Stockholm in 1890 there was one registered prostitute per 279 inhabitants (or about one per 80 males aged 15–64). In a small university town like Uppsala the registered supply was one per 430 inhabitants, in the larger towns the ratio ranged between 1:400 and 1:900 around 1900 (calculations from Lundquist 1982).

From the mid-eighteenth century the ratio of extra-marital births increased in Western Europe. The tendency was general, but its trajectory was very uneven, in the timing and, even more, in the height of its curve. In England it had oscillated between 2 and 4 per cent since 1550, but then it rose to about 6 per cent of all births by 1800 (Laslett 1980: 19). In Paris the ratio was around 10 per cent in the first third of the eighteenth century, climbing to a century peak at one-quarter of all births in 1765–74, then falling off somewhat in the pre-revolutionary and revolutionary period, before rising to new heights from late Napoleonic times and the Restoration (Meyer 1980: 252). In Sweden, births out of wedlock made up a little more than 2 per cent of all births in 1750–75, growing to 5 per cent in the 1790s (SCB 1999: table 3.6). Under very different economic, political and religious conditions a fascinating process of changing human intimacy began. Processes of secularization and of proletarianization may be suspected.

This process of 'bastardy' peaked before the story of this book, in England as early as 1845, and in most of Europe it was going down from about 1880. In most of the capital cities it became a major phenomenon, making several figures for the year 2000 pale by comparison. In Paris, 'capital of the nineteenth century', a third of all births for the later part of the century were outside marriage, by the end of it a good quarter (Meyer 1980: 252; Walle 1980: 267n; Ratcliffe 1996: 338n). In 1850, half of all births in Habsburg Vienna were out of wedlock, and almost half (46 per cent) in Stockholm (Matovic 1980: 336). Munich had also half of its children born outside marriage in 1860, and the provincial capital of Carinthia (Klagenfurt) holds perhaps a European record for a community of some size, with 69 per cent extra-marital births in 1870–74 (Mitterauer 1983: 150n, 23).

London was unusual in this context, and very different also were the British industrial cities. London, including its proletarian East End, was always below the national average, which itself was internationally low, culminating at 7 per cent. London never reached much above 4 per cent of 'illegitimate' children, and Manchester went only a few decimals above 6 per cent (Laslett 1980: 63).

From the late nineteenth century, the illegitimate ratio declined. France had its national peak in about 1900, Sweden in 1910, and Portugal in 1930, but other Western countries peaked before 1900 (Shorter *et al.* 1971: fig. 1). By 1880 Munich had gone down to 28 per cent, Berlin to 13 per cent, Paris to 28 (Knodel and Hochstadt 1980: table 12.1; Walle 1980: 267n), and by 1901–10 no longer half but only a third (36 per cent) of Stockholm babies entered the world outside marriage (SCB 1917: table 24). But where the social transformation had not settled, the figures were still very high. In 1898, 50 per cent of all births to Orthodox mothers in St Petersburg were out of wedlock (Mitterauer 1983: 151n).

Before venturing into the difficult task of explaining the variations of Western illegitimacy, with its strong and specific sub-national variations, let us consider the international picture around 1900 (see Table 4.3).

The international picture puts Austria, Portugal and Scandinavia – with Finland and Norway only half-way in – in one corner, of high extra-marital births, and the Balkans, Russia (in spite of St Petersburg and other Russian cities), the Netherlands, and Anglo-America in the other. In between, at the higher end are found Czechoslovakia, France Germany, Hungary and Romania, and at the lower end England and New Zealand, Spain and Switzerland. The centre, if there is one, is occupied by Australia, Italy and Poland. This is not quite a conventional line-up of states, in terms of welfare or otherwise. A

Table 4.3 The percentage of children born out of wedlock among live births in Europe, and in ex-British settlements, 1896–1900

Country	(%)	Country	(%)
Austria	14	Poland	6
Belgium	8	Portugal	12
Bulgaria	0.4[a]	Romania	9
Czechoslovakia	10[b]	Russia	3
Denmark	10	Spain	5
Finland	7	Sweden	11
France	9	Switzerland	5
Germany	9	England and Wales	4
Greece	1[c]	Scotland	7
Hungary	9	Canada (Ontario)	2
Iceland	16	US whites	1.5[d]
Italy	6	US blacks	12.5[d]
Netherlands, the	3	Australia	6
Norway	7	New Zealand	4[e]

Sources: USA: Smith (1980: table 17.1); other countries: Hartley (1975: tables 4–5)

Notes:
a 1901–5; b 1916–25; c 1921–30; d 1920; e whites only.

similar behaviour among US blacks, Portuguese and Swedes has not often been noticed either.

The regional pattern is also noteworthy, both because of the wide intra-national variation (Shorter *et al.* 1971: map 1), and because of its shape. It is sometimes, but not always, an outcome of industrialization and urbanization. In some countries, a high proportion of extra-marital births is above all an urban phenomenon: in France, Italy, Russia and, on the whole, in the Habsburg monarchy (Walle 1980; Mitterauer 1983: 29). In Sweden in 1901–10, extra-marital birth was primarily a capital-city custom, although with some-what more than 300,000 inhabitants Stockholm was far from a metropolis. While the national proportion was 13 per cent of all births, in Stockholm it was 36 per cent. But the countryside of a couple of the northern provinces had ratios equal to or just above the urban ratio exclusive of Stockholm, at 16.6 per cent (calculations from SCB 1917: table 24).

In Germany there was no urban gradient tendency: in the eastern and central parts of the country, rural illegitimacy was higher than urban, while it was the other way around in western areas. Nor did Berlin have a particularly high rate, actually having a lower rate than Königsberg or Breslau (Knodel and Hochstadt 1980). In Britain the relationship was rather the inverse. Extra-marital births were lower in London, and in Manchester and many other cities, than the national average, and highest in some 'rogue counties' (Laslett 1980) like Cumberland, Norfolk and Nottinghamshire, or even more so in Radnorshire and Montgomeryshire in Wales (Hollingsworth 1981: table II). Peter Laslett (1980: 29ff, 63f) concluded for nineteenth- to early twentieth-century England a case 'general inferiority of the urban population in illegitimacy'.

If urbanization, industrialization, and general level of economic development provide no straightforward accounts for the continental variations of extra-marital births, the same is true of religion. High and low rates can be found among Catholic, Protestant and Orthodox Christians. The extremely high rates in some large Catholic areas – most of Austria, Bavaria and northern Portugal – are surprising, while the low rates of Brittany or Ireland are perhaps not.

To fully explain the pattern of illegitimacy is beyond the aims of this study, but it throws a challenge to our understanding of the socio-sexual order, in the present as well as the past, which cannot be passed by. When Michel Foucault (1976) attacked what he called 'the repressive hypothesis', the notion of a modern era of sexual repression, seeing the period instead as an 'incitement to discourse' on a polymorph sexuality, he was hardly thinking of the hetero-sexual practices of Austrian and Icelandic labourers or Portuguese peasant youth. However, the integration of their deviant sexuality into closely knit, basically religious rural societies testifies to a complexity of the Western European sex–marriage complex, which might be taken as a practical counter-part to the discursive configuration, with which Foucault was concerned.

A significant proportion of births out of wedlock was an inherent possibility of the Western European family system. The late marriage rule left a long period between puberty and legitimate sexuality, on average more than a decade. The system further included a considerable amount of subtlety in its handling of pre-marital sex. Pre-nuptial conception might sometimes be sneered at, but was in many contexts basically respectable. The Christian betrothal rule, especially in Scandinavia, contributed to almost-legitimate coupling before the wedding night. A widespread pattern of pre-marital mingling of youth of both sexes, in the Germanic rural peripheries above all – in Scandinavia and in the Alpine regions – including customs of ritual night courting (Wikman 1937), gave opportunities for popular courtship. It was expected not to involve sexual intercourse, but sometimes did. Pre-nuptial conception was not surprisingly frequent in early modern Western Europe, amounting to one legitimate first birth of eight in France in the mid-eighteenth century, and one third of all English first births within wedlock in the early nineteenth century (Wrigley 1987: 284–85).

Furthermore, household formation in northwestern Europe gave young unmarried people ample opportunities to meet. This was the custom of the young entering service in other households, as maids, servants, labourers or apprentices, and was common among the sons and daughters of farmers and not only among the property-less (Hajnal 1982). This labour circulation was a way of evening the labour supply of farmers' households across the life-cycle, and for the young was a means to an income, out of which they could save for future marriage.

Births outside marriage can come to cohabiting couples as well as to single mothers, and the social dynamics behind the two is very different. In Paris in the 1880s, between a fifth and a quarter of births out of wedlock seem to have been to cohabitees (Walle 1980: 267, 269). Adult marriage, complex, and partly intrinsically ambiguous Christian marriage norms (as noted above) could in transitional times of weakening old social controls lead to intricate combinations of marriage and non-marriage. Among couples registering banns in Stockholm in the 1860s, i.e. going through the Lutheran marriage procedure, only 55 per cent lived apart and had no pre-marital children. That is, only half of this norm-following population corresponded to the conventional expectations. A good 40 per cent were already cohabiting (having the same address). About a tenth of all the couples getting married had non-marital children, half of whom were born in cohabitation (Matovic 1980: table 15.2). In nineteenth-century Paris among the popular classes about a third of couples seem to have been cohabiting before getting married (Ratcliffe 1996: 336).

We are confronting a large-scale process of change, beginning in the late eighteenth century and subsiding in the late nineteenth century. An explanation has to cover the span of the whole process. The enormous variation of the same process also has to be accounted for. But even though we are dealing with a large-scale, fascinatingly opaque process, we should also keep a sense of proportion. Even in a country scoring high on extra-marital fertility like Sweden, the actual number of women bearing a child outside marriage was a small minority. In the decade of 1901–10 the percentage of unmarried women in the highest risk group, aged 20–30, giving birth to a child was four (SCB 1944: table F).

Let us begin by touching on a special cause of variation, national and international, which has not been subject to systematic analysis but which clearly has a bearing on the explanation, procedures of registration and of categorization. How is marriage legally defined, and how is it registered? How are births categorized and registered?

Take the example of Paris. French family legislation, with its requirement of notarized parental consent (for men under 30 and women under 25), and French/Parisian administrative regulations made a proper marriage prohibitively expensive for poor people. Just the cost of the paperwork for a civil marriage could require more than one month's wages for a poor working couple (Fuchs 1992: 101–2). British marriages, as we saw above, were much easier than this, with easy urban residence registration and administrative privacy. There also developed a low-key urban plebeian marriage, further helped by an easy civil procedure from 1837 (Gillis 1985: ch. 7). A good part of the remarkable difference between English and continental cities must have derived from different legal–administrative procedures (Laslett (1980) apparently did not think so, but he offered no alternative explanation for the exceptionally flourishing marriage life among the urban proletariat of England). The Scottish ratio of extra-marital births was consistently higher than the English, three percentage points in 1911, and Scottish vital registration was known to be more careful than the English, while Scots (like continental) law allowed for 'bastards' to be legitimated by subsequent marriage. On the other hand, the puzzle remains, that while the British countryside was rather similar to mainstream Europe – with the ten highest English/Welsh counties having an illegitimacy ratio of 12 per cent in 1901, and 30 per cent in 1861 (Hollingsworth 1981: table II) – London and other cities stayed very much lower.

The Anglo-Saxon common law tradition included a presumption that a couple living together and not denied respectability by their local community, were de facto married. This assumption is very different from civil law conceptions – or from canon law countries with births registered in the baptismal records of the Church – and is clearly one of the reasons for the low proportions of illegitimacy in the Anglo-Saxon New Worlds. After Independence, American courts and legislators extended the inherited presumption of matrimony and legitimacy (Grossberg 1985: 201ff).

The dynamics of change had three major channels to operate through; a change of orientation among the actors, alterations of the normative order of sexual controls, and through material–structural changes of the possibilities of sexual encounters and of the prospects of marriage. Their relative importance and their modes of combination are likely to haver varied greatly over time and place.

About the orientations of the actors 100 to 200 years ago we have little direct evidence to go by. Whether one should, with the eminent historian Edward Shorter (1977: 86ff), talk of a 'sexual revolution' in this sense from the late eighteenth to mid-nineteenth century still seems to be more a question of belief in a hypothesis than of a conclusive verdict. But two points may be made, both indicating that actors' orientations were changing.

First, a certain, partial process of secularization was going on, a weakening of obedience to the rites of the Church, which would increase the chances of a weakened commitment to official Christian sexual morals. In France, for instance, from the mid-eighteenth century the increase of illegitimacy and of the number of pregnant brides is accompanied by a lower demand for masses for the dead and a lower recruitment to nunneries (Vovelle 1985: 37ff). Secularization was uneven and non-linear, but the tendency towards it meant that extraordinary religious efforts were needed to keep traditional sexual mores. Such efforts left their traces in the territorial demography of the Protestant revivalism, in the early nineteenth-century United States (Smith 1980: 373ff), in southwestern Norway and evangelized provinces in Sweden (e.g. the exceptional northern province of Västerbotten), in re-invigorated Calvinism-cum-Catholicism in the Netherlands and Switzerland, or in intensely Catholic Tirol (Mitterauer 1983: 36) or Brittany.

Secondly, the decline of extra-marital births coincided with a continental wave of fertility decline (see Part III). This is plausibly a good indicator that the practice of birth control by the sexual actors accounts for at least part of the decline (cf. Shorter *et al.* 1971).

The normative order of sex and marriage had several aspects in pre-modern and early modern Europe. Cisleithanian Austria, Bavaria and Iceland, for instance, had regulations to prevent or to make it difficult for servants to marry, the idea being that they could not be expected to afford a household of their own (Mitterauer and Sieder 1982: 123; Pinson 1992). From the other side, poor law authorities had an interest in preventing single motherhood, claiming parish support, so in Protestant countries, for instance in England (Stone 1995: part IIB) and in Sweden (Jarrick and Söderberg 1998: 98ff), ecclesiastical courts sentenced single fathers and mothers to marriage. Extra-marital sexual intercourse was a punishable criminal offence, although, of course, was not often prosecuted outside well-policed villages and towns.

It may at any rate be taken as a sign of a more tolerant sexual order, that extra-marital sex between two single adults was explicitly de-criminalized in the late eighteenth century. In 1769 the Enlightenment Prime Minister Pombal took it off the list of crimes in Portugal (Kuznesof 1991: 244). In Sweden the public church shaming for extra-marital intercourse was abolished in 1741, and in 1810 the latter was taken off the statute books. In 1779 the Swedish Diet gave an unmarried woman the right to bear anonymously (in another locality) (Jarrick 1997: 87f), and all over Europe, from Paris to St Petersburg, there were foundling institutions where unwanted children could be left anonymously (in practice this was almost a legalization of infanticide, given the grotesque death rates of these institutions: over 90 per cent in the eighteenth century, and in 1902 still 72 per cent in Moscow, while the Parisian rate by then had gone down to 20–30 per cent (Tilly *et al.* 1992: 12)).

The timing of the loosening of the normative order of sexuality differed somewhat across Europe, and for England, Lawrence Stone (1977) has pointed to a permissive phase from about 1670 to 1790, followed by a more repressive one till about 1860. French historians have generally pointed to the seventeenth century as the classical age of a Christian marriage order (Smith 1986: 74–5). The second half of the eighteenth century was clearly a period of significant normative change.

The possiblity of monitoring the normative order was radically altered in the nineteenth century. The enormous growth of mobility, due to commercialization of agriculture and industrialization, by steamers and trains as well as on foot, is understated by the process of urbanization, which increased from 16 to 41 per cent of the European population between 1800 and 1900 (Bairoch 1997: vol. II, 193ff).

However, the most important channel of change was probably class re-structuration, working itself out in and through variable national administrative, legal and ecclesiastical procedures, and through a variety of local customs and economic conditions. Proletarianization broke the mould of European marriage. The bulk of the sexual change was brought about by young proletarians. The marriage rules guarded membership of respectable society, which in the countryside first of all meant access to land. What set new processes in motion was a rise in the landless population.

Sexually, proletarianization meant that a large number of young men and women went to work in extra-familiar contexts, with no property to inherit, and uncertain, distant, meagre prospects of forming a stable marital household. Their numbers were rapidly rising, as a result of declining mortality, enclosures and other erosions of subsistence agriculture, and serf emancipation in the East. The demand for them was also mounting, from larger-scale commercial agriculture – a key feature of the extreme bastardy in Alpine eastern Austria, and later in Romania – from proto-industrial house production, from city and railway builders, forestry companies, from urban middle classes wanting servants, and from the beginnings of industry.

In the countryside the new proletarian conditions and sexual opportunities were intertwined with local peasant cultures, such as very late marriages-cum-headship inheritance in Alpine Austria, late marriages and outmigration in minifundist northern Portugal, or unchaperoned youth mingling in northern Scandinavia. In the cities, the maids recruited directly from the countryside with no urban kin, and independent textile industry women constituted a non-closeted youth population with their male counterparts, journeymen and labourers. The migration streams created local gender imbalances and itinerant workers with exit options, which also undermined normative courtship, betrothal and marriage.

Industrialization then turned the trend of loose sexuality and unstable unions downwards. Wages from industrial productivity created a new, 'respectable' working class, whose women upon marriage could withdraw from being a poorly paid maid or a factory girl and live on her husband's 'family wage', perhaps supplemented by an income from part-time odd jobs. In any case, a regularly employed industrial worker was a much better marriage prospect than a casual labourer, with whom marriage might mean only subordination and no economic security.

The re-stabilization of European marriage fittingly started in mid-nineteenth-century Britain, where industrialization had gone furthest. With the settlement of industrialism, English workers began to marry with gusto, and white weddings (Gillis 1985: ch. 8). Higher wages and more stable employment were also conducive to a married agricultural proletariat. And, not least, a good part of the pre-industrial proletariat moved to the Americas and to Oceania (see Mitterauer 1983; Levine 1984; Seccombe 1995).

The low rate of illegitimacy in the countries of British settlement is noteworthy, and testifies to the strength of their marriage institution in spite of dispersal over vast areas. But, as pointed out above, it also derives from a legal–administrative presumption of legitimacy. Pre-nuptial conception was considerable though. In the last four decades of the eighteenth century and in the three decades from 1880 to 1910, about a quarter of (a sample of) recorded American marriages involved a birth within 8.5 months of the wedding (Smith 1980: table 17.4).

Slaves, on the other hand, were legally barred from marriage, as it would have interfered with the slave-owner's property rights (Grossberg 1985: 130ff). How much this bears upon Afro-American sexual and family relations today is a very controversial issue. Orlando Patterson (1998) is the most distinguished scholarly advocate for its decisive importance. But whatever the significance of this, the history of the black American family has not been linear. In the period after the Civil War there was a major marriage boom among the now ex-slaves, encouraged by the authorities of the Reconstruction.

Around 1900, the difference in marriage rate, informal unions, and matrifocal households with absent fathers was not very large between whites and blacks, especially if blacks were compared with poor whites (Gutman 1976: 270ff, 375ff, 447ff, 496ff; Jones 1985: 336–37). Eighty-nine per cent of rural white children in the USA were then living with their two parents, and 75 per cent of rural black children. In the urban setting the difference was larger, 87 and 59 per cent, respectively. Most single mothers were widows, 79 per cent of the whites and 72 per cent of the blacks (Gordon and McLanahan 1991: 104, 106). But the grinding poverty of family share-cropping and the brutal rule of the master race was going to take its toll of rural southern black families. By the time of the first national figures on extra-marital births (1916–25) there was a substantial racial difference, as seen in Table 4.3, with 1.5 per cent among whites and 12.5 per cent among blacks – but their class structure was also very different.

As a convict colony, early Australia had some similarities to the West Indian slave colonies, and the family pattern of the former resembled the latter. In 1806, for instance, the overall rate of Australian illegitimacy was 56 per cent, of which the convict women provided virtually everything (Carmichael 1996: 284). But British policy with regard to Australia soon shifted. From the 1830s, assisted immigration of free settlers began on a large scale, especially favouring women. The originally penal colony was anxious about gaining respectability. In 1901 about 90 per cent of Australian women aged 45–49 were married, a good 60 per cent were married before 30 (McDonald 1975: 133–34), and the illegitimacy rate stood at 6 per cent (Carmichael 1996: 287).

The Creole Americas and their non-marriage

'The family based on formal marriage was the exception, not the rule, in Bahía', its historian has written (Borges 1992: 46), referring to a situation in a major centre of the world 150–200 years ago. This may include a bit of poetic licence, but it was significant enough. A partial household survey of 1855 showed that half of the households consisted of cohabitation unions. And it did strike a perceptive mid-nineteenth-century British traveller, Richard Burton, that Brazilians had a 'strange aversion to marriage', referring most directly to Minas Gerais, another major Brazilian state (Freyre 1933/1970: 309).

Brazil was by no means exceptional in Latin America in this respect. In Mexico City in 1900 barely one-third of births were legitimate (Blum 1998: 268n); only a third of women above 15 were married, and in the country as a whole less than half (about 45 per cent) (McCaa 1993: 622, 624; 1994: 30). According to one author, 80 per cent of sexual unions in the capital of Mexico were consensual unions (Sánchez Korrol 1999: 88).

Nineteenth-century Latin America had a large number of matrifocal, female-headed households: about a third of the total in Mexico City and in São Paolo, and well over half in Asunción and Vila Rica, the two main towns of Paraguay (figures from the first half of the century; Potthast-Jutkeit 1991: 229; 1997: 123n).

The low end of Creole American specificity around 1900 is made up by Argentina and Uruguay, reshaped by a swell of Latin European late nineteenth- to early twentieth-century immigration, with a much more even sex ratio (1.7 males to 1 female in Argentina in 1895) than the colonial pattern (Sánchez-Albornoz 1986: 137). In 1910 extra-marital births constituted a good fifth of all Argentinian births and in 1900 a good fourth of all births in Uruguay and almost half in the Andean provinces of Argentina (Lavrín 1995: 147–48). The lowest, i.e. Costa Rican,[5] ratios of 'bastardy' in Latin America and the Caribbean are about twice the highest national ratio in Europe of the period, and more than ten times the ratio in Anglo-North America. In comparison with the main European countries, the extra-marital fertility rate in the Rio de la Plata region was four to five times that of Spain and Italy.

The West Indian colonies of plantation slavery, which had prohibited marriage among slaves, and in Jamaica also among white bonded servants, were at the other extreme. Although Emancipation led to marriage and established it as a conceivable normative ideal, marriage was a post-procreation stage, which one might or might not reach in life. The lowest ever recorded ratio of 'illegitimacy' in Jamaica over a century of statistics by birth status was in the first registration, in 1878. Then 59 per cent of all babies were born out of wedlock. In 1896–1900 the share had crept up to 63 per cent (Hartley 1980: 387). Upon their annexation of Puerto Rico US officials were shocked by the dissolute sex–marriage complex on the island. Reforms were rushed in to combat the problem. Civil marriage free of charge was instituted by decree in 1899. In 1900 all ministers, rabbis and judges were given the right to marry, and in 1902 all marriages (including Catholic ones) were classified as civil contracts, divorceable for adultery, cruelty or abandonment. This was all to little avail as, for the time being, the ratio of illegitimacy stayed at about 50 per cent (Findlay 1998).

Iberian colonial America and the West Indies were the stage of the largest-scale assault on marriage in history. Its heritage was carried into the twentieth century, and it has not (yet) been overtaken by the recent Western European turn to informal coupling, even in Scandinavia. In the 1850s, and 1860s something between a third and half of the population of Salvador, Bahía, never married (Borges 1992: 46), whereas in the EU of the birth cohort of 1960 only 20–25 per cent are expected never to marry, and in Sweden a third (European Commission 2000: 96).

Colonialist penetration and plantation slavery were the main battering-rams of this unique sexual regime, but in interaction with a number of other factors and forces. In their major centres the Iberian colonists were cohabiting with Indian populations, who were neither killed off, chased away or locked up in reservations, as in Anglo-America. Originally, *conquistadores* married for-mally with aristocratic Indian women, but with the destruction of the Indian aristocracy and with imperial insistence on racial purity this soon became difficult and rare. Official doctrine was also increasingly fearful of and hostile to 'unequal' marriages, by which was meant both class and racial differences. Informal liaisons developed instead, and their offspring facilitated inter-racial carnal relations in the next generation, and so forth, over centuries of *mestizaje*.

The colonial economy of Iberian America was starkly class-divided. It was based on large-scale mining, mainly in today's Mexico, Bolivia, Peru and Brazilian Minas Gerais, and on vast landed estates or cattle ranches, all operated by large numbers of servile or semi-servile Indian proletarians. Alongside the colonial economy – to whose second leg, the plantation, we shall return below – was the subsistence agriculture of Indian communities, with more family stability and their own extra-colonial rules and procedures. Colonial family farming was exceptional though, till the share-cropping schemes of coffee cultivation in nineteenth-century São Paolo. To this 'bastardy-prone' class structure was added the popular impoverishment in much of nineteenth-century Hispanic America, from the devastations of the wars of independence and from the traumatic infancy of the new nations, with its break-up of ecclesiastical and bureaucratic structures (cf. McCaa 1994: 30).

A demographic basis of the mestizo development was a continuous shortage of white women, Iberian America and Brazil in particular having a much more lopsided sex imbalance than in Anglo-America. Furthermore, far from all white women were available for marriage. Patriarchal fathers had good reasons of expected dowries and inheritance divisions not to push all their daughters onto the marriage market, and convents provided an attractive alternative. Among the poor white there was another reason too. The Church prohibited marriage with close kin, e.g. cousin marriages and uncle–niece marriages, but in most colonial towns and outposts most conceivable spouses tended to be related. Dispensations could be obtained from the Church, but they were not cheap to poor people.

Marriage and birth registration were in the hands of the Church, which undertook a very impressive enterprise of converting and protecting the Indians. However, its administrative resources always remained far below the number of priests needed to ensure the enforcement of its own rules. Financial overstretch aggravated the situation by driving priests to demand what the locals regarded as exorbitant fees for their services. Marriage, rather than baptism, was then foregone or postponed – and baptisms then furnished the source for distinguishing marital and extra-marital births. Until a late nineteenth-century revival in the central regions of Latin America, the Catholic Church was moreover much weakened by national independence. It was never strong in the periphery of the vast Americas, as in so-called Central America, in the Andes, or in the interior of the Rio de la Plata region. Obligatory civil marriage, in Mexico from 1857 and in Brazil from 1890, made matters worse, by adding a new procedure without legitimacy among the religious populations.

In the Andean region, moreover, the Creole family system connected with an ancient Indian form of marriage, with which it shares certain traits: the possibility of sexual experimentation, relatively easy dissolution, and a tendency to avoid or to postpone official legitimation. Anthropologists have often referred to this Andean marriage form as 'trial marriage', locally known, in Quechua, as *watanaki* or *servinakuy* (Price 1965; Bolton 1980; Carter 1980). It goes back to Inca times, and was noticed by the Spanish conquerors. It predominates in the Quechua- and Aymara-speaking regions of Andean Peru and Bolivia, and similar forms of coupling may also be found in the Andes of central Colombia (Fals-Borda 1962) and in the northern mountain part of Chile (Martinic Galetovic 1991). *Watanaki* refers to a kind of betrothal involving cohabitation. There is no fixed duration, which may vary from a few months to many years. It may or may not include the birth of one or more children. It may end in a Catholic wedding or it may dissolve, then to be followed by another 'try'. Andean unions have a tradition of relative instability (Price 1965: 317; Lambert 1980: 24). Among the Mexican Indians, informal cohabitation was an indigenous custom apparently rather widespread among the lower ranks, who could ill afford the costs of a proper wedding (Basauri 1940: 99).

Plantation slavery, worked by Africans, was another mainstay of the colonial economy, in all the West Indies, the Brazilian northeast and, of course, the southern future United States. The slaves were in principle officially prohibited from marrying, but were on the other hand encouraged to breed. Slave girls were legitimate sexual prey for their owners, the owner's sons, and overseers. This kind of inter-racial sex was also common in the USA, in spite of the strict Anglo racial segregation in all other matters, including informal cohabitation. Again, a large new mixed population ensued, the mulattoes, and mulatto girls soon acquired a special sexual attraction among white men.

The sexual pattern of Creole America, from the Mason–Dixon Line to the Rio de la Plata, had its order, but it was dualistic, hierarchical and violent. The upper echelons of white society were governed by a particularly stiff patriarchy, keeping white women under strict surveillance, in colonial Iberian

America often in seclusion. White upper-class males, on the other hand, were admired among their peers for sexual exploits, including sex across the racial barriers. In Ibero- if not in Anglo-America it was common to keep a mixed-race mistress. To a woman of colour it was often a more rational option to be the mistress of a white, or whiter man, including being a single mother, than to marry a poor black or Indian man.

The white colonists provided important role models to other males. And what was the model? A virile, *macho* figure, sexually rapacious, and domineering in relations with women. On the plantations, the haciendas and the ranches, popular sexual experience had seldom been far from rape and the whip, and the Creole world tended to leave a heritage of sex-cum-violence. The white-set racial sexual hierarchy was pursued by mestizos and mulattoes in their relations to Indians and blacks.

The norm was racial endogamy, at times backed up legally. Elite status, particularly in the rich centres of Mexico and Peru, required so-called 'purity of blood' (*limpieza de sangre*). The norm against racial inter-marriage created a characteristic dual family system in Latin America, and in the British West Indies. It was graphically captured by the great Brazilian anthropologist Gilberto Freyre (1933/1970) in his summary of Brazilian slavery society in the close coexistence of *a Casa Grande* and the *senzala* (the mansion and the slave hut). One family system was an exclusive minority system for elite whites, with vigilant chaperoning of young virgins, an indissoluble Christian marriage, discrete seclusion of married women, and strong *patria potestas* (legal fatherly power). This was basically an Iberian variant of the Western European Christian family. Another was for the popular classes, ethnically mixed, informal, with unclear boundaries, with considerable instability, phallocratic rather than patriarchal, with a significant and sometimes strong matrifocality and with a relatively high proportion of female-headed families. Toleration, with contempt, of popular deviance might even include polygyny into the mid-twentieth century, as in an Indian/mestizo village in the Mexican state of Tlaxcala (Nutini 1965).

Among the poor outside the traditional Indian communities, households tended to matrifocality, built by a woman and her children. It may come out of women's hopes for sexual upward mobility or refusal to be trampled upon by an economically good-for-nothing, and from wishes for freedom from burdens and responsibility by male sexual predators.[6]

Creole sexual customs were old and strong. The conquest of Indian women was even aided by the relatively loose sexual mores of the Iberian northwest (Portuguese Tras-os-Montes, Spanish Galicia and Basque country), from where many of the first colonists came (Brettell and Metcalf 1993; McCaa 1994: 16ff), and established enough to have been noticed but left with resignation to further episcopal consideration by the Portuguese Crown at the height of the Counter-Reformation, right after the Council of Trent, the bishops of the time claiming that the tropical climate 'made chastity impossible' (Kuznesof 1991: 243). It seems to have made it impossible even within the Church itself: in mid-nineteenth-century Bahía, Borges (1992: 241) found that while nuns were kept well walled in, priests and monks were tacitly expected to form illegitimate families.

In 1900, Latin America and the Caribbean had the most complex and multi-faceted socio-sexual order of the world. The duality of family systems runs through the Andean-Caribbean hemisphere. Formal, virgin marriage was the highest ideal, and a number of virgins were always strictly chaperoned, alongside male polycoity as a normal and respectable side-show. But Creole marriage presupposed social equality of the partners, a secure socio-economic status of the couple, and a relatively easy access to a priest and/or a civil magistrate. Only a minority of the population was in conditions where all three criteria were fulfilled. So alongside marriages, there were informal unions of various kinds, a significant number of which were likely to lead to marriage at some later age. There were basically stable Indian unions according to local rituals, and there were many single mothers.

Although ideal, it seems that marriage did not in 1900 have an actual dominance in the patterns of sexuality, households and family in Latin America and the Caribbean, reaching northwards from Rio Grande to São Paolo and south-central Brazil, to Rio Paraná south of Paraguay, and, across the Andes, to Chile, where, as a borderline case, a good third of all children were born outside marriage (Lavrín 1995: 146). In Mexico, Central America, the Caribbean region, including its mainland coasts, the Andean countries, northeastern and north-central Brazil, and in Paraguay, about half or more of children were born out of wedlock, and fully formal marriage constituted hardly more than half of all sexual unions, and in several areas less.[7]

Changes were under way, however, which had already transformed the sexual order of the Southern Cone. The economic and the demographic structures which had given rise to Creole non-marriage were being eroded or mutated.

Slavery had finally been abolished: in the French Empire with the Haitian and French Revolutions, in the British Empire in 1833, in the USA in 1865, in Puerto Rico in 1874, in Cuba in 1884, and in Brazil in 1888. Family sharecropping was pushed in the US south and in southern Brazil (Stolcke 1988), whereto a large transfer of black labour from the northeast had begun already before the abolition of slavery (Sánchez-Albornoz 1986: 127). A new, less sexually imbalanced mass immigration was entering the area, the Southern Cone in particular. Steamships, railways and new export markets brought new wealth, which hardly alleviated the poverty of the poor, but the changed socio-economic infrastructure was pulling the mat from under the old rulers. Servile labourers were beginning to get exit possibilities, and the new exports were calling for more skilled workers. Spanish reaction in Cuba and Puerto Rico had been replaced by modernizing American imperialism, the Brazilian Republic was just starting out, and the Mexican Revolution was ten years ahead.

The global significance of marriage in 1900

Marriage divided the world in 1900. Creole America, Western Europe, and the North American and Oceanian offshoots of Western Europe differed starkly from the rest of the world in 1900. In the latter, marriage was the central status of adulthood, into which every normal person was expected to enter. A handful of poor unfortunates among a hundred males might be left out, in China and in parts of Africa, but hardly more. The East Asian notion of marriage was wide enough to accommodate different statuses and arrangements, such as 'minor wives', given as children to the family of her future husband, or intra-family concubines. Until its late Japanese import from the West, the notion of 'illegitimate birth' was lacking or at most marginal. Virtually all children were legitimate. Marriage included polygamy among Indian Brahmins and Muslim upper classes almost everywhere, and was a mass phenomenon in Africa – made demographiclly possible by much earlier female marriages.

Girls had no youth in South Asia, in Java, in some parts of China, and large parts of West Asia, and Africa. In some regions they were married off before reaching puberty. In most of Asia and Africa girls married in their teens, if not earlier. Only in Japan, the Philippines and in Eastern Europe was the mean age at first female marriage about 20 plus. Boys, on the other hand, often had to wait till their twenties.

Young pre-marital sex seems to have had some space in Southeast Asia and in parts of sub-Saharan Africa and in late Meiji Japan, but was difficult and most likely rare in other parts of the world. For other sex outside marriage there were certain more or less institutionalized channels. To the highest elites, there were certain specialized supply routes of slave or tribute girls, of Circassians to Istanbul and Cairo, and to Javanese courts from certain districts of western Java. There was, of course, prostitution on varying scales and in different forms, including sex work as bonded labour, in Siam (Barmé 1999) and in early Meiji Japan. The penetration of Western imperialism and commerce promoted large-scale port city prostitution, for example in Surabaya, Yokohama, Shanghai and Tanger.

Western Europe, from Portugal to Finland deviated clearly from the Eurasian pattern. Women married in their late twenties and 10 to 20 per cent never married. Having a child outside marriage had become quite common in the nineteenth century – both in many big cities of continental Europe and in specific but widely spread rural areas – but was on the decrease in 1900. Extra-marital births nevertheless constituted 10 per cent or more of all in Austria, Denmark, Portugal and Sweden – two Catholic and two Protestant countries. North America and Oceania had a variant of the Western European sex–marriage complex, with slightly lower marriage age, less celibacy, and fewer 'bastards'.

The Ibero-American elite had a Western European marriage pattern too, and a late nineteenth-century wave of European mass immigration was establishing it on a broader scale in the Southern Cone of the Americas. But the legacy of sexual conquest, informal inter-racial encounters, slavery, Indian marginalization, and of general popular poverty and exclusion had created a situation from Mexico to Paraguay, where formal marriage was a normative ideal but in fact only one form of sexual union and household among others.

5 Marital trends of the twentieth century

The rise of the Western honeymoon

The historical nineteenth-century decline of marriage in Western Europe continued into the twentieth century, carried by the last birth cohorts of the former. In terms of permanent female celibacy the tendency peaked by the end of the first third of the new century. Among Western European women born between 1880 and 1900, one out of eight (France, Germany) to one out of four (Finland, Ireland) never married (Table 5.1).

Table 5.1 Peaks of Western European female celibacy

Country	Dates	Never married (%)[a]
Austria[b]	1910, 1934	18.8, 17.0
Belgium	1856, 1880	19.2, 18.9
Denmark	1921, 1930	15.6, 15.6
Finland	1940, 1930	28.0, 24.6
France	1851, 1891	14.2, 13.1
Germany	1939, 1950	13.2, 12.6[c]
Ireland	1946, 1951	25.7, 25.7
Italy	1951, 1961	14.3, 13.8
Netherlands, the	1920, 1909	15.2, 15.0
Norway	1930, 1946	21.8, 21.8
Portugal	1890, 1864	22.2, 21.7
Spain	1787/97, 1950	17.2, 15.2
Sweden	1930, 1940	22.5, 22.2
Switzerland	1870, 1941	20.4, 19.7
UK: England and Wales	1921, 1931,	16.4, 16.4
UK: Scotland	1931, 1911	21.5, 20.9

Sources: England 1541–1871: Wrigley and Schofield (1981: 260); France eighteenth and nineteenth centuries: Henry and Houdaille (1978: tables 5 and 6); Portugal: Livi-Bacci (1971: 40); Spain: Reher (1997: 154); Sweden 1750: SCB (1969: table 18); for the rest: P. Flora *et al.* (1987: 215ff).

Notes:
a Proportion never married in the age group of 45–54.
b Territory of the twentieth-century Republic.
c Federal Republic.

The age of industrial marriage

The second third of the twentieth century constitutes the 'Marriage Age' in modern Western European history. Never before, since the mid-eighteenth century in France (Henry and Houdaille 1978), at least since the early eighteenth century in Sweden (SCB 1969: table 18), at least since the eighteenth century in Denmark and Norway (Flora *et al.* 1987: 170ff, 194ff) and since at least mid-sixteenth-century England (Wrigley and Schofield 1981: 428) had such a large proportion of the population married. Why were so many individuals and couples suddenly drawn into marriage?

Who were these people, what do we know about them, and their background? At least a few things are known, even at the macroscopic, semi-continental level of this analysis. We know that the marriage rate (and age) in Western Europe had for long been a means of adapting to the changing conditions of life: fewer and later marriages after experiences of bad times, more and earlier ones after better times. The people who started to push up the Western European marriage rate in the mid-1930s, in some countries already in the 1920s, were born in 1890–1910, that is, the children of what in their age of possible marriage became known '*la belle époque*', a period of accelerated economic growth, and also of poverty reduction by the first wave of massive out-migration overseas (see Maddison 2001). They were also more or less the first generation coming out of general schooling, although Bible-reading northern Protestantism had long ago established quasi-universal literacy. Thirdly, the newly-weds were very often second-generation urbanites, growing up after the dislocations of the nineteenth-century thrusts of rapid industrialization and urbanization.

In short, the new people attracted to marriage were a generation of competence and, presumably, self-confidence with an experience of economic improvement. As we shall go into later, this was also the generation that made birth control a main feature of marriage.

While the increase of marriage was virtually universal in Western Europe in the second third of the twentieth century – Iceland, where it occurred in the first third and then declined, and Spain, where the marriage rate of 1900–4 was reached again only in 1955–59 (Mitchell 1998c: table A6), are the most noteworthy exceptions – there was, of course a substantial amount of national (and regional) variation, of timing as well as of magnitude. Inside the broad economic–cultural context some political factors are discernible, apart from the discreet and obscure operation of local customs.

The end of the two world wars generally led to an immediate rise of marriage. But the extent to which the bliss of peace inaugurates a new trend varies a lot. The end of World War I did this only in two countries really, in Belgium and in France, the main victors of the war and reached late by the world crisis of 1929. In England, a peacetime rate of marriage higher than that of 1900–13 becomes discernible from the late 1920s and is established by the end of the next decade. The end of World War II caused a jump into marriage among the countries earlier at war, like in Spain after the disastrous colonial war of 1898. In Italy the short-wave oscillations of the inter-war period continued, with a new, higher level setting only in the 1960s, when at last the proportion married surpassed that of the 1860s and 1870s (Livi-Bacci 1977: 57). Emigration resumed its importance after the war as an alternative to marriage, as in Portugal, where marrying occurred more only in the second half of the 1960s, and in Spain. Emigration, and its causes of poverty, is a major factor affecting twentieth-century marriage. It also depressed the Irish rate of marriage until the end of the marriage boom period.

There are some remarkable moves of the marriage trends, which seem to derive rather immediately from political changes. One is the jump in German marriages in 1933, turning the trend upwards for the rest of the 1930s, to a level surpassing the euphoria of Unification of 1871, and only marginally overtaken in the early post-war years. In Austria, the twentieth-century record year of marriage is 1938, the year of *Anschluss* to Nazi Germany, and after the war a long period of marriage settles (Table 5.2). In Denmark a new upward trend also starts in 1933, in Sweden in 1934, and in Norway in 1936. In all five cases the reason is likely to be the same. The resourceful birth cohorts of 1900–14 reveal a glimpse of an economic dawn beyond the Depression, in Central Europe a window opened by Nazism, in Scandinavia by Social Democracy. To the Portuguese the Revolution of the Carnations brought hopes of happiness.

Even where marriages had been more frequent earlier, figures from the 1960s and early 1970s were extraordinarily high. In France the marriage frequency of 1971–72 was surpassed only by the immediate post-war years, of 1919–22 and 1945–49. Since the Unification of Italy, Italians had married more frequently than they did in 1972–74 only immediately after World War I, in 1920–21. The Swedish marriage rate in 1965–66 had, since the last Swedish post-war period, in 1810–11, only been surpassed in 1944–47.

Table 5.2 Years of peak numbers marrying in Western Europe since 1815

Country	Year(s)	Country	Year(s)
Austria	1938	Netherlands, the	1970
Belgium	1946, 1970	Norway	1968
Denmark	1965	Portugal	1975
Finland	1946–47	Spain	1900, 1956
France	1920, 1946	Sweden	1946
Germany	1962[a]	Switzerland	1969
Greece	1965	UK: England and Wales	1972
Ireland	1973	UK: Scotland	1966
Italy	1920–21, 1973		

Sources: The main source is Flora *et al.* (1987: ch. 2), which basically covers the period of 1815, sometimes 1840 – Italy since 1862 – to 1975, and which measures the number of people marrying per 10,000 non-married people aged 15–49. Greece, Portugal and Spain are not included, for which Mitchell (1998c: table A6) is used, going back to 1900 and measuring a crude marriage rate, per 1,000 population. For these countries since 1960, and for all countries after 1975, checks have been made with Council of Europe (2001b: fig. G2.2 and table T2.1).

Note:
a West Germany, with a marrying rate equal to the peak after World War I: 1,020 and 1,023 persons marrying per 10,000 non-married persons aged 15–49, respectively.

Western Europeans came to marry earlier as well as more. The female mean age at first marriage reached a historical low in the period 1960–75. In Italy and Spain this was only a fraction below the marriages of 1900 (see Table 4.1); in England and Germany women in the early 1970s married on average about four years earlier than they did in 1900, and in France, the Netherlands and Sweden, three years earlier (Festy 1979a: 69; Council of Europe 2001a: table T2.3).

With increasing marriage, extra-marital births declined. Prior to their recent rise they had reached their national maximum on the European continent in 1930, when Austria had 27 per cent of its births outside marriage, and Sweden (in 1929) 17 per cent (in neither case was this the same as the number of extra-marital births per fertile unmarried woman, which had peaked much earlier). Sweden had its lowest ratio after 1850 in 1945–49, 9 per cent of all births, about the same time as Switzerland on a 3 per cent level, Austria in 1965 at 11 per cent. France also had its historical low after 1815 in 1961–65 (4.3 per cent), and Germany since 1871 in 1966–67 (4.6 per cent). Belgium, Denmark, Ireland, the Netherlands, Norway and Scotland all had their lowest recorded ratios of 'illegitimacy' in the 1950s, Portugal and Spain in 1970. Only England and Wales deviate from the pattern, with a special twentieth-century low in 1920, and with a basically constant 4 per cent ratio in the first half of the twentieth century, rising slightly and slowly after World War II (Hartley 1975: table 4; Flora *et al.* 1987: ch. 2; Council of Europe 2001a: table T3.2).

The (mainly) Anglo New World followed largely the same developmental pattern in the twentieth century as did Western Europe: that is, a declining propensity to marriage and in the first decades, at least in Australia, a rising marriage age among the cohorts born in the second half of the nineteenth century. In 1920–21, 12 per cent of American and 17 per cent of Australian women had never married by the end of their fertile period (Spiegelman 1968: table 8.7; McDonald 1975: tables 40, 43). Then there was a mid-century marriage boom, which among white US women born in the 1920s and 1930s left only 5 per cent unmarried by the age of 50, in Canada about 6 per cent, and in Australia only 4 per cent (Festy 1979b: table 4; Trewin 2001: 195). The median female age at first marriage went down to 20 years in the USA in 1960, a decline of almost four years (3.7) since 1900 (Haines 1996: table 3), and in Australia and Canada to 21 (in the 1960s and 1970s) (Spiegelman 1968: table 8.8; Festy 1979b: 713–14; Trewin 2001: 195). In 2000, the American median, which is usually lower than the mean, had shot up to 25 (US Census Bureau 2001d).

Less time-lagged changes may be gauged by looking at the nuptiality of young women. The American record then shows a strong increase from 1940 to 1970, a fall back to the previous turn of the century by 1980, and thereafter a new era (Table 5.3).

In terms of extra-marital births, the North American (and New Zealand) record is similar to the English, with the very lowest ratio at the beginning of the twentieth century, but still just below 4 per cent in both the USA and

Table 5.3 Percentage married among American women aged 20–24,
1900–2000

Year	(%)	Year	(%)
1900	47	1950	66
1910	50	1960	70
1920	52	1970	64
1930	52	1980	44
1940	52	1990	32
		2000	27

Sources: 1970 and 2000: US Census Bureau (2001d: table 5); the rest: Haines
(1996: table 2; Haines gives a slightly lower figure – 1970, 61.5 per cent).

Canada in the early 1950s, before starting to mount gradually. Australia has
the same trough in 1951–52, but that is then lower than the early twentieth-
century figures (Hartley 1975: table 5).

The marriage boom had little effect on the racial endogamy of US marriages,
and none at all on the racist marriage legislation, put in place after slavery
and the Civil War, in the south and in the west. The US Supreme Court had in
1879 accepted the constitutionality of racist bans of marriage, as marriage was
not a right of US citizens (McIntyre 1995: 22). In their draconian prohibition
of marriage with a person of 'one fourth or more of Negro or mulatto blood',
these laws were more stringent in their racial demarcation than the Nazi
German Nuremberg Laws, according to which (§5) a 'Jew' was someone who
had at least three 'fully Jewish grandparents'. A Jewish '*Mischling*' (half-blood),
having two 'fully Jewish' grandparents, would have to ask permission to marry
a German (Bergmann 1940: I, 148n).

In 1967 an inter-racial couple, with the unbelievably apt surname of
Loving, were married in Washington DC, and moved to live in the state of
Virginia. They were then brought to court for violating the state ban on inter-
racial marriage, and convicted at all state levels. But at last, the time for
change had come, and in *Loving* v. *Virginia* the US Supreme Court struck down
the Virginia legislation. The right to adult heterosexual marriage had finally
been established in the USA (Clark and Glowinsky 1995: 130ff).

What should be underlined from this section is that the third quarter of the
twentieth century, the usual background of comparison to current developments, was a special period in modern Western population history. Those two
to three decades were *the* age of marriage and of intra-marital sexuality in
modern Western history.

The mid-twentieth century was also the zenith of the housewife family. In
Sweden in 1900 there were about 69 gainfully employed women per 100
housewives of economically active men, 90 in 1930, 60 in 1950, and 110 in
1965 (SCB 1914: table 14; Therborn 1981: table 73). British female labour
market participation was also at its secular ebb in 1950 (Gallie 2000: table
8.6), and the Dutch in 1960 (Pott-Buter 1993: table 2.2).

Eastern European marriage and the irony of Communism

In 1900, as we saw in Chapter 2, most of what later became Communist Europe for a period, had virtually universal marriage and an average female age at first marriage of around 20. Eastern Europe was part of the Eurasian marriage pattern. The East–West divide was maintained, by and large, till World War II. But the wars and the Revolution had their effects in Russia.

The female mean age at first marriage increased by two years from peace-time 1897 to those who entered the marriage market right after World War I and the Civil War, the birth cohort of 1900. It reached its maximum, at 25 years, for the cohorts of the 1920s, the brides of the soldiers and the victims of World War II. By the cohort of 1960, the young generation of the *perestroika*, the Russian marriage was back at 1897 levels (21.7 and 21.4 years, respectively). Also the proportion never married was, of course, affected by the disasters of violence, as many more men than women were killed. In the 1920 cohort it went up to the Western European level of 10 per cent never married, returning to 4 per cent with the 1940 cohort, after which cohabitation slowly began to change the pattern, as in the West. A third of Russian women were widowed by the age of 32 in the birth cohort of 1910 (Scherbov and van Vianen 2001). Among men, marriage remained universal, 96.5 per cent were married by the age of 45 in 1959. At that time, 14 per cent of Russian births were outside marriage, going down to 11 per cent in the late 1960s and staying there till the mid-1980s, about half of them recognized by their father (Avdeev and Mounier 1999: 648, 653).

In October 1918 a revolutionary family law established civil marriage. But in the wake of the revolutionary upheaval there were also many informal unions, which when they broke up led to conflicts about child support. After an extensive debate, the regime then adopted a new marriage law in 1926, which provided the same rights and obligations to couples of unregistered cohabitation. This broad view of cohabitation began to narrow in the 1930s, and in 1944 a strict legal distinction between marriage and non-marriage ensued, and thereby also between legitimate and illegitimate children; statistics were not made public (on the Soviet marriage debate, see the documentation compiled by Schlesinger (1949), cf. Geiger (1968: 93ff)).

It is interesting that the relative Eastern European marriage pattern was maintained throughout the Communist period, once the tremendous war losses of Russia were overcome. As there were major changes dismantling patriarchy (as noted above), and as the old inheritance rules lost their meaning with de-agrarianization and socialization, the reproduction of the marriage pattern cannot be seen only as some manifestation of Communist 'neo-traditionalism'. Moreover, the institution of marriage in the Communist part of Germany also received an Eastern tinge during the decades of the GDR. By 1950 the Czech lands had also adopted the more Eastern custom of quite early marriages, previously characteristic of Slovakia (Fialová 1994).

Let us first look at the outgoing marriage record of Eastern European Communism (Table 5.4). The East–West distinction in 1900 (Table 4.1) is still there eight to nine decades later. Whatever Communism did, it did not do away with marriage, and as we shall see below this conclusion is also valid for Cuba and East Asia. No Western European country had a higher or equal marriage rate to Communist Eastern and East-Central Europe. Portugal had a rate of 0.79. Between the two Germanies there is a clear divide since 1975, with the Easterners being more keen to marry. Greece represents non-Communist Eastern Europe, and is similar to by then at most semi-Communist Yugoslavia, but less so to Bulgaria and Romania.

After the early Bolshevik embrace of all kinds of heterosexual unions, Soviet Communism developed a concern with marriage as part of a post-revolutionary order, a perspective inculcated in later generations of Communists. After the fertility crisis of the 1960s, Eastern European Communism embarked upon an active and ambitious programme to boost the birth rate (see Chapter 6), of which marriage promotion was a part. A key mechanism seems to have been the non-market allocation of housing, which, given the scarcity, was favouring married couples.

Marriage promotion did not mean any repression of extra-marital sexuality and fertility, however. Whereas West Germany in 1985 had 9 per cent of its births outside marriage, East Germany had 34 per cent. To the Greek rate of 1.8 per cent corresponded the Romanian of 3.7 per cent and the Bulgarian of 11.7 per cent. Among eight future Council of Europe member countries which in 1960 had more than a tenth of their live births outside marriage, only three were non-Communist: Austria, Iceland and Sweden. But history and religion were also weighing upon cross-national differences. In 1985, Austria had 22 per cent, and Hungary 9 per cent. Deeply Catholic Communist Poland had 5 per cent extra-marital babies born in 1985, and deeply Catholic capitalist Ireland had 8.5 per cent (Council of Europe 2001a: table T3.2).

Table 5.4 East–West European marriages in 1985 (total female first marriage rate)

Country	Rate[a]
Russia	0.97
Other Communist Eastern Europe[b]	0.88
Communist Central Europe[c]	0.90
East Germany	0.74
Greece	0.83
Austria	0.60
West Germany	0.60
UK	0.66

Source: Council of Europe (2001a: table T2.2).

Notes:
a The rate runs from 0 to 1 and indicates the proportion of women, who at the current distribution of nuptials among age groups are likely to marry at least once before the age of 50.
b Unweighted averages of Bulgaria, Slovakia, Hungary, Romania and Yugoslavia.
c Unweighted average of Czech Republic and Poland.

Knots are tied in Latin America

As we saw above, Latin American and Caribbean nuptiality held the low record of the world around 1900. But we also noted that changes were under way. The propensity to marry did then rise substantially in the twentieth century, although available data do not allow us to draw a continuous curve of change.

Brazilian statistics took a long time to develop, and the country is therefore not even included in B.R. Mitchell's (1998) American compendium. But already before 1900 major forces of transformation were under way, with the country tilting from the old slavery region of the northeast to the settler areas of the south. Immigration changed the ethnic composition of the country. In 1890 blacks and browns made up 56 per cent of the population, in 1940 36 per cent (Burns 1993: 317). The country industrialized, grew and developed economically. It seems likely that legal marriage was established as the dominant institution of sexual relations in Brazil in the first decades of the century. In 1949 the then Federal District (Rio de Janeiro) registered only 13 per cent of births outside marriage (Hartley 1975: table 3). By 1960, Brazil had with Chile and Uruguay the strongest marital order in Latin America (Rosero-Bixby 1996: table 7.2; cf. Oliveria and Berquó 1990: table 8).

Mexico had a more enduring Caribbean/Indo-Creole legacy of family informality. But Mexican marriage rates picked up in the 1920s, and even more in the 1930s, with the stabilization-cum-radicalization of the Revolution, leaving the Caribbean rates of three to four marriages per thousand population for a rate of six to seven, similar to the Canadian rate (Mitchell 1998a: table A6). The marriage rate registered was also affected by the defeat of the Catholic rebellions and the mounting pressures of the secular state. In 1930, officially, marriage constituted only half of all sexual unions (Table 5.5). But that was in part because the state did not recognize purely religious marriages.

In the 1930s all clergy were prohibited from marrying anyone who did not have a civil marriage licence, and in the early 1940s a massive state campaign was launched for the legalization of 'free unions' (Tuñón 1997: 15). As consensual unions tend to turn into marriages – or to dissolve – a fourth of all Mexican sexual unions in 1982 began as informal cohabitation (Oliveira 1995: 286n). Between a fourth and a fifth of all Mexican births in 1955–65 took place outside marriage (Hartley 1975: table 2).

Chile had a notable rise of nuptiality already in the 1920s, and a peaking marriage rate of on average ten per thousand population for the three years of

Table 5.5 Sexual unions in Mexico in 1930 and 1970 (as a percentage of all unions)

	Religious and/or civil marriage	*Religious marriage only*	*Consensual union*
1930	48	28	24
1970	77	8	15

Source: Calculations from Bridges (1980: 312).

1928–30. Extra-marital births, which had approached 40 per cent in the second decade of the century, went down to 23 per cent by the end of the 1940s (Lavrín 1995: 146). Argentina since 1910 never had the low Caribbean rates, but it had its best years of marriage in the 1940s. In Uruguay, similar to Argentina, the rate rose towards the end of the 1930s, and then again after 1945.

Crude marriage rates of seven per thousand were reached in Venezuela only in the 1970s, and barely so in Colombia (Mitchell 1998a: table A6). In 2000, marriage overtakes cohabitation in Colombia only among women aged 35–39 or older, while in Peru this happens with the 30–34 age group (Demographic and Health Surveys). Colombia and Venezuela both contain a wide variety of family types and of sexual relations, due to different ethnic cultures and ecological conditions, from the Afro-Creole Caribbean coast to the Indo-Hispanic Andes or the frontier savannah of the Venezuelan south (see further, e.g., Angulo Novoa 1980; Pollak-Eltz 1980).

In Central America – with the West Indies the core of informal coupling in the Americas, and in the world – in the early 1970s, marriages still constituted just below half of all unions (including women aged 15–49) in El Salvador, Guatemala and Panama. They made up a little more than half in Honduras, 60 per cent in Nicaragua and 84 per cent in Costa Rica (Marin Lira 1981: table 2). In the Dominican Republic in 1975, marriages made up only a third of sexual unions (World Fertility Survey).

As was pointed out above, Creole informal pairing is the product of an unequal imposition of colonial religion and colonial law, sustained after Independence by the continuing coloniality of the white or mestizo state, and by the expanded reproduction of mass poverty. So while a good half of non-Indian Guatemaltecan women in union were married, only 40 per cent of Indians were, and in Panama almost half of non-Indian women were formally married, while 7 per cent of Panama Indians were (Marin Lira 1981: table 5).

In the Caribbean, there were established distinctions between three types of serious sexual unions. Marriage, the ideal, was in fact seldom entered into before a settled middle age, if that stage was ever reached. Cohabitation, or common law union in English, *concubinage* in French, or *unión libre* in Spanish, was and is the predominant pattern. 'Visiting unions', in French *'union de type ami'*, or in Haiti sometimes *'plaçage'*, i.e. a special sexual relationship without cohabitation, was also frequent in the Franco- and Anglophone parts of the area (cf. Charbit 1987: 60) From the World Fertility Survey we have a picture of Jamaica in the mid-1970s (Table 5.6).

After the Revolution, the popularity of marriage rose in Cuba – historically part of the Caribbean pattern of loose sexuality and free unions – a change sometimes boosted by governmental campaigns and collectively organized mass weddings. The crude marriage rate jumped from a 1955–59 average of 4.6 (per thousand population) to 9.2 and 10.4 in 1960–61, falling back to a new low, at 6.2, in 1964, then culminating in the years 1968–72 at a four-year average of 11.7, on a par with the US rate in 1935–45 (Mitchell 1998a: table A6). By 1981, two-thirds of Cuban couples were legally married and one-third cohabiting (*'unidos'*) (Benítez Pérez 1999: table 19).

Table 5.6 Sexual unions in Jamaica, 1975–76 (women aged 15–49, percentage in type of union)

Age	Never in union	Separated and single	Visiting	Cohabitation	Marriage
All	11	15	20	26	29
15–19	40	11	33	14	1
20–24	12	13	33	29	12
25–29	4	16	17	35	28
30–34	2	14	11	33	40
40–44	1	17	10	22	51
45–49	2	25	7	18	48

Source: World Fertility Survey 1975–76.

By the end of the 1960s, the bulk of all births in the Caribbean region took place outside of marriage, three-quarters in Jamaica, two-thirds in Barbados, Dominican Republic, El Salvador, Guatemala, Haiti, Honduras and Panama, a good half in Nicaragua and Venezuela, a good 40 per cent in Guadeloupe–Martinique and in Trinidad – comparable to Paraguay and Peru in South America – and a quarter in Costa Rica, the Dutch Antilles and Puerto Rico, as in Argentina and Mexico. Cuban data are lacking, but would have been similar to those of Trinidad. In Latin America and the Caribbean only Chile (17–18 per cent) and Brazil (13 per cent) were below 20 per cent (Hartley 1975: tables 2 and 3).

In terms of marriages per year, it seems that the high season of Latin American marriage ended in the 1970s: in Venezuela and in Mexico – carried by the oil boom – in the second half of the 1970s, in Brazil in the 1960s (Oliveira and Berquó 1990: table 8; Torrado 1993: 79; Rosero-Bixby 1996: table 7.2; Mitchell 1998a: table A6). As in Europe, in Latin America marrying followed economic trends. It increased with the onset of industrial development, and tapered off with the economic crises and the political dictatorships towards the end of the century, kept up in Chile by the late dictatorial bull market of the second half of the 1980s.

The median marriage age has been at the low end of the Western European pattern. At the end of the marriage boom, it was 22–23 years of age for women of the Southern Cone, including Brazil, 20–21 for the rest of Latin America outside the Caribbean (Zavala de Cosío 1996: table 5.3). There, sexual unions, married or most frequently non-married, have always started very young, in the 1950s at 12–13 (Marín Lira 1981: table VI), and the mean age at first marriage was in the late teens in the early 1970s, save in Costa Rica, which follows the Latin American mainstream.

Even outside the Caribbean and the Andes, Latin America has maintained a coexistence and a registration of both formal and informal sexual unions. Uruguay, a country very strongly marked by Latin European immigration, from where almost all Indians have disappeared and where most of the blacks were killed as cannon fodder in the wars of independence, provides us with a most interesting official time series of marital and extra-marital births (Table 5.7).

Table 5.7 Extra-marital births in Uruguay 1900–2000
(as a percentage of all live births)

Year	(%)	Year	(%)
1900	26	1960	20
1910	27	1970	21
1920	29	1980	25
1930	28	1990	32
1940	26	2000	48
1950	18	–	–

Source: Instituto Nacional de Estadistica (2002), www.ine.gub.ur

The proportion of extra-marital births is extremely high throughout the century in comparison with Latin Europe, even with mainland Scandinavia. In Europe on a national level it is only matched (or overtaken) by the Icelanders. Uruguayan statistics lists all extra-marital births as products of 'consensual unions', with no distinction between those and single mothers. But culturally similar Argentina also had a quarter of its children born outside marriage in 1980, 16 per cent in consensual unions and 7 per cent to single mothers (Torrado 1993: 343). The table also indicates a negation of marriage in Uruguay, then showing a pattern similar to that of Western Europe, with a marriage boom in the second third of the century, and ending the century by apparently moving out of the secular orbit.

Asian ageing

Universal marriage was the Asian rule in 1900, and only very recently has there been some modifications in that respect. There was, then, no space for a marriage boom. The process of marital change was instead one of ageing.

India was strongly dedicated to child marriage, and kept a female average first marriage age (so-called singulate mean age at marriage, or SMAM) of under 14 until World War II, which should mean a median age of 11–12 (Xenos and Gultiano 1992: appendix table 1). As marrying off a girl before her first menstruation was religiously charged, attempts at change were hotly controversial, and fed into conservative nationalism. In 1927 the controversy got an inter-continental dimension by *Mother India*, a liberal critique of Indian culture, with a special focus on child marriages, by an American visitor, Katherine Mayo (1927). The Indian elite was incensed, and the shrill tone and fast pace of the book apparently included factual errors and cases of dubious representativity – of infected and wrecked girl mothers in hospital, for instance – but the problems were real enough.[1]

In 1929, the government of British India passed the Child Marriage Restraint Act, making the marrying of girls under 14 an offence. It was a restrained act, in that a child marriage was not a cognizable offence, and could ony be acted upon after a complaint was filed (Kapadia 1966: 154). But schooling and evolving custom did edge the marriage age upwards. In the decennial censuses of 1941 to 1961, the SMAM stood at around 15, then increased again in the 1960s, to 17 in the census of 1971, 18 in 1981, and 19 in 1991. The male average stayed at around 20 in 1891–1941, approaching 21 in 1951, and almost reaching 24 in 1991 (Xenos and Gultiano 1992; UN 2001). The last hold-out of child marriage is the north Indian state of Rajasthan, where 13 per cent of girls aged 10–14 were married in 1991 (Vijayanunni 1998: table 10).

In the successor states of British India, the maturing of marriage has made the greatest strides in Muslim Pakistan, where female SMAM was close to 18 in 1951, and 21.6 in 1991, whereas it has been slowest in Muslim Bangladesh, where it stood at 18 in 1991. Mainly Buddhist Ceylon/Sri Lanka had a different marriage regime. Women married at 18 in 1901, and at 20–21 from 1921 until the 1950s, whence it moved upwards towards 25.

Direct economic inter-family transfers on the occasion of marriage have remained very important in South Asia. They were never really abolished in Communist China, and with the re-introduction of capitalism they are coming back (Liu *et al.* 1997: 209; Lee and Wang 1999: 81), while they have, on the whole, become more ritual than substantial in other parts of Asia. In South Asia, on the contrary, they have risen in significance.

The traditional Hindu high caste, northern Indian practice of dowry spread in the last third of the century to southern India, to lower castes, and to Muslim Bangladesh and Pakistan, which, of course, historically had a common Hindu–Muslim culture (Bénéï 1996; Amin and Cain 1997; Menski 1998). Dowry values have gone up, also in relative terms. Attempts at legal prohibition – the Indian Dowry Prohibition Act of 1961 and Dowry Prohibition (Amendment) Act of 1984, and similar laws in Pakistan (1976, 1980), and Bangladesh (1980) – had no short-term effect at all (Menski 1998; Bhat and Halli 1999). But in the late 1990s the Indian Supreme Court and other courts have belatedly begun to act (Menski 1998). In the first half of the 1990s, dowry conflicts led to 5,000 registered killings of women each year in India, with a heavy concentration in the northern states of Uttar Pradesh and Harayana and in the federal district of Delhi (Thakur 1998: tables 1–2).

The sub-continent has an old tradition of female hypergamy strategies, of marrying upwards, a hierarchy of wife-takers over wife-givers, and a practice of ostentatious weddings, customs now updated to adapt to new forms of wealth accumulation, to high education, and migration abroad.

The reasons for the spread of the dowry, and for its inflation are a complex compound of cultural, economic and demographic elements. There is a spread of upper caste culture, sometimes referred to as 'Sanskritization', with the erosion of the ancient caste division of labour and segregation. There is a certain economic development, from the Green Revolution and urban middle-class growth, and money influx through remittances from migrant workers in the Gulf, which with the commodification of social relations fuel the inflation. Third, there is a demographic marriage squeeze or excess of potential brides – in spite of their low sex ratio at birth – tipping the negotiating balance in favour of the families of grooms, due to the decline of mortality. The decline of infant and child mortality means that younger cohorts are larger than older ones. With the South Asian custom of males marrying females 5–8 years younger, demography has tilted the marriage market in male favour, enhanced by an accumulated backlog of waiting brides. The rise of the female marriage age may be an adaption to this. Further, longer life expectancy has caused widowers virtually to disappear from the market, whereas they previously made up a fifth of grooms seeking brides. But by the end of the twentieth century, the belated fertility decline is beginning to change Indian marriage demography in the opposite direction, more favourable to women and to parents of daughters (Bhat and Halli 1999).

The Chinese marriage age did not change clearly till the late 1950s, but it was always higher than in India, although child betrothal was common among the poor in parts of China. In the rural lower Yangtze valley studied by the pioneer Chinese anthropologist Fei Hsiao-tong (1939: 52) in the mid-1930s, 90 per cent of the girls and 75 per cent of the boys were married by the age of 16. By 25, no women were unmarried, and only 8 per cent of the men. Child betrothal was frequent. Other non-representative surveys have found average female marriage ages of 17 to 19, lower in the north, higher in the south, in China of the first third of the twentieth century. Right after the Communist revolution, female SMAM was calculated as 17.5, with males on the average 6 years older. Then follow two jumps, to 19 in 1960–64, and, with the birth control policy and its pressure for later marriages, to a little above 22 in 1982, where it remained in 1995 (Lee and Wang 1999: tables 5.1, 5.4).

Twenty-two is the legal minimum age for women (25 for men) in the 1980 Marriage Law of China. The long Communist campaign against child and youth marriages has been met with tenacious resilience ever since the 1950s (Croll 1981: 67ff), and the officious, quasi-medical advice of the 1980s and 1990s for women not to marry before 24 or 25 (Evans 1997: 154ff) has not been much heeded.

The Japanese marriage age, which was 'Eastern European' rather than 'Asian' already before World War I, began to rise again from the late 1920s to a plateau at a female age of barely 25 in 1955 to 1980. Thereupon followed a strong rise from the late 1980s, up to the Western European figure of 28 in 1995 (East–West Center 2002).

Some time between 1940 and 1955 the marriage age went up in Taiwan and, most strongly, in South Korea, and from the late 1950s there was a steep rise, common also to Southeast Asia except Indonesia, and to Pakistan. By the end of the century, China, Indonesia, Pakistan and Central Asia had acquired marriage preferences similar to those of Eastern Europe, while the rest of East and Southeast Asia had come to resemble Western Europe in this respect. Bangladesh and India also had older brides – and a little older grooms – but remained in a class of their own (Xenos and Gultiano 1992; UN 2001).

The rule of universal marriage has basically been maintained through the century on a national level all over Asia, with a few recent possible exceptions, and the usual partial qualification of Catholic Philippines. Seven per cent of

Filipinas were permanently celibate in 1960 (Jones 1997: table 3.1). However, in some East and Southeast Asian megacities this rule was undercut in the last third of the century.

Outside Japan, Bangkok led the development, clear also in Singapore, and visible in Hong Kong, Kuala Lumpur and Taipei, but not in Jakarta, Manila or Seoul (Jones 1997: table 3.2). In Bangkok the share of female celibacy in the 45–49 year age group rose from 4.5 per cent in 1960 to 11.3 per cent in 1990, a classic 'Western European' proportion. In Singapore in 1996, the same meaasure reached 15.6 per cent (Quah 1998: table 3.1). It is educated women who are delaying or abstaining from marriage in these cities, a tendency starting with secondary education and continuing with tertiary. Educated males continue to marry vigorously (Jones 1997: tables 3.3–3.6; Quah 1998: table 3.4). Educated female celibacy, then, is a product of interacting female autonomy and phallocracy: some males fear a highly educated wife; many educated women fear a restraining marriage.

Sex outside marriage is mainly formal and informal concubinage, and commercial. After the first two decades in Japan, and apart from the convulsive years of wars and civil wars for independence in Indonesia, it has hardly left any traces in the Asian birth registers (Hartley 1975: table 6). At least until independence India had its *devadasi* temple prostitution (Andrews 1939: 75), and various forms of concubinage were common throughout East and Southeast Asia. Concubinage is still a widespread upper middle-class phenomenon, especially in Thailand. The sex industry was boosted by American military demand during the Vietnam war, and has become a significant branch of the Southeast Asian economy, especially in Thailand (Hull *et al.* 1999; Jackson and Cook 1999).

Systematic and reliable data for the West Asian/North African Muslim world are patchy before World War II. But the basic pattern was one of mid- to late teenage female marriages to males 5–10 years older. From the far from fully satisfactory Egyptian censuses of 1907, 1937 and 1947, a certain upward tendency of the female marriage age is discernible (Goode 1963: table III, 3–4). In Istanbul, women's marriage age increased by a year per decade since 1900, reaching 23 in the 1930s, narrowing the gender gap from 10 to 6 years (Duben and Behar 1991: 224, 241). But Istanbul was very different from the rest of Turkey, where the mean age of female marriage was still 19 in 1960. Nineteen was the SMAM for West Asia/North Africa as a whole around 1960, which may have meant that half of all girls in the region were married before the age of 18; grooms were about 5 years older (UN 1987: 346).

The region has then followed the Asian trend of older marriage. In Egypt in 1995 the average female age was 22 (UN 2001b), and in Turkey in 1998 it was 22.9 (Liljeström and Özdalga 2002: 274). In the Mahgreb the changes of the 1980s and 1990s have been spectacular. In the mid-1990s the Libyan age of women's marriage had gone up to 29, in Tunisia almost to 27, in Morocco and Algeria to 26. The universality of marriage has been less affected. Among the age group of 30–39, 84 per cent of Moroccan, 90 per cent of Algerian, and 96 per cent of Egyptian women were married (Tawila 1998). What it does mean, though, is that Arab women have a youth of their own, largely thanks to educational expansion.

Remarkable is the outcome of the Islamic Revolution in Iran in 1979 which in literal scriptural orthodoxy lowered the minimum marriage age for girls from 16 to 9. In Iran in 1996 there were about 50,000 married girls aged 10–14, and 2,000 divorcées and almost 3,000 widows in the same age group. But these were marginal fates, and the wind was blowing in the opposite direction (Table 5.8).

Mean age at first marriage was 19.5 before the Revolution, and 17 years after it was 22.1. The drive for education and modernization has turned out more powerful than the tradition of the Revolution, and Sharia law does not, of course, prescribe child marriage. Between 1986 and 1996 female literacy rose from 52 to 74 per cent (Abbasi-Shawazi 2000).

Marriage is an important institution in Asia, and an expensive one. Ostentatious emulation of weddings has called forth legal interventions against them, albeit without any obvious effect. South Korea passed a Family Ritual Code with that aim in 1969, strengthening it in 1973 (Kendall 1996: 68), Vietnam passed a similar one in 1986 (Pham Van Bich 1997), and Pakistan promulgated in 1997 a Marriages (Prohibition of Wasteful Expenses) Act (Menski 1998). Marriage was historically much more important as a necessary link in the generational chain, than as a sexual union. Marital fertility was considerably lower, at two or three children, in Asia than in Europe (Lee and Wang 1999: 86–87).

Contemporary Asian marriages are not likely to follow the way India's first President, Rajendra Prasad, began his marital life. In the middle of the night his mother would send a maid-servant to wake him up and take him to his wife's room. Before morning he had to be back in his own bed (Narrain 1970: 458). But separate conjugal sleeping quarters, parents sleeping with their children rather than with each other, or sharing a bedroom with other family members have survived into living memory and into our own times (see Mandelbaum (1970: 74ff) on India; Caudill and Weinstein (1970: 41) on the Japanese middle class; Parish and Farrer (2000: 263n) on contemporary China). In the early 1950s, the chance of a Korean marriage leading to a birth after 9–11 months was no more than 10 per cent, among Malays of Malaysia 17 per cent. A minor revolution of marital sex in the 1960s would increase the probability to one in three (Rindfuss and Morgan 1983: 261ff).

The Japanese family sociologist Fumie Kumagai (1995: 151) has recently characterized Japanese marriage as an 'unintegrated conjugal relationship'.

Table 5.8 Married girls in Iran aged 15–19, 1976–96

Year	(%)
1976	34
1986	34
2000	18

Sources: 1976–86: Abbasi-Shawazi (2000); 1996: Calculations from Iran, Statistical Center (2000–1: table 2.24).

African specificity through colonialism and national crises

African marriage is an intricate, colourful mosaic of rules, customs and practices, to the complexity of which no non-specialist can ever give justice (excellent overviews are given by Radcliffe-Brown and Forde (1950), Philips (1953/1969), Goody (1976), Oppong (1983), Kayongo-Male and Onyango (1984), Parkin and Nyamwaya (1987), Lestaeghe (1989) and Caldwell *et al.* (1992)). As noted above in the part on patriarchy, the overall pattern may be seen as divided by a diagonal line, between economically autonomous wives on the northwestern coast, often not even residing with their husbands all of the time, and wives as property of the family of their husbands, a predominant, if not universal, pattern in the southeast, from the Horn to the Cape. In between is a largely matrilineal belt of middle Africa, where wives have often been under the thumb of an elder brother, and where the husband is often a weak role-figure. In northern Nigeria and generally in the Muslim Sahel, a milder form of the West and South Asian seclusion of women has developed.

The African family was non-nuclear. Kin was always more important than spouse – siblings and maternal kin in matrilineal families, inter-male paternal kin and the father-in-law family in the patrilineal cases. According to several norms, individuals in a given marriage were substitutable. Mass polygyny, spread all over the continent, meant that wives in general were exchangeable: barren or otherwise undesirable wives could be replaced or supplemented by a sister; a dead husband was to be succeeded by his brother. In some customs a wife could 'marry' another woman to bear children for her, and for the husband and his kin, in others the husband's friends who belonged to his own initiation age group had some sexual access to his wife.

The African sexual order was less rigid than the Eurasian, also in relation to female sexuality, or, better, to the female body as a sexual object. Adultery, at least in Southern Africa, was a male offence, for which compensation had to be paid if he was caught. In patrilineal societies the man responsible was the one who had preyed upon another man's wife, in matrilineal ones it was the father of the sexually abused woman (Jeater 1993: ch. 6). African marriage had a strong proprietary character in the patrilineal societies of the east and the south, and of the Sahel, because of the payment of bridewealth by the groom to the bride's family.

Change of the African marriage has been slow in the past century, with hardly any major turns or new tendencies in the first half, except for the hinterlands of the colonial enclaves. The general thrust of secular change has not been nuclearization, contrary to the master narrative of family modernization and of William Goode's (1963) great work, even though such tendencies have taken place. Rather it is a move towards new variants of specific African complexity, for instance non-cohabiting marriages. The main populations of Ghana are matrilineal and more tied to their families of maternal origin than to their spouse. In a town of Ashanti, the largest ethnic group, in the 1970s, 45 per cent of married women were living together with their husbands, and the rest with their mothers – as their husbands lived with theirs, in the same town (Abu 1983: 161; see further Ardayfio-Schandorf 1996).

Polygyny has maintained itself well on a massive continental scale, although it has declined among impoverished cattle-breeders of the east, like the Gusii in western Kenya, or of the south, like the Tswana of Botswana (Table 5.9). South Africa has not been included in the surveys, and South African statistics do not register it, although statisticians are aware of it (Bullender 1997). In 1921, 14 per cent of married African men had more than one wife, in 1951 at most 9 per cent, and probably less. Around the turn of the previous century a third of traditionally married males in Natal were polygynous (Simons 1968: ch. VIII). Nor does Congo/Kinshasa appear in Table 5.9, where earlier surveys indicated a relatively low frequency of polygyny (Lestaeghe *et al.* 1989: table 6.19). Sudan is a border region between sub-Saharan Africa and the Arab world, and the social distance between Africa and Yemen, one of the most traditional Arab societies, is noteworthy.

Most polygamous are the West Africans, along the coast as well as inland in the Sahel. The highest scorers are countries of predominantly Muslim and/or indigenous African religion, and of patrilineal kinship. Polygamy is more rural than urban, but the difference is usually rather small. In Senegal, for instance, 51 per cent of rural wives and 44 per cent of urban women had at least one co-

Table 5.9 African polygyny around 2000

Percentage of married women 15–49 having at least one co-wife			
High score		*Low score*	
Burkina Faso	55	Burundi	12[a]
Guinea	54	Namibia	12
Benin	50	Rwanda	14
Senegal	49	Ethiopia	14
Mali	44	Kenya	16
Togo	43	Zambia	17
Chad	39	Zimbabwe	19
Niger	38	Gabon	22
Nigeria	36	Ghana	23
Ivory Coast	35	Mozambique	28
Uganda	33	Tanzania	29
Malawi	32		
Memorandum			
Northern Sudan	20[a]		
Yemen	7		
Nepal	6		
Madagascar	4		

Sources: All data are from the International Demographic and Health Surveys. Burundi, Malawi, Namibia, Rwanda and Sudan are taken from Timaeus and Reynar (1998: table 1); the rest are from the Demographic and Health Surveys (DHS) of 1996–2001.

Note:
a 1986–90.

wife; in Nigeria the corresponding figures were 38 and 31 per cent. A fifth of Nigerian women with a secondary education or more had a co-wife, and in Senegal a quarter (DHS 1996–2001).

The lowest scores of polygyny are all in the east and the south (Botswana should be in the vicinity of Namibia in this respect too) which were more under Christian and colonial influence, and also hit by economic marginalization through the encroachments of white settlers. But it should be noted that Catholic Burundi has a higher frequency of polygyny than Muslim Yemen. The matrilineal middle African belt from northern Mozambique to Gabon, and the Akan peoples of Ghana and part of Ivory Coast have a relatively low rate of polygyny by the generous African standard.

The current household structure of urban South Africa also points to a continuing African path of development, rather than a rapprochement to the Euro-American age of industrial marriage (Table 5.10). The extended, most frequently three-generation, family remains a major feature, and its weight is probably underestimated in Table 5.10, as one should suspect that a good number of the 'unspecified' households have some kind of extended form. But even discarding them, there are as many extended families and single-parent households as there are couples, with and without children.

A particular African form of family complexity is the fostering, lending and borrowing of children, usually among kin (Table 5.11). This is an ancient way of coping with changes in the family cycle, and with contingencies of various kinds. To the extent that it functions well, it means a wider net of support and affection for the children; to the extent that it does not, it must be traumatic. To my knowledge there is no firm evidence allowing a conclusion of which is the more important tendency.

Since the 1970s, a process towards later female marriages has got under way in most of Africa, except the savannah region in the west (DHS surveys). In the 1990s, the average marriage age of Hausa women in northern Nigeria was just under 15, with no trend between the birth cohorts of 1950 and of the 1970s (Heaton and Hirschl 1999: table 2). But it has not got very far elsewhere either; in Kenya, Tanzania, Uganda and Zimbabwe, for example, half or more of all girls married before the age of 20.

Except in Southern Africa the general rule of universal marriage has main-

Table 5.10 The household structure of the black population of South Africa, 1996 (%)

	Urban population	Rural population
Single adult	21	13
Couple, with/without children	32	22
Single parent with children	11	18
Extended family	23	30
Three or more unrelated adults	2	2
Unspecified	11	15

Source: Ziehl (2002a: table 9).

Table 5.11 Children aged 10–14 in African households with both
parents, and with no parent present, 1995–2000 (as a
percentage of all children in the age group)

	Both parents	Neither parent
Ethiopia	58	18
Ghana	41	25
Kenya	53	17
Nigeria	65	19
Senegal	57	22
Tanzania	50	24
Uganda	44	30
Zimbabwe	39	29
South Africa[a]	40	13
Memorandum		
Brazil	67	11
Indonesia	83	7
Sweden[b]	69	<1
Turkey	89	3
USA[c]	69	4

Sources: South Africa: Ziehl (2000: table 8.7); Sweden: SCB (2000: 55, 199);
USA: US Census Bureau 2001d: table CH-1; the rest: DHS data.

Notes:
a Black children under 7.
b 12-year-olds.
c Children under 18.

tained itself, although now complicated by temporary cohabitation and informal polygyny (see further below, pp. 212–15).

Three large-scale processes of change have crucially affected African
marriages in the course of the twentieth century: the uneven and crisis-ridden
economic development; accelerating urbanization; and the colonial legacy of
legal and normative pluralism in family matters.

The colonial economic development consisted of mining enclaves and new
cash-crop areas, with their labour force supply regulated by residential segregation and arbitrary administrative, later national boundaries, tied in with the
low-intensity coupling of the African family. The result was a pattern of long-
distance, long-term male labour migration, leaving wives behind in an increasingly impoverished hinterland of subsistence agriculture. On the largest scale
this grew up in Southern Africa, and from the Sahel down to the Ivory Coast.
The migration routes to and from the early colonial construction projects
became paths for the spread of venereal disease, and more recently for the
spread of AIDS (Caldwell *et al.* 1992).

The monetarization of the African economy meant also a monetarization of
the bridewealth, which, given the centrality of the latter in African marriage,
gave a push to the commodification of coupling. The general economic crisis
since the 1970s, aggravated by a speeding population growth has tended to
exhaust kinship solidarity without bases for new forms of family stability.

A second important process of social transformation has been urbanization,
accelerating rapidly, from a very low base, in the second half of the century

Table 5.12 The urban population of sub-Saharan Africa, 1900–2000 (as a percentage of the total population)

1900	1950	1975	2000
3	7	21	34

Sources: 1900–50: Bairoch (1988: 417, 430); 1975–2000: UNDP (2002: table 5).

(Table 5.12). The pre-colonial-cum-colonial legacy of urbanization in Africa meant a very different impact in western Africa compared to the rest. Although major western cities such as Lagos and Abidjan are colonial creations, there was in the west a pre-colonial urban and trading tradition, which made for a sex-balanced population, and legitimate female economic autonomy. In the east, the south and the centre, there was no such background, and the colonial urban population was overwhelmingly male, with few female activities other than prostitution and beer-brewing/bar-keeping (Southall 1961: ch. V). Since 1975 this has, more or less, been a crisis urbanization, under conditions of rotting infrastructure, informalization of the economy, precariousness, and slumming. This is a process which we should expect to lead more in the direction of the Caribbean and of the US ghettos, than to settled industrial conjugality.

Colonial rule in Africa left a normative dualism with respect to family and marriage. The colonial powers introduced statutory family laws or 'ordinances' according to their national and Christian traditions, but at the same time they also recognized African customs, and later compiled the latter into customary law. In spite of missionary efforts, 'ordinance marriages' were not a success, but they were on the statute books and in several ways more congenial to the nationalist modernist project of the Independence leaders, than the motley variety of 'tribal' customary law.

The first post-Independence wave of attempts at national reform and unification of family failed more or less completely. But inspired by the UN women's programmes, efforts in the 1990s have been more successful, unshackled by crumbling rural tradition, although their implementation is still in many places an open question (Philips and Morris 1971; Eekelaar and Nhlapo 1998).

The coexistence of two or more legal systems has made marital strategies and conflicts possible which have claimed to follow either this or that code, for what is a valid marriage, a ground for divorce and/or alimony, a right to inherit. As seen in the chapter on patriarchy, African customary law is very patriarchal, and recent tendencies at legal reform are strengthening the position of women generally, and of wives particularly. This is a change also working in favour of the couple.

The world of marriage in 2000

Contrary to what many may believe, in Western Europe about as many people are married today as a hundred years ago, i.e. in the specific sense of women ever married by the end of their fertile life-period (Table 5.13). The main

Table 5.13 Western European women never married by the age
of 45–49, *c.* 1900 and 2000 (as a percentage of age
group)

	1900	2000[a]
Austria	13	17
Belgium	17	12
Denmark	13	16
Finland	15	18
France	12	14
Germany	10	13
Ireland	17[b]	13
Italy	11	6
Netherlands, the	14	12
Norway	18	14
Portugal	20	4[c]
Spain	10	13
Sweden	19	27
Switzerland	17	20
UK	17[d]	8
Unweighted average	*15*	*14*

Sources: 1900: Hajnal (1965: 102); 2000: Eurostat (2000a: table F11).

Notes:
a The figure for 2000 refers to the proportion never married by 1999
in the age cohort born in 1955.
b 1891.
c Birth cohort of 1960.
d Great Britain.

change over the century is that Portugal and Italy have moved from a Western
European to an Eastern European marriage pattern. Over the century the
proportion marrying and non-marrying has changed in both directions,
leaving very little net change. Austria and Belgium even each other out, and
so do Sweden and the UK.

Both columns of Table 5.13 sum up family processes of the preceding half
century, from the time the women were born. Rather reliable marriage projections may be made for some younger birth cohorts. For the female cohorts
born in 1965, of whom most of those who are ever to marry have married
already, the marriage probabilities for Bulgaria, Russia and Portugal are
around 95 per cent, for ex-Czechoslovakia and for Hungary around 90 per
cent, for Belgium, Ireland, Italy and Spain just above 80 per cent, for
Denmark, Germany and the UK just below 80 per cent, for Finland, France and
Norway above 70 per cent. Swedish women are by far the least likely to marry –
about 60 per cent of those born in 1965 (Council of Europe 2001a: fig. G.2.4).

Although this will be a new experience for several countries, for France for
example, the only 1965 cohort which is outside the previous twentieth-century
Western European range of non-marriage is the Swedish (see Table 5.1).

In the United States too, the net change of marital status between 1900 and
2000 is minimal. In 1900, 7.8 per cent of women aged 45–54 had never

married, in 2000, 8.6 per cent had not (Haines 1996: table 2; US Census Bureau 2001d: table 5). Among women born in 1961–65 nine out of ten are estimated to marry, and 92 to 94 per cent of white US women, whereas Afro-American women are no more likely to marry than the Swedish (Goldstein and Kenney 2001). White Americans still have a slightly higher propensity to marry than shown in the US record of 1900, as well as higher than the cohort of Amerian women born in 1900.

There are some cultural indications of a particular Anglo New World attachment to marriage, within the Europe overseas settlement cultures. The (dis)agreement with two statements in a 1994 International Social Survey are interesting here. The first stated that in general married persons are more happy than non-married, the second that the main advantage of marriage was the economic security it provided. Australia, Canada and the USA were unique in this Old and New World European survey in yielding significant agreement with the first and little with the second. The agreement distribution to the first–second statements was 44–16 in Australia, 32–8 in Canada, 47–17 in USA, in contrast to 25–22 in Britain, 42–39 in Germany, 59–56 in Russia, and 33–34 in Spain (International Social Survey 1994).

In Eastern Europe virtually universal marriage was maintained in Bulgaria until the generation of women born after 1955. In Russia, the Czech Republic and Hungary of that generation 95 per cent will marry, in Slovakia above 90 per cent.

The distribution of the relative marriage age in Europe in 2000 is basically the same as in 1900, still following the Hajnal line from Trieste to St Petersburg (Table 5.14). Among the 33 countries included in Table 5.14 there are only two real overlaps: Greece east of the Hajnal line, with a rather late marriage age of 26.6; and Portugal in the west, where women marry at 25.2. Compared with the situation in 1900 (Table 4.1), the distance between Eastern and Western Europe has narrowed to about two years. Around 1900 the age difference between Britain and Russia, for example, was six years, in 1995 it was four. Mainly it is Eastern Europe which has moved, but the historical marriage system differences remain.

Table 5.14 Female mean age at first marriage in Europe in 2000, east and west of the Trieste–St Petersburg line (years of age)

	East of the line	*West of the line*
Range	21.0–26.6	25.2–30.2
Unweighted average	*23.8*	*26.8*

Source: Council of Europe (2001b: table T2.3).

Countries: *East*: Albania, Belarus, Bulgaria, Croatia, Greece, Hungary, Macedonia, Moldova, Romania, Russia (1995), Slovakia, Yugoslavia. Data for Bosnia (22.3 in 1990) and the Ukraine were missing. *West*: Austria, Belgium, Czech Republic, Denmark, Estonia, Finland, France, Germany, Ireland, Italy, Latvia, Lithuania, the Netherlands, Norway, Poland, Portugal, Slovenia. Spain, Sweden, Switzerland, UK.

What will happen to the younger generations, will depend on how long the post-Communist socio-economic crisis, for the majority of the populations, endures.

Currently, marriage is being postponed, and the conjunctural marriage rate has plummeted since the end of Communism. In the very unlikely case that the marriage halt of 2000 should be permanent, there are some countries in the Council of Europe (2001b: table T2.2) area where only a minority of women would ever marry: Armenia 34 per cent, Estonia 39 per cent, ex-GDR 47 per cent (in 1999), Georgia 41 per cent, Hungary 49 per cent, Latvia 40 per cent, and Slovenia 45 per cent. The impoverishment or uncertainty of post-Communist capitalism seems to be the main reason here, combined, outside the Caucasian disaster area, with features of an East-Central European, rather than Eastern European, family. In Russia in 1995, the marriage rate was still 0.75, and in 2000 Belarus and Romania had a rate of 0.64, Yugoslavia of 0.68, Macedonia of 0.83, but the Bulgarian rate had gone down to 0.52. Catholic Poland registered a rate of 0.63, while the secularized Czech Republic was down to 0.50.

But these conjunctural marriage rates can gyrate wildly in periods of rapid change, without necessarily indicating that a new pattern is being established. In the 1965 birth cohort, as we saw above, 90–95 per cent of Eastern European women will marry. No longer universal, this propensity to marry is still clearly higher than in Western Europe.

Let us now see what has happened to the universality of Asian and African marriages (Table 5.15). Some fissures in the Afro-Asian marriage institution have developed, in racially mixed and slummed South Africa above all, underestimated in Table 5.15 with the inclusion of unions of cohabitation, and in a few other African countries, such as Mozambique and Gabon, which will be touched upon below. The Vietnamese development is very recent, and may include some survey margin of error, but the figure refers to the genera-

Table 5.15 Marriage propensities in Africa and Asia, 1990–2000 (percentage of women never married by age 45–49)

Country	Year	(%)	Country	Year	(%)
Nigeria	1999	1.1	China	1990	0.2
South Africa	1991	10.6[a]	South Korea	1995	1.0
Egypt	2000	1.5	Zimbabwe	1999	0.6
Kazakhstan	1999	5.9	Turkey	1998	1.7
Bangladesh	1999/2000	0.0	Uzbekistan	1996	1.4
Pakistan	1991	2.0	India	1998/99	0.8
Myanmar	1997	12.1	Philippines	1998	6.6
Indonesia	1997	1.7	Thailand	1990	5.2
Vietnam	1997	9.9	Japan	1990	4.6

Sources: China, Japan, Korea, Pakistan, South Africa and Thailand are census data from UN (2001b); the rest are survey data from DHS.

Note:
a Includes informal unions.

tion of women who should have married during the American war. In these matters, as in so many others, little is known about what is going on in Myanmar, and there were hardly any signs of departure from universal marriage before the military coup closed the country in 1962 (Spiro 1977: ch. 6). The Buddhist country has a tradition of relative female autonomy and of marital informality, but UN data also show a strong gender imbalance of celibacy (only 5.7 per cent among males), which may indicate some particular migration patterns. We noted above that universal marriage is eroding in some big cities of Southeast Asia and Japan, but this has not progressed far in the biggest country of the region, Indonesia.

While Japanese marriages are getting later, and some will not happen at all, the marital propensity in Japan is still impressive from a European vantage-point, with 74 per cent of women aged 30–34 being married in 2000 (Japan Statistics Bureau 2001). It is even more impressive, or at least intriguing, as the Japanese do not seem to be very happily married. Surveyed in 1994, Americans were overwhelmingly happy in their marriage, 87 per cent, but only 42 per cent of the Japanese, who more often gave a neutral answer (Inoue 1998: table 2.5). The most populous regions of the world, China and South Asia, still keep marriage universal. In 1995, 98.8 per cent of Chinese women had married by the age of 30 (Lee and Wang 1999: table 5.2). Central Asia (with some qualifications for Slavic Kazakhstan), West Asia, North Africa and most of sub-Saharan Africa also have more or less universal marriage.[2]

Creole America has come closer to Western Europe, but is still standing out from Asia and Africa. Incomplete statistics and survey tendencies to merge marriage and informal sexual unions make an exact quantitative assessment difficult. Occasionally census numbers glimmer, though. Among the 199 politically delimited territories included in the UN marriage overview, the only ones in which less than two-thirds of women had been married by the end of their fertility were Caribbean countries and dependent territories, products of plantation slavery and indentured labour, giving rise to what we have here called the Afro-Creole family. In Jamaica, for instance, only 54 per cent had ever married, in Grenada 57 per cent and in Barbados 60 per cent (UN 2001b). For many similar Caribbean islands and countries, corresponding figures available are off target, as they include non-married cohabitation. Some South American countries, Colombia, Chile, Ecuador, Paraguay and Venezuala reported marriage rates in the range of 85–89 per cent, even by including informal unions.

No Western European country has by 2000 reached the Jamaican situation of 1990, but Sweden in 2010 is expected to resemble Barbados in 1990, with respect to marriage frequency. The West Indies keep a world lead in non-marriage.

In order to get a better comparative grasp of the Creole sex–marriage complex we may make more use of the Demographic and Health Surveys, supplementing them with rather comparable data from a Swedish survey (Table 5.16). While first marriages will not have ceased by the late thirties age group in Northwestern Europe and in the Americas, a characteristic pattern of

Table 5.16 Marital status of women aged 35–39 in Creole America and some other
countries for comparison (as a percentage of all in the age group)

	Never married	Married	Cohabiting	Not cohabiting	Widow/divorcée
Brazil (1996)	8.2	65.8	14.6	7.4	3.9
Colombia (2000)	10.0	41.7	27.7	17.1	3.4
Dom. Rep. (1996)	4.5	32.5	43.0	14.3	5.8
Guatemala (1998/9)	3.6	58.3	27.6	7.9	2.6
Nicaragua (1997/8)	3.2	37.7	35.4	21.1	2.6
Peru (2000)	9.1	52.6	26.1	9.6	2.5
Philippines (1998)	7.5	79.7	7.3	3.3	2.2
Nigeria (1999)	1.9	84.9	8.3	1.7	3.2
Sweden (1992/3)[a]	25.3[b]	62.9	14.8	22.2	11.5[b]

Sources: Sweden: FFS (Fertility and Family Surveys); the rest: DHS data.

Notes:
a Women age 38.
b Figures refer to singles or to previously married, but they are also included in the counting
of cohabitees and non-cohabitees.

singlehood–cohabitation–marriage will have crystallized. The most interesting,
and the most reliable, data are those for married, cohabiting and not cohabiting. While Brazil has become rather similar to Sweden, the Caribbean and the
Andean countries in the survey differ strongly even from the informal outlier
of Western Europe, not to mention their distance from their once colonial
relative or from the ancestral country of many Afro-American descendants.
But also within Creole America differences are substantial. The regional marriage to cohabitation ratio ranges from 2:1 in Peru to 0.75:1 in the Dominican
Republic. Sweden, with a 4:1 ratio, is closer to the Caribbean than to Nigeria
at 10:1 and the most informal part of Southeast Asia, with almost 11 marriages
to 1 cohabitation.

The main conclusion of this section can only be, that despite significant
regional variations, and in spite of informal experimentation among the
younger generations, mainly of Europe, the Americas and some parts of
Africa, marriage remains the dominant institution of the global socio-sexual
order. Any opposite argument would be provincial, at most.

Only in the Caribbean, the Andes, countries of Southern Africa, and
possibly Scandinavia is marriage seriously challenged by informal sexual
unions. Very generously calculated, one may say that among 40 per cent of
the world population a pluralistic pattern of sexual relations – with predominant marriage coexisting with cohabitation and (non-commercially)
sexually active singlehood – is within current practice. That would include
Europe, the Americas, sub-Saharan Africa, Oceania, Japan and some urban
enclaves of East and Southeast Asia. But 60 per cent of the world population
live in the rest of Asia and in North Africa. And in major parts of Latin
America, such as Brazil, Mexico, Argentina, Chile, as well as in the large cities

of continental Western Europe, there is more marriage and marital familism today than 150 years ago.

However, the social and the sexual contexts in which the hopes, the ideals, the norms and the practices of marriage unfold and operate are changing. In the final sections of this chapter we shall look into some contemporary currents of change.

The great disruption – and the smaller ones

Marriage and family are cherished themes of social conservatism, central to its conception of desirable order. Individual rights, of women and children above all, are viewed negatively, as a breakdown or at least serious threat to order. In the current world of the European family system, this conservatism is particularly strong in the United States, although, less surprisingly, facing a strong counterpoint of individualism as well. Francis Fukuyama (1999), plugged into a powerful circuit when he made 'soaring' divorce together with lower fertility and more crime, a key feature of a 'Great Disruption in the social values' and of 'breakdown of social order'.

This is not a work of ideological polemic, so there is no reason to argue further. But Fukuyama's book title provides a good pointer to the recent decline of *the* great disrupter of marriage and family life – death. While death is the final, great disruption, separation and divorce are smaller ones, however nasty a divorce litigation might be. Marriage has been extended by the strong decline of adult mortality and by the increased longevity of older people. This has given rise to a new couple, rare in the past, the 'empty nest' pair with another 20–30 years of marital life after the children have started out on their own (cf. Hareven 2000). But, more important, it has also provided more stable childhoods, a stability only very recently and incrementally affected by parental separation and divorce.

While not exactly representative, Sweden has never been held an outlier of extreme marital stability, so Swedish data may have some international relevance here (Table 5.17). In the cohort of the 1900s, 17 per cent experienced a parent's death before the age of 16, while less than 1 per cent experienced a parental separation. Among the children of the 1960s, 3 per cent had their lives disrupted by parental death, while 15 per cent saw their parents separate. Six per cent of the generation had parents who never lived together, in contrast to 1 per cent of the previous turn of the century (SCB 2002b: 36).[3]

Table 5.17 Children living with both parents until the age of 16: Swedish birth cohorts, 1900–83 (%)

		Children born in		
1900–9	*1930–39*	*1950–59*	*1960–69*	*1980–83*
69	74	83	76	66

Sources: 1980–83: SCB (2000: 55); other years: SCB (1992: 34).

In the United States, at the vanguard of 'European-family' divorce since the nineteenth century, there were more widowers than male divorcees until the 1970s, and more widows than female divorcees until 1997 (US Census Bureau 2001d: table HH-1). Also in Sweden, male divorcees overtook widowers as part of the total population only between 1970 and 1975. By 1998 Sweden still had more widows than divorcees (SCB 1999: table 1.7). It has been calculated that in 1900 the probability that an American marriage would be disrupted by death within 40 years was 67 per cent, but in 1976 it was 36 per cent. The risk of disruption by death or divorce was 71 per cent in 1900, and 60 per cent in 1976 (Uhlenberg 1993: table 4.4). The 'death-to-divorce transition' (Pinsof 2002) is a recent, non-equivalent phenomenon, and, from a global perspective, a provincial one.

In many parts of the world, the great disruption of death is still predominant. From the Demographic and Health Surveys of the late 1990s we get the following picture. Among middle-aged women (45–49), divorcee is a significant state only in three countries: on the Comoro Islands (12.0 per cent), in Ghana (11.8 per cent), and in Kazakhstan (9.9 per cent). If we add separation from former partner, and currently not living together with one, we should add all the nine Latin American countries to the set, with the highest proportions in Nicaragua (22.1 per cent), Colombia (21.0 per cent) and the Dominican Republic (18.6 per cent). A major country like Brazil had 9.7 per cent 'not living together' and 1.8 per cent divorced. But (not remarried) widows account for more than a tenth of all women aged 45–49 in 17 of the 47 countries. Nineteen per cent of this age group of women in Kenya and Cambodia are widows, 17 per cent in Chad, 16 per cent in Bangladesh, Cameroon, Egypt and Zimbabwe, 13 per cent in India and Indonesia. Death is the dominant disrupter of Asian marriages, and of marriages in most African countries.

In upper-caste India, widowhood is still equivalent to social death, although the ancient taboo of widow remarriage, or even of maintaining an ordinary life single, has been legally broken (see Chen 1998).

Historically, divorce was possible wherever marriage was not seen as a sacral union, i.e. outside the Hindu and the Catholic Christian worlds. The Orthodox and the Protestant currents of Christianity made divorce generally very difficult, accepting only a few grounds for it – refusal of sex, sexual adultery, desertion – and requiring elaborate and expensive procedures, for which the populace sometimes found its own substitutes. African customs also usually made divorce difficult and expensive, requiring back payment of the bride-wealth. Islam, Buddhism and the Sinic civilization of East Asia saw marriage as a worldy union, albeit (except to the Buddhists) a strong normative prescription, and therefore dissolvable. However, the patriarchal drive of these cultures made divorce mainly a male prerogative. Only under very special exceptions was it allowed to wives; impotence was one reason which the Islamic schools of jurisprudence accepted.

In the Christian countries, no-fault divorce began in Scandinavia: in Norway in 1909, and then, promoted by the Scandinavian Law Commission set up in the same year, in the Swedish Marriage Law of 1915. The Russian

Revolution installed a secularized and individualist conception of marriage and divorce in 1918, to retract it under Stalinist social conservatism from 1936, making divorce difficult and expensive. The USA harboured relatively generous divorce legislation from the mid-nineteenth century, but the principle of no-fault divorce had its first breakthrough only in 1969, in California, from where it spread immediately. In the same year, England, the most Catholic of the Protestant countries, adopted a secular notion of marriage, after its political leadership in 1936 had created a constitutional crisis, forcing the King to abdicate for his intention to marry a divorced woman.

In the Catholic lands there was an anti-clerical strand, going back to the French Revolution, which was in favour of divorce, particularly over wifely adultery, and which sometimes, as in the French Third Republic or after the Liberal revolutions in Latin America and Iberia, got the upper hand politically. But the Catholic opposition was adamant, and often bounced back. Therefore, the Italian referendum in 1974, which the secularists won, was a major breakthrough. Today only the states of Ireland and Chile refuse to allow divorce.

The princely state of Baroda was, in 1931, the first polity admitting divorce to Hindus, under certain restrictive conditions, followed by the province of Bombay in 1947. In 1955 India passed the Hindu Marriage Act, allowing no-fault consensual divorce (Beri 1992). In the rest of Asia and in Africa, divorce rights to be won were mainly women's rights, and were part of the dismantling of patriarchy, from the 1947 Japanese Civil Code under US occupation and the Communist Revolution in China to the democratic 1980s and 1990s in post-colonial Southern Africa.[4]

In historical practice, the highest ever recorded divorce rates were registered in the first half of the twentieth century, among Muslim Malays in contemporary Malaysia and Indonesia (Jones 1994). Moderately high rates around the previous turn of the century can be found in Japan and in Taiwan, where the rates then went down (Goode 1993: 220ff, 299ff), and may be suspected in parts of the West Asian/North African world, where there were high rates in the 1930s and 1940s (UN 1951: table 56 on Egypt in 1935; Roudolph-Touha 1979: 229 on Iran in the 1940s). In 1899 the Egyptian judge Qasim Amin (Emin 1899/1928) wrote that in the past 18 years three-quarters of Cairene marriages had been dissolved.

Among Christian countries, the USA had the most divorces by far, followed at a considerable distance by Switzerland, but the latter were much less frequent than in the high-divorce countries. The US crude divorce in 1920 was only half of the Japanese rate in 1890, and the other post-war US peak rate, in 1946, was lower than the Egyptian one of 1935 (UN 1951: table 25; US Census Bureau 1975: tables B216–20; Goode 1993: fig. 8.1).

We may get a sense of proportion of current divorce rates, by comparing them to mid-twentieth-century peak cases (Table 5.18). The extraordinary Malay rates were no conjunctural crisis phenomenon, but a century-old custom, according to the authority on the topic, the Australian demographer Gavin Jones (1994). It did not constitute a breakdown of social order, it was

Table 5.18 Crude divorce rates around the world, 1950–99 (1950–85 per thousand population over 15; 1990s per thousand population)

	1950	1965	1985	1998/99
Malays of Peninsular Malaysia	20.3	7.4	2.8	–
Singapore Malays	18.2	2.6	2.7	–
Muslims of Indonesia	15.1	11.0	1.5	–
Egypt	4.8	3.9	2.8	1.2
Iran	2.8	1.8	1.4	0.7
Turkey	0.6	0.7	0.6	0.5
USA	3.5	3.5	6.3	4.2
USSR	–	2.2	4.5	3.7[a]
West Germany	2.0	1.3	2.5	2.3
England and Wales	0.9	1.0	4.0	2.9[b]
Sweden	1.8[c]	2.0	–	2.4
Japan	–	–	–	1.9
Cuba	–	–	–	3.5
South Africa	–	–	–	3.7[d]

Sources: Sweden 1950–65: SCB (1967: tables 18 and 33); South Africa: Ziehl (2002b: table 89); the rest of 1950–85: Jones (1994: table 5.8); 1998/99: UN (2001a: table 25).

Notes:
a Russia.
b UK.
c Annual average 1951–55.
d 1993.

part of it. Marriages were early and parentally arranged, and a major part of the divorce regime seems to have been a Malay flexibility adjustment of rigid Muslim-cum-Hindu practices, of universal marriage by puberty, an outlet for individual incompatibility. Many of the divorces would rather have corresponded to broken engagements in Christian Europe, as they were not sexually consummated. Education, later marriages, more self-investment and autonomy in marriage, and nationalist–modernist public discouragement – making divorce dependent on administrative and judicial procedures, beginning in earnest in Singapore in 1957 and followed in Indonesia and Malaysia (Jones 1994: 246ff) – brought down the divorce regime. On another scale, the decline of divorce in Egypt and Iran, possibly also Japan and Taiwan, may have had similar forces behind it, including post-World War II judicialization of the ancient Muslim male right of repudiation, a process starting in Syria in 1953 (Esposito 1982: 93).

Crude rates are crude measures, not taking the different age and marital structures into account. Nor do the patchy Latin American statistics give any indication of the separation of the many informal unions, and from sub-Saharan Africa there is very little offical information. From the Demographic and Health Surveys we know that sexual unions, married or not, in some African countries have an instability similar to that in the Dominican Republic, or between the latter and Colombia (54–72 per cent in their first union): Ghana and Liberia in the west, Uganda and Tanzania in the east, and Zambia in the south. Nigeria, on the other hand, and Kenya have more stability, with 80 per cent of their fertile-age women in their first sexual union, similar to Indonesia, Morocco, Brazil and Peru, but less than the 94 per cent in Pakistan (Westoff *et al.* 1994: table 4.2).

But on the whole, the crude official data give a reasonably good view of the global pattern. Most divorce is found among the main protagonists of the Cold War: in the USA (4.2 per thousand population) and in the core successor states of the Soviet Union – Russia (3.7), Ukraine (3.6) and Belarus (4.6). Cuba (3.5) and South Africa are also among the highest divorcers of the world. Cuba apart, the highest comparable Latin American rates are those of Costa Rica and Uruguay (both 2.0). The 1998 Japanese figure (1.9) is higher than in 1900 (1.5), but lower than in 1890 (>2.5). The Chinese rate is also low: 0.8 in 1996 (in Beijing and Shanghai 1.7; Parish and Farrer 2000: 265). In India, divorce is still rare, too rare to be reported to the UN at least. According to the Demographic and Health Survey of India in 1999, 0.5 per cent of women aged 30–34 and 0.6 per cent of aged 35–39 were divorced.

When the data allow it, demographers have another way of measuring divorce, the so-called total divorce rate, which indicates the probability that existing marriages will break up by divorce some time within a certain period of duration – in Council of Europe calculations 30 years. At the East–West Center (2002) in Honolulu it has been estimated that one in five of Chinese, Japanese and Korean marriages will end in divorce under current tendencies, i.e. a total divorce rate around 0.20. We may keep that in mind while looking at some European figures (Table 5.19).

Half of all Russian, Swedish and American marriages seem likely to end in divorce. In Russia the jump upwards came after 1965 (from 0.19 to 0.34 in 1970), in Western Europe after 1970 or later. In 1970 the French rate was 0.12, the West German 0.15, the Swedish 0.23 and the British 0.16. The intra-European variation may be underlined, from a divorce risk of one in ten to one in two. In Europe as in the world as a whole, divorce has a very variable location in the socio-sexual order.

Table 5.19 Total divorce rates in Europe, 1995–2000

Country	Rate	Country	Rate
France	0.38	Russia	0.50
Germany	0.39	Spain	0.15
Italy	0.08	Sweden	0.55
Poland	0.17	UK	0.43
Memorandum			
USA 1980 (peak year)	0.59	USA 1985	0.55

Sources: USA: Mounier (1998: table 5); the rest: Council of Europe (2001a: table T2.5).

6　The return of cohabitation and the sexual revolution

Boundaries blurred: marriage and non-marriage

The institution of marriage has always, almost everywhere had its outlying areas, without obvious, demarcated and guarded borders. Terrains of marriage have not seldom been contested, and representatives of other institutions – political, religious, economic have at times been at a loss how to tread. In some parts of the world, with no religious interest in marriage and no civilian bureaucracy, like Siam and Burma a century or less ago, most people's marriages were no more than actual cohabitation. The African practice, still in use if no longer generally accepted, of protracted negotiations and payments of bridewealth, leaves a large number of relationships on a contestable ground between marriage and non-marriage. The colonial invention, and the post-colonial legacy, of legal pluralism, between statutory law and ethno-religious 'customary' law, give rise to possible rival claims of marriage and non-marriage, on occasions of separation or death. The concubine of the Sinic civilizations was a sexual role, less than a married wife but (usually) more than a mistress, not to speak of a side affair, with certain publicly recognized rights. Post-colonial Latin American law accommodated from early on the widespread custom of informal unions among the popular classes and the subordinate ethnicities.

Even where there were strong normative rules of early universal marriage, of girls in particular, there could be a remarkable porosity, through provision of exit holes. Above we noted the Malay Muslim custom of early mass divorce, most frequently within a year of marriage, and ideally before it had been sexually consummated, and the Shi'ite invention of the institution of 'temporary marriage', a fixed-term sexual contract, as their contribution to sexual flexibility.

Within Christianity there have been many different conceptions of what constitutes a marriage. The medieval Catholic Church held that 'consent alone' makes a perfectly valid marriage,[1] and until the formalization procedures at the sixteenth-century Council of Trent, 'clandestine marriages', or rather disputes arising from them, were a major problem of the sexual order (Joyce 1948: ch. 3). The definition of marriage was a protracted controversy of medieval Catholicism. This was then carried over into Anglicanism, and into Anglo-Saxon Puritan dissent, but not into the more bureaucratically ordered, continental European Lutheranism and Calvinism. In the Anglo-Saxon tradition there is the notion of 'common law marriage', referring to a marriage recognized by the local community without any ritual initiation or formal registration. England till 1753 and Scotland till 1940 had no official formal criterion of marriage, with the law accepting actual cohabitation as a legal marriage, something which was also the case in thirteen states of the USA (Glendon 1977), while others listed and treated cohabitation as a punishable, and in the early 1970s still punished, offence (Trost 1979: 180, referring to cases in South Dakota and Florida).

The sharpest line between marriage and non-marriage, for girls and women, with whom patriarchal societies were most concerned, has been drawn from the Indic civilization of South Asia – except for its matrilineal deviants in today's Kerala – to West Asia, Eastern Europe and the Mediterranean, with forays into pastoral peoples of East and Southern Africa.

Informal cohabitation – a purely consensual marriage – then, is an ancient Western European Christian practice, which was de-legitimized in early modernity, to surge forward in proletarianized and early industrial Europe, and then abandoned in the age of industrial marriage. In the last third of the twentieth century, simultaneously with the turn to de-industrialization, cohabitation was returning with a vengeance, primarily in its areas of historical origin.

The post-industrial landscape of Western coupling

What is currently happening in northwestern Europe and in parts of the white New World is, then, not unique. Outside the small well-ordered societies dear to traditional anthropologists, marriage has often been a messy business. Nevertheless, since its beginning in the 1960s we have been witnessing a dramatic change in the landscape of human coupling.

Marriage has become a variable, in a social, not just a statistical, sense. It is not simply declining. Rather, it has become a variegated phenomenon within and between Western societies. Among the fifteen countries of the European Union, the crude marriage rate, per thousand population, not taking ageing and other population changes into account, declined from 8.0 in 1960, 7.8 in 1965, 7.7 in 1970, 7.2 in 1975, to 6.3 in 1980 and 5.1 in 1995, whereabouts it has stayed since then (European Commission 2000: table F3). The European marriage decline is not shared by the USA, where the crude marriage rate of 1960 (8.5, going up to 9.2 in 1965) has maintained itself well, in part through divorce and remarriages – which in the mid-1980s made up almost half of all American marriages (Lee and Wang 1999: 184n) – reaching 8.9 in 1997 and 8.3 in 1998 (UN 2001a: table 23). The Canadian rate went down from 7.3 in 1960 to 5.4 in 1994 (Spiegelman 1968: table 8.6; UN 1999: table 23). In 1970, 22 per cent of American women aged 15 and older had never married, and 25 per cent in 2000, a modest decline (US Census Bureau 2001d: table 5).

The end of the European-family marriage boom, and the beginning of a marked decline in propensity to marry are remarkably synchronized across the Western part of the continent, and even across the oceans, including the North American and Pacific New Worlds, and at least parts of Latin America, such as Argentina and Venezuela. In Eastern Europe there is no clear pattern of marital decline until the 1990s, except in East Germany and Slovenia (Flora *et al.* 1987: ch. 2; Mitchell 1998c: table A6; Mounier 1998: table 4; Council of Europe 2001b: fig. G.2.2 and table T2.1).

By 1975 the first marriage rate was going down all over Western Europe north of the Alps and the Pyrenées, although the decline was not yet historical in Belgium, France and the British Isles. Outside Europe it was declining strongly in Australia and New Zealand, more cautiously in Canada and the USA (Mounier 1994: table 4; Coleman 2000: table 2.15; Council of Europe 2001b: table T2.1). By 1980 a significant, epochal change had occurred all over Western Europe, although from and to quite different levels of marriage.

The turn was sudden and dramatic. The cohorts born in the 1930s or early 1940s – in Italy the generation of 1955 – were the most married generation of modern Europe (European Commission 2000: table F10-11), and also the generation which had the longest marriages and spent the largest part of its life within marriage.[2] But the Swedish cohorts born after 1955 have the lowest marriage rates recorded in the country (SCB 1999: table 4.5). For other countries the same should apply for the cohorts of the 1960s and after.

It started in Sweden, in 1967. In 1968 the Swedish marriage rate was already at its lowest point since the post-Depression upturn in 1937, and in 1972–73 it was down to the Depression level. In terms of the 'total first marriage rate', the estimate of the percentage of women who will ever marry before the age of 50 went down from 95 in 1965 to 62 in 1970. Denmark followed closely, gently reducing its marriage frequency after its historical peak in 1965, coming down to its 1941 level in 1970. Finland also played a part in the Nordic cluster, while Norway waited until the second half of the 1970s.

In 2000 united Germany had a total marriage rate of 0.58, and France 0.62, the same as Italy had in 1999. Sweden in 2000 and the UK in 1999 had the same rate, 0.53, which in the Swedish case is a recovery from the trough of 1995–98. The Danish propensity to marriage was at its ebb in 1980, from which a vigorous comeback has occurred, from 0.53 to 0.79 in 2000 (Council of Europe 2001a: table T.2.2).

Behind the marriage rate statistics there are several socio-demographic processes at work, among which three currents have had a major significance. Postponement of marriage is the simplest, and has strong effects on the demographic measure. Informal cohabitation is another, which may operate either as part of marital postponement or as an alternative form of coupling, or both. Thirdly, there is a tendency to living single, which again may be an option in itself or a temporary state nested in other processes, of postponement, or of more frequent divorce/separation. A special variant of singlehood, is a de-linking of parenting from pairing, and the increase of single parenthood. The relative importance of these processes varies from country to country.

It should be emphasized that all three of these tendencies were integral parts of the modern Western European family system as it developed after the Middle Ages, and in particular from late eighteenth until the early twentieth century, with late marriages, a significant minority of the population never marrying, and extensive informal cohabitation among the popular classes in various social milieux, rural as well as urban.

In the EU, mean age of marriage reached its lowest point in 1975, at the globally advanced age of 23 for women, after which it has climbed above 27, to 27.3 in 1998. In Sweden in 2000 women marry on average only at the age of 30. The American median age for women's first marriage has risen from around 20 in the 1950s and 20.8 in 1970 to 25.1 in 2000 (US Census Bureau 2001d: table MS-2 and p. 9).

This recent postponement is fully within the modern variations of the Western European family system. In 1900 the average female marriage age was 27 in Austria and Sweden, and around 26 in Britain, Germany, the Netherlands and Norway (but 24 in the USA) (see Tables 4.1 and 4.2). Among the Swedish population in 2000, for instance, there were still fewer unmarried people above the age of 15 (38 per cent) than in 1900 (42 per cent) or in 1940 (39 per cent) (SCB 2001a: table 1.1).

Another major process behind the lowered rates of marriage is the rise of informal cohabitation. As we saw above, this is not a new phenomenon in Western Europe. In the major cities of the nineteenth century, from Paris to Stockholm, it was a widespread popular practice. It was common also in certain rural peripheries.

As a recent form of mass pairing it was pioneered in Sweden in the late 1960s, closely followed by neighbouring Denmark. From an estimate of 1 per cent of all Swedish couples in the 1950s, cohabitation had perhaps reached 7 per cent in 1969. By the time of the 1975 Swedish census, 11 per cent of all cohabiting couples (of all ages) were unmarried, and a sizeable majority (57 per cent) of cohabiting women aged 20–24. In Denmark about 8 per cent of all couples in 1974 were unmarried, and about half of all cohabiting women aged 20–24 in 1976. No non-Scandinavian country came anywhere near those figures then. In France, 11 per cent of cohabiting women aged 20–24 were not married, a figure reached in Britain only in 1980. But from the late 1970s the custom spread across central and northwestern Europe (Trost 1979: ch. 3; Kiernan 1996: table 2.2).

Why Sweden (and Scandinavia)? Why the late 1960s? Before entering into historical dispositions, we should not forget the moment of rupture. In the first half of the 1960s, marriage was at the peak of its popularity, even in Scandinavia. The total first marriage rate was of Asian proportions, around 1 in Denmark, up to 0.97 in Sweden, indicating a tendency to universal marriage. Then it plummeted rapidly, in Sweden from 0.94 in 1966 to 0.86 in 1967, and then further down, to 0.62 in 1970, and to 0.56 in 1972, before levelling off. The Danish curve was less steep, from 0.94 in 1967 to 0.82 in 1970, temporarily stabilizing after reaching 0.65 in 1973. In the two, somewhat more religious, and thereby somewhat more culturally conservative Nordic countries, Finland and Norway, unmarried cohabitation had actually (in Norway in 1902) or nearly (in Finland in 1938: Mahkonen 1988: 127–28) been criminalized by modern legislation. True, that legislation had become obsolete, but it was abolished only in 1972 (Bradley 1996: 215).

But there were, of course, good preconditions for a start in Sweden and Denmark. The early *démontage* of patriarchal family legislation, which was a common Scandinavian initiative for the second and third decades of the twentieth century, had firmly established an individualistic and egalitarian conception of the family. Appeals to religious morality and to transcendental 'family values' had no mainstream audiences. Denmark and Sweden had also become more generally, the most secularized, the least religious countries of Western Europe. Furthermore, the nineteenth- and early twentieth-century tradition of cohabitation seems never to have quite died out. During the marriage boom decades its incidence was little noticed, and postdatedly underestimated, because most of it was a short-term pre-marriage occurrence. From retrospective interviews in a fertility survey of 1981 it appears that a quarter of Swedish women born in 1936–40 had had a consensual union by the age of 25, i.e. in the late 1950s to early 1960s (Hoem and Rennermalm 1985: table 5).

Continuity with the past before the salad days of marriage is also indicated by the geo-social pattern of the new wave of cohabitation. It was most popular among young working-class women, in the northern forest provinces and, after them, in the Stockholm region. That was the same pattern as a century earlier, although then Stockholm informality was more outstanding (Trost 1979: table 3.11; Agell *et al.* 1980: ch. 8; Bernhardt and Hoem 1985).

There was further an unbroken tradition of relative youth independence, of early departure from the parental home. Gradually there had also emerged an adult abstinence from sexual surveillance. For instance, when universities began to expand from about 1960 it had become a complete non-issue that student dormitories should be sexually integrated. Swedish universities had no parental authority, as the American ones had, and there were no formal sexual restrictions, such as those that in March 1968 triggered the French student revolt. This does not necessarily mean that Swedish or Scandinavian youth and students were particularly sexually active. My impression is, rather not. The point is rather that young people who had finished their secondary school, which was becoming obligatory around this time, were treated as responsible adults. Youth independence is crucial, because informal cohabitation became a mass phenomenon first among people in their early twenties. In other countries it was won only later, after violent conflicts, and in southern Europe to this day it remains delimited by youth unemployment and an inaccessible housing market.

The 1960s in Scandinavia were years of an accelerating boom. In Sweden there was not only full employment, but a scarcity of labour. Urban housing was largely rented, and a public queuing system made it available even to young newcomers without 'social capital'. From the mid-1960s a large-scale programme of public housing construction was in force. The crucial political question, whether a rich society no longer needed a welfare state, or whether it was a rich society that finally could afford a welfare state for all, had been put to a decisive democratic test. The answer was the latter, most resoundingly by the Swedish electorate, in one referendum and four elections during

1957–64. One of the areas of rapid welfare state expansion in the second half of the 1960s was the public health care system, offering an expanding labour market, above all to working-class women. Between 1965 and 1970 overall female employment in Sweden grew by four percentage points, two-thirds of which were jobs as medical orderlies.

So, economic, social and cultural conditions were propitious, but why the sudden change just then? The surge of informal cohabitation as a public, increasingly long-term practice was part of a broader cultural change taking place in Sweden in the mid-1960s – a more general process of informalization, de-solemnization, de-ritualization. The process was international, carried by an emergent radical youth culture. But it had more cultural suddenness and depth in Sweden than anywhere else. At Lund University, the wearing of white tie and tails at the public doctoral examinations ceased, academic gowns having disappeared in times immemorial. The Swedish language also changed: in 1967 a progressive physican and prominent welfare state bureaucrat successfully amended the Swedish language and its manner of address in little more than a year. In contrast to most other Western European languages, including the other Scandinavian ones, Swedish did not have a proper pronoun for polite address, neither the universal 'you' of English, nor the more formal 'Sie' of German or 'vous' of French. Instead, various, more or less clumsy, forms of third-person address had to be used. If you knew the title or the name of the person, you could use that: 'Does the Director want . . .?' 'Does Mrs Anderson think . . .?' Swedish manners and Swedish language had by northern European standards of the twentieth century become remarkably formal (see Meyer (1999) on German impressions of Scandinavia in the 1930s). In the first half of the 1960s there were still published academic articles and books on the stiffness and formality of the Swedes. Then, within a few years, this ancient, complicated way of speaking was replaced by a virtually universal 'du', and Swedish official and public life became suddenly known for its informality (see Löfgren 1988). The Royal family is the only circle which cannot be properly addressed as 'du' – and for whom a third-person address, 'Does the king think . . .?', is used outside high rituals – but the Prime Minister, the Archbishop or any business executive can and are.[3]

The coming of a prosperous, egalitarian urban society made conventionality untenable. Informal cohabitation was part of this cultural change. By 2000 it had reached Scandinavian royalty, when the Norwegian Crown Prince made it publicly known that he was going to move in informally with the woman he loved (which he did, although he did also throw a full wedding half a year later). It later spread to children of the Swedish King.

Equality, and not the least gender equality and equality of options, was the main concern of the Swedish polity of the late 1960s, and the turn to cohabitation was immediately backed up politically and juridically. In 1969 the Social Democratic Minister of Justice gave the following official Directive for family law reform: 'New legislation ought [so far] as possible to be neutral in relation to different forms of living together and different moral views.' In

1973 legislation followed, which gave the partners of cohabitation certain rights on the basis of need to the joint residence in case of separation, similar to, but more restricted than, the rules on matrimonial residence. A more extensive law of cohabitee rights was passed in 1985 (see Bradley 1996: ch. 3).

It is noteworthy, that the more dramatic cultural rebellions of the late 1960s had a more delayed effect on marriage than Swedish reformism: May 1968 in France, pop culture in Britain, the social upheavals of Italy, the youth insurrection in West Germany, the crumbling of institutionalized religious loyalties in the Netherlands – none of them had any visible effects on the overall propensity to marry before the late 1970s (Council of Europe 2001b).

At the beginning of the twenty-first century, unmarried cohabitation has become a major practice of Northwestern Europe (save Ireland), North America and Oceania. First of all, cohabitation has become the main form of first union of sex and household. In the UK about 60 per cent of all first marriages are preceded by unmarried cohabitation (Coleman 2000: 60). Interestingly, the current relative prevalence of cohabitation in the UK resembles the pattern of extra-marital births a century or more ago. In both cases it is higher in Wales than in England, in the East Midlands than in the West Midlands or London (Hollingsworth 1981; Office for National Statistics 2002).

Among French women born in 1964–68 three-quarters had entered a union by the age of 24: 60 per cent as cohabitees, and 16 per cent had married without prior cohabitation. Out of a similar West German cohort 61 per cent had coupled by the age of 24, but only 18 per cent directly by marriage. In the American sample, by that age, four out of ten born in 1971–75 had embarked on an informal union and one of six had married without precedent cohabitation. In Sweden marriage without prior cohabitation has become a small minority strategy. Seventeen per cent of Swedish women born in 1964 who had married by the age of 28 did so without prior cohabitation.[4]

Out of all couples around 2000, cohabitees make up a third in Sweden, between a quarter and a fifth in Denmark and the UK, a tenth in Australia and Germany, and 6 per cent in the USA (Australian Bureau of Statistics 2000: table 'Living arrangements'; Coleman 2000: 60; Eurostat 2000b: 48; US Census Bureau 2001d: table 7; SCB 2002b: 19). In other words, marriage is still overwhelmingly dominating Western pairing.

In all the formative normative cultures sustaining the major family systems of the world, marriage was for procreation. As we saw above, the European upheavals of proletarianization and urbanization led to a very significant rupture in the links between marriage and parenting, and in the Creole cultures of the Americas such links were more exceptions than the rule. After the tide of marriage there developed in the last third of the twentieth century a new de-linking in the European family pattern (Table 6.1).

Looking back to 1900, there are some historical continuities in our new base year of 1960 (Table 6.1). The high scorers then, Austria, Iceland, Portugal and Sweden, are still on top in 1960, but the Portuguese rate is then beginning to fall, reaching 6.9 in 1970. The particularly low scorers, below 3 per cent, a century (or 80 years) ago, Greece, the Netherlands and Ireland, are still at the

Table 6.1 Trajectories of extra-marital births in Europe, North America and Oceania, 1960–2000 (as a percentage of all live births)

Low to low[a]		Low to high		Low to very high		High to high		High to very high	
Belgium	2.1–11.6[b]	FRG	6.7–17.7[c]	Bulgaria	8.0–38.4	Portugal	9.5–22.2	Austria	13.3–31.3
Croatia	7.4–9.0	Lithuania	7.3–22.6	Denmark	7.8–44.6	Russia	13.1–28.0	Estonia	13.7–54.5
Greece	1.1–1.9[c]	Netherlands, the	1.4–24.9	Finland	4.0–39.2	Yugoslavia	11.–24.3	ex-GDR	11.6–49.9
Italy	2.4–10.2	Romania	3.5[d]–25.5	France	6.1–41.7[c]			Iceland	25.3–65.8
Poland	4.5–12.1	Slovakia	4.7–18.3	Hungary	5.5–29.0			Latvia	11.9–40.3
Switz.	3.8–10.7	Spain	2.3–16.3	Ireland	1.6–31.8			Slovenia	9.1–37.1
				Norway	3.7–49.6			Sweden	11.3–55.3
				UK	8.0[d]–39.5				
Memorandum				Australia	4.8–28.7				
Turkey	4.4 (1990)			Canada	4.3–(25.6x)				
Japan	1.2 (1994)			New Z.	5.3–40.7y				
				USA	5.3–31.0				

Sources: Europe, incl. Turkey: Council of Europe (2001a: table 3.2); outside Europe, in 1960: Hartley (1975: table 59); USA, 2000: US Census Bureau (2001b: fig. 2); other countries in 2000: Mounier (2001).

Notes:
a 'Low' means <10 in 1960, <15 in 2000; 'high' means >10 in 1960, >15 in 2000; 'very high' means >25 in 2000. These, intrinsically arbitrary, limits are not used quite mechanically, but with an eye to a cut-off point between countries. Because Icelanders make a tiny population, their very high level in 1960 is not put in a column of its own.
b 1990.
c 1999.

bottom, now joined by Spain but abandoned by the Eastern European high frequency–low age marriers, Bulgaria and Russia. The historically always relatively low Anglo-Saxon rate of illegitimacy – facilitated by the ancient flexibility of common law – was still in place in 1960. And countries in between stayed in between, by and large.

If we take the twentieth century as a whole, there were three countries where extra-marital births never went clearly below 10 per cent – Austria, Iceland and Sweden – although Sweden was a borderline case, with a 1940s rate of 9.5, the lowest since the mid-1860s (Hartley 1975: table 4; SCB 1999: table 3.6). Greece was the only European country staying below 5 per cent, and Italy and Switzerland did not exceed 10 per cent from 1900 to 1999, only in 2000 (Hartley 1975: table 4; Council of Europe 2001a: table T3.2).

The 1960 to 2000 trajectories strike new paths. A common Nordic pattern was established, not surprisingly perhaps, but not self-evident from the situation in 1960, although the Icelanders have kept their lead, and the Swedes their second place. More surprising perhaps is that the first Irish enonomic boom in modern history resulted in illegitimacy soaring, from 8.5 per cent in 1985 and 14.5 per cent in 1990 to 31.8 per cent in 2000, while elections and referenda have kept the Catholic prohibitions of abortion and divorce in operation. It is also noteworthy that the gap between West (FRG) and East (ex-GDR) Germany has widened further in the 1990s. The current gulf between France and West Germany, with almost identical rates in 1960 but a 42:18 relationship in 1999, is also somewhat astonishing, although more innovativeness was to be expected in much more secularized France (see Therborn 1995: 272ff).

Among Western countries, Orthodox Greece has best preserved its traditional form of parenting. The strongly Catholic countries have been less successful in that respect, although only Ireland has fallen out of the mould. Poland and even more so, Italy and Croatia have kept extra-marital births well below current averages. Lithuania has a clearly different norm of parenting than secularized Latvia, not to speak of quasi-Nordic Estonia, and believing Slovakia maintains at least some distance to the little believing Czech Republic. Austria and, above all, Portugal, with their historically accepted proletarian or minifundist deviants from the law of the Church, have not followed the Scandinavians into sky-high levels of extra-marital fertility. Among the American religions, it is Fundamentalist Protestantism and Mormonism which are standing out as religious barriers to 'sinful' coupling, while mainstream Protestantism, Catholicism and (above all) Judaism have lost their morally cutting edge in this respect (Lehrer 2000: table 12.6).

In 1970 Russia and the United States had the same rate of extra-marital births, about 11 per cent, but since then the Americans have moved ahead in de-linking marriage and parenthood. The contrast with the other Slavic republics of the former Soviet Union is even more pronounced. Belarus had 19 per cent extra-marital children in 2000, the Ukraine 17 per cent. However, the American disparity with Russia is due to the size of Creole family patterns inside the USA. In 2000, white, non-Hispanic American women gave birth to

26 babies per hundred out of wedlock, i.e. about the same as Russian women (28 per cent). Hispanic women, most, but not all, from a background that we defined above as Creole, bore 30 per cent of their children outside marriage. Afro-Americans, on the other hand, were close to the top Scandinavian score with 62 per cent (Asian Americans had shed some of their Asian customs and become more like Catholic Poles, bearing 15 per cent outside marriage) (US Census Bureau 2001b: fig. 2).

Now, de-linking marriage and parenthood may happen in two very different ways. Either through single motherhood – or more rarely single fatherhood – or through informal coupling – including re-marriages and re-combinations of paired parenthood. The UN Fertility and Family Surveys of the 1990s make possible a systematic comparison in this respect. Table 6.2 refers to women in their early thirties i.e. just past the median age of first birth. They were interviewed between 1992 and 1999, most frequently in 1995, and were mostly born in the first half of the 1960s. The women of the early Swedish survey were born in 1959, the Germans in 1958–62.

The figures in Table 6.2 refer to first births in the late 1980s and early to mid-1990s, and therefore not to the same era as Table 6.1. But they tell us

Table 6.2 Mother's partnership situation at first birth in Europe and the Western New World in the 1990s

	Married	Cohabiting	Single
Austria	59	18	23
Belgium	91	5	4
Canada	83	15	2
Czech Republic	90	4	6
Denmark	26	50	24
Estonia (natives)	70	19	11
Estonia (Russian origin)	91	3	6
Finland	77	16	7
France	71	20	9
West Germany	74	7	19
Greece	95	1	4
Hungary	90	4	6
Italy	91	4	5
Latvia	83	9	8
Lithuania	85	2	13
Netherlands, the	89	8	3
Norway	62	23	15
New Zealand	73	9	18
Poland	84	2	14
Slovenia	70	15	15
Spain	92	3	5
Sweden	32	58	10
Switzerland	90	6	4
US	71	9	20

Source: UN Economic Commission for Europe, Family and Fertility Surveys (see Appendix).

Note:
The UK took no part in these surveys, and the Portuguese data were less than complete.

something important about the social behaviour behind the overall numbers of births outside marriage. Marriage remains a strong parenting institution, dominating everywhere, except in parts of Scandinavia. Denmark and Sweden, and Iceland,[5] form a group apart here, having substituted informal coupling for marriage as the parenting norm. It is true, we should expect births after the first child to have a higher likelihood of being within marriage, and also births to older women, than the 33-year-olds interviewed in the Swedish survey. In 2000 the partnership status of the mothers of all children born was: cohabiting 46 per cent, married 45 per cent, single 9 per cent (SCB 2001a: table 3.23).

Both in Table 6.2 and in the overview of all births, there is a relatively low proportion of single mothers in Sweden. It is a pattern clearly distinguishing Sweden from all other countries with a high rate of extra-marital births. In England and Wales in 1996 about 15 per cent of all births were to single mothers (calculated from Coleman 2000: 51–52). For the USA a mid-1990s (Mounier 1998: table 6; Fukuyama 1999: 44) estimate would yield about 25 per cent of all babies being born to single mothers.

If we concentrate on the relative importance of the non-marital status at the time of birth we can discern an Anglo-Franco-Scandinavian pattern, of high extra-marital birth rates dominated by cohabitation, a pattern to which Canada – Québec in particular (Wu 2000: fig. 4.4) – and ethnic Estonians also adhere. At the other end we see another high rate pattern dominated by singlehood. That is the American way, but New Zealand also clearly belongs to it, and most likely Ireland (given its low rate of overall cohabitation: European Commission 1996: table 2.1). Austria (to judge from the full range of cohort data) seems to have moved away from the American pattern to the rather balanced picture of Table 6.2.

Among the countries of relatively low rates of birth out of wedlock, there is also variation: a clear preference for cohabitation, represented by the Dutch; a rather even distribution of types of non-marital status; and finally a domination by single mothers. Poland, Lithuania and West Germany belong to the latter, the low-key American way, whereas Slovenia, and the still overwhelmingly marrying countries manifest the second variant. Russia, with a historical impregnation of quasi-universal, relatively young marriages, sustained by Bolshevik policies after the iconoclasm of the Revolution, has a relatively low incidence of cohabitation, lower in 1994 than the EU average in 1996. It has also a unique pattern, of cohabitation being most common, not among the youngest cohorts, but among women in their thirties and forties (Avdeev and Mounier 1999: table 8). This is most likely mainly after-divorce cohabitation, a phenomenon also well known in Western Europe, but there not of the same significance.

What emerges out of this seems to be that the secularized, individualistic countries take the path of cohabitation, whereas the more religious and familistic[6] ones, when they change out of their marriage cast, do so more by innovating or deviant singles. In post-Communist Eastern Europe, there was a strong increase of cohabitation among people in their twenties. In the secularized countries it was dramatic, in Latvia, Estonia, Hungary and Slovenia. It was modest in Catholic Lithuania, Poland and Slovakia, and insignificant in Russia, Ukraine and Bulgaria (UN Economic Commission for Europe 2002: table 6.2.2).

In 1996 the European Commission asked all adults (aged 16 or older) in the EU about their family status. Thanks to this large, representative survey we can get a general overview of the Western European family situation (Table 6.3). We may notice that marriage remains the dominant adult status all over Europe, that for the EU as a whole there are more widows and widowers than cohabitees and divorcees together – although this is an interview study and the most elderly are not included – and that the European family system still contains a lot of variation.

Current cohabitation outside the European family

While cohabitation has recently reached into Eastern Europe, it is still a rare, marginal and/or underground phenomenon in almost all of Asia and in North Africa. Marriage universalism has gone down in the metropolises of Eastern Asia, and the age at marriage has gone up. Even though there are few hard data on it, we should expect that a certain amount of informal coupling exists there. But it is still infrequent. In Japan, for instance, in 1997 only 8 per cent of women aged 30–34 and 5 per cent aged 25–29 had sexually cohabited (East–West Center 2002: 33).

Table 6.3 Family status of women in the EU, 1996 (percentage of all women aged 16 and older)

	Single	Married	Cohabiting	Divorced[a]	Widowed
Austria	23	48	4	10	16
Belgium	18	61	6	7	9
Denmark	22	43	17	7	12
Finland	21	42	10	13	14
France	22	43	12	11	13
East Germany	16	62	4	7	11
West Germany	19	55	2	8	17
Greece	19	65	0	2	14
Ireland	32	51	3	2[b]	13
Italy	37	49	2	2	10
Netherlands	22	54	7	8	9
Portugal	24	59	1	4	13
Spain	28	57	2	2	12
Sweden	27	41	15	7	10
UK	23	54	4	8	12
EU15	*24*	*52*	*5*	*6*	*13*

Source: European Commission (1996: table 2.1.b).

Notes:
a Divorced and separated.
b Separated only, divorce being prohibited.

In China in 1989, less than 1 per cent of all couples were cohabiting with neither a certificate nor a wedding. But as with everything Chinese, the absolute number is non-negligible, 5.4 million people. It is likely to have increased since then. Besides, there are the much more numerous unofficial marriages, of people marrying before the legal age, something condoned by many local officials (Ruan 1991: 162–63).

In the Caucasus, despite its current marriage strikes, the 2000 Demographic and Health Survey of Armenia failed to hear of any non-marginal cohabitation. A few per cent only, of the most prone age groups, were discovered in post-Soviet Central Asia in the late 1990s, probably mainly involving ethnic Russian women. Thailand was not included in the late 1990s wave of demographic surveys, so the Philippines was the only Asian country with some modest amount of informal sexual unions, barely 8 per cent of women aged 20 to 29.

Latin America and the Caribbean was the classical area of centuries of massive coupling outside the norms of the Church and of the law. So, what has happened? Brazil, because of its size, provides an important picture (Table 6.4). The colonial legacy of conjugal informality was overcome in the first half of the twentieth century, and among unions in existence in 1980, those contracted before 1950 included only 2 per cent without a formal marriage. After 1950, and after 1970 in particular, the proportion of consensual unions grew again, headed by the areas of Rio de Janeiro and the northeast (Oliveira and Berquó 1990: table 9), i.e. those parts of Brazil where the colonial and post-colonial customs had been most firmly planted and developed. In other words, a re-connection with family patterns before the mid-twentieth-century marriage boom seems to have occurred in Brazil as well as in Sweden.

In 2000 informal cohabitation dominated among the unions of Brazilian women only up to (and barely including) the age group of 20–24 (about 51 per cent), which means that in contrast to contemporary Scandinavia or France, formal marriage has not been crowded out of young unions.[7] In spite of strong religious currents, Brazil has become very secularized in marital affairs. Compare, for example, Portugal, where in spite of clear decline recently, Catholic marriages made up 60 per cent of marriages concluded in 2001 (INE Portugal 2002). Also in Mexico young marriages are maintaining themselves in relation to cohabitation, at least as registered by the census.

Table 6.4 Forms of sexual union in Brazil, 1960–2000 (percentage distribution of different forms of unions, from the age of 15 in 1960–1980, from the age of 12 in 2000)

	Religious marriage	*Civil and religious marriage*	*Civil marriage*	*Consensual union*
1960	20	61	13	7
1970	14	65	14	7
1980	8	66	17	12
2000	4	50	17	28

Sources: 1960–80: Oliveira and Berquó (1990: table 8); 2000: IBGE (2000: table 1.4.2).

Among Mexican women aged 20 to 29 who are in a union, which two-thirds of them are, about one-quarter are cohabiting and three-quarters are married (INE Mexico 2002).

Because of its historical importance in the region – and the ecclesiastical classification of baptisms – Latin American censuses have often registered informal cohabitation, before Statistics Sweden pioneered it in Europe in 1975. The term used varies: 'free union', 'consensual union', 'living together' (*convivientes*), etc. From recent censuses we may get an overview of the current Latin American situation, and how it has changed (Table 6.5). The 1980 data show an enduring significance of informal unions almost everywhere. The main exception was Chile, where only 4 per cent of registered unions were 'consensual'. Uruguay, which might have been a candidate for exception, was not, given the fact that a quarter of children in 1980 were born in consensual unions (INE Uruguay 2000).

The criteria used by the different national census bureaux are not likely to be identical, so cross-national comparisons should be cautious. Basically, the variations express the different strength and penetration of the ecclesiastical orders and of the civil registers, which in turn are dependent both on twentieth-century political-cum-religious history, and on the inherited ethnic mix and stratification. Mass poverty is an important prop of informal coupling (cf. Ortmayr 1996). The highest rates are to be found in the Caribbean, except where it is kept down, as in Trinidad or Guyana, by a sizeable Hindu population. In Haiti in 1982, two-thirds of sexual unions were unmarried, in the Dominican Republic more than half, in Jamaica and Central America 40–50 per cent (Tremblay 1988). In the Demographic and Health Surveys of the late 1990s, the researchers on Haiti make no distinction between marriage and non-marriage, but for the Dominican Republic non-married cohabitation

Table 6.5 Cohabitation in Hispanic America, *c.* 1980 and 2000 (percentage of couples in non-married union)

	1980	*2000*
Argentina	12	18
Bolivia	n.a.	24
Chile	4	6
Colombia	28	41
Costa Rica	18	25
Cuba	36	37 (1995)
Ecuador	27	33
Guatemala	45	37
Mexico	16	19
Paraguay	20	23 (1990)
Peru	24	32 (1993)
Venezuela	33	n.a.

Sources: Cuba: Benítez (1999: table 19); Paraguay 1990, Demographic and Health Survey, reported in Westoff *et al.* (1994: table 3.1); 1980: Tremblay (1988: national tables); 2000: census data online from the national statistical offices, see Appendix.

dominates unions up to the age of the mid-forties, and in Nicaragua up to about the age of 35.

The national distributions still tend to manifest traditional cleavages, as we also noted above in the case of Brazil. In Mexico, for instance, the highest frequency of informal unions is in the Indian periphery of Chiapas, the lowest in Hispanic Guanajuato, and the capital is at the national average. In Peru it is more a rural than an urban phenomenon, and Lima is well below the national average (26 per cent against 32 per cent), and most informal unions are located in Cajamarca in the Andean north. The city of Buenos Aires in Argentina also has a somewhat lower rate of cohabitation than the country as a whole.

Sub-Saharan Africa is another part of the world with a significant informal sexual order, although not as important as in the Americas. Sub-Saharan Africa was traditionally a continent of virtually universal, family-regulated marriage. However, as indicated initially in this chapter, the protracted complexity of African marriage negotiations, the remarkably little significance attached to the wedding ritual (Goody 1976: 10), and the usually very weak conjugal bond might operate as preparing the ground for a wide informalization of pairing. Speaking of West Africa, but mainly of the non-Muslim coast, and of the matrilineal Akan peoples of Ghana in particular, the great anthropologist Meyer Fortes (1978: 29) asserted decades ago that 'Consensual, free and casual unions from which children result are of wide occurrence'.

For contemporary Africa, international surveys provide the best sources, in particular the Demographic and Health Surveys of the late 1990s. In the late 1980s surveys, it appeared that marriage in Liberia resembled the Caribbean, with marriage overtaking informal unions only among women aged above 40 (Westoff *et al.* 1994: table 3.1). In the late 1990s, among women aged 20–24, informal cohabitation dominates over marriage only in two countries surveyed – to which this time non-surveyed Botswana should probably be added (Westoff *et al.* 1994: table 3.1) – Gabon and Mozambique, but there in proportions of 3.5:1. It is a major custom also in Uganda, Ivory Coast and Ghana (there a major increase since 1988), constituting about a third of all unions in the age group, and making up a quarter of pairing in Madagascar and in Cameroon.

Cohabitation is rather rare in Nigeria – a finding of the surveys of both 1990 and 1999 – and even rarer in the predominantly Muslim countries of the west, in Catholic Burundi and Ruanda (surveyed in 1987 and 1992, respectively: Westoff *et al.* 1994: table 3.1), in still traditionally Christian Ethiopia, in spite of its ill-fated military revolution, in very patriarchal Kenya, and, somewhat more surprisingly, given its 'copperbelt' and its proximity to the matrilineal belt of central Africa, Zambia (again a reconfirmation of an earlier survey pattern, of 1992). In modernized but classically sternly patriarchal Zimbabwe, informal cohabitation made up a tenth of the unions of 20–24-year-old women.

Cohabitation does not seem to be a major phenomenon in South Africa. In 1996 8 per cent of the population aged 25–29 were 'living together', a fifth of all couples in that age group, 11 per cent of all couples in the 35–39 age bracket (Ziehl 2002b: table 4). Single living and matrifocal households are more important among the black and coloured populations than consensual unions. Among the mothers of non-white children born in Johannesburg in 1990, 52 per cent never married, and 9 per cent were cohabiting six years later (Barbarin and Richter 2001: 141). In 1996 Market Research Africa found that more than half of a random sample of women in urban 'townships' were living without a male partner in the household (Bullender 1997: 2).

Behind the national averages are major ethnic, as well as 'racial', differences. Informal cohabitation is very common among, for instance, the matrilineal Akan people of Ivory Coast and Ghana. In the former case, in 1980 for about 60 per cent of women their first union was informal, whereas among patrilineal ethnic groups it was only 20 per cent (Gage-Brandon 1993). It may be added that Gabon and the northern parts of Mozambique belong to the matrilineal belt of Central Africa. The more complex gender relations of traditional matrilineality seem to be one factor of contemporary African variation in informal coupling.

The sexual revolution

In the West, the last third of the twentieth century saw a sexual revolution, much talked about. What did it actually entail? Furthermore, to what extent was there a global sexual revolution?

The Western revolution

Culturally and legally, there was, first of all, a secularization of sexuality, liberating it from religious or other aprioristic normative rulings as 'sinful' or otherwise condemnable outside marriage and for sheer pleasure without intentions of procreation. According to Philip Larkin (1967/1988: 167), the English poet, it all began in 1963, *Annus Mirabilis*, between the acquittal of the publishers of *Lady Chatterley's Lover*, put on trial in Britain in 1960, and the Beatles' first LP. Bans on contraceptives were finally lifted, with the *Griswold* v. *Connecticut* case in the USA in 1965 and the repeal of national anti-contraceptive legislation in France in 1967 as legal landmarks. De-tabooing of homosexuality was another manifestation of change, to which we shall return below.

Technological innovations greatly facilitated a de-linking of sex and procreation. The pill hit the American market in 1960, and the Swedish one in 1964. Intrauterine contraceptive devices became available in Sweden in 1967.

The actual revolution was, of course, practice itself. It manifested itself most clearly in earlier and more pre-marital sexual debuts. While the age of marriage moved upwards, the age of first sexual intercourse moved downwards. The practice of pre-marital sex widened significantly.

Sex is a most private practice, and all surveys, not only the pre-representative ones of Kinsey and others, have to be taken with caution, the more so because of the thrill of sex even entering the statistical tables. Surveys of delicate and private issues such as sexual behaviour are fraught with methodological problems, which means that all comparisons, especially between countries but also between different surveys of the same country, have to be read with caution. There are problems of representativity – of sampling and response rates, of sensitivity of answers to the exact wording of questions and to the context of the questionnaire or interview. In times of change the manner of reporting matters more than usual, for instance the median age or mean age, calculated on the basis of which age group. The size of the problem may be dramatized by the findings of a comparison of three highly professional US surveys on adolescent sexual behaviour. After standardizing their age categories, the three surveys reported the proportion of adolescent sexual experience in 1995 as 52 per cent, 44 per cent and 36 per cent, respectively (Santelli *et al.* 2000).[8] In Africa, age answers have been found to include a certain amount of inconsistency, including, mainly in Kenya, a number of women appearing to have had their first child before their first sexual intercourse (Meekers 1993a). Nevertheless, broad trends and patterns may be discerned with fair accuracy, and many of the special sexual surveys have been made with sophisticated attention to the problems involved.

In Britain, for instance, the median age of first sexual intercourse decreased from 21 for women born in the 1930s and 1940s, to 17 for women born between 1966 and 1975 (Wylie *et al.* 1997: 1314). By 2000, the median age of first sex for British girls born in 1975–84 had gone down to 16, the same as for boys, with a quarter of them starting before the legal age of 16, and 90 per cent by the age of 19 (Wellings *et al.* 2001). A median age of 16–17 was the dominant range in northwestern Europe of the 1990s. From the 1980s, in Britain only since the mid-1990s, there seems to have occurred a stabilization around that age (cf. Bozon and Kontula 1997; Winaver 2002).

In the USA, in the period 1958 to 1969, about one in four 18-year-old women had experienced sexual intercourse. Then there was a jump, to almost half (43–46 per cent) in the 1970s, from 1972 and on, to 54 per cent in 1981 (Beeghley 1996: fig. 2). Among the whole group of teenage American women, about a third had pre-marital sex in the early 1970s, and about half in the 1980s and 1990s, and among non-Hispanic blacks 60 per cent (Singh and Darroch 1999). In a national sample of 1992 of the birth cohorts of 1953–74, 53 per cent of US women had had sexual intercourse before the age of 18 (Joyner and Laumann 2001: table 1.1).

In the mid-1990s the age of sexual debut rose in the USA, clearly for boys, and most probably somewhat also for girls. Among high school students aged 15–17, in the Youth Risk Behavior Surveys the proportion ever having had sexual intercourse was, in 1991, 56 per cent for boys and 51 per cent for girls, and 47 and 48 per cent, respectively, in 1997. Another survey reported the same tendency (Santelli *et al.* 2000: table 3).

In Finland, 6–9 per cent of women born between 1933 and 1942 had sex before the age of 18; among those born after 1972 the corresponding figure was 55–60 per cent, and between a quarter and a fifth of them had sex before 16 (Kontula and Haavio-Mannila 1994). In Sweden the median age of women's sexual debut is about 16, and this seems to have been the case since the birth cohorts of the late 1950s (Lewin *et al.* 1998: table 8.4).

The lowering of the age of first intercourse can be regarded as an established fact. Together with recent marriage postponement, as noted above, the period of pre-marital sex has clearly widened. From births out of wedlock and before nine months after the wedding we know that pre-marital sex was very frequent in early twentieth-century Europe. But pre-marital intercourse was usually with your prospective spouse, and extra-marital births actually occurred among a small minority of women, even in a country with a more or less national constant of 10 per cent extra-marital births, like Sweden. Now we are dealing with a majority of women, and men, sexually active before marriage. For some countries, the mid-1990s European Fertility and Family Surveys give us some comparative indications (Table 6.6).

The data for Finland, Sweden and the UK in Table 6.6 are not quite comparable with the rest, but should be a reasonable approximation. The decimal places of the survey data are, of course, surrounded by margins of error. Around 2000 the median period of female pre-marital sex would be about eight years in the USA, twelve years in the UK, and fourteen years in Sweden (looking at the youngest cohorts of the sex surveys and the mean age of first marriage in 2000). The difference between these countries and Eastern and Southern Europe is substantial, eight to ten years in the Swedish case, six to eight years in the British in the 1990s.

More life-space for sex has also meant more sexual partners. In the Finnish studies, the average number of sexual partners during the last twenty years among women aged 18–54 rose from three in 1971 to six in 1992. A median measure, less sensitive to the sexually hyperactive, shows a Swedish increase of the median number of partners for women from 1.4 to 4.6 from 1967 to 1996, for men from 4.6 to 7.1.

Table 6.6 Periods of female pre-marital sex: Europe, the USA and New Zealand in the mid-1990s (cohorts born 1960–65; years between median age of first intercourse and of marriage)

Country	Years	Country	Years
Belgium	4.0	Norway	8.1
Czech Rep.	2.8	Poland	1.8
Finland	(9)	Portugal	2.8
France	5.7	Slovenia	3.1
Greece	4.1	Spain	4.2
Italy	5.2	Sweden	(12)
Latvia	1.7	Switzerland	7.9
Lithuania	1.8	UK	(8)
New Zealand	5.3	USA	4.1

Sources: Sex initiation in Finland: Kontula and Haavio-Mannila (1994: 201); Sweden: Lewin *et al.* (1998: table 8.4); UK: Wylie *et al.* (1997: 1314); marriage age in 1995 for these countries: Council of Europe (2001a: table T2.3); other countries: UN Economic Commission for Europe, Family and Fertility Survey 1990s.

More than anything else, this is what the sexual revolution has brought: a long period for pre-marital sex, and a plurality of sexual partners over a lifetime becoming a 'normal' phenomenon, in the statistical as well as in a moral sense.

In Southern Europe (including France), the traditional pattern of much earlier sexual activity among males than among females is still in force, sustained by a small pool of sexually accessible women, prostitutes and others. The median age of first intercourse among males born in the second half of the 1960s was significantly lower than that for females, by 1.5 years in Greece, 1.8 years in Italy, 2.3 years in Portugal, and 1.5 years in Spain. In Sweden, by contrast, the median for the same group was basically the same, although with a slightly higher male age, 0.3 year for those born in 1966–72 and 0.8 for the cohorts of 1962–71 (Bozon and Kontula 1997: tables 1 and 2).

The fragile comparative data we have seem to indicate that the Finns are the most sexually active among the Western peoples. In comparison with France, the UK and the USA, data from the early 1990s show that Finnish men and women were significantly less likely to have had no sexual partner in the past year, and more likely to have had two or more partners. Swedes also have to concede the Finnish primacy in this respect (Lewin *et al.* 1998: 76). The US pattern has a bimodal aspect, with a high percentage without sexual experience in the past year (Kontula and Haavio-Mannila 1994: 206). In the early 1990s, a rather large proportion of Americans were still virgins upon marriage: in the age group of 25–34, 12 per cent of American men and 17 per cent of American women, as compared to 4 per cent and 7 per cent among Britons (Michael *et al.* 2001: table 12.1). Finnish sexual frequency did not increase in the 1971–92 period, though (Kontula and Haavio-Mannila 1995: 71).

A considerable amount of sex takes place outside, not just before, marriage or cohabitation. In the Finnish sample of 18–54-year-olds, the proportion of women having had an 'affair' increased from 9 to 19 per cent, among men from 24 to 44 per cent between 1971 and 1992. In the latter year, 15 per cent of men and 10 per cent of women reported that they had had an affair in the previous twelve months. Among Swedes in a 'stable union' the corresponding figures in 1996 were 8 per cent for women and 12 per cent for men (Kontula and Haavio-Mannila 1994: 207; Lewin *et al.* 1998: 76). It may be noted that, first, sexual double morality remains in Scandinavia, and, second, that the gap has become relatively small, with a gender ratio of extra-union sexual affairs of 1.5:1.[9] In the Anglo-Saxon world, extra-marital sexuality was less common (in the early 1990s), engaged in by less than 5 per cent of British and American men, and less than 3 per cent of women. For the younger age groups, the proportion is slightly higher, but not much: 5 per cent in the male group aged 25–34, 2 and 1 per cent of the British and American female group, respectively (Michael *et al.* 2001: table 12.1).

Eastern Europe, as noted above, has a very short period of pre-marital sex, but this changed in the 1990s with increased non-marital cohabitation. Anecdotal evidence indicates that, at least in the late Communist period, East-Central Europe was often enthusiastically engaged in extra-marital sex. The

Czech novelist Milan Kundera wrote about it in *The Unbearable Lightness of Being*, and the perceptive Hungarian sociologist Ivan Szelenyi also observed it (oral communication 2002).

Homosexuality is still a very minor variation of human sexual behaviour. In the USA in 1992, 4.5 per cent of men and 3–4 per cent of women said they had experienced homosexual sex after the age of 18 (Joyner and Laumann 2001: table 1.1; Michael *et al.* 2001: table 12.1). In the past year, 2.4 per cent of American men and 1.0 per cent of America women had a homosexual experience, and 1.1 per cent of British men and 0.4 per cent of British women (Michael *et al.* 2001: table 12.1). Among the Finns the experiences were remarkably similar, with 4 per cent having ever had a homosexual partner, and in the past year 1.3 per cent (Kontula and Haavio-Mannila 1994: 207). In the Swedish sample 2.8 per cent of the men and 2.1 per cent of women said they had had a homosexual experience, while 1.8 and 3.2 per cent, respectively, refused to answer the question (Lewin *et al.* 1998: table 9.5).

A freer and more open sexuality has also enriched marriage. The very good and fully representative Finnish study shows a significant increase in sexual satisfaction and in marital happiness between 1971 and 1992, and a disappearance of difference in male–female appreciation of sex up to about the age of the late thirties. Then female sexual pleasure begins to taper off. The Finnish data also show that women are the main winners of the sexual revolution. Male sexual satisfaction remained about the same in 1971 and in 1992, but women's pleasure increased much more over the two decades (Kontula and Haavio-Mannila 1995: 101ff).

A sexual geography of the world around 2000

The sexual revolution is not universal. Changes of sexual behaviour are not to be excluded anywhere, but often they are no more than minor variations of a given sexual regime. And it should not be forgotten that sexual practices have always had their outliers, their minorities of incessant seducers and of celibates, their professionals and their masters of ostentatious consumption, their devotees of special tastes. Here we are concerned with sexual mainstreams only.

By the 1990s, major sexual changes had occurred only in sub-Saharan Africa, apart from the West. Changes of major scope may be under way in Japan, in Taiwan, and in some big Asian cities, but as yet they are not comparable to those of northwestern Europe and North America. Latin America and the Caribbean have all the time had a more positive and informal approach to sex than the North Atlantic Puritans, but because of that, and also because of the remaining effects of formalization and stabilization following upon mid-twentieth-century economic development, dramatic changes are hard to detect. The extreme rigidity and control in South Asia and in West Asia/North Africa seem, on the whole, to have loosened somewhat, but only within its own walls of discretion.

The vast expanse of African sexuality

African customs well pre-dated the Western sexual revolution, in regarding sex as a legitimate human pleasure. The often intricate marriage rules often included a considerable flexibility for pre- and extra-marital sex, provided discretion and particular taboos were respected. Biological paternity has always been strongly subordinate to social father's rights, located in the lineage. The value of pre-marital chastity is part of most African culture too, but as a rule placed well below values of fertility and working capacity (cf. Caldwell *et al.* 1998).

Sexual informality is difficult to compare with any systematicity and precision. However, Africa shows no clear trend to earlier sexual debuts. Because of early marriage customs, the large majority of African women born around 1950 were sexually experienced by the age of 18, Rwanda and Zimbabwe being the only known exceptions (Blanc and Way 1998). The African age of marriage is still low in a global context, with a majority married by the age of 20, but there has been a rise in the female age. The age of sexual debut has also risen in some countries. In Nigeria, for instance, 59 per cent of the birth cohorts of 1966–70 had had sexual intercourse by the age of 18, but among girls born in 1970–74 the percentage was 49. From a northwestern European vantage-point this is now rather late.

Table 6.7 reveals that, in contrast to the female experience in Asia, there is little coincidence of first sex and of marriage. Even in the Muslim Sahel and southern Sahara the relationship between sex and marriage is variable, close in Niger and Chad, clearly separated in Burkina Faso and Mali. Many more African than Asian teenage girls have sexual experience, and, above all, many more have pre-marital sex. African girls do have a youth of their own, in contrast to most South Asian girls, and their mobility and their sexuality are clearly less circumscribed than they are to their West Asian or North African sisters.

In the country set in Table 6.7, an odd case is Catholic Rwanda (under ideal data circumstances most likely to have been joined by Catholic Burundi). At the other end are Botswana and Namibia, standing in also for other Southern African populations, demonstrating a hiatus between sex and marriage. Under the local conditions of the age of AIDS, this has been a lethal mix. In KwaZuluNatal in 1999 a quarter of girls aged 14 to 15 had had sex in the past 12 months, and 50 per cent of those aged 16–19. Indian girls were least likely to have had sexual experience, Africans the most, and the whites in between, in a ratio of 1:2.5:5 (Kaufman *et al.* 2001).

Many African teenagers become mothers, about a fifth of all, and in some countries up to a third. In South Africa a national survey in 1998 found that 30 per cent of 19-year-old girls had given birth (Kaufman *et al.* 2001). Marriage age varies enormously, with teenage marriages ranging from 50 to 8 per cent of the girl population.

The tradition of polygyny, and of long female post-partum abstinence periods – during long breast-feeding, 14–15 months in Ivory Coast and Nigeria on average, with a median of a year – have made parts of Africa,

Table 6.7 Teenage African women in the 1990s and their sexual experience (girls aged 15–19, as a percentage)

	Ever had sex	*Ever been married*	*Ever given birth*
Bénin	53	29	20
Botswana[a]	66	6	24
Burkina Faso	65	36	25
Central African Rep.	62	42	28
Chad	55	49	30
Ivory Coast	73	28	29
Ethiopia	31	30	13
Ghana	38	13	12
Kenya	56	17	17
Madagascar	57	34	37
Malawi	n.a.	41	27
Mali	66	50	34
Mozambique	69	47	30
Namibia	42	8	18
Niger	64	62	36
Nigeria	n.a.	27	18
Rwanda	14	10	8
Senegal	34	29	18
Tanzania	n.a.	27	20
Togo	61	20	16
Uganda	62	50	34
Zambia	58	25	24
Zimbabwe	32	23	16

Source: Demographic and Health Surveys 1990s, for Botswana 1988.

Note:
a 1988.

particularly on the western coast, the world centre of extra-marital sex. A study from Yorubaland in southern Nigeria calculated that only 40 per cent of sexual activity there in the 1980s took place inside marriage (Orubuloye *et al.* 1997). A larger Yoruba study in the mid-1990s, rural as well as urban, found that a tenth of married males had had extra-marital sex in the last month, and another fifth 'recently' (Orubuloye *et al.* 1997). Ivory Coast is another African hot-spot of informal sex. In a large-scale demographic survey in 1994, a fifth or more married men had had extra-marital sex in the past two months, the proportion increasing with polygyny (Ali and Cleland 2001).

Non-married sexual activity is high in Africa. If we take Brazil as a high Latin American yardstick, with 16 per cent of never-married women sexually active in the last month, we may get an idea of African activity. Twice the Brazilian score, a third of never-married women had been active in the past four weeks in three African countries – Cameroon, Ivory Coast and Gabon – and almost a quarter in Togo and Mozambique. Nigeria stood close to Brazil. But Africa is not of one piece. There were also countries with little non-marital sex: Ethiopia and Niger with less than 2 per cent of women active, Senegal and Zimbabwe with about 5 per cent.

The other side of this is a low sexual activity within marriage. In the 1996–2001 round of Demographic and Health Surveys, African countries had less sexual activity within marriage than other parts of the world. Of recently married women (0–4 years), (just) less than half had been sexually active for the last month in Benin, Burkina Faso, Ghana, Guinea and Togo, and around 60 per cent in Nigeria and the Ivory Coast. These figures may be compared to three-quarters sexually active in Kyrgyzstan, Peru and the Philippines, and above 80 per cent in Brazil, Indonesia and Uzbekistan.

Informal cohabitation is very common in some countries, and rare in others. To the former belong Mozambique, where it dominates among all age groups, Gabon where it prevails till the age of 35, and more qualifiedly Rwanda, Uganda, Ghana and the Ivory Coast, making up 20–29 per cent of the marital status of women aged 20–24. On the hand, it is almost non-existent in Niger, Senegal, Zambia, Ethiopia, Malawi and Mali. It is rare also in Nigeria: 4 per cent of 20–24-year-olds were cohabiting in 1999, which, however, might be accounted for by more exclusive criteria than in the countries with high incidence.

Summing up the above, we may distinguish four variants of the socio-sexual order in current Africa, along the axes of polygamy and sexual informality (Table 6.8). The intention is not to classify all African countries, but to provide a map of orientation. Huge and diverse Nigeria should perhaps be allocated twice, with the north probably more at ease in the low informality group, but the source used here operates with national categories only. The other parentheses indicate some other qualification. The Ivory Coast is very much a country of informal sex, but the prevalence of polygyny is not very high in the African context. Inversely, polygyny is not very low in Ghana and Gabon.

The upper left quadrant of Table 6.8 is made of West African countries with traditions of strong female autonomy, within patrilineal kinship, and with a strong influence of indigenous African religion. In the upper right quadrant are two kinds of countries. One is the southern group, with polygyny pushed back by Christianity and economic marginalization, and informality promoted by the disruptions of long-distance labour migration and of urban slumming driven by apartheid. The other group consists of largely matrilineal countries with always especially weak conjugal bonds, reinforced by the dislocations of the African crisis since the 1970s. The lower left quadrant has countries adding some of the

Table 6.8 Current African sexual orders

Informality	Polygyny	
	High	Low
High	Benin, Burkina Faso, Togo (Ivory Coast) (Nigeria south)	Botswana, Namibia, South Africa (Gabon, Ghana)
Low	Niger, Senegal (Nigeria north)	Ethiopia, Zambia, Zimbabwe

Source: Demographic Health Surveys 1996–2001.

Muslim rigour to the African customs of polygynous patriarchy. Finally, in the lower right quadrant we see a combined influence of Christianity and the typical East and South African stern father's right tradition.

While not an exhaustive explanation, religion, pre-modern kinship and contemporary economics will provide us with the basic coordinates of the African socio-sexual order.

Asian ways: control and/or discretion

Sexuality and marriage in Asia (and North Africa) are still basically channelled within a clearly defined framework. But we may distinguish two major variants on the threshold of the twenty-first century. There is one variant of strict control of female sexuality, in poor South Asia still largely by moving girls directly from childhood to marriage, in West and Central Asia and North Africa by means of tight controls on youth cultures. But in East and large parts of Southeast Asia there is now a second Asian variant with considerable sexual freedom and youth autonomy, but still also a widespread sense of decorum and discretion, as well as traditional normative inhibitions – of course outside the commercial sex circuits.

In Turkey in the late 1990s, school authorities sent suspect girls for virginity tests, and if found to be non-virginal the girls were expelled from school, including young women of the age of student nurses. Only in 2002, before the last election, did the Turkish Ministry of Education withdraw such expulsion from the educational system (Ilkkaracan 2002: 763–64). Most girls do not have any youth in South Asia, and not very much in Indonesia, Central and West Asia/North Africa either, although a few young women smoking water pipes may be seen in gender-mixed upper class cafés in Cairo (remarked on by the *New York Times*, 22 October 2002).

Considering Table 6.9, regionally, the young age at Indonesian marriage, reflecting a historical tradition, is more or less unique in Southeast Asia, while significant for being the pattern of the biggest country by far (cf. Xenos and Gultimano 1992; Jones 1997). The West Asian/North African countries in Table 6.9 represent only one part of their region. The other part has seen a rapid recent rise of the marriage age. Interestingly, this other group includes Islamist Iran, where in 1996 only 19 per cent of girls aged 15–19 were married, down from 34 per cent in 1976. In 1979 the ayatollahs reduced the minimum legal age of marriage for girls from 16 to 9 but this has had only ritual significance (Abbasi-Shawzi 2000). According to the Demographic Health Surveys, a quarter of Jordanian and barely a third of Moroccan girls born around 1970 had been married by age 20. Algeria had also married off hardly a quarter of its women at that age (Tawila 1998).

National figures for a huge country like India, of course, include a consider-able amount of variation. From the 1991 census we find that the proportion of girls married in the 15–19 age group ranged state-wise from 55.3 per cent in Bihar to 4.6 per cent in the tiny state of Goa. Because of its early marriages, northern India, while not giving any room for pre-marital female sex, has a

Table 6.9 Girls married by age 18 and 20 and female median age at marriage in South
Asia and in some other countries of young marriage and strict sexual control
(girls aged 20–24 in the 1990s)

	Married by age 18 (%)	Married by age 20 (%)	Median age at marriage (years)
South Asia			
Bangladesh	68.5	77.1	15.3
India	61.6	85.7	17.1
Pakistan	31.6	48.9	>20
Southeast Asia			
Indonesia	29.6	47.0	>20
Central Asia			
Kazakhstan	18.5	44.5	>20
Kyrgyzstan	21.2	58.4	19.5
Uzbekistan	15.3	55.7	19.8
West Asia/North Africa			
Egypt	26.8	41.4	>20
Saudi Arabia	–	48	–
Turkey	23.3	41.1	>20
Yemen	49.2	62.6	18.1

Sources: Saudi Arabia (1987): Tawila (1998); other countries: Demographic and Health Surveys.

post-marital lapse of 1–2 years before sex. From a large sample survey in
1980–81 we learn that the female average age of marriage in Bihar and
Rajasthan was 13.5 and 13.4 years, respectively, while the age of sexual
consummation was 14.8 and 15.4 (Sinha 1987). And these Indian states are no
rural backwaters: Bihar at the time had 70 million inhabitants and Rajasthan 34
million.

Education slows down both sex and marriage. A girl with at least secondary
education could escape a teenage marriage almost everywhere except in Mali,
and with rather less than a 50 per cent probability in Bangladesh or Central
Africa (Alan Guttmacher Institute 1998: table 1). In Indonesian Jakarta in
1990, a good quarter of women with a tertiary education were still unmarried
at the age of 30–34 (Jones 1997: table 3.3).

East and Southeast Asia are still largely governed by youth decorum, without the severe surveillance of South and West Asia, but nevertheless, by
relatively late, mostly post-teen sexual debuts, marginal cohabitation, and rare
extra-marital births. Japan, with its historical socio-economic edge, is the
pace-setter, and China, because of its weight, is the paradigm. South Korea has
the strongest traditional institutions. For instance, in the autumn of 2001, the
Korean Constitutional Court declared that the criminalization of adultery was
still valid law, although it recommended the legislator to change it (*DPA/ Neues
Deutschland*, 26 October 2001: 7).

Japan is heading the trend of late marriage in Asia, starting from a level of
relatively late marriage 80–100 years ago. The Japanese census of 2000 found
that 54 per cent of Japanese women aged 25–29 had never married. This does

not necessarily amount to single and independent living, however. The 1995 census reported that 74 per cent of never-married women aged 20–39 were living with their parents. Sexual debuts are also relatively late. A representative survey of 12–22-year-olds in 1993 found a median age of 20–21 (Althaus 1997). This would yield a female period of pre-marital sex of about ten years, but a period, as we noted above, little manifested in pre-marital pregnancy or in informal cohabitation. Some student data indicate something of the process of change: in 1974, 11 per cent of female Japanese university students had had sexual intercourse, in 1986 26 per cent, and in 1995 43 per cent (Hatano 1997: 805). By contrast, in China in 1989–90 only 6 per cent of female university students had sexual experience (Ruan 1997: 384), and in four universities of Egypt in 1996 only 3 per cent (Tawila 1998).

China had a median female marriage age a little above 22 in 1990 (the official minimum age), with the first quartile having married just before 21 (Zeng 2000: 94). Until recently, unconventional sex was penally repressed, such as college cohabitation (in 1987) and a sexual commune in Shanghai (in 1988) (Ruan 1991: 161). Since then China, and its pre-Communist capital of sex, Shanghai, in particular has 'opened up', with a wide repertoire of possible sexual encounters on offer (Farrer 2002). But how much real action there is, outside some small avant-garde milieux, is not easy to ascertain.

In the largest sexual survey of China to date, conducted in 1989–90, for example, only one fifth of college students questioned gave an answer. Half of those who did answer had ever had sexual intercourse (Liu *et al.* 1997: ch. 3). Married couples, rural and urban, were more prone to answer. The median age of first intercourse was about the same as the median age of marriage, and 90 per cent had their first sexual encounter with their spouse (Liu *et al.* 1997: 236ff). A study of Anhui province in 1997 found the same pattern, first inter-course and marriage almost coeval in time, although a good quarter of men and a fifth of women reported pre-marital sex. Ninety-five per cent had their first intercourse with their spouse (Liu *et al.* 1998).

Most Korean industrial workers in Seoul in their twenties (in 1996) had sexual experience, but only after the age of 20. Thirty per cent of female export-zone workers (aged 15–29), a tenth of them under duress, had sexual experience at an average age of 20. Two per cent of female and 15 per cent of all Vietnamese university students had experienced sex in 1996 (Anon. 2000: table 1). In the mid-1990s, about a tenth of Filipinas and about a fifth of Thai teenage women had experienced sexual intercourse, and then overwhelmingly after marriage (Singh *et al.* 2000: fig. 1; Lee 2002: 132). Among an early 1990s Malaysian adolescent national sample, aged 15–21, only 9 per cent had ever had a sexual experience (Zulkifli *et al.* 1995). Among Jakarta university students aged 20–24, 11 per cent had had sexual intercourse (Utomo 2002: table 11.3). Only in Taiwan, Korea and Japan is Asian sexual experience pre-marital (cf. East–West Center 2002: 61).

Asian prostitution is not only an export industry, it plays a major role in domestic masculinity, particularly in Thailand. About half of Thai males make their sexual debut with a prostitute, and most of them have been with one.

Commercial sex is also a major experience in male experience in the Philippines, in Vietnam, in India, and most probably in other parts of East and Southeast Asia (Savara and Sridhar 1992; Kanbargi and Kanbargi 1996; Anon. 2000).

Noteworthy is also the relatively high frequency of male homosexuality in several Asian samples, of highly variable representativeness. Most representative is a survey of Thai army conscripts in 1996, finding that about 10 per cent had had homosexual sex (Kitsiripornchai *et al.* 1998). There is also a seemingly representative Filipino urban sample of 1994 yielding 6 per cent gays or bisexuals (D'Agnes *et al.* 1995) Among a clearly non-representative Indian sample of readers of a men's magazine, of those with sexual experience, 37 per cent had had homosexual intercourse (Sarava and Sridhar 1992). While abstaining from trying to assess any truly representative figure of national populations, we may have reason to admit a higher Asian incidence of homosexual acts. If so, this case is probably to be interpreted as a manifestation of misogyny and of limited access to 'respectable' women.

Creole inequalities

Latin America is the world's most unequal region economically. The inequality of the sexual order has been institutionalized from early colonial times. The informal unions still coexist with official Catholic conservatism, currently manifested in the extremely restricted abortion rights across the region (UN 1999), and in the enduring prohibition of divorce in Chile. But within this distinctive Creole dualism, much stronger than that in the northern USA, there is also a centre–periphery division, of a territorial as well as class character. The Caribbean and Chile make up the two current poles of national socio-sexual orders, with a complex patchwork in between, checkered by sub-national regions, ethnicities/races and class.

Sex begins, for the median Latin American girl born in the 1970s, around 19, similar to Southern Europe and later than in the North Atlantic region. Except for Brazil there has been no lowering trend from the cohorts of the 1940s. Median age at first sexual union is two years later, between 21 and 22 (Heaton *et al.* 2002: tables 1–2). Marriage is later, but still early in comparison with Europe. In Chile in 2000 mean female age at first marriage was 26 years, but it was well below 24 in Mexico in 1998, which is more regionally repesentative. In age terms, Latin American marriage resembles the Eastern European custom.

Within the hemisphere, the earliest transitions to sexual intercourse, sexual union and birth may be found in eastern Bolivia, in the Peruvian *selva*, in southwestern Nicaragua (from Managua to the Pacific), in Brazilian Mato Grosso and Amazonas, in Ecuador, in the Colombian Andes and on its Caribbean coast, in Central America (save Costa Rica), and in Mexico outside the central high plateau (Heaton *et al.* 2002: fig. 1) (Table 6.10). On the whole, these are regions largely populated by Indians or at least with significant Indian cultural tradition.[10] The same pattern holds for the northern and the

Table 6.10 Teenage Latin American women in the 1990s and their sexual experience (percentage of girls aged 15–19)

	Ever had sex	*Ever been married* [a]	*Ever given birth*
Bolivia	20	12	12
Brazil	33	17	14
Colombia	30	15	14
Dominican R.	33	29	18
Guatemala	25	23	17
Haiti	–	17	11
Nicaragua	36	33	22
Paraguay	30	15	14
Peru	20	13	11

Source: Demographic and Health Surveys 1990s.

Note:

a 'Married' here usually includes cohabiting.

southern peripheries of Argentina (Torrado 1993: table 7.1). Those areas are also poor and underdeveloped, but Heaton and his collaborators had controlled for education and rurality.

The later sexual debut in Latin America, compared to Africa and to north-western Europe and North America, was also the finding of recent studies of adolescents in Buenos Aires and Mexico City, indicating a median age of around 18. Boys started a year earlier, in Buenos Aires half of them through prostitutes (Fleiz-Bautista *et al.* 1999; Nechi *et al.* 2000).

By and large, Latin American women enter into sex, marriage and children later than their African counterparts, although there is some area of overlap. Sex and sexual unions start early in adolescence in some parts of the region, in the Caribbean and among several Indian populations. A sizeable proportion of Jamaican girls are already sexually active at the age of 12–13 (Eggleston *et al.* 1999; Wyatt *et al.* 1999); 45 per cent of Jamaican girls had become pregnant by the age of 19 (McFarlane *et al.* 1994). But in the early 1970s cohorts of Haiti and the Dominican Republic the median age was about 19. At least in the Latin Caribbean, the amount of sexual activity is not impressive in an international context; in Haiti and Nicaragua it is well below the Latin American average, and very much below the married sex frequency of Central and Southeast Asia. Brazilians are the most sexually active in Latin America.[11] The median age of cohabitation or marriage has risen, with girls' education, but was in the mid-1990s still below 20 in the Dominican Republic and just above it in Haiti. In Cuba, which since the revolution has a more marital sexual order, the mean age at first marriage was 18 years (for women) in 1987 (Benítez Pérez 1999: table 2).

Parenting becomes in part de-linked from procreation. In Haiti in the mid-1990s only about 40 per cent of children aged 10–14 were growing up with both their parents, in the Dominican Republic barely a half, and in Nicaragua little more than a half. Thirty per cent of Haitian children in that age group had no parent in their household, a situation applying to 23 per cent of Dominican and 14 per cent of Nicaraguan children (Demographic and Health Surveys).

In the mid-twenty-first century, Brazil, as we saw above, formalized its sexual order, bringing down informal unions and out-of-marriage births, more than in Argentina and Uruguay or Mexico, not to speak of the Andean countries. But informal cohabitation has staged a most vigorous comeback in the last two decades. Only Chile is currently outside the old Creole family system, and becoming rather similar to Latin Europe.

The Indo-American norms of early and officially informal unions differ from the more fluid pattern of the Caribbean. In Guatemala, for instance, 70 per cent of children aged 10–14 grow up with both their parents, which is about the norm in Latin America. Also normal is that a tenth of the children are living without a parent in the household (Demographic Health Surveys). Outside the Caribbean, Latin American marriages are not particularly unstable, though not on a par with South Asian (Westoff *et al.* 1994: table 4.1). The formal divorce rate is mostly very low, in countries like Brazil and Mexico at 0.60 and 0.48, respectively. In 1998 there were 6.5 Mexican divorces per 100 marriages. Uruguay had a Western European rate of 2.01 per thousand population in 1998 (INE Uruguay 1999: tables 2.10 and 2.11; UN 2001a: table 25).

Marriages or informal unions are often embedded in complex households. Extended, non-nuclear households made up a fifth of Argentinian, Brazilian and Colombian households in the mid-1990s, about a quarter of Chilean and Mexican households, and well above a third of households in Paraguy and Venezuela (UN ECLAC 1997: 131).

Four 'Western' variants

Let us end this tour of the world by summing up some aspects of the current socio-sexual order, particularly its youth–adulthood interface, in Europe, North America and white Oceania, regions by cultural tradition often referred to as 'the West' – a label which is conveniently brief, although geographically ambiguous and traditionally often exclusive of some parts of Europe.

The northwestern European pattern of informal coupling and individualism

Sex starts early, 16 being about the median for both boys and girls, but adolescent births are rare, 10 per thousand women aged 15–19 in France and Finland, 8–9 in Belgium, Denmark, the Netherlands and Sweden (Singh and Darroch 2000: table 2: data from the mid-1990s). Mean age at first birth is in the late twenties, around 29 in Belgium, Britain and France, 27–28 in Finland and Sweden. Cohabitation is the rule before marriage, and is a major form of coupling generally. In Scandinavia it is equal to marriage in parenting the first child. Single parenting is not at a very high level, and has actually gone down in Sweden in recent decades. Marriage is late, after the first birth, in Scandinavia at the age of 30 for women. Marriage instability is high, including some of the highest divorce rates in Europe.

The 'ideal typical' populations of this socio-sexual order are the Nordic ones, the Danish, Icelandic and Swedish in particular. But what makes it a major European variant, and not just an Arctic outlier, is that, by and large, it is also featured in France, the Low Countries, and, with more qualifications of more single parents and less cohabitation, Britain.

Germanic Central Europe, which its closest eastern neighbours may now be about to join in socio-sexual as well as in economic matters, is also part of the northwestern pattern of early youth independence and late marriage. But it has been more hesitant in its embrace of informal cohabitation, and of non-marital parenting in particular. A stronger lingering religious influence is a likely reason, and in East Germany the legacy of the Communist promotion of marriage, a functional equivalent to the churches of West Germany. Austria, Germany and Switzerland may so far be considered a conservative variant of the northwestern European socio-sexual order, of which Denmark and Sweden then might be considered the radical wing.

The Southern European shadow of the parental household

This variant is rather similar across the southern belt of Europe, from Greece to Portugal. Young people tend to stay with their parents till they marry, which now happens rather late, in a range of averages from 25 in Portugal to 28 in Italy and Spain. Extended families of two generations of adults are not uncommon. Sex begins later than in the north, at 19–20 for women born in the 1960s, and has a gendered pattern, with boys starting a year or two earlier. Regional intra-south differences are also important. Between Emilia-Toscana on one hand, and the Mezzogiorno south of Naples, there is a two-year median debut difference, with the more chaperoned southern women, of course, coming out last (Billari and Borgoni 2002). Cohabitation is marginal, single parenting somewhat less so, but low by current European standards. The divorce rate is low to extremely low (Italy).

The unstable Eastern European marriage order

The Eastern European tradition of early and almost universal marriage survived the Bolshevik Revolution, the Stalinist terror and industrialization, and the post-Stalinist social development. But whether it will survive the re-introduction of capitalism and the concurrent upheavals is uncertain. In the 1990s the marriage-dominated order is still there, though, above all in Russia, Ukraine, Belarus, the Balkans, and in Catholic Lithuania, Poland and Slovakia. Marriages are relatively early, among women in their early twenties. While the marriage rate has plummeted with the post-Communist crisis, cohabitation is still rather rare in these countries. Among the 18 to 45 age group there were in 1999, in the Eastern Europe of Russia, Ukraine, Belarus, Romania and Bulgaria, clearly more married couples, much fewer cohabitees, significantly fewer singles, and more residents with parents than in Western Europe, with East-Central European countries, from Lithuania to Croatia, in between. Estonia, Latvia and Hungary are similar to the northwestern European pattern (Lestaeghe and Surkyn 2002: tables 1 and 2).

Divorce rates are high in most parts. Sex starts relatively late, and the interval of pre-marital sex is the shortest in Europe. To move directly from one's parental home to marriage is normal, and marriage, at least in Russia, has very often entailed living with parents or parents-in law as well – as was the custom of pre-Communist times.

American dualism of marriage and non-marriage

The USA has a socio-sexual order which is significantly different from any of the European variants, although, like its earlier specificities, these too might be regarded as part of intra-systemic variation. In terms of its current social organization of sexuality, what is characteristic of the USA is a dualism of marriage and its opposites, of early youth independence and of early marriage, of marital virginity and adolescent fertility, of married family values and single parenting, of marriage and of divorce, of ostentatious public display of the nuclear family and of the extended sexuality of matrifocal ghetto 'random families', with their 'roving hands' of 'mothers' husbands, boyfriends' brothers or grandfathers and uncles' (LeBlanc 2003: 12).

The median age of sexual debut was probably somewhat higher in the USA in the 1990s than in parts of northwestern Europe, and the marriage age was lower, as we noted above. The female singulate mean age at marriage (SMAM) was 26.0 in 1995 (UN 2001a: table 2a), and the median female age in 2000 was 25.1 (US Census Bureau 2001d: table MS-2). The period of pre-marital sex was thus smaller. More noteworthy, however, is the finding that about a fifth of American 18–24-year-olds, and about one in seven of 25–34-year-olds were virgins upon marriage, in contrast to almost nobody (5 per cent) in Britain (Michael *et al.* 2001: table 12.2). While interesting in itself, and reinforced by a Fundamentalist Protestant movement for pre-marital sexual abstinence, this datum should be seen together with statistics on teenage births.

In the mid-1990s, among European countries and countries of the former British Empire, the USA had the second highest rate of teenage births, 54.4 per 1,000 women aged 15–19, overtaken by Caucasian Armenia and closely followed by Ukraine. England, with the highest Western European rate, scored 28.4, while France and Germany were more representative having 10–12.5 births per thousand teenage girls. Sweden produced 7.7. Even the white American teenage birth rate (38), and the state low of New Hampshire (29) is above any Western European level. Two-thirds of American teenage pregnancies are reported as unwanted, which indicates faulty sexual education and deficient access to contraceptives, as well as general social weakness or disadvantage among a section of the American population. With the arrival of reliable contraceptives, teenage pregnancies and births went down after 1970, but in contrast to Western Europe that process levelled off in the USA after 1975 (see further Singh *et al.* 2000).

Cohabitation is not uncommon as a trial marriage – a third to 40 per cent of the high school cohort of 1972 practised it (Brien *et al.* 1999: 546) – but it tends to be a shortlived interim status (cf. Mosher and Bachrach 1996). Among all couples it is less widespread at one point in time than in Germany. For children it is much less important than single parenting.

The United States has one of the highest (crude) marriage rates of the world, higher than any country in Europe, and approximated there only by Albania and Belarus at 7.4 and 7.0 marriages, respectively, per thousand population in 1998 compared with the US rate of 8.3 (UN 2001a: table 23). Part of the reason for the US record is its high divorce rate, the highest in the world after Belarus (UN 2001a: table 25), which in conjunction with a high re-marriage rate produces a large number of marriages overall. The desire to re-marry is also a desire to marry.

The American order of sexuality is unique in the sense that the other white heirs of the British Empire – Australia, Canada and New Zealand – follow more closely the northwestern European pattern.

While the borderlines may be arguable, adolescents growing up are clearly facing very different entries into sexuality, adulthood and new family formation. And these entries vary not only between family civilizations, but also within the 'Western' one.

From outlaw to married citizen: a note on rights to homosexuality

A remarkable turn in the history of marriage began in the final decade of the twentieth century, the official institutionalization of same-sex marriage, or 'part-nership'. While socially and sexually still more of symbolic than of substantial significance, it does indicate how much the socio-sexual order has mutated since the trial of Oscar Wilde. It is also a noteworthy tribute to the institution of marriage.

Recognition of homosexuality as a legitimate form of sexuality was part of the Western sexual revolution. It was now de-criminalized, where it was still an offence, and in 1973 it was struck off the list of mental disorders of the American Psychiatric Association. In 1975 the US Civil Service Commission lifted its ban on employing homosexuals. Soon discrimination against homo-sexuals was made an offence instead. Equality with regard to 'sexual orientation' was on the rules for the appointment of mayors in the Netherlands in the 1980s, for instance. A major international breakthrough was its inclusion in the new post-apartheid South African Constitution, in the latter's interim version of 1993, and in the final Bill of Rights of 1996. The Anglican Archbishop Desmond Tutu moved the issue in the Constitutional Assembly, and said: 'It would be a sad day for South Africa if any individual or group of law-abiding citizens . . . would find that the Final Constitution did not guarantee their fundamental human right to a sexual life, whether heterosexual or homosexual' (Steyn 1998: 408n).

But what is interesting in our particular context here, has been the gay and lesbian demand for marriage rights, and the partial acceptance of their demand. Most progress has been made in Northern Europe, where it has received a basically favourable hearing from the secular pluralism now charac-teristic of these countries. There has been more resistance in England, the

Anglican tradition of which has remained largely immune to the unprejudiced humanism of the anti-apartheid leader Archbishop Tutu. In the 1996 *J.* v. *S.T.* transsexual case, Lord Justice Ward of the Court of Appeal, after quoting nineteenth-century colleagues in support, concluded, that 'single-sex unions remain proscribed as fundamentally abhorrent to this notion of marriage' (Katz 1998: 494–95).

In the United States, opinion is sharply polarized, between, on one hand, resourceful and well-organized homosexual communities, and a strong Christian Fundamentalism on the other. The courts have been a main arena of conflict, with variable outcomes. In 1986 the US Supreme Court, in the *Bowers* v. *Hardwick* case, ruled state criminalization of homosexuality was legitimate. In June 2003 the same court reversed its position, striking down a Texas law criminalizing homosexuality. For rights of homosexual partners, most of the gains so far have been local, by municipal ordinances and by some county and state agencies. The city of San Francisco issued an ordinance in 1991 on same-sex 'domestic partnerships', including provision of a civil wedding ceremony (Zicklin 1995; Wardle 1998: 387n). In 1993 the Hawaii Supreme Court raised the stakes by arguing, in *Baehr* v. *Lewin*, that denying a marriage licence to a same-sex couple was a discrimination which could be legitimate only on the ground of compelling state interest. The US Congress then passed the Defence of Marriage Act three years later, explicitly defining marriage as a heterosexual union. The next round was won by the other side in 1999, when the Vermont Supreme Court in a unanimous decision held that the legal 'benefits and protections' of married couples could not be denied same-sex couples. After a legislative battle, Vermont then adopted in 2000 a Civil Union Act, a kind of registered de facto homosexual marriage, a 'registered partnership' as it is most often called (Bonauto 2001). In the autumn of 2003, the highest court in Massachusetts opened the door to same-sex marriage. Earlier that same year the highest court in Ontario had legalized homosexual marriage in that province.

On the level of national legislation or jurisdiction, same-sex partnerships were first institutionalized in Scandinavia, like so much else of modern family change. Swedish authorities had since the 1970s recognized some general cohabitee rights to same-sex cohabitees, and this was made more systematic in the 1987 Cohabitee (Joint Home) and Homosexual Cohabitees Acts. The first national legislation of 'registered partnerships' between same-sex partners was passed in Denmark in 1989, and provided a model for the other Scandinavian countries (Bradley 1996; Lund-Andersen 2001). In the Netherlands a law on registered partnerships has been in effect since 1 January 1998, and France has had a '*Pacte civil de solidarité*' since 1999, aimed also at solidary personal relations other than homosexual ones.

The Netherlands is the first, and so far only, national jurisdiction providing homosexuals with a civil marriage. Rapid secularization from the mid-1960s led to the strong decline of the Confessional political parties, which had been key players in every Dutch government since 1918. In the 1990s the now merged Catholic and mainstream Calvinist party was outside the government, which provided political preconditions for radical cultural moves, in a tolerant, pluralistic society. After some vacillation the Social Democratic-cum-Liberal government introduced a bill on homosexual marriage in 1999, which was passed the year after, and took effect in 2001 (Waaldijk 2001).

The German Social Democratic–Green government passed a law of 'Life Partnerships', in force since August 2001. The Christian Democratic opposition challenged it in the Constitutional Court, alleging a breach of the German Constitution's 'special protection' of marriage and the family. In a five to three vote in July 2002 the Court dismissed the complaint, with the motivation that marriage, in the old Christian sense, was not infringed upon by the right to set up other recognized partnerships.

While the principle has won in Northern Europe and South Africa, the battle for new rights to marry goes on, and there are also non-resolved ceremonial and adoption issues in the first group of countries. The major family law reforms of the 1990s in Japan (Matushima 1998) and in Russia (Khazova 1998), and the new Chinese family legislation (Chiu 2001) bypassed the issue. In India, (male) homosexuality is still a criminal offence (Saxena 2001: 380). In Brazil, a bill, from the Labour Party opposition, was tabled before the 2002 elections, but not was not acted upon (Dealtry 2001) (see the broad overview of Wintemute and Andanaes 2001).

Marriage is not disappearing. It is changing.

Part III

Couples, babies and states

Subject to imprisonment of one to six months and a fine is 'anyone who, with an anti-conception aim has . . . divulged or offered to reveal procedures proper to prevent pregnancy, or to facilitate the use of such procedures'.
(French law of 31 July 1920, cited in Dhavernas 1978: 144–45)

Husband and wife are in duty bound to practice family planning.
(The Marriage Law of the People's Republic of China 1980, article 12, cited in Women of China 1987: 6)

The twentieth century was going to be the 'century of the child' according to the prophecy and hope on its threshold by the then world-famous Swedish feminist writer Ellen Key (1900). Like all prophets, Ellen Key may be interpreted as having shown the truth before anybody else. The singularity of the child has come true in most of Europe and large parts of East Asia, even in parts of South Asia. The 'little emperors' of current one-child-policy China, once the world's most elaborate centre for the veneration of fathers, in the Confucian tradition of 'filial piety', indicate more vividly the change of the world, than, say the UN Convention on the Rights of the Child.

In the course of the twentieth century, children became more costly, more scarce, more valuable, more unruly, more powerful. It has been a long and sinuous process, which has not even touched all countries of the world yet. But it is rolling on seemingly irresistibly. It reached the heartlands of the Islamic world in the 1980s and most parts of sub-Saharan Africa in the course of the 1990s. By that time it had spread widely throughout other parts of the world.

The dark side of this, even for non-patriarchs, is the greying of the world, the ageing of Europe, East Asia and Southern Cone America, the beginning of the 'dying out' of Germans, Italians, Swedes, Russians and most other Eastern Europeans, where more people die each year than are born.

In the Swedish countryside, it was my parents and their generation, born between 1890 and 1910, who made the big leap. My small-farmer paternal grandparents, born around 1870, had seven children surviving into adulthood (and eight into adolescence), and my big-farmer maternal grandparents also had seven. Of these fourteen children, one never married (and had no child), one only married after fertile age, two were (or had spouses who were) infertile, one had three children, one had one child only, and eight had two children. The latter included my parents, who after my little sister's death at the age of six months, settled down with one child. In the village where I grew up in the 1940s, the only peers I had with more than one (or two) sibling(s) were children of two clearly marginalized, 'backward' labourers' families, which comprised four or five children. No one was more prolific than that. Following my parents, with more insecure steps on a more slippery path of family-building, I also have two children, something which is now behind recent European developments.

7 Fertility decline and political natalism

In order to maintain a population, you need, migration apart, a little more than two children per woman during her fertile age (to take mortality and infertility into account). Alone among the most developed countries of some size, the USA is currently keeping a fertility rate (virtually) at 2.1. At the beginning of the twenty-first century, in all Europe only two small countries are reproducing themselves demographically, Albania and Iceland. In the fifteen countries of the European Union the current (2001) total fertility rate (TFR) is 1.47 per woman. East Asia is also below net reproduction, although the still relatively young Chinese age structure will keep the population of China growing slowly for some time, while Japan is heading for natural population decline quite soon. Fertility rates approximating that of my grand-mothers', of six children or more, can now be found only in the poorest parts of sub-Saharan Africa and in the most conservative countries of the Muslim world, in Afghanistan and in Yemen.

A hundred years earlier, France was unique, in the world as well as in Europe, in having the lowest birth rate, a TFR of 2.8 (Table 7.1). Married French women gave birth to four children on average, also the lowest in the world at the time. American fertility was a distant second. Within marriage, Western European women were very fertile, up until World War I. But change was coming rapidly and widely. By 1903, half of all Europe's provinces had experienced at least a 10 per cent decline in marital fertility (Coale 1986: 38).

Data and estimates outside the 'Western world' for this point in time are more uncertain or simply lacking. But what is available shows a higher fertility in the other family systems, although the distance was not overwhelming (Table 7.2). The Western European marriage system kept total fertility sub-stantially lower than in Eastern Europe, Asia and Africa. Within marriage, however, Scandinavian women were as fertile as their Indian sisters, and more fertile than Chinese women.

The world's demographic transition 1750–2050

In the long-view history of humankind, the secular decline of fertility is part of a longer and wider process, known among demographers as the 'demographic transition'; that is, a period of rapid population growth in a move, a 'transi-

Table 7.1 Total and marital fertility rates in the Western European family system
around 1900 (average number of children born per woman and per married
woman, respectively, during her lifetime)

Country	Period	TFR[a]	MFR[b]
France	1899–1903	2.8	4.1
	1904–8	2.7	4.0
USA[c]	1900–10	3.8	5.2
	1905–10	3.6	4.8
Australia	1907–15	3.9	5.9
Austria	1895–1900	5.1	7.0
Canada	1906	4.8	–
Denmark	1895–1900	4.2	7.1
	1906–15	3.6	6.0
England and Wales	1901	3.5	6.2
	1911	2.9	5.5
Finland	1906–15	4.1	6.9
Germany	1901–5/1876–80[d]	4.8	7.7
Italy	1903	4.4	–
Netherlands, the	1908–12/1906–13[d]	4.1	7.3
Norway	1889–92	4.4	7.9
	1916–20	3.4	6.1
Spain	1900	4.9	–
Sweden	1901–10	3.8	7.0
	1911–20	3.1	5.8

Sources: All marital fertilty rates and all total rates except for Canada, Germany, Italy, Spain
and Sweden are taken from Haines (1990: table 1); Canadian, German and Italian total
fertility: Chesnais (1992: 543); Spanish rates calculated from Reher (1997: 179), according to
the transformation multiplier given by Coale *et al.* (1979: 212); Swedish total fertility: SCB
(1999: 70).

Notes:
a Number of live births per woman aged 15–49.
b Number of live births per married woman aged 20–44. The technical term is TMFR 20–44.
c As estimated by Michael Haines. An earlier estimate by William Grabill gave for 1905–10 a
   TFR of 3.7 and an MFR of 5.0.
d The first period is that of TFR, the second of MFR.

tion', from a low-growth system of high fertility and high mortality (with
possibly crisis periods of decline) to another low-growth system of low fertility
and low mortality. The demographic transition was given a theoretical status
in the mid-1940s by F.W. Notestein (1945), director of the important and
resourceful Office of Population Research in Princeton (USA), as a demographic variant of what later became known as 'modernization theory'.

The economic and social developments of industrialization drove mortality
down, causing accelerated population growth. However, 'urban industrial
society' led to a new ideal of a small family, which then more gradually
brought fertility down too. The theory of demographic transition was an
elegant, important, far-reaching and plausible notion, which has had, and still
has, a tremendous impact on development policies in the world since World
War II, above all on North American and Western European conceptions of
Third World development. However, like most grand theories of the social

Table 7.2 Total and marital fertility rates outside the Western
European family around 1900 and early twentieth
century

	Period	*TFR*	*MFR*
Russia	1897	7.1	
Argentina	1895	7.0	
Peru	1876–1940	5.8	
China[a]	1929–31	5.5	6.2
Japan	1920	5.4	
India	1891–1911	5.8	7.1
Egypt	1937	6.4	
Namibia[b]	1930	8.0	

Sources: Japan: Chesnais (1992: appendix tables A2.1 and A2.3);
Russia: author's calculation from the special indices used by Coale
et al. (1979: 16, 124, 212); Argentina: Pantelides (1996: table 19.2);
Peru: Ferrando and Aramburú (1996: 417); China: Lee and Wang
Feng (1999: 85); India: Bhat (1989: 111); Egypt: Fargues (1989: 152);
Namibia: Notkola (1996: 298).

Notes:
a 22 provinces.
b Ovamboland.

world of humans, it has had considerable problems with the irregular varieties
of human behaviour. As a theory of explanation and of prediction it is now
widely questioned, while the concept itself still appears to make some sense as
a broad descriptive trajectory of great historical significance.[1] Its conception of
a pre-transition stable equilibrium, though, is being increasingly abandoned in
favour of one made up of long-term cyclical swings (e.g. Wrigley 1978; Wrigley
and Schofield 1981; Crook 1989).

If the current population trends, as estimated by the Population Division of
the UN Secretariat, hold, we can date the demographic transition in the world
as the three centuries between 1750 and 2050. Between 1500 and 1750 world
population grew at about 0.2 per cent per year, and at 0.25 per cent between
1700 and 1750. Then a new demographic era began, in Europe, but helped to
statistical visibility by a cyclical Asian upturn. The growth rate climbed to 0.4
per cent annually for the second half of the eighteenth century.

The Euro-Asian coincidence was due to the prosperity of eighteenth-
century China, with the consolidation of the Qing dynasty. By the mid-
nineteenth century this population growth had led to strong pressure on
available resources and technology, and a century of civil wars and invasions
lowered Chinese population growth to pre-transition levels (Ho 1959). The
population of China grew from about 150 million in 1700 to 'perhaps' 313
million in 1794 – which would mean an annual increase of almost 0.8 per cent
– and then to 450 million in 1850. By 1953, when a more reliable census
system had been re-established, a population of 583 million was counted. For
India and Japan, by contrast, the eighteenth century was a bad time. The
Indian population seems to have recovered in the nineteenth century, but
India was on a stable course of population growth only after 1921 (Dyson

1989). At its first census, in 1881, India had 194 million inhabitants, in 1981, 703 million. What happened in Japan mattered much less to world and Asian population, but a series of famines hit the country hard in the eighteenth century, and only in the second third of the nineteenth century did Japanese population growth reach early transition level (Taeuber 1958; Saito 1996). The Japanese population numbered about 35 million in the 1870s.

During the nineteenth century the population of the earth grew by 0.5 per cent a year. In spite of the world wars and other man-made disasters, the twentieth century saw human population increase by 1.3 per cent annually. On a global scale, population growth peaked historically in the third quarter of the twentieth century, at a rate of almost 2 per cent per year. In the last quarter of the century it fell back to 1.6 per cent. UN (1998, 2000b) predictions yield a growth rate for the first quarter of the twenty-first century of about 0.8 per cent and for the second of 0.4 per cent. Then we would be back at the 1750–1800 growth rate (Biraben 1979; Livi-Bacci 1992: 31), with most probable prospects of stagnation or decline.

The demographic transition has, of course, been a very uneven process. The population of the Americas began to grow again in the eighteenth century after the genocidal conquest, but the numerical effects of the latter were not overcome until well into the first half of the nineteenth century, through immigration. The slave-raided population of Africa also seems to have declined in the seventeenth and the eighteenth centuries. The transition, in the sense of accelerated population growth, began in Northern and Southern Africa in the late nineteenth century, in tropical Central Africa only in the 1920s (Coquery-Vidrovitch 2003).

Europe led the way to higher long-term population growth, and in Europe the UK. All through the nineteenth century the UK population, in spite of imperial emigration, increased at an annual rate of 1.2 per cent, with its high in the first half of the century, at 1.3 per cent. But for Europe as a whole, population growth culminated in the first decade of the twentieth century, about half a century before the world as a whole, at 1.0 per cent for 1900–1913, also a period of very extensive emigration (Livi-Bacci 1999: 174–75). The latter was part of the reason for European population growth stopping at about half of the increase of the poorer parts of the world in the third quarter of the twentieth century, but only a part – the family system was at least as important.

The theory of demographic transition is plagued by three fundamental, still largely unresolved questions. Why did mortality decline (in some areas at some point in time)? Why did fertility decline (in some areas at some point in time)? What comes first, mortality or fertility decline? The second issue has attracted most controversial energy by far. From the perspective of the institution of the family, fertility decline is clearly the most pertinent variable, as it is the process most amenable to family decision.

Fertility control is an ancient human wisdom, which could be practised in different ways. Before modern contraceptive devices there have been at least four major ways of keeping sexuality and fertility under control. Two are direct, by deliberate individual action. First, coitus interruptus, marital coital frequency, and other restrictive sexual practices constitute one important way. Another method has been abortion and infanticide, especially female infanticide. In medieval and modern Europe this method was on the whole marginal or secondary. More effective were institutional regulations which indirectly but importantly impinged upon the rate of human fertility, of which there have been two major types, one concentrated on access to marriage, i.e. to legitimate sex, the other on restraints on intra-marital and post-marital sex. Geoculturally, we may here distinguish between a Western European and an Afro-Asian approach.

The Western European way was regulation of entry into marriage. A married couple was normatively required to be able to set up a household of their own, outside the roof of their parents. Pre-industrial European society had established a relatively low fertility pattern by late marriages and a significant proportion of the population never marrying, at least one in ten. Once in the haven of marriage, however, European couples tended to be quite fertile.

Outside Western Europe and Creole America, marriage was virtually universal, and usually well before the bride was 20, as we saw in Chapter 4. Total fertility could be held back, like in India, by mortality: often big spousal age gaps, a large number of widows, and strict taboos against widows remarrying. The theoretically conceivable fertility resulting from this marriage pattern was further significantly reined in by limitations of marital fertility. The segregated life spheres of boys and girls, men and women, including, in some customs, separate sleeping quarters for wife and husband, and the family arrangement of marriage, often with large age differences among spouses – in brief the lack of marital intimacy – are likely to have kept coital frequency down. Polygyny tended to limit the fertility of married women sharing the same husband. Norms about long periods of breast-feeding – for up to two to three years – and/or of post-partum sexual abstinence, and prohibitions of (35 to 40-year-old) grandmothers from being sexually active, and of widow remarriage kept Afro-Asian marital fertility within bounds (see, e.g., Goody 1976, 1990; Caldwell 1982).

The bitter Chinese mid-nineteenth-century diarist Wang-shih-to proposed in the 1850s a whole barrage of measures against what he saw as the overpopulation of China: female infanticide en masse, the drowning of the weakest children of both sexes, more nunneries, postponed marriage age for both sexes, prohibiting widows from remarrying, propagation of the use of drugs which would sterilize women, extra taxation on families with more than one or two children.[2]

The cultural boundaries of the two systems of institutionalizing fertility control were in fact less tight than John Hajnal, the discoverer–theorist of the 'European marriage system', once thought. The ongoing Euro-Asian Project on Population and Family History has found Western European-type marriage regulation in parts of pre-modern Japan (Hayami and Ochiai 1996). Above all, however, it has brought out, in China as well as in Japan, important intra-marital adaptations, through spacing of births and infanticide (Alter *et al.* 2000; Wang and Tsuya 2000).

The two institutional complexes of fertility control were far from equal in their limitation effects. African, American and Asian total fertility rates (TFR) of six or seven children per woman, common in the post-1945 period of widespread demographic statistics, have hardly ever been recorded on a national scale in Western Europe. In the 1750s, French women had on average 5.5 children and English women about 4.8, the same as Swedish women. The Swedish national population registers, which, uniquely, go back to 1749, never recorded a national TFR of 5 of more. The reconstructed French series peaked in the 1750s. The only Western European country with a registered national TFR of 6 or more is England, for the years of 1805 to 1824. Some countries increased their fertility in the last third of the nineteenth century, up to five children per woman or slightly more in Finland (sporadically), Germany, Italy, the Netherlands and Spain.

Eastern Europe had another pattern, with a TFR of nearly 7 in Russia by the turn of the nineteenth and twentieth centuries, and 6 in Hungary in 1830, only a little less in 1890. The historically relatively low level of fertility is a Western European, not a 'Western' phenomenon: the United States had a TFR of well above 7 in 1800, Canada one of 6.8 for women born around 1840, and Australia a TFR of 5.7 (Festy 1979a: table 5; Coale 1986: 17–18; Chesnais 1992: 323, and tables A2.1–3; SCB 1999: table 3.3).

Both these two later approaches, of Western European access to first marriage regulation and of Afro-Asian intra-marriage and remarriage control, were anchored in collective social institutions, above and around the sexed couples and individuals. Modern demographic regimes meant an emancipation of copular and of individual decision-making.

Before continuing into modernity, it should be stressed that the various combinations of pre-modern fertility reductions have subjected human fertility to severe social controls. The maximum fertility of a human population has been estimated at 15 children (Bongaarts 1978), which has never been reached by any known population, although individual women are known to have had 15 children and more, including some in Northern Europe. The highest recorded population fertility comes from a Protestant Christian sect in North Dakota, the Hutterites, who therefore were used as a baseline for the Princeton European Fertility Project (Coale and Watkins 1986). Hutterite women bore about 10 children. The highest fertility ever recorded for ethnically or politically defined populations is 8. Historically, missionary parish records from Ovamboland in current Namibia yield a fertility rate of about 8 around 1930 (Notkola 1996: 298), and survey estimates from Jordan and a few African countries (Malawi, Kenya, Zimbabwe) in the early to mid-1960s, also show a maximum rate of 8 (World Bank 1990: table 27).

Deliberate quantitative family planning seems to have started in the seventeenth or early eighteenth century among privileged families of Europe, be they ruling dynasties, British and French peers, Swedish noblemen, or Western European urban Jewry (Livi-Bacci 1986; cf. Fauve-Chaumoux 2001).[3]

On a more popular level, controlled fertility decline began in northwestern France in the late eighteenth century and spread in the country, bringing the French TFR definitely below the four child level in the 1830s (Chesnais 1992:

ch. 11). The USA had a spectacular decline of fertility in the course of the nineteenth century, beginning in New England in the first decade of the century and in the country as a whole ten years later, gathering national momentum after 1820. On the threshold of the twentieth century US women were delivering only 3.8 children on average. In Europe, only France and England and Wales were below that level then. Australian and, more slowly, Canadian fertility was also coming down significantly in the nineteenth century (Potter 1968: table 1; Festy 1979a: 231ff; Chesnais 1992: tables A2.1–3).

Two waves of fertility decline

In modern human history there are two major international waves of fertility decline. The first rolled from the 1880s to the 1930s. The mid-nineteenth-century slight recuperation of the French fertility rate ended in the mid-1870s, and gradual decline resumed. A number of Western European countries had their highest late-nineteenth-century birth rates in the mid- to late 1870s: Austria, Belgium, England and Wales, Finland, Germany, the Netherlands, and Norway. Then the tide turned, after 1876 in France, after 1877 in England and Germany (Flora *et al.* 1987: ch. 1, national tables; Chesnais 1992: tables A2.1–2; cf. the deeper but less clear picture in Coale 1986). A multinational European decline had begun.

Whatever more long-term economic and socio-cultural shifts at work, there was something conjunctural to the sudden, synchronized change, which because of its modest immediate size appears as a turning-point only with hindsight. Strongly suspect is the Depression of the 1870s, following upon the financial crash of 1873. The Western European family system had a long history of economic adaptation, mainly through postponement of marriage. The marriage rate of England, France and Germany did, in fact, plummet in the last years of the 1870s (Flora *et al.* 1987: 180, 184, 207). But what started as a traditional reaction to an economic downturn, soon acquired the dynamic of a new demographic era.

It was a 'civil society' movement, against the state and against all established churches, which all condemned it, with mounting stridence and increasing inefficacy. The pioneering forays of French and US couples became an international wave when joined by other Western Europeans, and by other European settlers overseas. It was boosted by the spectacular Bradlaugh–Besant contraceptives trial in England in 1877, which spawned a mass diffusion of contraceptive knowledge, also overseas (cf. Caldwell 1999: 503; see further below). On the eve of the 1930s Depression, a total fertility decline of at least one child per woman from a nineteenth-century peak had occurred all over Europe, both East and West, and in the major European overseas settlements, from Canada to Argentina (but no country on the American continent between Rio Grande and Rio de la Plata), from South Africa to Australia, and in Cuba (then under strong US influence) but nowhere else, although Japan was on the margin, with a decline of one child by the end of the 1930s (Coale *et al.* 1979: figs.1.1 and 1.2; Chesnais 1992; Guzmán *et al.* 1996; Mitchell 1998a).[4]

The second wave started almost a hundred years later, in the final third of the twentieth century. In the Third World, this move was pushed by the state, often upon recalcitrant or at least sceptical populations. There were some forerunners – Taiwan since the mid-1950s, Singapore since the late 1950s, and South Korea and Taiwan from about 1960 more vigorously, with some changes also in Barbados and Puerto Rico – but the wave rose in the second half of the 1960s (World Bank 1978: table 15; 1990: table 27; Rele and Alam 1993; Mitchell 1998a,b). By 1980, significant – in some countries like China, drastic – changes had swept Latin America and most parts of Asia and North Africa. From the mid-1960s a second branch of the second wave was surging in the richer world, driven by a different dynamic. We shall deal with that further below.

Most of the figures for demographic shift shown in Table 7.3. have some decimal margin of error, but the picture is clear and non-controversial. Something historical and dramatic happened in most families of the Third World soon after the mid-1960s. Far from all countries are tabulated, only the main regional representatives, of which a few have been included to show the limits of the first 10–15 years of the second international wave of fertility decline. The process of change caught all Latin America, all East and Southeast Asia, Central Asia (Jones and Grupp 1987: table 2.11) except Afghanistan, South Asia save Pakistan, major chunks of West Asia, such as Iran and Turkey, and all North Africa except Libya. Change had begun in the oil sheikdoms of the Arab Gulf, but *Mashrek*, the eastern Arab world, was one of the two regions of the world still mainly unaffected by fertility changes by 1980. Sub-Saharan Africa was the other part, where births had gone down only in South Africa and in Zimbabwe.

In accordance with the theory of demographic transition, a decline in death rates generally preceded the decrease of births, more generally and more clearly than in the first wave (Walle 1986; Walle and Knodel 1986; World Bank 1990: table 27; Chesnais 1992: 140ff; Mitchell 1998a,b,c: table A6). However, there was not necessarily a linear decline of births. As in several instances of the first wave, birth rates and fertility first rose in many countries, probably as a result of better health (Coale and Freedman 1993 on China and Taiwan; Carvalho and Rodriguez Wong 1996 on Brazil; World Bank 1990: table 27 on African countries). Sometimes there could be, as in Bolivia (Torrez Pinto 1996), a rural increase simultaneously to an urban decline.

There is a fascinating parallel in the rapid sweep of change in Europe between 1880 and 1930, from England to Bulgaria, from Portugal to Russia, on one hand, and in the Third World in the last decades of the twentieth century, from Mexico to Mongolia and Myanmar, via Kenya and Nigeria. In both cases there was a process rapidly cutting through and across state boundaries, levels of industrialization, urbanization, and levels of income, across religions, ideologies and family systems. Between 1970/1975 and 1995/2000, the fertility rate in the Third World, or in what the UN calls 'All developing countries', declined by 40 per cent, from 5.4 to 3.1 children per woman (UNDP 2002: table 5). In Europe a similar trajectory took place in England and Wales, in

Table 7.3 The demographic shift: fertility decline in Third World countries, 1965–80 (total fertility rates)

	1965	1980
East Asia		
China	6.1–6.4[a]	2.2–2.5[a]
South Korea	4.9	2.6
Southeast Asia		
Indonesia	5.5	4.3
Malaysia	6.3	4.2
Myanmar	5.8	4.6–4.9[b]
Sri Lanka		
Thailand	6.3	3.8
South Asia		
Bangladesh	6.8	6.1
India	6.2	5.0
Pakistan	7.0	7.0
West Asia		
Iran	7.1	6.1–6.5[c]
Iraq	7.2	6.5
Syria	7.7	7.4
Turkey	5.8	4.2
North Africa		
Egypt	6.8	5.1
Morocco	7.1	5.6
Sub-Saharan Africa		
Ivory Coast	7.4	7.4
Kenya	8.0	8.0
Nigeria	6.9	6.9
South Africa	6.1	4.9
Zimbabwe	8.0	6.8
Latin America		
Brazil	6.0	4.4
Chile	4.8	2.7
Colombia	6.5	3.8
Mexico	6.7	4.5

Sources: For Africa and for many countries in Asia and Latin America and the Caribbean, the data are estimates from surveys, which means a certain margin of error and uncertainty. The two basic sources are, for 1965, World Bank (1990: table 27), and for 1980, World Bank (1992: national tables). These data are checked with Latin American ones from Guzmán *et al.* (1996), and wherever the World Bank sources deviate from the Guzman *et al.*, the latter is used. This is the case with Brazil above all, for which I have relied on Carvalho and Rodriguez Wong (1996: 377). Asian data have been checked with Leete and Alam (1993) with Sanderson and Tan (1995), and with Cleland (1994: 55–82). Cleland has also been used for checking African data.

Notes:
a   The lower estimates are from Sanderson and Tan (1995: 220), the higher from the World Bank (1992).
b   The higher estimate is from Cleland (1994: 58), the lower from Rele and Alam (1993: 20).
c   The higher estimate is by the UN and used by Cleland (1994: 62), who gives reasons for believing it might be too low; the lower estimate is from the World Bank (1992: 330).

Sweden, and in Germany from the 1870s to 1914, i.e. in 34 years. Worldwide, human fertility stood at 4.9 children in the 1960s, on the threshold of the plunge, and is now, 40 years later, down to 2.7 (Eurostat 2002: table A3).

Some Third World developments in 20–25 years had no European precedent for drama: in Algeria the fertility rate fell from 7.4 to 3.2 children per woman, in Brazil from 4.7 to 2.3, in Indonesia from 5.2 to 2.6, Kenya from 8.1 to 4.6, Mexico from 6.5 to 2.8, Thailand from 5.0 to 2.1, Vietnam from 6.7 to 2.5. The Chinese experience was the most dramatic of all, going from a rate of 5.8 in 1970 to 2.3 ten years later (Lee and Wang 1999: 85). Yet, the difference in velocity between the two demographic waves is much smaller than, say, the difference between the steamer or the telegraph and the jet plane or the e-mail.

In terms of the number of children, the two waves of fertility decline have by 2000 brought most of the world, outside sub-Saharan Africa and the northern parts of South Asia, to around a two-to-three child norm (Table 7.4).

For quite some time, a small nuclear family, established in France in the 1890s, was an exclusive ideal of Europeans, only hesitantly carried over into their overseas settlements. By 1965, the Japanese were the only non-Europeans who had adopted it. Then, in the last third of the century there was an explosive, almost worldwide interest in it.

Table 7.4 The timing of the two-to-three child norm worldwide[a]

Date	Country
By 1900	France
By 1914	England and Wales
By 1930	Australia, Belgium, Central Europe,[b] Scandinavia, (Australia), (USA)
By 1950	Bulgaria, Southern Europe[c], Uruguay, USSR, Japan[d]
By 1965	The Netherlands, rest of Eastern Europe (save Albania), Portugal,[e] Australia, Canada,[f] USA
By 1980–85	Ireland, New Zealand, Chile, Cuba, China, Mauritius, Caucasus republics, North and South Korea, Singapore, Taiwan
By 2000	Albania, Argentina, Brazil, Colombia, Costa Rica, Dominican Republic, Jamaica, Mexico, Panama, Trinidad, Iran, Israel, Lebanon, Tunisia, Turkey, Kazakhstan, non-northern India[g], Indonesia, Mongolia, Myanmar, Sri Lanka, Thailand, Vietnam

Sources: Generally up to 1985: Chesnais (1992: tables A2.4, A2.6, A.2.7). Historically also, Eastern Europe: Coale *et al.* (1979: 10–11); pre-1990 Caucasus and Central Asia: Jones and Grupp (1987: table 2.11). From 1965 also, World Bank (1990: table 27); UNDP (2002: table 5).

Notes:
a Operationalized as a total fertility rate below 3. Parentheses around the country name means that the norm was later revoked.
b Austria, Czechoslovakia, Germany, Hungary, Switzerland.
c Greece, Italy, Spain.
d Actually only in the first years of the 1950s.
e By 1968.
f By 1966.
g States from Gujarat in the central-west to Orissa in the central-east and south, Tamil Nadu, Kerala, Andhra Pradesh and, on the margin, Karnataka.

Who remains outside this norm? All Africa, from Cape Town to Cairo, except for secularized Tunisia, although Egypt and South Africa are both close to it; the Islamic heartlands of West Asia (except the little enclave of Kuwait), but not supposedly 'fundamentalist' Iran, nor, less surprisingly, officially secularized Turkey; Central Asia, Kazakhstan apart, Islamic South Asia, the strongly Hindu belt of northern India, Muslim Malaysia and the Catholic Philippines have not yet adopted a two-to-three child norm. Latin America has been very late in changing its fertility pattern, and there are still nine Latin American countries, virtually all part of what may be called the Indo-Creole family system, which have not clearly entered the small-family world, although Ecuador, Peru and Venezuela are standing on the threshold.

The ideal or the expected – the survey questions vary – number of children is currently about two children in Europe, North and South America, usually a little above rather than below (Fertility and Family Surveys of the 1990s). Three children have become the ideal of South, Central and Southeast Asian, as well as of Egyptian and of Latin Caribbean women. Africa stands out, with ideals of four in Kenya and Zimbabwe, eight in Chad and Niger, and six in Nigeria (Demographic and Health Surveys of the late 1990s).

Family systems and their fertility

When the second wave of fertility fall began, the first wave was still something of an enigma. Why Western Europeans and Western European settlers decided to limit their number of children radically is still a question without a full answer, in spite of a great amount of sophisticated demographic and historical research. Clearly, it was not industrialization and urbanization which set the process in motion. The two major pioneers, France and USA, were over-whelmingly agrarian. Nor, it seems, was large-scale compulsory schooling a necessary precipitant. Nor was the process mortality-driven, as a fall in infant mortality sometimes succeeded, sometimes preceded, and sometimes accompanied the fall in fertility. And French rates of mortality, both infant and general, remained high by Western European standards well into the twentieth century (Walle 1986; Chesnais 1992: tables A3.3 and A4.2).

The new wave has added questions of its own, and systematic comparisons of the two have hardly been attempted yet, although Jean-Claude Chesnais (1992) has brought them together in a magisterial work. There is no longer any neat explanation at hand.

What appears to be both the most plausible and the most widely accepted general theory of fertility decline seems to be taken only half-seriously by its own author. That is the great Australian demographer J.C. Caldwell's (1982) theory of inter-generational wealth flows. Caldwell's argument in a nutshell is that fertility is high when children are an asset to their parents and to other members of older generations, with labour services, income and other sources of 'wealth' mainly flowing from children to parents and other elders. Fertility is limited when children become a net cost, having to be fed and clothed, and provided for, and not expected to give much in return, either as children –

because they are at school – or as adults – because they are likely to move away and live lives of their own. The same year as that elaborate theoretical formulation appeared in book form, Caldwell, who has combined demography with anthropological fieldwork, published an article reporting a close-up study of fertility decline in rural Karnataka, India. Only towards the end of the article do Caldwell and his co-authors pose their own theoretical question: 'Finally . . . Has the wealth flow . . . really been reversed? . . . Perhaps the only conclusion that either local people or the researcher can reach is that the marginal value of each extra child is impossible to determine' (Caldwell *et al.* 1982: 722).

Crucial questions of how to analyse this kind of change process among a large number of individuals were raised more than a third of a century ago in an oft-quoted article by Professor Gösta Carlsson, dealing with the late nineteenth- to early twentieth-century fertility decline, in his characteristic thoughtful, penetrating, understated, somewhat inconclusive manner. Carlsson (1966: 173, 174) suggested a 'shift from innovation to adjustment theory . . . [with] less emphasis on birth control and its means, and more emphasis on motivation and social situation'. In the behaviourist language of the time he also suggested a focus more on 'response' than on 'stimulus', that is, in 'the process of communication, internal psychological processes connected with attitude change, the laws of human perception, conditioning and learning, and primary group and community structure'. The weakness of his still very valuable argument, I think, is his bland notion of 'adjustment' – as the alternative to technical innovation and diffusion – which fails to convey anything of the profound changes in people's most intimate everyday life.

Chesnais' (1992: 513) general conclusion, that there 'is a close relation between fertility and socioeconomic development at a given date' is only remotely corroborated by his own data and specific analyses.

However, that explanatory theories may have difficulties in front of the bewildering variety of humankind does not mean that the epochal decline of fertility is random or unintelligible. The statistical records, the clever and painstaking reconstructions by demographic historians of patchy registers, and a strong current of high-level, multidisciplinary research, not only by demographers but also by historians, anthropologists, economists and sociologists, provide us with a meaningful picture.

A framework of interpretation is something more modest and more soft than an explanatory theory. Here it is intended as a composite of social logic and a set of plausible hypotheses, derived from a careful but limited sifting of the evidence.

A framework for grasping the most intriguing aspect of the demographic transition, the decline of fertility has to focus on the motivation of individuals, couples and family members more generally, inserted in a flow of history. Why do they decide to part from the ways of their fathers and mothers and restrict their fertility? Secondly, how did it come about, that individuals and couples came to make these intimately private decisions roughly at the same time as millions of other individuals and couples? In other words, it is necessary to relate intimate motivation to large-scale social change.

We do not know the motivations of all these individuals of the two great historical waves of fertility decline, nor those of their forerunners. What we might do is to reconstruct some meaningful motivational logic, broad enough to cover a wide range of possible reasons, but sharp enough to be useful for historical analyses of change. In this vein, I think that birth control by the potential progenitors themselves, i.e. of marital – or more generally within-union – fertility has two necessary preconditions for becoming a mass phenomenon. Note that I am here not talking about institutional birth regulations, for example through restrictions on marriage and remarriage, and I am referring to pre-emptive birth control, not to infanticide.

Birth control, in the just-mentioned sense, expresses a control of nature or 'fate', and of one's own life-course. It means an assertion of power, the power to shape one's own future. It presupposes, first of all, *a sense of personal mastery*. A veteran of Barbados family planning expressed well what is involved: 'People today have prospects in life, hopes they want to realize' (Handwerker 1989: 120). By contrast, in the World Fertility Surveys of the mid-1970s and early 1980s about a third of married women asked in African countries or in Bangladesh, for example, could or would not give any numerical answer to the question of how many children they would like to have: 'It depends on God', or 'It depends on my husband', they answered (cf. UN 1987: 51ff).

The possibility of shaping one's own future is what a 'modern' culture and 'modernization' are about, having shed ethnocentric institutional trappings. Fertility control is a manifestation of modernity. A modern futurism of family formation may come from different sources and take different forms, like other aspects of modernity.

However, in this, strictly temporal, sense of modernity, there is no fixed number of children which can be claimed to be 'modern'. Instead, an elementary assumption of human rationality should lead us to the second prerequisite of pre-emptive birth control, *a sense of benefit* from having fewer children. Note that the argument is not a structural cost–benefit argument, but one of benefits being perceived. A sense of benefit provides a tight logic, but makes life difficult for empirical tests of theory by allowing for a number of possible lags and discrepancies between a structured situation and its perception. The logical argument does point to a crucial empirical historical reference, though. The perception of the costs and benefits of children has to change for fertility change to take place.

The two key variables here – a sense of personal mastery and a sense of benefit from birth control – are shaped by three sets of determinants or, alternatively, at three levels of determination: cultural, structural and familial. The family system, the major world variants of which we identified in Chapter 1, defines the rights and duties, the burdens and the benefits of family members. The social structure arranges people into positions in an economic and political system, into classes in short, and connects these positions to family ones. Cultural determination here refers above all to the shaping of life-meanings, life-perspectives and life-goals across or challenging structural and family positions.

In the waves of fertility decline, there seem to have been two processes of determination at work. One was a cultural process, changing people's life-conceptions, and the role of children in their lives, across a wide geographical and social spectrum. The other was a structural-cum-familial one, providing thresholds of initiation and patterning pioneers and resisters, forerunners and laggards of birth control. Although they did have structural and familial preconditions, the strong cultural character of the waves could explain the weakness of structural variables, such as industrialization and urbanization, which so baffled the first post-war generation of researchers into European fertility decline. On the other hand, the evidence also shows abundantly that class, social skills like literacy, and urbanity have weighed heavily on fertility differences at a given point in time during the transition.

The processes of determination operate through human agency. At the most immediate level of fertility, this is, of course, the individual and the couple, but here we are interested in vast, macro-social phenomena, 'waves' of fertility change. A crucial agency, then, is the key agent of the simultaneity of change.

Among the three determinants, the family system is the most stable one, and on the whole the one paid least attention to so far, although the family (and social) position of women is increasingly singled out as a key to the process of change. As a system of demographic and social reproduction it has no inherent dynamic of change, apart from the equilibrating adjustments which seem to be inherent in most family systems. As noted above, family institutions are patterned not only by broad normative systems; they also include variants by local custom, which further adds to the inertia of the family set-up. But family systems differ in their openness to external change. Furthermore, as long as the family is the predominant regulator of the off-spring of human sexuality – which is still the case – all important fertility changes have to take place through the family system.

Generally speaking, there are in this context two decisive features of family systems, their *normative content* and their *decision structure*. The evaluative and normative charge of human progeny is the most directly pertinent part of the former in this context. How important is the life and the number of children to a given family system and its norm source? But relevant norms also include those of inheritance and of gender relations. Who in the family benefit(s) from a large number of children, and who from a small one? Secondly, there is the legitimate decision structure. Who decides about marriage and about children within marriage – adult children, parents, parents-in-law, grandparents, kin elders, husband, wife?

Social structure distributes mastery and submission, skills and dependencies. It also allocates the costs and benefits of children to families. However, major processes of structural change, say industrialization or the rise of capitalism, tend to have divisive effects of mastery and subjection, and often of the cost–benefit of children as well. It should be no wonder, then, that linear models of effects tend to yield modest results. In contrast to family systems, social structures of power and production tend to have an inherent dynamic or dialectic. Structural change is an important motor of historical change.

However, historical experience of fertility decline seems to have led to a fairly widespread, if by no means unanimous, conclusion: that structural change has not been the prime, or the only prime mover of fertility change in modern times. Within each wave, and among forerunners, structural location determines adoption and inertia, but for the jump to one wave or the other, we have to look elsewhere.

The above discussion would then land us on the cultural terrain, which is rather problematic, given the heterogeneity of the notion of culture and the often vaporous character of cultural change. On the other hand, we know what cultural change to look out for. That is, a culture of possible personal change of life-course, and one conveying, directly or indirectly, the relative costs of many children. We also know that we are interested here in mass, not in elite, culture, which should bring our attention to mass experiences and mass communication. There is no reason to adopt an idealist stance of arguing culture as the prime mover of history. My personal hunch is that cultural changes tend to have structural origins, but that processes of diffusion and of imitation or resistance – working themselves out through a crucial agency to be identified – tend to make cultural changes non-concordant in time and space with structural ones.

With the help of the framework above, I think we may understand the main lines of fertility decline in the world. Let us first sum it up graphically in Figure 7.1. The anonymous key variable 'Crucial agency' will be identified in the empirical analyses below, and listed in Table 8.7. The important contextual variables are kept out of the figure for the sake of simplicity, but they will also be brought out below.

Beginnings and the Western European family

The Western European family system produced three firsts of birth control: the first known modern social groups significantly cutting down their fertility; the first two nations of substantial fertility decrease; and, third, the first international mass wave of birth control. The urban patriciate of Florence, Geneva, Genoa, Milan and possibly other cities, the urban Jewry of Leghorn, Florence

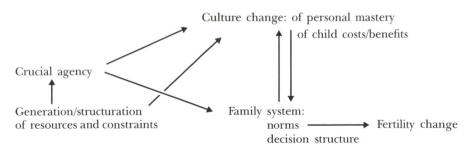

Figure 7.1 A framework for understanding fertility control.

and other Italian cities, British and French peers, the Swedish nobility, and the ruling dynasties of Europe, all began a major restriction of their legitimate fertility after 1700, the Genevan patricians as early as the seventeenth century or before (Livi-Bacci 1986).[5]

The ruling families of Europe set an example. Marriages in those families between 1500 and 1699 produced about six children (per married man), but marriages concluded between 1700 and 1749 generated only five children, and for the century of marriages during 1750–1849, 4.6 children. Among the princely children of the sixteenth to eighteenth centuries inclusive, only two of three survived to the age of 15, however. Marriage restrictions also reduced potential fertility. Princesses married in the sixteenth century on average just above the age of 20, and later at 22 or 23. Among princesses who survived to the age of 30, a third of those born in 1480–1679 had not married, and a quarter of those born in 1780–1879. Forty per cent of the princes who survived puberty never married in the sixteenth and seventeenth centuries (Peller 1965: 88–90, 94).

The internationally trend-setting French high aristocracy limited itself to 2.8 legitimate children in its marriages concluded in the first half of the eighteenth century (Lévy and Henry 1960: 820). The more peripheral Swedish nobility manifested an interesting intra-class pattern in the seventeenth and early eighteenth centuries: a very high marital fertility for the first noble generation, seven to nine children, strongly reduced fertility for subsequent noble generations, five to six children, with the old aristocracy in between. A modest general decline of fertility began with the birth cohorts of the 1720s (Elmroth 1981: 150ff).

France and the USA preceded other nations through showing significantly fallen birth rates by 1830, preceding all others by half a century or more. Finally, there came the all-European wave of fertility decline in 1880 to 1930, the first international wave of the world.

Family and class, family and revolution, family and social movements seem to account for the three firsts of birth control. Most probably, its decision structure was the key to the capacity for change of the Western European family system. The unique Western European combination of adult marriages and neolocality left married behaviour, including fertility, fully in the hands of the couple, subject, of course, to the religious and other norms of the community. That all decisions within marriage were normally taken by mature couples running their own households must have made change more easy than in family systems where dependent children were married off by their parents and even after marriage remained under the authority of the older generation in some form of extended family. Through its regulation of who can marry and when, this Western European family system had for centuries been adjusting itself to good and bad times, expanding marriage opportunities after experiences of good times, contracting them after bad ones (Wrigley and Schofield 1981).

The religious fundament of the Western European family at least contained more potential openings to fertility change than some other major norm systems of the world. The norms of monogamy, of legitimate inheritance, and against infanticide put the issue of heirs into focus within a more narrow range of options than in, say, polygamous systems. The Christian view of sexuality as sinful or, within marriage, a base instinct, and the rationalist Protestant (or rationalist Jewish) notion of a conscience-controlled virtuous life-course could, with some theological logic, be extended to marital birth control, particularly if the latter did not mean 'safe sex' but self-control of one's sexual urges. The one who first formulated 'the population problem' in respectable European discourse was, after all, an Anglican clergyman, Thomas Malthus (1798).

To the Catholic Church this had long been anathema, however. In conservative Catholic bulwarks like Brittany and Quebec well into the twentieth century, priests visited fertile-age families which had no pregnancy to show in 24 months, reminding them of their marriage duties (Segalen 1992: 241). In nineteenth-century France, priests complained about the 'sin of Onan' (coitus interruptus) being practised (Walle 1978: 290); indeed such practices had been condemned in the *Cathechism of Married People* by Father Féline in 1782 (Freyer 1965: 36). The Catholic Church has all the time maintained its opposition to contraceptive devices. In the twentieth century the strong stand of Catholicism and of fundamentalist Protestantism against medical abortion has also been a constraint on birth control.

It mattered also to the relatively limited resilience of Christian family norms, that all the established churches of European Christianity were on the opposite side of the forces of modernity, the latter coming from the fields of science, philosophy, economy and politics in the uniquely endogenous rise of modernity in Europe. Every victory of modern 'enlightenment' therefore meant a weakening of church control, and in that sense an advance of 'secularization'. In all other areas of the world, including the Americas – the North in particular – the external–internal aspects of the modernity–antimodernity conflicts gave organized religion a chance to realign itself with forces of the modern (see Therborn 1992, 1995: chs 1–2). Among the Christian churches weakened by modernism, mainstream Protestantism was most open to influence from it, and Catholicism endowed with most powers of resistance.

What made Europe's princes, aristocrats of several countries, and patricians of the European city belt restrict their fertility in the eighteenth century, while the top of the British aristocracy, the ducal families, actually increased its fertility (Hollingsworth 1965: table 26), I do not know. But other things being equal, it might be expected that a control of legitimate offspring should start among those whose social standing included the highest sense of mastery. This was also the social class which had most to gain from a calculated transmission of property and power, and most to lose from non-control.

But let us not forget that this is a rationality within a particular system of inheritance and lordship. That rationality does not apply where high, including the highest, office was not, or little, dependent on uniquely legitimate descent, as in the Muslim or Sinic empires with their legitimating harems or concubinage and their systems of ascent through different forms of adoption, or in sub-Saharan Africa, whose sacred kings are associated with fertility (cf. Jacobsson-Widding 2000).

The two nations at the vanguard of marital birth control had two things in common: they were both variants of the Western European family system, and they had experienced a thoroughgoing modern social revolution. Whatever happened in Britain in the mid- or late seventeenth century had no equivalent to the radical novelties – political, religious, legal – of the French Revolution, nor to the enormous popular mobilizations in France, both during the Revolution itself and during its imperial successor state. The American Revolution was ideologically less radical, but it also involved massive popular participation, and it ushered in a period of hectic and profound social change. A leading contemporary historian has referred to 'an explosion . . . of entre-preneurial energy, of religious passion, and of pecuniary desires' (Wood 1992: 232).

In both France and the USA, large numbers of people had realized from experience that new ways of life were possible, and new ways of charting one's own life-course, as the American and the French Revolutions did not mean massive and brutal uprooting and dislocations, in marked contrast to the British Industrial Revolution. When their fertility decline set in, both France and the USA were predominantly rural and pre-industrial countries.

Class and local tendencies of fertility control before the revolutions have been spotted. But it was only in the 1830s that French fertility fell below the range of pre-modern Swedish variation, of 4.1 to 5.0 children for 1750–1900 (Chesnais 1992: 323; SCB 1999). American fertility decline is remarkable, not for an early attainment of a low level, but for two things: for an early onset of a sustained downward trend; and, secondly, for an early birth control within marriage. The crude American (white) birth rate was at an estimated 41 in 1860, down from 55 in 1800 (Coale and Zelnik 1963), a rate of Eastern European proportions (Serbia had a rate of 42 in 1862–63: Chesnais 1992: table A1).

Counter-revolutionary Canada was not touched by the revolutionary family practices of the USA (until much later, with the rest of Europe). The Latin American revolutions of independence did not open up new social opportu-nities for the population at large. On the contrary, the devastation of the prolonged wars, followed by civil wars, meant in many places a decline of development. The lot or the prospects of the masses of landless labourers and poor subsistence peasants did not ameliorate. The whole of independent Brazil was marked by slavery at least as much as the US south, and at a much lower level of literacy.

The paths of fertility decline are still intriguing, though, both in France and the USA. Common and most clear is that the process was led by the most pros-perous parts of the countries: by the Paris Basin, but not by the city of Paris, by the regions of Guyenne in the southwest and Normandy in the northwest of France, and by Massachusetts and New England generally in the USA. They also had a relatively high literacy, but in France the departmental correlation between literacy and early fertility decline was found to be insignificant. In both countries there was a tendency for urbanites to practise more birth control, but the tendency was not very strong; nor was it necessarily associated with secularization.

The Puritans of New England had developed a religious conception of a sexually controlled marriage life. This was never part of Catholic Church doctrine, but the French association of secularization and early family planning is weak. Bas-Normandie, one of the regions in the vanguard, had been little affected by the weakening of organized religion in eighteenth-century France (Walle 1978; Wrigley 1987; Guest 1990). French data also show a significant, but not overwhelming, mid-nineteenth-century correlation between low fertility and equal inheritance rights among children (Berkner and Mendel 1978: 322). As could be expected, American family planning was associated with the decreasing abundance of land, which by European standards, of course, remained abundant (Easterlin *et al.* 1978; Vinovskis 1981: ch. 5). That the old Western European method of fertility control, through nuptiality, was in some kind of communication with the new method of within-marriage birth control is indicated by their appearing as alternatives in nineteenth-century France. At least at the *département* (province) level there was a tendency for within-marriage control to be associated with high marriage rates and low marriage age (Walle 1978: 274ff).

Again, pertinent questions remain unanswered. But the combination of family system and experience of revolutionary change provides a micro- as well as a macro-frame of intelligibility.

The movement of European fertility decline

The amazing wave of European fertility change from 1880 to 1914 and its extension in time to 1929 (and the new situation of the Depression), and in space to the other major European overseas settlements, is best understood as related to a vast social movement claiming social change, and practising social change. The labour movement, with its several variants – Marxist, Anarcho-Syndicalist, Labourite – was central to this 'great movement', but there were many others too: movements of religious dissent and turning away from religion, of the search for knowledge, political parties of Liberalism, farmers' and peasants' movements, popular nationalism in Eastern Europe and in some of the Western peripheries like Norway and Ireland. These were the years of the emergence of mass-circulation newspapers, and of the accessibility of railways and steamboats to the popular masses, migrating to cities and overseas.

Contraception was among the new subversive ideas propagated. Already by the first decades of the nineteenth century, contraception had ceased to be a secret knowledge and practice of high society ladies, experienced prostitutes or leisured libertines, known to the public only through writings of moral condemnation. Pre-emptive birth control became Radical propaganda, in England and in the USA. The English pioneer seems to have been Francis Place, a master-tailor and a veteran of the Jacobin London Corresponding Society. John Stuart Mill in his youth participated in the distribution of handbills propagating birth control (Freyer 1965: chs 4–5). In the United States, in which nineteenth-century Radicalism had much more free space than anywhere in Europe, a public movement for birth control got underway in the

1830s, with Robert Dale Owen, the son of the British social reformer Robert Owen, as one of the most prominent figures. The issue was later taken up by leading American feminists, such as Elizabeth Cady Stanton (Brodie 1994).

The first impact of contraceptive propaganda in Britain seems to have been negligible. But the tide turned with a famous trial in 1877. An American book on birth control from the 1830s, the free-thinking Bostonian physician Charles Knowlton's *Fruits of Philosophy*, had been judged obscene by an English court. The free-thinking Radicals Charles Bradlaugh and Annie Besant took it upon themselves to republish it, which called forth another trial, amply covered by the new popular journalism. Their case was seen favourably by the Lord Chief Justice, and both they and the book were in the end acquitted. But the main effect was that 125,000 copies of the contentious book were sold, and that contraception was made a public issue in Britain, now on a massive scale. The trial also spawned foreign-language translations of the book (Freyer 1965: ch. 16).

The issue of birth control was peripheral to the Marxist labour movement. Marx himself had been full of scorn for Malthus, and the neo-Malthusian activists usually belonged to a non-Marxist stream of anti-clerical Radicalism of the tradition of Place and Bradlaugh or, for example, the Swedish economist Knut Wicksell. Within the labour movement propagation of birth control was more important to Anarchism. The Marxists wanted to focus on the contradictions of capitalism and on the latter's replacement by a socialist economy. The 'population question' would be solved by the emancipation of women. Nevertheless, family planning was clearly a part of the social vision of the mainstream labour movement. This is how the issue was put by the foremost leader of the Second International, the leader of German Social Democracy August Bebel (1879/1979: 405–6), in his *Woman and Socialism*, after the *Communist Manifesto* the most widely read Marxist publication of the time: 'Intelligent and energetic women – exceptions apart – have as a rule no propensity to give life to a large number of children, "as a gift of God", and to spend their best years in life in pregnancy or with a child at her breast.' In the German Reich before 1914 the association of support for Social Democracy with a 'rationalization of sexual life' was noticed by the great German demographer of the period, Julius Wolf.

Wolf (1912: 91, 101) further emphasized the question of modernity, in the form of position on tradition. Social Democracy, he said, is 'the enemy of tradition in this [fertility] as well as in every area'. The stance of the variants of Christianity he summed up in the following: 'in the Greek Orthodox faith we see the uncritical reception of *tradition*, in Catholicism its deliberate recognition, in Protestantism the critique of it, in atheism its rejection.' The particularly rapid decline of births among the German and Austrian-Hungarian Jews, Wolf (1912: 161) also saw as a result of the success of 'the rationalist argument' among them. This was the period of strong assimilationist and secularist tendencies among Central European Jewry.

Later demographers have also occasionally paid attention to the relationship between fertility change, on one hand, and movements of social and cultural change on the other, of secularism and socialism above all. Ron

Lestaeghe and Chris Wilson (1986) have especially drawn our attention to the polarization of Catholic countries under modernist challenge, in contrast to the mainstream Protestant accommodation. Some areas secularized early, generating both birth control and political secularism, others became hedged in as fortresses of Catholic tradition and fertility, like French Brittany, Belgian Flanders, German Westphalia, Italian Veneto.

Cultural cleavages in the Catholic lands could also give rise to puzzling correlations, such as higher literacy rates being associated with higher fertility and slower fertility decline, found both in Portugal and in Spain. The reason is that illiteracy was high among the labourers on the big estates in Alentejo and Andalucia and similar regions, who had never been properly controlled by the Church, and who secularized early. Among the small farmers of northern Portugal and central Spain, on the other hand, the Church was deeply and firmly rooted, and schooling was also more widespread.

The connection between birth control and left-wing politics, and between right-wing politics and absent or late birth control has been very clear on the Iberian Peninsula. At the time of the Spanish Civil War, for instance, the core of Republican Spain – Catalonia, Valencia, Madrid – had then been practising marital birth control for half a century or more, while the heartland of Franquismo, Castile-León, had not yet started. In the revolutionary years in Portugal in 1974–75, the centre of counter-revolutionary resistance was in the north-northeast, where marital fertility only went into a downward trend after 1960 (Braga) or slowly began to decline only in the Depression (Livi-Bacci 1971: 127ff, table 16; Reher 1997: 184 and map 6.14). Through low nuptiality, and a concomitant high rate of illegitimacy, the northern Portuguese small farmers kept their fertility under some control, however.

Fundamentalist bastions excepted, which might also include Dutch Calvinist 'Gereformeerden', birth control swept the European continent in half a century, the speed of the process varying with the effects of religion, urbanity and class.

The high-fertility Eastern European family system was probably most affected by changes in the conditions of the peasantry, the overwhelming majority of the population. The Eastern European system shared the sanctity of marriage, monogamy, legitimate inheritance, and the norm against infanticide with the rest of Christianity. It differed in its widespread practice of arranged marriages, condoned by Orthodox disinterest in consent, in its norms of early and universal marriage, a patrilocal dependence of young couples and in its sometimes extended families, as in the Balkan *zadruga*. The abolition of serfdom in Russia (in 1861) and the early twentieth-century promotion of family farms eased the pressure towards fertility maximization of the old system of communal serfdom (Moseley 1959/1976; Czap 1976; Johnson 1976). But only the cataclysm of Stalinist collectivization brought Russian birth rates down to turn-of-the-century Western European levels (Coale *et al.* 1979; Livi-Bacci 1993).

The expulsion of the Turks with subsequent Slavic settlement, the upheavals of the Balkan wars and of World War I, and post-war land reform shook the Balkan peasant population and its social relations. The late nineteenth-century agrarian crisis, in the wake of competition from New World producers, the maelstrom of wars from 1912 to 1918, and then finally the Depression extinguished the *zadruga*. Eastern Europe had to carry most of the costs of the European wave of nationalism and of the European 'world wars', and a good part of the fertility decline there was an adjustment to adversity, under new social and cultural conditions (Erlich 1966; Botev 1990).

However 'East', this was still part of Europe, though. The Germanic labour movement spread to, stimulated and supported the Eastern European one, from Russia to Bulgaria, and modern nationalism reached the peasantry. And all the time, of course, the upper crust of Eastern Europe, from St Petersburg to Sofia, was under strong Western European, French and German, influence. Christian Orthodoxy, for its part, was all the way anti-modernist, but without much moral power of its own, separate from the *knout* of the state.

Under the overall arc of modernist questioning of traditional practices and authority, the context and the reasons for birth control could be very different.

How the preconditions of marital fertility control could operate in different modes and milieux during the European wave – and its belated aftermath – and thereby escape strong correlations with any single indicator is illustrated beautifully by a historical anthropological study of a laggard Sicilian town. Jane and Peter Schneider (1992) distinguish three different demographic transitions there. The first occurred among the landowning gentry, around 1900. It occurred in response to the economic crisis following upon American grain imports into Italy, and to a perceived lack of suitable migration alternatives for the class. Fertility control worked through coitus interruptus, marital abstinence, and the occasional abortion in Palermo. Husbands compensated themselves by extra-marital philandering, among domestic servants, local peasant women and urban prostitutes.

The artisan transition took place in the inter-war period, among literate, secularized, politically radical artisans reacting against the sudden closure of emigration outlets, through US legislation. Many had learnt birth control from French colleagues in Palermo. These radical artisans came to regard birth control through coitus interruptus as a skilled art, practised in companionship with their spouses.

The landless labourers turned to family planning only in the 1950s, then often as small farmers.

> The more or less new and neo-technic house [financed by remittances from new, postwar emigration], associated with the revolt against domestic service and the possibility for working-class respectability, plus the simultaneously rising cost of children . . . [through the advent of schooling inter alia.] . . . Sicilian *braccianti* have a straightforard answer to question why they now practice contraception: it is the only way to have a decent life. Before their struggle [for land after Fascism and World War II] and the land reform, no better life seemed possible.
>
> (Schneider and Schneider 1992: 171)

Whereas in the case of the groups and nations in the vanguard it has been impossible to find any clear sign of a change in the costs and benefits of children preceding or accompanying the onset of birth control, the European wave around the turn of the previous century had an important connection in this nature. Continental fertility decline followed rather closely after the institution of compulsory public schooling, which was much more effective than often circumvented child labour legislation in raising the cost of children. The nation-state and the labour movement here supported each other in keeping children at school and out of work. After earlier, more insouciant beginnings, uniform public primary education was established across most of Western Europe in the 1870s and 1880s, although religious–secular strife delayed a decision in Belgium till 1914 (Therborn 1993: 248–49).

In 1910 the pre-revolutionary municipal government of Moscow instituted four years of compulsory schooling for the city's children. By 1911 almost half of the enrolment was made up of girls (Koerner 1976: 288). The Revolution then brought education to the whole country. In Bulgaria, the proportion of literate Orthodox brides rose from 21 per cent in 1901–5 to 67 per cent in 1921–25 (Botev 1990: 118). By the 1930s, Albania was the only country in Europe where more than half of the population was illiterate, and only Greece, Portugal and Yugoslavia had 40 per cent or more (but less than 50 per cent) illiterate. In the 1930s Bulgaria had barely a third, and the poorer European countries (such as Italy, Poland, Romania and Spain) had between a fifth and a quarter of their adult population unable to read. Northwestern Europe (with a lacuna of Irish data) from France to Finland, and Central Europe from Switzerland to Hungary was almost fully literate, in some sense (UN 1949/1950: table 163; UNESCO 1964: table 4). In 1939 Soviet Russia had a literacy rate of 87 per cent (Bideleux 1985: 227).

English Chartism of the 1830s and 1840s, the world's first mass labour movement, took on board a conception of domesticity of women and children supported by a male 'family wage'. The trade union movement fought with philanthropists against child labour, and schooling and child labour legislation gradually became effective in keeping children out of the labour market. By the turn of the twentieth century, the idea that children should be at school had stuck among the 'respectable' English working class. Only to the relatively well-paid miners, with their closed communities of manliness, did this situation of parent–child relations not mean a propensity for birth control (Szreter 1996: 312, 52ff).

The Western European family system, a vast pan-European social movement of modernism linking up with Eastern Europe, a continental movement of public schooling, and a normatively weak traditionalism of the Orthodox periphery seem to account for the world's first international wave of fertility control.

Damming a tide: governmental birth promotion

European governments were not accepting birth control among their peoples hands down. Condemnation, repression and positive incentives to breed were attempted, with varied but at most modest success.

The United States, originally the most liberal country but always also a centre of Protestant Christian fundamentalism, led the way, with a law of 1873 banning any federal distribution of and advertisement for contraceptives. After their successful lobbyist, this and related legislation were known as the Comstock laws, referring to a Protestant crusader and professional militant of a Committee for the Suppression of Vice, an offshoot of the New York Young Men's Christian Association. The Comstock laws were deadly serious, even if lacking in totalitarian effectiveness; Comstock was appointed a special agent for the US Post Office with powers of mail inspection and of mail seizure (Brodie 1994: 259ff).[6]

In England, efforts to suppress information on contraception – by the Church of England in 1908, for instance – never became successful, which also had its effects in the British Empire, except in Canada which in 1892 had gone the American way. But in the rest of Western Europe the authorities moved in with prohibitions of various rigour, in Sweden in 1910 (re-legalized in 1938), in the Netherlands in 1911, in Denmark in 1913, in France most strictly in 1920, also spilling over into the colonies (cf. Caldwell 1966), in Belgium in 1923, and in Fascist Italy in 1926 (cf. Gauthier 1996: table 2.5).

On Christmas Eve 1930 Pope Pius XI added his voice against contraception, condemning it (within marriage), by any means, as an 'infringement of the law of God and of nature', in his Encyclica *Casti connubii* (paragraphs 54ff). He reminded his flock that according to Saint Augustine, 'Onan, son of Juda', had been killed by God (Rodriguez 1964). In Germany, where the birth control movement had a particularly vigorous development, all the birth control centres were closed down by the Nazis. But contraceptives were not explicitly prohibited until a police ordinance of January 1941. This Himmler ordinance against contraceptives was repealed in West Germany only in 1961, nine years later than its repeal in Austria (Glass 1968: 131).

Positive pro-natalist public policies of any significance emerged only in the 1930s. True, some relevant policies had developed earlier, in other somewhat different contexts, mainly trying to cope with the effects of proletarianization. The rise of social insurance from the 1880s had led to paid maternity leave – in Germany from 1883, and in most of Western Europe by World War I. After the war, schemes of assistance for mothers and indigent children spread over the relatively developed world of that time, including the USA and Japan. The 'family wage', enough to support a wife and three children, became an institutional concept in the Australian industrial arbitration system from 1907. French employers, beginning in the 1890s and more widely after World War I, took to the idea of a family allowance supplement to wages, as a means to manage wage cuts and rejection of general nominal wage increases. The regulation and equalization, among employers, of these schemes led on to publicly instituted allowances. From experimental nineteenth-century pedagogy and from philanthropy came the first daycare for pre-school children, the *Kindergarten* and, in France, the so-called *Ecoles maternelles* (Lam *et al.* 1992; Gauthier 1996: ch. 3).

The continuous decline of the birth rate in the 1920s, following upon an important pre-war plunge, reached alarming proportions in the early 1930s.

The decline was most pronounced in two areas, in which the total fertility rate fell by about one child per woman, or more, between 1920 and 1930: north-western Europe, consisting of England, Scotland and Wales, but not Ireland, and Scandinavia, including Finland; and Central Europe, consisting of Austria, Czechoslovakia, Germany and Hungary, but not so much Switzerland. Italy, just barely, and Bulgaria, more strongly, attached themselves to these two areas. France, by contrast, had a more modest decline now, of 0.4. Among the overseas European settlements, the US total fertility rate decreased most, by 0.7 (Chesnais 1992: tables A2.3 and A1.5).

The new, positive population policy of the 1930s had three centres of ideas and implementation. Chronologically first, getting into action in the late 1920s, was Fascism and, more generally, imperialist expansionism. This was a revamping of an old idea, prominent under Mercantilism, that the size of the population was a crucial basis of state power. Mussolini expressed it in a speech in 1927 with characteristic bombast and brutality: 'To count for something in this world, Italy must have a population of at least 60 millions when she reaches the threshold of the second half of this century.' 'With a declining population a country does not create an empire, but becomes a colony' (quoted from Glass 1936: 34; De Grazia 1993; cf. Treves 2001). In 1950 Italy had a population of 47 million.

The Japanese government, which previously had entertained worries of over-population, adopted the same view in the 1930s, setting their target at 100 million (but in 1950 Japan had a population of 83 million). Nazi Germany qualified its natalist policies by eugenics and racism, backed up by an extensive sterilization programme. Indeed, in the officious Ten Commandments for Choosing a Partner, the first, and two others, were racist: 'Remember you are German!' was the first commandment, and only as the tenth came a rather vague 'Hope for as many children as possible' (Koonz 1988: 189). When the war was on, and the eugenic sterilizations undertaken, natalism was more unrestrained: 'The essential thing for the future is to have lots of children', Hitler (who himself had none) said to his own circle in October 1941 (Pine 1997: 98).

Authoritarian, largely anti-modern but also nationalist familism was another major impulse of family policy. This was a strong tradition of French Conservatism, at least since Frédéric Le Play and the Second Empire, worried by the early decline of the French birth rate, and even more so after the defeat of 1871. It drew very much upon official Catholic thought and was not, as such, confined to France. Politically it was important in Belgium and Portugal, and in Spain after the outcome of the Civil War. This body of thought often contained racist arguments – as did the French natalist bestseller of the 1930s, Alex Carrell's *L'Homme, cet inconnu* (1935) – but its main concern, apart from raising the birth rate, was not eugenics. It was 'strengthening the family', a code-word for strengthening patriarchy, emphasizing the husband as *chef de famille*, prohibiting divorce, keeping women from the labour market, even restricting girls' education (Muel-Dreyfus 1996: 87ff).

Thirdly, natalist family policy also developed left of centre, as part of a programme of social reform and social engineering. This was the achievement of Alva and Gunnar Myrdal and of the reception of their *Crisis in the Population Question* (1934) by Swedish Social Democracy – as well as by the parties to the right. With the other sources the social reform conception shared a concern with the nation and its demographic future, but it owed nothing to imperialism, racism and familism. It was a small, sheltered country's domestic perspective. In its originality it combined three major features. One was a feminist individualism, very much ahead of its time, arguing for voluntary parenthood with the legalization of contraception and liberalization of abortion, and strengthening of women's rights on the labour market. A second was a modernist social engineering, dedicated to raising 'the quality' of children, not by breeding but by the provision of social services in kind. The third and smallest component was a eugenic sterilization programme, directed not only against people with severe hereditary diseases but also against blatantly 'irresponsible' parents, i.e. high-fertility paupers. The latter two sets of proposals were very favourably received – although the benefits-in-kind programme, from housing and maternal education to children's clothes, was eventually scaled down in favour of cash allowances – while the first owed its passage to the package as a whole, and to the brilliant energy of the Myrdals (Myrdal 1941; Kälvemark 1980).

Among these three kinds of natalist policies in the 1930s, the Nazi German variant of Fascism and state aggrandisement was the most important, because of the weight of Germany and because of its length of serious implementation. In this area, as in so many others, Fascist Italy was more rhetoric than reality. The Conservative French was the least significant, because the main French package of policies, enshrined in a magisterial Code de Famille, was adopted only in 1939. It laid the basis for post-war French natalism, but by then active family policies were developing in many countries, from varying national premises. Sweden inspired the other Scandinavian countries, and its policies were at least studied in the Anglo-Saxon world through translations of the Myrdals' work and implemented vigorously from the last years of the decade (Glass 1936, 1940).

Whatever their rationale, did these public policies for raising the birth rate have any visible impact? Their aim at raising the growth of population might have three main targets: the rates of marriage, of birth, and of mortality. The French focused almost exclusively on the birth rate and, like Germany and Italy, primarily on high-order parities, i.e. on providing incentives for (some) women to have many children. Germany, Italy and Sweden made the marriage rate their priority target, without necessarily saying so. After Mussolini's speech in 1927, Italy introduced marriage incentives into its taxation system, discriminating against bachelors and childless couples. Germany in 1933 set up a system of public marriage loans, originally meant more as an alleviation of unemployment and as an incentive for women to withdraw from the labour market, but from 1936 it operated as a general marriage support, for those judged racially and medically fit to marry. Italy and Sweden, from the beginning of 1938, adopted the general idea of marriage loans. No one seems to have made infant and child mortality an issue, although it was, of course, to be affected by the extension of maternity clinics and care which tended to be part of the population programmes, particularly in Germany and Sweden.

Infant mortality rates showed most inter-war improvement. But could the latter in any way be attributed to population policies? Between 1909–11 and 1919–21 Italian infant mortality fell from an annual average of 151 per thousand to 128; the corresponding figures for 1928–30, after Fascist interventions, were 115, and 103 for 1938–40. Percentagewise, from 15 to 10 per cent, as well as in absolute terms, Fascist power had a decelerating effect on mortality decline. For Germany the same time series is 175, 137, 88 and 65; here, Weimar democracy provided most change. The Swedish series is 73, 65, 57 and 40 (Chesnais 1992: table A4.2). Social Democratic Sweden is alone in having an accelerating trend, which of course does not necessarily mean a causal effect. Other factors may have been at work, and in fact the pace quickened during the year 1932, i.e. before the Social Democrats got into office, and well before any population policy.

As far as births are concerned, Fascist Italy never recovered the pre-Fascist birth rate, which except for the war years and their immediate aftermath, (1915–19), oscillated between 30 and 33 for 1900–22. The slope was continuously downwards, with a slight recuperation in 1938–40, blipping upwards to an average of 23.6 from a 1936 trough of 22.4. Total fertility rate stood at 3.9 in 1922 and at 3.1 in 1940. In Germany, on the other hand, there was a trend-break: from a bottom mark of 14.7 in 1933 the German birth rate crawled up to 20.4 in 1939. The achievement was modest though, taking Germany back to the sunny days of the Weimar Republic, with a rate of 20.7 for 1924–25, but below those of the early 1920s. The fact that the rate went back to a level somewhat above that on the eve of the Depression (18.3 in 1928–29), indicates that Nazism did make a difference, by its successful employment policies and, perhaps, by its population policy. Sweden also changed the slope of the curve in the late 1930s, but here it is less clear whether we can speak of a trend-break, other than by looking into the mirror of the 1940s. In 1939–40 the Swedish birth rate was just back at where it was before the crisis, at 15.3, from a conjunctural trough of 13.7. The total fertility rate of 1939 was still below that of 1929–30 (Chesnais 1992: tables A1.5 and A2.3).

Finally we have the marriage rates (Mitchell 1998c: table A6), the birth effects of which may lag behind by several years in countries with extensive private family planning. Personal taxes have always played a minor part in Italy, and there are no visible macro-effects of the Fascist taxation policy on the marriage rate. In 1927 the Italian marriage rate stood at 15.2 per thousand population, a rate it never reached again, except for 1937, directly after the Abyssinian war. It went down to 12.8 in 1932 and ended at 14.8 for 1938–39. Both the German and the Swedish marriage rates went up after the crisis, ending in 1937–38 in Germany at the same level as in 1928–29 (the jump to the 1922 level in 1939 may have been related to the mobilization for war). The first year of the full effect of the new marriage loans, 1934, also saw a temporary upward jump. Swedish marriages in the second half of the 1930s went to a record high of the century. Again, something important had happened.

In both the German and the Swedish cases, population policies, through marriage loans above all, seem to have taken effect; however, it appears impossible to say how much. Anyway, the policy contribution was hardly decisive. German as well as Swedish propensities to marry reversed a downward trend in the mid-1920s. The new upturn was then interrupted by the Depression and resumed its march after 1932. The Swedish bounce was stronger than the German, 1934 apart, but the Swedish willingness to marry began accelerating in 1934, which was the year the Myrdals' book was published but before any concrete family policy measures. A similar turn of the marriage rate in the 1920s also occurred in the UK, the other Nordic countries and, less clearly, in Central Europe. The northwestern European and overseas 'marriage boom', which John Hajnal (1953b) signalled, comparing the periods of 1925–34 and 1935–50, actually started in Europe, but not in North America, in Hajnal's first period. It was this marriage boom, of 'industrial marriage', which, in full swing, led to the baby boom of the 1940s.

Concluding so far, the sum total of the demographic effects of the population policies of the 1930s seems to be either zero (Italy) or minor (Germany and Sweden).

After World War II there were two significant variants of birth-promotion policies. The first one, instituted immediately after peace broke out, was a modernized, more general social policy-oriented, less explicitly patriarchal version of the French natalist tradition. The other was deployed in Communist Europe from the late 1960s. With the positive fertility effects of the marriage boom, post-war Nordic Social Democracy lost interest in demography, although general child allowances became part of their growing welfare states. Issues of children and family resurfaced in this political tradition only in the 1970s, as part of a feminist movement for gender equality.

French social policy after the war was characterized by a uniquely generous system of child and family allowances. In 1949–50 the latter constituted in France about 4.5 per cent of national income, to be compared with 1.7 per cent in Sweden and 0.7 per cent in the UK. For a two-child family French child allowances corresponded to almost a fifth of the average male manufacturing wage, as against a tenth of it in Sweden and a twenty-fifth in the UK (ILO 1961: tables 3 and 8; Gauthier 1996: table 4.4).

How much direct effect this child support had, I dare not say. However, it seems implausible that it did not have some positive effect. During 1946–60 French women had one of the highest fertility rates in Western Europe, after the Dutch and the still rather pre-modern Finnish, Irish and Portuguese. In the 1920s other Western European countries, headed by England, had overtaken France in the descent to low fertility. But the post-war bounce back from the fertility of 1936–40 to that of 1946–50 was stronger in France than anywhere else in Western Europe: an absolute increase of the fertility rate by 0.91 child. After 1945 the French fertility rate was for the rest of the century higher than that of the current European Union as a whole, though clearly below that of North America and Oceania in the 1950s and 1960s (Chesnais 1992: tables A2.4–5). French fertility had started to stabilize in the 1920s, but the post-war record may be considered a historical trend-break, after two hundred years of French pioneering fertility decline in Europe and the world. There seems to be no strong reason for disbelieving that the generous child support policies contributed to this turn.

The new wave of fertility decline in Europe from the 1970s was generally met in the West with indifference, resignation or passive complaint. Not even in France was there any vigorous policy response, although the left-wing government from 1981 did not break with the national tradition of natalism. The relative significance of child allowances had been allowed to slip during the Fifth Republic, to 5 per cent of the average male manufacturing wage for a two-child family in 1980, raised somewhat under Mitterrand to 7 per cent (Gauthier 1996: 166; Muller-Escoda and Vogt 1997).

It was only in Communist Eastern Europe that active counter-measures were taken. Communist de-Stalinization meant more freedom also in the area of sexuality and family. From the mid-1950s abortion was re-legalized and divorce was made easier. At least in East-Central Europe information about modern birth control and family planning was now actively distributed. Combined with enormous increases in female higher education and industrial and professional employment, this new possibility of choice sent Eastern European birth figures down rapidly, while they were still rising in Capitalist Europe.

Beginning in Hungary, in 1959, and Czechoslovakia and spreading all over the bloc, a whole set of birth-promoting policies were set in motion in the course of the 1960s and, more vigorously, the 1970s. They were occasionally repressive, against abortion and contraception, as in Romania, or negligent of sexual and contraceptive education, as in the USSR, but more often and in general they provided positive incentives. Early marriage was stimulated by generous marriage loans and grants, and a housing allocation discriminating against single persons; fertility was encouraged by long and generous paid maternity and infant care leave, and by substantial child allowances. In 1967 the latter corresponded to a third of the average wage in Czechoslovakia and Hungary, a quarter in Bulgaria and Romania (Ferge 1979: 214–15). Considerable social investments in childhood were also made: virtually universal free daycare of children (Edwards 1985: 30; Riazantsev *et al.* 1992: 26), extensive sports facilities, leisure organization, and vacation centres for children.

The effects of these policies could be discerned clearly, although they did not manage to turn the downward trend of fertility. In spite of having almost all adult women employed, and in contrast to Western Europe, Communist Europe succeeded in slowing down, and in some cases stopping the decline of births in the 1970s and 1980s (Table 7.5).

It is only in comparison with non-Communist Europe and in view of the strong downward tendencies, that Communist birth promotion appears effective, stopping the decline in the 1960s and slowing it down in the 1970s and in the first half of the 1980s. The importance of the measures undertaken is underlined by the fact that in spite of the renewed slide in the 1980s, the earlier birth rate bottom was never reached again under Communism or only in its final agony. The USSR had its lowest historical fertility rate in 1981, and

Table 7.5 Fertility in Communist and in Capitalist Europe, 1951–85 (total fertility rates, unweighted group averages)

	1951–55	1956–60	1961–65	1966–70	1971–75	1976–80	1981–85
Communist	2.92	2.62	2.36	2.35	2.24	2.20	2.08
Central	2.17	2.42	2.63	2.39	1.83	1.53	1.48
Nordic	2.53	2.61	2.61	2.28	1.93	1.68	1.61
Western	2.57	2.71	2.87	2.57	2.06	1.74	1.70
Southern	2.64	2.59	2.68	2.65	2.54	2.23	1.78

Source: Calculated from Chesnais (1992: table A2.5).

Definitions:
Communist Europe: Bulgaria, Czechoslovakia, GDR, Hungary, Poland, Romania, USSR, Yugoslavia. Central Europe: Austria, FRG, Switzerland. Nordic Europe: Denmark, Finland, Norway, Sweden. Western Europe: Belgium, England and Wales, France, the Netherlands. Southern Europe: Greece, Italy, Portugal, Spain.

it then climbed slowly upward with *perestroika* (Besemers 1980; Jones and Grupp 1987; Grasland 1990; Chesnais 1992: table A2.4).

Then, with the collapse of Communism, this coupling of family and employment through a whole complex of socio-economic institutions and policies also broke down, sending Eastern European fertility plummeting for a decade. For example, Russian fertility went down from 1.90 in 1990 to 1.23 in 1997, Polish from 2.04 in 1990 to 1.29 in 2001, Czech from 1.89 to 1.14, and Hungarian from 1.87 to 1.32 (Eurostat 2002: table J8; UNDP 2002: table 5).

But the most dramatic change of all occurred in the country that disappeared, the German Democratic Republic (GDR), which in the early 1950s and then again throughout the 1970s and 1980s had a higher fertility rate than West Germany. From 1.73 in 1985 and 1.57 in the GDR's last year (1989), fertility plunged to 0.83 in 1992 and then further to 0.77 for 1993 and 1994, crawling up to 0.93 in 1996, and to 1.09 in 1998. The crude birth rate was 5.1 children born per thousand population in 1994 (Mounier 1998: table 2; Grünheid and Roloff 2000: table 11; cf. Conrad *et al.* 1998). These figures constitute the lowest ever – in war as well as in peacetime – recorded fertility rate of any substantial population, while the West German rate remained basically stable, at 1.39 in 1989, 1.34 in 1994, and back to 1.41 in 1998. In 1916 French fertility amounted to 1.21, and German in 1945 to 1.53. The lowest Depression rate was noticed in Sweden, at 1.70 (Chesnais 1992: tables A1.5, A2.3–4).

How permanent the 'birth strike' of women in ex-Communist Europe will turn out to be is anybody's guess. And how should its plausible explanatory components be weighted? Life-course postponement of marriage/partnership and of giving birth? Effects of selective emigration? Adaptations to Western European standards of career and consumption, for which children appear an unwanted burden? Adaptations to loss of social infrastructure for children, of employment, and to an uncertain future? What is important in this context is that Communism has played an important part in family history in many ways, including in damming the current of birth decline.

In summary, governmental birth promotion has not been without effects, but they have been relatively modest. They have mainly consisted of either sustaining a social trend already initiated without it, like the family policies of Germany and Sweden in the 1930s and of France in the 1950s, or of slowing down and even bringing to a temporary halt an unwanted birth decrease. Opposite policies, of birth control, have often, but far from always, been much more effective.

8   The politics and sociology of birth control

Family systems and the second wave of fertility control

In the second half of the twentieth century, the trajectory of fertility outside the 'West' has been shaped largely through an interaction of family systems and public population policies, constrained or facilitated by socio-economic structuration of literacy, urbanity and general (in)equality. The snag of modern history has been, that many of the traditional vital barriers to fertility – mortality, morbidity, malnutrition – and traditional restrictive norms have been eroded, before new norms of small families asserted themselves. In most parts of the Third World, the immediate response to post-World War II economic and medical developments was a rise of fertility, from enhanced fecundity and from the erosion of post-marital taboos.

Among the non-Western European major family systems of the world, there were four plausible candidates for the succession of birth control. Closest at hand, from a cultural point of view, was the Latin American Creole family, coming out of the encounters of Iberian and Indian family relations, with additions of African slavery, but normatively a New World variant of European Latinity. When the Western European movement swept along Eastern Europe, the Southern Cone of the Americas, and the European settlers from South Africa to New Zealand, most of Latin America, from Chile and Brazil to Mexico, resisted it for quite some time. As will be elaborated below, a major reason for that continuing lag seems to be the inegalitarian social structure. Among the Latin American Creole families we might expect the more Euro-American variant to follow Europe and North America more rapidly than the more Indo-mestizo variant.

The Afro-American variant of the Creole family is another candidate. Normatively rudimentary, with a weak parental control structure, matrifocal rather than patriarchal, and fundamentally unstable, this family of the Caribbean and of US blacks lacked strong normative barriers to fertility control and had clear female benefits of the latter. The instability of sexual unions meant in itself a limit to fertility. But non-propertied or non-middle-class Afro-Creole males had no benefits to expect from fertility control, as they left their children in the charge of their mothers. Rather, it was a cost, as offspring proved your virility. Creole women had to be extraordinarily resourceful in order to establish a pattern of birth control under such circumstances. That was, on the whole, very difficult before the advent of, knowledge about, and access to the diaphragm, the intrauterine device or the pill. Some fertility control did establish itself in Cuba in the inter-war period, uniquely in the Caribbean, for reasons still not quite clear, but probably related to US influence. Literacy was predominant, as in Jamaica and Puerto Rico, and female mobilization and general social conditions, as measured by mortality rates, were more advanced than in the rest of the West Indies (cf. Miller 1991: 90ff; Mitchell 1998a: table A6). But post-World War II fertility was generally high in the Caribbean, rising significantly in Jamaica, and in Cuba after the 1959 revolution. Eastern European fertility rates, like those of Bulgaria in the early 1930s, were reached definitely in the Caribbean only in the late 1960s in Puerto Rico and in Trinidad, and in Cuba in the 1970s (Chesnais 1992: table A2.7; Mitchell 1998a: table A6).

Leaving the Americas, we should expect two Asian candidates to early birth control, the Southeast Asian Buddhist-cum-Malay Muslim family, and the East Asian one, deriving from ancient Sinic civilization.

Generally characteristic of the Southeast Asian family was a relatively permissive normative system. Buddhism was generally uninterested in marriage, and Southeast Asian Islam had been considerably mellowed by Malay custom. The colonial Catholic Church of the Philippines had been notoriously reactionary – and as such a main target of early Filipino patriotism – but half a century of vigorous American occupation and English-language education had seriously weakened the Church's hold of its flock (Anderson 1998: chs 9–10).

Malay girls married very young, but their marriage included the right to divorce. And by the mid-twentieth century the Malay rate of divorce was, as we noted above, by far the highest in the world. In the Therawada Buddhist world of Burma/Myanmar, Ceylon/Sri Lanka, and Siam/Thailand, on the other hand, there was a widespread practice of more or less adult marriage by choice. Southeast Asian women were also relatively literate by mid-century, above all in the US-educated Philippines, where female illiteracy was below 50 per cent, better than most of the high-fertility countries of Latin America, although well behind Chile, Costa Rica and Cuba. About half of Ceylonese women and a third of Burmese and Thai women were literate. Malay women were less fortunate, less than one in five in Malacca was literate in 1947. In this respect, Ceylonese women were similar to Mexican and somewhat better off than Brazilian (UNESCO 1964: table 4). Southeast Asia was to correspond to its potential.

While the Creole and the Southeast Asian family systems may be regarded as interstitial or hybrid, the East Asian had a long and proud history of its own. In spite of its strongly patriarchal character, the East Asian family system had in fact erected less formidable barriers to birth control than the South Asian, the West Asian-cum-North African, or the sub-Saharan African. Outside its patrilineal and patriarchal core it was more normatively pragmatic than the other family systems. Female sexuality was strictly controlled, but without the South Asian and Malay norm of marriage by menarche at the latest, nor involving seclusion or veiling. Marriage was an obligation to one's ancestors, but not a sacred institution, as in Catholicism or Hinduism. Fertility was not a value to be maximized as in the African worldview, nor were children 'gifts of

God', and as such beyond human control, as in Hindu, Muslim and Christian piety. Abortion and infanticide were viewed pragmatically, rather than as moral principles (with regard to female infanticide this was a stance in common with the Hindu family). Finally, the normative structure of the East Asian family system had little of specialized, authoritative norm defenders – few priests, few monks, no specialists in sacred law, no chiefs. The East Asian normative system had hardly any extra-family props at all with any autonomy from the state.

The decision structure was strongly patriarchal, investing fathers, or grandfathers, with decisive power. In terms of paternal power East Asia was second to none. Filial piety and submission was indeed the highest Confucian virtue. Marriages were generally arranged by the parental generation. However, some young women of East Asia in the first half of the twentieth century had more of two resources for autonomous decision-making than most of their Afro-Asian sisters: age and literacy, resources handed down by tradition and reinforced in early modernity. Literacy and schooling are important for two reasons in this context, it will be remembered. Schooling increases the cost of children, if for no other reason then at least by keeping them out of work. Literacy, usually the effect of previous schooling, affects the family decision structure by augmenting the resources and the sense of mastery of young brides and of young couples.

Among East Asian cultures, the Japanese stood out at the beginning of the twentieth century in several respects, not only militarily since the defeat of the Chinese in 1895, but also in aspects of their family system. Japanese women married relatively late, as adults; on average Japanese women married in 1920 at the age of 21 (Xenos and Gultiano 1992: appendix table 1).

Another distinctive trait was literacy and schooling. By the mid-nineteenth century about 40 per cent of Japanese boys and about 10 per cent of Japanese girls were 'receiving some kind of formal education outside of their home' (Dore 1965: 254). Meiji Japan introduced compulsory schooling in the 1870s, and by 1900 half of all children were actually attending school. In 1910 enrolment was 98 per cent and actual attendance 85 per cent (Waswo 1988: 544, 560), more than in southwestern, not to speak of Eastern, Europe at the time.

Even though the Japanese were ahead, a relatively high rate of literacy characterized early twentieth-century East Asian civilization as a whole. In pre-revolutionary China 30 to 45 per cent of males and 2 to 10 per cent of women are held to have been literate. Primary school enrolment in 1949 was 25 per cent (raised to 85 per cent by 1965; Pepper 1987: 186; 1991: 578). By the end of the 1930s, a third of Koreans and a quarter of Taiwanese were literate (Bideleux 1985: table 3). But in 1950, 40 per cent of Taiwanese women and 60 per of Taiwanese men were literate, and in 1955 two-thirds of South Korean women and seven-eighths of South Korean men were (UNESCO 1964: tables 4, 9).

Around 1950 the literacy difference between China and ex-colonial India was not very significant. Less than 10 per cent of Indian women and a third of Indian men were literate by 1951, and primary school enrolment in India was

21 per cent. The main difference took place after the revolution and independence, respectively. In 1960, Indian primary school enrolment was still only at
32 per cent.

The Muslim families of once Soviet Central Asia should be expected to be
relatively amenable to change, given the anti-traditional ambience of the
USSR. The same should hold for Kemalist Turkey. In both cases we are referring to societies that had experienced half a century of strong, official
modernist influence.

By contrast, the Arab-Muslim, the African, and the South Asian family
systems could all be expected to be highly resistant to fertility change. Neither,
by mid-century, left any room for innovative female or young couple decisions.
Girls were very tightly controlled and married off, as children in South Asia
and at least before adulthood in the Arab-Muslim world. African societies
tended to be less preoccupied with controlling female sexuality, and the
female marriage age differed considerably, although all the African countries
of the 1980s World Fertility Survey had married off the overwhelming
majority of their women by the age of 20 (UN 1987: 9). However, in compensation, so to speak, the supra-individual family alliance aspect of marriage,
symbolized by the transfer of bridewealth, was, on the whole, even more
strong in sub-Saharan Africa than in North Africa/West Asia and in South Asia.
High fertility was a value in itself in most African societies, as indicated by the
few quantitative sources available, the missionary parish records. Subsistence
agriculture or landless labouring have no obvious immediate benefits from
birth control. None of these societies provided any mass female literacy. The
Muslim world and Indian civilization were certainly literary cultures, but of a
very elitist kind, and African civilization was mainly oral.

By the time of the World Fertility Surveys of the mid-1970s, fertility changes
were underway in some parts of the world, but the desired number of children
indicates noteworthy differences on the threshold of the second world international movement of fertility decline (Table 8.1). The special position of
children in the African value system of the 1970s is underlined by the fact that
the only other country with women wanting more children than the least
natalist Black African country was Mauritania, a predominantly Arab-Berber
country in the border region of North and sub-Saharan Africa. As Sudan is
also a border country (with a mean desire for 6.3 children), only one fully
Arab-Muslim country had a desirable fertility on a par with the lowest African
countries (Ghana and Lesotho) – Syria with a mean wish for 6.1 children. The
fatalist abdication from any numerical wish, which yields a statistical
understatement of the number of children desired, is also very much African
and Yemenite. If we take away Yemen and the two Arab-African border countries, on average only 5 per cent of the women of the five other Arab-Muslim
countries had no idea of desired family size. Among the other countries and
regions, the variations are small, and should not be elaborated, in view of the
margins of error involved. But perhaps the low number of children wanted in
the two most typically Afro-Creole countries should be noted, 4 children in
Jamaica, 3.5 in Haiti.

Table 8.1 Desired number of children in family regions of the world, mid- to late 1970s (unweighted averages)

	Mean	Range	Per cent giving no number
Sub-Saharan Africa	7.3	8.3–6.0	19.1
Arab-Muslim world	5.1	8.7–4.1	14.7
Andean America	4.3	5.1–3.8	0.6
Caribbean	4.2	4.7–3.8	0.2
South Asia	4.1	3.9–4.2	11.0
Southeast Asia	4.1	4.4–3.7	1.7
East Asia (Korea)	3.2		1.0

Source: Re-calculations from UN (1987: table 29)

Regions:
Sub-Saharan Africa: Benin, Cameroon, Ivory Coast, Ghana, Kenya, Lesotho, Senegal. Arab-Muslim world: Egypt, Jordan, Mauritania, Morocco, Sudan, Syria, Tunisia, Yemen. Andean America: Colombia, Ecuador, Mexico, Paraguay, Peru. Caribbean: Costa Rica, Dominican Republic, Guyana, Haiti, Jamaica, Panama, Trinidad and Tobago, Venezuela. South Asia: Bangladesh, Nepal, Pakistan. Southeast Asia: Indonesia, Malaysia, Philippines, Sri Lanka, Thailand.

Japan by the mid-twentieth century was somewhere between Europe and the rest of Asia in fertility as in other aspects of social and economic development. Japan provided, so to speak, a hinge between the first and the second wave of fertility control. Though Japanese fertility was slowly coming down in the 1920s and 1930s, it did not quite follow the Eastern European decline, except for a plunge in 1938–39, recuperating during the war and immediately after the war. Then, in the 1950s, Japan became a global trend-setter with a prosperity fertility around and below the rate of reproduction. By about 1960 Japan was definitely down to that level of two children per woman, having had a rate of 4.3 in 1948–49, and by the mid-1970s Japan was settled on a long-term level below reproduction fertility. What had happened?

The process was a mixture of the spontaneous European process and non-European post-war population policy. There clearly was a widespread desire for a two- or three-child family, as in the European wave around the beginning of the century. There was a mass-media discussion in 1946–47 about the population issue under the new bleak post-imperialist post-war conditions, and 'overpopulation' had, of course, earlier been a nationalist argument for imperialist expansion. The demand became effective, rapidly and dramatically due to three governmental decisions. One was the new Civil Code of 1947, pushed by the American occupants. It abolished the patriarchal 'house' (*ie*) and instituted legal gender equality. Second, pre-war principled but ineffective governmental natalism was now reversed. In 1948 a new 'Eugenic Protection Law' was passed, replacing the natalist one of 1940, legalizing abortion on generous conditions, including economic. Third, in the early 1950s, the public health authorities trained consultants on contraception, 31,000 by the end of 1953, and mass education meetings on contraception were conducted.

Contraceptive practices, mainly condoms and abstinence or coitus inter-ruptus, spread rapidly among Japanese couples. By 1954 more than 40 per cent of married women aged 25–39 reported contraceptive practice in their marriage. Most efficient was abortion, which more than quadrupled between 1949 and 1953. The latter year, 35 per cent of all Japanese conceptions ended in abortion. And abortions continued to rise: in 1954 for three live births there were two induced abortions, meaning that 40 per cent of all conceptions were aborted (Taeuber 1958: 272ff; Mosk 1979; Muramatsu 1996).

What happened to diminish fertility around the world following Japan in the 1950s? Not much before the 1960s, but then it started, more or less in predictable order (Table 8.2). On the whole, the character of the world's major family systems, and their historical context, outlined above, is capable of predicting rather well, in broad non-statistical terms, the range of fertility change, from the Western European to the African family system. After Europe, East Asia, Southeast Asia and Creole America led the way. Soviet influence brought later independent states of Caucasus and Central Asia closer to Europe in family terms than would have followed from their pre-Communist geoculture alone. By 1970–75, save for war-torn Vietnam, all East Asia, all Afro-Creole America except Haiti (with a historically relatively low fertility), all Euro-Creole countries and, by the end of the 1970s, all of Southeast Asia had embarked on a lower-fertility way of life. The timing of change, however, was more spread out among the Indian/mestizo countries of Latin America, between the three major countries of South Asia, and among the Arab nations.

The populations of the African family were the last to move. Pioneering Southern Africa and Kenya apart, sub-Saharan Africa joined the bandwagon only in the 1990s, and many countries there are still missing. The latter tend to be the poorest, least developed, often war-torn parts of the continent, including nine of the ten lowest-ranking countries on the UNDP world list of human development. But they also comprise sparsely populated, traditionally high-sterility middle Africa, like relatively resourceful Gabon, and a relatively well-operating country from the high-fertility lakes region of East Africa, such as Uganda.

Assessing the waves: Europe and the Third World

The second, intercontinental wave of fertility control after 1965 was explicitly state-led, and it was deliberately global, debated among global elites and after some time pushed by worldwide operators, the World Bank, the UN, USAID and other donors. Therefore, it could establish itself faster, more heavily, and across more family systems than the first wave. True, it did not strike out of the blue, but was connected to societal developments – in their turn, of course, affected by politics – of schooling and literacy, urbanization, mass communi-cation, general economic resources, and changed life-course aspirations. Direct state intervention was also less important in Creole America than in Africa and Asia, although it became active there too, in Colombia and Mexico as well as in Jamaica. But it played no intended part in Cuban fertility decline and only

Table 8.2 Timing of extra-European post-World War II fertility decline by geocultural family system (timing of trend to fertility decline of at least 0.5 child)[a]

Year	Country
1950–55	East Asia: Japan
	Soviet West/Central Asia: Georgia[b]
1960/65 to 1965–70	East Asia: Korea, Taiwan, and city-states of Hong Kong and Singapore
	Southeast Asia: Malaysia, Philippines, Sri Lanka
	Creole America: Barbados, Brazil, Chile, Colombia, Costa Rica, Trinidad, Venezuela
	Soviet West/Central Asia: Armenia, Azerbaidjan, Kazakhstan
1970–75	East Asia: China
	Creole America: Dominican Republic, Jamaica, Ecuador, El Salvador, Panama, Peru
	West Asia/North Africa: Egypt, Lebanon, Tunisia, Turkey
	Sub-Saharan Africa: South Africa
1975–80	Southeast Asia: remaining countries, Cambodia, Indonesia, Myanmar, Thailand
	Creole America: Honduras, Mexico, Nicaragua
	South Asia: India
	Soviet West/Central Asia: Kyrgyzstan, Uzbekistan
	West Asia/North Africa: Bahrein, Iran, Iraq, Kuwait, Morocco, Qatar, UAE
1985–90	East Asia: Vietnam
	South Asia: Bangladesh
	Soviet West/Central Asia: Tadjikistan, Turkmenistan
	West Asia/North Africa: Algeria, Jordan, Syria,
	Creole America: all remaining countries
	Sub-Saharan Africa: Zimbabwe, Kenya
After 1990 only	South Asia: Pakistan
	West Asia/North Africa: Libya, Saudi Arabia, all remaining except Yemen
	Sub-Sahara Africa: Nigeria and majority of countries
Missing by end of twentieth century	West/Central Asia: Afghanistan, Yemen
	Sub-Saharan Africa: Angola, Burundi, Central African Republic, Chad, (both) Congos, Equatorial Guinea, Ethiopia, Gabon, Guinea-Bissau, Liberia, Mali, Mozambique, Niger, Rwanda, Sierra Leone, Uganda.

Sources: Cleland (1994); Ross *et al.* (1988: table 3); UNDP (2002: table 5); Mitchell (1998a, b: table A6; Jones and Grupp (1987, table 2.11).

Notes:
a When fertility rates are missing, a trend decline of the crude birth rate by at least five points has been used instead.
b Then Soviet Georgia had by the late 1950s a fertility rate similar to that of Russia, 2.6.

a modest one in Brazil (Mundigo 1996). State policies and programmes often provided a decisive initial push, but on other occasions their role was more of a facilitator, responsive to more or less inarticulate demand.

Fertility decline or 'the demographic transition' is still a controversial and in several respects elusive object of demographic explanations. A recent state-of-the-art review (Bulatao 2001) listed eight key explanatory factors on offer and seven theoretical approaches. The key explanatory factors were: mortality reduction, reduced economic contributions from children, opportunity costs of child-bearing (in relation to other activities), family transformation (to conjugal units), vanishing cultural props for child-bearing (religion, lineages), improved access to effective fertility regulation, marriage delay, diffusion of ideas and practices. The theoretical approaches enumerated included: a demographic approach, focusing on the effect of mortality reduction; a historical approach, in which socio-economic development, contraceptives, and diffusion of low-fertility ideals are highlighted in the examples Bulatao refers to; a multivariate sociological approach, combining mortality reduction, falling demand for children, and increasing ability to regulate fertility; a psychological approach concentrating on the argument that individuals have to be ready, willing and able to control their fertility; an economic approach, centring on the changing costs of children; a gender perspective, stressing that fertility change is retarded or facilitated by different social systems of control and subordination of women; and a policy perspective, emphasizing birth control programmes, and indirect effects of other state interventions.

As most of these approaches are exemplified by some of the best demographers of the world (Caldwell 2001; Casterline 2001; Cleland 2001; Kaa 2001; McNicoll 2001; Mason 2001; Tsui 2001), they all make good sense, while abstaining from any tight explanatory model.

But statistically most impressive is an approach not listed or represented in the special issue of *Population and Development Review* (Bulatao 2001): a human ecology model presented by Edward Crenshaw and associates (2000). It purports to explain Third World changes in total fertility during 1965–90, whereby it reaches an impressive 90 per cent of the variation accounted for. The significant explanatory variables of the best-fitting model are: the fertility and the child mortality rates in 1965 plus their quadratics to capture curvilinear effects; service-sector labour-force-cum-GDP importance; agrarian land/labour ratio-cum-agrarian labour force size in 1960; export share of GDP in 1970; ethnic homogeneity; and family planning effort in 1982.

How to assess the explanation and understanding value of this contribution is not that easy, primarily because it gives an explanation of something which is unknown, and something which did not exist. The annual rate of fertility change is something extrapolated from a set of irregular, non-annual fertility surveys. To calculate an average annual rate of change means, then, to assume a process of continuous fertility change for 1965 to 1990, which did not happen in a large number of countries. Second, its devotion to 'universalist, abstract theory' means that it does not address the question of historical timing, of 1965 and of the last third of the twentieth century, while the ecological variables used are chosen for their fitting to this particular period. Third, the authors' cavalier dismissal of gender variables is hardly convincing, particularly in view of the massive individual data evidence of differential fertility at different levels of female education. The authors discard their two gender variables – female secondary school enrolment in 1970 and female

non-agrarian employment in 1970 – upon finding that their effects independent of economic structure and child mortality become statistically insignificant. The issue is not further probed into, and gender relations are dismissed
as '*symptoms* of more fundamental macro-organizational processes' (Crenshaw *et
al.* 2000: 387, original emphasis). Finally, although the 60-odd sample of countries is tested for robustness (by so-called jack-knife regression), it may need a
note of caution for its exclusion of China, among others, and because the
authors threw out Congo/Kinshasa as an outlier, with its large 'service' sector.

For all its statistical marksmanship, this is hardly a decisive explanation of
fertility change. But its two key variables of social ecology are worth remem-
bering. The size of a problematic land–labour ratio – mystifyingly named
'demographic inheritance' – was a visible variable in the early fertility decline
in Eastern Asia (Japan, South Korea, Taiwan, Java), and provided a belated
push for it in poor Bangladesh, while retarding it in most of Africa. The
service-sector variable indicates, in a Third World context, a social structure
shaken out of its traditional agrarian mould, even if still poor, which is why it
is a better social predictor than GDP level. As the European road to development by industrialization is not repeated, to the same extent, anywhere
(Therborn 1995: 65ff), what Crenshaw *et al.* (2000) call 'industrial dominance'
is also less significant.

Against the state and with the state

The perspective adopted here is that of a sociological historian in front of the
two vast, modern international waves of fertility decline. Time is, then, important, and so are the commonality/difference of the two waves, and the pattern
of diffusion. While obviously related, these concerns differ from those of the
demographic mainstream, as well as from ahistorical economic or ecological
interests.

The first wave, as noted, seems to have been driven by a vast, multi-faceted
social movement of dissent, of individual aspiration, and of strivings for
collective emancipation. It was spawned by the French and the American
Revolutions, and sustained by mass migration, proletarianization, industrialization and urbanization, and carried by movements of religious dissent, of
labour, of women, of Radicals of whatever cause. In time the first wave of
modern fertility change was coeval with the rise and spread of the labour
movement, then emerging as a major social force all over Europe. It was also
contemporary to the rise of the first modern mass medium, the popular press.
Through the latter the Annie Besant trial for contraceptive information, for
instance, became an intercontinental public event. The first wave was opposed
by every single state.

Nineteenth-century infant mortality history varied, in trajectories as well as
in levels. In England and the Netherlands the rate was about the same in the
1890s as in the 1830s. The Russian record starts in the 1860s, and shows no
trend. The Belgian and the French rates did not change their path after the
1840s. In Austria, Germany and Scandinavia, on the other hand, infant mortal-

ity was trending downwards in the second half of the century (Chesnais 1992: table A4.1). In the decades around 1900, the parental costs and benefits of European children were crucially affected by the establishment of compulsory schooling, and by the concomitant effectiveness of laws against child labour (see Therborn 1993).

What in the second wave corresponds to the social movement of dissent and of emancipation is the developmentalist state, deriving from post-Depression economics, the outcome of World War II and from the anti-colonial revolution. National short-term economic performance and economic growth became measurable, and politically a government responsibility. Colonial peace and 'civilization' were replaced by 'development', by independent states, culturally supported by metropolitan disciplines of development, economic, social, political and, increasingly focused, demographic.

The Europe-wide social movement was succeeded by a developmentalist globalism, pushed by, first, a small coterie of economists and demographers, and then gathering momentum through metropolitan aid agencies, the World Bank and the UN machinery. This was only possible after a significant de-traditionalization and secularization of Western politics, something which took place gradually and unevenly in the decades after World War II, led by the Protestant countries of northwestern Europe.

The sense of personal mastery, which we have put forward as a key variable of birth control, could be delegated by the developmentalist state, as well as arising out of participating in a social movement. Much fewer resources would then be required of the individual. But it would require, that the state could provide, with cultural respect, cheap and effective means of contraception. Post-war developmentalism had led to generous resources being made available in rich countries for contraceptive research. By 1960, and the years before, an array of effective contraceptives were available. As well as the pill, launched onto the American market in 1960, there were also intrauterine devices (IUDs), and easy female and male sterilization. A new sense of sexual mastery was conveyed from above to the poor, the illiterate and the downtrodden by the development of easily manageable, cheap contraceptives in the course of the 1950s that could be used by poor populations with little motivation or self-confidence.

The post-colonial developmentalist state emerged in Asia in the late 1940s, and spread through Africa in the first half of the 1960s, though there more as an idea than as reality. By the 1960s a new stage of world demographic history was set. Successful anti-colonialism and the new macro-economics of develop-ment, coming both from Soviet planning and from post-Depression Western mainstream, had led up to developmentalist states. Two more things were still in short supply for a global wave of birth control to start rolling: elite conviction and state capacity. It would take until the early 1980s before the great majority of the governors of the globe were convinced that birth control was a crucial component of any development strategy. Secondly, even con-vinced political elites were still lacking politico-administrative capacity, even with foreign aid, for implementing family planning among their sceptical populations. As observed more closely below, this was something which for long was frustrating the early South Asian programmes.

Economic-cultural resources of the population, on one hand, and state purpose and efficacy, on the other, are to some extent exchangeable within this framework, and not only between the two historical waves. In the second wave, urbanization, post-agrarian employment, GDP, and female literacy were, on the whole, much higher in Latin America than in Asia or Africa. State interventions on fertility, on the other hand, while present and significant from the mid-1960s onwards, were generally weaker and less focused.

National independence and developmentalism also altered the cost–benefit schedule of children. Schooling was given a new push, although with very uneven effectiveness. Global medicine and hygiene brought mortality down, increasing the population pressure on developmentalist politicians as well as on parents. Mass communication began to develop, with its message of different life options, first by transistor radio, later by television.

Whereas the first wave only covered variants of the European family – and the Japanese at its tail end – the second wave rolled over all the other family systems. Again, our framework postulates a trade-off, as different family systems can be expected to have variable resilience to fertility change. Thus, the religiously anchored South Asian, West Asian/North African, and African – with strong lineages and alien states – family systems should be expected to be more resistant to change, than the state-dependent patriarchy of East Asia and the interstitial Southeast Asian and Creole American families.

The data of Table 8.2 show a pioneering role of the vigorous states of developed, and crowded, East Asia, the most developed countries of Southeast Asia, and the culturally open, relatively resourceful countries of Creole America. Together with a couple of special African cases, the least resource-developed parts of Africa, and of West and Central Asia form the end of the caravan.

While developmenalist states and, at times, external-donor-supported non-governmental societies, like Bangladesh, may provide a sense of fertility mastery, a massive post-colonial expansion of education has both altered the cost–benefit of having a large number of children, and pointed to new life-course horizons for educated young adults.

The second wave of fertility decline took place in the context of a drastic overall fall in mortality after World War II, with mortality decline accompanying and succeeding as well as preceding fertility decline. This meant that had both fertility and mortality continued at their rates of 1950–55, the world population would have been roughly the same in 2000 as it actually turned out to be. The distribution would have been somewhat different, but not dramatically so. The rich world would have had 180 million more people, and so would China. There would have been 140 million more Africans, and 100 million fewer Indians. But if the change in life expectancy had not been met by a fertility response, the poor part of the world would now have had two billion more people (Heuveline 1999: 691).

How much of this birth reduction is due directly to family planning and how much to other factors, which may also come from developmentalist policies, such as female schooling or land reform (cf. McNicoll 2001), is unknown and subject to controversial estimates. Among leading demographers, current high estimates are that between a third and a half of Third World fertility decline between 1950 and 2000 were due to birth control policies, but lower indications are also fielded (Tsui 2001: 195; cf. Heuveline 2001: 389ff). No statistical modelling is likely to settle this complicated issue to the satisfaction of all experts.

But it does seem clear that state family planning was decisive in rapidly bringing down fertility in the large Asian countries, of East, Southeast, South and West Asia, and in Africa where it was aided by the squeeze of population growth from lowered mortality and economic decline in the 1980s and 1990s (see the example of Cameroon: Eloundou-Enyegue *et al.* 2000). In countries of Latin America there were also almost simultaneous cultural changes pointing in the same direction, but birth control programmes made a crucial difference here also (see, for example, Parrado (2000) on Colombia and Venezuela).

As the 180-degree turnaround of state and public policies is a major part of the second wave of fertility decline, it deserves a special analysis.

The political demography of family planning

Until the second half of the twentieth century all governments were interested in increasing their populations, if they thought about population at all. Immigration colonization policies apart, this meant a governmental interest in families having more children. French fertility decline was seen by leading politicians as a national tragedy, particularly after French defeat in the Franco-Prussian war of 1870–71. French families were not producing future soldiers enough for the coming revenge. We noted above how most European governments met the first wave of birth control with prohibitions of contraceptives and contraceptive information.

It could happen that a tendency to overpopulation was noticed, as by Thomas Malthus in England, but there was no policy remedy. A Chinese educational commissioner Hung Liang-chi (1746–1809) noticed the problem in China at about the same time, when the country was undergoing rapid population growth which nineteenth-century pre-modern China was not going to be able to cope with, unlike modernizing England. But, he asked:

> Does the government have remedies? The answer is that its methods are to exhort people to develop new land, to practice more intensive farming, . . . to prohibit extravagant living and the consumption of luxuries . . . . During a long reign of peace the government could not prevent the people from multiplying themselves, yet its remedies are few.
>
> (Ho 1959: 272)

Hung's conclusion was repeated by social scientists on the topic almost two hundred years later (cf. Carlsson 1966) – and not without reason. The inter-war European governmental policies to promote more births had not been a clear success, to put it mildly.

The relationship of government power and human procreation was reversed after 1950, with Asian governments blazing the trail, egged on by certain significant non-governmental or small governmental forces in North America and Western Europe. It is a fascinating story of global politics, national politics and demography, which, as far as I know, has not yet met its master historian, although there is a great, unpublished, sociological dissertation on the international side of the story (Barrett 1995; cf. the bibliographical essay by Connelly 2003).

There had been an international birth control movement since the beginning of the century, generally radical and secularized – pace the very conservative Reverend Malthus – but also with some roots in non-established Anglo-Saxon Protestantism. Rather early it also managed to reach out to some intellectual and political elites of South and East Asia. Annie Besant, whom we encountered above in her 1877 trial on contraception, went to India, and was even for a year (in 1908) elected President of the Indian Congress, the, then very moderate, national movement. Margaret Sanger, the leading US birth control propagandist, was invited to Japan and China in the early 1920s, and given rapt receptions. A decade later she was also invited to India, where a Neo-Malthusian League had been formed in the late 1920s, and where the princely government of Mysore in 1930 had set up what arguably was the world's first governmental birth clinic (Raina 1966: 113).

Birth control remained highly controversial after World War II, however. By then, it had become a reasonable and respectable view and practice in secularized and/or Protestant societies of Western Europe and North America. Swedish Social Democratic natalism of the 1930s was unique for its time by easing restrictions on contraceptives in the name of voluntary parenthood, and post-war Swedish international aid from the late 1950s tended to specialize in family planning. Birth control was given official endorsement in Britain by a Royal Commission report on population in 1949 (Glass 1966: 190n). But it was still anathema to Catholicism. The Communist powers, like German Social Democratic orthodoxy before World War I, regarded it as a side issue, often as a cover for economic conservatism. West Germany retained the Nazi anti-contraceptive rulings until 1961 (Glass 1966: 193–94). In 1959 US President Eisenhower rejected the recommendation of a presidential policy committee that the USA, on request, should assist countries which wished to implement policies for reducing population growth: 'So long as I am President, this government will have nothing to do with birth control' (Chamie 1994: 37). The French post-war governments retained the anti-contraceptive legislation of the 1920s. Between 1957 and 1967 eleven bills by the left-wing opposition proposing changes to this were defeated (Dhavernas 1978: 150).

It was in these mined waters that a dedicated band of US demographers, Protestant philanthropists (like John Rockefeller III), development economists, and below-top-level policy-makers set out to conquer the world for birth control, with some help from the UK and from the secularized Lutheran social engineers of Scandinavia.

The stratagems deployed, using 'research' as a spear of policy, global network-building, lavish cross-national finance, private as well as public, etc. are of little pertinence to our story here, however fascinating as an early example of global 'governance'. But we should pay attention to the barometer of international cultural–political change.

The international scene had for long been frustrating to the birth controllers. Catholic representatives to UN bodies put up a strong, and for a long time quite successful, fight against any support of birth control. In 1951, a motion from Italy, Lebanon and Belgium got the World Health Organization (WHO), which had burnt its fingers supporting Indian population policy, to refrain from dealing with population issues for quite some years. When family planning came before the UN Economic Committee in 1962, the matter was put off the agenda four times and then was put on a night session, from which

> the Polish chairman had a diplomatic illness and disappeared, and the French under-secretary felt he had something better to do, . . . the Argentinean said that he couldn't possibly discuss such a matter as this, . . . the Irish gentleman said he would be put in jail . . . the Italian said that probably his country would not be able to give money, even to the UNICEF, if they heard that the UN was concerned with . . . helping countries to curb their population.
>
> (Barrett 1995: 181, 227)

In the late 1950s, Australian broadcasting officials were apparently trying to dissuade Gunnar Myrdal (1968: 1474n) from approaching the topic of birth control in South Asia in a public radio lecture. Myrdal, a former Social Democratic cabinet minister in (voluntary) exile as a senior UN economist, later Nobel Laureate, was both the most brilliant, the most cosmopolitan and the most quintessential of secularized Protestant Scandinavian social engineers.

The trajectory of international policy-making opinion can be traced by looking at the post-World War II world population conferences from Rome in 1954 to Cairo in 1994.

The Rome Conference was organized by the UN together with the International Union for the Scientific Study of Population. For its time it was a big scientific conference, with 435 experts from 74 countries. At the centre of the discussions was the theory of demographic transition, pushed by Frank Notestein and the Princeton Population Office, disputed by scholars from the Communist countries. Policy was too delicate to approach directly.

The next big occasion was the Second World Conference on Population in Belgrade in 1965, with 852 participants. By now there was a more general agreement that there was a population problem, but was birth control the right answer? Or economic re-organization? Should the UN be involved in family planning? On the first question, there was still a major divide. As far as the second was concerned, the door had been opened in the course of the early 1960s for the UN to be able to help upon request.

The Bucharest conference in 1974, official and post-scientific, took place against the background of Third World frustration with the UN 'Development

Decade' of the 1960s, and in particular with the US combination of reduced development aid and official pushing of population control. Western drafts of a contraceptive plan of action were deleted, but again the relevance of population issues to socio-economic development was agreed upon (Finkle and Crane 1975).

Global official opinion turned between 1974 and 1984. In Mexico City the Fourth World Population Conference decided to call upon governments 'as a matter of urgency' to make family planning services 'universally available'. Latin American opinion had begun to shift in 1967 (see below). In the run-up to the Mexico event, regional conferences in Africa (in Arusha) and in the Arab world (in Amman) had given the official green light to birth control (Chamie 1994). The 1994 Cairo Conference was not without controversy, but it centred mainly on abortion, and the Vatican found itself increasingly isolated, against 'artificial' contraception as well as against abortion (McIntosh and Finkle 1995).

The Protestant Christian global establishment, in the body of the World Council of Churches, endorsed family planning in 1961, as had the Church of England earlier in 1958. Authoritative Catholic opinion shifted in the days of the Second Vatican Council and the papacy of John XXIII from explicit, anathemic condemnation to studied interest. But in 1968, with the *Humanae Vitae Encyclica* of Pope Paul VI, the Church restated, in milder words, its traditional negativity to 'artificial' birth control, a negativity maintained under the reign of Pope John Paul II.

In spite of resistance, the winds of change strengthened from the beginning of the 1960s. In 1961 the US government – under the country's first Catholic President – announced that it would subsidize foreign birth control programmes, and the American president of the World Bank, Eugene Black, made a dramatic call for birth control: without it 'hope of economic progress in the populous countries of Asia and the Middle East should be abandoned' (Barrett 1995: 219–20). In the same year West Germany deleted anti-contraceptive legislation; in January Tunisia had already abolished such legislation, bequeathed to it by French colonialism (Daly 1966: 151). In France itself, it was only in 1967 that it was abolished, not for principled reasons but mainly because it was recognized by the Gaullist government as ineffective (Dhavernas 1978: 152).

In contrast to the case of the first wave of birth control, the second wave owed significantly to contraceptive innovations. Intrauterine devices, mainly the so-called Lippes loop, but also the Ota ring and the Zipper ring, spread extra-clinically in the first half of the 1960s, and so did oral contraceptives, 'the pill'. The latter was developed in the USA, tried out in Puerto Rico, and launched on the US market. In January 1965 there were about twice as many pill users in the USA as in the rest of the world. Latin America was the second market, and the pill early on became the main contraceptive of the Arab-Muslim world. IUDs were crucial in East Asia, in South Korea and Taiwan. Vasectomy, male sterilization, was a new practice, important in South Korea and India above all. Female sterilization had been used en masse before World

War II, in eugenics programmes from the USA to Nazi Germany. Abortion was, of course, an old practice, however illegal, but after World War II it became a major means of legitimate birth control in East Asia, beginning, as we saw above, in Japan (Lawrence 1966; Levin 1966; Satterthwaite 1966).

National programmes, their conditions, and their equivalents

Government programmes for reducing population growth constitute an innovation of the second half of the twentieth century. They were pioneered in South Asia, but were for long frustrated there; they had their first success in East Asia in the 1960s, spreading early to (parts of) Arab-Muslim North Africa and to the westernmost tip of Asia, and passing their crucial test of programme effectiveness in Southeast Asia. They always played a secondary role in Latin America, which had its own combination of a much belated Euro-American cultural movement and late twentieth-century conditions, although having some decisive interventions to show there, and in the Caribbean. It took a long time for them to get official endorsement in sub-Saharan Africa, and even longer to get a popular hold. But by the end of the century they were operating.

State developmentalism is in itself a manifestation of a sense of mastery of nature, and it is the more convincing the more it is generating resources and providing services of education and health. Through their single-mindedness, well-managed authoritarian regimes tend to have an initial advantage in changing the reproductive behaviour of a population, and reproductive change downwards is much easier – because more directly effective and less costly to the parents – than upwards.

State interventions can also alter the relations of power within the family. As Caldwell *et al.* (1982: 718) conclude from their South Indian study: 'The state does a good deal to counterbalance, both in the case of birth control and in the treatment of sick children, the influence of males and the elderly.' Once development gets going, new horizons open, through mass communication and through possibilities for discretionary consumption, to individual decisions.

India was the first country, in its First Five-Year Plan of 1951–56, to adopt birth control as a national public policy. Alone in independent Asia, India had an elite continuity across the divide of the 1940s, of the Pacific War to Japan, of the Communist Revolution to China. By the 1930s the new generation of Congress leaders had become convinced that India was facing a 'population problem', in the sense of too much or too much growth. Jawaharlal Nehru and his more strident rival Subhas Chandra Bose agreed on this. In world history, this was a novelty, nationalist leaders thinking that the nation was running the risk of becoming too large (Visaria and Chari 1998: 55).

After Independence, the Indian government made family planning a governmental policy. However, the issue remained controversial. Gandhi had been ambiguous, in favour of sexual abstinence, but against contraception. Many of Gandhi's high-profile followers were fully against family control. Nehru seems never to have committed himself explicitly in public to birth control (Myrdal 1968: 1510–11; Demeny 2001). The Planning Commission of the First Five-

Year Plan hoped for periodic abstinence, 'the rhythm method', because it would mean 'avoiding enormous expenditure' as well as 'securing the ethical values that community life would gain by the self-imposed restraint' (Myrdal 1968: 2152). This idea of costless communitarianism was, of course, self-deluding idealism, and the 'soft state' of India was going to prove itself strikingly ineffective in bringing about any fertility decline, although there were a couple of early provincial instances of birth control from the late 1940s, in Kerala and among Punjabi landholders (Das Gupta 2001; Dyson 2001). In hindsight this is not so surprising, in the light of its incapacity of bringing schooling to the people. And in the mid-1960s, Gunnar Myrdal (1968: 1473) had to conclude, sadly, in his monumental *Asian Drama*, that 'no country in South Asia has yet been able to affect any measurable reduction in fertility rates'. It should be noted that Myrdal's 'South Asia' included what is here, and in many other places, called Southeast Asia.

The programme was stepped up in the second half of the 1960s, with UN and Ford Foundation help. From American management monitoring the idea was adopted of assigning birth control workers with specific targets of method acceptance – so many condoms, IUDs, sterilizations, etc. – which became a practice of ridicule (Visaria and Chari 1998: 63). The overall target of a birth rate of 25 per thousand population in 1973, was actually hardly even approached. The crude Indian birth rate in 1973 was 35 (Mitchell 1998b: 74). In fact, Indian birth controllers were swimming against the current in the first decades after Independence. Reduced mortality meant fewer widows, and less traditional life-conceptions shortened previously prolonged periods of breast-feeding: both tendencies, and perhaps better health, tended to push birth rates upwards (Dyson 1989: 185ff). The ideals of the Anglicized urban elite did not penetrate the vast countryside of the sub-continent. Particularly resistant were the strongly patriarchal, largely illiterate states of the north, Uttar Pradesh, Madhya Pradesh, Rajasthan and Bihar, as well as the north-western state of Harayana (cf. Malhotra and Reeve 1995; Visaria and Visaria 1995: 22).

In the 1970s sterilization campaigns – mainly for vasectomy on men – were launched, which under 'emergency' rule in 1975–76 escalated into mass compulsion. When Indira Gandhi's government fell, in 1977, there was an immediate but not very long backlash against birth control. Indian fertility rates had begun to fall in the second half of the 1970s, and the decline continued after that. In the early 1990s the birth rate fell below 30 (Chesnais 1992: 554).

The Anglophile elitist but elected government of Ceylon – later, under more populist Buddhist regimes, known as Sri Lanka – took an early, cautious and low-profile interest in birth control, concluding an agreement in 1958 with the Swedish government about help from the latter in starting pilot projects of action-cum-research. The input of this programme was rather modest, but conditions – traditionally adult marriages, high literacy, no strong religious objections – were favourable, and the birth rate of the island went down gradually, from about 40 in 1951 to 36 in 1961 and to 30 in 1971 (cf. Kinch 1966).

In the early 1960s several committed Western birth controllers hoped for progress under the new military dictator of Pakistan, Ayub Khan, who since 1959 had vigorously endorsed birth control, which was written into Pakistan's new plan from 1960. However, Ayub himself and his regime did not last long, and family planning became politically compromised under his successors after Ayub's disastrous war with India over East Bengal (Lush *et al.* 2000: 15–16). Family planning took effect in Pakistan only by the mid-1980s.

The military dictatorship of South Korea, which seized power in May 1961, was the first clearcut case of birth control success. The turn from old traditions of military statecraft was signalled by the fact that it was this military government which repealed the law prohibiting the importation and manufacture of contraceptives. A centrally organized, highly publicized campaign, mainly using a new IUD, the Lippes loop, got going from 1962, with US and, somewhat later, Swedish aid. By 1968 the crude birth rate had declined from 42 in 1960 to 33. The total fertility rate, which stood at six children in 1960 went down to 4.5 for the second half of the 1960s (fertility rates from Coale and Freedman (1993) and from Chesnais (1992: 554); see further Cha 1966; Kim 1969)).

In Taiwan, also under emergency military law, the programme had a lower political profile and was running from 1964. But the seal of government approval was stamped on it as early as 1954, when the Family Planning Association of China was officially chartered by the Ministry of the Interior. Taiwan was very densely populated, even more so than South Korea and Japan, and like Japan its population was swollen by the outcome of war, here by Guomindang refugees after their defeat in the Chinese civil war. All three countries also had a large, recently propertied class of farmers, benefiting from post-war land reform. Taiwanese family planning was an immediate success, riding on an already downward wave of fertility, which between 1950 and 1963 had brought the birth rate down from a peak of 50 in 1951 to 36. By 1968, 30 per cent of married women aged 20–24 had an IUD (Chow 1969: 35, 40).

The colony of Hong Kong relied on 'civil society' initiatives even more than Taiwan, but the pre-war Eugenics League turned into the Family Planning Association (both upper-class, heavily expatriate organizations), received government subsidies from 1955, and effectively pushed birth control with lavish media support (Chun 1966: 73, 79–80).

While the late Japanese fertility reduction had relied mainly on legalized abortion and condoms, Korea, Taiwan and Hong Kong were the world leaders in adopting IUDs. By mid-1965, one out of 53 females of all ages from infancy and above had an IUD in Taiwan, one of 55 in South Korea, and one of 61 in Hong Kong (calculations from Levin 1966: 489). No other country in the world was close to this.

Singapore, a civilian, but hardly kid-gloved government, developed from 1966 a wide battery of penalties and incentives, including housing and maternity leave, for discouraging high fertility (Kangaratnam 1969; Coale and Freedman 1993). Malaysia followed in the mid-1960s, the Philippines and Thailand about 1970, the former under civilian, the latter under military dictatorship. In 1975, the bloodiest military dictator of Asia, General Suharto, installed governmental family planning in Indonesia (Lim 1966; Tsui 1985; Thomas and Grindle 1994; Leete 1996).

In Western Asia, the Turkish military government had begun preparing for family planning in 1963, making it policy in 1965 (Metner 1966). In North Africa, Tunisia turned in 1962 to the American Ford Foundation and the Population Council for advice, and began a concerted effort in 1963–64, publicly backed by the secularized President Bourguiba (Daly 1966). Nile-centred, desert-surrounded Egypt was, of course, the 'Middle Eastern' country with the most obvious problem of overpopulation, an issue taken notice of by Egyptian scholars in the 1930s. The nationalist military revolution of 1952 meant that the issue was taken seriously and brought to high-level study from 1953 onwards. Family planning was endorsed in the National Charter of 1961, promulgated by President Nasser. However, only in 1965 was birth control made public policy (Husein 1966; Ibrahim and Ibrahim 1998).

This military interest in birth control was a historical novelty. These dictators and authoritarian rulers (except Nasser) were all attached to, and often much dependent on, the United States. It seems that the American connection was a crucial channel whereby governmental birth control was effectively established in the world. A key figure in Guomindang Taiwan was the chairman of the Sino-American Joint Commission on Rural Reconstruction, Chiang Mon-lin (Chow 1969: 36). With the Vietnam war the Thai military regime of Sarit Thanarat and his successors (1958–73) aligned itself closely with the USA.

How important these US-oriented developmentalist dictatorships or authoritarian regimes were in the second wave of fertility control is still debatable (Leete 1996: 152). But it was the rural success in Taiwan, Korea, Malaysia, Thailand and Indonesia which disproved prevailing assumptions about fertility on one hand, and industrialization, urbanization and GDP level, on the other. A late 1970s estimate concluded that of the fertility decline between the early 1960s and the early 1970s, 28 per cent in Taiwan was due to the family planning programme, 37 per cent in South Korea, 47 per cent in Thailand, and 57 per cent in Singapore (estimates by S.-E. Khoo and B.P. Chai, reported by Raimundo 1993: 44).

The hidden American hand was probably crucial in parts of East and Southeast Asia, but the Chinese Communists, faced with a very different demographic situation than the Russians, were also concerned with population growth rather early, although the spectacular breakthrough of Chinese birth reduction came in the 1970s. In 1956 the Chinese government explicitly endorsed birth control, without making an orchestrated campaign of it. The recommended method was a turn towards a Western European type of family, with late marriages. Official discourse was backed up by quasi-medical arguments that a woman's 'internal system' was not fully mature until the age of 25 (Evans 1997: 42). At least among the urban population this was quite effective. In a sample from China's five biggest cities, about two-thirds of women who married in 1950–53 were under 21, but among those who married in 1958–65 only one-fifth were, and between 1966 and 1982 hardly anybody married under the age of 21 (Zang 1993: 38; cf. the somewhat more gradual rural change reported by Sanderson and Tan 1995: 113). Through mechanisms apparently not yet known, Shanghai had a spectacular decline of fertility in the last years of the 1950s, from a total fertility rate of about 5.5 to just above 3. If these figures are correct, this was more rapid than the, somewhat later, decline in Singapore and Hong Kong (cf. Taeuber and Orleans 1966; Leete and Alam 1993: 244).

While the Shanghai curve shows a strong fertility decline from 1955 to 1959, slowing down in the 1960s and flattening out in the 1970s, the national urban configuration is very different. It shows a conjunctural plunge in 1958–60, the years of the disastrous 'Great Leap', a temporary recovery in the early 1960s, followed by a precipitous decline until stabilization during the Cultural Revolution, and thereafter a gradual decline during the 1970s. Rural and national curves differ in their lack of the mid-1960s decline (Sanderson and Tan 1995: 114).

After the most convulsive phase of the Cultural Revolution, birth control was pushed by the Chinese authorities from 1971: 'later [births], longer [spacing], fewer [children]'. Pressured couples responded vigorously to these campaigns, implemented mainly with IUDs and, secondarily, female sterilization, supported by a massive supply of abortions, well exceeding the number of live births in the course of the 1970s. The predominant pattern was 'parity-specific control', that is a very significant decline in the propensity to move from one child to a second, in urban areas, and from two children to three, in both rural and urban areas (Feeney 1994: 129; Sanderson and Tan 1995: 115). The effect was dramatic. In 1970, the overall Chinese birth rate was about 34 per thousand population, the same as in the mid-1950s; in 1973 it stood at 28, and by 1979 it had gone down to 18 (Aird 1982: 269). Not all of this change was voluntary. Local abuses were flagrant enough for the central leadership to intervene, with a campaign against coercion in 1978, but the pressure for birth control was maintained, so the signals from the centre were contradictory. In 1980 party leader Hua Guofeng again castigated 'impermissible' compulsion in the implementation of the population policy (Aird 1982: 285–86).

It was upon this success that the Chinese government in 1979 adopted a one-child policy, backed up with financial penalties and official pressures towards sterilization and to abortion of 'excessive' pregnancies. While on the whole effective, its actual implementation and outcomes have been more moderate than the policy proclaimed (see, for example, the provincial insights provided by Greenhalgh (1993) and Li (1995)). The 1980 target of a population not exceeding 1.2 billion in 2000 was not reached, exceeded by 66 million in 1999, and the actual fertility rate for 1995–2000 was 1.8 children (UNDP 2002: table 5).

When embarking in the early 1970s upon their policies of drastic fertility reduction, the Chinese leaders could draw upon a popular tendency already manifest in the cities, but the use of the campaign apparatus of the ruling Communist Party provided both ruthlessness and effectiveness. Family planning meant a politically planned demography, with birth quotas coming from the national plan centre and then specified down to annual birth quotas for work units and neighbourhoods. Article 12 of the 1980 Marriage Law stipulated that: 'Husband and wife are in duty bound to practice family planning'. Enormous pressure, not seldom including outright coercion, was deployed. The maintenance of IUDs was checked by X-raying. Non-authorized pregnancies were under great pressure to be aborted. However, the Marriage Law, with its female minimum age of 20, pulled the carpet from under the 1970s campaigns for 'late marriages', meaning from the age of 24, and the socioeconomic changes, with their much enhanced scope for private initiatives, tended to weaken the bullying power of the party machine.

In more closed and authoritarian China the coercive abuses never became a great scandal – unlike the mass sterilization camps of the mid-1970s in more open India – although occasionally they became flagrant enough for central condemnation. But the process happened to be watched by a Stanford PhD student in Guangdong in the early 1980s, Steven Mosher (1983, 1993), who with the help of Catholic media and of *Reader's Digest* conveyed shrill horror stories to the US public. There the stories plugged into the local, hotly controversial abortion debate, and this intervention led to the ironic result that opposition to birth control in China became, in January 1990, a valid reason for political asylum in the USA, the country which more than any other has pushed (non-coercive) birth control in the world.

The caution of elected politicians, in India, Ceylon/Sri Lanka or in Kenya (see below), and their contrast to the abrasive explicitness of, say, Ayub Khan, or the full-scale commitment of the military regimes of Park Chung Hee in South Korea, Chiang Kai-shek in Taiwan, Thanom and Praphat in Thailand, Suharto in Indonesia, and of the tough-minded civilian authoritarian governments of Lee Kuan Yew in Singapore, Tunku Abdul Rahman in Malaysia, or Ferdinand Marcos in the Philippines, and the Communist authorities of China and Vietnam, is striking.

Kenya is the India of Black Africa in terms of family planning, the governmental pioneer and for a long time cautious and frustrated. The idea was developed by an outgoing colonial civil servant and was adopted by one of the leading politicians of independent Kenya, Tom Mboya, Minister of Planning and Development, and launched as a policy programme in 1967, with considerable foreign assistance, from Rockefeller's Population Council above all. President Kenyatta refrained from committing himself, and the whole programme had a rather low domestic profile until the mid-1980s, under the Moi Presidency. No visible effects were discovered until the census of 1989 (Ajayi and Kekovole 1998). Husbands, and males generally, had for long been hostile to birth control. One district study in the early 1970s found that most of the women who dropped out of the family planning programme did so because of opposition from clan or lineage elders (Oohiambo 1995). The dramatic size of the decline of the fertility rate, from 7.7 in 1984 to 6.7 in 1989, from survey data, has been criticized for sampling bias (Jensen 1996: 100ff), but the trend, upward since Independence as in India, had definitely turned at last.

The first major drop in sub-Saharan fertility occurred in Southern Africa and owed much to the wider spread of education and health services, further helped by the separation of couples through extensive male labour migration, rather than to specific public programmes of family planning. Zimbabwe and the more special cases of Botswana – diamond-rich, small population, very extensive labour migration – and the black population of South Africa led the way in bringing about a very substantial fertility decline between the mid-1970s and the mid-1980s (UNDP 1999a: table 'Demographic trends'). Anglo-Saxon birth control clinics had been introduced during the colonial government of Rhodesia, and a developed network of pharmacies and health clinics provided contraceptives. The white minority government provided 'field educators'. By the late 1980s, about twice as many women in Zimbabwe as in Kenya were using contraceptives (Kokole 1994: 83; Scribner 1995: 39; Jensen 1996: 102).

The peoples of Zimbabwe are generally very patriarchal (on the majority Shona, compare Meekers (1993b) and Jacobsson-Widding (2000)), but a strong (mainly Protestant) Christian missionary tradition of schooling turned out to be more important. By 1960 at least half of all girls were enrolled in primary schooling, and after Independence in 1980 a major educational drive brought full enrolment in a few years. In the late 1980s some third of girls were in secondary education. Botswana had a parallel educational expansion, whereas Kenya, which had a lead in primary education in 1980, stagnated afterwards. In 1990 the crucial secondary school enrolment in Kenya was less than half that of Zimbabwe and Botswana. In West Africa, the economic and political crises after 1980 led to a decline in school enrolment in the ensuing decade (Scribner 1995: table III: 3).

Most of Africa is, of course, not at risk of being overpopulated with regard to availability of land, and the Francophone and Francophile elites were for long deaf to all mention of family planning (Caldwell 1966: 165ff; Kokole 1994: 82). A couple of the more stable and modestly prosperous Francophone countries have also had special reasons for being uninterested. Ivory Coast and Gabon have actually faced a scarcity of labour and, in particular the former, are heavily dependent on foreign migrant labour. Sparsely populated, mineral-rich Gabon is furthermore part of the region of the continent suffering from pathological sterility, with a fertility rate in 1975 estimated at 4.3, rising to 5.4 ten years later.

So far, the traditional, still largely reproduced, low fecundity of Central Africa has been left out, as it manifests an undesired childlessness of a significant portion of unlucky women. Surveys from the 1950s showed a proportion of childless women, at the end of their fertile period, in populations of virtually universal marriage, of one in five in Congo (Leopoldville/Kinshasa, and Brazzaville) in 1960–61, of one-third in an area of Cameroon, one in eight in Mozambique, and one in ten in Angola (Brass *et al.* 1968: 67ff). The 1978 World Fertility Survey in Cameroon indicated that 28 per cent of women aged 50–54, i.e. born in the 1920s, were childless, and 15 per cent of women aged 45–49, born in the 1930s (cf. Larsen 1989).

At Arusha in Tanzania in 1984, African government representatives, preparing for the world conference on population in Bucharest, adopted a resolution that 'Governments should ensure the availability and accessiblity of family planning services to all couples or individuals seeking such services freely or at subsidized prices' (Chamie 1994: 43). In 1989 Nigeria launched a policy of birth control, and in the first half of 1990s long-reluctant governments, like those of Senegal and Ivory Coast, began to promote contraception (International Planned Parenthood Federation 1999).

Neither politically nor economically have most Africans had much reason to feel a new sense of mastery after Independence. Children and kin have remained the most reliable source of security in a brutalized world, where the winning lots have been few. Slowly, however, towards the end of the century, education was accumulating and media images of life-style options began to appear, and donor-aided governments supported fertility control.

In Latin America, a new population file was opened in 1967. There were two events, mutually ignored by their specific chroniclers. In April the International Planned Parenthood Federation held its Seventh World Conference in Santiago de Chile, benevolently inaugurated by the Catholic (Christian Democratic) President of the country, Eduardo Frei (Romero 1969). In September there was a more official, inter-governmental Organization of American States (OAS) conference in Caracas. Characteristic of the sensitivity of the issue at the time, it had no high-status political presence, neither from the host country nor from the OAS. Nevertheless, it was an important coming together of key officials, as well as scholars, putting birth control on the Latin American agenda. The rapporteur of the conference was a few years later the major designer of Mexico's policy of family planning, when President Echeverría reversed policy in 1972 and the year after replaced the natalist Mexican Population Law of 1936 with one of birth control (Mundigo 1996: 198–99; Brambila 1998).

Chilean studies of the early 1960s showed a massive frequency of (illegal) abortions, and the theological thaw in the Vatican turned Catholic public opinion in a more positive direction vis-à-vis birth control, primarily but not only in Chile. The progressive Primas of the Chilean Church, Cardinal Silva Herzog, expressed his support (Romero 1969: 138). The Frei government of Chile (1964–70) was also a period of major social modernization, with land reform and massive health improvements bringing down the high infant mortality rate from 108 to 79. The Chilean birth rate declined from an average of 34.5 in 1960–64 to 29.6 for 1965–69, and the fertility rate fell from 5.3 to 4.4 (Chackiel and Schkolnik 1996: table 1.1). With Costa Rica – the other most Euro-Creole country in Latin America, after the early birth controllers of Argentina and Uruguay – Chile had the strongest birth reduction of the 1960s in Latin America.

However, in the Americas of the 1960s, it was the Afro-Creole countries of Barbados and Trinidad–Tobago which had the fastest reduction, from birth rates of 32.4 and 38.4 in 1959–60 to 20.5 and 25.3 in 1969–70, respectively. By 1970 their fertility rates were down to 3.0 and 3.6 respectively. In the Latin

Caribbean the second half of the 1960s saw significant, but less dramatic, reductions of fertility in the Dominican Republic, Puerto Rico and Venezuela. Jamaica, where family planning policy started in the mid-1960s, was a decade later, as was the more gradual decline in poverty-stricken Haiti (World Bank 1992: national tables; Chackiel and Schkolnik 1996: table 1.1; Mitchell 1998a: table A6). Barbados and Trinidad managed rather early, before the rest of the Caribbean and before Mauritius, to re-orient their traditional, no longer profitable sugar plantation economy to manufacturing and tourism, which opened new opportunities to the new generations, especially to women (cf. Handwerker 1989).

Brazil, as late as the 1960s, had no reliable vital statistics, and the fertility estimates differ. The Latin American Demographic Center estimated (in 1995) a Brazilian fertility decline from five-year averages of 6.2 for 1950–65 to 5.3 for 1965–70 (Chackiel and Schkolnik 1996: table 1.1). This seems to be an exaggeration. Brazilian demographers give a quinquennial rate of 5.8 for 1965–70 and an annual rate of 5.8 for 1970 (Carvalho and Rodriguez Wong 1996: table 21.3; Martine 1996: 48). The main fall occurred in the 1970s.

Brazilian change was mainly a cultural process, although the military dictatorship from 1965 took a permissive stance on birth control. Schooling, from the birth cohort of 1940 onwards, rapid proletarianization, urbanization, large-scale internal northeast–south migration in the 1950s and 1960s, and mass media developments in the 1960s and 1970s altered the context and prospects of coupling and family formation. The extension of private health services committed, for economic reasons, to births by caesarean section, provided an institutional anchorage for birth control by female sterilization. Abortion was also frequent, although basically illegal.

Whereas Brazil has an important component of Afro-Creole families, the other big country of Latin America, Mexico, harbours an Indian variant of the Creole family system. From Paraguay to Mexico, these family systems were later and more gradual in their fertility decline until 1975, than were the Euro- and the Afro-Creole ones. In 1973 Mexico, with an elective one-party system, adopted a public birth control programme, judged the most vigorous in Latin America, together with that of Colombia (Mundigo 1996: 205). Swimming with a cultural current it was a great success: Mexican fertility declined from 6.4 in 1972 to 4.5 in 1980 (World Bank 1992: 418).

Latin American fertility decline started late in the timescale of social development, 150 years after national independence, and then at levels of GDP, de-agrarianization, urbanization and literacy much higher than in Asia and Africa. The stark inequalities of the region meant that there was neither much sense of personal mastery of one's life among the masses, nor much of a national development conception – as distinctive from elite 'civilization' – among the rulers. As we saw above, contemporary education differentials of fertility are larger in Latin America than in other world regions, and so are rural–urban differentials.

Without any exception among the 33 countries of the international Demographic Health Surveys of 1985–92, rural women have significantly more children than urban. In ten Latin American countries in the 1980s – including Brazil, Colombia, and smaller countries – city women had on the (unweighted) average 2.3 fewer children than their rural sisters. The urban–rural divide was less in North Africa, at 1.9 children, and in sub-Saharan Africa, at 1.4. Urbanity and education work both by postponing (later on also by avoiding) marriage and by more fertility control inside marriage. Marital fertility therefore differs less along education and residence lines than total fertility, but still very markedly in Latin America. Married urban women in Mexico and Peru, for instance, had 2.4 more children than married women in the countryside over the same period of marriage, in Brazil 1.6 (Muhari 1994). On the whole, it seems that the late fertility decline in (most of) Latin America and its relatively slow downward trend are due largely to the stark inequalities of the subcontinent – educational, urban–ural ethnic and class inequalities. Also the World Fertility Surveys of the 1970s found the widest urban–rural differences in Latin America (Singh and Casterline 1985: table 9.5).

Moving against oneself?

The second wave of fertility decline in the more developed world

The second international wave of fertility decline also touched the rich world, in the last third of the twentieth century. In size it was not comparable to that of the Third World, and could not be because of the already lowered fertility, but it was important because it fell well below the rate of population replacement. It was definitely not promoted by governments, although in contrast to the first wave, only in Eastern Europe was there any defensive governmental action (mentioned above). Where demand for it was needed, abortion was liberalized and contraceptives made fully legal. But John Caldwell (2001) is right in highlighting the coincidence as an important instance of global change to be explained.

In Table 8.3 we are dealing, first of all, with different trajectories. Eastern European fertility was continuously falling from its brief post-war recovery, most probably due to the difficulties of combining having children with the push for high female labour force participation. But the fall was slowed down after 1965 or 1970, precipitating with the restoration of capitalism in the 1990s. Japanese fertility plummeted after 1949, with government promotion – adapting to the end of imperialist expansion – and the 1965 figure is part of a slight, and temporary, recovery after a slump in the first half of the 1960s.

The fertility rates of the New Worlds of European settlement, for their part, were declining from quite high levels, which peaked in the USA in 1957 at 3.77 children per woman (the highest rate on its twentieth-century record), in Canada in 1959 at 3.94, and in Australia in 1961 at 3.55. The fastest US decline took place between 1961 and 1965, with a decline of 0.7 child in four years. The American rate, but not the Australian or Canadian, then recovered significantly after 1980, almost returning at least to replacement level.

Table 8.3 Total fertility rates in the developed world, 1965–2000

	1965	1970	1980	2000
Western Europe				
France	2.84	2.47	1.95	1.89
(West) Germany	2.51	1.99	1.45	1.36
Italy	2.66	2.43	1.64	1.21
Scandinavia[a]	2.62	2.05	1.65	1.72
Spain	2.94	2.88	2.20	1.24
UK	2.86	2.43	1.89	1.65
Eastern Europe				
Poland	2.69	2.26	2.26	1.34
Russia	2.12	2.00	1.86	1.21
North America and Oceania				
Canada	3.15	2.33	1.71	1.6[b]
USA	2.93	2.48	1.82	2.0[b]
Australia	2.97	2.85	1.94	1.8[b]
East Asia				
Japan	2.14	2.13	1.75	1.4[b]

Sources: Europe: Council of Europe (2001a: table T3.3); outside Europe, 1965–80: Chesnais (1992: table A2.4); 1995–2000: UNDP (2002: table 5).

Notes:
a Average of Denmark, Finland, Norway and Sweden.
b Average 1995–2000.

In Western Europe, finally, 1965 was more or less the peak of post-war fertility, from which two downward routes may be distinguished. One trend, seen in Northern–Central–Western Europe, was an early plunge after the peak, in the second half of the 1960s, followed by a certain stabilization, or even slight recuperation after 1980–85; Austria, Germany, Switzerland (reaching lowest), Scandinavia, the Low Countries, France and the UK are examples. The southern trajectory, taken by Greece, Italy, Spain and, less clearly, Portugal, declines later, after 1975–80, and then continues downhill until around 1995, after which it flattens out.

In terms of the economics of children, the Northern European–North American fertility decline of the 1960s and early 1970s was a historical novelty. This was the first time that a significant fertility decline accompanied accelerated prosperity, following upon a long decade of growth. The effect of bad times remained – as seen most clearly in Sweden and Finland in the early to mid-1990s and, dramatically, in the impoverishment of the bulk of Eastern European and Caucasian populations after 1989–91 – but on a new schedule.

Leaving out further consideration of the Eastern European experience in this context, and concentrating attention on Western Europe and the USA, there are four obvious commonalities of this part of the second wave. Of global impact is the launch of new contraceptives: the pill hit the US market in 1960, and Western Europe four or five years later. Global also is the onslaught on patriarchy by the rise of feminism and the women's movement. Global, thirdly, is the expansion of female education in this part of the world, the universalization of secondary and the wide expansion of tertiary education. More specific is the increase of female labour-force participation, driven, not – as later in many poor countries – by poverty, but by a new life-course priority of independent income, of interesting work, and of a career.

Between 1960 and 1970 labour-force participation among women aged 20–24 rose by 11 percentage points in the USA, and by 8 in Denmark and Sweden. In the age group 25–54 the Scandinavian change was spectacular – a Danish increase of 19 percentage points in ten years, and in Sweden 17 points. The Norwegian rate rose from a low base by 10 percentage points, and the Finnish from a very high one by almost 9 points. Only Australia and Canada were close to the highest Scandinavian figures, 17 and 12 points, respectively. The US, French, British, Italian and German ones were more modest: seven, seven, six, five, and three points, respectively.

After the war, Germany had a sizeable female contingent on the labour market, particularly teenagers, and while total female labour-force participation actually declined slightly in West Germany after 1960, education increased instead. The proportion of West German teenage girls on the labour market went down from 76 per cent in 1960 to 55 per cent in 1970. Though female education continued to lag after male in the Federal Republic, there was a large expansion, of tertiary as well as secondary education. By 1975, the share of German women aged 20–24 years in full-time education was third in an OECD ranking, after the USA and Scandinavia (OECD 1979).

Female higher education then continued to rise rapidly in the rich world. By the end of the twentieth century there were substantially more women in higher education than men (in Norway and Sweden 40 per cent more) in all the most developed countries except Japan and Switzerland, where they were 15–25 per cent fewer, and in Germany, where they were almost equal. Young women are entering the twenty-first century more highly educated than men in several other parts of the world too: in Eastern Europe, in Latin America (though not yet in Mexico and Chile) and the Caribbean, in Southeast Asia, Turkey, and the oil-rich Arab states including Saudi Arabia. South Asia and most of Africa (as well as China) are still outside this educational gender revolution, and are likely to keep the momentum of fertility change in remaining relatively high-fertility countries (UNDP 2002: table 24)

This second, developed world branch of the second wave has an international social movement as its crucial agency, but operating under varying conditions. The relative weight of the compound of factors is likely to have differed. New, cheap, accessible contraceptives were clearly significant, not just the pill, but also IUD, sterilization and highly functional diaphragms. One of the most clinching arguments for the importance of contraceptives is Caldwell's (2001: table 2) observation that the 1960s saw fertility declining among the indigenous populations of South Africa, Canada and New Zealand, and somewhat later in Australia. On the other hand, new contraceptives were not necessary. As Caldwell pointed out, US fertility began to decline before the pill; furthermore, contraceptive use was widespread in the developed world before the pill (Frejka and Ross 2001: 234ff), and simple methods had brought fertility below replacement in northwestern Europe before World War II.

A non-mechanical way of disentangling the dynamics of the rich-world branch of the second wave might be to decompose it. A full comparative schedule is not available for this, but let us sort out a few components. Who were the women who restricted their childbearing? The Council of Europe (2001b) provides us with some noteworthy data, which I have supplemented with recent Swedish demographic statistics.

The largest decline of child-bearing occurs in the female age-group of 20–24, with the category of 25–29 a distant second. Percentagewise the decline tends to be largest among teenagers, but they did not contribute many children in the European family system. This pattern indicates an effect of higher education and of a new desire to enter the labour market before any full-time family commitment. Contraceptives then meant that education and a job were not necessarily asexual options.

When the birth decline set in, it tended to affect women of all ages, which points to some common contraceptive and/or labour market determinant. However, what distinguished the northwestern from the Southern European path was that in the former countries, although not in Germany really, there was a compensatory fertility after the age of 30, by the early 1990s (in Germany there was a diminishing birth reduction at older ages but no compensation). In the UK, for instance, women above 30 gave birth more in 1990 than in 1970. Swedish women born in 1965 had more babies at the age of 25 or above than women born in 1940.

This difference should most probably be seen as affected by a much larger provision of child-care as well as of part-time jobs, than in Southern Europe, thereby making it much easier to combine children and employment. This may account for the noteworthy fact that whereas the OECD fertility rate in 1980 was negatively associated with female employment and female tertiary education, in 1998 it was positively correlated (Castles 2003).[1]

Another pattern of fertility change is the categorical birth distributions among women. Childlessness as a large-scale phenomenon was pioneered in West Germany, by the birth cohort of 1955. Finally childless were about a tenth of Western European women in the mid- to late twentieth century, but the West German generation of 1955 brought it to 22 per cent (Eurostat 2002: table E12). Among American women born in 1954–60 the 2000 US census found a similar rate of childlessness, 19 per cent. Third or higher-order children were 29 per cent of all births in West Germany in 1960 and 42 per cent of all Dutch births. In 1999–2000 they make up 18 per cent in both countries, and the decline of higher-than-two-order births surpassed the total birth decline in the Netherlands, while making up less than half the decrease in Germany.

The 'total fertility rate' (TFR) is a very conjectural measure and very sensitive to changes of age at childbirth. Between 1970 and 2000, the mean age at Western European first childbirth rose by about 4 years, and women's mean age at first marriage increased by 5 years (Eurostat 2002: tables E10, F9). Let us therefore look at completed fertility by age cohorts, actual and, for the youngest, estimated (Table 8.4). The rapid fertility decline in northwestern

Europe after 1965 was largely a postponement of, rather than an abstention from, having children. The most drastic changers were not so much those born in the 1940s (the '1968ers'), but their children. The table also means that the total fertility rates of the 1980s and 1990s underestimated the actual number of children born to the generations of the 1950s and the 1960s (cf. Bongaarts 2001b: table 1).

Birth deficits: unintended low fertility

Around 2000 in the Council of Europe (2001a: table T3.6) area, only Iceland and Turkey, and possibly Albania, are producing enough children to replace their current generations. In the long run this will spawn a number of social problems, of ageing and fewer people to shoulder the burdens of pensions and caring, of declining populations, aggravating the costs of ageing and diminishing the politico-economic clout of the countries affected.

However, not only the socio-politico-economic effects of this are unintended. Individuals and couples are going against their own desires, or they are at least holding their satisfaction below ideal. In this sense, there is a kind of 'moving against oneself' in the developed world branch of the second wave of fertility decline. Actual fertility rates do not correspond to the desires and expectations of individuals and couples. Table 8.4, with estimated completed fertility up to the female of generation 1965, and the current well- below-replacement rates of fertility should be compared to the expected family size of young Europeans (Table 8.5). Males of the same generation have about the same expectations of children, but sometimes one decimal place lower. In terms of expectations and ideals, it is Germany, and not Southern Europe as in TFR tables, which stands out, for reasons that go back at least to the mid-1950s generation. But also in Germany, actual outcome is clearly below expectations.

From Table 8.5, and from earlier surveys such as an EEC one in 1979 (Girard and Roussel 1982: table 1), it is clear that the actual number of children born to women of the late 1950s, the 1960s and most likely the 1970s was lower than the number expected and wanted. The recent decline of Western fertility,

Table 8.4 Completed fertility in Europe by female birth cohorts

Country	First cohort with <2 children		Fertility of 1965 birth cohort
	Birth year	*Fertility*	
France	1965	1.92	1.92
(West) Germany	1940	1.97	1.48
Italy	1950	1.88	1.67 (1960)
Russia	1940	1.94	1.65
Scandinavia	1950	1.97	1.96
Spain	1955	1.90	1.76 (1960)
UK	1960	1.97	1.87

Source: Council of Europe (2001a: table T3.7).

Table 8.5 Expected number of children by young European and American women

	Latest birth cohort	*Number of children expected*
France	1969–73	2.1
Germany	1967/68–72	1.8
Italy	1971–75 (and 1961–70)	2.1
Spain	1975–77 (and 1955–75)	2.2
Sweden	1969	2.4
Switzerland	1970–74	2.2
USA	1971–75	2.3

Source: Fertility and Family Surveys 1990s (table 24).

then, is not the outcome of a desire for fewer children. Rather, it largely derives from a changed set of women's priorities. First an education, then a job, and then a family. That is, the same priority list as of old for males of the European family system. But then for some, a suitable partner may be hard to find, or the career may enter into a 'hot' phase, and there may not be time enough to bear two children (cf. Pérez-Díaz *et al.* 2000: ch. 4; SCB 2001b).

Alone (with Iceland) among the rich countries, the USA is maintaining a fertility rate close to net reproduction, even though below the number of children expected. This is mainly due to the recent mass Hispanic immigration, producing a fifth of all American births in 2000 (US Census Bureau 2001b), and to the Afro-American contribution (Table 8.6). The USA differs demographically from Europe and Japan because of its wider openness to external, and above all extra-continental immigration. From 1980 to 1999, US fertility rose from 1.84 to 2.08, i.e. virtually up to replacement level, mainly because of immigration. Germany, with a 1998 fertility rate of 1.4, got 14.3 per cent of its new-born babies from its foreign population of 8.9 per cent, too little to balance native barrenness (Statistisches Bundesamt 2000: table 3.24.2). Euro-American women have about the same fertility as French or Scandinavian women.

Summing up: the routes to fertility decline – convergent or divergent?

We might sum up the long, winding, and complex world history of mass fertility decline by highlighting the main processes and their contexts. The

Table 8.6 Ethnic fertility in women in the USA, 1999

Ethnicity	*Fertility*
European descent	1.85
Asian	1.93
Afro-American	2.15
Hispanic	2.98
All US	2.08

Source: Hacker (2000: 14).

crucial agencies of Figure 7.1 can now be identified, and the contexts spelled out (Box 8.1). Like all brief summaries, this is, of course, a good deal stereotypical, and the relative weight of the variables is still often hypothetical. Nevertheless, I do think that the crucial common variables and the most significant differences of a complex, 200-year-long historical process are highlighted in Box 8.1 below.

Box 8.1 World routes of fertility decline

Mass pioneers, first third of the nineteenth century
　　Family range: post-revolutionary French and American couples
　　Process: socio-cultural, outside the state
　　Socio-economic context: commercial agriculture
　　Political context: revolutions
　　Cultural context: first secularization or religious dissent and anti-traditionalist
　　　　individualism
　　Higher sense of personal mastery: enhanced by revolutionary change
　　Higher costs of children: farm inheritance costs
　　Crucial agency: national social movement
　　Family system channel: conjugal decision

First wave (1880–1930)
　　Family system range: European, all major variants; East Asian Japanese, as
　　　　latecomer
　　Process: socio-cultural against the state
　　Socio-economic context: de-agrarianization, mass migration, mortality decline
　　Political context: movements of dissent and protest
　　Cultural context: first secularization, mass circulation newspapers
　　Higher sense of personal mastery: breaks of socio-economic and cultural moulds
　　Higher costs of children: compulsory schooling
　　Crucial agency: conglomerate of international social movements of dissent
　　Family system channel: conjugal decision under beginning of erosion of patriarchy

Second wave (1965–2000)
　A. Third World
　　Family range: eventually all so far unaffected, beginning with East Asian and
　　　　Southeast Asian, and ending with Arab-Muslim, Muslim South Asian, and
　　　　African
　　Process: state developmentalism, in Asia and Africa with foreign Western aid
　　Socio-economic context: development economics, de-agrarianization, rapid
　　　　population growth
　　Political context: post-colonial independence, global population policy, gradually
　　　　global feminism
　　Cultural context: availability of contraceptives for low-motivated mass use,
　　　　transistor radio, TV
　　Higher sense of personal mastery: largely derived from state and other external
　　　　helpers, sometimes by land reform, little by national independence per se
　　Higher costs of children: from lowered mortality and growing schooling
　　Crucial agency: the state, in South Asia and Africa also foreign donor
　　　　organizations; socio-cultural movements significant in Latin America, and
　　　　elsewhere, once the state impetus took root
　　Family system channels: by-passing, undermining patriarchal decision structures

B. *Most developed world*
> *Family range:* European in all its variants, Japanese
> *Process:* socio-cultural movement, with state toleration
> *Socio-economic context:* unprecedented prosperity, de-industrialization, expansion of higher education
> *Political context:* rise of feminism
> *Cultural context:* mass modernism, second secularization, invention of female-controlled contraceptives
> *Higher sense of personal mastery:* women's emancipation from patriarchy and couples' from a priori traditionalism
> *Higher costs of children:* increased 'opportunity costs' in relation to higher education, an independent income, and to a career
> *Crucial agency:* women's movement in broad and loose sense
> *Family system channel:* individual decisions in post-patriarchal relations.

The role of the state and the character of the family system constitute the major divides between the first and the Third World second intercontinental waves of birth control. The first wave was everywhere against state policy, and was carried only by European family systems, with the latter's core in Western Europe, off-shoots under different conditions in overseas settlements, and, conversely, a rather different Eastern variant, affected by assimilating conditions. The second had always either the active promotion or at the very least the benevolent support of the state. It finally covered all the remaining world family systems, but at least the South Asian and the African proved themselves capable of strong resistance. In view of widespread stereotypes, the relatively receptive reactions of Arab Muslim families and of non-Arab West Asian Muslims, from Turkey to Iran, are worth noticing, as well as the fact that Indonesian Muslims embraced birth control at the same time as Mexican Christians.

The two currents of the second wave had very different economic contexts – development hopes or frustrations versus successfully achieved prosperity – and were carried by very different agencies, by states and their foreign helpers, on one hand, by a socio-cultural movement tolerated, but not at all furthered, by the state, on the other. However, they also had features in common, new contraceptives, rapid educational expansion – although at different levels – and an increasingly global feminism.

The family system has been a crucial variable in both waves, but always operating in specific historical socio-political settings. The 'demographic transition' is not a linear process of individuals and couples on a certain level of mortality and socio-economic development, but a complex, historically situated social process, inserted in family systems, class relations, socio-cultural movements, and states.

The sense of mastery, crucial to decision-making about birth control, drew upon two major historical sources. A collective, and individualized, modernism was one, bred originally from high class, then from social revolution, later from mass modernist movements, or from mass media. In the developed world second wave it was further enhanced by post-industrial individualism, and by de-patriarchalization and feminism. The other was a state-induced civic opportunity-cum-obligation, deriving from new economic developmentalist doctrines and, in some cases, from preoccupations with very high density of population. Either way, the families of the world changed crucially.

In everyday human life, the secular decline of fertility, in conjunction with the postponement of death at all ages, has created new, or much more common 'non-traditional', domestic situations, and new life-course stages: the deliberately childless couple, the only-child-childhood, the empty-nest middle-aged couple (Hareven 2000: 138), the single elderly person household (cf. Gundy 1999). We shall come back to the family challenges of the future.

With respect to the number of children, the families of the world have not become of one kind. But we may finally ask, are they becoming more or less similar, or different? Among the Western families of Table 7.1, the century 1900–2000 saw the absolute differences, in total fertility rates, diminish, but the relative differences, in relation to the lower average, actually increased slightly. For the fourteen countries of Table 7.1, average TFR went down from 4.2 to 1.6 children per woman. The absolute spread, measured by the standard deviation, diminished from 0.60 to 0.23 but the coefficient of variation, tapping relative dispersion, increased from 0.14 around 1900 to 0.15 in 1995–2000 (calculated from Table 7.1 and UNDP 2002: table 5).

The more interesting question, however, is what has happened on the global level (Table 8.8). Here there is a data problem: for the first half of the past century, available fertility data are very patchy. In order not to give undue weight to countries for which data are available, our analysis will be restricted to a small set of major countries, for which there are data at least from the earlier part of the twentieth century if not from 1900. For Africa and Latin America, no major country with a sufficiently long time series was found, and instead the following decisions were made.

For Latin America, there is a long time series for Argentina – in the eyes of Argentines certainly a major country, even though its population weight is much lighter than that of Brazil and Mexico. But Argentina had a demographic development very different from most of its neighbours. Peru, for which historical demographic estimates back to the late nineteenth century exist, seems to be a much better proxy. It then turns out that that historical estimate (5.8) is almost identical to the overall Latin American rate around 1950, estimated at 5.9, so I have opted for using the latter as an estimate of fertility in 1900, as one alternative. From the crude birth rates, we know that fertility in Latin American countries moved both up (for example Colombia, Mexico, Venezuela) and down (for instance Argentina, Chile, Uruguay) between the early part and middle of the twentieth century (Mitchell 1998a: table A6). But given the weight of Brazil (a good quarter of the hemispheric population in 1900, like Mexico), we may also pay attention to an uncertain Brazilian estimate of a fertility rate of 7.7 in 1903, going down to 5.9 in 1950 (Berquó 2001: table 2). An alternative Latin American estimate for 1900 will then be 6.5, midway between Brazilian and Hispanic estimates. As Table 8.7 shows, the statistical effect of the different estimates is slight.

Table 8.7 Fertility in major countries or regions of the world, 1896/1900–1995/2000
(total fertility rates, children per woman)

	1896–1900	*1950–55*	*1995–2000*
Germany	5.0	2.4	1.3
USA	3.8	3.4	2.0
Russia	7.1	2.9	1.2
Japan	5.4[a]	2.8	1.4
China	5.5[b]	6.0	1.8
India	5.8	6.0	3.3
Egypt	6.4[c]	6.6	3.4
Latin America	5.9–6.5[d]	5.9	2.7
Sub-Saharan Africa	6.0–6.5[d]	6.0–6.5[d]	5.8

Statistics[e]
A. Latin America at 5.9 and Africa at 6.5 in 1900–55

Mean	5.8	4.7	2.5
S.d.	0.90	1.68	1.39
C.v.	0.16	0.36	0.55

B. Latin America at 6.5 in 1900, Africa at 6.5

Mean	5.8	unchanged	unchanged
S.d.	0.94	unchanged	unchanged
C.v.	0.16	unchanged	unchanged

C. Latin America at 5.9 in 1900, Africa at 6.0 in 1900–55

Mean	5.7	4.7	2.5
S.d.	0.87	1.63	0.39
C.v.	0.15	0.35	0.55

D. Latin America at 6.5 in 1900, Africa at 6.0

Mean	5.7	unchanged	unchanged
S.d.	0.91	unchanged	unchanged
C.v.	0.16	unchanged	unchanged

E. Latin America at 5.9 in 1900, Africa excluded

Mean	5.6	4.5	2.1
S.d.	0.91	1.66	0.83
C.v.	0.16	0.37	0.39

Sources: 1896–1900 and 1950–55: Germany, USA and Japan: Chesnais (1992: appendix tables A2.1 and A2.3); Russia (1900): author's calculation from the special indices used by Coale *et al.* (1979: 16, 124, 212); Latin America and Peru: Ferrando and Aramburú (1996: 417); Brazil (see text): Berquó (2001: table 2); China: Lee and Wang (1999: 85); India: Bhat (1989: 111); Egypt: Fargues (1989: 152); Africa: Coale and Lorimer (1968: table 4.2); van de Walle (1968: table 5.32); World Fertility Surveys (1980s); Cameroon, Ghana, Lesotho, Nigeria, Senegal; 1995–2000: UNDP (2002: table 5).

Notes:
a 1920.
b 22 provinces 1929–31.
c 1937.
d Estimated by backward extrapolation, see text.
e Statistics: Mean is unweighted, S.d.=standard deviation, C.v.=coefficient of variation.

For sub-Saharan Africa, there are only incomplete data for mid-century. The first large-scale reliable data are from the World Fertility Surveys of the 1970s, while there is a set of expert estimates from the 1950s. Unknown are the fertility effects of the ravages of the late nineteenth-century colonial conquests, which in Congo cannot be assumed insignificant by 1900. Nevertheless, in the first decades of the twentieth century, the population of sub-Saharan Africa began to grow again (Caldwell 1985; Coquery-Vidrovitch 2003), and before modern birth control fertility rates tended to be rather stable. On the basis, then, of the early demographic estimates and the World Fertility Survey data, African fertility has been extrapolated backwards, as most likely to have been in the 6–6.5 range, with a reservation for possible colonial disruption in 1900, but not long after.

Globally, the twentieth-century fertility history is divergent. In this respect the world's families are becoming increasingly different. In absolute as well as in relative terms, dispersion is higher around 2000 than a hundred years earlier. By mid-century, the absolute differences were still larger, though. The uncertainties about Africa and Latin America do not affect the robustness of this result, as shown by the five statistical parts of Table 8.8. The same result as in Table 8.7 comes out of a calculation of dispersion among fourteen regions of the world for the period 1950/55–1990/95 identified by Caldwell (2001: table 1): a decrease of the standard deviation (from 1.74 to 1.33) and an increase of the coefficient of variation (from 0.37 to 0.46).

The twentieth century of the Christian or Common Era saw the historical peak of population growth, in its third quarter, and it also contained a unique historical turn to deliberate, peacetime below-reproduction fertility among the world's leading countries. In the second third of the century, history's most ambitious birth promotion programmes were launched, and in the last third unique and forceful state interventions for birth restriction. By the early twenty-first century the world as a whole is heading back to a pre-1750 slow growth pattern of human population. The era of the demographic transition is closing.

Conclusions
The century gone, the century coming

In the preceding chapters we have followed, over more than a century, three sets of family processes across the planet, the trajectory of the rights and powers of fathers and husbands, of patriarchy in short, the vicissitudes of marriage and of extra-marital sexual coupling, and the shifting life course of human fertility. What we found then is not going to be repeated here. Instead, we shall try to conclude by an explanatory overview of the global dynamics of family change in the period studied, and by a brief assessment of the sum of changes.

The global dynamics of family institutional change

All over the world, the institution of the family has changed in the course of the past century. Some changes have been epochal – the erosion of patriarchy, the worldwide establishment of birth control, and some large populations setting out to natural decline. Sex and marriage have changed radically before, and their mutations in the twentieth century do not yet amount to a new global era. But from a provincial European or North American outlook, the sexual revolution and informal coupling are about to take unprecedented dimensions.

While family change has been universal, the starting-point, the timing, the pace, and the amount of change of the three dimensions of family relations studied in this book have differed greatly across the globe. Even within regions changes have varied widely, like patriarchy in Western Europe, marriage in Southeast Asia, or fertility in Latin America and in South Asia. To grasp and to convey one pattern of global secular change, then, is a daunting task.

Figures of change

The concrete overall change pattern is different among our three clusters of variables. The twentieth-century history of patriarchy is basically one of step-wise decline, begun at different points in time across the world. The first breakthrough came in the 1910s, by broadly consensual reform in Scandinavia, by violent revolution in Russia. The late 1940s and early 1950s provided another important ladder of descent, this time centred in East Asia – in Japan under American occupation and in China through Communist Revolution. The Communist takeover of Eastern Europe meant that the bell tolled for institutionalized patriarchy there too. Without being implemented in the short term, the UN Declaration of Human Rights signalled an important global constitutional victory against patriarchy. Finally the years following upon '1968', in particular the years around 1975 (the International Women's Year), released a worldwide wave against the special powers and privileges of husbands and fathers, with the first breaks coming in Western Europe and North America, but leaving no part of the planet untouched.

Marriage change has the shape of an inverted V in Western Europe and the Americas. That is, referring to marriage frequency which rose towards mid-century, and descended in the last third of it. After the convulsions of colonial conquest and slavery in the Americas, including post-Independence crises in Hispanic America, and of proletarianization in Western Europe, a marital stabilization began in the late nineteenth century, carried by industrialization and economic development, which continued into the post-World War II boom, with some brief conjunctural effects of the world wars and the Depression. Before the end of the unprecedented boom and prosperity, marriage in these regions took a new, downward path, aided by the new economic crisis of Latin America. Scandinavia, with its old flexibility of marriage, has been in the vanguard.

In the rest of the world, the high flat plateau of virtually universal marriage has been basically maintained, until the post-Communist plunge in Eastern Europe. Some big Asian cities and Southern Africa provide recent exceptions, of marital decline. In terms of age, there is a J-shaped age curve of later female marriage, though less clear in sub-Saharan Africa than in North Africa and all over Asia.

Fertility declined in two different international waves, after pioneering mass change in post-revolutionary France and the USA in the early nineteenth century. One, covering all Europe and the European settlements overseas, started after the Depression of the 1870s and ran into the Depression of the 1930s. The other was global and rolled in the last third of the century, at different pace in different parts of the world. In between there was a significant contra-flow of recovered fertility in the first wave countries, and significant oscillations have continued in recent years, for instance in Scandinavia and the United States.

However, with all three variables and their trajectories, there are three common noteworthy features. First, they are all patterned, in timing, pace and amount of change, by the family system. Second, they are temporally uneven, with clearly discernible breaking points, statistical as well as legal, and with periods of no or insignificant change alternating with ones of rapid transformation. Third, often, but not always, they are remarkably synchronized in space, into international or intercontinental waves of change, or at least of attempts at change.

On a more abstract, analytical level, this means that family change in the twentieth century has been neither evolutionary nor unilinear, findings which run counter to mid-twentieth-century 'modernization' as well as to early twentieth-century evolutionism. But how then to get at the cadence of global family change? The approach adopted here might be summed up as a global analysis of institutional change of family systems, i.e. a three-pronged explanation, looking at the family systems, their most pertinent characteristics and their mutability/resilience (including that of their cultural props), at processes of institutional change, and at the global dynamics involved.

Family systems and the process of institutional change

Family systems do not seem to possess an intrinsic dynamic – their changes are exogenous, coming from outside. But the historical line-up about 1900 of major family systems in the world differed in their baseline characteristics, and in their adaptability or resistance to new challenges. The Western European family was by far the least patriarchal in a very patriarchal world. Alone in the world, Catholic Christianity insisted on marriage by consent only, qualified by the Protestant Fathers and down-pedalled by the Orthodox clergy, but nevertheless an important European legacy of its Middle Ages. Western Europe had a marriage system with an old flexibility in responding to good and bad economic times, which in 1900 had been under severe strain from nineteenth-century proletarianization and rapid urbanization. Its neolocal pattern of household formation meant that fertility decisions were basically in the hands of the couples themselves. A major restraint was the religious enthronement of a patriarchal family of uncontrolled fertility, and there was also the patriarchy of the early modern French Revolution, expressed in the Napoleonic Civil Code, which was the model for all Latin Europe and America, and for the Netherlands.

The Eastern European variant was much more patriarchal, including a patrilocal household norm, and involved virtually universal marriage. In some ways it was more similar to the Asian systems than to the Western European. But in contrast to the former, Eastern Europe was monogamous, had a relatively symmetrical fault-divorce right, and did not practise female seclusion. Although marriages were usually parentally arranged, the Christian norm of consent was part of the Orthodox tradition too. A weak spot was the heavy state dependency of the Orthodox Church.

The East Asian family, and its Chinese variant in particular, was the most explicitly and elaboratedly patriarchal of all, with respect and deference to the father and to patrilineal ancestors, 'filial piety' the highest moral value. Marriage was universal and heavily husband-dominated. Fertility concentrated on reproducing the male bloodline. The family had a much more central place in the value system than in the countries of universalistic religions, as the main religious practice was ancestor worship. The East Asian family had grown up under the protection of ancient and splendid states, upon which its values largely depended as there was no significant clergy. Outside its core father–son relationship the East Asian family system included, or was open to, a certain secular pragmatism.

The South Asian family system was much more religiously charged and regulated, by caste rules of purity against pollution, largely affecting the Muslim population of the subcontinent as well. Norms were strictly patriarchal and male-dominating, but without the typical East Asian father–son focus. Particularly in the northern part of the region Muslim and Hindu tradition merged in institutionalizing female seclusion. Marriage was universal, regulated by strict rules of endogamy and exogamy, and a religious paternal duty. Fertility belonged to the patrilineal household. The diffuse but pervasive Hindu religion, which also includes an ancestry cult, had an ancient tradition of reproducing itself independent of political power.

The geoculture of West Asia/North Africa comprised the heartlands of Islam, and this is where the Muslim family developed, like Christianity in Europe, although both are universalistic and proselytizing religions that have spread to other regions and cultures as well. In a comparative perspective, this is a patriarchy particularly concerned with the sexual control of women, including seclusion and veiling, as well as universal marriage, while allowing married women economic rights denied in common law, for instance. Household norms are patrilocal. Jurisprudence and theology are very much intertwined in Islam, and family matters are of great and detailed concern to it. Family change is therefore very religiously sensitive, and Islam has a large clergy. On the other hand, Islam has no real church hierarchy, and its highest authorities have always been dependants of the highest political ruler.

The African family combines an explicit gender hierarchy with a traditionally unique amount of female autonomy, above all as West African traders, but also as agriculturalists. Mass polygyny usually meant that each of the wives of the patriarch has her own household within the compound. Conjugal relations are correspondingly thinner than in other parts of the world. Fertility is a very important value – reinforced by the high land-labour ratios of the continent – and belongs to the lineage. The indigenous sexual order was unaffected by the Christian notion of sin or the male Muslim fear of uncontrolled female desire, and therefore more open to change. The institution developed with neither state nor clergy, but rooted in the local authority of chiefs and among the elders of the lineage.

Buddhist nonchalance in family matters, and Malay and other customs of the region, made Southeast Asia an interstitial geoculture of family relations in Asia, basically less patriarchal, and less sexually controlled. Tradition included a sexual objectification of women though, such as sexual slavery in Siam and concubine donations in Java. Marriage was universal, with a norm of strong parental involvement, but relatively informal – because of the virtual absence of Buddhist marriage rites, or because of a Malay custom of formal but de facto trial marriage, with an enormous rate of divorce when our story begins. Bilateral kinship made the male heir issue less important, and fertility as such was not particularly value-charged. The family system had no strong political or clerical props, although the Muslim *ulemas* have to be taken into account, as well as the Catholic Church of the Philippines, re-invigorated in the twentieth century.

The hierarchical ethnic relations of the slave plantations, the haciendas, and the Iberian mining in the Americas created a special, interstitial system of sex and family relations, which we have called the Creole system. It involved a tightly patriarchal ruling class culture, usually tighter than patriarchy in its Western European continent of origin, and a phallocratic popular culture of informal sexuality, frequent non-marriage, and widespread matrifocal households. It was sustained by racist power, ethnic hierarchy and mass poverty.

As institutions, family systems may be seen as equilibria, where social definitions correspond to social visions, rights and advantages correspond to powers, and disadvantages and duties to dependence and lack of resources. Institutional change should be seen as a two-phase process. First a disturbance of the institutional equilibrium, which may arise from inherent contradictions, but which in the family case is most likely to be exogenous – opening new vistas, challenging existing powers, providing new resources and options to the disadvantaged, in short destabilizing a given social set of arrangements. This disruption may or may not be coped with by re-equilibrating, re-stabilizing mechanisms. If it is, then change is aborted. But if not, there arises the need for a second phase of change, a phase of setting a direction of change and of organizing the institution anew, in brief a phase of new institutional direction. If this second phase succeeds we have institutional change. If not, there be will be a shorter or longer period of anarchy, after which the institution in question will either change (including disappear) or relapse into its previous form. The main point here is that the relationship between disturbance and re-direction can vary widely, in the cause and the size of the disturbance, the force of re-equilibration, the velocity and the efficacy of new institutional direction.

Institutional change – which we may distinguish from 'change of an institution', referring to any alteration of a given institution, a disturbance of its equilibrium, an erosion of its hold – would indicate the establishment of a new institutional order and temporary equilibrium, through a re-organization of the challenged institution, by a re-allocation of its place and significance in the broader social order, through its replacement by a new institution, or by its abolition into irrelevance.

To the extent that the above makes sense, it follows that modern institutional change includes (a) crucial moment(s) of normative decision, decisive moments when a process of de-institutionalization or of institutionalization is sent along one path or the other. This is the political, or the judicial, moment, to which I think also family history and family sociology should pay attention. Even a sexual revolution challenging a marital sexual order has its judicial or political moments, in the USA *Griswold* v. *Connecticut* (1965, contraceptives) and *Roe* v. *Wade* (1973, abortion), for instance.

On a macro-level, these moments are moments of legislation, judicial verdicts, or of authoritative religious exegesis, of papal encyclicae or of an imam *fatwa*, for example. But they exist also at a micro-level, the moment a breach of institutional norms ceases to make offence or to lead to social marginalization, such as, for example, young women going out alone, married women working outside the house, males taking care of children or doing household chores, cohabitation without marriage, a birth out of wedlock, homosexuality.

In this vein we might explicate the secular trajectory of the family systems by taking note of the disturbances of the equilibria, of possible restoring mechanisms, and of the direction of institutional change.

An attention to global dynamics, then, means paying attention to the most important challenges and disturbances facing the different family systems of the globe, and to what extent the former are related to each other, capable of bringing about waves of family change. As this is not a general global history, but a history of the family, our search for the global dynamics will start out from the family systems and from what we have learnt about their strains, challenges and change.

The Creole family pattern was an early modern invention, out of the colonial thrust of the sixteenth and the seventeenth centuries. The *conquistadores,* the *haciendados* and the plantation slave owners, from Virginia to Bahía, and their exploitees may lay claim to pioneering modern family change in the world. However, that was before the proper beginning of this book. After the Creoles, in the vanguard of family change was Western Europe. The Western European elite from the seventeenth century – in Calvinist Geneva from the mid-sixteenth century, and the French population beginning in the late eighteenth century – pioneered birth control, which in the 1880s turned into a continental wave, with a parallel development in the USA starting in the first decades of the nineteenth century. The dismantling of patriarchy, and the provision of important rights to wives and children, began in Scandinavia in the 1910s. So did the late twentieth-century informalization of sexual coupling, soon but unevenly fanning out all over the wide world of the European family system.

Over the century there have been least changes in the families of South Asia, West Asia/North Africa, and sub-Saharan Africa. But all family systems, throughout their changes, have tended to preserve specific characteristics. For all its patriarchal norms, the European family system had always recognized some legitimate public space to women, something which always struck eighteenth- and nineteenth-century Ottoman, Arab and Asian visitors to Europe and America. In East Asia, there is still a strong sense of obligation to parents, even though ancient 'filial piety' has been eroded. Parental arrangement of marriages, a traditional Hindu duty, is still entrenched in contemporary South Asia, and even in the Indian diaspora. The sexual control of women remains a central concern of the West Asian/North African family institution, and a key component of current patriarchal backlash. The African family has always held fertility as a central value – superordinate to son–daughter distinctions and to biological fatherhood. In modern times it has been the most resilient to birth control and to the two-to-three child norm. Its massive polygyny has adapted itself surprisingly well to urban conditions. The interstitial families of Southeast Asia and of Creole America have by definition less of a core tradition, but the paternal powers in the former and the male-dominated informal sexuality of the latter are still being reproduced. Indonesia still has an explicit husband-headship of the family, and marriage remains a minority practice in Jamaica and the Dominican Republic, for instance.

While the comparative sociology of family systems makes a Western European vanguard of late modern change something to be expected, its complex dynamics needs to be unravelled.

Trajectories and their properties

The Western European rule of new household formation upon marriage, the European mores of legitimate descent, and the Christian taboo on infanticide – although the eighteenth- and nineteenth-century foundling system with its abominable mortality actually came close to it – brought the issue of the number of descendants into view. The fact that it was the two countries of modern social revolution, France and the USA, which first made birth control a popular pursuit – after the propertied elites of Western Europe – and the fact that birth control was pushed by and developed in milieux supporting radical social movements in the late nineteenth and early twentieth century, make plausible a hypothesis of modern popular birth control as driven by social revolution and radical social movements. Governments and churches of all kinds were always opposed. No wonder, then, that birth control did not spread with European imperialism.

The actual dynamics of change is often a combination of contingent conjunctures and structural trends. The onset of the European wave of birth control seems to have been determined by the financial crash of 1873 and its depressive aftermath. It was greatly helped by the famous contraceptives trial in England in 1877, relayed by an emergent mass circulation press, and linked by the continental spread of the Marxist labour movement and other radicalisms. It was structurally sustained by the continental wave of compulsory schooling and of legislation against child labour, both raising the cost of children to parents. The great Princeton European Fertility Project found little economic or habitation (urbanization) leverage in European fertility change. The dynamic appears to have been politico-cultural instead.

In terms of patriarchy and of marriage, Western Europe in 1900 is rather an area of restoration, of institutional recuperation, than of institutional change. Nineteenth-century proletarianization – driven by population growth as well as by capitalist expropriation – and rapid urbanization had seriously disrupted the socio-sexual order, expressed in high rates of cohabitation and extra-marital births over major parts of the European continent, less so in Britain, but that at least in part for reasons of procedure and registration. However, already in the approach to 1900, European marriage and patriarchy were recuperating after the initial dislocations of economic modernity, heavily supported by all established cultural institutions, and largely by counter-cultural labour institutions too. The new forms of informal coupling had been practised preponderantly, if not exclusively, by the poor and the uprooted, and they nowhere reached a moment of legitimacy, until 75–100 years later. Successful industrialization provided an economic basis for a re-stabilization and a re-institutionalization of the working-class family.

Around 1900, European and US imperialism was a central part of the world process, manifested in the 'opening up' of East Asia, conquests and threats in Indo-China, the competition for Iran, the British control of Egypt, the 'scramble' for Africa, the US seizure of Cuba, Puerto Rico and the Philippines, and in German forays into the Pacific. No part of the world was beyond imperialist interest and menace. In this situation, perceptive and nationally concerned intellectuals of conquered or threatened countries were questioning their family and sexuality patterns in view of the imperialist challenges. Excessive patriarchy and male domination were often singled out as at least one of the reasons for inferiority to the West. Very little came out of this, though – the most important positive result was the Japanese pursuit of girls' schooling. The reformist intellectuals had no political clout, the imperialist powers themselves pushed family traditionalism as part of 'indirect rule', and the most popular nationalist response tended to be reactionary.

Apart from developments in Western Europe, and its New World offshoots, the only important family process of change running in the world of 1900 was the undermining of the Creole family pattern. The abolition of slavery had ended the prohibition of Afro-Americans to marry, and the new waves of immigration were weakening the relative importance of the old slavery regions of the US south and of the Brazilian northeast.

In Western Europe and North America, patriarchy was also becoming challenged from the middle class, while the popular classes were increasingly drawn to it. The new communications of telephone, telegraph and newspapers, and the expansion of teaching had created new possible labour markets to middle-class women. Middle-class demands of female economic autonomy were being raised. Class polarization had also weakened paternal solidarity. In 1889 both England and France passed legislation against maltreatment of children, mainly with poor, brutalized and alcoholic fathers in mind.

The Scandinavian early twentieth-century reformers – of children's rights, of husband–wife equality, and of no-fault divorce rights – did not believe that they were changing the world. Rather, they saw themselves as enlightened adapters to new times. Economic growth had been vigorous since the last quarter of the nineteenth century, but Scandinavia was still a rustic outlier of Europe, with a political system very archaic in Sweden and in Finland until 1905. What made Scandinavia a family avant-garde, in the 1910s and 1920s as well as in the 1960s and 1970s, was its late, sudden and economically efficacious political modernization and secularization.

Scandinavian patriarchy never entered into powerful early modern cultures, like that of the French Revolution, English common law, or German nationalism, but remained part of an archaic, pre-modern social system. This weakness of early modern traditions was soon to pave the way for social democracy, a key political player in the family changes of the 1960s and 1970s. The classical Lutheran state churches of Scandinavia had been strongly patriarchal in every sense, backed up by states defining themselves as defenders of the faith. But bureaucratic state churches were ill-equipped to deal with proletarianization and with urbanization. One sector of the new popular classes was lost to new evangelical movements, which at the time were too divided and/or too anti-establishment to offer any patriarchal prop, and another to agnostic or atheistic social movements. Secularization took its time, and did not succeed before 1900. But by the 1910s, as in the 1960s and 1970s, there was no longer any loud ecclesiastical voice of patriarchy, or later on even of formal marriage.

The Scandinavian reforms of the 1910s had hardly any direct international repercussions, nor had, more surprisingly, the coeval Chinese and Mexican revolutions. But the Bolsheviks, who introduced free marriage choice, husband–wife equality and no-fault divorce in Russia at the end of the decade, certainly did. With a certain historical irony, this Communist legacy spread amazingly around the world. 'World Communism' was not just a right-wing hysteria. It did push radical family change in Eastern Europe and in East Asia after World War II. It inspired radical family reform in Cuba in the 1960s and 1970s. An uninhibited, atheistic socio-cultural modernism, coming out of the European Enlightenment and the European Marxist labour movement, provided the drive for family revolution, against stiff resistance from patriarchal peasantries.

In power Communism was a strong supporter of marriage, and in its later age it was very much engaged in fertility, pushing birth promotion in Eastern Europe with some relative success, and launching dramatically – and brutally – effective birth control in China and Vietnam. As a women's movement it was behind the initiative of the UN International Women's Year, and in the shape of the Communist government of Poland it launched the process leading up to the UN Convention of the Rights of the Child.

For 70 years, from 1917 till 1989, when the UN Child Convention was adopted, Communism was an important part of the global dynamic of family change, with a very impressive achievement in terms of influence and impact, the value of which may, of course, be esteemed in different ways. But because of its vanguard role, the actual implementation of its stipulations could take at least a generation, as they did in Russia and in China, where parental control of marriages slipped only slowly. And because of the politically dictatorial character of Communism, its family policies also included political discrimination and insensitive state expediency.

The two world wars and the worldwide 1930s Depression did challenge family systems in many parts of the world – but not everywhere – either directly by throwing societies out of normalcy, or indirectly by undercutting or terminating political regimes. Their effects in Africa, in West Asia/North Africa and in Southeast Asia were relatively negligible.

After World War I women won the right to vote in Northern Europe, but family changes outside of Scandinavia were not substantial. The end of World War I highlighted the continued humiliation of China, calling forth the May Fourth Movement of modernist nationalist rebellion, including an explicit family challenge. But no decisive politico-judicial moment occurred to the Chinese family before 1950. The fall of the Ottoman Empire led on to the Kemalist Turkish revolution which, apart from its influence on Iran, remained an oddity in the Islamic world, and its writ of family reform did not run far outside the metropolis of Istanbul and the bureaucratic neighbourhoods of Ankara.

The Depression was probably most important as a backdrop, or as a dark hole from which the way out of it shone brighter, immediately stimulating marriages and births in Germany, Sweden and Austria, under very different political auspices. It was the background to the post-World War II prosperity that sent Western Europeans, North Americans, Australians and even Latin Americans into record rates of marriage. The old economic adaptability of the Western European marriage system was still in operation, now reacting faster than before.

World War II issued into a very important constitutional moment, in Japan, in Germany, and in the UN. Patriarchy was for the first time seriously and explicitly challenged by an international mainstream – by the victorious Anti-Fascist coalition. Change was not instantaneous even in those three cases, but a new path was struck. 'Love marriages' gradually became the norm in Japan. The West German Constitutional Court did not let the Conservative Christian political majority off the hook before the constitutional clause of gender equality became manifest in legislation. The UN Declaration of Human Rights did not receive legislative implementation, but its gender equality proclamation provided the basis for later important UN efforts with respect to women's rights and children's rights.

As in northwestern Europe after World War I, the vote to Latin European women after World War II did not amount to significant family change. Asian independence from colonialism spawned general equality constitutional clauses without any significant impact, like the African Independence of the 1960s.

Intellectual discourse apart, the colonial and the anti-colonial family impact has been severely limited (after the invention of Creolity). The long-distance, long-term labour migration established in Southern Africa, and reinforced by apartheid racism, has been one of the most important colonial effects, and a disruptive one. Sometimes the resilience of family patterns among the colonized is remarkable, such as the large-scale survival of polygamy among African Christians. The racist duality of rulers and natives, characteristic of colonialism, left the native family basically uncolonized, and limited severely its penetration by missionaries and by secular apostles of family change.

There have been several pertinent global movements in the twentieth century including, for instance, the first feminist wave, which included a pan-Pacific meeting in Honolulu in 1928 (Wollacott 1999), and the first movement for birth control, whose representatives were fêted both in India and in China of the 1920s. But, Communism apart, their influence was very limited, usually confined to small elite groups. The post-World War II birth control movement slowly but skilfully managed to change that, working through donor agencies of secularized Protestant philanthropy in the USA and public agencies of northwestern Europe, some Third World political leaders, and gradually through the World Bank and the UN. The second wave of fertility decline in the Third World owed enormously to this composite movement. It both sponsored and was helped by a technological breakthrough of cheap and easy contraceptives, simple and reversible sterilization, the intrauterine device and the pill.

The movement of 1968 set on course a worldwide voyage of change. In its Western European and North American homelands it throve on the expansion of female higher education, which provided the 'special forces' of feminism. But it was relayed by the UN machinery of conferences, networks and publications, which also provided global agendas or 'Plans of Action', and spawned new government agencies in most countries, charged with new concerns of gender and family issues. Female education globally leapt forward, and upwards, into higher education, including in the Gulf States and other parts of West Asia/North Africa. Structurally, the wave of de-patriarchialization and delayed marriages of 1968 onward was also sustained by post-industrial labour market developments in the rich world, landing women in good seats of the service economy, and, much more cautiously and indirectly, by an expansion of female textile and electronics industrial labour in Asia and in other parts of the Third World.

So far, the effective family changes, birth control apart, have not been dramatic in Asia or Africa. But changes of world culture – into a broadly pro-feminist, pro-individualist stance, highlighted by the mid-1990s UN conferences in Cairo and Beijing – and the new educational and economic developments pose serious challenges to remaining patriarchy and to male-dominated family collectivism. On the other hand, the male-dominated family was reinforced in the last third of the past century in a strong Islamic religious revival, often with intense patriarchal preoccupations, and, less effectively, in surges of Christian, Jewish and Hindu fundamentalism, and in currents of Eastern European post-Communism. The victory of US Christian fundamentalism in stopping the Equal Rights Amendment in the 1970s now appears rather Pyrrhic.

Ex-Communist Europe is moving closer to the Western pattern, meeting the post-Communist economic depression with large-scale postponement of marriage and plummeting birth rates. But the classical European family divide, running from Trieste to St Petersburg, going back for more than a thousand years to the early Middle Ages, is still visible in 2000. Those post-Communist parts which previously belonged to the Western family pattern are rapidly adopting the current Western practice of informal cohabitation. Anti-Communist anti-feminism does not seem to have made much headway.

The profound and protracted economic crisis and the gaping inequalities of Africa seem to generate a tendency towards Creolization, of phallocratic sexuality and matrifocal households. At the same time, specific African patterns are being reproduced, like mass polygyny and high (though lowered) fertility, while being transformed by family planning and legal reforms strengthening the position of wives and daughters.

The secular tendency towards a formalization and stabilization of the Creole family in Latin America was reversed in the last quarter of the century. Here an interactive cultural and economic dynamic may be suspected, cultural influences from Western Europe and North America affecting middle-class

Latin America, while large sectors of the popular classes saw their whole social existence eroded or threatened by the long economic crisis.

Family change has been uneven, in time as well as in space. Its dynamic has been multidimensional, cultural and political as well as economic. Its topography has the ruggedness of conjunctures, rather than the smooth slope of growth curves. Its planetary extension is less the outcome of common universal forces than the result of global linkages and of global movements.

Our findings have shown that the world's family patterns and sexual relations remain varied. All the main family systems of the world have changed over the past century, but they are all still here. In the case of the European family, we have also been able to discern how internal variations, of marriage age and of informal cohabitation, have re-emerged along the same lines after vast and profound societal transformations.

But could it be said that, after all, in spite of persistent important differences, the family patterns of the world have become more similar? With respect to the variables investigated here, the answer to that question is: no. The complex, multi-faceted clusters of relations and practices studied do not make any exact measurement easy. In the case of fertility, quantitative precision is possible, though the historical database contains a margin of error. As we saw above, in Table 8.8, fertility developments have made the major parts of the world more different in 2000 than they were around 1900. The so far delimited stretch of the sexual revolution and of informal coupling has certainly not made the socio-sexual order converge across the globe. Again, the trajectories rather seem to diverge, between still almost universal marriage and strict controls of legitimate sexuality in Asia, and the Western tendency of the last three decades, of less marriage and more sex.

The patriarchal outcome is somewhat different. The radical changes in the populous core area of patriarchy, East Asia, and the coming together of Europe in a post-patriarchal – if by no means gender-equal – family are important tendencies of convergence. While the rights of daughters, sisters and wives in the northern regions of South Asia are now (relatively speaking) probably further below those of their European sisters than they were in 1900, the convergent tendency appears to carry more weight. If so, the main direct reason of convergent de-patriarchalization was not the work of a 'feminist world spirit', but the specific outcome and aftermath of World War II in Japan and in China.

Times coming

One century is enough for this book. To grasp it we have had to go back, not only to the nineteenth century, and its processes of fertility and marital change and embryonic questioning of patriarchy, but also to the population movements of the early European Middle Ages and to the conquest of the Americas. But what can we see of the twenty-first century from its threshold of past changes? Let us start with the two least hazy and hazardous pictures, i.e. with the outlook for fertility and for patriarchy, although it should not be forgotten that no future can claim absolute certainty or full clarity.

Beyond 'transition': ageing and geopolitical demographic shifts

If and when we have family patterns in which the population no longer is reproducing itself, we have left the epoch of 'transition' from one supposed equilibrium into another one. That is the current situation of the 'more developed regions' of the world as a whole, although it is too early to tell whether this will settle. The UN Population Fund (UNFPA 2002) estimates a total fertility rate in the rich world for 2000–5 of 1.5 child per woman. Below the long-term replacement rate of 2.1 is also China (1.8) and South Korea (1.5). The USA is the only significant part of the developed world that is roughly on replacement level (US Census Bureau 2001a: table 74) – mainly due to the fertility of Hispanic and other recent immigrant women – while South Korean fertility is down to 1.5. Russian and Ukrainian populations are already declining, while immigration is still offsetting the natural decrease of Germany and Italy (Council of Europe 2001a: table T0.2). In Asia, save Japan, it will take decades for the fertility rate to translate into population decline, because of age structures with large fertile cohorts.

A new demographic era of non-catastrophic population decline may be dawning. Famines, epidemics, floods, volcanoes and wars have taken their toll in the past, but that large populations by individual choice do not reproduce is an epochal historical change. In Western Europe the pattern is being established in peacetime and under conditions of great prosperity, although conjunctural oscillations are still visible, and were significant in the Scandinavian depression of the early 1990s.

Whether this will actually happen is far from certain, but a stable population end-point after the 'demographic transition' is no longer tenable as a basic framework for population analysis (cf. Bongaarts 2001b). A population decline in the next fifty years, if it occurs, will only befall parts of the world. Global population will go on growing – unless there is some planetary disaster. And current tendencies in the areas now bent on decline are not beyond reversibility. European fertility rates recuperated after their Depression trough, and in several countries a recovery set in after the 1970s fall, including a return to replacement level in the USA. Furthermore, the current European total fertility rate figures exaggerate recent change by not taking simple postponement of births into account, and we noted above that the two-child norm is still embraced by European women and couples – although not quite in Germany. Natalist public policies have not always been ineffective in the past, and the supply of childcare services has made possible the noteworthy current OECD positive cross-national correlation between fertility and women's labour-force participation (Castles 2003; cf. Kögel 2002). In other words, population decline, even in the rich world, is far from determined. The means of public policies provide a possible equilibrating mechanism, not included in standard demographic theory. Whether they will be deployed will depend on public debate and on the priorities of political decision-making.

There are at least three sets of arguments for an active population policy. The strongest, from an individual and democratic point of view, is that current difficulties of combining work and family lead to sub-optimal solutions, where a significant number of individuals end up having fewer children than they had wanted. Hitherto, that argument has played a marginal role in the public discussion. Second, and more frequently used, is the argument of generational relay: that is, securing a future population base sufficient for providing pensions and care to the current generation later in its life. Out of fashion these days, but nevertheless pertinent, is a third, national/regional argument about the demography of geopolitics, geoeconomics and geoculture. Shrinking and ageing populations are vulnerable, not only in power games, but also in the sustainability of their economic well-being, and of their cultural preferences.

For the two latter purposes, although somewhat less so for the last one, immigration is a functional alternative to birth facilitation. Traditionally closed or out-migrating countries like Germany, Italy, Japan, Korea and Spain, all with family systems geared to housewife motherhood, are facing some especially difficult, and inevitably controversial, choices here.

In case current demographic tendencies should not change radically, important population shifts will occur – of the geographic distribution of world population, and of the age structure of national populations. The figures of long-term estimates should always be read with a wide margin of error. But we are no doubt heading for major regional tilts of population weight. Continuing the fertility rate of 1995 for a hundred years and assuming a stable population, by the turn of the next century there would only be about 14 million Germans (instead of 82 million) left, and about 35 million Japanese (instead of 125 million) (McDonald 1997: 1–2). While that is a demographic calculation exercise, showing the possible long-term effects of an unhampered process, there are also more realistic prognoses (Table 9.1).

In its December 2003 prognosis, the UN Population Division predicts in its 'medium scenario' that the human population will peak around 2075 at 9.2 billion and then decline slowly to 8.5 billion (www.un.org/esa/population).

Europe, Japan and Russia are bent on becoming the demographic losers of the new century. From contemporary projections of population and of economic growth, China may come to dwarf its Russian and Japanese neighbours. In 1900 Europe housed a quarter of the world's population, in 2000 one-eighth, and in 2050 it is predicted to harbour only one-fifteenth of the human beings of the earth. South Asia, and perhaps also sub-Saharan Africa, are heading for overtaking East Asia as the most populous regions of the world. The natural riches of Africa and the demonstrated productive capacity of India make it not inconceivable that their population weight may in the end get an economic base to stand on. The West Asian/North African heartland of Islam is likely to become a demographically heavyweight player, although the educational changes just started may bring down the current estimates. Anyway, the balance of power in the world will be affected, not only by the distribution of missiles and other weapons of mass destruction, but also by population movements.

So far, ageing has attracted much more attention than population decline and shifts of demographic weight. Even under assumptions of continued immigration and of some recuperation of the fertility rate, the future of Europe and

Table 9.1 Regional population prospects of the world, 2000–50 (millions)

	Prognosticated population in 2050	*Change 2000–50*
Sub-Saharan Africa	1680	+1045
Latin America and Caribbean	806	+280
Northern America	438	+120
USA	397	+111
Eastern Asia	1665	+173
China	1462	+177
Japan	109	−19
South Asia[a]	2345	+933
India	1572	+547
Pakistan	344	+199
Southeast Asia	800	+170
Indonesia	311	+97
West Asia and North Africa[a]	920	+457
Europe[b]	603	−123
Russia	104	−44
World	*9322*	*3186*

Source: UN (2001b).

Notes:
a Afghanistan and Iran here transferred to West Asia.
b Enlarged EU and the Balkans.

Japan looks rather grey. By 2000, there were already more people of the age of 65 and older than there were children under 15 in Japan, and also in Germany, Greece, Italy and Spain. In 2015 this appears likely to be the case over the whole of Europe (UNDP 2002: table 5). The UNFPA (2000: table A11) predicts that in 2050 one Japanese of three will be aged 65 or more, and almost one among three (29 per cent) of the inhabitants of the current European Union, with a median age of 49 and 48, respectively. The US prognostic is one in five being 65 or older.

A major task of twenty-first-century social science will be to look into how enormously different age structures will affect social, cultural, economic and political relations. In 2000, 30 per cent of world population were children, ranging from 14–15 per cent in Italy, Japan and Germany, to 45 per cent in Nigeria, and in sub-Saharan Africa as a whole, reaching the 50 per cent mark in Yemen and a few African countries. In 2015 the range is estimated to run between 12–13 per cent in the most child-poor countries and 42–43 per cent for Africa, with some countries still going up to 50 per cent. By contrast, the whole world in 2000 had 7 per cent of its population aged 65 or older, forecast to increase by 1 per cent until 2015, when one Japanese out of four will be 65+, one German in five, and 19 and 14 per cent of the UK and US population, respectively (UNDP 2002: table 5). Ageing is, above all, a Euro-Japanese problem.

Dim prospects of patriarchy

Patriarchy still governs most of Asia (particularly in the west), most of Africa, parts of the Andes and the Balkans, and leaves its shadows in significant parts of

East Asia. Where fathers and husbands do not rule, phallocracy or asymmetric male sexual power may dominate the socio-sexual order, as in popular Creole societies or in the swollen slum cities of Africa. Even if, for this particular occasion, we leave out the political economy of gender inequality and concentrate on family and sexual relations, patriarchy and its younger brother phallocracy are major phenomena of the twenty-first century. There is little basis for a prediction that they will definitely be gone by 2091, for the bi-centenary of the first edition of Edward Westermarck's *The History of Human Marriage*.

However, the prospects for patriarchy are certainly far from bright. With the ageing of the median voter, democratic politics will be increasingly attentive to the needs of old people, admittedly, but that is more likely to manifest a dependence on support than family power. Symptomatic, even if geoculturally particular, is the 1996 Chinese Law for the Protection of the Rights and the Interests of the Elderly. While including exhortative stipulations reminiscent of filial piety, the main thrust of the law is to make the elderly a protected species in the storms of the Communist market economy. Obligations of younger family members to support their elderly are made clear, backed up with legal sanctions and speedy judicial redress. Perhaps the most telling paragraph is §18, which deals with a post-patriarchal problem: 'the freedom of marriage of the elderly is protected by law. Children or other relatives may not interfere in the divorce, remarriage or life after marriage of the elderly'. The Revolution set out to protect the freedom of the young to marry against the interference of their parents. Now, the Chinese legislator sees a need to protect the freedom of the elderly against the interference of their children.

Another indicator of how ancient patriarchy is being eroded was provided by Indian television in the autumn of 2002. The sacred Indian paternal/parental prerogative of arranging children's marriages was turned into a TV show, with arrangements made before the cameras of the TV studio. It is, of course, the symbolic profanation of Hindu marriage which is significant here, not the real one, which is no more than a raindrop in an ocean.

Patriarchy has become officially illegitimate across the whole world. The UN Convention on the Elimination of All Forms of Discrimination Against Women came into force in 1981 and has been ratified by most countries. The exceptions are Afghanistan, Somalia, the Gulf States and the USA, which also in this respect finds unacceptable any international rule it has not dictated itself but whose national judiciary no longer sustains gender discrimination. The forces of female education, of labour market openings, of public politics, international networking, and mass culture are all gnawing at the remaining pillars of patriarchy. Above we saw the limitation of backlash as powerful as that embodied in the Islamic Republic of Iran. On the other hand, exits from patriarchy require resources – of schooling, jobs and income. Patriarchy is now entrenched in the poor parts of the world, and the pace of its demise will depend very much on the future vigour of their economic development.

Under the new conditions of birth control, patriarchal discrimination against daughters is creating a special problem for future generations, a sexual imbalance. Lingering East Asian son preferences initiated a rise in the male-to-female ratio of children in the late 1980s, not only in China but also in Taiwan, less sharply in Hong Kong, and in South Korea on a par with China. In mainland China this change was apparently in part brought about by infanticide and by under-reporting girls to the birth-planning as well as birth-registering authorities, whereas selective abortion was the overwhelming method in other areas. Foetal gender assessment became available on a large scale on the Chinese mainland only in the 1990s (Park and Cho 1993; Das Gupta *et al.* 2000). In 1995, the Chinese sex ratio at birth was 117 boys for 100 girls (Li and Peng 2000: table 6.3), while the South Korean 2001 census showed a slightly lowered ratio of 109 to 100.

India is another country of 'missing girls'. The Indian census of 2001 found more missing than preceding censuses, reporting 108 boys per 100 girls for the 0–6 years age group (for a methodological and data-critical discussion of this, see Bhat 2002). A normal human distribution at birth is about 105–6 boys per 100 girls.

In the long run, this discrimination against daughters is likely to be self-defeating, in the sense of raising the scarcity value of girls.

Gender inequality can be predicted a longer life expectancy than patriarchy, because of its deep embeddedness in structurally gendered income patterns and in ancient asymmetries of family responsibilities. However, it was significantly cut down in the second half, and especially in the last third, of the past century. There seem to be no strong reasons for doubting that that process of equalization can continue. At least on the level of rhetoric and of official policies, greater opportunities for women has become one of the few issues on which states and inter-state organizations, from the EU and the World Bank to the UN General Assembly, can agree.

Complexities and conflicts of the future socio-sexual order

To what extent will the family, in the sense of long-term coupling, marriage, and parenting, continue to structure the socio-sexual order? To what extent will the Western sexual revolution have an impact on the whole world? Let us start from an angle opposite to our study of the past, from the individualism of single living, fleeting relationships, 'plastic sexuality', brought up in recent Western public discussion. Much of the debate may be provincial, local even, looking no further than into one or a few rich-world, big-city milieu(x), but the issues are general.

Solitude and contingency: after industrial standardization

Are we heading for a century of solitude? Hardly. Single householding is likely to go on increasing, but the phenomenon is much more circumscribed than is usually realized.

As a form of life of more than marginal significance, single living today is largely confined to the rich world, and a couple of ageing, formerly rich countries in Latin America. Indeed even in the OECD countries, it has not spread far in Southern Europe. In the Demographic and Health Surveys of 43 Third World countries in the 1990s, 1 to 2 per cent of individuals were living alone (Bongaarts and Zimmer 2001: table 1). In Latin America of the mid-1990s, only in Argentina and Uruguay did one-person households constitute more than 8 per cent of all (reaching 15 per cent). Everywhere, except in Argentina, there were more extended families than single households: in Brazil 16 per cent extended families, 8 per cent singles, and in Mexico 19 per cent and 6 per cent, respectively (UN ECLAC 1997: table VI.1.1).

Also in the EU in 1999 there were many more people living in households with three or more adults than living alone: 25 and 12 per cent, respectively, and in the UK 20 and 13 per cent. Only in Scandinavia were there more singles than people in multi-adult families. If to singles were added single parents and their children, the balance would become 20 to 21 per cent in the UK, but remain basically unchanged in the EU at 25 to 16 per cent (Eurostat 2001: 115). Now, 'adults' here include offspring from the age of 16 if in the labour force and above 24 if economically active but living with (a) parent(s). But even in a more conventional counting of complex/extended families, a third of the countries of the EU – Greece, Ireland, Luxemburg, Portugal and Spain – have more people actually living in such families than alone (Eurostat 2000b: 50). But then there were (in 1995) in the UK twice as many people in one-person households.

The extension of singleness is exaggerated by counting households only, as all other households have more members. Around 2000, one-person households make up a good quarter of all households in the EU, North America, Japan and Australia, but one-tenth (USA, Japan) to one-ninth (EU, Britain) of the population (Coleman 2000: table 2.22; Eurostat 2000: 49; Japan Statistics Bureau 2001; Trewin 2001: 194; US Census Bureau 2001c: table 2). In Sweden, the Western tendency to solitude is doubled: in 1999, 44 per cent of all households had only one member, who made up 26 per cent of the population aged above 15 (SCB 2002a: 21). It has a tradition to build on: in 1900 a quarter of all Swedish households were single, corresponding to a tenth of the population aged 15 and over (SCB 1999: tables 1.9, 1.2). But this means no more than that 15 per cent of the Swedish population aged 35–54 are living alone at any one moment, and 85 per cent are not (SCB 2002b: table SR1).

Behind single living and its increase is, first of all, what we may call generational economics, an interaction of generation dependence and economic resources. Independent youth leaves its parental home before forming a new family (or couple), and independent elderly, most often widows, maintain their own households. Such generation independence, or generation individualism, is an old feature of the northwestern European family, although solitary households were more common on the continent from France to Scandinavia than in the British Isles (Wall 1989: table 7). General prosperity makes this possible more widely, but specific housing market conditions may keep young people in their parental home, as in Southern Europe, or restrain several single elders in Japan from moving in with their son.

Secondly, there is what labour-market students would call frictional loneliness: that is, the single living between one coupling, marriage or cohabitation, and another. Finally, there are structural and voluntary singleness, the relative importance of which is little known. 'Structural' would here mean a skewing of coupling markets in such a way that some men or women are excluded or find available matches unattractive. Lower-class males are sometimes excluded in some such way, and highly educated women in patriarchal societies sometimes see the existing marriage alternatives as unappealing.

Single living is no late twentieth-century invention, but an old component of the northwestern European family system. Post-World War II dismantling of the patriarchal 'house' (*ie*) gradually spread it to Japan. In the near future it is not likely to become a major feature of other non-European family systems, but if the current economic crisis there is overcome, it is likely to increase substantially in Eastern Europe. Its ongoing gradual advance in the West will probably continue, without leading to any very fundamental change. Swedish experience shows the flexibility of the northwestern European family, combining high rates of singleness, extra-marital births and non-married cohabitation with above-EU-average fertility, infrequent single parenthood, and two-thirds of teenage children growing up with both their parents.

The sexual revolution was not an assault on marriage and long-term coupling. It was an assertion of the right to sexual pleasure, before marriage and outside marriage, as well as inside it. As we noticed above, marriage was sexually enriched too. Cohabitation developed as trial marriage, and as secularized and informal pairing, which legislators and courts have made increasingly marriage-like. The family never died, in contradiction to a once famous counter-cultural psychiatrist (Cooper 1971), and the communes and experimentation with sexual plasticity never went beyond a bohemian fringe. By the late 1990s, the Right to Marriage had become a central slogan of gays and lesbians.

The core of romantic freedom and commitment in the modern European (and New World) family system was not broken, and is still there for the future. In the USA, for instance, marital happiness, while falling slightly in the mid-1980s, remained at its high level from the beginning of the 1970s, and married people stayed much more happy than non-married ones (Waite 2000: figs 19.1 and 19.2). In a large German survey in 2000, 70 per cent of young people aged 12–25 held that one needed a family to be happy (Linssen *et al.* 2002: 58).

What came out of the '1968' changes was not so much the beginning of an end to the Western socio-sexual order, as an end to the twentieth-century industrial standardization of it, and of the human life-course in general: an end to a temporary standardization around a low-level (but above replacement) homogenization of birth rates, compulsory standard education (with a tiny elite supplement), a maintenance of strict sexual norms combined with increased possibilities of avoiding sexual accidents, a high marriage rate, and marrying concentrated to a short and historically early age-span, a prosperous decrease of inequality among class households, a wide, inter-class social diffusion of bourgeois family norms and housewife marriage, with the coming of liveable pensions and of standardized retirement. In the two decades right after World War II this pattern of homogenization and standardization reached its zenith. Since then all these features have become more variable.

For the Western European family in particular, what happened did not lead to some 'aftermath of the family', but rather to a return to its modern historical complexity, including non-marriage as well as marriage, variable age at marriage, informal cohabitation and extra-marital births. In terms of lone parenthood, Britain had by 1981 returned to the English proportions of 1551–1705, although now driven by divorce rather than by death (Wall 1989: table 5). This complexity, of course, includes a number of new, or previously rare or marginal, forms: the dual-income couple; the deliberately childless couple, which seems to have been pioneered on a significant scale in West Germany (Eurostat 1999: 108–9); the only-child childhood; the empty-nest middle-aged couple (cf. Hareven 2000); and the single elderly person household (cf. Gundy 1999).

This recovered complexity may come to include a tendency to a conservative re-ordering, pleaded by Fukuyama (1999), as well an extension of Giddensian 'pure relationships'. But it is unlikely within the foreseeable future to be seriously reduced by either. Complexity is likely to remain, and with it a contingency of sexual relations, partnerships and family forms, around a modal pattern of long-term, institutionalized heterosexual coupling.

But it is a complexity rent by contradictions and conflicts. The fall of patriarchy has given rise and prominence to a set of contradictions or hard issues with which people are wrestling, and to which there are no easy solutions at hand.

All surveys point to there being a strong desire both to embark on a career and to form a family, including having children. But how to combine them is a difficult task, which many people have not yet been able to solve satisfactorily. One implication of this was that in the 1990s fewer children than desired were born.

Many taboos about sex have disappeared, and there is earlier, more frequent and, it seems, better sex than before. On the other hand, the new sexual openness has not taken away the longing for deep, lasting and exclusive emotional bonding.

Thirdly, there is at the same time a demand for and an enjoyment of individual autonomy and an actual family dependence, which in many countries has rather increased in recent years. Young people tend, for economic and housing reasons, to live longer with their parents, although the level of this parental dependence varies greatly among countries, and a growing proportion of old and longer-living people become dependent on children or other relatives, for social and physical reasons.

Finally, sexual and personal relations are subject to processes of commodification, which clash both with erotic equality and with romantic commitment. In many respects this is also a historical return to the earlier modern ages of mass prostitution, now updated as sex industry and sex tourism. Seemingly more novel are tendencies to auto-commodification in contemporary youth and para-entertainment cultures: corporeal exhibition, sexual display, using one's own person as a social stage actor, a personal marketing for extrinsic exchange relationships. The careful rearing of the French *courtesanes* has a more popular succession.

None of these conflicts is necessarily fatal or even threatening to the existing institutional set-up. They only indicate that the future will have its problems too.

Different rules and practices of marriage and sexuality have remained in the world. By and large they became more different in the past century. The evidence available to me does not provide any firm ground for predicting whether that divergence will continue, stop, or be reversed. But important differences are very likely to remain in the coming decades. What will probably also happen is a growth of diversity of sexual relations and of coupling within the large Asian family cultures. Pre-marital non-commercial sex and informal pairing will become less rare. Whether the African socio-sexual order will stabilize in some mutated form or slip further into Creole-like phallocracy and matrifocality will depend crucially on its economic development. Economic prospects will also strongly affect whether Latin American family and sexual relations will become similar to their Western European contemporaries or to their nineteenth-century past.

But in the end, the best bet for the future is on the inexhaustible innovative capacity of humankind, which eventually surpasses all social science.

Appendix

A note on primary sources

The references in the text and their listing in the Bibliography section show the empirical supports upon which this work rests. However, primary sources sometimes have a notational pattern which differs from the literary standard, and which therefore may appear clumsy or unclear in a standard reference system, like the one used in this book. Therefore, a few words on the basic primary sources utilized may be in order.

Apart from the vast literature resorted to, there are three kinds of primary sources here: legal collections – of laws, including in the German and Swedish cases their parliamentary preparation, of UN Conventions and, in the American case, of decisive court decisions; official statistics – censuses and other statistical series, national and international; and a set of international demographic surveys, from the 1970s to the first years of the twenty-first century.

The statistics speak for themselves, and nowadays they usually exist in on-line as well as in printed versions. Here use has been made of both, depending on what has been most convenient in each case. Electronic addresses for the Latin American census data used in Table 6.5 are:

Argentina: http://www.indec.mecon.ar/webcenso
Bolivia: http://www.ine.gov.bo/beyond/esn/ReportFolders
Chile: http://www.ine.cl/cd2002/index.php
Colombia: http://www.dane.gov.co/inf_est/censo_demografia.htm
Costa Rica: http://www.inec.go.cr
Ecuador: http://www.inec.gov.ec/interna.asp?inc=enc_tablas_graf&idEncuesta=7
Guatemala: http://www.segeplan.gob.gt/ine/index.htm
Mexico: http://www.inegi.gob.mx/est/default.asp?c=2412

Most of the legal collections can be, and have been, referred to in a standard format. But two specialities of legal references should be noted. Both express a veneration for pioneers. In legal scholarship, and in German law in particular, there is a tradition of officious legal commentary being subject to expanded reproduction by later scholars, meaning, for instance, that the original commentary on the German Civil Code of 1896 by J. von Staudinger is continued long after his death, and then titled 'Staudinger's Commentary' xth edition.

German legal scholarship has also enriched international knowledge by compiling and translating laws from all over the world. Since World War II, these compilations have been running both as national series under a founding author's name, such as Leske-Loewenfeld, or as a collection of continuous updates, like Bergmann and Ferid. In law libraries they are identified under the names of their founding editors. Bergmann and Ferid is a continuously updated collection of laws on marriage and childhood, translated into German, and provided with a brief history of legislation, but no commentary.

A third major primary source of this study are international demographic surveys. The first was a series of World Fertility Surveys, carried out in the 1970s and reported in the 1980s. Demographers have made special reports from them, which sometimes have been referred to, e.g. Cleland and Hobcraft (1985), but the primary reports were released, in mimeographed format, by the International Statistical Institute in The Hague. The Demographic and Health Surveys of the 1980s and 1990s, up to early 2000, may be accessed through Macro International, Calverton, Maryland, USA (http://www.measuredhs.com/). The Population Council in New York has also made available special data on adolescents from the Demographic and Health Surveys (www.Popcouncil.org).

In Europe, the UN Economic Commission for Europe sponsored in the 1990s a series of Fertility and Family Surveys (http://www.unece.org/ead/pau/ffs/ffs_standtabframe.htm). The companion American survey is not in the same public domain. I gained access to it through the kind collegiality of Dr Erik Klijzing of Bielefeld University (erik.klijzing@uni-bielefeld.de).

Notes

Part I Patriarchy: its exits and closures

1 Modernities and family systems: patriarchy around 1900

1 This twenty-first-century English does not convey the late nineteenth-century German solemnity of what the wife had to direct, *das gemeinschaftliche Hauswesen*.

2 The Ezhavas were the upper tier of untouchability; below them were the slave castes. This caste organized one of the first successful caste movements of social reform in India, starting in the late nineteenth century. Later this movement carried over into the Communist Party, which is unusually strong in Kerala, in independent India alternating in government with the Congress Party (Jeffrey 1992: ch. 8; Ramachandran 2000: 100ff).

3 For a wonderful analysis of the novel and its fate in English translations, see B. Anderson, *The Spectre of Comparisons* (London, Verso, 1998, chs 10 and 11). Rizal, who is remembered and revered as 'the First Filipino', was executed by the Spanish in 1896. The lascivious friars of Rizal's novel were not just a standard anticlerical theme of a Catholic country. The early modern nationalism of the Filipinas owed much to a peculiar split and conflict within the Catholic Church. Because of the scarcity of ordinary priests, Filipino parishes had long been manned by friars from religious orders, Franciscans and Dominicans above all, outside the normal episcopal line of command. As bishops began recruiting native priests, the ecclesiastical contest acquired ethnic overtones. With the support of the conservative Spanish Governors-General the friars kept the upper hand. The countdown to the uprising of the 1890s began with the execution in 1872 of three Filipino priests, accused of sedition. Believers in their innocence included the Archbishop, who refused to excommunicate them and instead had the bells tolled for the executed.

4 China did have a press at this time, but more an official gazette than a free one. I owe this point to my Uppsala colleague, the eighteenth-century literary historian Marie-Christine Skuncke.

5 Another noteworthy part of this policy was the inclusion of five girls in the important Iwakura embassy-cum-study mission to the United States and Europe in 1871–73 (Sievers 1983: 12).

6 The legal text used here is a contemporary English translation by a German lawyer in Tokio, J. Jönholm (1898).

7 The sweeping condemnation of the Meiji Family Code, that 'The wife had no legal capacity at all and was listed as an "incompetent" in the Civil Code', put forward by Hiroshi Oda, Sir Ernest Satow Professor of Japanese Law at the University of London (Oda 1992: 232) is not quite warranted.

8 As the neo-Confucian Dean of the Todai Law School, Hozumi, put it, 'The ancestors of my ancestors is the Sun Goddess. The Sun Goddess is the founder of our race, and the throne is the sacred house of our race' (Pyle 1998: 126).

9 Samuel Smiles' *Self-Help, with Illustrations of Conduct and Perseverence*, which first appeared in London in 1859, was a tremendously successful pedagogical tract of liberal individualism, full of anecdotal examples from a vast range of areas, industrial invention and entrepreneurship, art, science, military exploits of British imperial commanders, etc. It was written primarily for young men of the ambitious Victorian working and middle classes. In its introduction it also hinted at what we would now call a 'theory of development', dismissing the importance of institutions, laws and nationality, and instead emphasizing the assiduity, energy and virtue of the individuals of the nation. It was this theory of development which appealed to Asian and North African readers.

2 A long night's journey into dawn

1 At least one major reason for this absence were the bitter political fights with the Catholic Church, and the fear of the anti-clerical liberals, or Radicals as they were usually labelled, for clerical sway over women, which made the male liberals of Catholic countries unconcerned with a public role for women, and then also for family changes for the promotion of such roles.

2 My reading of the laws and of legislative process is mainly from the Swedish parliamentary records for 1915 and 1920. A brief overview in English, including of the Nordic context, is given in Melby *et al.* (2001). See further Bradley (1996).

3 It is typical of clerical resignation at the time, that in the Swedish First Chamber debate of 1915, one of the really right-wing ultras, Sam Clason, in his speech against the new marriage bill, referred only hypothetically to what wisdom would come out if 'the men of the Church' were asked. The latter were not actively expressing opposition.

4 The overall female labour force participation rate was somewhat higher in Turkey than in Iran, but for the latter country there are no statistics on how many of these economically active women are 'family helpers'.

5 Although put into a minority, the Communist countries stayed in the drafting process of the Declaration, and gave it a reluctant legitimacy by abstaining in the final vote, rather than voting against it.

6 This rule, which derived from the French legal tradition – from which it had been expunged in 1933 – was not meant as a parental veto, and could be brought to court if disputed. Rather, it was a norm of filial piety, an *acte respectueux* (an act of respect) (Coester-Waltjen and Coester 1997: 16n). The norm was around in the preparations of the German Civil Code in the 1890s, but was finally rejected and did not make it into the Code of 1896.

3 The patriarchal burden of the twenty-first century

1 In the candle ceremony, the bride and the groom each light a candle from a candle at their parents' table, and then together light the other candles of the room. In the more explicit flower presentation, they bow to their parents, as an expression of gratitude, which may also be expressed verbally, and then present their mother with a bouquet of flowers, and their father with a carnation in his lapel.

Part II Marriage and mutations of the socio-sexual order

1 Four of them refer to variations of a father's gift of his virgin daughter in marriage. They are the four virtuous forms. Then there is the variant of bridewealth given by the groom. At the bottom of the list are abduction of the girl, and seduction by stealth. The latter two are clearly illegal, and subject to punishment, but may have legal marriage effects nevertheless, if the proper rites are performed. For a modern reader, the most interesting way of procuring a wife is the *Gandharva* variant, sixth

only on the eight-point scale of virtue, and clearly blameworthy. That is the 'voluntary union of a maiden and her lover' (Mayne 1953: 121).

2 In Gary Becker's (1991) major economic *Treatise on the Family* there is, however, a conspicuous silence on the sexual economy, in spite of chapters 2 and 3 on polygamy/monogamy and on 'assortative mating'.

3 Strictly speaking, there was one other valid ground for a wife-initiated divorce. Upon reaching puberty a girl who had been given in marriage by someone other than her father or grandfather could ask for a divorce, provided that her marriage had not been consummated (Esposito 1982: 78).

4 Both regard marriage as a dissolvable contract, and a religious duty. Jewish law originally allowed husbands up to four wives, and invested divorce rights exclusively in the former. Both had a principle of voluntary marriage, but allowed children to marry at the first signs of puberty, i.e. when still fully dependent on their father. Judaism moved on from there, though. A Synod in Mainz (960–1028) allowed for divorce by mutual consent, and for a wife's right to sue for fault divorce (Bergmann 1926: ch. IV).

4 Sex and marriage in 1900

1 Involving Annie Besant, not (closely) related to Walter Besant.

2 Actually, the first volume (*The Inversion of Sex*) appeared in 1896, in a German translation as *Das konträre Geschlechtsgefühl*, and the first English edition of it, of 1898, was bought up before appearing (Ellis 1939: 351).

3 The study of sexual behaviour developed in the Weimar Republic between the wars, by Magnus Hirschfeldt and Wilhelm Reich, and in Britain from the late 1930s, but the real empirical breakthroughs were studies directed by the American entomologist Alfred Kinsey, and published in 1948, on male sexual behaviour, and in 1953 on women (Kinsey *et al.* 1948, 1953). Sexuality never became a mainstream of social, psychological or medical research, but the Kinsey tradition lived on to produce a series of replicas.

4 At least at the provincial level: all Italy was 'Western' by this time, although the south married earlier and had fewer permanent celibates than the national average. The lowest age at first female marriage in 1901 was in Basilicata, at 21.7, with a female rate of permanent celibacy of 8.7 per cent. Abruzzi had less celibacy and a higher marriage age, 6.4 and 23.6 per cent, respectively (Barbagli 1984: 498). Spain had the largest internal variation of marriage patterns in Western Europe, and parts of it, mainly in Castilia-León and in Aragón, had 'Eastern' customs of almost universal marriage, but the marriage age was usually 'Western European': out of 476 judicial districts in 1887, the lowest mean age of first female marriage was 21 (Reher 1997: 155).

5 In Central America, Costa Rica (300,000 inhabitants in 1900) has tended to a lower rate of illegitimacy than its neighbours – only 20 per cent of births out of wedlock in 1910, but the mulatto Atlantic province of Limón and the cattle hacienda Pacific region of Guanacaste had about 60 per cent (Perez Brignoli 1981: 487). In four parishes of Paraguay in the 1850s, the proportion of children out of wedlock ranged from 55 to 76 per cent (Potthast-Jutkeit 1991: 226).

6 While the Creole family system as such has hardly been analysed in its totality, the literature on its key features is enormous. The works which have taught me most include, on slavery societies: Freyre (1933/1970), Martinez-Alier (1974), Patterson (1967, 1998), Borges (1992), Wyatt-Brown (1986), Morris (1995), Stolcke (1992); on *mestizaje* societies: Potthast-Jutkeit (1991, 1997), McCaa (1993, 1994), Kuznesof (1991), Arrom (1985), Lavrin (1978, 1989), Navarro and Sánchez Korrol (1999); an instructive demographic comparison is provided by Charbit (1987); interesting insights into Indian–mestizo relations may be found in Fals Borda (1962), Gutierrez de Pineda (1976), Tumin (1952), Hawkins (1984), Price (1965) and Mayer and Bolton (1980).

7 This assessment is based (cited sources on Mexico, Brazil, West Indies, Paraguay, and the Southern Cone, apart) on an extrapolation backwards of somewhat later birth (Hartley 1975: tables 2 and 3) and marriage statistics (Mitchell 1998: table A6) from Central America and the Andean countries, and overviews (Das and Jesser 1980; Marin Lira 1981; Deere 1990: 98).

5 Marital trends of the twentieth century

1 An experienced, Indophile British missionary, C.F. Andrews (1939) wrote a well-reasoned, circumspect rebuttal of Mayo.
2 Sometimes pressure may be applied. In November 2000 the Sharia Implementation Board of the Nige state in Nigeria proclaimed that unemployed single women had to either marry or leave the state (Muhammad 2001).
3 In the 1900s cohort about 10 per cent left their parental home before the age of 16, to earn their living.
4 William Goode (1993) has written a major overview of divorce in the world, and there are at least two very good recent Anglo-Saxon histories, by Lawrence Stone (1995) and by Roderick Philips (1991). An explanatory account of late twentieth-century OECD changes is given by Frank Castles (1993). On pioneering Scandinavia, English readers will appreciate the skillful and very knowledgeable work of David Bradley (1996), although mainly focused on later developments of Nordic family law. The legal context is provided by the key figure of the Scandinavian Law Commission, the Danish professor Viggo Bentzon (1924–26).

6 The return of cohabitation and the sexual revolution

1 *Contractus perfectus est per solum consensum*, as Church doctrine put it.
2 These data derive from demographic life-tables and have been calculated by Robert Schoen and associates. They refer to Belgium and Sweden, but, give or take a few years of birth, they should hold for most of Western Europe (Schoen and Urton 1979: tables 4–5; Devos 1999: tables 18–19).
3 The Swedish welfare state played a significant, initiating role in the process of change. One of the most publicized and influential 'du reforms' was made in 1967 by an incoming Director-General of the National Health Board, calling a meeting of all its employees and declaring that from now on everyone should address the Director-General, and everybody else, as 'du'.
4 Unless stated otherwise, the sources used on cohabitation in the 1990s derive from the Fertility and Family Surveys, undertaken in the 1990s by the UN Economic Commission for Europe and the UN Population Fund.
5 On average for 1996–2000, 51 per cent of Icelandic babies had cohabiting parents, 36 per cent had married parents, and 13 per cent had a mother living single (Hagstofa Islands, 2002, www.stat.ice.is).
6 In East Germany, Russia, and in other Communist countries, there had developed a kind of state familism, with vigorous natalist policies and a tight housing allocation clearly favouring married couples.
7 The 1996 Demographic and Health Survey of Brazil gives a much lower figure for cohabitation, about a third of all unions.
8 A plausible explanation for part of the discrepancy seems to be that the lower figure came from interviews made in the home, whereas the highest figure derived from a self-administered questionnaire filled in at school.
9 A Mexico City study around 1990 found a 5:1 ratio of male to female adultery (de la Peña and Toledo, source unknown).
10 Heaton *et al.* found one exception, the Guaraní-speaking region of southern Bolivia, an Indian culture with a norm of sexual lateness.
11 The way this is measured by the Demographic and Health Surveys of the mid- to

late 1990s is a question about whether the person (women only) has been sexually active or not in the past 4 weeks. Argentina and Mexico were not part of the eight Latin American samples.

Part III Couples, babies and states

7 *Fertility decline and political natalism*

1 For some recent assessments, see Bulatao and Casterline (2001), Alter (1992), Chesnais (1992), C. Renshaw *et al.* (2000), van de Kaa (1996), Kirk (1996) and Szreter (1996).
2 Here cited from Ho 1959: 274–75. Wang Shih-to was an impoverished merchant who wrote this diary while a captive of the Taiping rebels in 1855–56. Ho used the 1881 edition of his diary.
3 How much their early birth control was due to their class is not clear from Livi-Bacci's treatment of the Jews, although he notices that the rural Jews of Italy, for whom early modern birth records have been found, did not limit their offspring. In Russia urban Jews had a higher fertility than the rest of the urban population (Coale *et al.* 1979: 78ff).
4 There might also have been a decline in some other parts of the Caribbean as well as Cuba, and birth rates there tended to be lower than in continental Latin America. However, Mitchell's (1998a) birth rates do not support this; nor do the early 1950s fertility data reported in Guzmán *et al.* (1996: 5) bear out Chesnais' (1992: 108) low birth rates for the Caribbean in 1925.
5 Already in 1566 the Genevan publisher and humanist Henri Estienne Jr referred to noble ladies not having to resort to abortion or infanticide, because they were using 'several preventives which keep them from becoming pregnant', cited by Freyer (1965: 31).
6 For 1880, for instance, Comstock proudly reported the seizure and destruction of '24,225 pounds of books and sheet stock', and 64,094 'rubber articles for immoral use'. He had, he said, a register of the names and addresses of 901,125 people receiving goods from 'smut dealers' (Brodie 1994: 281).

8 *The politics and sociology of birth control*

1 The interesting reversal of the traditional Catholic association with higher fertility than Protestants, which Castles noticed for OECD countries between 1980 and 1998, occurred in the US in the 1970s to early 1980s, there largely due to later and less frequent marriage (Mosher and Bachrach 1996: 13).

Bibliography

Abbasi-Shavazi, M.J. (2000) 'Effects of Marital Fertility and Nuptiality on Fertility Transition in the Islamic Republic of Iran 1976–1996', Canberra: The Australian National University, Research School of the Social Sciences, Demography Program.

Abbott, Ph. (1981) *The Family on Trial. Special Relationships in Modern Political Thought*, University Park and London: Pennsylvania State University Press.

Abraham, K. and Kumar, K.A. (1999) 'Sexual Experiences and Their Correlates Among College Students in Mumbai City, India' *International Family Planning Perspectives* 25,3: 139–46, 152.

Abu, K. (1983) 'The Separateness of Spouses: Conjugal Resources in an Ashanti Town', in C. Oppong (ed.), *Female and Male in West Africa*, London: George Allen & Unwin.

Afshar, H. (1993) *Women in the Middle East*, London: Macmillan.

Agarwal, B. (1994) *A Field of One's Own*, Cambridge: Cambridge University Press.

Agarwal, B. (1998) 'Widows versus Daughters or Widows as Daughters? Property, Land, and Economic Security in Rural India', in M. Alter Chen (ed.), *Widows in India*, New Delhi and London: Sage Publications.

Agell, A., Forsman, G. and Ingebrand, G. (1980) *Äktenskap eller samboende*, Stockholm: Liber.

Ahmad, A. (1998) 'Women in Malaysia', Manila: Asian Development Bank, Country Briefing Paper.

Aijmer, G. and Ho, V. (2000) *Cantonese Society in a Time of Change*, Hong Kong: The Chinese University Press.

Aird, J. (1982) 'Population Studies and Population Policies in China', *Population and Development Review* 8.

Ajami, F. (1981) *The Arab Predicament*, Cambridge: Cambridge University Press.

Ajayi, A. and Kekovole, J. (1998) 'Kenya's Population Policy: From Apathy to Effectiveness', in A. Jain (ed.), *Do Population Policies Matter?*, New York: Population Council.

Akerlof, G. (1998) 'Men Without Children', *The Economic Journal* 108: 287–309.

Alan Guttmacher Institute (1998) *Into A New World. Young Women's Sexual and Reproductive Lives*, New York: Alan Guttmacher Institute.

Albisetti, J. (1996) 'Female Education in German-Speaking Austria, Germany, and Switzerland, 1866–1914', in D. Good *et al.* (eds), *Austrian Women in the Nineteenth and Twentieth Centuries*, Providence, RI, and Oxford: Berghahn Books.

Ali, M. and Cleland, J. (2001) 'The Link Between Postnatal Abstinence and Extramarital Sex in Côte d'Ivoire', *Studies in Family Planning* 32,3: 214–29.

Alpern Engel, B. (1976) 'Mothers and Daughters: Family Pattern and the Female Intelligentsia', in D. Ransel (ed.), *The Family in Imperial Russia*, Urbana, Chicago and London: University of Illinois Press, 44–59.

Alter, G. (1992) 'Theories of Fertility Decline: A Non-Specialist's Guide to the Current Debate', in J. Gillis *et al.* (eds), *The European Experience of Declining Fertility, 1850–1970*, Oxford: Blackwell.

Alter, G. *et al.* (2000) 'Beyond Malthus: Reproductive Strategies in Asia and Europe before the Demographic Transition', presented at the Population Association of America, Los Angeles, March 23–25, 2000.

Althaus, F. (1997) 'Most Japanese students do not have intercourse until after adolescence', *Family Planning Perspectives* 29: 145–46.

Amin, S. and Cain, M. (1997) 'The Rise of Dowry in Bangladesh', in G. Jones *et al.* (eds), *The Continuing Demographic Transition*, Oxford: Clarendon Press.

Amin, S. and Lloyd, C. (2002) 'Women's Lives and Rapid Fertility Decline: Some Lessons from Bangladesh and Egypt', *Population Research and Policy Review* 21: 275–317.

Andersen, I. (1998) 'Cohabitation and Registered Partnership in Scandinavia – The Legal Position of Homosexuals', in J. Eekelaar and T. Nhlapo (eds), *The Changing Family*, Oxford: Hart Publishing.

Anderson, B. (1998) *The Spectre of Comparisons*, London: Verso.

Anderson, G. (ed.) (1997) *The Family in Global Transitions*, St Paul, MN: World Peace Academy.

Andrews, C.F. (1939) *The True India*, London: George Allen and Unwin.

Angulo-Novoa, A. (1980) 'The Family in Colombia', in M.S. Das and C. Jesser (eds), *The Family in Latin America*, New Delhi: Vikas Publishing House.

Anon. (2000) 'The Context of Young People's Sexual Relations', *Progress in Reproductive Health Research* 53: 2–3.

Aphornsuvan, T. (1998) 'Slavery and Modernity: Freedom in the Making of Modern Siam', in D. Kelly and A. Reid (eds), *Asian Freedoms*, Cambridge: Cambridge University Press.

Appiah, K. (1992) *In My Father's House*, Oxford: Oxford University Press.

Applbaum. K. (1985) 'Marriage with the Proper Stranger: Arranged Marriages in Metropolitan Japan', *Ethnology* XXXIV: 37–51.

Ardayfio-Schandorf, E. (ed.) (1996) *The Changng Family in Ghana*, Accra: Ghana Universities Press.

Arrom, S. (1985) *The Women of Mexico City, 1790–1857*, Stanford: Stanford University Press.

Asian Development Bank (2000) 'Women in Pakistan', Manila: Programs Department paper.

Asian Development Bank (2001) 'Women in Bangladesh', Manila: Programs Department paper.

Australian Bureau of Statistics (2000) *Australian Social Trends 2000. Family – National summary tables* [www. abs.gov.au/ausstats/abs].

Avdeev, A. and Mounier, A. (1999) 'La Nuptialité Russe', *Population* 54,4–5: 635–76.

Badran, M. and Cooke, M. (1990) 'Introduction', in M. Badran and M. Cooke (eds), *Opening the Gates*, London: Virago.

Baer, J. (1996) *Women in American Law*, New York and London: Holmes and Meier.

Bainham, A. (ed.) (1995) *The International Survey of Family Law*, The Hague: Martinus Nijhoff.

Bairoch, P. (1988) *Cities and Economic Development*, London: Mansell Publishing.

Bairoch, P. (1997) *Victoires et Déboires*, 3 vols, Paris: Gallimard.

Barakat, H. (1993) *The Arab World, Society, Culture, and State*, Berkeley: University of California Press.

Barbagli, M. (1984) *Sotto Lo Stesso Tetto,* Bologna: Il Mulino.

Barbarin, O. and Richter, L. (2001) *Mandela's Children*, New York, London: Routledge.

Barceló, R. (1997) 'Hegemonia y Conflicto en la ideologia porfiriana sobre el papel de la mujer y la familia', in S. Monte Gonzales and J. Tuñon (eds), *Familias y Mujeres en Mexico*, Mexico D.F.: Colegio de México.

Barmé, S. (1999) 'Proto-feminist Discourses in Early Twentieth Century Siam', in P. Jackson and N. Cook (eds), *Genders and Sexualities in Modern Thailand*, Bangkok: Silkworm Books.

Barnes, T. (2002) 'Virgin Territory? Travel and Migration by African Women in Twentieth-Century Southern Africa', in J. Allman *et al.* (eds), *Women in African Colonial Histories*, Bloomington: Indiana University Press.

Baron, B. (1991) 'The Making and Breaking of Marital Bonds in Egypt', in N. Keddie and B. Baron (eds), *Women in Middle Eastern History*, New Haven and London: Yale University Press, 275–91.

Baron, B. (2000) 'The Making of the Egyptian Nation', in I. Blom *et al.* (eds), *Gendered Nations*, Oxford: Berg, 137–58.

Barrett, D. (1995) *Reproducing Persons as a Global Concern: The Making of an Institution*, Stanford Sociology PhD Thesis, Ann Arbor, MI: UMI Dissertation Service.

Barrig, M. (2001) *El Mundo al revés: imágenes de la mujer indígena*, Buenos Aires: CLACSO.

Barrow, C. (1996) *Family in the Caribbean*, Kingston and Oxford: Ian Randle and James Currey.

Bartley, K. (1998) *Barnpolitik och barnets rättigheter*, Göteborg: Sociologiska institutionen, Göteborgs Universitet.

Basauri, C. (1940) *La población indígena de México*, Ciudad de México: Secretaría de Educación Pública.

Basu Malwade, A. (1999) 'Fertility Decline and Increasing Gender Imbalance in India, Including a Possible South Indian Turnaround', *Development and Change*, 30,2: 237–63.

Beasley, W.G. (1990) *The Rise of Modern Japan*, New York: St Martin's Press.

Bebel, A. (1879/1979) *Die Frau und der Sozialismus*, Berlin: Dietz Verlag.

Beck-Gernsheim, E. (1998) *Was Kommt nach der Familie?* Munich: C.H. Beck.

Becker, G. (1991) *Treatise on the Family*, Cambridge, London: Harvard University Press.

Beeghley, L. (1996) *What Does Your Wife Do?*, Boulder, CO: Westview Press.

Behar, C. (1995) 'The Fertility Transition in Turkey: Reforms, Policies, and Family Structure', in C.M. Obermeyer (ed.), *Family, Gender, and Population in the Middle East*, Cairo: The American University in Cairo Press.

Behrman, J., Duryea, S. and Székely, M. (1999) 'Decomposing Fertility Differences Across World Regions and Over Time: Is Improved Health More Important than Women's Schooling?', *Working Paper 406* Washington, DC: Inter-American Development Bank.

Bélanger, D. and Khuat Thu Hong (2001) 'Parents' Involvement in Children's Marriage', in J. Kleinen (ed.), *Vietnamese Society in Transition*, Amsterdam: Het Spinhuis.

Bénéï, V. (1996) *La dot en Inde un fléau social?* Paris: Karthala.

Benitez Perez, M.E. (1999) *Familia Cubana*, La Habana: Editorial de Ciencias Sociales.

Bentzon, V. (1924–26) *Familieretten I–II*, 2 vols. Copenhagen: G.E.C. Gad.

Berathung (1896) *Berathung, Zweite und dritte, des Entwurfs eines bürgerlichen Gesetzbuchs im Reichstage*, Stenographische Berichte, Berlin: J. Guttentag.

Berelson, B. (ed.) (1969) *Family Planning Programs*, New York: Basic Books.

Berelson, B. *et al.* (eds) (1966) *Family Planning and Population Programs*, Chicago: Chicago University Press.

Berg, M. (1994) *Seldas andra bröllop*, Göteborg: Etnologiska föreningen i Västra Sverige.

Bergmann, A. (1926/1928) *Internationales Ehe- und Kindschaftsrecht* (1st edn), Berlin: Verlag des Reichsbundes der Standesbeamten Deutschlands. 3 vols (vols 1, 2, 1926, vol. 3, 1928).

Bergmann, A. (1938/1940) *Internationales Ehe- und Kindschaftsrecht* (2nd edn), Berlin: Verlag für Standesamtswesen, 2 vols (vol. 1 1938, vol. 2 1940).

Bergmann, A. and Ferid, M. (1955–) *Internationales Ehe- und Kindschaftsrecht*, Frankfurt: Verlag für Standeswesen. See Appendix.

Beri, B.P. (1992) *Law of Marriage and Divorce in India*, New Delhi: Eastern Book Company.

Berkner, L. and Mendel, F. (1978) 'Inheritance Systems, Family Structure, Demographic Pattern in Western Europe, 1700–1900', in C. Tilly (ed.), *Historical Studies of Changing Fertility*, Princeton, NJ: Princeton University Press.

Berkowitz, N. (1999) *From Motherhood to Citizenship: Women's Rights and International Organizations*, Baltimore: Johns Hopkins University Press.

Bernhardt, E. and Hoem, B. (1985) 'Cohabitation and Social Background: Trends Observed for Swedish Women Born Between 1936 and 1960', *European Journal of Population* 1: 375–95.

Bernhardt, K. (1996) 'A Ming-Qing Transition in Women's History? The Perspective from Law', in G. Hershatter *et al.* (eds), *Remapping China*, Stanford: Stanford University Press, 42–58.

Berquó, E. and Xenos, P. (eds) (1992) *Family Systems and Cultural Change*, Oxford: Clarendon Press.

Besemers, J. (1980) *Socialist Population Politics*, New York: M E. Sharpe.

Beuys, B. (1980) *Familienleben in Deutschland*, Reinbek bei Hamburg: Rowohlt.

Bhat, P.N.M. (1989) 'Mortality and Fertility in India, 1881–1961: a Reassessment', in T. Dyson (ed.), *India's Historical Demography*, London: Curzon Press.

Bhat, P.N.M. (2002) 'On the Trail of "Missing" Indian Females', *Economic and Political Weekly* 21: 5105–18.

Bhat, P.N.M. and Halli, S. (1999) 'Demography of Brideprice and Dowry: Causes and Consequences of the Indian Marriage Squeeze', *Population Studies* 53: 129–48.

Bideleux, R. (1985) *Communism and Development*, London and New York: Methuen.

Billari, F. and Borgoni, R. (2002) 'Spatial Profiles in the Analysis of Event Histories: An Application to First Sexual Intercourse in Italy', *International Journal of Population Geography* 8: 261–75.

Binstock, H. (1998) 'Hacia la igualdad de la mujer', Santiago de Chile: CEPAL/ECLAC, SMYD No. 24.

Biraben, J.N. (1979) 'Essai sur l'évolution du nombre des hommes', *Population* 34.

Blackburn, R. (1997) *The Making of New World Slavery*, London: Verso.

Blackburn, S. and Bessell, S. (1997) 'Marriage Age: Political Debates on Early Marriage in Twentieth Century Indonesia', *Indonesia* 63: 107–35.

Blanc, A. (2001) 'The Effect of Power in Sexual Relationships on Sexual and Reproductive Health: An Examintion of the Evidence', *Studies in Family Planning* 32,3: 189–213.

Blanc, A. and Way, A. (1998) 'Sexual Behavior and Contraceptive Knowledge and Use among Adolescents in Developing Countries', *Studies in Family Planning* 29,2: 106–16.

Blom, I. and Tranberg, A. (1985) *Nordisk lovoversikt. Viktige lover for kvinner ca. 1810–1980*, Oslo: Nordisk Ministerråd.

Blum, A.S. (1998) 'Public welfare and child circulation, Mexico City, 1877 to 1925', *Journal of Family History* 23: 240–71.

Boahen, A. (ed.) (1985) *General History of Africa. VII*, London, Berkeley and Paris: Heinemann/ University of California Press/Unesco.

Boahen, A. (1989) *African Perspectives on Colonialism*, Baltimore, MA: Johns Hopkins University Press (paperback edn).

Bodde, D. and Morris, C. (1967) *Law in Imperial China*, Cambridge, MA: Harvard University Press.

Bolton, R. (1980) 'El proceso matrimonial Qolla', in E. Mayer and R. Bolton (eds), *Parentesco y matrimonio en los Andes*, Lima: Fondo Editorial.

Bonauto, M. (2001) 'The Freedom to Marry for Same-Sex Couples in the United States', in R. Wintemute and M. Andenaes (eds), *Legal Recognition of Same-Sex Partnerships*, London: Hart.

Bonfield, L., Smith, R.M. and Wrightson, K. (eds) (1986) *The World We Have Gained*, Oxford: Basil Blackwell.

Bongaarts, J. (1978) 'Framework for analyzing the proximate determinants of fertility', *Population and Development Review* 14: 105–32.

Bongaarts, J. (2001a) *Household Size and Composition in the Developing World*, New York: Population Council.

Bongaarts, J. (2001b) *The End of the Fertility Transition in the Developed World*, New York: Population Council.

Bongaarts, J. (2002) *The End of the Fertility Transition in the Developing World*, New York: Population Council.

Bongaarts, J. and Barney, C. (1998) 'Introduction and Overview', *Studies in Family Planning* 29,2: 99–105.

Bongaarts, J. and Zimmer, Z. (2001) *Living Arrangements of Older Adults in the Developing World: An Analysis of DHS Household Surveys*, New York: Population Council.

Boomgaard, P. (1981) 'Multiplying Masses: Nineteenth Century Population Growth in India and Indonesia', in M. Hasan *et al.* (eds), *India and Indonesia from the 1830s to 1914: the Heyday of Colonial Rule*, Leiden: Brill.

Borges, D. (1992) *The Family in Bahia, Brazil 1870–1945*, Stanford: Stanford University Press.

Bose, S. and Jalal, A. (1997) *Modern South Asia*, London: Routledge.

Boserup, E. (1970) *Woman's Role in Economic Development*, London: George Allen and Unwin.

Botev, N. (1990) 'Nuptiality in the Course of the Demographic Transition: The Experience of the Balkan Countries', *Population Studies* 44: 107–26.

Botiveau, B. (1993) *Loi islamique et droit dans les sociétés arabes*, Paris: Karthala.

Boulanger, F. (1990) *Droit Civil de la Famille*, Paris: Economica.

Bozon, M. and Kontula, O. (1997) 'Initiation sexuelle et genre: comparaison des évolutions de douze pays européens', *Population* 52: 1367–99.

Bradley, D. (1996) *Family Law and Political Culture*, London: Sweet and Maxwell.

Bradley, D. (1998) 'The Antecedents of Finnish Family Law', *Journal of Legal History* 19.

Bradley, D. (1999) 'Comparative Family Law and the Political Process: Regulation of Sexual Morality in Finland', *Journal of Law and Society* 26: 175–91.

Brambila, C. (1998) 'Mexico's Population Policy and Demographic Dynamics: The Record of Three Decades', in A. Jain (ed.), *Do Population Policies Matter?*, New York: Population Council.

Brass, W. *et al.* (1968) *The Demography of Tropical Africa*, Princeton, NJ: Princeton University Press.

Brettell, C. and Metcalf, A. (1993) 'Family Customs in Portugal and Brazil: Transatlantic parallels', *Continuity and Change* 8: 365–88.

Bridger, S. (1987) *Women in the Soviet Countryside*, Cambridge: Cambridge University Press.

Bridges, J. (1980) 'The Mexican Family', in M.S. Das and C. Jesser (eds), *The Family in Latin America*, New Delhi: Vikas Publishing House.

Brien, M., Lillard, L. and Waite, L. (1999) 'Inter-Related Family-Building Behaviors: Cohabitation, Marriage, and Nonmarital Conception', *Demography* 36: 535–51.

Brodie, J.F. (1994) *Contraception and Abortion in Nineteenth-Century America*, Ithaca, NY: Cornell University Press.

Buckley, P. (ed.) (1993) (ed.), *Chinese Civilization: A Sourcebook*, New York: The Free Press.

Buckley, P. (2003) *Women and the Family in Chinese History*, London: Routledge.

Bulatao, R. (2001) 'Introduction', *Population and Development Review* 27 Supplement: 1–15.

Bulatao, R. and Casterline, J. (eds) (2001) 'Global Fertility Transition', *Population and Development Review* 27 Supplement.

Bullender, D. (1997) 'The Debate about Household Headship', Pretoria: STATSSA.

Bürgerliches Gesetzbuch vom 18 August 1896 (1907) München: Becksche Verlagsbuchhandlung.

Burgess, E. and Locke, H. (1945) *The Family*, New York: American Book Company.

Burguière, A. *et al.* (eds) (1986) *Histoire de la famille*, 3 vols, Paris: Armand Colin.

Burns, E.B. (1993) *A History of Brazil*, New York: Columbia University Press.

Buxbaum, D. (ed.) (1978) *Chinese Family Law and Social Change*, Seattle: University of Washington Press.

Byrnes, R.F. (ed.) (1976) *Communal Families in the Balkans: the Zadruga*, Notre Dame: University of Notre Dame Press.

Cady, J. (1958) *A History of Modern Burma*, Ithaca, NY: Cornell University Press.

Caldwell, J.C. (1966) 'Africa', in B. Berelson *et al.* (eds), *Family Planning and Population Programs*, Chicago: Chicago University Press.

Caldwell, J.C. (1982) *Theory of Fertility Decline*, London: Academic Press.

Caldwell, J.C. (1985) 'The Social Repercussions of Colonial Rule: Demographic Aspects', in A. Boahen (ed.), *General History of Africa. VII* London, Berkeley, Paris: Heinemann/University of California Press/Unesco.

Caldwell, J.C. (1999) 'The Delayed Western Fertility Decline: An Examination of English-Speaking Countries', *Population and Development Review* 25,3: 479–513.

Caldwell, J.C. (2001) 'The Globalization of Fertility Behavior', *Population and Development Review* 27 Supplement: 93–115.

Caldwell, J.C. *et al.* (1982) 'The Causes of Demographic Change in Rural South India: A Micro Approach', *Population and Development Reviews* 8: 718.

Caldwell, J.C., Caldwell, P. and Quiggin, P. (1989) 'The Social Context of Aids in Sub-Saharan Africa', *Population and Development Review*, 15,2: 185–234.

Caldwell, J.C., Caldwell, P. and Orubuloye, I. (1992) 'The Family and Sexual Networking in Sub-Saharan Africa: Historical Regional Differences and Present-Day Implications', *Population Studies* 46,3: 385–410.

Caldwell, J.C. *et al.* (1998) 'The Construction of Adolescence in a Changing World: Implications for Sexuality, Reproduction, and Marriage', *Studies of Family Planning* 29,2: 137–53.

Caldwell, J.C. *et al.* (2000) 'Female Genital Mutilation: Conditions of Decline, *Population Research and Policy Review* 19: 233–54.

Caldwell, J.C., Phillips, J. and el-Khuda, B. (2002) 'The Future of Family Planning Programs', *Studies in Family Planning Programs* 33,1: 1–10.

Cannell, F. (1999) *Power and Intimacy in Christian Philippines*, Cambridge: Cambridge University Press.

Carlsson, G. (1966) 'The Decline of Fertility: Innovation or Adjustment Process?' *Population Studies* 20,2: 149–74.

Carmichael, G. (1996) 'From Floating Brothels to Suburban Semirespectability: Two Centuries of Nonmarital Pregnancy in Australia', *Journal of Family History* 21: 281–315.

Carter, W.E. (1980) 'El matrimonio de prueba en los Andes', in E. Mayer and R. Bolton (eds), *Parentesco y matrimonio en los Andes*, Lima: Fondo Editorial.

Carvalho, J.A.M. de and Rodriguez Wong, L. (1996) 'The Fertility Transition in Brazil: Causes and Consequences', in J. Guzmán *et al.* (eds), *The Fertility Transition in Latin America*, Oxford: Clarendon Press.

Cassina de Nogara, A. (1989) *Las Feministas*, Montevideo: Instituto Nacioal del Libro.

Casterline, J. (1999) *The Onset and Pace of Fertility Transition: National Patterns in the Second Half of the Twentieth Century*, New York: Population Council.

Casterline, J. (2001) 'The Pace of Fertility Transition: National Patterns in the Second Half of the Twentieth Century', *Population and Development Review* 27 Supplement: 17–52.

Castles, F.G. (1993) 'Why Divorce Rate Differ: Law, Religious Belief and Modernity', in F. Castles (ed.), *Families of Nations*, Aldershot: Dartmouth.

Castles, F.G. (2003) 'The World Turned Upside Down: Below Replacement Fertility, Changing Preferences and Family-friendly Public Policy in 21 OECD Countries', *Journal of European Social Policy* 13: 209–27.

Caudill, W. and Weinstein, H. (1970) 'Maternal care and infant behavior in Japanese and American urban middle class families', in R. Hill and R. König (eds), *Families in East and West*, Paris, The Hague: Mouton.

Cha, Yon Keun (1966) 'South Korea', in B. Berelson *et al.* (eds), *Family Planning and Population Program*, Chicago: Chicago University Press.

Chackiel, J. and Schkolnik, S. (1996) 'Latin America: Overview of the Fertility Transition, 1950–1980', in J. Guzmán *et al.* (eds), *The Fertility Transition in Latin America*, Oxford: Clarendon Press.

Chakravarti, U. (1990) 'Whatever Happened to the Vedic *Dasi*? Orientalism, Nationalism and a Script for the Past', in K. Sangari and S. Vaid (eds), *Recasting Women: Essays in Indian Colonial History*, New Brunswick, NJ: Rutgers University Press, 73–78.

Chamie, J. (1994) 'Trends, Variations, and Contradictions in National Policies to Influence Fertility', in J. Finkle and A. McIntosh (eds), 'The New Politics of Population: Conflict and Consensus in Family Planning', *Population and Development Review* 20 Supplement: 37–50.

Charbit, Y. (1987) *Famille et Nuptialité dans le Caraïbe*, Paris: Presses Universitaires de France.

Chatterjee, P. (1990) 'The Nationalist Resolution of the Women's Question', in K. Sangari and S. Vaid (eds), *Recasting Women: Essays in Indan Colonial History*, New Brunswick, NJ: Rutgers University Press.

Chen, M.A. (ed.) (1998) *Widows in India*, New Delhi: Sage.

Chesnais, J.-C. (1992) *The Demographic Transition*, Oxford: Clarendon Press.

Chiang, Lan-hung Nora (2000) 'Women in Taiwan: Linking Economic Propesperity and Women's Progress', in L. Edwards and M. Roces (eds), *Women in Asia*, Ann Arbor: University of Michigan Press.

China, People's Republic of, National Bureau of Statistics (2001) *Communiqué on Major Features of the 2000 Population Census* [www.stats.gov.cn/english/p2000].

Chiu, M. (2001) 'Contextualizing the Same-Sex Erotic Relationship: Post-Colonial Tongzhi and Political Discourse on Marriage Law in Hong Kong and Mainland China', in R. Wintemute and M. Andanaes (eds), *Legal Recognition of Same-Sex Partnership*, London: Hart.

Chiu, V. (1965) *Marriage Laws and Customs of China*, Hong Kong: The Chinese University of Hong Kong.

Chloros, A.G. (ed.) (1978) *The Reform of Family Law in Europe*, Deventer: Kluwer.

Chow, L.P. (1969) 'Taiwan: Island Laboratory', in B. Berelson (ed.), *Family Planning Programs*, New York: Basic Books.

Chowdhury, I. (1998) *The Frail Hero and Virile History*, Delhi: Oxford University Press.

Chun, D. (1966) 'Hong Kong', in B. Berelson *et al.* (eds), *Family Planning and Population Program*, Chicago: Chicago University Press.

C.J.S. (*Corpus Juris Secundum*) (1944) *A Complete Restatement of the Entire American Law*, vol. 41, St Paul, MN: West Publishing.

Clark, H. and Glowinsky, C. (1995) *Cases and Problems on Domestic Relations*, St Paul, MN: West Publishing.

Cleland, J. (1994) 'A Regional Review of Fertility Trends in Developing Countries: 1960 to 1990', in W. Lutz (ed.), *The Future of World Population*, London: Earthscan.

Cleland, J. (2001) 'The Effects of Improved Survival on Fertility: A Reassessment', *Population and Development Review* 27 Supplement: 60–92.

Cleland, J. and Hobcraft, J. (eds) (1985) *Reproductive Change in Developing Countries*, Oxford: Oxford University Press.

Coale, A. (1986) 'The Decline of Fertility in Europe since the Eighteenth Century as a Chapter in Human Demographic History', in A. Coale and S.C. Watkins (eds), *The Decline of Fertility in Europe*, Princeton NJ: Princeton University Press.

Coale, A. and Freedman, R. (1993) 'Similarities in the Fertility Transition in China and Three Other East Asian Populations', in R. Leete and I. Alam (eds), *The Revolution in Asian Fertility*, Oxford: Clarendon Press.

Coale, A. and Lorimer, F. (1968) 'Summary of Estimates of Fertility and Mortality', in W. Brass *et al.* (eds), *The Demography of Tropical Africa*, Princeton, NJ: Princeton University Press.

Coale, A. and Watkins, S.C. (eds) (1986) *The Decline of Fertiliy in Europe*, Princeton, NJ: Princeton University Press.

Coale, A. and Zelnik, M. (1963) *New Estimates of Fertility and Population in the United States: A Study of Annual White Births from 1855 to 1960 and of Completeness of Enumeration in the Censuses from 1880 to 1960*, Princeton, NJ: Princeton University Press.

Coale, A., Anderson, B. and Herm, E. (1979) *Human Fertility in Russia since the Nineteenth Century*, Princeton, NJ: Princeton University Press.

Coester-Waltjen, D. and Coester, M. (1997) 'Formation of Marriage', in *International Encyclopedia of Comparative Law*, Tübingen and Dordrecht: Mohr Siebeck and Martinus Nijhoff.

Coleman, D. (2000) ' Population and Family', in A.H. Halsey (ed.), *Twentieth-Century British Social Trends*, Basingstoke: Macmillan.

Coleman, D.A. (2002) 'Populations of the Industrial World – A Convergent Demographic Community?, *International Journal of Population Geography* 8: 319–44.

Committee on the Status of Women in India (1974) *The Status of Women in India*, New Delhi: Government Publications.

Conklin, A. (1997) *A Mission to Civilize*, Stanford, CA: Stanford University Press.

Connelly, M. (2003) 'Population Control in History: New Perspectives on the

International Campaign to Limit Population Growth', *Comparative Studies in Society and History* 45,1: 122–47.

Conrad, C. *et al.* (1998) 'East German Fertility After Unification: Crisis or Adaptation?', *Population and Development Review* 22: 331–58.

Cooper, D. (1971) *The Death of the Family*, London: Penguin.

Coquery-Vidrovitch, C. (1997) *African Women: A Modern History*, Boulder, CO: Westview Press.

Coquery-Vidrovitch, C. (2003) 'Evolution démographique de l'Afrique coloniale', in M. Ferro (ed.), *Le livre noir du colonialisme*, Paris: Robert Laffont.

Cordell, D. and Gregory, J. (eds) (1987) *African Population and Capitalism*, Wisconsin: The University of Wisconsin Press.

Corpus Juris Secundum (1944) *A Complete Restatement of the Entire American Law as Developed by All Reported Cases*, St Paul, MN: West Publishing.

Cosar, F.M. (1978) 'Women in Turkish Society', in N. Keddie and L. Beck (eds), *Women in the Muslim World*, Cambridge, MA: Harvard University Press.

Coulson, N. and Hinchcliffe, D. (1978) 'Women and Law Reform in Contemporary Islam', in N. Keddie and L. Beck (eds), *Women in the Muslim World*, Cambridge, MA: Harvard University Press.

Council of Europe, (2001a) *Recent Demographic Developments in Europe*, Strasbourg.

Council of Europe (2001b) *Demographic Yearbook 2001* [http://www.coe.int/t/e/social-cohesion/population/Demographic_Year_Book].

Crenshaw, E. *et al.* (2000) 'Demographic Transition in Ecological Focus', *American Sociological Review* 65: 371–91.

Cretney, S.M. (1998) *Law, Law Reform and the Family*, Oxford: Clarendon Press.

Cretney, S.M. and Masson, J.M. (1990) *Principles of Family Law*, London: Sweet & Maxwell.

Croll, E. (1981) *The Politics of Marriage in Contemporary China*, Cambridge: Cambridge University Press.

Croll, E. (1990) 'Like the Chinese Goddess of Mercy. Mrs. Little and the *Natural Foot Society*', in D. Goodman (ed.), *China and the West: Ideas and Activists*, Manchester: Manchester University Press.

Croll, E. (1995) *Changing Identities of Chinese Women*, Hong Kong: Hong Kong University Press.

Crook, D. (1959) *Revolution in a Chinese Village*, London: Routledge and Kegan Paul.

Crook, N. (1989) 'On the Comparative Historical Perspective: India, Europe, the Far East', in T. Dyson (ed.), *India's Historical Demography. Studies in Famine, Disease and Society*, London: Curzon Press.

Crusen, G. *et al.* (1937) *Das Eherecht der europäischen Staaten und ihrer Kolonien* (2nd edn), Berlin: Carl Heymanns Verlag.

Czap, P. (1976) 'Marriage and the Peasant Family in the Era of Serfdom', in D. Ransel (ed.), *The Family in Imperial Russia*, Urbana, Chicago and London: University of Illinois Press.

D'Agnes, L. *et al.* (1995) 'Sexual Practices and Patterns of Urban Filipino Males: Implications for HIV Intervention Programs', available at Popline Record [http://db.jhuccp.org./dbtw-wpd].

Dai Kejing (1990) 'The Social Significance of Marriage and the Family in China', in S. Quah (ed.), *The Family as an Asset*, Singapore: Times Academic Press.

Daly, A. (1966) 'Tunisia', in B. Berelson *et al.* (eds), *Family Planning and Population Programs*, Chicago: University of Chicago Press.

Das, H.H. and Mahapatra, S. (1996) *The Indian Renaissance and Raja Rammohan Roy*, Jaipur: Pointer Publishers.

Das, M.S. (ed.) (1991) *The Family in The Muslim World*, New Delhi: M. D. Publication.

Das, M.S. and Jesser, C. (eds) (1980) *The Family in Latin America*, New Delhi: Vikas Publishing.

Das Gupta, M. (2001) 'Synthesizing Diverse Interpretations of Reproductive Change in India', in Z.A. Sathar and J. Philips (eds), *Fertility Transition in South Asia*, Oxford: Oxford University Press.

Das Gupta, M. *et al.* (2000) 'State Policies and Women's Autonomy in China, The Republic of Korea, and India, 1950–2000: Lessons from Contrasting Experiences', Washington D.C.: World Bank, Gender and Development Working Paper Series No. 16.

Davies, C.E.P. (1957) 'Matrimonial Relief in English Law', in R.H. Graven and F.R. Crane (eds), *A Century of Family Law*, London: Sweet & Maxwell.

Davis, D. (1993) 'Urban Households: Supplicants to a Socialist State', in D. Davis and S. Harrell (eds), *Chinese Families in the Post-Mao Era*, Berkeley: University of California Press.

Davis, K. (1951) *The Population of India and Pakistan*, Princeton: Princeton University Press.

Davison R. (1990) *Essays in Ottoman and Turkish History, 1774–1923*, London: Saqi Books.

Dealtry, M. (2001) 'Brazil's Proposed "Civil Unions Persons of the Same Sex": Legislative Inaction and Judicial Reactions', in R. Wintemute and M. Andenaes (eds), *Legal Recognition of Same-Sex Partnerships*, London: Hart Publishing.

Deere, C. (1990) *Household and Class Relations*, Berkeley, Los Angeles: University of California Press.

De Grazia, V. (1993) 'Patriarcado fascista: las italianas bajo el gobierno de Mussolini, 1922–1940', in G. Duby and M. Perrot (eds), *Historia de las mujeres*, Madrid: Taurus.

Deliège, R. (1997) *The World of the Untouchables*, Dehli: Oxford University Press.

Delumeau, J. and Roche, D. (1990) *Histoire des Pères et de la Paternité*, Paris: Larousse.

Demeny, P. (2001) 'Intellectual Origins of Post-World War II Population Policies in South Asia', in Z.A. Sathar and J. Philips (eds.) *Fertility Transition in South Asia*, Oxford: Oxford University Press.

D'Emilio, J. and Freedman, E. (1988) *Intimate Matters*, New York: Harper & Row.

Demographic and Health Surveys. See Appendix.

Devos, I. (1999) 'Marriage and Economic Conditions since 1700: The Belgian Case', in I. Devos and L. Kennedy (eds), *Marriage and Rural Economy*, Ghent: BREPOLS.

Dhavernas, O. (1978) *Droits des femmes pouvoir des hommes*, Paris: Seuil.

DHS (Demographic and Health Surveys). See Appendix.

Dikötter, F. (1995) *Sex, Culture and Modernity in China*, London: C. Hurst & Co.

Dixon, R. (1971) 'Explaining Cross-Cultural Variations in Age at Marriage and Proportions Never Marrying', *Population Studies* 25,2: 215–33.

Dollard, J. (1937/1957) *Caste and Class in a Southern Town*, Garden City, NY: Doubleday Anchor Books.

Domenach, J.L. and Hua, Chang-Ming (1987) *Le Marriage en Chine*, Paris: Presses de la Fondation Nationale des Sciences Politiques.

Domingo, L. and King, E. (1992) 'The Role of the Family in the Process of Entry to Marriage in Asia', in E. Berquó and P. Xenos (eds), *Family System and Cultural Change*, Oxford: Clarendon Press.

Donzelot, J. (1977) *La Police des familles*, Paris: Ed. de Minuit.

Dore, R.P. (1958) *City Life in Japan*, London: Routledge and Kegan Paul.

Dore, R.P. (1965) *Education in Tokugawa Japan*, Berkeley: University of California Press.

Dower, J. (1999) *Embracing Defeat*, Harmondsworth: Penguin.

Dozon, J-P. (1986) 'En Afrique, la famille la croisée des chemins', in A. Burgière *et al.* (eds), *Histoire de la famille*, vol. 3, Paris: Armand Colin.

Dube, L. (2001) *Anthropological Explorations in Gender*, New Delhi: Sage Publications.

Duben, A. (1982) 'The Significance of Family and Kinship in Urban Turkey', in C. Kâgitcibasi (ed.), *Sex, Roles, Family, and Community in Turkey*, Indiana: Indiana University Turkish Studies.

Duben, A. and Behar, C. (1991) *Istanbul Households*, Cambridge: Cambridge University Press.

Dupâquier, E. *et al.* (eds) (1981) *Marriage and Remarriage in Populations of the Past*, London, New York: Academic Press.

Dyson, T. (ed.) (1989) *India's Historical Demography*, London: Curzon Press.

Dyson, T. (2001) 'Birth Rate Trends in India, Sri Lanka, Bangladesh, and Pakistan: A Long Comparative View', in Z.A. Sathar and J. Philips (eds), *Fertility Transition in South Asia*, Oxford: Oxford University Press.

Dyson, T. and Moore, M. (1983) 'On Kinship Structure, Female Autonomy, and Demographic Behavior in India', *Population and Development Review* 9,1: 35–60.

East–West Center (2002) *The Future of Population in Asia*, Honolulu.

Easterlin, R. *et al.* (1978) 'Farm and Farm Families in Old and New Areas: The Northern States in 1860', in T.K. Hareven and M.A. Vinovskis (eds), *Family and Population in Nineteenth Century America*, Princeton, NJ: Princeton University Press.

Ebrey, P.B.E. (2003) *Women and Family in Chinese History*, London: Routledge.

Edwards, G.E. (1985) *GDR Society and Social Institutions*, Basingstoke: Macmillan.

Edwards, L. and Roces, M. (eds) (2000) *Women in Asia*, Ann Arbor: The University of Michigan Press.

Edwards, W. (1989) *Modern Japan Through its Weddings*, Stanford: Stanford University Press.

Eekelaar, J. and Nhlapo, T. (eds) (1998) *The Changing Family*, Oxford: Hart Publishing.

Eggleston, E., Jackson, J. and Hardee, K. (1999) 'Sexual attitudes and behavior among young adolescents in Jamaica', *International Family Planning Perspectives* 25: 78–84, 91.

Ehmer, J. (2002) 'Marriage', in D. Kertzer and M. Barbagli (eds), *Family Life in the Long Nineteenth Century*, New Haven, London: Yale University Press.

Einhorn, B. (1993) *Cinderella Goes to the Market*. London: Verso.

Ellis, H. (1939) *My Life*, Boston: Houghton Mifflin.

Ellman, M. (2000) 'The Social Costs and Consequences of the Transformation Process' in UN Economic Commission for Europe, *Economic Survey of Europe*, New York and Geneva: United Nations.

Elmroth, I. (1981) *För kung och fosterland*, Lund: CWK Gleerup.

Eloundou-Enyegue *et al.* (2000) 'Are there crisis-led fertility declines? Evidence from Cameroon' *Population Research and Policy Review*, 19: 47–72.

Emin [Amin], Q. (1899/1928) *Ueber die Frauenemanzipation*, Stuttgart.

Enqinün, I. (2000) 'Turkish Literature and Self-Identity: From Ottoman to Modern Turkish', in K. Karpat (ed.), *Ottoman Past and Modern Turkey*, Leiden: Brill.

Erlich, V. (1966) *Family in Transition*, Princeton, NJ: Princeton University Press.

Eschenburg T, (1983) *Jahre der Besatzung 1949–1949*, Stuttgart: DVA, Wiesbaden: Brockhaus.

Esposito, J. (1982) *Women in Muslim Family Law*, Syracuse, NY: Syracuse University Press.

European Commission (1996) *Eurobarometer* no. 45, Brussels.

European Commission (2000) *European Social Statistics. Demography*, Luxembourg.

Eurostat (1999) *Demographic Statistics, 1960–1998*, Luxembourg.

Eurostat (2000a) *European Social Statistics, Demography*, Luxembourg.
Eurostat (2000b) *The Social Situation in the European Union 2000*, Luxembourg.
Eurostat (2001) *The Social Situation in the European Union 2001*, Luxembourg.
Eurostat (2002) *Statistiques sociales européennes Démographie*, Luxembourg.
Evans, Grubbs, J. (2002) *Women and the Law in the Roman Empire*, London and New York: Routledge.
Evans, H. (1997) *Women and Sexuality in China*, Cambridge: Polity Press.
Evans, R. (1979) *The Feminists* (rev. edn), London: Croom Helm.
Eyrumlu, R. (2001) *Modernisering och Islam i Iran och Turkiet*, Angered: Invand-Lit.
Fals-Borda, O. (1962) *Peasant Societies in the Colombian Andes*, Gainesville: University of Florida Press.
Fanon, F. (1952) *Peau Noire Masques Blancs*, Paris: Èditions du Seuil.
Fanon, F. (1962) *l' an v de la révolution algérienne*, Paris: Maspero.
Fargues, Ph. (1989) 'The Decline of Arab Fertility', *Population: An English Selection* 44: 1.
Farrel Brodie, J. (1994) *Contraception and Abortion in Nineteenth-Century America*, Ithaca, NY: Cornell University Press.
Farrer, J. (2002) *Opening Up. Youth Sex Culture and Market Reform in Shanghai*, Chicago, London: Chicago University Press.
Fauve-Chaumoux, A. (2001) 'Familles Urbaines et Maternité Consciente au XVIII Siècle: Reims entre Genève et Rouen', in A.L. Head-König *et al.* (eds), *Famille, parenté et reseaux en Occident*, Genève: Société d'histoire et d'archéologie de Genève.
Fazlhashemi, M. (1999) *Exemplets makt*, Stockholm: Brutus Östling.
Feeney, G. (1994) 'Fertility in China: Past, Present, Prospects', in W. Lutz (ed.), *The Future Population of the World*, London: Earthscan.
Fei, Hsiao-Tung (1939) *Peasant Life in China*, London: Routledge.
Feng, W. and Tsuya, N. (2000) 'Comparative Reproductive Regimes in the Past. A Eurasian Perspective', presented at Population Association of America, Los Angeles, March 23–25, 2000.
Ferge, Z. (1979) *A Society in the Making*, Harmondsworth: Penguin.
Ferrando, D. and Aramburú, C. (1996)'The Fertility Transition in Peru', in J.M. Guzmán *et al.* (eds), *The Fertility Transition in Latin America*, Oxford: Clarendon Press.
Ferro, M. (1967) *La révolution de 1917*, 2 vols, Paris: Aubier.
Fertility and Family Surveys. See Appendix.
Festy, P. (1979a) *La Fecondité des Pays Occidentaux de 1870 a 1970*, Paris: Presses Universitaires de France.
Festy, P. (1979b) 'La Fécondité en Amérique du Nord', *Population* 4,5: 767–800.
Fialová, L. (1994) 'Changes of Nuptiality in Czech Lands and Slovakia, 1918–1988', *Journal of Family History* 19: 107–15.
Findlay, E. (1998) 'Love in the Tropics: Marriage, Divorce, and the Construction of Benevolent Colonialism in Puerto Rico, 1898–1910', in G. Joseph, C. Legrand and D. Salvatore (eds), *Close Encounters of Empire*, Durham and London: Duke University Press.
Finkle, J. and Crane, B. (1975) 'The Politics of Bucharest: Population, Development, and the New Inernational Economic Order', *Population Development Review* 1: 87–114.
Finlay, H.A. (1979) *Family Law in Australia*, Sydney: Butterworths.
Fischer, M. and Lyon, W. (2000) 'Marriage Strategies in Lahore: Projections of a Model Marriage on Social Processes', in M. Böck and A. Rao (eds), *Culture, Creation and Procreation*, New York, Oxford: Berghahn Books.

Fisher, W. (1980) *The Soviet Marriage Market*, New York: Praeger.

Fischer, W. *et al.* (1985) *Handbuch der europäischen Wirtschafts- und Sozialgeschichte* Bd. 5, Stuttgart: Klett-Cotta.

Fleiz-Bautista, C. *et al.* (1999) 'Conducta sexual en estudiantes de la Ciudad de México', *Salud Mental* 22: 14–19.

Flekköy, M. (1993) *Children's Rights*, Gent: Universiteit Gent.

Flora, P. *et al.* (1987) *State, Economy, and Society in Western Europe 1815–1975*, Frankfurt, London: Campus Verlag.

Fonseca, C. (1991) 'Spouses, Siblings and Sex-Linked Bonding: A Look at Kinship Organization in a Brazilian Slum', in E. Jelin (ed.), *Family, Household and Gender Relation in Latin America*, London: Kegan Paul International.

Fortes, M. (1978) 'Family, marriage and fertility in West Africa', in C. Oppong *et al.* (eds), *Marriage, Fertility, and Parenthood in West Africa*, Canberra: Australian National University.

Foucault, M. (1976) *Histoire de la sexualité 1. La volonté de savoir*. Paris: Gallimard.

Fowler-Salamini, H. (2002) 'Women Coffee Sorters Confront the Mill Owners and the Veracruz Revolutionary State, 1915–1918', *Journal of Women's History* 14,1: 34–63.

Franklin, B. (ed.) (1995) *Children's Rights*, London and New York: Routledge.

Frejka, T. and Ross, J. (2001) 'Paths to Subreplacement Fertility: The Empirical Evidence', *Population and Development Review* 27 Supplement: 213–54.

Freyer, P. (1965) *The Birth Controllers*, London: Secker & Warburg.

Freyre, G. (1933/1970) *The Masters And The Slaves*, New York: Alfred A. Knopf.

Fries, L. and Matus, V. (1999) *El derecho. Trama y conjura patriarchal*, Santiago de Chile: LOM.

Frykman, J. (1993) *Horan i bondesamhället*, Stockholm: Carlssons.

Fuchs, R. (1992) *Poor and Pregnant in Paris*, New Brunswick, NJ: Rutgers University Press.

Fukuyama, F. (1999) *The Great Disruption*, New York: The Free Press.

Gage-Brandon, A. (1993) 'The Formation and Stability of Informl Unions in Côte d'Ivoire', *Journal of Comparative Family Studies* 24: 219–33.

Gallie, D. (2000) 'The Labour Force', in A.H. Halsey (ed.), *Twentieth-Century British Social Trends*, Basingstoke: Macmillan.

Gandhi, M.K. (1948) *The Story of my Experiments with Truth*, Washington: Public Affairs.

Ganghofer, R. (ed.) (1992) *Le droit de famille en Europe*, Strasbourg: Presses Universitaires des Strasbourg.

Gaunt, D. (1983) 'The Property and Kin Relationships of Retired Farmers in Northern and Central Europe', in R. Wall (ed.), *Family Forms in Historic Europe*, Cambridge: Cambridge University Press.

Gauthier, A.H. (1996) *The State and the Family*, Oxford: Clarendon Press.

Geertz, H. (1961) *The Javanese Family*, New York: The Free Press of Glencoe.

Geiger, K. (1968) *The Family in Soviet Russia*, Cambridge, MA: Harvard University Press.

Giddens, A. (1992) *The Transformation of Intimacy*, Cambridge: Polity Press.

Gillis, J. (1975) *Youth and History*, New York and London: Academic Press.

Gillis, J. (1985) *For Better, For Worse. British Marriages, 1600 to the Present*, Oxford: Oxford University Press.

Gillis, J. (1997) *A World of Their Own Making*, Oxford: Oxford University Press.

Ginsborg, P. (2002) 'Measuring the Distance: The case of the Family, 1968–2001', *Thesis Eleven* 68: 46, 63.

Girard, A. and Roussel, L. (1982) 'Ideal Family Size, Fertility, and Population Policy in Western Europe', *Population and Development Review* 8,8: 323–45.

Glass, D.V. (1936) *The Struggle for Population*, Oxford: Clarendon Press.

Glass, D.V. (1940) *Population Policies and Movements in Europe*, Oxford: Clarendon Press.

Glass, D.V. (1966) 'Western Europe', in B. Berelson *et al.* (eds), *Family Planning and Population Programs*, Chicago: Chicago University Press.

Glass, D.V. (1968) 'Family planning programmes and action in Western Europe', in E. Szabady (ed.), *World Views of Population Problems*, Budapest: Akadémiai Kiadó.

Gledhill, A. (1968) 'Community Property in the Marriage Law of Burma', in J.N.D. Anderson (ed.), *Family Law in Asia and Africa*, London: George Allen & Unwin.

Glendon, M.A. (1977) *State, Law and Family*, Amsterdam: North-Holland Publishing Company.

Glendon, M.A. (1989) *The Transformation of Family Law*, Chicago: The University of Chicago Press.

Glendon, M.A. (2001) *A World Made New*, New York: Random House.

Goldstein, J. and Kenney, C. (2001) 'Marriage Delayed or Marriage Forgone? New Cohort Forecasts of First Marriage for U.S. Women', *American Sociological Review* 66: 506–19.

Göle, N. (1995) *Republik und Schleier*, Berlin: Babel.

Goode, W. (1963) *World Revolution and Family Patterns*, New York: Free Press of Glencoe.

Goode, W. (1993) *World Changes in Divorce Patterns*, New Haven: Yale University Press.

Goody, J. (1976) *Production and Reproduction*, Cambridge: Cambridge University Press.

Goody, J. (1990) *The Oriental, the Ancient and the Primitive*, Cambridge: Cambridge University Press.

Goody, J. (2001) *La famille en Europe*, Paris: Seuil.

Goonsekere, R.K.W. (1979) 'Family Law in Sri Lanka', in J. Sihombing and H.A. Finlay (eds), *Lawasia Family Law Series*, vol. 1, Singapore: Singapore University Press.

Goonesekere, S. (1995) 'Realizing Gender Equity through Law: Sri Lanka's Experience in the Post-Nairobi Decade', in *Facets of Change. Women in Sri Lanka 1986–1995*, Colombo: Centre for Women's Research.

Gordon, L. and McLanahan, S. (1991) 'Single Parenthood in 1900', *Journal of Family History* 16,2: 97–116.

Grasland, C. (1990) 'Systèmes démographiques et systèmes supranationaux: La fécondité européenne de 1952 á 1982', *European Journal of Population* 6: 163–91.

Graveson, R.H. (1957), 'The Background of the Century', in R.H. Graveson and F.R. Crane (eds), *A Century of Family Law*, London: Sweet & Maxwell.

Graveson, R.H. and Crane, F.R. (eds) (1957) *A Century of Family Law*, London: Sweet & Maxwell.

Green, D. (1999) *Gender Violence in Africa*, New York: St Martin's Press.

Greenhalgh, S. (1985) 'Sexual Stratification: The Other Side of "Growth with Equity" in East Asia', *Population and Development Review* 11,2: 265–314.

Greenhalgh, S. (1993) 'The Peasantization of the One-Child Policy in Shanxi', in D. Davis and S. Hurrell (eds), *Chinese Families in the Post-Mao Era*, Berkeley: University of California Press.

Grossberg, M. (1985) *Governing the Hearth*, Chapel Hill and London: University of North Carolina Press.

Groves, E. (1944) *The American Woman*, New York: Emerson.

Grtossen, J.M. (1986) 'Switzerland: Further Steps Towards Equality', *Journal of Family Law* 25: 255–59.

Grünheid, E. and Roloff, J. (2000) 'Die demographische Lage in Deutschland 1999 mit dem Teil B "Die demographische Entwicklung in den Bundesländern – ein Vergliech"', *Zeitschrift f. Bevölkerungswissenschaft* 25: 3–150.

Guest, A. (1990) 'What Can We Learn About Fertility Transitions from the New York State Census of 1865', *Journal of Family History* 15: 49–69.

Gundy, E. (1999) 'Living Arrangements and Health of Older Persons in Developed Countries', New York: UN Population Division Paper.

Guo Zhigang (2000) 'Family Patterns', in Peng Xizhe and Guo Zhigang (eds), *The Changing Population of China*, Oxford: Blackwell.

Gutierrez de Pineda, V. (1976) *Estructura, función, y cambio de la familia en Colombia*, Bogotá: Asociación Colombiana de Facultades de Medicina.

Gutman, H. (1976) *The Black Family in Slavery and Freedom, 1750–1925*, Oxford: Basil Blackwell.

Guy, D. (1985) 'Lower-Class Families, Women and the Law in Nineteenth-Century Argentina', *Journal of Family History* 10,3: 318–31.

Guy, D. (1998) 'The Pan American Child Congresses, 1916 to 1942: Pan Americanism, Child Reform, and Welfare State in Latin America', *Journal of Family History* 23,3: 272–91.

Guzmán, J. *et al.* (eds) (1996) *The Fertility Transition in Latin America*, Oxford: Clarendon Press.

Guzmán, V. (2001) 'La institucionalidad de género en el estado: Nuevas perspectivas de análisis', Santiago de Chile: CEPAL/ECLAC SMYD No. 32.

Hacker, A. (2000) 'The Case Against Kids', *New York Review of Books* 19.

Haddad, Y. (1998) 'Islam and Gender: Dilemmas in the Changing Arab World', in Y. Haddad and J. Esposito (eds), *Islam, Gender and Social Change*, New York: Oxford University Press.

Hafström, G. (1970) *Den svenska familjerättens historia*, Lund: Studentliteratur.

Hahang, E. (1992) *Tradition et Modernité du Mariage en Thailande*, Bangkok: Edition Duang Kamol.

Haines, M. (1990) 'Western Fertility in Mid-Transition: Fertility and Nuptiality in the United States and Selected Nations at the Turn of the Century', *Journal of Family History* 15,1: 23–48.

Haines, M. (1996) 'Long-Term Marriage Patterns in the United States from Colonial Times to the Present', *The History of the Family* 1: 15–40.

Hajnal, J. (1953a) 'Age at Marriage and Proportions Marrying', *Population Studies* 7,2: 111–36.

Hajnal, J. (1953b) 'The Marriage Boom', *Population Index* 19: 80–101.

Hajnal, J. (1965) 'European Marriage Patterns in Perspective', in V.D. Glass and D.E.C. Eversley (eds), *Population in History*, London: Edward Arnold.

Hajnal, J. (1982) 'Two Kinds of Preindustrial Household Formation System', *Population and Development Review* 8,3: 449–94.

Hamilton, G. (1990) 'Patriarchy, Patrimonialism, and Filial Piety: a comparison of China and Western Europe', *British Journal of Sociology* 41,1: 77–104.

Hampson, S. (2000) 'Rhetoric or reality? Contesting definitions of women in Korea', in L. Edwards and M. Roces (eds), *Women in Asia*, Ann Arbor: University of Michigan Press.

Handwerker, P. (1989) *Women's Power and Social Revolution. Fertility Transition in the West Indies*, London: Sage.

Hane, M. (1984) 'Fukuzawa Yukichi and Women's Rights', in H. Conroy (ed.), *Japan in Transition: Thought and Action in the Meiji Era, 1868–1912*, London and Toronto: Associated University Presses.

Hareven, T. (2000) *Families, History, and Social Change*, Boulder, CO: Westview Press.

Hareven, T. and Plakans, A. (eds) (1996) *The History of the Family*, Greenwich, CT: JAI Press.

Harrell, S. (1993) 'Geography, Demography, and Family Composition in Three South-western Villages', in D. Davis and S. Harrell (eds), *Chinese Families in the Post-Mao Era*, Berkeley: University of California Press.

Hartley, S.F. (1975) *Illegitimacy*, Berkeley: University of California Press.

Hartley, S.F. (1980) ' Illegitimacy in Jamaica', in P. Laslett, K. Oosterveen and R.M. Smith (eds), *Bastardy and its Comparative History*, London: Edward Arnold.

Hatano, Y. (1997) 'Japan', in R. Francoeur (ed.), *The International Encyclopedia of Sexuality*, vol. 1, New York: Continuum.

Hawkins, J. (1984) *Inverse Images*, Albuquerque: University of New Mexico Press.

Hawkins, S. (2002) '"The Women in Question": Marriage and Identity in the Colonial Courts of Northern Ghana, 1907–1954', in J. Allman *et al.* (eds), *Women in African Colonial Histories*, Bloomington: Indiana University Press.

Hayami, A. (1980) 'Illegitimacy in Japan', in P. Laslett, K. Oosterveen and R.M. Smith (eds), *Bastardy and its Comparative History*, London: Edward Arnold.

Hayami, A. and Ochiai, E. (1996) 'Family Patterns and Demographic Factors in Pre-Industrial Japan', *EurAsian Project on Population and Family History*, Kyoto: International Research Center for Japanese Studies.

Haydon, E.S. (1960) *Law and Justice in Buganda*, London: Buttterworths.

Heaton, F., Forste, R. and Otterstrom, S. (2002) 'Family Transitions in Latin America: First Intercourse, First Union, First Birth', *International Journal of Population History* 8: 1–15.

Heaton, T. and Hirschl, T. (1999) 'The Trajectory of Family Change in Nigeria', *Journal of Comparative Family Studies* 30: 35–56.

Helwig, G. (1982) *Frau und Familie in beiden deutschen Staaten*, Köln: Verlag Wissenschaft und Politik.

Hendry, J. (1981) *Marriage in Changing Japan*, London: Croom Helm.

Henriques, F. (1968) *Modern Sexuality*, London: Macgibbon and Kee.

Henry, L. and Houdaille, J. (1979) 'Celibat et âge au marriage aux XVIIIe et XIXe siècles en France', *Population* 34: 2–79, 403–43.

Henry, L. and Houdaille, J. (1978) 'Célibat et âge au mariage aux XVIIIe et XIXe siècles en France. I. Célibat définitif ', *Population* 33: 43–84.

Heuveline, P. (1999) 'The Global and Regional Impact of Mortality and Fertility Transitions, 1950– 2000', *Population Development Review* 25,4: 681–702.

Heuveline, P. (2001) 'Demographic Pressure, Economic Development, and Social Engineering: An Assessment of Fertility Declines in the Second Half of the Twentieth Century' *Population Research and Policy Review* 20: 365–96.

Heydt-Coca, M.v.d. (1999) 'When Worlds Collide: The Incorporation of the Andean World into the Emerging World-Economy in the Colonial Period', *Dialectical Anthropology* 24: 1–43.

Hicks, E. (1996) *Infibulation*, New Brunswick, NJ: Transaction.

Higman, B. (1991) 'The Slave Populations of the British Caribbean: Some Nineteenth-Century Variations', in H. Beckles and V. Shepherd (eds), *Caribbean Slave Society and Economy*, Kingston and London: Ian Randle and James Currey.

Hill, R. and König, R. (eds) (1970) *Families in East and West*, Paris: Mouton.

Hilton, A. (1983) 'Family and Kinship among the Kongo South of the Zaïre River from the Sixteenth to the Nineteenth Centuries', *The Journal of African History* 24: 145–61.

Hintze, P. (ed.) (1995) *Die CDU-Parteiprogramme*, Bonn: Bouvier.

Hirakawa, S. (1998) 'Japan's Turn to the West', in B.T. Wakabayashi (ed.), *Modern Japanese Thought*, Cambridge: Cambridge University Press.

Hla Aung (1968) 'The Effect of Anglo-Indian Legislation upon Burmese Customary

Law', in D. Buxbaum (ed.), *Family Law and Customary Law in Asia*, The Hague: Martinus Nijhoff.

Hochschild, A. (2000) *King Leopold's Ghost*, Basingstoke: Papermac.

Hoem, J. and Rennermalm, B. (1985) 'Modern family initiation in Sweden: Experience of women born between 1936 and 1960', *European Journal of Population* 1: 81–112.

Hollingsworth, T.H. (1965) 'A Demographic Study of the British Ducal Families', in D.V. Glass and D.E.C. Eversley (eds), *Population in History*, London: Edward Arnold.

Hollingsworth, T.H. (1981) 'Illegitimate births and marriage rates in Great Britain 1841–1911', in J. Dupâquier *et al.* (eds), *Marriage and Remarriage in Populations of the Past*, London, New York: Academic Press.

Hoodfar, H. (1995) 'Population Policy and Gender Equity in Post-Revolutionary Iran', in C.M. Obermeyer (ed.), *Family, Gender, and Population in the Middle East*, Cairo: The American University in Cairo Press.

Hoodfar, H. (1997) 'The Impact of Male Migration on Domestic Budgeting: Egyptian Women Striving for an Islamic Budgeting Pattern', *Journal of Comparative Family Studies* 28,2: 73–98.

Ho Ping-ti (1959) *Studies on the Population of China, 1368–1953*, Cambridge, MA: Harvard University Press.

Hopper, H. (1996) *A New Woman of Japan*, Boulder, CO: Westview Press.

Hourani, A. (1983) *Arabic Thought in the Liberal Age 1798–1939*, Cambridge: Cambridge University Press.

Htun, M. (2002), 'Puzzles of Women's Rights in Brazil', *Social Research* 69,3: 733–51.

Hull, T., Sulistyaningsih, E. and Jones, G. (1999) *Prostitution in Indonesia*, Jakarta: Pustaka Sinar Harapan.

Hume, D. (1742/n.a.) 'Rise and Progress of the Arts and Sciences', in *Essays, Literary, Moral, and Political*, London: Ward, Lock and Tyler.

Hunecke, V. (1994) 'The Abandonment of Legitimate Children in Nineteenth-century Milan and the European Context', in J. Henderson and R. Wall (eds), *Poor Women and Children in the European Past*, London and New York: Routledge.

Husein, H. (1966) 'United Arab Republic', in B. Berelson *et al.* (eds), *Family Planning and Population Programs*, Chicago: Chicago University Press.

Huxley, A. (1988) 'Burma: It works, but is it law?', *Journal of Family Law* 27: 23–37.

Ibrahim, S.E. and Ibrahim, B.L. (1998) 'Egypt's Population Policy: The Long March of State and Civil Society', in A. Jain (ed.), *Do Population Policies Matter?*, New York: Population Council.

IBGE (2000) *Censo Demográfico 2000*. Instituto Brasileiro de Geografia e Estatistica [www.ibge.gov.br/home/estatisticapopulacao/censa2000].

Iliffe, J. (1995) *Africans: The History of a Continent*, Cambridge: Cambridge University Press.

Ilkkaracan, P. (2002) 'Women, Sexuality, and Social Change in the Middle East and the Maghreb', *Social Reseach* 69,3: 753–79.

ILO (1961) *The Cost of Social Security 1949–1957*, Geneva.

INE México (2002) *Estado conyugal*, Instituto Nacional de Estadística [http://dgcnseyp.inegi.gob.mx].

INE Portugal (2002) *General Statistical Data*, Instituto Nacional de Estatistica [http://www.ine.pt/prodserv/indicadores/quadros_eng.asp?CodInd=20].

INE Uruguay (1999) *Nacimientos occurridos y registrados según la forma conyugal de las madres*, Instituto Nacional de Estadística, Montevideo [http://www.ine.gub.uy/banco%20de%20datos/soc_estadisticasvitales/Nac_por_uni%F3n_cony%20.xls].

INE Uruguay (2000) Instituto Nacional de Estadística [www.ine.gub.uy].

Inoue, S. (1998) 'Family Formation in Japan, South Korea, and the United States', in K.O. Mason *et al.* (eds), *The Changing Family in Comparative Perspective: Asia and the United States*, Honolulu: East–West Center.

International Planned Parenthood Federation (1999) *Country Profiles* [www.ippf.org/regions/countries].

Ipaye, O. (1998) 'The Changing Pattern of Family Structure in Nigeria', in J. Eekelaar and T. Nhlapo (eds), *The Changing Family*, Oxford: Hart Publishing.

Iran, Statistical Center of (2000–01), *Statistical Yearbook*, Teheran.

International Social Survey (1994) [http://www.cis.es/boletin/11/est3.html].

al-Jabartî, A. (1979/1798–1801) *Journal d' un notable du Caire durant l' expédition francaise 1798–1801*, Paris: Albin Michel.

Jabbra, G. and N. (eds) (1992) *Women and Development in the Middle East and North Africa*, Leiden, New York: E. J. Brill.

Jackson, L. (2002) '"When in the White Man's Town": Zimbabwean Women Remember Chibeura', in J. Allman, S. Geiger and N. Musisi (eds), *Women in African Colonial Histories*, Bloomington and Indianapolis: Indiana University Press.

Jackson, P. and Cook, N. (1999) *Genders and Sexualities in Modern Thailand*, Chiang Mai: Silkworm Books.

Jacobson, A. (1967) *Marriage and Money*, Uppsala: Studia Ethnographica.

Jacobson, A. (1977) *Försörjerskan*, Stockholm: Sida.

Jacobson-Widding, A. (2000) *Chapungo: The Birth that Never Drops a Feather. Male and Female Identities in an African Society*, Uppsala: Acta Universitatis Uppsaliensis.

Janiewski, D. (1996) 'Southern Honour, Southern Dishonour: Managerial Ideology and the Construction of Gender, Race, and Class Relations in Southern Industry', in J.W. Scott (ed.), *Feminism and History*, Oxford and New York: Oxford University Press.

Japan Foreign Press Center (1994) *Japanese Families*, Tokyo.

Japan Statistics Bureau (2000) *1995 Population Census of Japan*, Results of Special Tabulation on Living with Parents, Tokyo [www.stat.go.jp/English/data/kokusei/1995].

Japan Statistics Bureau (2001) *Population Census. Summary of Prompt Sample Tabulation – Results* [www.stat.go.jp/english/data/kokusei/2000].

Japan Statistics Bureau (2002) *Japan Statistical Yearbook 2002*, Tokyo.

Jaramillo, A. (1980) 'The Ecuadorian Family', in M. Das and C. Jesser (eds), *The Family in Latin America*, New Delhi: Vikas Publishing House.

Jarrick, A. (1997) *Kärlekens makt och tårar*, Stockholm: Norstedts.

Jarrick, A. and Söderberg, J. (1998) *Odygd och vanära*, Stockholm: Rabén Prisma.

Javillonar, G. (1979) 'The Filipino Family', in M. Singh Das and P. Bardis (eds), *The Family in Asia*, London: George Allen & Unwin.

Jayawardena, K. (1986) *Feminism and Nationalism in the Third World*, London: Zed Books.

Jeater, D. (1993) *Marriage, Perversion, and Power*, Oxford: Clarendon Press.

Jeffrey, R. (1992) *Politics, Women and Well-Being. How Kerala Became 'A Model'*, London: Macmillan.

Jejeebhoy, S. (1998) *Women's Education, Autonomy, and Reproductive Behaviour: Experience from Developing Countries*, Oxford: Clarendon Press.

Jejeebhoy, S. (2001) 'Women's Autonomy and Reproductive Behaviour in India', in Z.A. Sathar and J. Philips (eds), *Fertility Transition in South Asia*, Oxford: Oxford Universty Press.

Jejeebhoy, S. and Sathar, Z. (2001) 'Women's Autonomy in India and Pakistan: The Influence of Religion and Region', *Population and Development Review*, 27,4: 687–712.

Jensen, A.-M. (1996) *Fertility – Between Passion and Utility*, Dr. polit. thesis, Oslo University Department of Sociology and Human Geography.

Johnson, G. (1993) 'Family Strategies and Economic Transformation in Rural China: Some Evidence from the Pearl River Delta', in D. Davis and S. Harrell (eds), *Chinese Families in the Post-Mao Era*, Berkeley: University of California Press.

Johnson, R.E. (1976) 'Family Relations and the Rural–Urban Nexus: Patterns in the Hinterland of Moscow, 1880–1900', in D. Ransel (ed.), *The Family in Imperial Russia*, Urbana, Chicago, London: University of Illinois Press.

Johnson, S. (1995) *The Politics of Population*, London: Earthscan Publications.

Jones, E. and Grupp, F. (1987) *Modernization, Value Change and Fertility in the Soviet Union*, Cambridge: Cambridge University Press.

Jones, G. (1994) *Marriage and Divorce in Southeast Asia*, Oxford: Oxford University Press.

Jones, G. (1997) 'The Demise of Universal Marriage in East and Southeast Asia', in G. Jones *et al.* (eds), *The Continuing Demographic Transition*, Oxford: Clarendon Press.

Jones, G. (1999) 'The Population of Southeast Asia', Canberra: ANU, Working Papers in Demography.

Jones, G. (2002) 'The Changing Indonesian Household', in K. Robinson and S. Bessell (eds), *Women in Indonesia*, Singapore: Institute of Southeast Asian Studies Press.

Jones, G. and Leete, R. (2002) 'Low Fertility is Attained', *Studies in Family Planning* 33,1: 114–26.

Jones, G. *et al.* (eds) (1997) *The Continuing Demographic Transition*, Oxford: Clarendon Press.

Jones, J. (1985) *Labor of Love, Labor of Sorrow*, New York: Basic Books.

Jönholm, J. (1898) *The Civil Code of Japan*, Tokyo.

Jörberg, L. and Krantz, O. (1976) 'Scandinavia 1914–1970', in C. Cipolla (ed.), *The Fontana Economic History of Europe. Contemporary Economies Part 2*, London: Collins/Fontana.

Joyce, G.H. (1948) *Christian Marriage* (2nd edn), London: Sheed and Ward.

Joyner, K. and Laumann, E. (2001) 'Teenage Sex and Sexual Revolution', in E. Laumann and R. Michael (eds), *Sex, Love and Health in America*, Chicago: University of Chicago Press.

Juárez, F. and Llera, S. (1996) 'The Process of Family Formation during the Fertility Transition', in J.M. Guzmán *et al.* (eds), *The Fertility Transformation in Latin America*, Oxford: Clarendon Press.

Juliver, P. (1978) 'Women and Sex in Soviet Law', in D. Atkinson *et al.* (eds), *Women in Russia*, New York: Harvester Press.

Kaa, D.J. van de (1996) 'Anchored Narrative: The Story and Findings of Half a Century of Research into the Determinants of Fertility', *Population Studies* 50: 389–432.

Kaa, D.J. van de (2001) 'Postmodern Fertility Preferences: From Changing Value Orientations to New Behavior', *Population and Development Review* 27 Supplement: 294–330.

Kabeheri-Macharia, J. and Nyamu, C. (1998) 'Marriage by Affidavit: Alternative Laws on Cohabitation in Kenya', in J. Eekelaar and Th. Nhlapo (eds), *The Changing Family*, Oxford: Hart Publishing.

Kälvemark, A-S. (1980) *More Children of Better Quality?*, Uppsala and Stockholm: Almqvist & Wiksell International.

Kamerman, S. and Kahn, A. (eds) (1997) *Family Change and Family Policies in Great Britain, Canada, New Zealand, and the United States*, Oxford: Clarendon Press.

Kanbargi, R.M. and Kanbargi, S. (1996) 'Sexually transmitted diseases in Bangalore city: some findings from an exploratory study', *Journal of Family Welfare* 42: 30–7.

Kandiyoti, D. (1982) 'Urban Change and Women's Roles in Turkey: an Overview and

Evaluation', in C. Kâgitcibasi (ed.), *Sex Roles, Family, and Community in Turkey*, Indiana: Indiana University Turkish Studies.

Kangaratnam, T. (1969) 'Singapore: Meeting the Test', in B. Berelson (ed.), *Family Planning Programs*, New York: Basic Books.

Kanowitz, L. (1973) *Sex Roles in Law and Society*, Albuquerque: University of New Mexico Press.

Kapadia, K.M. (1966) *Marriage and Family in India*, London: Oxford University Press.

Karvé, I. (1953) *Kinship Organisation in India*, Poona: Deccan College.

Kasensup, P. (1956) 'Reception of Law in Thailand, A Buddhist Society', in M. Chiba (ed.), *Asian Indigenous Law*, London: KPI.

Kaser, K. (1995) *Familie und Verwandtschaft auf dem Balkan*, Wien: Böhlau Verlag.

Kaser, K. (2000) *Macht und Erbe*, Vienna: Böhlau.

Katz, S. (1998) 'The United States', in A. Bainham (ed.), *The International Survey of Family Law 1998*, The Hague: Kluwer.

Kaufman, C. *et al*. (2001) 'Adolescent Pregnancy and Parenthood in South Africa', *Studies in Family Planning* 32,2: 147–60.

Kaufman, C. *et al*. (2002) *How Community Structures of Time and Opportunity Shape. Adolescent Sexual Behavior in South Africa*, New York: Population Council.

Kaufmann, F.-X. *et al*. (eds) (1997–2002) *Family Life and Policies in Europe*, vols 1–2, Oxford: Clarendon Press.

Kayongo-Male, D. and Onyango, P. (1984) *The Sociology of the African Family*, London, New York: Longman.

Keddie, N. (1991) 'Introduction: Deciphering Middle Eastern Women's History', in N. Keddie and B. Baron (eds), *Women in Middle Eastern History*, New Haven and London: Yale University Press.

Kendall, L. (1996) *Getting Married in Korea*, Berkeley: University of California Press.

Kenyatta, J. (1938/1961) *Facing Mount Kenya*, London: Mercury Books.

Kertzer, D. (2002) 'Living with Kin', in D. Kertzer and M. Barbagli (eds), *Family Life in the Long Nineteenth Century, 1789–1913*, New Haven and London: Yale University Press.

Kertzer, D. and Barbagli, M. (eds) (2002) *Family Life in the Long Nineteenth Century 1789–1913*, New Haven, London: Yale University Press.

Key, E. (1900) *Barnets århundrade*, Stockholm: Bonniers.

Key, E. (1911) *Love and Marriage,* New York: G.P. Putman's Sons.

Khazova, O. (1998) 'The New Codification of Russian Family Law', in J. Eekelaar and T. Nhlapo (eds), *The Changing Family*, Oxford: Hart Publishing.

Kiernan, K. (1996) 'Partnership Behavior in Europe: Recent Trends and Issues', in D. Coleman (ed.), *Europe's Population in the 1990s*, Oxford, Oxford University Press.

Kim, Taek Il (1969) 'South Korea: Enlightened Leadership and Enlightened Parents', in B. Berelson (ed.), *Family Planning Programs*, New York: Basic Books.

Kinch, A. (1966) 'Ceylon', in B. Berelson *et al*. (eds), *Family Planning and Population Programs*, Chicago: Chicago University Press.

Kinsey, A., Pomeroy, W. and Martin, C. (1948) *Sexual Behavior in the Human Male*, Philidalphia: W.B. Saunders.

Kinsey, A., Pomeroy, W., Martin, C. and Gerhard, P. (1953) *Sexual Behavior in the Human Female*, Philadelphia and London: W.B. Saunders.

Kipnis, A. (1997) *Producing Guanxi,* Durham and London: Duke University Press.

Kirk, D. (1996) 'Demographic Transition Theory', *Population Studies* 50: 361–87.

Kirk, M. *et al*. (eds) (1975) *Law and Fertility in Europe*, Liege: Ordina.

Kitching, G. (1983) 'Proto-Industrialization and Demographic Change: A Thesis and Some Possible African implications', *Journal of African History* 24,2: 221–40.

Kitsiripornchai, S. *et al.* (1998) 'Sexual Behaviour of Young Men in Thailand: Regional Differences and Evidence of Behavior Change', *Journal of Acquired Immune Deficiency Syndromes and Human Retrovirology* 18: 282–88.

Knodel, J. and Hochstadt S. (1980) 'Urban and Rural Illegitimacy in Imperial Germany', in P. Laslett, K. Oosterveen and R.M. Smith (eds), *Bastardy and its Comparative History* London: Edward Arnold.

Koerner, D. (1976) 'Urban Families, Working-Class Youth Groups, and the 1917 Revolution in Moscow', in D. Ransel (ed.), *The Family in Imperial Russia*, Urbana, IL: University of Illinois Press.

Kögel, T. (2002) *Did the Association Between Fertility and Female Employment Within OECD Countries Really Change its Sign?*, Rostock: Max Planck Institute for Demographic Research.

Koker, J. de (1998) 'African Customary Family Law in South Africa: A Legacy of Many Pasts', in J. Eekelaar and T. Nhlapo (eds), *The Changing Family*, Oxford: Hart Publishing.

Kokole, O. (1994) 'The Politics of Fertility in Africa', in J. Finkle and A. McIntosh (eds), *The New Politics of Population: Conflict and Consensus in Family Planning*, New York and Oxford: Oxford University Press.

Kolendra, P. (1987) *Regional Differences in Family Structure in India*, Jaipur: Rawat.

Kono, A.Y. (1970) *The Evolution of the Concept of Matrimonial Consent in Japanese Law*, Tokyo: Monumenta Nipponica.

Kontula, O. and Haavio-Mannila, E. (1994) 'Sexual Behavior Change in Finland during the Last 20 Years', *Nordisk Sexologi* 12: 196–214.

Kontula, O. and Haavio-Mannila, E. (1995) *Sexual Pleasures. Enhancement of Sex Life in Finland, 1971–1992*, Aldershot: Dartmouth.

Koonz, C. (1988) *Mothers in the Fatherland*, London: Methuen.

Kopola, N. (2001) *The Construction of Womanhood in Algeria*, Stockholm: Stockholm University Department of Political Science.

Korea National Statistical Office (2001) *Korea Statistical Yearbook 2001*, Seoul.

Krishnan, P. (2001) 'Culture and the Fertility Transition in India 'Helsinki: UNU/Wider, Discussion Paper No. 2001/7.

Krupinski, J. and Stoller, A. (eds) (1980) *The Family in Australia*, Bushcutters Bay: Pergamon Press.

Kumagai, F. (1995) 'Families in Japan: Beliefs and Realities', *Journal of Comparative Family Studies* 26: 136–62.

Kurczewski, J. (1994) 'Privatizing the Polish Family after Communism', in M. Maclean and J. Kurczewski (eds), *Families, Politics, and the Law*, Oxford: Clarendon Press.

Kuznesof, E. (1991) 'Sexual Politics, Race, and Bastard-Bearing in Nineteenth Century Brazil: A Question of Culture or Power?', *Journal of Family History* 16: 241–60.

Kwon, I. (1999) 'The New Women's Movement in 1920s Korea: Rethinking the Relationship Between Imperialism and Women', in M. Sinha *et al.* (eds), *Feminisms and Internationalism*, Oxford: Blackwell.

Lahrichi, F.S. (1985) *Vivre musulmane au Maroc*, Paris: Librairie Générale de Droit et de Jurisprudence.

Lalive, P. and Keppler, B. (1968) 'Schweizerisches Eherecht', *Leske-Loewenfeld Das Eherecht der europäischen und der assuereuropäischen Staaten*, Teil I, Köln: Carl Heymanns Verlag.

Lam, M. *et al.* (eds) (1992) *Child Care in Context*, Hove and London: Lawrence Erlbaum Associates.

Lambert, B. (1980) 'Bilateralidad en los Andes', in E. Mayer and R. Bolton (eds),

Parentesco y matrimonio en los Andes, Lima: Pontifícia Universidad Católica del Perú, Fondo Editorial.

Lang, O. (1946) *Chinese Family and Society*, New Haven: Yale University Press.

Lardinois, R. (1986a) 'L'ordre du monde et l'institution familiale en Inde', in A. Burguière *et al.* (eds), *Histoire de la Famille*, vol. 2, Paris: Armand Colin.

Lardinois, R. (1986b) ' En Inde, la famille, l 'Etat, la femme', in A. Burguière *et al.* (eds) Histoire de la Famille, vol. 3, Paris: Armand Colin.

Larkin, P. (1967/1988) *Collected Poems*, London: The Marvell Press and Faber and Faber.

Larsen, U. (1989) 'A Comparative Study of the Levels and Differentials of Sterility in Cameroon, Kenya, and Sudan', in R. Lestaeghe (ed.), *Reproduction and Social Organization in Sub-Saharan Africa*, Berkeley: University of California Press.

Laslett, P. (1965/1971) *The World We Have Lost* (2nd edn), London: Methuen.

Laslett, P. (1977) *Family Life and Illicit Love in Earlier Generations*, London and New York: Cambridge University Press.

Laslett, P. (1980) ' Introduction: Comparing Illegitimacy over Time and between Cultures', in P. Laslett, K. Oosterveen and R.M. Smith (eds), *Bastardy and its Comparative History*, London: Edward Arnold.

Laslett, P. (1983) 'Family and Household as Work Group and Kin Group: Areas of Traditional Europe Compared', in R. Wall (ed.), *Family Forms in Historic Europe*, Cambridge: Cambridge University Press.

Laslett, P., Oosterveen, K. and R.M. Smith (eds) (1980) *Bastardy and its Comparative History*, London: Edward Arnold.

Lavrin, A. (ed.) (1978) *Latin American Women*, Westport, CT: Greenwood Press.

Lavrin, A. (ed.) (1989) *Sexuality and Marriage in Colonial Latin America*, Lincoln and London: University of Nebraska Press.

Lavrin, A. (1995) *Women, Feminism, and Social Change*, Lincoln and London: University of Nebraska Press.

Lawrence, K. (1966) 'Current Laboratory Studies on Fertility Regulation: Evaluation of Their Possibilities', in B. Berelson *et al.* (eds), *Family Planning and Population Programs*, Chicago: University of Chicago Press.

Le Play, F. (1855) *Les ouvriers européens*, Paris: Imprimerie Impériale.

Le Play, F. (1866) *La réforme sociale en France* (2nd edn), Paris: E. Dentu.

Le Play, F. (1871) *L'organisation de la famille* Tours: Mame.

Le Play, F. (1982) *On Family, Work, and Social Change*, in C.B. Silver (ed), Chicago and London: University of Chicago Press. LeBlanc, A.N. (2003) *Random Family*, New York: Scribner.

Le Thi Quy (2000) *Prevention of Trafficking in Women in Vietnam*, Hanoi: Labour and Social Affairs Publishing House.

Lee, J. and Wang Feng (1999) *One Quarter of Humanity*, Cambridge, MA: Harvard University Press.

Lee, Mei-lin, and Sun, Te-Hsiung (1995) 'The Family and Demography in Contemporary Taiwan', *Journal of Comparative Family Studies* XXVI,1: 101–15.

Lee, R. (2002) 'Social and Cultural Contexts of Single Young Men's Heterosexual Relationships: A View from Metro Manila', in L. Manderson and P. Liamputtong (eds), *Coming of Age in South and Southeast Asia*, Richmond, Surrey: Curzon Press.

Leete, A. (1996) *Malaysia's Demographic Transition*, Oxford, Singapore, New York: Oxford University Press.

Leete, R. and Alam, I. (eds) (1993) *The Revolution in Asian Fertility*, Oxford: Clarendon Press.

Lehrer, E. (2000) 'Religion as Determinants of Entry into Cohabitation and Marriage', in L. Waite (ed.), *The Ties that Bind*, New York: Aldine de Gruyter.

Lenin, V.I. (1917/1947) 'The tasks of the proletariat in our revolution', in *Selected Works*, vol. 2, Moscow: Foreign Languages Publishing House.

Lenin, V.I. (1922/1947) 'The fourth anniversary of the October Revolution', in *Selected Works*, vol. 2, Moscow: Foreign Languages Publishing House.

Lesthaeghe, R. (ed.) (1989) *Reproduction and Social Organization in Sub-Saharan Africa*, Berkeley: University of California Press.

Lesthaeghe, R. and Surkyn, J. (2002) 'New Forms of Household Formation in Central and Eastern Europe: Are they Related to Newly Emerging Value Orientations?', Brussel: Vrije Universiteit, Interface Demography.

Lesthaeghe, R. and Wilson, C. (1986) 'Mode of Production, Secularization, and the Pace of Fertility Decline in Western Europe, 1870–1930', in A. Coale and S.C. Watkins (eds), *The Decline of Fertility in Europe*, Princeton, NJ: Princeton University Press.

Lett, D.P. (1998) *In Pursuit of Status*, Cambridge, MA: Harvard University Press.

Lev, D. (1978) 'Remarks on Family Law Change in Post-Revolutionary Indonesia', in D. Buxbaum (ed.), *Chinese Family Law and Social Change*, Seattle and London: University of Washington Press.

Levasseur, A. (1976) *The Civil Code of the Ivory Coast*, Charlottesville, VA: The Michie Company.

Lévi-Strauss, C. (1949/1969) *The Elementary Structure of Kinship*, London: Eyre & Spottiswoode.

Levin, H. (1966) 'Distribution of Contraceptive Supplies through Commercial Channels', in B. Berelson *et al.* (eds), *Family Planning and Population Programs*, Chicago: University of Chicago Press.

Levine, D. (ed.) (1984) *Proletarianization and Family History*, New York: Academic Press.

Lévy, C. and Henry, L. (1960) 'Ducs et pairs sous l'Ancien Régime', *Population* 15,5.

Levy, M. (1949) *The Family Revolution in Modern China*, Cambridge, MA: Harvard University Press.

Lewin, B. *et al.* (1998) *Sex i Sverige*, Stockholm: Folkhälsoinstitutet.

Lewis, J. (2001) *The End of Marriage?*, Cheltenham: Edward Elgar.

Librando, V. (1978) 'In Italy', in A.G. Chloros (ed.), *The Reform of Family Law in Europe*, Deventer: Kluwer.

Li, Jiali (1995) 'China's One-Child Policy: How and How Well Has It Worked?', *Population and Development Review* 21: 563–85.

Li Shuchang (1988/1901) *Carnet de notes sur l'Occident*, Paris: Editions de la Maison des sciences de l'Homme.

Li Yinhe (1994) *Rural Women in China*, Rome: IFAD.

Li Yongping (2000) 'Age and Sex Structure', in Peng Xizhe and Guo Zhigang (eds), *The Changing Population of China*, Oxford: Blackwell.

Li Yongping and Peng Xizhe (2000) 'Age and Sex Structures', in Peng Xizhe and Guo Zhigang (eds), *The Changing Population of China*, Oxford: Blackwell.

Liljeström, R. and Tuong Lai (eds) (1991) *Sociological Studies on the Vietnamese Family*, Hanoi: Social Sciences Publishing House.

Liljeström R. and Özdalga, E. (2002) *Autonomy and Dependence in the Family*, Istanbul: Swedish Research Institute in Istanbul.

Lim, M. (1966) 'Malaysia and Singapore', in B. Berelson *et al.* (eds), *Family Planning and Population Programs*, Chicago: Chicago University Press.

Limanonda, B. (1995) 'Families in Thailand: Beliefs and Realities', *Journal of Comparative Family Studies* XXVI,1: 67–81.

Linssen, R. *et al.* (2002) 'Wachsende Ungleichheit der Zukunftschancen? Familie, Schule und Freizeit als jugendliche Lebenswelten', in Deutsche Shell (Hrsg.) *Jugend 2002 14. Shell Jugendstudie,* Frankfurt a.M.: Fischer.

Litten, G.K. (1984) *Colonialism, Class and Nation,* Calcutta: K.P. Bagchi & Co.

Liu, D. *et al.* (1997) *Sexual Behavior in Modern China,* New York: Continuun.

Liu, H. *et al.* (1998) 'A study of sexual behaviour among rural residents of China', *Journal of Acquired Immune Deficiency Syndrome and Human Retrovirology* 19: 80–88.

Livi-Bacci, M. (1971) *A Century of Portuguese Fertility,* Princeton, NJ: Princeton University Press.

Livi-Bacci, M. (1977) *A History of Italian Fertility During the Last Two Centuries,* Princeton, NJ: Princeton University Press.

Livi-Bacci, M. (1986) 'Social-Group Forerunners of Fertility Control in Europe', in A. Coale and S. Cotts Watkins (eds), *The Decline of Fertility in Europe,* Princeton, NJ: Princeton University Press.

Livi-Bacci, M. (1992) *A Concise History of World Population,* Oxford: Blackwell.

Livi-Bacci, M. (1993) 'On the Human Costs of Collectivization in the Soviets Union', *Population and Development Review* 19: 743–66.

Livi-Bacci, M. (1999) *Europa und seine Menschen,* Munich: C.H. Beck, 174–75. (Orig. edn, 1998, *La popolazione nella storia d'Europa,* Rome: Laterza).

Loewenfeld, E. and Lauterbach, W. (1963–72) *Das Eherecht der europäischen und aussereuropäischen Staaten,* Cologne: Carl Heymann.

Löfgren, O. (ed.) (1988) *Hej, det är från försäkringskassan,* Stockholm: Natur och Kultur.

Lohlé-Tart, L. (1975) 'Law and Fertility in Belgium', in M. Kirk *et al.* (eds), *Law and Fertility in Europe,* Liege: Ordina.

Lomnitz, L. and Perez-Lizaur, M. (1991) 'Dynastic Growth and Survival Strategies: The Solidarity of Mexican Grand-Families, in E. Jelin (ed.), *Family, Household and Gender Relation in Latin America,* London: Kegan Paul International.

Lugard (1922/1965) *The Dual Mandate in British Tropical Africa* (5th edn), London: Frank Cass.

Lund-Andersen, I. (2001) 'The Danish Registered Partnerships Act, 1989: Has the Act Meant a Change in Attitudes?', in R. Wintemute and M. Andanaes (eds), *Legal Recogniton of Same-Sex Partnerships,* London: Hart Publishing.

Lundquist, T. (1982) *Den disciplinerade dubbelmoralen: studier i den reglementerade prostitutionens historia i Sverige 1859–1918,* PhD thesis, Historiska Institutionen, Göteborg University.

Lush, L., Cleland, J. *et al.* (2000) 'Politics and Fertility', *Population Research and Policy Review* 19: 1–28.

Lynd, R. and Lynd, H. (1929/1956) *Middletown,* New York: Harcourt, Brace & World.

McCaa, R. (1993) 'The Peopling of Nineteenth-Century Mexico: Critical Scrutiny of a Cesured Century', in J. Wilkie, C.A. Contreras and C.A. Weber (eds), *Statistical Abstract of Latin America,* vol. 30, Los Angeles: UCLA Latin American Center Publications.

McCaa, R. (1994) 'Marriageways in Mexico and Spain, 1500–1900', *Continuity and Change* 9: 11–43.

McDonald, P. (1975) *Marriage in Australia,* Canberra: ANU Department of Demography.

McDonald, P. (1997) 'Gender Equity, Social Institutions, and the Future of Fertility', Canberra: Australian National University, Working Papers in Demography no. 69.

McFarlane, C.P., Friedman, J.S. and Morris, L. (1994) *1993 Contraceptive Prevalence Surveys, Knowledge and Attitudes Towards Family, Contaceptives, and AIDS Volume II,* Washington, DC: National Family Planning Board.

McGaffey, W. (1983) 'Lineage Structure, Marriage and the Family among the Central Bantu', *Journal of African History* 24,2: 173–86.

Macias, A. (1982) *Against all Odds*, Westport, CT, London: Greenwood Press.

McIntosh, A. and Finkle, J. (1995) 'The Cairo Conference on Population and Development: A New Paradigm?', *Population and Development Review*, 21: 223–60.

McIntyre, L. (1995) 'Law and the Family in Historical Perspective: Issues and Antecedents', *Marriage and Family Review* 21: 5–30.

Mackie, V. (1998) 'Freedom and the Family: Gendering Meiji Political Thought', in D. Kelly and A. Reid (eds), *Asian Freedoms*, Cambridge: Cambridge University Press.

MacMahon, D. (2001) *Enemies of the Enlightenment*, Oxford: Oxford University Press.

McNicoll, G. (1992) 'Changing Fertility Patterns and Policies in the Third World', *Annual Review of Sociology* 18: 85–108.

McNicoll, G. (2001) 'Government and Fertility in Transitional and Post-Transitional Societies, the Fertility Transition', *Population and Development Review* 27 Supplement: 135–59.

Maddison, A. (2001) *The World Economy: A Millennial Perspective*, Paris: OECD.

Magnani, R.J. *et al.* (1995) 'Men, marriage and fatherhood in Kinshasa, Zaire', *International Family Planning Perspectives* 21,1: 19–25.

Mahkonen, S. (1988) 'From Control of the Family to Its Autonomy', in A. Victorin (ed.), *Scandinavian Studies in Law 32*, Sockholm: Stockholm Institute of Scandinavian Law.

Makdisi, G. (1981) *The Rise of Colleges. Institutions of Learning in Islam and in the West*, Edinburgh: Edinburgh University Press.

Makhlouf, C. (1995) *Family, Gender, and Population in the Middle East*, Cairo: The American University in Cairo Press.

Malhotra, A. (1991) ' Gender and Changing Generational Relations: Spouse Choice in Indonesia', *Demography* 28,4: 549–70.

Malhotra, A. and Reeve, V. (1995) 'Fertility, Dimensions of Patriarchy, and Development in India', *Population and Development Review* 21,2: 281–305.

Malhotra, A., Vanneman, R. and Kishor, S. (1995) 'Fertility, Dimensions of Patriarchy, and Development in India', *Population and Development Review* 21: 281–305.

Malthus, T. (1798) *An Essay on the Principle of Population*, London: J. Johnson.

Mamdani, M. (1996) *Citizen and Subject*, Princeton, NJ: Princeton University Press.

Mandelbaum, D. (1970) *Society in India*, Berkeley: University of California Press.

Manderson, L. and Liamputtong, P. (2002) *Coming of Age in South and Southeast Asia*, Richmond, Surrey: Curzon Press.

Mango, A. (2002) *Atatürk*, New York: The Overlook Press (paperback edn).

Mani, L. (1993) 'The Female Subject, the Colonial Gaze: Reading Eyewitness Accounts of Widow Burning', in T. Niranjana *et al.* (eds), *Interrogating Modernity. Culture and Colonialism in India*, Calcutta: Seagull.

Marcus, A. (1989) *The Middle East on the Eve of Modernity. Aleppo in the Eighteenth Century*, New York: Columbia University Press.

Marecek, J. (2000) '"Am I a woman in these matters?": some notes on Sinhala nationalism and gender in Sri Lanka', in T. Mayer (ed.), *Gender Ironies of Nationalism*, London: Routledge.

Marín Lira, M.A. (1981) 'Les unions consensuelles en Amérique Latine: l 'Amérique Centrale', in J. Dupâquier *et al.* (eds), *Marriage and Remarriage in Populations of the Past*, London, New York: Academic Press.

Marr, D. (1981) *Vietnamese Tradition on Trial 1920–1945*, Berkeley: University of California Press.

Martine, G. (1996) 'Brazil's Fertility Decline, 1965–95', *Population and Development Review* 22.

Martinez-Alier, V. (1974) *Marriage, Class and Colour in Nineteenth-Century Cuba*, Cambridge: Cambridge University Press.

Martinic Galetovic, M.D. (1991) 'El concubinato y figuras afines: un caso de marginalidd jurídica', in E. Barrios Bourie (ed.), *Familia y personas*, Santiago de Chile: Editorial Jurídica de Chile.

Mason, K.O. (1997) 'Explaining Fertility Transitions', *Demography* 34,4: 443–54.

Mason, K.O. (1998) 'Wives' Economic Decision-Making Power in the Family', in K.O. Mason *et al.* (eds), *The Changing Family in Comparative Perspective: Asia and the United States*, Honolulu: East–West Center.

Mason, K.O. (2001) 'Gender and Family Systems in the Fertility Transition', *Population and Development Review* 27 Supplement: 160–76.

Massell, G. (1978) 'Family Law and Social Mobilization in Soviet Central Asia: Some Comparisons with the People's Republic of China', in D. Buxbaum (ed.), *Chinese Family Law and Social Change*, Seattle and London: University of Washington Press.

Mathabane, M. (1995) *African Women*, London: Hamish Hamilton.

Matovic, M. (1984) *Stockholmsäktenskap.Familjebildning och partnerval i Stockholm 1850–1890*, Stockholm: Stockholm Universitet, Historiska Institutionen.

Matovic, M.R. (1980) 'Illegitimacy and Marriage in Stockholm in the Nineteenth Century', in P. Laslett, K. Oosterveen and R.M. Smith (eds), *Bastardy and its Comparative History*, London: Edward Arnold.

Matsushima, Y. (1998) 'The Development of Japanese Family Law from 1898 to 1997 and its Relationship to Social and Political Change', in J. Eekelaar and T. Nhlapo (eds), *The Changing Family*, Oxford: Hart Publishing.

Mayer, E. and Bolton, R. (eds) (1980) *Parentesco y Matrimonio en los Andes*, Peru: Pontificia Universidad Católica del Perú, Fondo Editorial.

Mayer, J. (1980) 'The Family in Brazil', in M.S. Das and C. Jesser (eds), *The Family in Latin America*, New Delhi: Vikas Publishing House.

Mayne, J. (1953, 1974–5) *Mayne's Treatise on Hindu Law and Usage* (11th edn) by Chandrasekhara Aiyar, Madras: Higginbothams.

Mayo, K. (1927) *Mother India*, London: Jonathan Cape.

Mbiti, J. (1989) *African Religions and Philosophy* (2nd edn), London: Heinemann.

Meekers, D. (1993a) 'Immaculate Conceptions in Sub-Saharan Africa', Pennsylvania: Pennsylvania State University.

Meekers, D. (1993b) 'The Noble Custom of Roora: The Marriage Practices of the Shona of Zimbabwe', *Ethnology* XXXII.

Meijer, M. (1971) *Marriage Law and Policy*, Hong Kong: Hong Kong University Press.

Meijer, M. (1978) 'Marriage Law and Policy in the People's Republic of China', in D. Buxbaum (ed.), *Chinese Family and Social Change*, Seattle and London: University of Washington Press.

Melby, K., Pylkkänen, A., Rosenbeck, B. and Carlsson Wetterberg C. (eds) (2001) *The Nordic Model of Marriage and the Welfare State*, Copenhagen: Nordic Council of Ministers.

Mencius (1963) *Mencius*, translated, arranged, and annotated by W.A.C.H. Dobson, London: Oxford University Press.

Mensch, B. *et al.* (2000) *Socialization to Gender Roles and Marriage Among Egyptian Adolescents*, New York: Population Council.

Menski, W. (ed.) (1998) *South Asians and the Dowry Problem*, London: Trentham Books.

Mernissi, F. (1978) 'The Patriarch in the Moroccan Family: Myth or Reality?', in J. Allan (ed.), *Women's Status and Fertility in the Muslim World*, New York: Praeger.

Metner, T. (1966) 'Turkey', in B. Berelson *et al.* (eds), *Family Planning and Population Programs*, Chicago: Chicago University Press.

Meyer, F. (1999) 'Men og kvinner i Skandinavia på 1930–talet', in A. Warring (ed.), *Kön, religion og kvinder i bevaegelse*, Roskilde: Kvinder på tvaers, Roskilde Universitetscenter.

Meyer, J. (1980) ' Illegitimates and foundlings in pre-industrial France', in P. Laslett, K. Oosterveen and R.M. Smith (eds), *Bastardy and its Comparative History*, London: Edward Arnold.

Mezger, E. (1967) 'Das Eherecht Frankreichs', in *Leske-Loewenfeld Das Eherecht der europäischen und der assuereuropäischen Staaten*, Teil I, Cologne: Carl Heymanns Verlag.

Michael, R. *et al.* (2001) 'Private Sexual Behavior, Public Opinion, and Public Health Policy Related to Sexually Transmitted Diseases: A US–British Comparison', in E. Laumann and R. Michael (eds), *Sex, Love and Health in America*, Chicago: University of Chicago Press.

Mill, J.S. (1817) *History of British India*, vol. 1, London.

Mill. J.S. (1869/1970) *The Subjection of Women*, Cambridge, MA: MIT Press.

Millar, J. (1771) *The Origin of the Distinction of Ranks*, London.

Miller, F. (1991) *Latin American Women*, Hanover and London: University Press of New England.

Minces, J. (1978) 'Women in Algeria', in L. Beck and N. Keddie (eds), *Women in the Muslim World*, Cambridge, MA: Harvard University Press.

Minturn, L. (1993) *Sitas's Daughters*, New York and Oxford: Oxford University Press.

Mintz, S. and Kellogg, S. (1988) *Domestic Revolutions*, New York: The Free Press.

Mir-Hosseini, Z. (1993) 'Women, Marriage and the Law in Post-Revolutionary Iran', in H. Afshar (ed.), *Women in the Middle East*, Basingstoke: Macmillan.

Mitchell, B.R. (1998a) *International Historical Statistics. The Americas* (4th edn), Basingstoke: Macmillan.

Mitchell, B.R. (1998b) *International Historical Statistics. Africa, Asia & Oceania 1750–1993* (3rd edn), Basingstoke: Macmillan.

Mitchell, B.R. (1998c) *International Historical Statistics. Europe 1750–1993* (4th edn), Basingstoke: Macmillan.

Mitchell, J. (1966) 'Women – the Longest Revolution', *New Left Review* 40: 11–37.

Mitchell, T. (1988) *Colonising Egypt*, Cambridge: Cambridge University Press.

Mitterauer, M. (1983) *Ledige Mütter*, Munich: C.H. Beck.

Mitterauer, M. (1986) *Sozialgeschichte der Jugend*, Frankfurt: Suhrkamp.

Mitterauer, M. and Sieder, R. (1982) *The European Family*, Oxford: Basil Blackwell.

Miyoshi, M. (1979) *As We Saw Them*, Berkeley, Los Angeles, London: University of California Press.

Mody, P. (2002) 'Love and the Law: Love-Marriage in Delhi', *Modern Asian Studies* 36,1: 223–56.

Montagu, M. (1994/1716–18) *The Turkish Embassy Letters*, London: Virago.

Montgomery, M.R., Cheung, P.P.L. and Sulak, D.B. (1988) 'Rates of Courtship and First Marriage in Thailand', *Population Studies* 42: 375–88.

Morgan, E. (1944/1966) *The Puritan Family*, New York: Harper Torchbooks.

Morgan, P. (1996) 'Buddhism', in P. Morgan and C. Lawron (eds), *Ethical Issues in Six Religious Traditions*, Edinburgh: Edinburgh University Press.

Morris, C. (1995) *Becoming Southern*, New York and Oxford: Oxford University Press.

Morris, H.F. (1968) 'Marriage Law in Uganda: Sixty Years of Attempted Reform', in J.N.D. Anderson (ed.), *Family Law in Asia and Africa*, London: George Allen & Unwin.

Morris, H.F. and Reid J.S. (1972) *Indirect Rule and The Search for Justice*, Oxford: Clarendon Press.

Morton, W. (1962) *Woman Suffrage in Mexico*, Gainesville: University of Florida Press.

Moseley, P. (1959/1976) 'The Russian Family: Old Style and New', in R.F. Byrnes (ed.), *Communal Families in the Balkans: the Zadruga*, Notre Dame: University of Notre Dame Press.

Mosher, D. and Bachrach, C. (1996) 'Understanding U.S. Fertility: Continuity and Change in the National Survey of Family Growth, 1988–1995', *Family Planning Perspectives* 28,1: 1–29.

Mosher, S.W. (1983) *The Broken Earth: The Rural Chinese*, New York: Free Press.

Mosher, S.W. (1993) *A Mother's Ordeal: One Woman's Fight Against China's One-Child Policy*, New York: Harcourt Brace Jovanovich.

Mosk, C. (1979) 'The Decline of Marital Fertility in Japan', *Population Studies*, 33: 19–38.

Mosk, C. (1983) *Patriarchy and Fertility: Japan and Sweden, 1880–1960*, New York: Academic Press.

Mounier, A. (1998) 'The demographic situation of Europe and the developed countries overseas', *Population: An English Selection* 10,2: 447–74.

Muel-Dreyfus, F. (1996) *Vichy et l'éternel feminine*, Paris: Seuil.

Muhammad, A. (2001) 'Nigeria: Spinsters Flee to Barracks in Minna' [http//:www.jendajournal.com/jenda/vol.11.1/sharia.html].

Muhari, P. *et al.* (1994) *Socioeconomic Differentials in Fertility*, Calverton, MD: Macro International Inc.

Muller-Escoda, B. and Vogt, U. (1997) 'France: the Institutionalization of Plurality', in F-X. Kaufmann *et al.* (eds), *Family Life and Family Policies in Europe*, vol. 1, Oxford: Clarendon Press.

Müller-Freienfels, W. (1978) 'Soviet Family Law and Comparative Chinese Developments', in D. Buxbaum (ed.), *Chinese Family and Social Change*, Seattle and London: University of Washington Press.

Mundigo, A. (1996) 'The Role of Family Planning Programmes in the Fertility Transition of Latin America', in J. Guzmán *et al.* (eds), *The Fertility Transition in Latin America*, Oxford: Clarendon Press.

Muramatsu. M. (1966) 'Japan', in B. Berelson *et al.* (eds), *Family Planning and Population Programs*, Chicago: Chicago University Press.

Murthi, M. and Guio, A.C. (1995) 'Mortality, Fertility, and Gender Bias in India: A District-Level Analysis', *Population and Development Review* 21,4: 745–82.

Musisi, N. (2002) 'The Politics of Perception or Perception as Politics? Colonial and Missionary Representations of Baganda Women, 1900–1945', in J. Allman *et al.* (eds), *Women in African Colonial Histories*, Bloomington: Indiana University Press.

Myrdal, A. (1941) *Nation and Family*, London: Kegan Paul.

Myrdal, A. and Myrdal, G. (1934) *Kris is befolkningsfrågan*, Stockholm: KF's Förlag.

Myrdal, G. (1968) *Asian Drama*, 3 vols, New York: Pantheon.

Nahm, A. (1993) *Introduction to Korean History and Culture* Elizabeth, NJ and Seoul: Hollym.

Nandy, A. (1983) *The Intimate Enemy*, New Delhi: Oxford University Press.

Narrain, D. (1970) 'Interpersonal relations in the Hindu family', in R. Hill and R. König (eds), *Families in East and West*, Paris, The Hague: Mouton.

Nasir, J. (1990) *The Islamic Law of Personal Status*, London: Graham and Trotman.

Natsoulas, T. (1998) 'The Politicization of the Ban on Female Circumcision and the Rise of the Independent School Movement in Kenya', *Journal of African and Asian Studies* xxxiii,2: 137–55.

Natsukari, Y. (1994) 'A Structural Study of Spouse Selection in Japan', in Lee-Jay Cho and M. Yada (eds), *Tradition and Change in the Asian Family*, Honolulu: East–West Center.

Navarro, M. (1999) 'Women in Pre-Columbian and Colonial Latin America and the Caribbean', in M. Navarro and V. Sánchez Korrol (eds), *Women in Latin America and the Caribbean*, Bloomington, Indianapolis: Indiana University Press.

Navarro, M. and Sánchez Korrol, V. (1999) *Women in Latin America and the Caribbean*, Bloomington, Indianapolis: Indiana University Press.

Nawar, L., Lloyd, C. and Ibrahim, B. (1995) 'Women's Autonomy and Gender Roles in Egyptian Families', in C.M. Obermeyer (ed.), *Family, Gender, and Population in the Middle East*, Cairo: The American University in Cairo Press.

Ncube, W. (1998) 'Defending and Protecting Gender Equality and the Family under a Decidedly Undecided Constitution in Zimbabwe', in J. Eekelaar and T. Nhlapo (eds), *The Changing Family*, Oxford: Hart Publishing.

Nechi, S., Schufer, M. and Mendez Ribas, J.M. (2000) 'Adolescentes de la ciudad de Buenos Aires: su paso hacia la vida sexual adulta', in E.A. Pantelides and S. Bott (eds), *Reproducción, salud y sexualidad en America Latina*, Buenos Aires: Biblos.

Nelson, C. and Koch, F. (eds) (1983) *Law and Social Change in Contemporary Egypt*, Cairo: Cairo Papers in Social Science.

Nhlapo, T. (1998) 'African Family Law under an Undecided Constitution – The Challenge for Law Reform in South Africa', in J. Eekelaar and T. Nhlapo (eds), *The Changing Family*, Oxford: Hart Publishing.

Notestein, F.W. (1945) 'Population – the long view', in T.W. Schultz (ed.), *Food for the World*, Chicago: Chicago University Press.

Notkola, V. (1996) 'Parish Records from Namibia 1925–1990 – An Attempt to Analyze Fertility and Mortality in Ovamboland', *Yearbook of Population Research in Finland* 33: 295–305.

Noulte, S. and Hastings, S.A. (1991) 'The Meiji State's Policy Toward Women, 1890–1910', in G.L. Bernstein (ed.), *Recreating Japanese Women, 1600–1945*, Berkeley and Los Angeles: University of California Press.

Nowaihi, M. (1979) 'Changing the Law on Personal Status within a Liberal Interpretation of the Sharia', in C. Nelson and E. Koch (eds), *Law and Social Change in Contemmporary Egypt*, Cairo: Cairo Papers in Social Science.

Nutini, H.G. (1965) 'Polygyny in a Tlaxcalan Comunity', *Ethnology* 4: 123–47.

Oda, H. (1992) *Japanese Law*, London: Butterworths.

Odén, B. (1991) 'Relationer mellan generationerna', in B. Ankarloo (ed.), *Maktpolitik och husfrid*, Lund: Lund University Press, 85–116.

OECD (1979) *Demographic Trends 1950–1990*, Paris: OECD.

OECD (2002) *OECD Employment Outlook*, Paris: OECD.

Office for National Statistics (2002) *General Household Survey*, [www.statistics.gov.uk/STATBASE] (2002–12–03).

Oheneba-Sakyi, Y. (1999) *Female Autonomy, Family Decision Making, and Demographic Behavior in Africa*, Lewiston, Queenstown, Lampeter: Edwin Mellen Press.

Oliveira, M. and Berquó, E.(1990) 'A Familia no Brasil', *Ciências Sociais Hoje*, 1990: 30–64.

Oliveira, O. de (1991) ' Migration of Women, Family Organization and Labour Markets in Mexico', in E. Jelín (ed.), *Family, Household and Gender Relations in Latin America*, London: Kegan Paul International.

Oliveira, O. de (1995) 'Experiencias matrimoniales en el México urbano: la importancia de la familia de orígen', *Estudios Sociológicos* 13,38: 283–308.

Oliver, R. and Atmore, A. (1994) *Africa since 1800* (4th edn), Cambridge: Cambridge University Press.

Ono, K. (1989) *Chinese Women in a Century of Revolution, 1850–1950*, Stanford: Stanford University Press.

Oohiambo, O. (1995) *Men and Fertility in Kenya*, PhD Thesis, Ann Arbor, MI: UMI Dissertation Services.

Oppler, A. (1976) *Legal Reform in Occupied Japan*, Princeton, NJ: Princeton University Press.

Oppong, C. (ed) (1983) *Female and Male in West Africa*, Boston and Sydney: George Allen and Unwin.

Orubuloye, O., Caldwell, J. and Caldwell, P. (1997) 'Men's sexual behaviour in urban and rural Southwest Nigeria': Its Cultural, Social and Attitudinal Context, *Health Transition Review* 7: 315–28.

Ortmayr, N. (1996) 'Illegitimacy and Low-Wage Economy in Highland Austria and Jamaica', in M.J. Maynes *et al.* (eds), *Gender, Kinship, Power*, New York and London: Routledge.

Ortmayr, N. (1997) 'Church, Marriage, and Legitimacy in the British West Indies (Nineteenth and Twentieth Centuries)', *The History of the Family* 2: 141–70.

Osterhammel, J. (1998) *Die Entzauberung Asiens*, Munich: C.H. Beck.

Palmer, M. (2000) 'Caring for Young and Old: Developments in the Family Law of the People's Republic of China, 1996–1998', in A. Bainham (ed.), *The International Survey of Family Law*, Bristol: Jordan Publishing.

Pantelides, E. (1996) 'A Century and a Quarter of Fertility Change in Argentina: 1869 to the Present', in J.M. Guzmán *et al.* (eds), *The Fertility Transition in Latin America*, Oxford: Clarendon Press.

Parawansa, K.I. (2002) 'Institution-Building: An Effort to Improve Indonesian Women's Role and Staus', in K. Robinson and Sh. Bessel (eds), *Women in Indonesia*, Singapore: Institute of Southeast Asian Studies.

Parish, W. and Whyte, M.K. (1978) *Village and family in Contemporary China*, Chicago: University of Chicago Press.

Parish, W. and Farrer, J. (2000) 'Gender and Family', in Wenfang Tang and W. Parish (eds), *Chinese Urban Life under Reform*, Cambridge: Cambridge University Press.

Park, Chai Bin, and Cho, Nam-Hoon (1993) 'Consequences of Son Preferences in a Low-Fertility Society: Imbalance of the Sex Ratio at Birth in Korea', *Population and Development Review* 21,1: 59–84.

Park, Insook Han, and Cho, Lee-Jay (1995) 'Confucianism and the Korean Family', *Journal of Comparative Family Studies*, XXVI,1: 116–35.

Parkin, D. and Nyamwaya, D. (eds) (1987) *Transformations of African Marriage*, Manchester: Manchester University Press.

Parrado, E. (2000) 'Social Change, Population Policies, and Fertility Decline in Colombia and Venezuela', *Population Research and Policy Review* 19: 421– 57.

Patterson, O. (1967) *The Sociology of Slavery*, London: MacGibbon & Kee.

Patterson, O. (1982) *Slavery and Social Death*, Cambridge, MA: Harvard University Press.

Patterson, O. (1998) *Rituals of Blood*, Washington, DC: Civitas Counterpoint.

Pearl, D. 1979, *A Textbook on Muslim Law*, London: Croom Helm.

Peller, S. (1965) 'Births and Deaths among Europe's Ruling Families since 1500', in D.V. Glass and D.E.C. Eversley (eds), *Population in History*, London: Edward Arnold.

Pemberton, J. (1994) *On The Subject of 'Java'*, Ithaca and London: Cornell University Press.

Pepper, S. (1987) 'Education', in D. Twitchelt and J. Fairbank (eds), *The Cambridge History of China*, vol. 14, Cambridge: Cambridge University Press.

Pepper, S. (1991) 'Education', in D. Twitchelt and J. Fairbank (eds), *The Cambridge History of China*, vol. 15, Cambridge: Cambridge University Press.

Pérez-Brignoli, H. (1981) 'Deux siècles d'illégitimité au Costa Rica 17701974', in J. Dupâquier *et al.* (eds), *Marriage and Remarriage in Populations of the Past*, London and New York: Academic Press.

Pérez-Díaz, V., Chuliá, E. and Valiente, C. (2000) *La familia española en el 2000*, Madrid: Fundación Argentaria.

Person, E.S. (1999) *The Sexual Century*, New Haven: Yale University Press.

Pham Van Bich (1999) *The Vietnamese Family in Change*, Richmond, Surrey: Curzon Press.

Pharr, S. (1977) 'Japan', in J. Giele and A. Smock (eds), *Women – Roles and Status in Eight Countries*, New York: Wiley.

Pharr, S. (1987) 'The Politics of Women's Rights', in R. Ward and Y. Sakamoto (eds), *Democratizing Japan*, Honolulu: University of Hawaii Press.

Philips, A. (1953/1969) *African Marriage and Social Change*, London: Frank Cass.

Philips, A. and Morris, H.F. (1971) *Marriage Laws in Africa*, London, New York, Toronto: Oxford University Press.

Phillips, R. (1991) *Untying the Knot*, Cambridge: Cambridge University Press.

Pietilä, H. and Vickers, J. (1990/1996) *Making Women Matter* (3rd edn), London: Zed Books.

Pine, L. (1997) *Nazi Family Policy, 1933–1945*, Oxford, New York: Berg.

Ping-ti Ho, (1959) *Studies on the Population of China, 1368–1953*, Cambridge, MA: Harvard University Press.

Pinsof, W. (2002) 'The Death of "Till Death Us Do Part"', *Family Process*, 41,2: 135–58.

Pinson, A. (1992) 'The Evolving Icelandic Household in the shift from Pastoralism to Ranching', *Journal of Family History* 17: 47–67.

Pius XI, (1964) 'Casti Connubii', in F. Rodriguez (ed.), *Doctrina Pontificia III Documentos sociales*, Madrid: Biblioteca de Autores Cristianos.

Pollak-Eitz, A. (1980) 'The Family in Venezuela', in M.S. Das and C. Jesser (eds), *The Family in Latin America*, New Delhi: Vikas Publishing House.

Pott-Buter, H.A. (1993) *Fact and Fairy Tales about Female Labor, Family and Fertility*, Amsterdam: Amsterdam University Press.

Potter, J. (1968) 'American Population in the Early National Period', in P. Deprez (ed.), *Population and Economics*, Winnipeg: University of Manitoba Press.

Potthast-Jutkeit, B. (1991) 'The Ass of Mare and Other Scandals: Marriage and Extramarital Relations in Nineteenth-Century Paraguay', *Journal of Family History* 16: 215–39.

Potthast-Jutkeit, B. (1997) 'The Creation of the Mestizo Family Model', *The History of the Family* 2,2: 123–39.

Price, R. (1965) 'Trial Marriage in the Andes', *Ethnology* 4: 310–22.

Pyle, K. 1998, 'Meiji Conservatism', in B.T. Wakabayashi (ed.), *Modern Japanese Thought*, Cambridge: Cambridge University Press.

Quah, S. (ed.) (1990) *The Family as an Asset*, Singapore: Times Academic Press.

Quah, S. (1998) *Family in Singapore* (2nd edn), Singapore: Times Academic Press.

Quale, R. (1988) *A History of Marriage Systems*, New York: Greenwood Press.

Quataert, D. (1991) 'Ottoman Women, Household, and Textile Manufacturing, 1800–1914', in N. Keddie and B. Baron (eds), *Women in Middle Eastern History*, New Haven and London: Yale University Press.

Quatre premiers congrès mondiaux de l'Internationale Communiste 1919–1923 (1934/1969), Paris: Maspero.

Radcliffe-Brown E. and Forde, D. (eds) (1950) *African Systems of Kinship and Marriage*, London, New York: Oxford University Press.

Rahman, F.H. (1995) *The Status of Rural Women in China*, Rome: IFAD.

Raimundo, C. (1993) 'Cost-Efficiency and Effectiveness of Programmes', in UN Economic Commission for Asia and the Pacific, *Family Planning Programmes in Asia and the Pacific*, New York: United Nations.

Raina, L. (1966) 'India', in B. Berelson *et al.* (eds), *Family Planning and Population Programs*, Chicago: University of Chicago Press.

Ramachandran, R. (1989) *Urbanization and Urban Systems in India*, New Delhi: Oxford University Press.

Ramachandran, V.K. (2000) 'Kerala's Development Achievements and Their Replicability', in G. Parayil (ed.), *Kerala. The Development Experience*, London: Zed Books.

Ratcliffe, B. (1996) 'Popular Classes and Cohabitation in Nineteenth-Century Paris', *Journal of Family History* 21,3: 316–50.

Rattray, R.S. (1923) *Ashanti*, Oxford: Clarendon Press.

Ray, B. (ed.) (1995) 'The Freedom Movement and Feminist Consciousness in Bengal, 1905–1929', in B. Ray (ed.), *From the Seams of History: Essays on Indian Women*, Oxford: Oxford University Press.

Reher, D. (1997) *Perspectives on the Family in Spain Past and Present*, Oxford: Clarendon Press.

Reid, A. (1988–93) *Southeast Asia in the Age of Commerce, 1450–1680*, 2 vols, New Haven and London: Yale University Press.

Rele, J.R. and Alam, I. (1993) 'Fertility Transition in Asia: The Statistical Evidence', in R. Leete and I. Alam (eds), *The Revolution in Asian Fertility*, Oxford: Clarendon Press.

Remez, L. (1998) 'In Turkey, Women's Fertility is Linked to Education, Employment and Freedom to Choose a Husband', *International Family Planning Perspectives* 24,2: 97–8.

Riazantsev, A. *et al.* (1992) 'Child Welfare and the Socialist Experiment: Social and Economic Trends in the USSR 1960–90', *Innocenti Occasional Papers*, Florence: Unicef.

Ricklefs, M. (1981), *A History of Modern Indonesia*, Basingstoke: Macmillan.

Rieg, A. (1992) 'Traits fondamentaux de l'evolution du droits des régimes matrimoniaux dans l'Europe du XXe siècle', in R. Ganghofer (ed.), *Le droit de la Famille en Europe*, Strasbourg: Presses Universitaires de Strasbourg.

Rindfuss, R. and Morgan, S. (1983) 'Marriage, Sex, and the First Birth Interval: The Quiet Revolution in Asia', *Population and Development Review* 9,2: 259–78.

Robertson, B.C. (1995) *Raja Rammohan Ray*, Delhi: Oxford University Press.

Robinson, C.A. (1999) *Tradition and Liberation*, Richmond, Surrey: Curzon Press.

Robinson, K. (2000) 'Indonesian Women- from *Orde Baru* to *Reformasi*', in L. Edwards and M. Roces (eds), *Women in Asia*, Ann Arbor: University of Michigan Press.

Robinson, K (2002) *Women in Indonesia*, Singapore: Institute of Southeast Asian Studies.

Rodriguez, F. (ed.) (1964) *Doctrina Pontificia*, vol. 3, Madrid: Editorial Católica.

Romero, H. (1969) 'Chile: The Abortion Epidemic', in B. Berelson (ed.), *Family Planning Programs*, New York: Basic Books.

Rosero-Bixby, L. (1996) 'Nuptiality trends and fertility transition in Latin America', in J.M. Guzmán *et al.* (eds), *The Fertility Transition in Latin America*, Oxford: Clarendon Press.

Ross, J., Rich, M. *et al.* (1988) *Family Planning and Child Survival*, New York: Center for Population and Family Health, Columbia University.

Roudinesco, E. (2002) *La Famille en désordre*, Paris: Fayard.

Roudolph-Touha, J. (1979) 'Marriage and Family in Iran', in. M. Singh Das and P. Bardis (eds), *The Family in Asia*, London: George Allen & Unwin.

Roy, R.M. (1823/1999) 'Letter to Lord Amherst, governor-general in council', in L.

Zastoupil and M. Moir (eds), *The Great Indian Education Debate*, Richmond, Surrey: Curzon Press, 110–13.

Ruan Fung-fu (1997) 'China', in R. Francoeur (ed.), *The International Encyclopedia of Sexuality*, vol. 1, New York: Continuum.

Ruan, Fang-fu (1991) *Sex in China*, New York and London: Plenum Press.

Rugh, A. (1984) *Family in Contemporary Egypt*, Syracuse, New York: Syracuse University Press.

Ruiz-Domènec, J.E. (2003) *La ambición del amor*, Madrid, Buenos Aires: Aguilar.

Rwezaura, B. (1998) 'The Proposed Abolition of *De Facto* Unions in Tanzania: A Case of Sailing against the Current', in J. Eekelaar and Th. Nhlapo (eds), *The Changing Family*, Oxford: Hart Publishing.

Sachs, A. and Wilson, J.H. (1978) *Sexism and the Law*, Oxford: Martin Robertson.

Saito, O. (1996) 'Famine and mortality in the Japanese past: wth special reference to the eighteenth and nineteenth centuries', *EurAsian Project on Population and Family History*, Kyoto: International Research Center for Japanese Studies.

Sanasarian, E. (1992) 'The Politics of Gender and Development in the Islamic Republic of Iran', in J. Jabbra and N. Jabbra (eds), *Women and Devlopment in the Middle East and North Africa*, Leiden: E.J. Brill.

Sánchez Albornoz, N. (1986) *The Population of Latin America. A History*, Berkeley: University of California Press.

Sánchez-Korrol, V. (1999) 'Women in Nineteenth- and Twentieth-Century Latin America and the Caribbean', in M. Navarro and V. Sánchez-Korrol (eds), *Women in Latin America and the Caribbean*, Bloomington and Indianapolis: Indiana University Press.

Sanderson, W. and Jee-Peng Tan (1995) *Population in Asia*, Washington, DC: The World Bank.

Santelli, J. *et al.* (2000) 'Adolescent Sexual Behavior: Estimates and Trends from Four Nationally Representative Surveys', *Family Planning Perspectives* 32,4: 156–65, 194.

Sarkar, L. (1977) 'Law and the Status of Women in India', *Columbia Human Rights Law Review* 8,1: 95–122.

Satterthwaite, A. (1966) 'Oral Contraceptives', in B. Berelson *et al.* (eds), *Family Planning and Population Programs*, Chicago: University of Chicago Press.

Savara, M. and Sridhar, C.R. (1992) 'Sexual behaviour of urban, educated Indian men: results of a survey', *Journal of Family Welfare* 38: 30–43.

Saxena, P. (2001) 'Same-Sex Partnerships and Indian Law: Climate for a Change', in R. Wintermute and M. Andenaes (eds), *Legal Recognition of Same-Sex Partnerships*, London: Hart Publishing.

SCB (Statistics Sweden) (1914) *Statistisk Årsbok*, Stockholm.

SCB (1917) *Befolkningsrörelsen 1901–10*, Stockholm.

SCB (1944) *Befolkningsrörelsen 1931–40*, Stockholm.

SCB (1967) *Historisk statistik för Sverige. Del 1. Bofolkning* (2nd edn) Stockholm.

SCB (1969) *Historisk statistik för Sverige, Del II*, Stockolm.

SCB (1992) *Levnadsförhållanden*, 71, Stockholm.

SCB (1999) *Befolkningsutvecklingen under 250 år*, Stockholm.

SCB (2000) *Barn och deras familjer 1999*, Stockholm.

SCB (2001a) *Befolkningsstatistik del 3*, Stockholm.

SCB (2001b) *Varför föds det så få barn?*, Stockholm.

SCB (2001c) *Befolkningsstatistik del 4, 2000*, Stockholm.

SCB (2002a) *Befolkningsåret 2001*, Stockholm.

SCB (2002b) *Familj, sociala relationer, barn*, Stockholm.

Schapera, I. (1950) 'Kinship and Marriage among the Tswana', in A.R. Radcliffe-Brown and D. Forde (eds), *African Systems of Kinship and Marriage*, London: Oxford University Press.

Scherbov, S. and Van Vianen, H. (2001) 'Marriage and Fertility in Russia of Women Born between 1900 and 1960: A Cohort Analysis', *European Journal of Population* 17: 281–94.

Schoen, R. and Urton, W. (1979) *Marital Status Life Tables for Sweden*, Stockholm: SCB.

Schlesinger, R. (ed.) (1949) *The Family in the USSR*, London: Routledge and Kegan Paul.

Schneider, J. and Schneider, P. (1992) 'Going Forward in Reverse Gear: Culture, Economy, and Political Economy in the Demographic Transitions of a Rural Sicilian Town', in J. Gillis *et al.* (eds), *The European Experience of Declining Fertility*, Oxford: Blackwell.

Schoppa, K. (2000) *Modern Chinese History*, New York: Columbia University Press.

Schwab, D. (2001) *Familienrecht*, Munich: C.H. Beck.

Schwarz, H.-P. (1986) *Adenauer. Der Aufstieg 1876–1952*, Stuttgart: DVA.

Scribner, S. (1995) *Policies Affecting Fertility and Contraceptive Use: An Assessment of Twelve Sub-Saharan Countries*, Washington, DC: World Bank Discussion Papers.

Scott, H. (1978) *Kan socialismen befria kvinnan?* Stockholm: Liber (English edn: Does socialism liberate women? 1974).

Seccombe, W. (1995) *Weathering the Storm*, London: Verso.

Segalen, M. (1992) 'Exploring a Case of Late French Fertility Decline: Two Contrasted Breton Examples', in J. Gillis *et al.* (eds), *The European Experience of Declining Fertility* Oxford: Blackwell.

Seidensticker, E. (1983) *Low City, High City*, New York: Alfred Knopf.

Sen, G. *et al.* (eds) (1994) *Population Policies Reconsidered. Health, Empowerment, Rights*, Cambridge, MA: Harvard University Press.

Sevenhuisen, S. (1987) *De orde van het vaderschap*, Amsterdam: Univesitei van Amsterdam, Proefschrift.

Shah, A.M. (1998) *The Family in India. Critical Essays*, London: Sangam Books.

Sharabi, H. (1970) *Arab Intellectuals and the West: The Formative Years, 1875–1914*, Baltimore and London: Johns Hopkins University Press.

Sharabi, H. (1988) *Neopatriarchy*, New York, Oxford: Oxford University Press.

Shorter, E. (1977) *The Making of the Modern Family*, London: Fontana/Collins.

Shorter, E., Knodel, J. and Walle, E. v.d. (1971) 'The Decline of Non-marital Fertility in Europe, 1880–1940', *Population Studies* 25,3: 375–93.

Showalter, E. (1960/1992) *Sexual Anarchy. Gender and Culture of the Fin de Siècle*, London: Virago Press.

Sievers, S. (1983) *Flowers in Salt The Beginnings of Feminist Consciousness in Japan*, Stanford: Stanford University Press.

Simons, H.J. (1968) *African Women*, Evanston, IL: Northwestern University Press.

Sinclair, J. (1998) 'Way of Seeing – "Lawyering" for a New Society in South Africa', in J. Eekelaar and T. Nhlapo (eds), *The Changing Family*, Oxford: Hart Publishing.

Singh, S. and Casterline, J. (1985) 'The Socio-economic Determinants of Fertility', in J. Cleland and J. Hobcraft (eds), *Reproductive Change in Developing Countries*, Oxford: Oxford University Press.

Singh, S. and Darroch, J. (1999) 'Trends in Sexual Activity Among Adolescent American Women: 1982–1995', *Family Planning Perspectives* 31,5: 212–19.

Singh, S. and Darroch, J. (2000) 'Adolescent Pregnancy and Childbearing: Levels and Trends in Developed Countries', *Family Planning Perspectives* 32: 14–23.

Singh, S. *et al.* (2000) 'Gender Differences in the Timing of First Intercourse: Data from 14 Countries', *International Family Planning Perspectives* 26: 21, 28, 43.

Sinha, M. *et al.* (eds) (1999) *Feminisms and Internationalism*, Oxford: Blackwell.

Sinha, R.K. (1987) *A Study of Recent Marriage Patterns in Two Less Developed Sites in India, Rajasthan and Bihar*, Bombay: International Institute for Population Sciences.

Siu, H. (1993) 'Reconstituting Dowry and Brideprice in South China', in D. Davis and S. Harrell (eds), *Chinese Families in the Post-Mao Era*, Berkeley: University of California Press.

Skinner, W. (1997) 'Family Systems and Demographic Processes', in D. Kertzer and T. Fricke (eds), *Anthropological Demography*, Chicago: University of Chicago Press.

Sklar, J.L. (1974) 'The Role of Marriage Behaviour in the Demographic Transition: The Case of Eastern Europe Around 1900', *Population Studies* 28,2: 231–47.

Sloth-Nielsen, J. and Van Heerden, B. (1998) 'Signposts on the Road to Equality: Towards the New Millennium for Parents, Children and Families in South Africa', in J. Eekelaar and T. Nhlapo (eds), *The Changing Family*, Oxford: Hart Publishing.

Smiles, S. (1859/1866) *Self-Help, with Illustrations of Conduct and Perseverence* (rev. edn), London.

Smith, D.S. (1980) 'The long cycle in American illegitimacy and prenuptial pregnancy', in P. Laslett, K. Oosterveen and R.M. Smith (eds), *Bastardy and its Comparative History*, London: Edward Arnold.

Smith, R.M. (1986) 'Marriage Processes in the English Past: Some Continuites', in L. Bonfield, R. Smith and K. Wrightson (eds), *The World We Have Gained*, Oxford: Basil Blackwell.

Socolow, S. (1989) 'Acceptable Partners: Marriage Choice in Colonial Argentina, 1778–1810', in A. Lavrín (ed.), *Sexuality and Marriage in Colonial Latin America*, Lincoln and London: University of Nebraska Press.

Soewondo, N. (1977) 'Law and the Status of Women in Indonesia', in *Law and the Status of Women*, New York: United Nations; also published as *Columbia Human Rights Law Review* 8,1: 123–40.

Solari, A. and Franco, R. (1980) 'The Family in Uruguay', in S.M. Das and C. Jesser (eds), *The Family in Latin America*, New Delhi: Vikas Publishing House.

Southall, A. (1961) 'Introductory Summary', in A. Southall (ed.), *Social Change in Modern Africa*, London and New York: Oxford University Press.

Speizer, I. (1999) 'Men, Marriage, and Ideal Family Size in Francophone Africa', *Journal of Comparative Family Studies* 30: 17–34.

Spence, J. (1990) *The Search for Modern China*, New York and London: W.W. Norton.

Spiegelman, M. (1968) *Introduction to Demography*, Cambridge, MA: Harvard University Press.

Spiro, M. (1977) *Kinship and Marriage in Burma*, Berkeley, Los Angeles, London: University of California Press.

Spitzer, L. (1972) 'The Sierra Leone Creoles, 1870–1900', in P. Curtin (ed.), *Africa and the West*, Madison: University of Wisconsin Press.

St John Stevas, N. (1957) 'Women in Public Law', in R.H. Graveson and F.R. Crane (eds), *A Century of Family Law*, London: Sweet & Maxwell.

Statistisches Bundesamt (2000) *Statistisches Jahrbuch 2000*, Wiesbaden.

Staudinger, J.V. (1908) *J.V. Staudingers Kommentar zum Bürgerlichen Gesetzbuch und dem Einführungsgesetze* (3rd/4th edn), Band IV, Munich: Schweitzer Verlag.

Staudinger, J.V. (1995) *J.V. Staudingers Kommentar zum Bürgerlichen Gesetzbuch und dem Einführungsgesetze* (13th edn), Buch I, Berlin: Sellier de Gruyter.

Stearns, P. (2000) *Gender in World History*, London and New York: Routledge.

Steiner, H. and Alston, P. (1996) *International Human Rights in Context*, Oxford: Clarendon Press.

Stephen, L. (1997) *Women and Social Movements in Latin America*, Austin: University of Texas Press.

Stevenson, L. (1991) *The Victorian Homefront. American Thought and Culture 1860–1880*, New York: Twayne.

Steyn, E. (1998) 'From Closet to Constitution: The South African Gay Family Rights Odyssey', in J. Eekelaar and T. Nhlapo (eds), *The Changing Family*, Oxford: Hart Publishing.

Stockard, J. (1989) *Daughters of the Canton Delta*, Stanford: Stanford University Press.

Stolcke, V. (1988) *Coffee Planters, Workers and Wives*, Basingstoke: Macmillan.

Stolcke, V. (1992) 'The Slavery Period and its Influence on Household Structure and the Family in Jamaica, Cuba, and Brazil', in E. Berquó and P. Xenos (eds), *Family System and Cultural Change*, Oxford: Clarendon Press.

Stoler, A.L. (1996) 'Carnal Knowledge and Imperial Power: Gender, Race, and Morality in Colonial Asia', in J.W. Scott (ed.), *Feminism and History*, Oxford and New York: Oxford University Press.

Stoler, A.L. (1997) 'Sexual Affronts and Racial Frontiers: European Identities and the Cultural Politics of Exclusion in Colonial Southeast Asia', in F. Cooper and A.N. Stoler (eds), *Tensions of Empire*, Berkeley, Los Angeles and London: University of California Press.

Stone, L. (1977) *The Family, Sex and Marriage in England 1500–1800*, London: Weidenfeld and Nicolson.

Stone, L. (1995) *Road to Divorce*, Oxford: Oxford University Press.

Supreme Court of Japan (1959) *The Civil Code of Japan*, Tokyo.

Supriadi, W.C. (1995) 'Indonesia', in A. Bainham (ed.), *The International Survey of Family Law*, The Hague: Martinus Nijhoff.

Suret-Canale, J. (1971) *French Colonialism in Tropical Africa 1900–1945*, London: C. Hurst & Company.

Suryakusuma, J. (1996) 'The State and Sexuality in New Order Indonesia', in L. Sears (ed.), *Fantasizing the Feminine in Indonesia*, Durham and London: Duke University Press.

Szlezak, A. (1994) 'Families, Politics and the Law', in M. Maclean and J. Kurcewski (eds), *Families, Politics and the Law*, Oxford: Clarendon Press.

Szreter, S. (1996) *Fertility, Class, and Gender in Britain, 1860–1940*, Cambridge: Cambridge University Press.

Taeuber, I. (1958) *The Population of Japan*, Princeton, NJ: Princeton University Press.

Taeuber, I. and Orleans, L. (1966) 'Mainland China', in B. Berelson *et al.* (eds), *Family Planning and Population Programs*, Chicago: Chicago University Press.

al-Tahtawi, A. (1990) 'Family Reform Comes Only Through the Education of Girls', in M. Badran and M. Cooke (eds), *Opening the Gates*, London: Virago.

al-Tahtawi, R. (1834/1989) *Ein Muslim entdeckt Europa*, Munich: C.H. Beck.

Tai Yen-hui (1978) 'Divorce in Traditional Chinese Law', in D. Buxbaum (ed.), *Chinese Family Law and Social Change*, Seattle, London: University of Washington Press.

Tan, L. and Peng, X. (2000) 'China's Female Population', in X. Peng and Z. Guo (eds), *The Changing Population of China*, Oxford: Blackwell.

Tang, W. and Parish, W. (2000) *Chinese Urban Life Under Reform*, Cambridge: Cambridge University Press.

Tashjian, V. and Allman, J. (2002) 'Marrying and Marriage on a Shifting Terrain: Reconfigurations of Power and Authority in Early Colonial Asante', in J. Allman *et al.* (eds), *Women in African Colonial Histories*, Bloomington and Indianapolis: Indiana University Press.

el-Tawila, S. (1998) 'Youths in Population Agenda: Concepts and Methodologies', Cairo: The American University in Cairo, Working Paper.

Teng, S. and Fairbank, J.K. (1954) *China's Response to the West, a Documentary Survey 1839–1923*, Cambridge, MA: Harvard University Press.

Tenhunen, S. (1998) 'Urban Hierarchies in Flux: Arranged Intercaste Marriages in Calcutta', in A. Parpola and S. Tenhunen (eds), *Changing Patterns of Family and Kinship in South Asia*, Helsinki: Finnnish Oriental Society.

Tessler, M. *et al.* (1978) 'Tunisian Attitudes toward Women and Child Rearing', in J. Allman (ed.), *Women's Status and Fertility in the Muslim World*, New York: Praeger.

Thakur, H. (1998) 'Preface', in W. Menski (ed.), *South Asians and the Dowry Problem*, London: Trentham Books.

Therborn, G. (1981) *Klasstrukturen i Sverige 1930–80*, Lund: Zenit.

Therborn, G. (1992) 'The Right to Vote and the Four World Routes to/through Modernity', in R. Torstendahl (ed.), *State Theory and State History*, London: Sage.

Therborn, G. (1993) 'The Politics of Childhood: The Rights of Children in Modern Times', in F. Castles (ed.), *Families of Nations*, Aldershot: Dartmouth.

Therborn, G. (1995) *European Modernity and Beyond*, London: Sage.

Therborn, G. (1996) 'Child politics: dimensions and perspectives', *Childhood* 3,1: 29–44.

Therborn, G. (2003) 'Dimensions and Processes of Global Inequalities', in A.-M. Orla-Bukowska and G. Skapska (eds), *The Moral Fabric of Contemporary Societies*, Leyden: Brill.

Therborn, G. (ed.) (2004) *Inequalities of the World*, London: Verso.

Thobie, J. (1991) 'La France Coloniale de 1870 á 1914', in J. Thobie and G. Meynier (eds), *Histoire de la France Coloniale*, Paris: Armand Colin.

Thobie, J. and Meynier, G. (1991) *Histoire de la France Coloniale*, Paris: Armand Colin.

Thomas, J.A. (1998) 'Naturalizing Nationhood: Ideology and Practice in Early Twentieth-Century Japan', in S. Minichiello (ed.), *Japan's Competing Modernities*, Honolulu: University of Hawaii Press.

Thomas, J. and Grindle, M. (1994) 'Political Leadership and Policy Characteristics in Population Policy Reform', in J. Finkle and A. McIntosh (eds), *The New Politics of Population: Conflict and Consensus in Family Planning*, New York and Oxford: Oxford University Press.

Tilly, C. (1984) 'Demographic Origins of the European Proletariat', in D. Levine (ed.), *Proletarinization and Family History*, Orlando, FL: Academic Press.

Tilly L. and Scott, J. (1987/1978) *Les femmes, le travail et la famille*, Paris: Rivages/Histoire (translated from the English, *Women, Work and Family*).

Tilly, L. *et al.* (1992) 'Child Abandonment in European History: A Symposium', *Journal of Family History* 17,1: 1–23.

Timaeus, I. and Reynar, A. (1998) 'Polygynists and Their Wives in Sub-Saharan Africa: An Analysis of Five Demographic and Health Surveys', *Population Studies* 52: 145–52.

Timur, S. (1978a) 'Determinants of Family Structure in Turkey', in J. Allman (ed.), *Women's Status and Fertility in the Muslim World*, New York: Praeger.

Timur, S. (1978b) 'Socioeconomic Determinants of Differential Fertility in Turkey', in J. Allman (ed.) *Women's Status and Fertility in the Muslim World*, New York: Praeger.

Tiwon, S. (1996) 'Models and Maniacs', in L. Sears (ed.), *Fantasizing the Feminine in Indonesia*, Durham and London: Duke University Press.

Todd, E. (1990) *L' invention de L'Europe*, Paris: Seuil.

Tohidi, N. (2002) 'The Global Intersection of Feminism in Muslim Societies: The Cases of Iran and Azerbaijan', *Social Research* 69,3: 851–87.

Tomka, B. (1999) 'The Development of the Family in 20th Century Hungary and Western Europe: Convergence or Divergence?', Szeged: University of Szeged (manuscript).

Torrado, S. (1993) *Procreación en Argentina*, Buenos Aires: Ediciones de la Flor.

Tórrez Pinto, H. (1996) 'Bolivia: The Social and Geographic Context of Trends in Fertility', in J.M. Guzmán *et al.* (eds), *The Fertility Transition in Latin America*, Oxford: Clarendon Press.

Tremblay, H. (1988) *Families of the World. Vol. 1 The Americas and the Caribbean*, New York: Farrar, Straus and Giroux.

Treves, A. (2001) *Le nascite e la politica nell'Italia del Novecento*, Milan: Editori Universitarie di Lettere Economia Diritto.

Trewin, D. (2001) *Yearbook Australia*, Canberra: Australian Bureau of Statistics.

Trost, J. (1979) *Unmarried Cohabitation*, Västerås: International Library.

Tsui, A.O. (1985) 'The Rise of Modern Contraception', in J. Cleland and J. Hobcraft (eds), *Reproductive Change in Developing Countries*, Oxford: Oxford University Press.

Tsui, A.O. (2001) 'Populations Policies, Family Planning Programs, and Fertility: The Record', *Population and Development Review* 27 Supplement: 184–204.

Tsuya, N. and Bumpass, L. (1998) 'Time Allocation between Employment and Housework in Japan, South Korea, and the United States', in K.O. Mason *et al.* (eds), *The Changing Family in Comparative Perspective: Asia and the United States*, Honolulu: East–West Center.

Tu Wei-ming (1998) 'Probing the "Three Bonds" and "Five Relationships" in Confucian Humanism', in W. Slote and G. De Vos (eds), *Confucianism and the Family*, Albany: State University of New York Press.

Tucker, J. (1991) 'Ties That Bound Women in Eighteenth and Nineteenth Century Nablus', in N. Keddie and B. Baron (eds), *Women in Middle Eastern History*, New Haven and London: Yale University Press.

Tumin, M. (1952) *Caste in a Peasant Society* Princeton, NJ: Princeton University Press.

Tuñon, J. (1997) 'Del modelo a la diversidad: Mujeres y familias en la historia mexicana' in S. Monte Gonzales and J. Tuñon (eds), *Familias y mujeres en México*, Mexico D.F.: Colegio de México.

Turshen, M. (2002) 'Algerian Women in the Liberation Struggle and the Civil War', *Social Research* 69,3: 889–911.

Twitchelt, D. and Fairbank, J. (eds) (1987) *The Cambridge History of China*, vol. 14, Cambridge: Cambridge University Press.

Twitchelt, D. and Fairbank, J. (eds) (1991) *The Cambridge History of China*, vol. 15, Cambridge: Cambridge University Press.

Uberoi, P. (1999) *The Family in India: Beyond the Nuclear Versus Joint Family Debate*, Delhi: Institute of Economic Growth.

Udegbe, B. (2001) 'Female (In)dependence and Male Dominance in Contemporary Nigerian Families', Paper presented at the Workshop on Global Processes, Cape Town, South Africa, December 2001.

Uhlenberg, P. (1993) 'Death and the Family', in A. Skolnick and J. Skolnick (eds), *Family in Transition*, New York: Harper Collins.

Ungari, P. (1970) *Il diritto di famiglia in Italia*, Bologna: Il Mulino.

UN (United Nations) (1949/1950) *Statistical Yearbook 1949/1950*, New York.

UN (1951) *Demographic Yearbook*, New York.

UN (1975) *Meeting in Mexico*, New York.

UN (1976) *Report of the World Conference of the International Women's Year*, New York.

UN (1977) *Law and the Status of Women*, New York. Also published by Columbia Human Rights Law Review.

UN (1980) *Report of the World Conference of the United Nations Decade for Women: Equality, Development and Peace*, New York (mimeographed).

UN (1987) *Fertility Behavior in the Context of Development*, New York.

UN (1989) *Convention on the Rights of the Child*, New York.

UN (1991) *The World's Women 1970–1990*, New York.

UN (1998) *World Population Prospects* (internet edn).

UN (1999) *World Abortion Policies*, New York.

UN (2000a) *The World's Women 2000*, New York.

UN (2000b) *Long-Range World Population Projections* [www.unfpa.org].

UN (2001a) *1999 Demographic Yearbook*, New York.

UN (2001b) *The State of World Population* [www.unfpa.org].

UNDP (United Nations Development Programme) (1999a) *A Worsening Record on Gender Equality, Eastern Europe*, New York.

UNDP (1999b) *Human Development Report, Eastern Europe* [www.undp.org].

UNDP (2002) *Human Development Report*, New York.

UN Economic Commission for Europe (2002) *Economic Survey of Europe 2002 No.1*, New York, Geneva.

UN Economic Commission for Latin America and the Caribbean (ECLAC) (1988) *The Decade for Women in Latin America and the Caribbean*, Santiago de Chile.

UN ECLAC (1997) *Social Panorama of Latin America*, Santiago de Chile.

UNESCO (1964) *Statistical Yearbook 1964*, Paris.

UNFPA (2000) *Replacement Migration*, New York: UN.

UNFPA (2002) *The State of the World Population* [www.unfpa.org].

UNICEF (1999) *Women in Transition*, Florence.

US Census Bureau (1975) *Historical Abstract of the United States*, Washington, DC.

US Census Bureau (2001a) *Statistical Abstract of the United States*, Washington, DC.

US Census Bureau (2001b) *Fertility of American Women* [www.census.gov/population].

US Census Bureau (2001c), *Households and Families: 2000* [www.census.gov/population].

US Census Bureau (2001d) *America's Families and Living Arrangements* [www.census.gov/population].

Utomo, I.D. (2002) 'Sexual Values and Early Experiences among Young People in Jakarta', in L. Manderson and P. Liamputtong (eds), *Coming of Age in South and Southeast Asia*, Richmond, Surrey: Curzon Press.

Valk, M.H. van der (1939) *An Outline of Modern Chinese Family Law*, Leiden: Faculteit der Rechtsgeleerdheid.

Veblen, T. (1899/1953) *The Theory of the Leisure Class*, New York: Mentor Books.

Vellenga, D.D. (1983) 'Who is a Wife? Legal Expressions of Heterosexual Conflicts in Ghana', in C. Oppong (ed.), *Female and Male in West Africa*, London: George Allen & Unwin.

Vijayanunni, M. (1998) *State Profile 1991 India*, New Delhi: Registrar General and Census Commisioner India.

Vinovskis, M. (1981) *Fertility in Massachusetts from the Revolution to the Civil War*, New York: Academic Press.

Visaria, L. and Visaria, P. (1995) 'India's Population in Transition', *Population Bulletin* 50: 22.

Visaria, P. and Chari, V. (1998) 'India's Population Policy and Family Planning Program: Yesterday, Today and Tomorrow', in A. Jain (ed.), *Do Population Policies Matter?* New York: Population Council.

Visaria, P. and Visaria, L. (1995) 'India's Population in Transition', *Population Bulletin* 50,3: 1–51.

Vogel, A. (1989a) 'Familie', in W. Benz (ed.), *Geschichte der Bundesrepublik Deutschland* vol. 3, Frankfurt: Fischer.

Vogel, A. (1989b) 'Frauen und Frauenbewegung', in W. Benz (ed.), *Geschichte der Bundesrepublik Deutschland*, vol. 3, Frankfurt: Fischer.

Vovelle, M. (1985) *La mentalité révolutionnaire*, Paris: Messidor/Editions sociales.

Waaldijk, K. (2001) 'Small Change: How the Road to Same-Sex Marriage Got Paved in the Netherlands', in R. Wintemute and M. Andenaes (eds), *Legal Recognition of Same-Sex Partnerships*, Oxford and Portland: Hart Publishing.

Waite, L. (2000) 'Trends in Men's and Women's Well-Being in Marriage', in L. Waite *et al.* (eds), *The Ties That Bind*, New York: Aldine de Gruyter.

Waite, L. *et al.* (eds) (2000) *The Ties That Bind*, New York: Aldine de Gruyter.

Walby, S. (1990) *Theorizing Patriarchy*, Oxford: Blackwell.

Wall, R. (1989) 'Leaving Home and Living Alone: An Historical Perspective', *Population Studies* 43: 369–89.

Walle, E. van de (1968) 'Marriage in African Census and Inquiries', in W. Brass *et al.* (eds), *The Demography of Tropical Africa*, Princeton, NJ: Princeton University Press.

Walle, E. van de (1978) 'Alone in Europe. The French Fertility Decline until 1850', in C. Tilly (ed.), *Historical Studies of Changing Fertility*, Princeton, NJ: Princeton University Press.

Walle, E. van de (1980) 'Illegitimacy in France during the nineteenth century', in P. Laslett, K. Oosterveen and R.M. Smith (eds), *Bastardy and its Comparative History*, London: Edward Arnold.

Walle, E. van de (1986) 'Infant Mortality in the European Demographic Transition', in A. Coale and S.C. Watkins (eds), *The Decline of Fertility in Europe*, Princeton, NJ: Princeton University Press.

Walle, E. van de and Knodel, J. (1986) 'Lessons from the Past: Policy Implications of Historical Fertility Studies', in A. Coale and S.C. Watkins (eds), *The Decline of Fertility in Europe*, Princeton, NJ: Princeton University Press.

Wallerstein, I. (1991) *Geopolitics and Geoculture*, Cambridge: Cambridge University Press.

Wang Feng and Tsuya, N. (2000), 'Comparative Reproductive Regimes in the Past: A Eurasian Perspective', paper presented at the Population Association of America Conference, Los Angeles.

Wang Gungwu (1991) *China and the Chinese Overseas*, Singapore: Times Academic Press.

Wang Zheng (1998) *Women in the Chinese Enlightenment*, Berkeley, University of California Press.

Wang, Zheng (2000) 'Gender, employment and women's resistance', in E. Perry and M. Selden (eds), *Chinese Society*, London and New York: Routledge.

Ward, R. and Yoshikazu, S. (eds) (1987) *Democratizing Japan*, Honolulu: University of Hawaii Press.

Wardle, L. (1998) 'Same-sex Marriage and the Limits of Legal pluralism', in J. Eekelaar and T. Nhlapo (eds), *The Changing Family*, Oxford: Hart Publishing.

Waswo, A. (1988) 'The Transformation of Rural Society, 1900–1950', in P. Duus (ed.), *The Cambridge History of Japan*, vol. 6, Cambridge: Cambridge University Press.

Welchman, L. (2001) 'Jordan', in A. Bainham (ed.), *The International Survey of Family Law*, Bristol: Jordan Publishing.

Wellings, K. *et al.* (2001) 'Sexual Behaviour in Britain: Early Heterosexual Experience', *The Lancet* 358: 1843–50.

Wells, R. (1980) 'Illegitimacy and bridal pregnancy in colonial America', in P. Laslett, K. Oosterveen and R.M. Smith (eds), *Bastardy and its Comparative History*, London: Edward Arnold.

Werth, L. (2000) 'Kinship, Creation, and Procreation among the Vagri of South India', in M. Böck and A. Rao (eds), *Culture Creation and Procreation*, New York and Oxford: Berghahn Books.

Westermarck, E. (1889) *The History of Human Marriage*, Part I, Helsingfors: Imperial Alexander University of Finland.

Westermarck, E. (1891) *The History of Human Marriage* (1st edn), London: Macmillan.

Westermarck, E. (1903) *The History of Human Marriage* (3rd edn), London: Macmillan.

Westermarck, E. (1921) *The History of Human Marriage* (5th edn), 3 vols, London: Macmillan.

Westoff, C. (1991) *Reproductive Preferences: A Comparative View*, Columbia: Institute for Resource Development/Macro System.

Westoff, C., Blanc, A. and Nyblade, L. (1994) *Marriage and Entry into Parenthood*, Demographic and Health Surveys Studies No. 10, Calverton, MD: Macro International Inc.

Whittaker, A. (1999) 'Women and Capitalist Transformation in a Northeastern Thai Village', in P. Jackson and N. Cook (eds), *Genders and Sexualities in Modern Thailand*, Bangkok: Silkworm Books.

Whyte, M.K. (1996) 'The Chinese Family and Economic Development: Obstacle or Engine', *Economic Development and Cultural Change* 45,1: 1–30.

Wichiencharoen, A. and Netisastra, L.C. (1968) 'Some Main Features of Modernization of Ancient Family Law in Thailand', in D. Buxbaum (ed.), *Family and Customary Law in Asia*, The Hague: Martinus Nijhoff.

Wikman, R. (1937) *Die Einleitung der Ehe*, Åbo: Åbo Akademi.

Winaver, D. (2002) 'Sexe et sentiments', *Gynécologie, Obstétrique, Fertilité* 30,4: 303–7.

Winslow, A. (ed.) (1995) *Women, Politics, and the United Nations*, Westport, CT: Greenwood Press.

Wintemute, R. and Andanaes, M. (eds) (2001) *Legal Recognition of Same-Sex Partnership*, Oxford: Hart Publishing.

Wit de, J. (1996) *Poverty, Policy and Politics in Madras Slums*, New Delhi: Sage Publications.

Wolf, A. (1985) 'Chinese Family Size: A Myth Revitalized', in Hsieh Jih-chang and Chuang Yin-chang (eds), *The Chinese Family and Its Ritual Behavior*, Taipei: Academia Sinica.

Wolf, A. and Huang, Ch. (1980) *Marriage and Adoption in China, 1845–1945*, Stanford: Stanford University Press.

Wolf, J. (1912) *Der Geburtenrückgang. Die Rationalisierung des Sexuellebens in unserer Zeit*, Jena: Gustav Fischer.

Wollacott, A. (1999) 'Inventing Commonwealth and Pan-Pacific Feminisms: Australian Women's Internationalist Activism in the 1920s-1930s', in M. Sinha, D. Guy and A. Wollacott (eds), *Feminism and Internationalism*, Oxford: Blackwell.

Women of China (1987) *New Trends in Chinese Marriage and the Family*, Beijing: China International Book Trading.

Wood, E. (1997) *The Baba and the Comrade*, Bloomington and Indianapolis: Indiana University Press.

Wood, G. (1992) *The Radicalism of the American Revolution*, New York: Alfred Knopf.

World Bank (1978) *World Development Report 1978*, New York: Oxford University Press.

World Bank (1990) *World Development Report 1990*, New York: Oxford University Press.

World Bank (1992) *World Tables*, Washington, DC.

World Bank (1997) *World Development Report 1997*, New York: Oxford University Press.

World Bank Development Research Group (2000) *State Policies and Women's Autonomy in China, The Republic of Korea, and India 1950–2000*, Washington, DC.

World Fertility Surveys. See Appendix.

Wrigley, E.A. (1978) 'Fertility Strategy for the Individual and for the Group', in C. Tilly (ed.), *Historical Studies in Changing Fertility*, Princeton, NJ: Princeton University Press.

Wrigley, E.A. (1987) 'The Fall of Marital Fertility in Nineteenth Century France: Exemplar or Exception?', Wrigley, E.A., *People, Cities, and Wealth*, Oxford: Basil Blackwell.

Wrigley, E.A. and Schofield, R.S. (1981) *The Population History of England*, London: Edward Arnold.

Wu, Zheng (2000) *Cohabitation: an Alternative Form of Living*, (Studies in Canadian Population), Oxford and New York: Oxford University Press.

Wu, Zheng, and Baer, D. (1996) 'Attitudes Toward Family and Gender Roles: A Comparison of English and French Canadian Women', *Journal of Comparative Family Studes* XXVII: 437–52.

Wyatt, G. *et al.* (1999) 'Correlates of First Intercourse Among Women in Jamaica', *Archives of Sexual Behavior* 28: 139–57.

Wyatt-Brown, B. (1986) *Honor and Violence in the Old South*, New York: Oxford University Press.

Wylie, K. *et al.* (1997) 'United Kingdom', in R. Francoeur (ed.), *The International Encyclopedia of Sexuality*, 3 vols, New York: Continuum.

Xenos, P. and Gultiano, S. (1992) 'Trends in Female and Male Age at Marriage and Celibacy in Asia', Honolulu: East-West Center, Papers of the Program on Population.

Xinran (2002) *The Good Women of China*, London: Chatto and Windus.

Xu, X. (1998) 'Convergence or Divergence: The Transformation of Marriage Relationships in Urban America and Urban China', *Journal of African and Asian Studies* 33,2: 181–204.

Yang, C.K. (1965/1959) *Chinese Communist Society: The Family and the Village*, Cambridge, MA: The MIT Press.

Yerasimos, S. (ed.) (1992) *Istanbul 1914–1923*, Paris: Editions Autrement.

el-Zanaty, F. *et al.* (1996) *Egypt Demographic and Health Survey 1995*, Cairo: National Population Council.

Zang Xiaowei (1993) 'Household Structure and Marriage in Urban China, 1900–1982', *Journal of Comparative Family Studies* XXIV,1: 35–79.

Zastoupil, L. and Moir, M. (eds) (1999) *The Great Indian Education Debate*, Richmond Surrey: Curzon Press.

Zavala de Cosío, M. (1996) 'The Demographic Transition in Latin America and Europe', in J.M. Guzmán *et al.* (eds), *The Fertility Transition in Latin America*, Oxford: Clarendon Press.

Zeng Yi (2000) 'Marriage Patterns in Contemporary China', in Peng Xizhe and Guo Zhigang (eds), *The Changing Population of China*, Oxford: Blackwell.

Zicklin, G. (1995) 'Deconstructing Legal Rationality: The Case of Gay and Lesbian Family Relationships', *Marriage & Family Law Review* 21: 55–76.

Ziehl, S. (2000) 'Families and Households in South Africa', Grahamstown: Rhodes University, Department of Sociology and Industrial Sociology.

Ziehl, S. (2002a) 'Globalization and Family Patterns: A View from South Africa Grahamstown: Rhodes University, Department of Sociology and Industrial Sociology.

Ziehl, S. (2002b) 'Trends in Marriage and Divorce in South Africa', Grahamstown: Rhodes University Department of Sociology and Industrial Sociology.

Zulkifli, S.N., Low, W.Y. and Yusuf, K. (1995) 'Sexual activities of Malaysian Adolescents', *Medical Journal of Malaysia* 50: 4–10.

Index

abolitionism 32, 36
abortion: Asia, East 262, 275; Catholic
    Church 200; Chile 282; China
    279; Poland 127; selective 123, 233,
    311
Abyssinia 56
Adivar, Halide Edip 70, 87
adultery 14; Africa 118, 177;
    criminalization 216; divorce 134;
    Islam 135; in literature 139
Afghanistan 112
Africa: adultery 118, 177; bridewealth
    192; Christianity 49; cohabitation
    214; colonialism 46–51, 180, 181;
    family 105, 177, 298; gender
    equality 116, 117–18; Islam 49;
    kinship 47, 142, 177; literacy 79;
    marriage 135, 177, 179, 184, 212;
    matrilineality 179; patriarchy 14,
    129–30; polygyny 177, 212–15, 298;
    pre-marital sex 144, 212; sexual
    unions 190–91, 213; urbanization
    180–81
Africa, Southern 49, 177
Africa, sub-Saharan: age at marriage
    143; agrarian 129; cohabitation
    206; fertility decline 281; fertility
    rate 294; kinship 142; patriarchy
    107; state birth control 275
Africa, West 14, 47–48, 178–79
African Charter on Human and
    People's Rights 116
Agarwal, Bina 5
agrarian sector 129, 239
agriculture 22, 78
AIDS 111, 180, 212
Albania 126, 251, 288

Algeria 40, 114–15, 141, 175, 215
Ali, Muhammad 68
Alter, George 5
American Child Institute 91
American Civil War 36
Amin, Qasim 53, 69, 77
ancestor veneration 121, 261–62, 297
Anderson, B. 318n3
Anderson, Gordon 5
anti-colonialism 40, 269–70, 304
anti-feminism backlash 102, 105, 127
Argentina: Civil Code 33; cohabitation
    206; extra-marital birth 156, 170,
    172; fertility decline 292; marriage
    18–19; women students 31; women's
    voting rights 99
Arinori, Mori 59
Armenia 204
Asia 184, 215–18
Asia, Central 107, 204, 263
Asia, East: abortion 262, 275; birth
    control 261–62, 275; family 58–65,
    297; filial piety 300; literacy 262;
    patriarchy 72, 108; polygyny 300;
    secularization 78–79
Asia, South: colonialism 41–46; family
    297–98; fertility rate 263; gender
    equality 306; marriage 108–12,
    216; patriarchy 107, 129; polygamy
    41
Asia, Southeast: birth control 261;
    divorce 51, 52; extra-marital birth
    216; family 51–56; patriarchy
    51–56, 123–26, 130
Asia, West 112–13, 129–30, 298
Asian Marriage Survey 124
Atatürk, Kemal 77, 88

Australia 19, 101, 155, 165–66, 234
Austria 147, 153, 164, 165, 200, 202

Bali 54
Balkans 28, 126, 249–50
Bangladesh 110, 173
Barbagli, Marzio 5
Barrett, D. 273
Barrios, Domitila 103
Bavaria 147, 153
Bebel, August 20, 25, 26, 76, 83, 248
Beck-Gernsheim, E. 2
Becker, Gary 5, 320n2
Belgium 165
Belgrade World Conference on
    Population 273
Bello, Andrés 30
Bengal 39, 49–50
Besant, Annie 19, 235, 248, 268, 272
Besant, Walter 137
Bhat, P.N. Mari 5
birth control 272, 277–78; Asia, East
    261–62, 275; Asia, Southeast 261;
    autonomy 269m241; Catholic
    Church 249, 272; China 120–21,
    272, 278–80; class 243–44;
    Communism 272, 279–80; Creole
    family 260–61; Cuba 261;
    developmentalist state 278; Europe,
    Eastern 250; Europe, Western
    243–44; feminism 304; France 301;
    Korea, South 123; labour
    movements 248, 251; Latin America
    275, 282; marriage 246; Mexico
    282; modernization 241; Nigeria
    282; Pakistan 277; state 275, 294;
    Tanzania 282; USA 247–48, 301;
    see also contraception; family
    planning
birth promotion policies 256–59, 294
Black, Eugene 274
Blackstone, W. 131
Boissonade, Gustave 60
Bolshevik Revolution 76, 84, 85, 168,
    303
Borges, D. 159
Borges, Jorge Luis 138
Boserup, Esther 5
Botswana 118, 206, 281
Bradlaugh, Charles 235, 248

Bradley, David 5
Brazil: Civil Code 90; cohabitation
    204, 220; Constitution 104;
    education 283; family migration
    30; fertility decline 283, 292;
    Golden Act 36; marriage 158, 169;
    non-marriage 156; sugar
    plantations 35; women's voting
    rights 92
breast-feeding 212, 233
brideprice 49, 117
bridewealth 51, 120, 177, 180, 192,
    263, 319–20n1
Britain: birth control 272; Chartism
    251; cohabitation 198; extra-marital
    birth 149, 150; family 6, 15;
    Guardianship Act 101;
    Guardianship of Infants Act 86;
    homosexuality 137; India 39,
    43–44; industrialization 24;
    marriage 19, 194; Married Women's
    Property Acts 17, 71–72, 101;
    Matrimonial Causes Act 78, 86;
    Matrimonial Homes Act 101;
    Matrimonial Proceedings and
    Property Act 101; pre-marital sex
    208; Prevention of Cruelty to, and
    Better Protection of Children Act
    18; women students 31; *see also*
    England; Scotland; Wales
British East India Company 40
Bucharest World Conference on
    Population 273–74
Buddhism 52, 123, 134, 261, 298
Bulatao, R. 267
Bulgaria 29, 98, 251
Burger, Warren 101
Burgess, E. 1
Burguière, André 5, 10
Burma 51, 53, 55, 123, 125
Burton, Richard 156
Burundi 179, 206

Cairo World Conference on Population
    274
Caldwell, C. 177
Caldwell, J. 5, 275–76, 284, 286–87,
    294
Caldwell, J. C. 239–40
Calvinism 55, 192

Cambodia 51, 53
Cameroon 206, 281
Canada 34, 165, 193, 234
Caribbean: cohabitation 204, 205;
extra-marital birth 171; fertility rate
261, 282–83; Hinduism 34; seuxal
relations 170, 219; state birth
control 275; *see also individual
countries*
Carlsson, Gösta 240, 271
Carrell, Alex 253
Cassin, René 99
Catholic Church 319[2]n1; abortion
200; birth control 249, 272; celibacy
148; child-bearing 245; divorce
189, 200; education 97; endogamy
157; family planning 274; marriage
21, 133–34, 158, 192, 297;
Philippines 174–75, 261, 298;
polygyny 179; women 31–32
celibacy 21, 23, 147, 148, 162, 175
Central America 170–72
Ceylon 53, 56
Chartism 251
chastity 159–60
Chesnais, Jean-Claude 5, 239, 240
child marriage 66, 120, 140, 141, 143,
172–74
Child Marriage Restraint Act 172
Child Protection Act 81
childbirth 220, 245, 260, 267, 287–88;
see also extra-marital birth
childcare 252, 287
children: African households 180; of
concubines 61, 138, 140;
cost/benefit 227, 239–40, 241, 270,
282; family systems 242; legitimacy
138; mortality 110, 174; parents
13, 17–18, 26–27, 33, 52–53, 109,
219; *see also* child marriage;
illegitimacy
children's rights 81, 302
Chile: abortion 282; Civil Code 30,
33; cohabitation 205, 220; divorce
189; extra-marital birth 170;
fertility rate 282; marriage 18;
marriage rates 169–70; Pinochet
Constitution 104–5; women
students 31; women's voting rights
99

China: abortion 279; birth control
120–21, 227, 278–80; birth control
movement 272; cohabitation 204;
Communism 62, 93–95, 119, 129,
272, 279–80; concubinage 63, 192;
divorce 63–64, 94; dowries 143;
family 63, 78, 86–87, 225; fertility
rate 231, 233, 279; foot-binding 8,
14, 18, 64–65, 71; infanticide 63;
land reform 95; marriage 63, 119,
132, 217; Marriage Law 93–94, 120,
174, 280; May Fourth Movement
303–4; mourning rites 14, 63;
never-married women 139; Opium
War 57; patriarchy 14, 62–63;
polygyny 140; population growth
231, 271, 308; prostitution 121;
Protection of the Rights and the
Interests of the Elderly 310; sex
ratios 120–21; sexual behaviour
survey 217; wedding customs 121
Chiu, V. 131
Chou En-lai 94
Christianity: Africa 49; betrothal 151;
Coptic 114; divorce 188;
Fundamentalists 29; militant 39;
missionaries 18, 55; Moluccas
51–52; polygyny 215; sexuality 245;
see also Catholic Church;
Protestantism
class 21, 23, 154, 159, 243–44; *see also*
working class
Coale, Ansley 5
coffee plantations 30
cohabitation: Africa 206, 214; Brazil
204, 220; Britain 198; colonialism
204; cross-country comparisons 195,
202–7, 220; Europe, Eastern 167,
202–3, 305; Europe, Western 147,
305; extra-marital birth 151, 202;
France 198; inter-racial 157; Italy
221; Japan 203; Latin America
170, 204–5; marriage 104, 186, 193,
194; Scandinavia 195–98; Thailand
204; USA 222–23
Colombia 35, 99, 170
colonialism 37–40; Africa 46–51, 180,
181; Asia, South 41–46;
cohabitation 204; family 18, 38, 40,
54, 304; India 39, 43–44, 45–46;

inter-racial relations 158–59;
Marriage Ordinances 51; patriarchy
50
Communism: birth control 272,
279–80; China 62, 93–95, 119, 129,
272, 279–80; Cuba 76; Europe,
Eastern 74, 127, 167–68; family
76, 303; marriage 167; Russia
83–85
Comoro Islands 188
Comstock laws 252
concubinage 175; children of 61, 138,
140; China 63, 192; colonialism 38;
Egypt 68; Japan 59
Confucianism 14, 52, 74, 119, 120,
134–35, 227
Congo 48, 49, 117, 281
contraception 227, 301; Besant 19,
137, 235; cross-country comparisons
252, 264–65; education about 247,
268, 281; fertility decline 139,
286–87; fertility rate 232–33;
methods 207–8, 261, 269, 274–75,
304–5; pre-marital sex 207; *see also*
birth control
convents 157, 233
Costa Rica 156, 170, 282, 320[4]n5
Crenshaw, Edward 267–68
Creole society 36, 72, 158, 305–6,
320[4]n6; Afro-American 34, 35,
260–61, 263–64, 282–83; birth
control 260–61; extra-marital birth
200–1; family 36, 72, 158; Freetown
50; Indo-Creoles 34–37; marriage
185, 186; non-marriage 156–60;
patriarchy 35, 299, 300, 302; race
36–37; sexual relations 158–59;
undermined 302
Cretney, Stephen 86
Cuba: birth control 261; Communism
76; Family Code 104; fertility
decline 265–66; marriage 168, 170,
219; sugar plantations 35; women
students 31; women's voting rights
92
Czech Republic 167, 200
Czechoslovakia 98, 257, 258

Danton, G. J. 15
dating culture 86, 139

daughters: convents 157, 233;
discrimination against 8, 14, 310;
infanticide 14, 45, 63, 120–21, 233,
262; inheritance rights 14, 28, 61,
71, 96, 121; prostitution 59, 63;
rights 33, 306
death of partner 188
Defense of Marriage Act (US) 224
Deliège, Robert 112
Demographic and Health Surveys 204,
205–6, 214, 215, 283–84, 312
demographic transition 9, 111,
229–30, 232–33, 236, 266–67
Denmark 26, 77; extra-marital birth
165; marriage 80, 164, 194;
women's vote 82
de-patriarchalization 73, 76, 101–2,
106, 112, 292
developmentalist state 269–70, 278
Deventer, C.Th. van 55
Disraeli, Benjamin 15
divorce 5, 7; adultery 134; Asia,
Southeast 51, 52; Catholic Church
189, 200; China 63–64, 94;
Christianity 188; Egypt 114, 189;
Europe, Eastern 222; Fukuyama
187; Ghana 188; Goode 320[5]n4;
Hinduism 189; Indonesia 189;
Islam 63, 66, 71, 132; Italy 221;
Japan 61, 189; Malaysia 123,
189–90, 192, 261; Poland 127;
Protestantism 134; Russia 84, 191,
303; Scandinavia 188–89; Sweden
187, 191; Turkey 88; USA 188,
189, 191, 223; wife-initiated 320n3
Divorce Law 81
Dominican Republic 170, 205–6, 219,
300
dominium 13
double standards 107, 210
dowries 5, 66–67, 109, 120, 143, 146,
173
Dutch East Indies 54, 55

East India Company 44
East Timor 54
economics 235, 303
Ecuador 32, 92, 105
Edinburgh Review 58
education: Afghanistan 112; Brazil

283; Catholic Church 97; colonialism 40; contraception 281; Egypt 114; gender 30–31, 59, 79, 82, 112, 138, 143, 216, 267–68, 286; India 46, 79; Islam 69–70; Japan 59, 143, 262; literacy 79, 262; marriage 216; Mexico 138; Russia 85, 251; secularization 24; Turkey 87, 88, 89; *see also* university education

Eekelaar, John 5

Efendi, Mehmet 57

Egypt: birth control 278; concubinage 68; divorce 114, 189; education 114; feminism 68–69; French occupation 67–68; Islam 114; marriage 113, 138–39, 175; modernization 67–68; never-married women 141; patriarchy 113–14; polygyny 141; Ramadan war 112

El Salvador 170

Ellis, Havelock 139

Emancipation Decree 28

employment: industrialization 22–23; non-agrarian 268; part-time 128; women 2, 90, 95, 100, 112, 143–44, 166, 197, 257, 286; *see also* labour

endogamy 108, 113, 157

Engels, Friedrich 83

England 193, 234, 236, 238

Enlightenment 21, 30, 56–57

Equal Rights Act (Germany) 97–98

Equal Rights Amendment (US) 102, 305

Estonia 85, 200, 202

Ethiopia 48, 79

ethnicity 54, 289

eugenics 253, 275

Euro-Asian Project on Population and Family History 233

Europe, Eastern: birth control 250; birth promotion policies 257–58; cohabitation 167, 202–3, 305; Communism 74, 127, 167–68; divorce 222; extra-marital birth 167; family 28–29, 249–50, 297; fertility decline 284–88; fertility rate 234, 258; marriage 142, 167–68, 183, 194, 221–22; never-married

women 142; pre-marital sex 210–11, 222

Europe, Western: birth control 243–44; cohabitation 147, 305; extra-marital birth 139, 148–52; family 15, 21–22, 243–44, 297, 300; fertility decline 285–86, 288–89; fertility rate 230, 234, 235, 258; growth 232; inheritance rights 146; marriage 144–55, 161, 163–65, 183–84, 193, 194, 195, 301; never-married women 145–46, 162, 182–83; part-time employment 128; population growth 232; post-patriarchy 126; prostitution 147, 148

European Commission 203

European Fertility and Family Surveys 209

Evans, R. 32

exogamy 42, 94, 108, 132

extra-marital birth: Argentina 156, 170, 172; Asia, Southeast 216; Australia 155; Caribbean 171; cohabitation 151, 202; cross-country comparisons 148–52, 165, 168, 170, 198–201; Europe, Eastern 167; Europe, Western 139, 148–52; Iceland 172; Mexico 156; race 155; Sweden 150, 151, 165; Uruguay 156, 170, 171–72; USA 165, 200

extra-marital sex 135, 153, 161, 168, 210, 213; *see also* cohabitation; sexual relations

family: Africa 105, 177, 298; Asia, East 58–65, 297; Asia, South 297–98; Asia, Southeast 51–56; children 242; China 63, 78; class 23–24, 244; colonialism 18, 38, 40, 54, 304; Communism 76, 303; Creole society 36, 72, 158, 320[4]n6; desired size 263–64, 292; economics 303; Europe, Eastern 28–29, 249–50, 297; Europe, Western 15, 21–22, 243–44, 297, 300; fertility decline 291, 296; gender relations 59, 86; headship 14, 60, 82, 88; as institution 1–2, 17, 295, 297–301;

Japan 122, 123; kinship 116; Latin
America 90–92; Ottoman Empire
303–4; proletariat 6, 22; religion
18, 28–29, 65–66, 245, 263, 298;
Scandinavia 78; state 260, 275–76;
typology 1, 3, 6, 10–12, 61, 107,
121, 123
family legislation 17, 18, 33–34
family planning 227, 233, 234, 241,
271–72, 280
family wage 23, 251, 252
Fanon, Frantz 38
fathers 2, 8, 13, 25; *see also* paternity;
patriarchy
Fei Hsiao-tong 174
feminism 19, 77; Algeria 114–15;
birth control 304; Bolsheviks 84;
Egypt 68–69; fertility decline 292;
France 25; gender equality 32;
Islam 112; Japan 59–60; Latin
America 31, 103; Mexico 90, 91;
patriarchy 8, 84, 285–86; Third
World 103–4; Turkey 70; university
education 305; USA 101
Ferro, Marc 83
fertility decline 234–39, 284–88;
Africa, sub-Saharan 281; Brazil
283, 292; contraception 139,
286–87; cross-country comparisons
236, 246, 253; Cuba 265–66;
Europe, Eastern 284–88; Europe,
Western 285–86, 288–89; family
291, 296; feminism 292; France
244, 246, 253, 271; global 289–91;
India 240; Japan 238, 265, 277;
Latin America 283, 292; motivation
240–41; non-Western Europe 266;
post-World War II 270–71; state
252–53, 265–66, 291–92; Third
World 237, 238; USA 244, 246
fertility rate 248, 260; Africa, sub-
Saharan 294; Asia, South 263;
Cameroon 281; Caribbean 261,
282–83; Chile 282; China 231, 233,
279; Congo 281; contraception
232–33; cross-country comparisons
229, 231, 234–35, 235, 293, 307;
economics 235; education of girls
267–68; ethnicity 289; Europe,
Eastern 234, 258; Europe, Western

230, 234, 235, 258; Gabon 281;
Germany 234, 258, 289; India 276;
inheritance rights 247; Ivory Coast
281; Japan 233, 235, 253, 264;
marriage 229, 233; mortality rate
232–33; polygyny 233; rural/urban
283–84; Russia 234, 249, 258;
Sweden 227–28, 234; taxation 233,
254; Turkey 89, 288; USA 229,
234, 235, 289
Figner, Vera 28
filial piety 119, 120, 227, 297, 300
Finland: fertility rate 234; marriage
80, 194; pre-marital sex 208; sexual
partners 210; women's vote 82
foot-binding 8, 14, 18, 64–65, 71
Forde, D. 177
Fortes, Meyer 206
Foucault, Michel 150
foundling institutions 153, 301
Fourieristes 25
France: anti-contraception 272; birth
control 301; birth promotion
policies 256–57; cohabitation 198;
extra-marital birth 152, 165; fathers
25; feminism 25; fertility decline
244, 246, 253, 271; fertility rate
229, 234–35; French Revolution 6,
14–15, 24–25, 36, 160; marriage
164, 194; student rebellion 100,
126, 198, 313–14
Freemasons 25, 31
Frei, Eduardo 282
Freud, Sigmund 137, 139
Freyre, Gilberto 159
Friedan, Betty 103
Fukuyama, Francis 2, 84, 187, 314
Fukuzawa Yukichi 59, 77
Fumie Kumagai 176–77
functionalism 4, 10
fundamentalism 29, 73, 200, 222, 224,
305

Gabon 206, 207, 214, 281
Gandhi, Mahatma 38, 95–96, 275–76
gay and lesbian rights 223–24, 313
gender 8–9, 35; child preferences 123,
310–11; education 28, 30–31, 59,
79, 82, 112, 138, 143, 267–68, 286;
European settlers 29–34; family 59,

86, 107; headship 104, 107, 112;
labour market 122; Latin America
99; life expectancy 110–11, 311;
literacy 262; wages 127–28; *see also*
inheritance rights; university
education
gender equality 32; Africa 116,
117–18; Asia, South 306; feminism
32; France 74, 92; Germany 97;
Ghana 118–19; Italy 98; Japan 74,
92; marriage 17; patriarchy 25;
Sweden 197–98
genital mutilation 8, 14, 50, 71, 106,
113
geoculture 10–11, 298
German Social Democracy 25, 27, 76,
83, 248
Germany: Civil Code 17, 26–27, 61;
Communism 167; Equal Rights Act
97–98; eugenics 253; extra-marital
birth 150; fertility rate 234, 258,
289; gender equality 97;
homosexuality 225; infant mortality
rate 255; marriage 164, 194, 255;
Nazism 253, 254, 255; women
students 31; World War II 74–75,
96–97
Ghana: cohabitation 206, 207, 214;
divorce 188; gender equality
118–19; marriage 131;
matrilineality 177–78
Giddens, A. 2, 314
Gillis, John 5, 19, 131
Glendon, Mary Ann 5, 99, 193
Goa 44, 215
Gökalp, Ziya 87, 88
Gold Coast 18, 49
Goode, William J. 3–4, 10, 320[5]n4
Goody, Jack 5, 46–51, 177, 206
Goos, Carl 79–80
Greece 28–29, 200
Greenhalgh, S. 279
Groza, Maria 103
Guangxu, Emperor 65
Guardianship Act (UK) 101
Guardianship of Infants Act (UK) 86
Guatemala 170, 220
Gultiano, S. 172

Haddad, Y.Y. 131

Haiti 36, 160, 205, 219, 263–64
Hajnal, John 144, 233, 256
Hanafi School 113, 132
Hardwicke Act 134
headship: family 14, 60, 82, 88;
gender 104, 107, 112; Indonesia
299
Hinduism: Arya Samaj organization
108; Caribbean 34; divorce 189;
inheritance rights 96; marriage
41–42, 131, 134; patriarchy 41; *see
also* widows
Ho Chi Minh 95
Hobbes, Thomas 15
homosexuality 211, 218; Britain 137,
207, 211; de-criminalized 223;
fundamentalism 224; gay and
lesbian rights 223–24, 313;
Germany 225; Thailand 218
Honduras 170
Hong Kong 277
Honolulu 191
household 60, 88, 121–22, 133, 146,
220; single person 194, 311–12; *see
also* family
Hozumi Yatsuka 60
Hume, David 21
Humphrey, John 99
Hung Liang-chi 271
Hungary 127, 128, 234, 257, 258
husbands 2, 13, 14, 18, 19, 27, 30, 91,
100–1
Hutterites 234

Ibsen, Henrik 20, 25, 77, 137
Iceland: extra-marital birth 172;
fertility rate 288; illegitimacy 81;
marriage 147, 153, 163;
patrilineality 46–47
illegitimacy 81, 140, 155, 157, 200,
320[4]n5; *see also* extra-marital birth
illiteracy 79, 249, 261
immigration 271, 308
incest taboo 7, 132
India 42–43; birth control movement
272; child marriage 141, 143,
172–74; Christian missionaries 18;
colonialism 39, 43–44, 45–46;
Committee on the Status of Women
105, 110; Dowry Prohibition Act

173; education 46, 79; fertility
decline 240; fertility rate 276;
homosexuality 218; infanticide 18,
110; intellectual elite 44; literacy
262–63; marriage 45, 108–9,
140–41, 215–16; missing girls 106,
311; nationalism 95–96; population
growth 231–32; prostitution 218;
state birth control policy 275–76;
sterilization 276, 280; widows 71,
141
Indonesia: child marriage 141; divorce
189; education for girls 216; gender
equality 96; headship 299;
marriage 124, 215; Suharto
dictatorship 124, 280
industrialization: employment 22–23;
labour migration 20; patriarchy 22,
24; population growth 230–31;
urbanization 3–4, 10, 78, 150;
working-class 154, 301
infant mortality 254–55, 268–69
infanticide: China 63; daughters 14,
45, 63, 120–21, 233, 262; India 18,
110; taboo 245, 301
infibulation 14, 50
inheritance rights: daughters 14, 28,
61, 71, 96, 121; Europe, Western
146; fertility rate 247; French
Revolution 6; Hinduism 96; Islam
66–67; monogamy 244–45;
patriarchy 13; widows 28, 121
International Planned Parenthood
Federation 282
International Women's Year 75, 76, 99,
102–3, 296, 303
Iran 40, 112, 115, 142, 176, 319[2]n4
Iraq 115
Ireland 165, 189, 200, 202
Islam 112; adultery 135; Africa 49;
divorce 63, 66, 71, 132; dowries
143; education 69–70; Egypt 114;
extra-marital sex 135; family 18,
65–66, 263, 298; inheritance rights
66–67; marriage 117, 134–35;
patriarchy 116; polygamy 66;
polygyny 179, 214–15; Sharia law
68, 69, 176; Shia 142; Sunni 18;
Turkey 88
Islamic Revolution 112, 115, 176

Israelis 112, 115
Italy: Abyssinia 56; cohabitation 221;
divorce 221; extra-marital birth
200; family 86; Fascism 253, 254,
255; fertility rate 234; gender
equality 98; infant mortality rate
255; marriage 164, 182, 221;
women students 31
Ivory Coast 105, 206, 207, 213, 214,
281

al-Jabarti, Abd-al-Rahman 67–68
Jamaica 35–36, 156, 171, 219, 263–64,
300
Japan: ambassador to US 57; birth
control movement 272; Civil Code
17, 138; cohabitation 203;
concubinage 59; Constitution 74,
92–93; contraception 264–65;
divorce 61, 189; education 59, 143,
262; employment 128, 143–44;
Eugenic Protection Law 264; family
122, 123; Family Code 119, 225;
feminism 59–60; fertility decline
238, 265, 277; fertility rate 233,
235, 253, 264; gender equality 74,
92; marriage 140, 174, 185, 216–17,
262, 304; Meiji Restoration 18,
58–59, 318n7; modernization
58–62; never-married women
139–40, 216–17; patriarchy 62;
population ageing 308–9;
population growth 231–32; post-
World War II 92–93, 96–97; sex
ratios 121
Java 51
John Paul II, Pope 274
John XXIII, Pope 274
Jones, Gavin 5, 189–90
Jones, William 44
Jordan 215, 234
Joyce, G.H. 134
Judaism 320n4

Kaa, Dirk van de 5
Kahn, Alfred 5
Kamerman, Sheila 5
Kang You-wei 18, 64–65, 138
Kartini, Raden Adjeng 56, 141
Karvé, Irawati 42–43, 134

Kaser, Karl 5, 144
Kaufmann, Franz-Xavier 5
Kayongo-Male, D. 177
Kazakhstan 188
Kemal, Mustafa 87–88
Kenya 118, 208, 280
Kertzer, David 5
Key, Ellen 137, 227
Kikuyu people 48, 50
Kinsey, Alfred 320[4]n3
kinship: Africa 47, 142, 177; bilateral
    298; Europe, Western 21; family
    116; Malaya 51; marriage 42;
    patriarchy 14
Kishida Toshiko 59
Klimt, Gustav 137
Knowlton, Charles 248
Kollontai, Alexandra 28
Korea 18, 139
Korea, South 123, 176, 217, 277, 280
Kumano Binzo 60
Kundera, Milan 211
Kuusinen, Hertta 76
Kuyper, Abraham 55

labour: colonialism 40; forced 40, 48;
    gender 122; Turkey 319[2]n4;
    women 2, 122, 286, 302; *see also*
    employment
labour migration 20, 49
labour movements 247, 248, 251, 301,
    303
land reform 90, 95
Laos 51, 53
Larkin, Philip 207–8
Laslett, Peter 5
Latin America 298–99; birth control
    275, 282; Civil Codes 30;
    cohabitation 170, 204–5; Creole
    family 305–6; family 90–92;
    feminism 31, 103; fertility decline
    283, 292; gender rights 99; inter-
    racial relations 159; marriage 161,
    169–72, 193–94, 218, 220; polygamy
    36; pre-marital sex 218, 219;
    prostitution 219; sexuality 218–20;
    single person households 312
Latin American Demographic Center
    283
Latvia 127, 200

Le Play, Frédéric 5–7, 13, 144, 253
Lee, James 5
Leibniz, G.W. 56
Lenin, V. I. 76–77, 83
Leo XIII, Pope 20, 26
Lestaeghe, Ron 5, 177, 248–49
Lévi-Strauss, Claude 133
Levy, Marion Jr 95
Lewis, J. 2
Li, Jiali 279
Li Shuchang 57
Liberalism 82
Liberia 206
Libya 175
life expectancy 110–11
literacy 79, 251, 262–63; *see also*
    illiteracy
Lithuania 200
Little, Mrs Archibald 64
Locke, H. 1
Locke, John 14, 15
Louis XVI 15
love 131, 132
Luther, Martin 80
Lutheranism 80, 151, 182, 192
Lynd, R. and H. 131

McArthur, General 74, 92–93
Macaulay, Thomas 44
McDonald, Peter 5
Madagascar 206
Malaysia: birth control 277; divorce
    123, 189–90, 192, 261; fertility rate
    176; kinship 51; marriage 124–25;
    politics 280; pre-marital sex 217
male breadwinner model 24
Mali 117
Malik, Charles 99
Malthus, Thomas 245, 248, 271
Mann, Thomas 23
Manu Code 41
manus 13
Marcos, Imelda 103
marriage 2, 7–8, 181–82, 296; Africa
    135, 177, 179, 184, 212; age
    differences 141; Asia, South
    108–12, 124–25; autonomy 93, 107,
    109–10; birth control 246;
    Buddhism 52, 134, 261; Catholic
    Church 21, 133–34, 158, 192, 297;

cohabitation 104, 186, 193, 194;
Communism 167; Confucianism
134–35; Creole society 185, 186;
death of partner 188; education
216; endogamy 108, 113, 157;
Europe, Eastern 142, 167–68, 183;
Europe, Western 144–55; exogamy
42, 94, 108, 132; fertility rate 229,
233; global significance 160–62;
Hinduism 41–42, 131, 134;
household 133, 146; as institution
30, 32; Islam 117, 134–35; Judaism
320n4; kinship 42; Latin America
18–19, 158, 161, 169–72, 220;
parents/children 61, 95, 107,
112–13, 125; patriarchy 79–80;
procreation 132, 198, 201, 202;
property 26, 81, 133; residence 41,
61, 111, 119–20, 123, 177–78, 233;
as sacrament 21; scandals 138–39;
sex 131–32, 153, 212, 214, 247;
virginity 210, 222; *see also individual
countries*
marriage, age at: Afghanistan 112;
Africa 143, 212; Asia, South 161,
215–17; Asia, Southeast 53, 56, 123,
125; China 140, 233; cross-country
comparisons 165, 183–84, 195;
Egypt 68; Europe, Eastern 142,
145; Europe, Western 145–46, 165,
221, 296; India 18, 140–41, 172–73;
Iran 115; Japan 61, 140, 262; Latin
America 218
marriage, types: arranged 41, 108,
110, 122; clandestine 192; common
law 193; contract 30, 32; customary
117; forced 121; homosexual
223–25, 313; inter-caste 18; inter-
racial 33, 166; love 108, 110, 122,
131, 132, 304; neo-local 146–47;
post-pubertal 19; pre-pubertal 45;
samurai tradition 61; temporary
142, 192
marriage loans 254–55, 256
marriage rate 169–71, 193–94, 255
Married Women's Property Acts (UK)
17, 71–72, 101
Marx, Karl 83, 248
Marxism 248, 301, 303
maternity leave 252

matrilineality 47–48, 177–78, 179
Matrimonial Causes Act (UK) 78, 86
Matrimonial Homes Act (UK) 101
Matrimonial Proceedings and Property
Act (UK) 101
Matthew, Gospel according to 13
Mauritania 263
Mayo, Katherine 172
Mazzini, Giuseppe 19
Meiji Restoration 18, 58–59, 318n7
men: domination 110; homosexuality
211, 218; sexual consumption 124;
sexuality 8; surplus 111; *see also*
fathers; gender; husbands
Mencius 135
mestizo populations 35, 157
Mexican Revolution 90–92
Mexico: birth control 282; Civil Code
33; cohabitation 204–5, 206; extra-
marital birth 156; family equality
105; feminism 90, 91; fertility
decline 292; Indian Creole family
system 283; land reform 90;
marriage 158, 169; part-time
employment 128; women's voting
rights 99
Mexico City World Conference on
Population 274
Mill, James 39
Mill, John Stuart 20, 25, 59, 77, 79,
247
Millar, J. 21
mining 49, 157
misogyny 112
Mitchell, B.R. 169
Mitchell, Juliet 2
Mitterauer, Michael 5, 144, 149
modernization 58–62, 67–68, 241
Moluccas 51–52
monogamy 21, 138, 244–45
Montagu, Lady 21, 67
Montesquieu, C.-L. 70
Morgan, Lewis Henry 83
Mörner, Magnus 34
Morocco 7, 70, 115, 175, 215
Morozov, Pavlik 84
mortality rate 230, 232–33; children
110, 174; infants 254–55, 268–69
Mosher, Steven 280
motherhood 98, 153, 201–2, 212

mourning rites 14, 63
Mozambique 206, 207, 214
Muhammed, Prophet 131
Multatuli (Dekker) 55
Mussolini, Benito 253, 254
Myanmar 123, 125, 185
Myrdal, Alva 254, 256
Myrdal, Gunnar 254, 256, 273, 276

Nakamura Masano 59
Namibia 48, 234
Nandy, Ashis 38
Napoleonic Civil Code 18, 21, 24, 27,
    117, 134, 297
natalism 253–54, 263, 307
nationalism 40, 67, 95–96
Natural Foot Society 64
Nazism 253, 254, 255, 272
Nehru, Jawaharlal 96, 275–76
Neo-Malthusian League 272
neo-patriarchalism 107
Netherlands, the 31, 55, 101, 165, 224,
    234
never-married women: China 139;
    cross-country comparisons 142, 165;
    Egypt 141; Europe, Eastern 142;
    Europe, Western 145–46, 162,
    182–83; Japan 139–40, 216–17;
    Russia 140; Sweden 182; USA 165,
    182–83
New Zealand 19, 31, 32, 165, 202
Nicaragua 170, 206, 219
Nigeria 117, 179, 206, 213, 214,
    282
night bundling 139
non-agrarian employment 268
non-marriage 9, 156–60, 185
Norway 80, 81–82, 164, 165, 194
Notestein, F.W. 230, 273
Nyamwaya, D. 177

October Revolution 74
Office of Population Research 230
Ombudsman for Children 81
Onyango, P. 177
Opium War 57
Oppong, C. 177
Organization of American States
    282
Orthodox Church 28, 297

Ottoman Empire 57, 66, 68, 87–89,
    142, 303–4
Owen, Robert Dale 248

Pahlavi, Ashraf 103
Pakistan 110, 173, 277
Palestine 116, 142
Panama 170
Paraguay 99, 156
Parental Code 81
parents: authority 100; children 13,
    17–18, 26–27, 33, 52–53, 109, 219;
    marriage 201, 202; marriage of
    children 20–21, 27, 61, 95, 107,
    112–13, 125; procreation 219;
    single 98, 153, 194, 313
Parkin, D. 177
Parsons, Talcott 4, 10
pater familias 23
paternalism 38, 100
paternity 81, 212; *see also* fathers
patriarchy 8, 13, 70–71, 129–30,
    309–11; Africa 14, 107, 129–30;
    Anti-Enlightenment 21; Asia, East
    72, 108; Asia, South 107, 129; Asia,
    Southeast 51–56, 123–26, 130;
    China 14, 62–63; colonialism 50;
    Confucianism 14; Creole society
    35, 299, 300, 302; customary law
    181; Egypt 113–14; feminism 8, 84,
    285–86; gender equality 32;
    Hinduism 41; industrialization 22,
    24; inheritance rights 13;
    institutional 295–96; Islam 116;
    Japan 62; kinship 14; marriage
    79–80; misogyny 112; Netherlands,
    the 101; Russia 14; secularization
    303; Sweden 26; urbanization 22
patrilineality 46–47, 63, 177–78
Patterson, Orlando 155
Paul VI, Pope 274
pauperization 20, 24, 55–56
people trafficking 127
Persia 56, 70
Peru 99, 105, 170, 206, 292
phallocracy 118, 305, 310, 315
Philippines: birth control 277–78;
    Catholic Church 54, 174–75, 261,
    298; cohabitation 204;
    homosexuality 218; illiteracy 261;

marriage 52–53, 141; mate selection 126; politics 280; property rights 51; prostitution 218

Philips, A. 177

Place, Francis 247

plantations 35, 55, 156, 158, 300

Plassey, Battle of 39

Poland 102, 127, 128, 200, 258, 303

polygamy: Africa, West 178–79; Asia, South 41; Islam 66; Latin America 36; Thailand 53; Turkey 88, 89

polygyny 14, 71, 141–42; Africa 177, 212–15, 298; Algeria 114–15; Asia, East 300; Catholic Church 179; China 140; Christianity 215; Egypt 141; fertility rate 233; Islam 179, 214–15; Tunisia 115; Turkey 141–42

population ageing 227, 288, 308–9

Population and Development Review 267

Population Division, UN 231

population growth 275; China 231, 271, 308; cross-country comparisons 231–32; global 232, 307; industrialization 230–31; state 251–59, 272; Third World 260

Portugal: cohabitation 204; extra-marital birth 165, 200; Goa 44; marriage 164, 182, 221

post-patriarchy 126, 127, 130

potestas 13

Prasad, Rajendra 176

pre-marital sex: Africa 144, 212; contraception 207; cross-country comparisons 208–9; Europe, Eastern 210–11, 222; Latin America 218, 219; Malaysia 217; youth 161

Prevention of Cruelty to, and Better Protection of Children Act (UK) 18

Princeton European Fertility Project 5, 301

procreation 132, 198, 219

proletarianization: family 6, 22; pauperization 20, 24; sexual habits 154; social security 252; urbanization 198, 301, 302–3

property rights 2, 26, 51, 81, 133

prostitution: Asia 217–18; China 121; daughters 59, 63; Europe, Western 147, 148; India 175, 218; Latin

America 219; rites of passage 138

Protestantism: Calvinism 55, 192; divorce 134; family 245; Lutheranism 80, 82, 151, 192; marriage of clergy 148; radicalism 25; USA 200; women 31–32; *see also* fundamentalism

Proust, Marcel 138

Puerto Rico 156–57

purdah 41, 110

race 35–37, 155

racism 253

Radcliffe-Brown, E. 177

Ramadan war 112

Ramirez, Maria Abella de 31

Ray, Rammohan 39–40, 44, 46, 49

religion 28–29, 73, 168

remarriage: divorcées 66; parenthood 201; widows 18, 45, 52, 64, 66, 141, 188, 233

Rerum novarum (1891 Encyclica) 20, 26

residence: marriage 41, 61, 111, 119–20, 123, 177–78, 233; youth 312, 314

Rizal, José 54, 318n3

Roman law 13

Romania 257–58

Rome Conference 273

Roosevelt, Eleanor 99

Rousseau, Jean Jacques 15

rural–urban migration 20

Rushdi, Eugénie Le Brun 69

Russia: Civil Code 28; Communism 83–85; divorce 84, 191, 303; education 85, 251; extra-marital birth 200; Family Code 85, 127; fertility rate 234, 249, 258; GDP 127; Land Code 84; marriage 85; never-married women 140; October Revolution 74; patriarchy 14; serfdom 249; widows 167; women's vote 82; *zadruga* 28, 46–47, 250; *see also* Soviet Union

Rwanda 206, 212, 214

Sachs, A. 101

Saint-Simonistes 25

Sanger, Margaret 272

sati 14, 18, 39, 44; *see also* widows

Scandinavia: children's rights 302;
cohabitation 195–98; divorce
188–89; family reform 78, 80;
marriage 296; Marriage Code
80–81; single person households
312; women's movement 82;
women's voting rights 303–4; *see also
individual countries*
Schneider, Jane and Peter 250
Scotland 21, 152, 165, 193
Scott, Joan 5, 23
Scottish Enlightenment 21
Second Congress of Feminine
Organizations and Institutions 137
secularization: Asia, East 78–79;
education 24; morals 153;
patriarchy 303; religion 73;
sexuality 207–8
Seneca Falls Declaration 32
Senegal 117, 178–79
Serbia 29
settlers 29–34, 147, 157, 235, 239, 284
sex industry 175, 314–15
sex ratios 111, 120–21, 311
sex trade 124, 127
sexual behaviour surveys 207–8, 217
sexual relations 1–2; abstinence 233;
Africa 190–91, 213; age at debut
208–10, 219, 222; autonomy 43;
Caribbean 170; class 23, 159;
commodification 314; consumption
124; Creole society 158–59;
diversity 315; domination 38;
emotion 314; informal 186–87,
306; inter-racial 54, 138; Jamaica
171; marriage 144–45, 153, 212;
partners 209–10; secularization
207–8; selection 7; university
education 217; USA 210, 222
sexuality: Africa 212–15; Asia 215–18;
Asia, Southeast 51; Christianity
245; class 21; double standards
107; Latin America 218–20;
pleasure 211, 313
Sharabi, Hisham 113
Sharia law 68, 69, 176
Shorter, E. 29–34, 152
Siam 51, 53, 56, 123
Sierra, Justo 138
Sierra Leone 50

Silver, Catherine Bodard 7
Singapore 51, 277, 280
single person households 194, 311–12
Sino-Japanese war 65
Sipilä, Helvi 102–3, 103
Sirota, Beate 93
Sklar, June 144
slavery 32, 35, 36, 48, 142, 155–56,
158
Slovakia 167, 200
Smiles, Samuel 69, 319n9
Smith, Adam 56–57
social security 252
Socialist Labour Movement 76
son preference 123, 310–11
South Africa 117, 118, 206–7
Soviet Union 74, 98, 189, 257–58; *see
also* Russia
Spain: age at marriage 221; birth
control 249; extra-marital birth
165; fertility rate 234; marriage
163–64; women students 31; *see also*
Latin America
Spencer, Herbert 69
Sri Lanka 105, 123, 126, 173, 276, 280
Stalin, Joseph 84–85
Stanton, Elizabeth Cady 248
state: birth control 275–76, 294; birth
promotion policies 256–59;
childcare 252; family 275–76;
fertility decline 252–53, 265–66,
291–2; marriage loans 254–55,
256; population growth 251–59,
272, 275
sterilization 233, 253, 274–75, 276,
279, 280
Stone, Lawrence 134, 153
Strindberg, August 137
student rebellion 100, 126, 198,
313–14
Sudan 263
sugar plantations 35
Suharto dictatorship 124, 280
Suslova, Nadezhda 28
Sweden: cohabitation 195–98; divorce
187, 191; extra-marital birth 150,
151, 165; fertility rate 227–28, 234;
gender equality 197–98;
guardianship of women 71; infant
mortality rate 255; language

changes 197; marriage 164, 194,
195, 255; Marriage Law 74, 77, 80,
188–89; never-married women 182;
parents/children's marriages
112–13; patriarchy 26; Penal Code
17–18; sexual partners 210; Social
Democracy 254; women students
31; women's vote 82
Switzerland 112, 165, 189
Syria 115, 263
Szelenyi, Ivan 211

al-Taimuriya, Aisha Ismat 68
Taiwan 122, 139, 174, 277, 278, 280
Tan Su-tung 65
Tanganyika 48
Tanzania 282
taxation/fertility rate 233, 254
teenage pregnancy 219, 222
temperance movements 19, 32
Thailand: birth control 277–78;
Buddhism 123; cohabitation 204;
colonialism 51; homosexuality 218;
marriage 18; Marriage Survey 125;
politics 280; polygamy 53;
prostitution 217–18; sex industry 175
Therborn, Göran 8, 18, 81, 102, 251,
268
Thianwan 53, 77
Third World 103–4, 236, 237, 238, 260
Tilly, Louise 5, 23
Todd, Emmanuel 6
Tolstoy, A. 137
trade unions 251
Treitschke, Heinrich V. 25
Trent, Council of 21, 133–34, 159, 192
Tunisia 115, 175, 274, 278
Turkey: Balkans 249–50; birth control
278; divorce 88; education 87, 88,
89; feminism 70; fertility rate 89,
288; Greek occupation 87; Islam
88; marriage 88–89, 175; polygamy
88, 89; polygyny 141–42; reforms
77; virginity 215; women's
employment 112, 319[2]n4; *see also*
Ottoman Empire
Tutu, Desmond 223, 224

Udegbe, Bola 117
Uganda 206, 214

United Nations Commission on the
Status of Women 76
United Nations Convention on the
Elimination of All Forms of
Discrimination Against Women 103,
105, 310
United Nations Convention on the
Rights of the Child 102, 105–6, 227,
303
United Nations Decade for Women
102, 103–4
United Nations Declaration of Human
Rights 75, 92, 98–99, 296, 304
United Nations Economic Committee
273
United Nations General Assembly 75
United Nations Population Fund 307
United Nations Secretariat Population
Division 231
United States of America: birth control
247–48, 301; black Americans 155;
cohabitation 222–23; contraception
252; dating culture 86; Defense of
Marriage Act 224; de-
patriarchalization 101–2; divorce
188, 189, 191, 223; Equal Rights
Amendment 102; European settlers
29–34; extra-marital birth 165, 200;
family law 86; feminism 101;
fertility decline 244, 246; fertility
rate 229, 234, 235, 289;
fundamentalism 305; marriage 2,
166, 193, 195, 223; never-married
women 165, 182–83; pre-marital sex
208; sexual relations 222; women
students 31; women's rights 19
university education: cross-country
comparisons 31, 128–29, 286;
feminism 305; sexual relations 217;
student rebellion 100; women 28,
30–1, 82, 89, 128–29
unmarried mothers 98, 153
urbanization: Africa 180–81;
industrialization 3–4, 10, 78, 150;
patriarchy 22; proletarianization
198, 301, 302–3
Uruguay: Civil Code 33; cohabitation
205; extra-marital birth 156, 170,
171–72; marriage 18, 220; women's
voting rights 92

Veblen, Thorstein 137
veil 40, 70, 71, 112, 298
Venezuela 35, 99, 105, 170
Vidyasagar, Isvaracandra 49
Vietnam 51, 52, 95, 125–26, 218
virginity 160, 210, 215, 222
Vivekananda, Swami 45
Voltaire 56
voting rights 32, 75, 82, 85, 92, 99, 303–4

wages 127–28, 154
Walby, S. 8
Wales 236, 238
Wallace, Alfred 7
Wallerstein, Immanuel 11
Wang Feng 5
Wang-shih-to 233
watanaki (trial marriage) 158
wedding customs 121
West Indies 156, 185
Westermarck, Edward 5–7, 132, 147, 310
Wicksell, Knut 248
widows 71, 134, 188; inheritance rights 28, 121; remarriage 18, 45, 52, 64, 66, 141, 188, 233; Russia 167; social death 42, 45
Wilde, Oscar 137, 223
Wilson, Chris 249
Wilson, J.H. 101
wives: beating of 71, 107, 118; husbands 18, 19, 27, 30, 91, 100–1; sexual autonomy 43; Siam 53; types 161
Wolf, Julius 248
Woman's Christian Temperance Union 19, 32, 137
women: Catholic Church 31–32; class 302; employment 2, 143–44, 166, 197, 257, 286; employment rights 90, 95, 100, 112; exclusion 28; guardianship 71; homosexuality 211; Protestantism 31–32; race 35–36; seclusion 71; status 21, 27, 33–34, 39, 45, 57, 116; subordination 111–12, 298; trafficking in 127; university education 28, 30–31, 82, 89, 128–29; veiling 40, 70, 71, 112, 298; voting rights 32, 75, 82, 85, 92, 99, 303–4; *see also* feminism; gender; motherhood; never-married women; women's rights
Women's International Democratic Federation 76
women's movement 82; *see also* feminism
women's rights 17; Atatürk 88; Lenin 76–77, 83; marriage 26; Mill 20, 25, 59, 77, 79; nationalism 40; New Zealand 19; United Nations 76, 103; USA 19
Woodhull, Victoria 33
working class 24, 154, 301
World Fertility Surveys 241, 263, 281, 294
World War II 163–64, 304

Xenos, P. 172

Yemen 179, 263
Yoshida, Prime Minister 93
Young Italy 19
youth 144, 161, 312, 314; pregnancy 219, 222
youth movements 19, 87
Youth Risk Behavior Surveys 208

zadruga 28, 46, 250
Zaïre 117
Zambia 117–18, 206
Zapatista movement 105
Zetkin, Clara 84
Zimbabwe 117–18, 206, 212, 281
Zionism 103